Security and Privacy Management, Techniques, and Protocols

Yassine Maleh
University Hassan I, Morocco

A volume in the Advances in Information Security,
Privacy, and Ethics (AISPE) Book Series

Published in the United States of America by
IGI Global
Information Science Reference (an imprint of IGI Global)
701 E. Chocolate Avenue
Hershey PA, USA 17033
Tel: 717-533-8845
Fax: 717-533-8661
E-mail: cust@igi-global.com
Web site: http://www.igi-global.com

Library of Congress Cataloging-in-Publication Data

Names: Maleh, Yassine, 1987- editor.
Title: Security and privacy management, techniques, and protocols / Yassine
  Maleh, editor.
Description: Hershey PA : Information Science Reference (an imprint of IGI
  Global), [2018] | Includes bibliographical references and index.
Identifiers: LCCN 2017048268| ISBN 9781522555834 (hardcover) | ISBN
  9781522555841 (ebook)
Subjects: LCSH: Computer networks--Security measures. | Privacy, Right of.
Classification: LCC TK5105.59 .S439235 2018 | DDC 005.8--dc23 LC record available at https://lccn.loc.gov/2017048268

This book is published in the IGI Global book series Advances in Information Security, Privacy, and Ethics (AISPE) (ISSN: 1948-9730; eISSN: 1948-9749)

British Cataloguing in Publication Data
A Cataloguing in Publication record for this book is available from the British Library.

All work contributed to this book is new, previously-unpublished material. The views expressed in this book are those of the authors, but not necessarily of the publisher.

For electronic access to this publication, please contact: eresources@igi-global.com.

Advances in Information Security, Privacy, and Ethics (AISPE) Book Series

Manish Gupta
State University of New York, USA

ISSN:1948-9730
EISSN:1948-9749

MISSION

As digital technologies become more pervasive in everyday life and the Internet is utilized in ever in-creasing ways by both private and public entities, concern over digital threats becomes more prevalent.

The **Advances in Information Security, Privacy, & Ethics (AISPE) Book Series** provides cutting-edge research on the protection and misuse of information and technology across various industries and settings. Comprised of scholarly research on topics such as identity management, cryptography, system security, authentication, and data protection, this book series is ideal for reference by IT professionals, academicians, and upper-level students.

COVERAGE

- Tracking Cookies
- Computer ethics
- Cookies
- Information Security Standards
- Access Control
- Security Classifications
- Telecommunications Regulations
- Privacy Issues of Social Networking
- Cyberethics
- Data Storage of Minors

IGI Global is currently accepting manuscripts for publication within this series. To submit a proposal for a volume in this series, please contact our Acquisition Editors at Acquisitions@igi-global.com or visit: http://www.igi-global.com/publish/.

Titles in this Series

For a list of additional titles in this series, please visit: www.igi-global.com/book-series

Security, Privacy, and Anonymization in Social Networks Emerging Research and Opportunities
B. K. Tripathy (VIT University, India) and Kiran Baktha (VIT University, India)
Information Science Reference • copyright 2018 • 110pp • H/C (ISBN: 9781522551584) • US $155.00 (our price)

Critical Research on Scalability and Security Issues in Virtual Cloud Environments
Shadi Aljawarneh (Jordan University of Science and Technology, Jordan) and Manisha Malhotra (Chandigarh University, India)
Information Science Reference • copyright 2018 • 341pp • H/C (ISBN: 9781522530299) • US $225.00 (our price)

The Morality of Weapons Design and Development Emerging Research and Opportunities
John Forge (University of Sydney, Australia)
Information Science Reference • copyright 2018 • 216pp • H/C (ISBN: 9781522539841) • US $175.00 (our price)

Advanced Cloud Computing Security Techniques and Applications
Ihssan Alkadi (Independent Researcher, USA)
Information Science Reference • copyright 2018 • 350pp • H/C (ISBN: 9781522525066) • US $225.00 (our price)

Algorithmic Strategies for Solving Complex Problems in Cryptography
Kannan Balasubramanian (Mepco Schlenk Engineering College, India) and M. Rajakani (Mepco Schlenk Engineering College, India)
Information Science Reference • copyright 2018 • 302pp • H/C (ISBN: 9781522529156) • US $245.00 (our price)

Information Technology Risk Management and Compliance in Modern Organizations
Manish Gupta (State University of New York, Buffalo, USA) Raj Sharman (State University of New York, Buffalo, USA) John Walp (M&T Bank Corporation, USA) and Pavankumar Mulgund (State University of New York, Buffalo, USA)
Business Science Reference • copyright 2018 • 360pp • H/C (ISBN: 9781522526049) • US $225.00 (our price)

Detecting and Mitigating Robotic Cyber Security Risks
Raghavendra Kumar (LNCT Group of College, India) Prasant Kumar Pattnaik (KIIT University, India) and Priyanka Pandey (LNCT Group of College, India)
Information Science Reference • copyright 2017 • 384pp • H/C (ISBN: 9781522521549) • US $210.00 (our price)

701 East Chocolate Avenue, Hershey, PA 17033, USA
Tel: 717-533-8845 x100 • Fax: 717-533-8661
E-Mail: cust@igi-global.com • www.igi-global.com

Table of Contents

Preface.. xvi

Acknowledgment.. xxi

Section 1
Security and Privacy Protocols and Cryptographic Algorithms

Chapter 1
A Lightweight Authentication and Encryption Protocol for Secure Communications Between
Resource-Limited Devices Without Hardware Modification: Resource-Limited Device
Authentication.. 1
Piotr Ksiazak, Letterkenny Institute of Technology, Ireland
William Farrelly, Letterkenny Institute of Technology, Ireland
Kevin Curran, Ulster University, UK

Chapter 2
Trust-Based Analytical Models for Secure Wireless Sensor Networks... 47
Aminu Bello Usman, Auckland University of Technology, New Zealand
Jairo Gutierrez, Auckland University of Technology, New Zealand

Chapter 3
Semantically Secure Classifiers for Privacy Preserving Data Mining... 66
Sumana M., M. S. Ramaiah Institute of Technology, India
Hareesha K. S., Manipal Institute of Technology, India
Sampath Kumar, Manipal Institute of Technology, India

Chapter 4
Building a Maturity Framework for Information Security Governance Through an Empirical
Study in Organizations... 96
Yassine Maleh, University Hassan I, Morocco
Mounia Zaydi, University Hassan I, Morocco
Abdelkbir Sahid, National School of Commerce and Management (ENCG), Morocco
Abdellah Ezzati, Faculty of Science and Technology (FST), Morocco

Section 2
Security and Privacy Management and Methods

Chapter 5
IT Security Risk Management Model for Handling IT-Related Security Incidents: The Need for a
New Escalation Approach 129
Gunnar Wahlgren, Stockholm University, Sweden
Stewart James Kowalski, Norwegian University of Science and Technology, Norway

Chapter 6
Security Visualization Extended Review Issues, Classifications, Validation Methods, Trends,
Extensions 152
Ferda Özdemir Sönmez, Middle East Technical University, Turkey
Banu Günel, Middle East Technical University, Turkey

Section 3
E-Health Security Management and Methodologies

Chapter 7
Compliance of Electronic Health Record Applications With HIPAA Security and Privacy
Requirements 199
Maryam Farhadi, Kennesaw State University, USA
Hisham Haddad, Kennesaw State University, USA
Hossain Shahriar, Kennesaw State University, USA

Chapter 8
Standards and Guides for Implementing Security and Privacy for Health Information
Technology 214
Francis E. Akowuah, Syracuse University, USA
Jonathan Land, The University of Tennessee at Chattanooga, USA
Xiaohong Yuan, North Carolina A&T State University, USA
Li Yang, The University of Tennessee at Chattanooga, USA
Jinsheng Xu, North Carolina A&T State University, USA
Hong Wang, North Carolina A&T State University, USA

Chapter 9
A Semiotic Examination of the Security Policy Lifecycle 237
Michael Lapke, University of Mary Washington, USA

Section 4
Intrusion Detection Systems

Chapter 10
Intrusion Detection Systems Alerts Reduction: New Approach for Forensics Readiness 255
Aymen Akremi, Umm Al-Qura University, Saudi Arabia
Hassen Sallay, Umm Al-Qura University, Saudi Arabia
Mohsen Rouached, Sultan Qaboos University, Oman

Chapter 11
Visualization Technique for Intrusion Detection 276
    Mohamed Cheikh, Constantine 2 University, Algeria
    Salima Hacini, Constantine 2 University, Algeria
    Zizette Boufaida, Constantine 2 University, Algeria

Chapter 12
False Alarm Reduction: A Profiling Mechanism and New Research Directions 291
    Salima Hacini, Constantine 2 University, Algeria
    Zahia Guessoum, Pierre et Marie Curie University, France
    Mohamed Cheikh, Constantine 2 University, Algeria

Section 5
Cyber Security and Malware

Chapter 13
Internet Crime and Anti-Fraud Activism: A Hands-On Approach 322
    Andreas Zingerle, Woosong University, South Korea
    Linda Kronman, Woosong University, South Korea

Chapter 14
Metamorphic Malware Detection Using Minimal Opcode Statistical Patterns 337
    Mahmood Fazlali, Shahid Beheshti University, Iran
    Peyman Khodamoradi, Aryanpour Schoul of Culture and Education, Iran

Chapter 15
Classification of Web-Service-Based Attacks and Mitigation Techniques 360
    Hossain Shahriar, Kennesaw State University, USA
    Victor Clincy, Kennesaw State University, USA
    William Bond, Kennesaw State University, USA

Compilation of References 379

About the Contributors 416

Index 424

Detailed Table of Contents

Preface.. xvi

Acknowledgment.. xxi

Section 1
Security and Privacy Protocols and Cryptographic Algorithms

Chapter 1
A Lightweight Authentication and Encryption Protocol for Secure Communications Between
Resource-Limited Devices Without Hardware Modification: Resource-Limited Device
Authentication... 1
Piotr Ksiazak, Letterkenny Institute of Technology, Ireland
William Farrelly, Letterkenny Institute of Technology, Ireland
Kevin Curran, Ulster University, UK

In this chapter, the authors examine the theoretical context for the security of wireless communication between ubiquitous computing devices and present an implementation that addresses this need. The number of resource-limited wireless devices utilized in many areas of the IT industry is growing rapidly. Some of the applications of these devices pose real security threats that can be addressed using authentication and cryptography. Many of the available authentication and encryption software solutions are predicated on the availability of ample processing power and memory. These demands cannot be met by most ubiquitous computing devices; thus, there is a need to apply lightweight cryptography primitives and lightweight authentication protocols that meet these demands in any application of security to devices with limited resources. The analysis of the lightweight solutions is divided into lightweight authentication protocols and lightweight encryption algorithms. The authors present a prototype running on the nRF9E5 microcontroller that provides necessary authentication and encryption on resource-limited devices.

Chapter 2
Trust-Based Analytical Models for Secure Wireless Sensor Networks... 47
Aminu Bello Usman, Auckland University of Technology, New Zealand
Jairo Gutierrez, Auckland University of Technology, New Zealand

In this chapter, the authors hypothesize that in the design of a trust-based routing protocol, the exploration of the peers' routing attributes could significantly improve trust evaluation accuracy. In this regard, they study the properties of complex networks and their impact on trust and reputation propagation and evaluation. They start by illustrating the structural transitivity in the network and its approximation.

They then proceed to present the theoretical and analytical relationship between trust and reputation model accuracy, average structural transitivity between peers, average shortest path between peers, and energy consumed by peers for trust and reputation propagation and evaluations. The experimental studies using simulation have further supported the results of the analytical study. In this chapter, the authors are paving a new angle of research on exploring the complex network properties impact on trust and reputation evaluation between wireless peers.

Chapter 3
Semantically Secure Classifiers for Privacy Preserving Data Mining.. 66
    Sumana M., M. S. Ramaiah Institute of Technology, India
    Hareesha K. S., Manipal Institute of Technology, India
    Sampath Kumar, Manipal Institute of Technology, India

Essential predictions are to be made by the parties distributed at multiple locations. However, in the process of building a model, perceptive data is not to be revealed. Maintaining the privacy of such data is a foremost concern. Earlier approaches developed for classification and prediction are proven not to be secure enough and the performance is affected. This chapter focuses on the secure construction of commonly used classifiers. The computations performed during model building are proved to be semantically secure. The homomorphism and probabilistic property of Paillier is used to perform secure product, mean, and variance calculations. The secure computations are performed without any intermediate data or the sensitive data at multiple sites being revealed. It is observed that the accuracy of the classifiers modeled is almost equivalent to the non-privacy preserving classifiers. Secure protocols require reduced computation time and communication cost. It is also proved that proposed privacy preserving classifiers perform significantly better than the base classifiers.

Chapter 4
Building a Maturity Framework for Information Security Governance Through an Empirical
Study in Organizations.. 96
    Yassine Maleh, University Hassan I, Morocco
    Mounia Zaydi, University Hassan I, Morocco
    Abdelkbir Sahid, National School of Commerce and Management (ENCG), Morocco
    Abdellah Ezzati, Faculty of Science and Technology (FST), Morocco

There is a dearth of academic research literature on the practices and commitments of information security governance in organizations. Despite the existence of referential and standards of the security governance, the research literature remains limited regarding the practices of organizations and, on the other hand, the lack of a strategy and practical model to follow in adopting an effective information security governance. This chapter aims to explore the engagement processes and the practices of organizations involved in a strategy of information security governance via a statistical and econometric analysis of data from a survey of 1000 participants (with a participation rate of 83.67%) from large and medium companies belonging to various industries. Based on the results of the survey regarding practices of information security management and governance, a practical maturity framework for the information security governance and management in organizations is presented.

Section 2
Security and Privacy Management and Methods

Chapter 5

IT Security Risk Management Model for Handling IT-Related Security Incidents: The Need for a
New Escalation Approach 129

Gunnar Wahlgren, Stockholm University, Sweden
Stewart James Kowalski, Norwegian University of Science and Technology, Norway

Managing IT-related security incidents is an important issue facing many organizations in Sweden and around the world. To deal with this growing problem, the authors have used a design science approach to develop an artifact to measure different organizations' capabilities and maturity to handle IT-related security incidents. In this chapter, an escalation maturity model (artifact) is presented, which has been tested on several different Swedish organizations. The participating organizations come from both the private and public sectors, and all organizations handle critical infrastructure, which can be damaged if an IT-related security incident occurs. Organizations had the opportunity to evaluate the actual model itself and also to test the model by calculating the organization's escalation capability using a query package for self-assessment.

Chapter 6

Security Visualization Extended Review Issues, Classifications, Validation Methods, Trends,
Extensions 152

Ferda Özdemir Sönmez, Middle East Technical University, Turkey
Banu Günel, Middle East Technical University, Turkey

Security visualization has been an issue, and it continues to grow in many directions. In order to give sufficient security visualization designs, information both in many different aspects of visualization techniques and the security problems is required. More beneficial designs depend on decisions that include use cases covering security artifacts and business requirements of the organizations, correct and optimal use of data sources, and selection of proper display types. To be able to see the big picture, the designers should be aware of available data types, possible use cases and different styles of displays. In this chapter, these properties of a large set of earlier security visualization work have been depicted and classified using both textual and graphical ways. This work also contains information related to trending topics of the domain, ways of user interaction, evaluation, and validation techniques that are commonly used for the security visualization designs.

Section 3
E-Health Security Management and Methodologies

Chapter 7

Compliance of Electronic Health Record Applications With HIPAA Security and Privacy
Requirements 199

Maryam Farhadi, Kennesaw State University, USA
Hisham Haddad, Kennesaw State University, USA
Hossain Shahriar, Kennesaw State University, USA

Electronic health record (EHR) applications are digital versions of paper-based patients health information. EHR applications are increasingly being adopted in many countries. They have resulted in improved quality in healthcare, convenient access to histories of patient medication and clinic visits, easier follow up of patient treatment plans, and precise medical decision-making process by doctors. EHR applications are guided by measures of the Health Insurance Portability and Accountability Act (HIPAA) to ensure confidentiality, integrity, and availability. However, there have been reported breaches of protected health identifier (PHI) data stored by EHR applications. In many reported breaches, improper use of EHRs has resulted in disclosure of patient's protected health information. The goal of this chapter is to (1) provide an overview of HIPAA security and privacy requirements; (2) summarize recent literature works related to complying with HIPAA security and privacy requirements; (3) map some of the existing vulnerabilities with HIPAA security rules.

Chapter 8
Standards and Guides for Implementing Security and Privacy for Health Information Technology 214

Francis E. Akowuah, Syracuse University, USA
Jonathan Land, The University of Tennessee at Chattanooga, USA
Xiaohong Yuan, North Carolina A&T State University, USA
Li Yang, The University of Tennessee at Chattanooga, USA
Jinsheng Xu, North Carolina A&T State University, USA
Hong Wang, North Carolina A&T State University, USA

In this chapter, the authors survey security standards and guides applicable to healthcare industry including control objective for information and related technologies (COBIT), ISO/IEC 27001:2005 (which has been revised by ISO/IEC 27001:2013), ISO/IEC 27002:2005 (which has been revised by ISO/IEC 27002:2013), ISO 27799:2008 (which has been revised by ISO 27799:2016), ISO 17090:2008 (which has been revised by ISO 17090:2015), ISO/TS 25237:2008, HITRUST common security framework (CSF), NIST Special Publication 800-53, NIST SP 1800, NIST SP 1800-8, and building code for medical device software security. This survey informs the audience of currently available standards that can guide the implementation of information security programs in healthcare organizations, and provides a starting point for IT management in healthcare organizations to select a standard suitable for their organizations.

Chapter 9
A Semiotic Examination of the Security Policy Lifecycle 237

Michael Lapke, University of Mary Washington, USA

Major security breaches continue to plague organizations decades after best practices, standards, and technical safeguards have become commonplace. This worrying trend clearly demonstrates that information systems security remains a significant issue within organizations. As policy forms the basis for practice, a major contributor to this ongoing security problem is a faulty security policy lifecycle. This can lead to an insufficient or worse, a failed policy. This chapter is aimed at understanding the lifecycle by analyzing the meanings that are attributed to policy formulation and implementation by the stakeholders involved in the process. A case study was carried out and a "snapshot in time" of the lifecycle of IS security policy lifecycle at the organization revealed that a disconnect is evident in the security policy lifecycle.

Section 4
Intrusion Detection Systems

Chapter 10

Intrusion Detection Systems Alerts Reduction: New Approach for Forensics Readiness.................. 255

Aymen Akremi, Umm Al-Qura University, Saudi Arabia
Hassen Sallay, Umm Al-Qura University, Saudi Arabia
Mohsen Rouached, Sultan Qaboos University, Oman

Investigators search usually for any kind of events related directly to an investigation case to both limit the search space and propose new hypotheses about the suspect. Intrusion detection system (IDS) provide relevant information to the forensics experts since it detects the attacks and gathers automatically several pertinent features of the network in the attack moment. Thus, IDS should be very effective in term of detection accuracy of new unknown attacks signatures, and without generating huge number of false alerts in high speed networks. This tradeoff between keeping high detection accuracy without generating false alerts is today a big challenge. As an effort to deal with false alerts generation, the authors propose new intrusion alert classifier, named Alert Miner (AM), to classify efficiently in near real-time the intrusion alerts in HSN. AM uses an outlier detection technique based on an adaptive deduced association rules set to classify the alerts automatically and without human assistance.

Chapter 11

Visualization Technique for Intrusion Detection 276

Mohamed Cheikh, Constantine 2 University, Algeria
Salima Hacini, Constantine 2 University, Algeria
Zizette Boufaida, Constantine 2 University, Algeria

Intrusion detection system (IDS) plays a vital and crucial role in a computer security. However, they suffer from a number of problems such as low detection of DoS (denial-of-service)/DDoS (distributed denial-of-service) attacks with a high rate of false alarms. In this chapter, a new technique for detecting DoS attacks is proposed; it detects DOS attacks using a set of classifiers and visualizes them in real time. This technique is based on the collection of network parameter values (data packets), which are automatically represented by simple geometric graphs in order to highlight relevant elements. Two implementations for this technique are performed. The first is based on the Euclidian distance while the second is based on KNN algorithm. The effectiveness of the proposed technique has been proven through a simulation of network traffic drawn from the 10% KDD and a comparison with other classification techniques for intrusion detection.

Chapter 12

False Alarm Reduction: A Profiling Mechanism and New Research Directions 291

Salima Hacini, Constantine 2 University, Algeria
Zahia Guessoum, Pierre et Marie Curie University, France
Mohamed Cheikh, Constantine 2 University, Algeria

Intrusion detection systems (IDSs) are commonly used to detect attacks on computer networks. These tools analyze incoming and outgoing traffic for suspicious anomalies or activities. Unfortunately, these generate a significant amount of noise complexifying greatly the analysis of the data. This chapter addresses the problem of false alarms in IDSs. Its first purpose is to improve their accuracy by detecting real attacks and by reducing the number of unnecessary alerts. To do so, this intrusion detection mechanism enhances the accuracy of anomaly intrusion detection systems using a set of agents to ensure the detection and the adaptation of normal profile to support the legitimate changes that occur over time and are the cause of many false alarms. Besides this, as a perspective of this work, this chapter opens up new research directions by listing the different requirements of an IDS and proposing solutions to achieve them.

Section 5
Cyber Security and Malware

Chapter 13
Internet Crime and Anti-Fraud Activism: A Hands-On Approach... 322
Andreas Zingerle, Woosong University, South Korea
Linda Kronman, Woosong University, South Korea

Scambaiting is a form of vigilantism that targets internet scammers who try to trick people into advance fee payments. In the past, victims were mainly contacted by bulk emails; now the widespread use of social networking services has made it easier for scammers to contact potential victims – those who seek various online opportunities in the form of sales and rentals, dating, booking holidays, or seeking for jobs. Scambaiters are online information communities specializing in identifying, documenting, and reporting activities of scammers. By following scambaiting forums, it was possible to categorize different scambaiting subgroups with various strategies and tools. These were tested in hands-on sessions during creative workshops in order to gain a wider understanding of the scope of existing internet scams as well as exploring counter strategies to prevent internet crime. The aim of the workshops was to recognize and develop diverse forms of anti-scam activism.

Chapter 14
Metamorphic Malware Detection Using Minimal Opcode Statistical Patterns................................... 337
Mahmood Fazlali, Shahid Beheshti University, Iran
Peyman Khodamoradi, Aryanpour School of Culture and Education, Iran

High-speed and accurate malware detection for metamorphic malware are two goals in antiviruses. To reach beyond this issue, this chapter presents a new malware detection method that can be summarized as follows: (1) Input file is disassembled and classified to obtain the minimal opcode pattern as feature vectors; (2) a forward feature selection method (i.e., maximum relevancy and minimum redundancy) is applied to remove the redundant as well as irrelevant features; and (3) the process ends by classification through using decision tree. The results indicate the proposed method can effectively detect metamorphic malware in terms of speed, efficiency, and accuracy.

Chapter 15
Classification of Web-Service-Based Attacks and Mitigation Techniques.. 360
Hossain Shahriar, Kennesaw State University, USA
Victor Clincy, Kennesaw State University, USA
William Bond, Kennesaw State University, USA

Web services are being widely used for business integration. Understanding what these web services are and how they work is important. Attacks on these web services are a major concern and can expose an organizations' valuable resources. This chapter performs a survey describing web service attacks.

The authors provide a taxonomy of web service vulnerabilities and explain how they can be exploited. This chapter discusses some of the approaches that make up best practices and some that are in the development phase. They also discuss some common approaches to address the vulnerabilities. This chapter discusses some of the approaches to be using in planning and securing web services. Securing web services is a very important part of a cybersecurity plan.

Compilation of References 379

About the Contributors 416

Index 424

Preface

INTRODUCTION

Information security and privacy issues have evolved at a rapid pace in the past two decades. Technology has gone through tremendous changes in terms of security, access techniques, protocols and standards, bandwidth usage and also the wide range of applications in all domains. Advances made as well as complexity have increased due to the introduction of different access technologies and tools, available services and models, and many other aspects of this evolution (Schou & Shoemaker, 2006). Yet, this progress is accompanied by more vulnerabilities, higher risks, increasing threats and sophisticated attacks (Von Solms, 2005). Due to the ubiquitous and pervasive nature of newly developed systems, there are new concerns and issues in information security and privacy related to financial confidentiality, Privacy Litigation, Electronic health and social networks (Bulgurcu, Cavusoglu, & Benbasat, 2010). Organizations and users need to understand the data and systems protection mechanisms thoroughly. Comprehensive knowledge of information security management, Technics and protocols are required not only for researchers and practitioners but also for policy makers, system managers, owners, and administrators (Moulton & Coles, 2003).

Although cryptography and security techniques have been around for quite some time, emerging technologies such the ones described above place new requirements on security with respect to data management. As the data is accessible anytime anywhere, according to these new concepts, it becomes much easier to obtain unauthorized data access. In addition, it becomes easier to collect, store and search for personal information and endanger the privacy of individuals (Moulton & Coles, 2003; Peltier, 2013).

In the context of these trends the forthcoming book on security and privacy management, techniques, and protocols will address significant issues in the field. Topics covered include Security and Network Management, Access control, Anonymity, Audit and Authentication and authorization financial privacy, unauthorized access to networks and information, Security and privacy in electronic communications, security models and protocols, Security and privacy in new trends technologies (IoT, Cloud, Big Data), Hacking, cyber-terrorism, and intrusion detection, and much more.

CHALLENGES

In today's rapidly changing and evolving environment, IT and security executives have to make difficult calculations and decisions about security with limited information (Dhillon, Syed, & Pedron 2016). They need to make decisions that are based on analyzing opportunities, risks and security. In such an environment, information security management and governance issues are at the forefront of any discussions for security organization's information assets, which includes considerations for managing risks, data and costs. Organizations, worldwide, have adopted practical and applied approaches for mitigating risks and managing information security program. The book contains 15 chapters on the most relevant and important issues and advances in applied information security management. The chapters are authored by leading researchers and practitioners in the field of information security from across the globe. The chapters represent emerging protocols and methods for effective management of information security at organizations.

The main goal of this project is to encourage both researchers and practitioners to share and exchange their experiences and recent studies between academia and industry. The overall objectives are:

- Study and analysis of different security and privacy protocols, solutions and methods.
- To improve the awareness of readers about: Security management, concepts, and privacy areas.
- To analyze and present the state-of-the-art of security and privacy management, techniques, and protocols and related technologies and methodologies.
- To highlight and discuss the recent development and emerging trends in security management, concepts, and privacy areas.
- To propose new models, practical solutions and technological advances related to security.
- To discuss new solutions related to security management, concepts, and privacy areas.

OBJECTIVE

The book aims to promote high-quality research by bringing together researchers and practitioners from academia and industry. This book will present the state of the art and the state of the practice of how to address the following unique security and privacy challenges facing emerging technologies. This book publication comprised of enhanced, expanded, and updated versions of articles published in 2014, 2015, 2016 volume year(s) of the International Journal of Information Security and Privacy. Additionally, to create a more robust publication, we are also incorporate some invited papers and new research-based chapters relevant to the overall theme of the journal.

TARGET AUDIENCE

The target audience of this book will be composed of professionals and researchers working in the field of information security and privacy in various disciplines, e.g. library, information and communication sciences, administrative sciences and management, education, adult education, sociology, computer science, and information technology. Moreover, the book will provide insights and support executives concerned with the management of expertise, knowledge, information and organizational development in different types of work communities and environments.

BOOK ORGANIZATION

The book is organized into five sections and 15 chapters. A brief description of each of the chapters follows:

Section 1: Security and Privacy Protocols and Cryptographic Algorithms

Chapter 1, "A Lightweight Authentication and Encryption Protocol for Secure Communications Between Resource-Limited Devices Without Hardware Modification: Resource-Limited Device Authentication," presents a prototype running on the nRF9E5 microcontroller which provides necessary authentication & encryption on resource limited devices.

Chapter 2, "Trust-Based Analytical Models for Secure Wireless Sensor Networks," studies the properties of complex networks and their impact on trust and reputation propagation and evaluation. The chapter explores the complex network properties impact on trust and reputation evaluation between wireless peers.

Chapter 3, "Semantically Secure Classifiers for Privacy Preserving Data Mining," focuses on the secure construction of commonly used classifiers. The computations performed during model building are proved to be semantically secure. The homomorphism and probabilistic property of Paillier is used to perform secure product, mean and variance calculations.

Section 2: Security and Privacy Management and Methods

Chapter 4, "Building a Maturity Framework for Information Security Governance Through an Empirical Study in Organizations," aims to explore the engagement processes and the practices of organizations involved in a strategy of information security governance. Based on the results of the survey, a practical maturity framework for the information security governance and management in organizations will be presented.

Chapter 5, "IT Security Risk Management Model for Handling IT-Related Security Incidents: The Need for a New Escalation Approach," uses a design science approach to develop an artifact to measure different organizations' capabilities and maturity to handle IT-related security incidents. In this chapter an escalation maturity model (artifact) is presented, which has been tested on several different Swedish organizations.

Chapter 6, "Security Visualization Extended Review Issues, Classifications, Validation Methods, Trends, Extensions," depicts and classifies a large set of earlier security visualization work using both textual and graphical ways. This chapter also contains information related to trending topics of the domain, ways of user interaction, evaluation and validation techniques which are commonly used for the security visualization designs.

Section 3: E-Health Security Management and Methodologies

Chapter 7, "Compliance of Electronic Health Record Applications With HIPAA Security and Privacy Requirements," provides an overview of HIPAA security and privacy requirements; summarizes recent literature works related to complying with HIPAA security and privacy requirements; and maps some of the existing vulnerabilities with HIPAA security rules.

Chapter 8, "Standards and Guides for Implementing Security and Privacy for Health Information Technology," gives a survey of security standards and guides applicable to healthcare industry including Control Objective for Information and related Technologies that can guide the implementation of information security programs in healthcare organizations.

Chapter 9, "A Semiotic Examination of the Security Policy Lifecycle," aims to understanding the lifecycle by analyzing the meanings that are attributed to policy formulation and implementation by the stakeholders involved in the process. A case study was carried out and a "snapshot in time" of the lifecycle of IS security policy lifecycle at the organization revealed that a disconnect is evident in the security policy lifecycle.

Section 4: Intrusion Detection Systems

Chapter 10, "Intrusion Detection Systems Alerts Reduction: New Approach for Forensics Readiness," proposes a new intrusion alert classifier, named Alert Miner (AM), to classify efficiently in near real-time the intrusion alerts in HSN. AM uses an outlier detection technique based on an adaptive deduced association rules set to classify the alerts automatically and without human assistance.

Chapter 11, "Visualization Technique for Intrusion Detection," proposes a new technique for detecting DoS attacks is proposed; it detects DOS attacks using a set of classifiers and visualizes them in real time. This technique is based on the collection of network parameter values (data packets) which are automatically represented by simple geometric graphs form in order to highlight relevant elements. Two implementations for this technique are performed, the first is based on the Euclidian distance, while the second one is based on KNN algorithm.

Chapter 12, "False Alarm Reduction: A Profiling Mechanism and New Research Directions," addresses the problem of false alarms in IDSs. Its first purpose is to improve their accuracy by detecting real attacks and by reducing the number of unnecessary generated alerts. To do so, this intrusion detection mechanism enhances the accuracy of anomaly Intrusion Detection Systems using a set of agents to ensure the detection and the adaptation of normal profile to support the legitimate changes that occur over time and are the cause of high rate of false alarms.

Section 5: Cyber Security and Malware

Chapter 13, "Internet Crime and Anti-Fraud Activism: A Hands-On Approach," categorizes different scambaiting subgroups with various strategies and tools. These were tested in hands-on sessions during creative workshops in order to gain a wider understanding of the scope of existing Internet scams as well as exploring counter strategies to prevent Internet crime. The aim of the workshops was to recognize and develop diverse forms of anti-scam activism.

Chapter 14, "Metamorphic Malware Detection Using Minimal Opcode Statistical Patterns," presents a new malware detection method which can be summarized as follows: Input file is disassembled and classified to obtain the minimal opcode pattern as feature vectors, a forward feature selection method, i.e., maximum Relevancy and Minimum Redundancy is applied to remove the redundant as well as irrelevant features, and the process ends by classification through using decision tree.

Chapter 15, "Classification of Web Service-Based Attacks and Mitigation Techniques," discusses some of the approaches that make up best practices and some that are in the development phase. We also discuss some common approaches to address the vulnerabilities. This paper discusses some of the approaches to be using in planning and securing web services. Securing web services is a very important part of a Cybersecurity plan.

Yassine Maleh
University Hassan I, Morocco

REFERENCES

Bulgurcu, B., Cavusoglu, H., & Benbasat, I. (2010). Information Security Policy Compliance: An Empirical Study of Rationality-Based Beliefs and Information Security Awareness. *Management Information Systems Quarterly*, *34*(3), 523–548. doi:10.2307/25750690

Dhillon, G., Syed, R., & Pedron, C. (2016). Interpreting Information Security Culture: An Organizational Transformation Case Study. *Computers & Security*, *56*, 63–69. doi:10.1016/j.cose.2015.10.001

Moulton, R., & Coles, R. S. (2003). Applying Information Security Governance. *Computers & Security*, *22*(7), 580–584. doi:10.1016/S0167-4048(03)00705-3

Peltier, T. R. (2013). *Information Security Fundamentals* (2nd ed.). Taylor & Francis. doi:10.1201/b15573

Schou, C., & Shoemaker, D. P. (2006). *Information Assurance for the Enterprise: A Roadmap to Information Security*. McGraw-Hill, Inc.

Von Solms, S. H. (2005). Information Security Governance - Compliance Management vs Operational Management. *Computers & Security*, *24*(6), 443–447. doi:10.1016/j.cose.2005.07.003

Acknowledgment

We would like to acknowledge all the people who have helped us in the completion of this book. It is a result of a concentrated and coordinated effort of 15 eminent authors who presented their knowledge and the ideas in the area of security and privacy management, techniques, and protocols. Therefore, first of all, we would like to thank them for their work. Without them, this comprehensive overview of security, privacy and trust technologies in modern data management would have never seen the light of day. Next, we would like to mention Prof. Imed Romdhani and Prof. Abdelkrim Haqiq. Their comments were helpful in making this a better book. Finally, we are very thankful to the team of IGI Global for accepting our book proposal and giving us the opportunity to work on this book project. Particularly, we are thankful to Colleen Moore (Editorial Assistant, Acquisitions), Jordan Tepper (Assistant Development Editor, Acquisitions), Jan Travers (Director of Intellectual Property and Contracts).

Yassine Maleh
University Hassan I, Morocco

Section 1
Security and Privacy Protocols and Cryptographic Algorithms

Chapter 1
A Lightweight Authentication and Encryption Protocol for Secure Communications Between Resource-Limited Devices Without Hardware Modification:
Resource-Limited Device Authentication

Piotr Ksiazak
Letterkenny Institute of Technology, Ireland

William Farrelly
Letterkenny Institute of Technology, Ireland

Kevin Curran
Ulster University, UK

ABSTRACT

In this chapter, the authors examine the theoretical context for the security of wireless communication between ubiquitous computing devices and present an implementation that addresses this need. The number of resource-limited wireless devices utilized in many areas of the IT industry is growing rapidly. Some of the applications of these devices pose real security threats that can be addressed using authentication and cryptography. Many of the available authentication and encryption software solutions are predicated on the availability of ample processing power and memory. These demands cannot be met by most ubiquitous computing devices; thus, there is a need to apply lightweight cryptography primitives and lightweight authentication protocols that meet these demands in any application of security to devices with limited resources. The analysis of the lightweight solutions is divided into lightweight authentication protocols and lightweight encryption algorithms. The authors present a prototype running on the nRF9E5 microcontroller that provides necessary authentication and encryption on resource-limited devices.

DOI: 10.4018/978-1-5225-5583-4.ch001

INTRODUCTION

Resource-Limited Wireless Device use is growing rapidly. This growth rate is expected to rise even higher when RFID transponders begin to replace Barcodes on a larger scale (Tanwar & Kumar, 2017). Some of the applications of these devices pose a security threat which can be addressed using cryptographic techniques (Kumawat et al., 2017). Most of the currently used cryptographic solutions are predicated on the existence of ample processing power and memory. These demands cannot be met by most ubiquitous computing devices, thus there is a need to apply lightweight cryptography primitives that meet security demands when considering devices with low resources.

A Risk Analysis of threats associated with the usage of Wireless Sensor Networks or RFID systems for the item-level stock control and temperature monitoring include the following:

- **Tag/Sensor Cloning:** A serious threat related to the counterfeiting of medicines with a high likely-hood of occurrence (Juels, 2005). Can be addressed with a strong encryption and authentication system.
- **Tag/Sensor Tracing:** A threat related to unauthorised Track & Trace of a Sensor/Tag movement throughout a given area, which has negative privacy implications. It can be addressed with a proper Authentication system that does not allow the disclosure of a Tag's/Sensor's unique ID (Sing et al., 2017).
- **Data Eavesdropping:** Unauthorized retrieval of sensor/tag data. A strong encryption algorithm provides a counter-measure to this threat (McBrearty et al., 2016).
- **Denial of Service Attack:** Affects the operation of the entire network or a group of Tags/Sensors. The likely-hood of occurrence can be regarded as medium. Such an attack would require appropriate hardware and in-depth knowledge of the radio protocol used. A proper Authentication system provides counter-measures to this threat.
- **Rogue-Data Injection:** An adversary can inject malicious data into the network causing improper configuration of the sensors for example. The probability of occurrence can be low as this kind of attack is not valuable to an adversary in most cases. A Mutual-Authentication system prevents accepting rogue data from unknown sources.
- **Cryptanalysis Attack:** Secret key discovery through a cryptanalysis attack on the authentication and/or encryption system's secret data. Such an attack compromises the whole security and leads to a full disclosure of all data. The likelihood of such an event is very low if the encryption key-space is large enough to prevent brute-force attacks (assumes unbreakable algorithm).

Figure 1 illustrates an example of a Risk Analysis concerning the threats associated with the usage of Wireless Sensor Networks or RFID systems for the item-level stock control and temperature monitoring. Typically, the application of security to wireless networks, such as the Wi-Fi Protected Access specification (Wi-Fi Alliance, 2003), requires complex mathematical computation and significant protocol data overhead. Since these requirements cannot be fulfilled by the types of Resource-Limited Devices used in Wireless Sensor Networks (WSN) and Radio Frequency-Identification (RFID) systems due to the constraints imposed by limited computational power, limited memory size and the requirement for low power consumption (Akyildiz et al. 2002; Patel & Shah, 2016), there is a need to provide a lightweight

Figure 1. Risk Analysis Example for the Pharmaceutical Industry

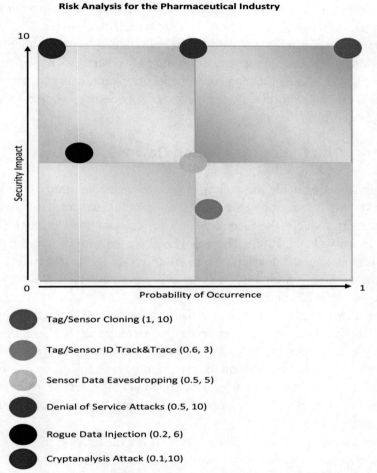

Risk Analysis for the Pharmaceutical Industry

Tag/Sensor Cloning (1, 10)

Tag/Sensor ID Track&Trace (0.6, 3)

Sensor Data Eavesdropping (0.5, 5)

Denial of Service Attacks (0.5, 10)

Rogue Data Injection (0.2, 6)

Cryptanalysis Attack (0.1,10)

The security impact is measured in the scale of 1 to 10, where 10 is the highest.

security mechanism that can be implemented within device specifications. The primary aspects of the security of data exchange are mutual authentication, confidentiality, integrity and availability (Menezes et al., 1997). Another important aspect of security especially in the context of Wireless Sensor Networks, is Data Freshness which ensures that the data received is fresh and the adversary cannot replay old messages. Weak data freshness ensures the order of messages, and strong data freshness allows additionally for the delay of the message estimation.

Our work examines the nature of inter-device security in the context Wireless Resource-Limited Devices by decomposition; splitting it into the sub-problems of authentication and encryption. These sub-problems address the key security issues identified in the literature (Schneier, 1996; Menezes et al., 1997; Mollin, 2007; Ranasinghe & Cole, 2008, Karlof et al., 2004).

AUTHENTICATION IN WIRELESS RESOURCE-LIMITED DEVICES

Mutual Authentication is a process of ensuring that all parties taking part in the communication can validate each other's identity. An intruder should not be able to masquerade as someone else (Schneier, 1996). The physical properties of the radio frequency communication channel (the ease of eavesdropping), computational efficiency and power consumption constraints (Akyildiz et al., 2002; Doherty et al., 2017) impose limitations on the range of authentication protocols which can be taken under consideration. The problem of authentication in the context of networking resource-limited devices is explained in the following sections.

Authentication With Resource-Limited Devices

The issue of Authentication in the networking of wireless resource-limited devices was given little attention until RFID systems became popular. As RFID systems are expected to be widely used for item-level tagging of consumer products, the Electronic Privacy Information Center (EPIC) take a keen interest in privacy and security (Juels, 2006). There is a need for the application of lightweight cryptographic primitives and protocols in the development of solutions for RFID (Sarma et al., 2003). Major threats to consumers are tracking (traceability) and inventory privacy (Juels, 2006). Under normal operating conditions, a tag reader will interrogate and read all tags in its proximity. Thus an unsecured RFID tag reveals its unique identifier in the absence of authentication between tag and reader. Any reader compliant with a given RFID specification can interrogate and identify the tag. In consequence, a person carrying a given tag, e.g. in a shopping bag, can be tracked around an area by a series of purposely located interrogators without the person's consent. If an unsecured tag conforms to the Electronic Product Code (EPC) specification, it also carries a unique identification of the item to which it is attached. This poses a threat in respect of itemising the contents of say, a shopping trolley, and identifying an individual's purchasing patterns (Leong et al., 2006).

Privacy, although drawing most of the attention, is not the only set of issues associated with the absence of an authentication mechanism (Korba et al., 2016). RFID systems and Wireless Sensor Networks are facing the threat of data forging and manipulation (Chung et al., 2016). Using commonly available equipment, an adversary can easily inject messages (Perrig et al. 2002), leading to false sensor readings. The majority of commonly used authentication mechanisms rely heavily on computationally intensive mathematical techniques requiring the manipulation of, for example, long keys. Resource Limited Devices share a number of constraints which in the case of RFID systems make the implementation of computationally intensive mathematical routines impossible due mainly to significant reduction in processor power and the absence of sufficient memory to store lengthy keys. A secondary argument is that an increase in the number of logic gates implemented on an Integrated Circuit dramatically increases the overall price per tag (Sarma 2001). Although Wireless Sensor Networks (WSNs) use more capable hardware they are also tightly constrained by power limitations (Cadger et al., 2016). WSN sensor battery life requirements force limited usage of the CPU and the radio bandwidth. Additionally, a node in a WSN is imbued with many tasks such as the Analogue to Digital Converter (ADC) readings interpretation, radio protocol handling, reprogramming behaviours etc., thus the code space left for security mechanism implementation is very limited. In recent years the field of lightweight security has emerged rapidly and is offering solutions mostly for RFID but also covering the area of WSNs (Vance et al., 2015). A number Ultra-Lightweight Authentication protocols have been developed which mainly target RFID but additionally, promise ways of providing a resource-saving authentication mechanism for Infrastructure Wireless Sensor Networks due to their computational simplicity and small data overhead (Juels, 2005; Chien, 2007; Peris-Lopez et al., 2009; Lee et al., 2009).

There are a number of attacks such as passive attacks, where the adversary eavesdrops on transmitted messages. In this case we assume that the adversary is not able to alter the messages or inject new ones and active attacks, where the adversary is able not only to eavesdrop the communication but also inject new messages or alter and replay the previous ones (Ferry et al., 2016). Physical invasive attacks are where the adversary has a physical access and toolset required to access the device's circuitry and for example read the EEPROM memory contents. While the physical access attack threat cannot be fully negated by a protocol, it has to be noted that the results of such an attack have to be minimised: a compromise of one tag/node should not compromise the security of other nodes/tags. It should not be possible to crack a node's previously recorded and stored communications with a recently discovered key. This requirement is known as data freshness. It is a requirement of RFID systems and Wireless Sensor Networks that it should not be possible to track nodes without express authority to do so. This is known as a Traceability (ID disclosure) Attack (Juels 2006). The attack is performed to obtain a device's unique ID number which can be further used to track the device's movements using an appropriate RF transceiver. The ID disclosure attack may be performed using passive or active methods and typically targets the authentication protocol as the ID has to be transferred in one of the protocol's messages (Ksiazak et al., 2015).

The success of full disclosure attack means that the entire security of the protocol has been compromised and all secret information used during the protocol flow is disclosed. This allows the adversary to fully impersonate (spoof) one of the devices taking part in the communication and effectively 'Clone' one of the nodes/tags. Typically a full disclosure attack requires active methods, but weak authentication protocols can be fully compromised using passive eavesdropping of consecutive rounds only (Bárász et al., 2007a). A de-synchronization attack is one of the most serious threats for an authentication protocol that is used in wireless networks. Synchronization means that both parties are aware of the status of the protocol and are able to continue executing the protocol with a normal flow. A de-synchronization attack breaks the protocol by altering the state of one (or both) of the parties authenticating each other in a way which renders further phases of the protocol not executable (Li & Wang, 2007). This kind of attack may effectively cause a denial-of-service of one or more nodes in the network.

Infrastructure Wireless Sensor Network (IWSN) Protocols

Ultralightweight protocols, which were designed for low-cost RFID systems, rely on minimalistic cryptography techniques and provide a viable alternative for securing a heavily constrained Infrastructure Wireless Sensor Network (IWSN) with minor modifications (Collotta et al., 2015). Other more computationally intensive schemes designed specifically for Wireless Sensor Networks (although filtered by the specific requirements of IWSN) or advanced RFID systems are also discussed next.

M²AP: Minimalist Mutual-Authentication Protocol

M²AP (Minimalist Mutual-Authentication Protocol) is an Ultralightweight Mutual Authentication Protocol (UMAP) (Peris-Lopez et al., 2006c). M²AP uses an index-pseudonym (IDS) to avoid disclosing device's ID which prevents the privacy issues (Traceability and Inventory) associated with both RFID and some applications of WSN, for example Wireless Body Sensor Networks (WBSNs). The IDS (96-bit long) is effectively an index to a record in a database storing tag-specific information. Each tag stores a key consisting of four concatenated 96-bit long parts (K = K1 II K2 II K3 II K4). It is assumed that the communication link between a reader and the back-end database is secure.

The protocol is divided into four main stages: tag singulation, mutual authentication, IDS updating and key updating.

- **Tag Singulation:** The reader sends a "hello" message and the tag replies with current IDS. The interrogator can now access a record in the database containing sub-keys K1-K4 associated with a given tag.

- **Mutual Authentication Is Split Into Two Distinct Parts:** Reader Authentication and Tag Authentication. In the first stage the reader generates two random numbers n1 and n2. The n1 and sub-keys K1 and K2 are used to generate A and B authentication sub-messages which are further concatenated (A II B). The following computation is performed during a round (n) for a tag(i):

$$A \parallel B = IDS_{tag(i)}^{(n)} \oplus K1_{tag(i)}^{(n)} \oplus n1 \parallel \left(IDS_{tag(i)}^{(n)} \wedge K2_{tag(i)}^{(n)} \right) \vee n1$$

where $\oplus$ = exclusive OR, = concatenation, $\wedge$ = logical AND, $\vee$ = logical OR.

The n2 number and K3 key are used to generate sub-message C (further used to update the IDS and the key K):

$$C = IDS_{tag(i)}^{(n)} + K3_{tag(i)}^{(n)} + n2$$

These sub-messages are then concatenated and sent to the tag (message = A II B II C). The next stage is the Tag Authentication. The Tag uses sub-messages A and B to authenticate the reader. The message C provides random number n2 which is used by the Tag to update the key K and the IDS. After a successful reader authentication, the tag sends a message comprising of two concatenated sub-messages D II E.

$$D = (IDS_{tag(i)}^{(n)} \vee K4_{tag(i)}^{(n)}) \wedge n2$$

$$E = \left(IDS_{tag(i)}^{(n)} + ID_{tag(i)} \right) \oplus n1$$

Sub-message D allows the reader to authenticate the tag. Part E is used to send the ID in a secure form.

- **IDS Updating:** In case of a successful authentication the reader and the tag update the index-pseudonym using the following operation:

$$IDS_{tag(i)}^{(n+1)} = \left(IDS_{tag(i)}^{(n)} + \left(n2 \oplus n1 \right) \right) \oplus ID_{tag(i)}$$

- **Key Updating:** After a completion of the IDS updating the reader and the tag have to update all 4 sub-keys K1-K4 using the following equations:

$$K1_{tag(i)}^{(n+1)} = K1_{tag(i)}^{(n)} \oplus n2 \oplus \left(K3_{tag(i)}^{(n)} + ID_{tag(i)} \right)$$

$$K2_{tag(i)}^{(n+1)} = K2_{tag(i)}^{(n)} \oplus n2 \oplus \left(K4_{tag(i)}^{(n)} + ID_{tag(i)} \right)$$

$$K3_{tag(i)}^{(n+1)} = \left(K3_{tag(i)}^{(n)} \oplus n1 \right) + \left(K1_{tag(i)}^{(n)} + ID_{tag(i)} \right)$$

$$K4_{tag(i)}^{(n+1)} = \left(K4_{tag(i)}^{(n)} \oplus n1 \right) + \left(K2_{tag(i)}^{(n)} + ID_{tag(i)} \right)$$

Peris-Lopez et al. chose only simple operations ($\oplus$, $\wedge$, $\vee$ and sum mod 2^{96}) forced by the computational power constraints of low-cost RFID tags and tag reading speed requirements (limited time for computation). He claims that the probability of ones and zeros in every sub-key is spread almost evenly and the Hamming distance between two consecutive keys $K1_{tag(i)}^{(n)}$ and $K1_{tag(i)}^{(n+1)}$ is 47.5 bits on average.

The protocol's author provided a security analysis of the proposal in terms of resistance to ID disclosure, Man-in-the-middle, replay attacks and Data Integrity assurance. The anonymity of the tag (ID hiding) is ensured by the usage of an index-pseudonym (IDS). The Data Integrity is guaranteed by the IDS and four sub-keys - the attacker would have to be able to modify these values on both the database and the tag, otherwise even a single bit manipulation would stop the protocol execution. The mutual authentication mechanism based on two random numbers refreshed with every iteration of the protocol renders the Man-in-the-middle attack impossible. The IDS and sub-keys updating mechanism aims to prevent Replay Attacks.

A passive attack (eavesdropping only) against the M²AP which is able to retrieve the IDS and all sub-keys by eavesdropping over a few consecutive runs of the protocol is possible (Bárász et al., 2007b). Weaknesses in M²AP include the usage of the bit-wise operations and the modulo 2^{96} addition which only implies that every bit affects only bits which are to the left of it and the least significant bit is independent of any other bits. Such operations are called triangular functions or T-functions and per Klimov and Shamir "A *T-function* is a mapping in which the *i*-th bit of the output can depend only on bits 0,1,..., *i* of the input"(Klimov & Shamir, 2004). Another weak aspect is the OR and AND operations used in messages B and D which can help to derive n1 and n2 values with the help of set and reset bits of IDS. The attacker can learn the ID, K1, K3, n1 and n2 after eavesdropping only two consecutive rounds of the M²AP which already allows for Traceability of the tag. K2 and K4 sub-key discovery requires eavesdropping more rounds but provides the attacker with the ability to impersonate the Tag or the Reader.

EMAP: An Efficient Mutual-Authentication Protocol

The EMAP Protocol (Peris-Lopez et al., 2006a) was developed as a result of weaknesses discovered in the M²AP Protocol (Bárász et al., 2007b). EMAP is similar to M²AP: It has the same four stages and uses IDS and four sub-keys K1-K4. The only changes which were applied were the mathematical operations used to construct sub-messages A, B, C, D, E and the formulas for updating the IDS and four sub-keys. The IDS updating formula was supposed to have better statistical properties than the M²AP as the entire number use bit-wise XORed with a random number n2. The key updating formulas now contain a parity function $\left(F_{p(x)}\right)$ which divides the 96-bit number into 24 4-bit blocks, calculates and outputs a parity bit for each block.

$$K1^{(n+1)}_{tag(i)} = K1^{(n)}_{tag(i)} \oplus n2 \oplus \left(ID_{tag(i)}\left(1:48\right) \| F_p\left(K4^{(n)}_{tag(i)}\right) \| F_p\left(K3^{(n)}_{tag(i)}\right)\right)$$

$$K2^{(n+1)}_{tag(i)} = K2^{(n)}_{tag(i)} \oplus n2 \oplus \left(F_p\left(K1^{(n)}_{tag(i)}\right) \| F_p\left(K4^{(n)}_{tag(i)}\right) \| ID_{tag(i)}\left(49:96\right)\right)$$

$$K3^{(n+1)}_{tag(i)} = K3^{(n)}_{tag(i)} \oplus n1 \oplus \left(ID_{tag(i)}\left(1:48\right) \| F_p\left(K4^{(n)}_{tag(i)}\right) \| F_p\left(K2^{(n)}_{tag(i)}\right)\right)$$

$$K4^{(n+1)}_{tag(i)} = K4^{(n)}_{tag(i)} \oplus n1 \oplus \left(F_p\left(K3^{(n)}_{tag(i)}\right) \| F_p\left(K1^{(n)}_{tag(i)}\right) \| ID_{tag(i)}\left(49:96\right)\right)$$

A de-synchronization attack and full disclosure attack are possible on LMAP (Li & Deng, 2007). As both protocols rely on a synchronization of IDS and keys stored on a tag and the back-end database therefore a full round of the protocol has to take place in order to keep synchronization on both sides. A man-in-the-middle de-synchronisation attack can be performed by changing the message C – by intercepting message (A II B II C) and XORing sub-message C with a series of zeros excluding the least significant bit set to 1 and forwarding the set of messages to the tag. The tag can still authenticate the reader as A and B remain unchanged, but it will get the wrong n2 number. Despite this the protocol will continue and the tag will reply with incorrect D and E messages; however, the reader will not be able to discover changes in D and will accept in all cases. It was shown that there is a 75% chance on average that the reader will accept an incorrect value E and update its database using original n2. The tag will do the same using incorrect n2 and both devices will lose synchronization. The full disclosure attack is based on a stateless nature of the tags - there is no way to save the state of the protocol execution on a tag. The attack consists of four stages, the first three of which are performed on a single protocol run and disclose all secret values apart from K2, K4 and the tag ID. The fourth stage requires approximately ($\log_2 m - 1$) runs to fully disclose tag's ID (m-bits long).

LMAP: A Real Lightweight Mutual Authentication Protocol

LMAP addresses weaknesses discovered in M²AP and EMAP (Peris-Lopez et al., 2006b). LMAP and EMAP share some similarities including the same size of the IDS and the same size and number of sub-keys. However, the Tag to Reader message (previously consisting of sub-messages D and E) was reduced only to a single message D. The rest of the sub-messages are now created using the following equations:

$$A = IDS^{(n)}_{tag(i)} \oplus K1^{(n)}_{tag(i)} \oplus n1$$

$$B = (IDS^{(n)}_{tag(i)} \vee K2^{(n)}_{tag(i)}) + n1$$

$$C = IDS^{(n)}_{tag(i)} + K3^{(n)}_{tag(i)} + n2$$

$$D = (IDS^{(n)}_{tag(i)} + ID_{tag(i)}) \oplus n1 \oplus n2$$

The IDS index-pseudonym is now created with the following operation:

$$IDS^{(n+1)}_{tag(i)} = (IDS^{(n)}_{tag(i)} + (n2 \oplus K4^{(n)}_{tag(i)})) \oplus ID_{tag(i)}$$

The sub-key K1 and K2 equations are identical to the ones proposed in M²AP:

$$K1^{(n+1)}_{tag(i)} = K1^{(n)}_{tag(i)} \oplus n2 \oplus (K3^{(n)}_{tag(i)} + ID_{tag(i)})$$

$$K2^{(n+1)}_{tag(i)} = K2^{(n)}_{tag(i)} \oplus n2 \oplus (K4^{(n)}_{tag(i)} + ID_{tag(i)})$$

The operations used to create the last two sub-keys K3 and K4 were slightly modified in comparison to M²AP and are as follows:

$$K3^{(n+1)}_{tag(i)} = (K3^{(n)}_{tag(i)} \oplus n1) + (K1^{(n)}_{tag(i)} \oplus ID_{tag(i)})$$

$$K4^{(n+1)}_{tag(i)} = (K4^{(n)}_{tag(i)} \oplus n1) + (K2^{(n)}_{tag(i)} \oplus ID_{tag(i)})$$

Weaknesses were discovered in both the LMAP and the M²AP protocols (Li & Wang, 2007). The vulnerabilities and possible attacks are similar to the EMAP security flaws (Li & Deng, 2007). Again, the main issue is related to the fact that the tag is not able to verify if the reader successfully received and verified message D, which may lead to a protocol de-synchronization. The de-synchronization attacks are practically identical to the one proposed earlier: message C alteration and messages A&B alteration attacks performed by XOring the message with zeros and one as the least significant bit. The probability of the success of the first attack remained at 50%. The full disclosure attack is slightly more difficult than in the case of the M²AP protocol. The attacker has to obtain the current IDS of the tag and then try all possible (A II B II C) messages by sending them to the tag and changing the j-th bit in A and B at each try. This reveals the n1 random number value and allows the calculation of K1 and K2. The rest of the secret values can be discovered by interacting with the reader and the tag one more time and then derived from the known sub-message creation equations and a simple algorithm described in (Li & Wang 2007). Several countermeasures were proposed, the most interesting one proposes a tag status storage mechanism preventing de-synchronization attacks: an additional status bit on the tag indicating whether a protocol has been successfully completed and two additional 96-bit memory spaces for storing n1 and n2 values used in the last protocol run. A Similar mechanism was included in (Peris-Lopez et al. 2006b) as a LMAP+ extension. Dispite these countermeasures, LMAP and M²AP are still susceptible to de-synchronization and full disclosure attacks (Chien & Huang 2007). With LMAP and M²AP, the attacker can flip some bits without being noticed by the reader or the tag so the protocol round would complete and both sides would update the IDS and keys with different n1 and n2 random numbers (Chien & Huang, 2007). A fully passive full disclosure attack is also possible against LMAP, which requires only eavesdropping a few (about 10) consecutive rounds of the protocol (Bárász et al. 2007a)l. Another weakness of the protocol is related to triangular functions properties (weak propagation of bits from left to right) (Bárász et al. 2007b).

SASI: Strong Authentication and Strong Integrity

The family of UMAP protocols (Peris-Lopez et al., 2006b) influenced the SASI (Strong Authentication and Strong Integrity) protocol (Chien, 2007). The tag has a unique 96-bit ID and pre-shares an index-pseudonym (IDS) and two keys K1 and K2 with a back-end database accessible by the reader (secure link assumed). In order to resist de-synchronization a state-verification has been employed: the tag stores two sets of (IDS, K1, K2) – the old values and the potential new values. In each protocol instance the reader may probe the tag twice: the first time the tag replies with its potential new IDS and if it was not found it may probe the tag again and this time the tag will use the old IDS value. The protocol flow is also like UMAP.

The protocol flow is also similar to UMAP family:

- The reader sends a "hello" message.
- The tag replies with its potential next IDS.
- The reader uses IDS to find a matched record in the database. It generates two random values n1 and n2 and uses stored keys K1 and K2 to generate messages A, B and C which are further concatenated and sent to the tag. The following equations are used to generate A and B:

$$A = IDS^{(n)}_{tag(i)} \oplus K1^{(n)}_{tag(i)} \oplus n1$$

$$B = (IDS^{(n)}_{tag(i)} \vee K2^{(n)}_{tag(i)}) + n2$$

Keys K1 and K2 are rotated using a rotation function 'ROT', which was not clearly specified in Chen's paper but revealed in (Hernandez-Castro et al. 2008) to be a Hamming rotation. The rotations are described as follows:

$$\bar{K}1 = ROT\left(K1 \oplus n2, K1\right)$$

$$\bar{K}2 = ROT\left(K2 \oplus n1, K2\right)$$

According to Hernandez-Castro et al. Chien intended to use a Hamming rotation $ROT\left(A, B\right) = A \ll wt\left(B\right)$, where $wt\left(B\right)$ stands for the Hamming weight of vector B. If a modular rotation $ROT\left(A, B\right) = A \ll B mod N$ was chosen, then the protocol would be susceptible to a passive attack proposed in (Hernandez-Castro et al. 2008). After rotations are performed, the rotated and original keys are used to form the message C:

$$C = \left(K1 \oplus \bar{K}2\right) + \left(\bar{K}1 \oplus K2\right)$$

The tag receives A II B II C and extracts n1 from A, and n2 from B. Then it performs the same two rotation functions as the reader in previous step, calculates message C and compares it with the received one. Upon successful verification the tag replies to the reader with a message D:

$$D = \left(\bar{K}2 + ID\right) \oplus \left(\left(K1 \oplus K2\right) \vee \bar{K}1\right)$$

After sending the message the tag updates the IDS and keys K1 and K2 using the following equations:

$$IDS_{old} = IDS; IDS_{next} = \left(\left(IDS + ID\right) \oplus \left(n2 \oplus \bar{K}1\right)\right)$$

$$K1_{old} = K1; K1_{next} = \bar{K}1$$

$$K2_{old} = K2; K2_{next} = \bar{K}2$$

After the message was received and successfully verified by the reader, the reader updates the IDS and keys entries using the same equations as the tag.

It is secure against de-synchronization attacks, ID disclosure attacks and it should provide privacy, anonymity, mutual authentication and forward secrecy (keeping the past communication secure even if a tag is compromised later) while retaining the ultra-lightweight properties (Chien, 2007). It requires a message length of 4L[1] and the total memory size on a tag of 7L as opposed to 6L in UMAP family protocols. There have been no published successful passive attacks against the SASI protocol using Hamming rotation function. However, several active attack possibilities were discovered. De-synchronization attacks on the SASI protocol include targeting the anti-de-synchronization mechanism of the SASI protocol: the possibility of re-trying the communication with the old IDS in case the next-possible IDS was not found in the database (Sun et al., 2008). A denial-of-service and ID disclosure attack is also possible (Cao et al., 2009). A de-synchronization, ID disclosure and a full disclosure attack against the SASI protocol is also achievable (D'Arco & De Santis, 2008).

Gossamer Protocol

The Gossamer Protocol (Peris-Lopez et al. 2009) is a recent entrant in the field of lightweight cryptography. It was built on the premise that many of the weaknesses in other approaches which use simple bitwise operations like AND, OR, XOR and modulo 2^{96} addition are T-functions (Klimov & Shamir 2004), and thus suffer from weak propagation of bits from left to right. Another weakness is the bias in the probability (75%) of obtaining a bit '1' when using bitwise AND operation. The Gossamer Protocol that is largely similar to the SASI protocol in general concept: each tag has a static identifier (ID), an index-pseudonym (IDS) and two keys K1 and K2 in memory. Additionally each tag is required to store two sets of the tuple (IDS, K1, K2): old value and the potential next value. It is assumed that the only mathematical operations that will be used are bitwise XOR, addition modulo 2^m and left rotation function $Rot(x, y)$. The rotation function performs a circular shift on the value of x by $(y \bmod N)$, positions to the left for a given N (96 in case of the EPC RFID). The most computationally expensive operation of generating two random numbers required in each protocol run is designed to be done on the reader side. An additional security layer is added with a lightweight function called *MixBits* (Hernandez-Castro et al. 2006) and uses only bitwise right shift. The protocol executes in three stages: tag identification, mutual identification and updating phase. The protocol requires exchanging four messages between the reader and the tag. Hello message length is not specified, the IDS and D messages are 96-bits long and the concatenated A II B II C message consist of three 96-bit long sub-messages. A total of 384 bits (excluding Hello message) needs to be transmitted during one protocol run. The Storage Requirements on the tag side are limited to 7 times the key-length (96-bits in the original specification) to hold two IDS, K1, K2 tuples and the static identifier ID. Each database record is required to story only one IDS, K1, K2 tuple and the static ID. The Gossamer Protocol prevents attacks as follows:

- **ID Disclosure Attack**: The notion of an index-pseudonym (IDS) and private keys K1 and K2 changed for every authentication session prevents disclosure of the unique identifier (ID) of the tag.
- **Full Disclosure Attack:** The secret data (ID, K1, K2) is always scrambled using two random numbers and sum, Mixbits and Rot functions before being transmitted over the wireless link.

- **De-Synchronization Attack:** Each tag stores (IDS, K1, K2) tuples used in a previous protocol run. In case of an unsuccessful update on the reader side in the last stage of the protocol (message D) the tag can be still identified using old values. The result is that both the tag and the reader can recover their synchronized state.

The requirement of *Data Freshness* is fulfilled by updating secret values K1, K2, n1 and n2 at each protocol run (see Figure 2). There are a number of attacks against the protocol (Ahmed et al., 2010). One is feasible if both random numbers n1 and n2 were equal to zero allowing the discovery of all secret values after eavesdropping two consecutive runs of the protocol. Another attack concerns a case where both K1 and K2 values are equal to zero, which leads to disclosure of all secret values during a single authentication round. A modification was proposed (Ahmed et al., 2010) however it has a flaw in that it renders the extraction of n1 and n2 impossible.

An attack on the original Gossamer protocol is feasible if both random numbers n1 and n2 were equal to zero permitting the discovery of K1 and K2 after eavesdropping two consecutive runs of the protocol. The values n1 and n2 are known to the reader. In A, $\mathrm{ROT}\left(\mathrm{IDS} + \mathrm{K1} + \mathrm{\grave{A}} + \mathrm{n1}, \mathrm{K2}\right) + \mathrm{K1}$ is rotated by n2 by the reader and likewise in B, $\mathrm{ROT}\left(\mathrm{IDS} + \mathrm{K2} + \mathrm{\grave{A}} + \mathrm{n2}, \mathrm{K1}\right) + \mathrm{K2}$ is rotated by n1. Messages A & B are exchanged with the tag. The tag's job is to extract the values n2 and n1 from messages A and B and to perform the appropriate inverse rotation to verify the remainder of the contents of messages A and B. However, in this modification, the tag is not aware of the value n1 or n2 and therefore cannot perform the inverse rotation to retrieve $\mathrm{ROT}\left(\mathrm{IDS} + \mathrm{K1} + \mathrm{\grave{A}} + \mathrm{n1}, \mathrm{K2}\right) + \mathrm{K1}$. This is a flaw that will not permit the completion of authentication. Another modification (Ahmed et al., 2010) concerning the MixBits function also has a weak effect on overcoming the problem of both random numbers n1 and n2 equalling zero. In the original Gossamer protocol, the mix-bits function exists during the creation of the new IDS and Key values. Where X and Y are the input 96-bit numbers and Z is the final result of the MixBits function. The weakness identified (Ahmed et al., 2010) is that if both of the MixBits input values (n1 and n2 in the first run) are equal to 0 then the result of the function is also equal to 0. As a

Figure 2. The Gossamer Protocol

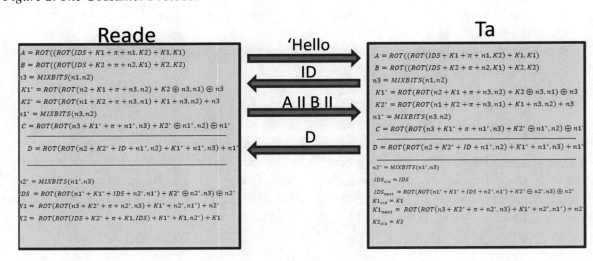

result all transformations are dependent on the Key values, the IDS and Pi. This weakens the effective security of the Gossamer Protocol. (Ahmed et al., 2010) proposed a modification however in a case where both n1 and n2 numbers are equal to zero, then the result of the MixBits function will be always the sum of numbers 1 to 32 which is 528.

SQUASH

SQUASH (short for SQUare-hASH) is an authentication mechanism based on a challenge-response scheme and Message Authentication Code (MAC) specifically for Resource Limited Devices (Shamir, 2008) such as RFID tags. The challenge-response scheme allows tag-to-reader authentication and does not address the ID disclosure issue (Shen, 2016). A strong one-way hashing function (H) is performed by the tag upon receiving a random challenge message (R). The reader shares the secret key S and performs the same calculation upon receiving the MAC to validate if a tag is legitimate. Most of the standard one-way hash functions such as SHA-1 (Eastlake & Jones, 2001) are primarily designed to be collision resistant as their main area of usage concerns digital signatures. The requirement for collision resistance typically adds complexity to the algorithm. Since a collision is not a security threat in a challenge-response scheme, the author proposed an algorithm based on the Rabin encryption scheme (Rabin, 1979). In the Rabin scheme the ciphertext (c) is computed as $c = m^2 \left(mod\, n\right)$, where (m) is a message and (n) is a product of at least two unknown prime factors. Shamir has shown how the calculation can be simplified using a step-by-step process that has no adverse effects on the strength of the security and has proposed a hardware implementation using mixing function (M) applied to the secret and challenge (S, R) and then the SQUASH function SQUASH(M(S,R)). The SQUASH function SQUASH(M(S,R)) as follows:

1. Start with j which is the index at lower end of the desired extended window of $t + u$ bits, and set carry to 0.
2. Numerically add to the current carry (over the integers, not modulo 2) the k products of the form

$$mv * m_{j-v\left(mod\, k\right)} \text{ for } v = 0, 1, 2, ..., k-1$$

3. Define bit cj as the least significant bit of the carry, set the new carry to the current carry right-shifted by one bit position, and increment j by one.
4. Repeat steps 2 and 3 $t + u$ times, throw away the first u bits, and provide the last t bits as the response to the challenge.(Shamir 2008)

The proposed SQUASH-128 hash function uses a modulus $2^{1277} - 1$, a 64-bit key S and a 64-bit challenge R to produce a 32-bit response. There is a vulnerability in this scheme with the key recovery attack known as "known random coins attack" against the Rabin scheme using 1024 chosen challenges (Ouafi & Vaudenay 2009). The "known random coins attack" allows an adversary to request many encryptions of the same plaintext and in consequence get the random coins. The attack is only effective if a linear mixing function is used, thus the security of SQUASH is still regarded as strong, assuming that a non-linear mixing function is used.

Encryption

Cryptography is the art and science of keeping messages secure (Schneier, 1996). An algorithm that has its security based on keeping its foundations secret is called restricted. Such a security system can be compromised through an information leak, reverse engineering (Harran et al., 2017). Quality control and standardisation cannot be maintained. The most common type of cryptography is the Secret-Key Cryptography (symmetric cryptography), where a message 'M' gets encrypted with encryption function E, using a key 'k' to generate a ciphertext 'c'. Therefore, c = E(k,M). The decryption function D should provide a way to recover the plaintext 'p' using the shared secret 'k', such that p = D(k,c) (Menezes et al. 1997). Resource-Limited Devices (RLDs) are highly constrained in terms of available memory and processing power. The reference platform nRF9E5 does not provide any hardware support for any encryption algorithm, thus the entire mechanism needs to be implemented in software. The most security critical aspect of wireless sensor operation is the reconfiguration of the nodes. An attack enabling an adversary to alter the control messages may lead for example to Denial Of Service (DOS) attacks affecting the entire network of sensors. It is assumed that the authentication system will guarantee frequent session key changes for the purpose of maintaining the data freshness. In consequence, the control messages have to remain safe for a relatively short period of time, until the next session key is exchanged. In most IWSN applications the data transferred by sensors will not be valuable to an attacker and will not require infinitely long secrecy. Given the analysis above, the encryption algorithm may be based on relatively short encryption keys.

Attacks can be generally divided into two categories - passive and active attacks. A special case of an active attack is a physical invasive attack - the adversary has a physical access and toolset required to access the device's circuitry and for example read the EEPROM memory contents. Since a full protection against these types of attacks requires advanced hardware (such as a sensor case destroying the EEPROM chip during opening), it is assumed that such attack cannot be prevented. The consequences of the physical invasive attack must be limited in such a way that the security of the entire system is not compromised when a single node's key is revealed and the past communication remains safe. This issue introduces a requirement to maintain session keys unique to each of the sensor nodes. Cryptography for low cost embedded devices has not been given much attention until recently such as the search for solutions easily implementable in hardware (Bogdanov et al. 2007, Eisenbarth et al. 2007, Poschmann et al. 2007) or focused on a software implementation efficient on low resource microcontrollers (Standaert et al. 2006, Wheeler & Needham 1994).

Tiny Encryption Algorithm (TEA) Family

The Tiny Encryption Algorithm (TEA) (Wheeler & Needham 1994) was the initial proposal of a family of algorithms - XTEA and Block TEA (Needham & Wheeler 1997) and XXTEA (Wheeler & Needham 1998). The main principle behind the TEA algorithm design was the simplicity of the implementation and the ease of translation to many programming languages (including Assembly). The initial proposal was a block cipher operating on 64-bit blocks with 128-bit key. Each of the identical 64 rounds of the algorithm uses only logical AND, OR, as well as bit-shift operations and addition/subtraction $Mod2^8$. The sample C-language source code consisted of less than 10 lines. The authors favoured large number of iterations over the complexity of the code. The set-up time is relatively short and there is no need to store any Look-Up-Tables (LUTs) in the memory.

The first weakness discovered in TEA was the fact that each key is equivalent to three others which effectively reduces the key size to 126 bits. This vulnerability was used to construct an attack against Microsoft's Xbox game console, which uses TEA as a hash function (Russell 2004). Since the initial proposal in 1994 several attacks were published, for example a Key-schedule cryptanalysis (Kelsey et al. 1997) and Related-key cryptanalysis (Kelsey et al. 1997). Wheeler & Needham addressed the issue mentioned above when proposing Block TEA and XTEA algorithms. The key schedule was revised and other computations (bit-shifts, XORs and additions) were rearranged to introduce the key material more slowly. The XTEA algorithm and it's block version Block TEA also suffer from weaknesses discovered by shortly after publication by Saarinen (Saarinen 1998): slow diffusion in the decryption direction exploited by chosen plaintext attack. Several other cryptanalysis attempts were also published in (Andem 2003, Hong et al. 2004, Ko et al. 2004, Lu 2009, Moon et al. 2002). The slow decoding propagation pointed by Saarinen was addressed by Wheelar & Needham in their XXTEA proposal as a short amendment to the Block TEA (Wheeler & Needham 1998). XXTEA operates on a block consisting of at least two 32-bit words using a 128-bit key. A single round of the algorithm can be viewed as operations on a word and its two adjacent words (previous and the next one). (Rinne et al. 2007) analysed the performance of several ciphers, including DES (Federal Information Processing Standards, 1993), AES (Daemen & Rijmen, 1999), IDEA, SEA (Standaert et al. 2006), HIGHT and the TEA family. The TEA family requirements in terms of the code space required, are among the lowest (after the IDEA algorithm) throughout all ciphers. The small code space footprint was achieved thanks to the lack of substitution tables common in other block ciphers. The XXTEA optimisation and performance analysis were also provided in (Jinwala et al. 2008) proving it to be a viable encryption algorithm for WSNs. Recently, a chosen-plaintext attack against the XXTEA requiring 2^{59} queries was discovered (Yarrkov, 2010). Here, advantage was taken of the fact that the number of full cycles to perform over each block is equivalent to $6 + 52 / n$, where n represents the number of rounds. If the block consists of at least 53 words then the number of cycles per word is reduced to only 6. This characteristic was used to perform differential cryptanalysis, where the difference was considered subtraction per word. The author described two attacks proving that XXTEA does not provide the intended 128-bit security.

Scalable Encryption Algorithm (SEA)

The Scalable Encryption Algorithm (SEA) (Standaert et al. 2006) provides low cost encryption implementable on resource limited processors. Similarly to the TEA family, it uses basic operations such as logical AND, OR, XOR, word/bit rotations, modular additions and a simple substitution box. Apart from the limited instruction set, the other design criteria were the low memory requirements and small code size. It is capable of "on-the-fly" key derivation.. The scalability of the algorithm is achieved through the flexibility in the size of the input parameters. There is one constraint on the size of the key/plaintext that n is a multiple of 6b ($n = x6b$). The minimum required number of rounds to provide security against well known attacks (assuming word size equal or greater than 8 bits) is:

$$\frac{3n}{4} + 2\left(n_b + \left(\frac{b}{2}\right)\right)$$

Figure 3 shows one encryption and key round, where R denotes the word rotation, r the bit rotation and S the substitution box ($S_T \blacklozenge \{0,5,6,7,4,3,1,2\}$ in C-like notation). The $C(i)$ represents an n_b-word vector with all words of a value 0 except the least significant word which value is equal to i. The Li and Ri represent left and right halves of the word or the key (KLi, RKi).

The performance of the algorithm was analysed using the Atmel AVR ATiny reference 8-bit CPU platform among others. The expected code size for a 96-bit key implementation was estimated at 386 bytes and the amount of clock cycles required for encryption/decryption was estimated at 17745. A performance analysis (Rinne et al., 2007) on AVR Atmel163 showed a code size of 2132 bytes for the 96-bit SEA (compared to 1160 bytes for XTEA) and the number of CPU cycles required to complete encryption/decryption was 9654 (compared to 6718 with XTEA). The performance and code space requirements of the XTEA algorithm look more promising than the SEA. However, due to the discovery of security weaknesses in XXTEA, the implementation of this algorithm will be abandoned in favour of the Scalable Encryption Algorithm in 96-bit version (Perrig et al. 2002).

RESOURCE-LIMITED DEVICES

The term Resource-Limited Device (RLD) describes a microcontroller device with significantly lower processing power and limited memory in comparison to a modern Personal Computer. This group of devices range from Radio Frequency Identification (RFID) transponders to a wide spectrum of embedded devices equipped with small (typically 8-bit) microcontrollers. Such devices are utilised in wireless sensor networking for example. This research focuses on the security of the communication over the radio channel, thus the area of research will be restricted to Wireless Sensor Networks and advanced RFID systems. The work here is predicated upon the application of the Nordic Semiconductors nRF9E5 Integrated Circuit (Nordic Semiconductors, 2009b) as the target device. This microcontroller was cho-

Figure 3. Encrypt/decrypt and key round of SEA

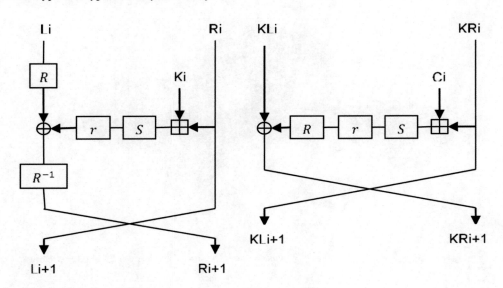

sen due to its low price (approximately 2$US per unit at quantities over 1000), integrated UHF radio transceiver and excellent power saving characteristics which make it an ideal solution for the design of a low-cost wireless sensor. The nRF9E5 entire chip will be referred to as a microcontroller and the Intel 8051-compatible Central Processor Unit - a subset of this system will be referred to as CPU or microprocessor.

IWSN

A typical Wireless Sensor Network consists of a set of Wireless Sensor Nodes and one or more Upload Stations (also referred to as Gateway Sensor Nodes or sinks) (Akyildiz et al. 2002) that provide a connection to a Host Computer on an external network (see Figure 4). The external network uses a communication media not available to the Wireless Sensor Nodes, such as Ethernet or a different RF technology. The most commonly used architecture (Ye et al. 2002) is an ad-hoc network where every sensor node either broadcasts the message to all other nodes (using an endless message repetition preventing mechanism) or uses a routing mechanism to forward the message to the upload station through a series of other sensor nodes used as 'hops'(Kamble et al. 2007). Once the upload station receives the message it is uploaded to the External Network. Such architecture is useful in applications where sensors are distributed in an unplanned manner (e.g. battlefield sensor network deployed from an aircraft) and messages can be sent unreliably with no confirmation of the delivery from the Upload Station (although the acknowledgement system can be implemented in this architecture if the routing mechanism allows that) (HINT Project 2010). All battery operated sensors (Slaves) attempt to connect to the Master device at a pre-programmed interval. The Master device uses an acknowledgement mechanism to guarantee the delivery of a single

Figure 4. Wireless Sensor Network Architecture

Classic WSN

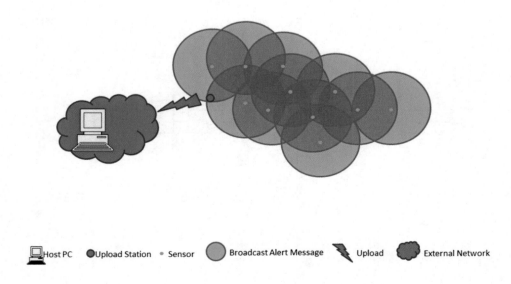

Host PC   ●Upload Station   • Sensor   Broadcast Alert Message   Upload   External Network

packet or an entire multi-packet transmission (depending on the configuration and packet type). Each Slave repeats the transmission attempt a pre-programmed number of times if an acknowledgement was not received. Repeaters are used to extend the coverage area of the network by forwarding each received packet to the Master (or other Repeater) and forwarding acknowledgements back to Sensors.

All devices using the radio link utilise a simple collision avoidance mechanism with a back-off system similar to Pure-Aloha Protocol (Abramson, 1970). Here every node listens to determine if the radio carrier is busy prior to a transmission attempt. If the carrier is sensed as busy then a node backs off for a random period of time before another transmission attempt. The main advantage of this architecture is the simplicity of communication between devices as no routing tables need to be maintained, even though the delivery of specific (user pre-defined) data packets can be confirmed by the acknowledgement mechanism. Thanks to this simplicity the radio-handling part of the software can be implemented within the limited code space and run efficiently on many Resource Limited Devices. However, this architecture is not ideal in environments, where Repeaters and Masters cannot be provided with a fixed power source. The other disadvantage is that as more slaves are introduced to the network performance degrades. The simplicity of the collision avoidance mechanism inhibits the use of many slaves because slaves share a common frequency channel for transmission.

Authentication and Encryption in IWSNs

Infrastructure WSNs experience common issues related to the use of modulated radio frequency spectrum (radio waves) as the communication medium: Eavesdropping is possible on any wireless link using virtually any radio transceiver tuned to a given frequency with the ability to demodulate the signal. The architecture assumes that the link between the Master and the Host is secure. The Repeaters are used only to receive and forward data packets, without processing them and act as radio range extenders. Repeaters will not perform any active role in the security mechanism. The only parties requiring mutual authentication and secured (encrypted) communication channel are the Master and the Slave. Since the encryption and decryption mechanism must be implemented on the Slave device, choosing such a mechanism must involve consideration of the limitationss. Ideally, the Master device will have an always-on, secured link with a Host (server) and this Host device can perform all the computationally heavy encryption and decryption-related calculations. In other words, the master can offload all computationally heavy tasks to a back-end server and accept returned values. This permits the processing power of the master device to be used to handle service requests from several slave devices, rather than becoming occupied with computations associated with authentication and encryption.

Resource Limited Devices Security Issues

The constraints imposed on possible implementations of security systems for RLDs can be categorised as Central Processor Unit (CPU) limitations, memory limitations, power consumption and cost barriers. The main CPU constraint in resource-limited devices is obviously the limited processing power of the processor. Passive RFID transponders (powered by an external interrogator) with a very limited number of logic gates on the circuit may be only capable of performing simple logical operations with one-bit values. More powerful embedded devices may be using 8-bit CPUs for example the Intel 8051 derivative nRF9E5 clocked at 12MHz, which is able to execute only 750,000 operations per second (assuming that 50% of operations require two CPU cycles and the remaining require one). The number of operations per second is not the only constraint relating to the processor. Another issue related to microcontrollers is the word size. The most commonly used cryptographic standards were designed to be implemented either in hardware (e.g. the first proposals of the Data Encryption Standard - DES (Federal Information Processing Standards 1993)) or more flexible using software. However, the majority of standards assume that 32-bit CPUs will be used, thus their mathematical basis and implementation is commonly optimized to use 32-bit (e.g. the Rijndael cipher (Daemen & Rijmen 1999)) or even 64-bit word. 8-bit microcontrollers would be forced to perform numerous instructions to handle 32-bit numbers manipulation, e.g. it takes approximately 35 CPU operations to multiply two 32-bit numbers on the 8051 8-bit CPU (Vault Information Services 2009).

Low-cost passive Electronic Product Code (EPC) RFID tags can have as little as 104 bits of non-volatile memory (EPCGlobal 2008) and may not even contain any Random-Access Memory. More advanced tags however, may be equipped with 1-2KB of memory. Microcontrollers are typically equipped with no more than 64KB memory, but this amount can be subject to limitations also due to 8-bit addressing issues causing slow access to some parts of the memory. Heavyweight cryptographic techniques using large keys (even 2048-bit in some RSA implementations) cannot be implemented in resource-limited device environments not only due to the amount of memory needed but also due to slow memory access times and limited read/write lifecycle.

NRF9E5 PROCESSOR AND SECURITY

The nRF9E5 single chip system uses an 8-bit microprocessor with an instruction set compatible with the industry standard 8051 processor. The instruction timing differs from the industry standard: each instruction uses 4 to 20 clock cycles instead of 12 to 48 in the standard. The hardware specification of the chip (Nordic Semiconductors 2009b) allows utilizing a 4-20MHz crystal oscillator to generate clocking signal on the circuit (shared by microcontroller, AD converter and radio transceiver). The crystal oscillator can be started and stopped as requested by software. While it is stopped, nRF9E5 uses the internal low power 4KHz RC oscillator which runs continuously (as long as 1.8V of power is supplied) and ensures that vital functions such as the wake-up timer are functioning even in deep power saving modes.

The microcontroller's architecture is 8-bit: each machine language opcode (operation code) is a single 8-bit value, which allows for 256 different instruction codes. Most of 8051's registers are 8-bit values, e.g. the Accumulator, each of the Register Banks. There are several special cases where a given register is referred to as 16-bit (such as the three Timers), but in fact these registers are addressed as two separate 8-bit registers often referred to as High and Low indicating which part of the 16-bit value they hold. The only truly 16-bit values that the 8051 handles are the Program Counter (PC) indicating the address of the next instruction to be executed and Data Pointer (DPTR) used for memory addressing. The CPU is only capable of performing basic mathematical operations on two 8-bit numbers at each cycle. There is no additional hardware support for calculation of numbers larger than 8-bit or any decryption/encryption coprocessors. In consequence manipulation of larger numbers requires numerous 8-bit calculations, for example a multiplication of two 16-bit numbers requires 9 CPU instructions. The 8-bit word size, relatively low CPU clock frequency and the lack of mathematical hardware coprocessors in the nRF9E5 narrow the area of possible security protocols and algorithms which can be successfully implemented to those that do not require exhaustive calculations (required by most of the Asymmetric Cryptography techniques) and those that are optimized for 8-bit values. In consequence, only lightweight authentication protocols and lightweight encryption algorithms are reviewed and analysed in this dissertation.

nRF9E5 Memory Structure and Security

The nRF9E5 microcontroller has 256 bytes of Internal Data Memory used as a RAM with fast access, 128 Special Function Registers (one byte each) used to set different operating modes of the CPU and the Radio Frequency Transceiver. Additionally, it contains 4 kilobytes of external on-chip RAM. The memory uses Harvard Architecture and is organized into six different memory spaces (see Erreur ! Source du renvoi introuvable.). It provides 128-bytes of directly addressable DATA RAM (8052 compatible) but may also be used to hold IDATA-addressed variables. The next 128 bytes are the IDATA memory area which is accessible through indirect addressing and effectively interleaves with the Special Function Register (SFR) which in turn is directly accessed. The entire 4K of memory (addresses above 0FFh) is accessible as an external XDATA memory but this area is shared with the CODE memory, so the use of XDATA variables effectively limits the available code space. The first of 256 bytes of XDATA can be addressed in paged mode and in this configuration, it is referred to as PDATA. Additionally, there is a small 512-byte ROM area located on-chip and containing bootstrap program executed automatically after power on or reset. The bootstrap loads the user program into on-chip 4K RAM from the off-chip external EEPROM memory required for operation. The manufacturer of the chip did not include any options to extend the RAM size above the 4KB - it is not possible to connect any additional external memory directly to the CPU pins. Additionally, the bootstrap program in ROM cannot be updated. The only memory size expanding option is to use an external EEPROM memory (generic 25320 with SPI) attached through one of the GPIO pins and interfacing through a common SPI bus. Accessing external memory through the SPI bus has major consequence on the performance of the CPU as each of the SPI read/write (performed byte-by-byte) operations takes several processor cycles. The CPU is not able to perform additional tasks while in this process. One of the major limitations is the fact that external EEPROM cannot be used to expand the possible program size. In consequence, the program code size is always limited to 4KB – the bootstrap program will ignore anything above 0FFFh address in EEPROM when loading the program. We provide a solution to overcome this limitation with the support of 8051 dedicated software Assembly Language Linker. Possible security implementations have to be filtered through the following constraints imposed by nRF9E5:

- **Limited Code/RAM Space:** The CODE and XDATA space are shared in this CPU's architecture, so variables and constants allocated here limit the overall code space. The existing Infrastructure WSN programs already occupy a vast amount of the code/RAM space (HINT Project 2010), so the algorithms/protocols have to be implementable with a minimum machine code size and there must be a limited need for variable memory allocation. In case the solutions used to overcome the memory limitations fail, the space for the machine code may be limited to approximately 200 bytes only (assuming that for an existing sensor program already occupies 95% of the available code space).
- **Extremely Slow Access to the External Non-Volatile Memory:** The reference platform utilizes 32Kb 25320 generic EEPROM. The amount of the data which needs to be accessed from the external EEPROM memory and the frequency of the access must be limited. This imposes restrictions on possible encryption key sizes and the usage of non-volatile protocol-specific data.

- **Hacking the EEPROM:** The EEPROM memory can be read by freely available EEPROM programmers, thus in the case of a physical access attack the amount of information disclosed cannot compromise the security of the entire system. This forces solutions without global pre-shared encryption keys. An example of a physical access attack compromising the security of the entire WSN using the TinySec Protocol (Karlof et al. 2004) was described in (Hartung et al. 2005).

Radio Transceiver and Security

The nRF9E5 single chip microcontroller integrates a nRF905 (Nordic Semiconductors 2009a) compatible Radio Frequency (RF) transceiver operating on 433/868/915MHz bands (sub-1GHz). The transceiver consists of a fully integrated frequency synthesizer, a power amplifier, a modulator and receiver chain with demodulator. The modulation type used in nRF905 is Gaussian Frequency Shift Keying (GFSK) with a data rate of 100kbps. The data bits are encoded and decoded using Manchester Encoding/Decoding and the effective symbol rate is limited to 50kbps (one symbol per two clock signals); however, no scrambling on the microcontroller is needed.

The transceiver uses SPI bus for reprogramming and data input/output. It is equipped with a circuit able to calculate the Cyclic Redundancy Check (CRC) checksum of the incoming or outgoing data packets. Transmitting (TX) and Receiving (RX) addresses can be 1 to 4-byte long and the data payload length may vary from 1 to 32 bytes.

Each data packet contains the following (see Figure 5):

- **Preamble:** Predefined 10-bit sequence used to adjust the receiver for optimal performance.
- **TX Address:** Programmable recipient's address with a length of 1 to 4 bytes.
- **Payload:** User data, length of the field configurable within 1 to 32 bytes range.
- **CRC:** 8 or 16-bit CRC checksum.

During the TX mode the packet is assembled automatically by the transceiver once the Payload and TX address is supplied – the CRC is calculated and added with a Preamble. After a transmission, the RF transceiver sets the Data Ready (DR) pin high, so the microprocessor can be notified of a finished transmission. In RX mode, the radio is used to listen for incoming transmissions and if one occurs the Carrier Detect (CD) pin is set high. After this action, the nRF905 analyses the Address field and discards the packet if it is destined for a different address or accepts it if the address matches, sets the Address Match (AM) pin high, reads in the payload to the buffer and verifies the CRC checksum. The way the RF transceiver handles incoming packet addressing (automatic packet discarding when the address does not match) imposes constraints on the possibilities of protection against traceability (ID disclosure related) attacks (Juels 2006). In consequence in a situation where the communication is initiated by the Master device the packet will need to hold a broadcast address and all Slaves should be able to temporarily

Figure 5. NRF9E5 packet structure

Preamble	TX Address	Payload	CRC

reconfigure themselves to accept such packets. A frequent usage of broadcast addressing may negatively impact the performance of the entire network (Ni et al. 1999). Another solution would require Slaves to ignore address mismatch and examine each packet which again reduces the performance of the network. The maximum Payload size of 32 bytes seems large but the bandwidth of only 50kbps has to be taken into consideration too. In the presence of multiple devices operating on the same frequency the transmission time has to be limited to avoid network congestion. It has to be noted also that the entire NRF9E5 consumes the highest possible amount of power during radio transceiver operations (up to 30mA at 10dBm output power comparing to 2.2mA when only the 8051 CPU is active), thus large data transfer, although possible, can severely degrade the sensor's lifetime. In consequence of the above limitations, the security system must impose low radio bandwidth requirements.

Code Banking on the nRF9E5

The major limitations of the reference platform nRF9E5 chip are the code space size and the lack of any coprocessors enhancing mathematical calculations. While the latter can be overcome by using less CPU intensive security protocols and algorithms, the program size and RAM limitations are hard to overcome without changing the entire microcontroller platform. A software solution to this issue using the concept of Code Banking with the native support of the 8051 Assembler Linker (similar solutions are available from KEIL (ARM Ltd. 2009a) and Raisonance (Raisonance SAS 2010) Integrated Development Environments) is proposed below.

The origin of the Code Banking concept (ARM Ltd. 2009b) comes from the 16-bit memory addressing limitation of the 8051 CPU. Due to the addressing bit width, the maximum memory which can be allocated is limited to 64Kb. The Code Banking mechanism permits and increases in the Code memory size up to 1MB (KEIL linker) or 4MB (Raisonance linker) by splitting the program into a Common Area section and a number of memory banks (see Figure 6). The Common Area (of a user-defined size s) and one of the Code Banks is loaded at a given time, so the microcontroller can effectively "see" and address 64KB of the Code memory. If a function makes a call to another function the linker generates a code performing that switch, called a Bridge. All bridges are located in the Common Area which remains the same regardless of which Code Bank is currently used. The full description of the assembly language routines performing bank switches and limitations such as interrupt vector handling are outside the scope of the document and can be found in Raisonance and KEIL linkers' documentation (ARM Ltd. 2009b).

A typical hardware design scenario permits connecting the memory directly to the CPUs I/O ports. In this case a bank switch process would only require changing the input/output port number to access different blocks of memory, where additional code banks are located. The Common Area must be duplicated across all memory blocks so it would still be accessible in the same form after changing the I/O ports.

In case of the reference platform with the nRF9E5 microcontroller, where it is not possible to connect any additional memory directly to the CPU, the Code Banking mechanism can be utilized to overcome the Code space limitation but in a manner different to the original design (see Figure 7). Instead of using the directly attached memory chip an external EEPROM connected to the SPI bus can be utilized to hold additional code banks. However, the I/O pin switching routine has to be replaced with a function that overwrites the code bank space in the on-chip RAM with the content of this bank located on the external EEPROM. Every bank switch will be a very slow process since the entire code bank binary file (2-3Kb) must be read through the SPI bus from the external EEPROM (see Figure 8). Experiments have shown that it takes 65 milliseconds to load a Code Bank of 2Kb in size (HINT Project, 2010).

Figure 6. Code Banking Layout

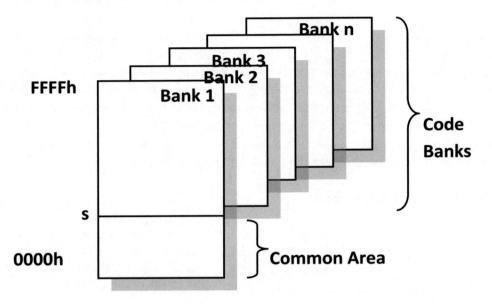

Figure 7. 8051 with 156Kb EEPROM attached to ports P0-P3

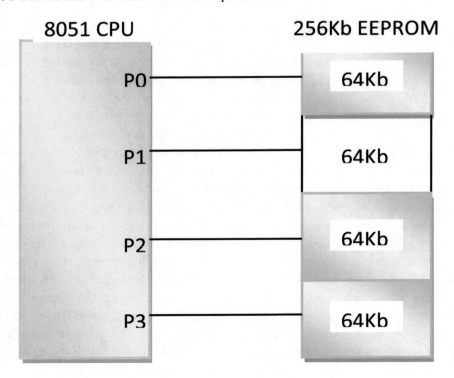

Figure 8. nRF9E5 code banking with an external SPI-accessed EEPROM

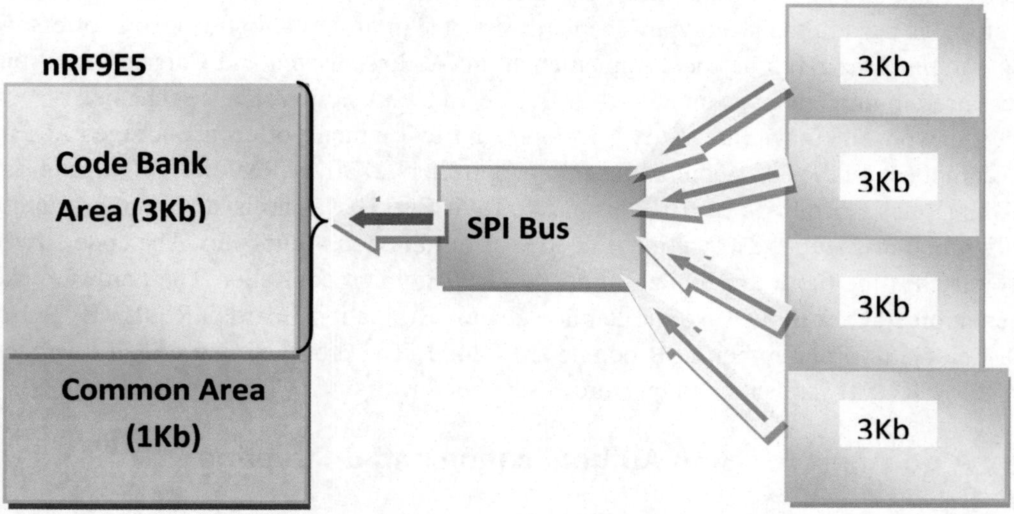

Despite the negative effect on the microcontroller's performance this mechanism permits the effective expansion of the available code space above 4Kb without any hardware modifications in the existing reference platform. This would allow providing a relatively large code space for the implementation of the security mechanism. The failure of this concept would result in significant code space limitations for the security algorithms and force the usage of slow –access EEPROM-located variables.

LIGHTWEIGHT AUTHENTICATION PROTOTYPE

The main development platform used is the Nordic Semiconductors nRF9E5 microcontroller that is used for both master and slave devices. The nRF9E5 has limited resources and this has implications for the implementation of authentication and encryption on these devices. This limitation is somewhat eased by (a) offloading computationally heavy tasks from the master to a back-end server, allowing the master to more effectively handle service requests from slave devices and (b) by improving code memory space using code banking. Neither of these enhancements has been used in this project. Since a vastly scaled down communication and radio protocol is used, the inherent memory of the nRF9E5 is sufficient to effectively run the security mechanisms. Variables that would otherwise be serviced from a back-end server have been hard-coded into master and slave, negating the use of the back-end server in the developed prototype. However, in a field implementation of secure sensor networking, where many slaves communicate with a master, it would be necessary to use a back-end server and overcome the code space limitations through code banking. Considering the limitations of the devices, a C language implementation was chosen instead of 8051 native Assembly code to allow faster porting to other platforms.

The main limitation of the nRF9E5 microcontroller in terms of the implementation was the maximum code size of only 4 kilobytes. The prototype was implemented to fit under this barrier. However, some protocol simplifications were needed to achieve small code space. The amount of RAM (256 bytes for both Data and Idata) was sufficient but almost entirely used by both master and slave prototypes. The radio transceiver embedded on nRF9E5 requires pre-configuration and manual handling of the OSI Model Data Link and upper layers. This generates another code space requirement; thus a simplified radio protocol is used in the prototype. The hardware design of the radio transceiver offers two useful tools that simplify the radio protocol implementation: Address Match and Carrier Detect bits. These tools were used to implement a simple Listen-Before-Talk collision avoidance scheme.

There are two well known Integrated Development Environments offering packaged Assembler and ANSI-C compilers for the 8051-compatible microcontrollers: KEIL (ARM Ltd., 2009a) and Raisonance RC51 IDEs (Raisonance SAS, 2010). Raisonance RKit Eval51 was utilised as it offers an 8051 compiler fully functional with the exception of a code size limited to 4 kilobytes. The code size limitation perfectly matches the hardware limitation of the nRF9E5 microcontroller. The hardware used in the implementation stage were two Nordic Semiconductor Evaluation Boards nRF9E5-EVBOARD with EEPROM emulator/programmer USB dongles nRF24E1. The programming dongles were controlled by the nRFPROG software supplied by Nordic Semiconductors.

Design: Algorithms for Both Authentication and Encryption

The prototype is designed to fit within 4 kilobytes of total code space available for programs on the nRF9E5 reference platform. The usage of code banking or other techniques overcoming the 4KB limitation is not considered in the prototype implementation. Instead some minor simplifications in the protocol (explained below) are used. The scope of the prototype is explained in Figure 9. The back-end database and PC Host software are outside the scope of the implementation – it will focus only on the 8-bit microcontroller code written in the C language with nRF9E5-specific radio transceiver handling functions.

The Gossamer lightweight authentication protocol was chosen to fulfil the requirement for mutual authentication between the Master and the Slave devices in Infrastructure WSN. It has proven security, low memory, computation requirements, and the expected simplicity of the implementation of all necessary mathematical operations on 8051-compatible CPU. The original design of the Protocol is simplified for the prototype implementation purposes in the following areas:

Figure 9. The Scope of the Implementation part

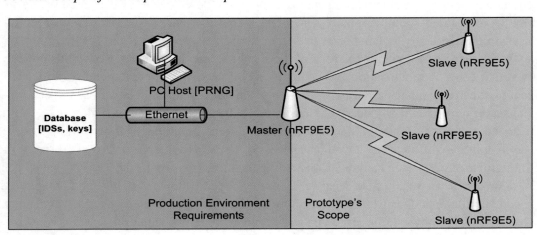

- The keys and IDS are not stored persistently on the Slave device due to code space overhead imposed by the EEPROM read/write routines. Upon each power loss, these values will be reset to the initial ones.
- **Master Side:** Random numbers n1 and n2 will be replaced by hard-coded values for experimentation purposes. The IDS of a sample Slave will also be hard-coded, so the back-end database will not be needed in the simplified model.
- **Slave Side:** In the original Gossamer Protocol, the Slave device sends the value D but there is no acknowledgement that D has been received and verified by the Master. The Slave then updates its keys and IDS and saves the previous IDS and key values. In a subsequent round, if the slave cannot verify value C, in which case authentication of the master will not have been a success, the slave can roll back to the previous keys and IDS values. This de-synchronization attack prevention mechanism has not been implemented in the simplified protocol.

Figure 10 shows the full round of the Gossamer authentication protocol adapted to the needs of the Infrastructure WSN. The main difference was the removal of the 'Hello' message as in IWSN the Slave device (Tag equivalent in standard Gossamer specification) initiates the communication. The Scalable Encryption Algorithm (SEA) was chosen as the encryption mechanism. SEA (96, 8) mode was used, meaning that the block and the key size of 96-bits and 8-bit word matching the word size on the nRF9E5. The choice of the algorithm can be justified by the lack of proven weaknesses in the algorithm and the fact that the algorithm can be implemented with a very limited code space by sacrificing the throughput of the encryption (number of words that can be encrypted over a given period of time). The reduced throughput of the algorithm is not a significant issue in the context of IWSN, where the amount of data transferred is very small in most cases.

Another advantage of this algorithm is its scalability which permits increasing key and word sizes to 192 bits without major modifications of the code. This can be applied in cases where the 96-bit security is not regarded as strong enough. Since the Gossamer authentication protocol exchanges two new 96-bits keys at each round, one of these keys can be used as an encryption key for the SEA (96,8) algorithm during one communication session between the Master and the Slave. Both the Master and the Slave programs were written in two separate modules: Master.c and Slave.c. Each of the modules contains Initialization (UART timers, radio), Utilities Block (UART handling, SPI handling), Radio Handling Block (TX and RX), Gossamer functions and SEA functions.

The Gossamer Protocol implementation uses the main gossamerMaster and gossamerSlave loops. All 96-bit values are implemented as an array of 12 unsigned characters (one byte each) in Big-endian (Most Significant Bit first) notation. The IDS, ID, K1, K2 and Pi values are initialized on the startup of the main loop, thus on every power-loss they are reset to the hard-coded values. The XOR two 96-bit numbers function loops through all elements in the array and performs a bitwise exclusive OR operation on them one-by-one.

The bitRotation function performs circular bit rotation of a 96-bit number by a Modulo96 of a second number passed as a second parameter. This function uses four sub-functions to perform the bit rotation:

Figure 10. Gossamer Protocol Adapted to the Infrastructure WSN

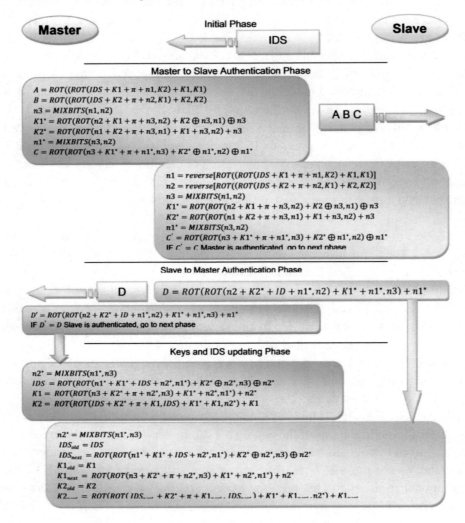

- **getModulo96:** Returns Modulo96 of a 96-bit number passed in the array of 12 one-byte elements. The function uses a command and conquer approach. Starting from the lowest element a Modulo96 of each element (split into two 4-bit numbers and multiplied by 256) is calculated one-by-one and added to the overall result. At each iteration, the overall result is reduced Modulo96.
- **bitShift:** Performs circular bit-shift (up to 7 places) of each element in the array in both directions. Depending on the direction the remainder of the shift is appended to the lower or upper element.
- **indexShift:** Rotates the elements of the array by up to 11 positions left or right. It takes advantage of the arrayReverse function and a formula assuming that the array is split into two sub-arrays A and B (A.B), where the size of array A is the number of places the elements are to be rotated. The formula is as follows:

B.A = reverse(reverse(A).reverse(B)).

- **arrayReverse:** Reverses the elements in the array (array[beginning] becomes array[end] and so on).

The bitRotation function calculates the Modulo96 of the first argument (array to be rotated by) and then analyses the result to verify if bitShift and indexShift functions need to be called and calls them accrodingly. The MixBits function implements the Gossamer author's recommendation shown in Figure 11.

```
Z = MixBits (X, Y)
Z = X
FOR counter = 0 to 32
Z = (Z>>1) + Z + Z + Y
ENDFOR
```

The function uses two arrays passed as parameters and a temporary array returned with the result. Functions described above (additionMod96 and bitShift) are utilized. The SEA (96, 8) implementation uses a word size of 8-bits (unsigned char) with a block and key size of 96-bits. Both are passed as an argument in a form of a 12-element array of unsigned characters. The main components of the SEA implementation are the following functions: cryptographic round, the key round, the S-Box, the bit-rotation, the word-rotation and the main SEA wrap-up function. In this prototype, the key used in encryption will be either k1 or k2 updated by the Gossamer function at each authentication round. Per SEA author's suggestions the S-Box can be applied bitwise to any 3 elements of a block-half currently being processed (for blocks of 96-bits). Since there are 6 one-byte elements in each half of the block the S-Box can be applied on two different set of words. (Standaert et al. 2006) suggested a function ('i' equals 0 or 1) shown in Figure 12.

```
void seaSBOX (unsigned char data *block, unsigned char i)
{
block[3*i] = (block[3*i+2] && block[3*i+1]) ^ block[3*i];
block[3*i+1] = (block[3*i+2] && block[3*i]) ^ block[3*i+1];
block[3*i+2] = (block[3*i] || block[3*i+1]) ^ block[3*i+2];
}
```

Figure 11. MixBits Function pseudocode

```
Z = MixBits (X, Y)
Z = X
FOR counter = 0 to 32
Z = (Z>>1) + Z + Z + Y
ENDFOR
```

Figure 12. Code: SEA S-Box

```
void seaSBOX (unsigned char data *block, unsigned char i)
{
block[3*i] = (block[3*i+2] && block[3*i+1]) ^ block[3*i];
block[3*i+1] = (block[3*i+2] && block[3*i]) ^ block[3*i+1];
block[3*i+2] = (block[3*i] || block[3*i+1]) ^ block[3*i+2];
}
```

The seaWordRotation function performs circular right- or left-rotation of the block-half array elements by one place. The Gossamer indexShift function can be re-used to save the code space but this function was also implemented to make the SEA module independent and re-usable without the Gossamer functions overhead. The seaCryptRound function performs one round encryption or decryption round using left and right half of the block and one half of the key - left or right depending on the round. This function implements the following SEA equations: F_E encryption function and F_D decryption function (below).

Fe (Li, Ri, KeyHalf) = RightWordRot (Li) XOR bitRotation (sbox(Ri+ KeyHalf))

Fd (Li, Ri, KeyHalf) = LeftWordRot (Li XOR bitRotation (sbox(Ri+ KeyHalf)))

The function takes advantage of previously described word rotation, bit rotation and substitution box functions. The seaKeyRound function performs one round of the key scheduling. These rounds are interleaved with encryption/decryption rounds. Each key round performs the following key scheduling function.

Fk(KLi-1,KRi-1,Ci) <=> KRi = KLi-1 XOR RightWordRot(bitRot(sbox((KRi-1)+Ci)))

The function takes advantage of previously described word rotation, bit rotation and substitution box functions. The main SEA(96, 8) function takes two 12-byte parameters: block and key. (Standaert et al. 2006) advised that the minimum safe number of encryption/decryption rounds can be calculated using the following formula:

$$\frac{3n}{4} + 1 + 2\left(\frac{n}{2b} + \left(\frac{b}{2}\right)\right), where\, n = plaintext\, size\left(96\,bits\right); b = word\, size\left(8\,bits\right)$$

The odd result in case of SEA (96, 8) is 93. The main function runs interleaved encryption (or decryption) and key scheduling round 46 times. After the initial 46 rounds the key halves are swapped and another further 46 rounds are executed. After the 92nd round another one encryption/decryption round runs - the key is in its final state already. It must be noted that this final state of the key is identical to its initial state, thus no additional memory locations are needed to store a temporary key at each round. After the last round the block halves need to be swapped and the execution of the algorithm stops.

The experimental implementation takes Gossamer K1 key as an encryption key for the SEA algorithm. After a successful authentication round the Master encrypts a message using K1 and sends it to the Slave. The Slave decrypts the message using K1 and outputs it to the UART.

EVALUATION

The system was tested using the same hardware and software as in the implementation stage. During the testing stage two nRF9E5-EVBOARD development boards with nRF24E1 EEPROM programmers were used. The EEPROM programmers were connected over the USB link and the UART input/outputs from the development boards were connected through serial cables to the RS-232 ports on the development PC running Microsoft Windows XP Operating System. Since the RC51 compiler used does not offer nRF9E5-compatible debugger, the debugging was performed on-device using manually written debug messages sent to the UART I/O.

One Round Step-By-Step Test

The goal here is to verify the proper functioning of all core functions used by the Gossamer Authentication Protocol and the SEA encryption/decryption algorithm. Both the Master and the Slave programs are pre-configured with a Gossamer Protocol test data and set to output the data at each of the modifications so that the result can be verified with a 'paper-test' (manual calculation). The integer-to-ascii (itoa) function will be employed to output the data to the UART in a human-readable form. The SEA algorithm was tested step-by-step due to a large number of rounds. Instead, a result of the entire encryption and decryption loop is displayed (see Figure 13, Figure 14 and Figure 15).

unsigned char idata Pi[12] = { 0x32, 0x43, 0xF6, 0xA8, 0x88, 0x5A, 0x30, 0x8D, 0x31, 0x31, 0x98, 0xA2 };

unsigned char idata IDS[12] = { 0x01, 0x01, 0x01, 0x01, 0x01, 0x01, 0x01, 0x01, 0x01, 0x01, 0x01, 0x01 };

unsigned char idata ID[12] = { 0x44, 0x44, 0x44, 0x44, 0x44, 0x44, 0x44, 0x44, 0x44, 0x44, 0x44, 0x44 };

unsigned char idata k1[12] = { 0x10, 0x10, 0x10, 0x10, 0x10, 0x10, 0x10, 0x10, 0x10, 0x10, 0x10, 0x10 };

unsigned char idata k2[12] = { 0x20, 0x20, 0x20, 0x20, 0x20, 0x20, 0x20, 0x20, 0x20, 0x20, 0x20, 0x20 };

unsigned char idata n1[12] = { 0x22, 0x22, 0xFF, 0xFF, 0x22, 0x22, 0x22, 0x22, 0x22, 0x22, 0x22, 0x22 };

unsigned char idata n2[12] = { 0x23, 0x23, 0x00, 0x00, 0x23, 0x23, 0x23, 0x23, 0x23, 0x23, 0x23, 0x23 };

unsigned char idata Pi[12] = { 0x32, 0x43, 0xF6, 0xA8, 0x88, 0x5A, 0x30, 0x8D, 0x31, 0x31, 0x98, 0xA2 };

unsigned char idata IDS[12] = { 0x01, 0x01, 0x01, 0x01, 0x01, 0x01, 0x01, 0x01, 0x01, 0x01, 0x01, 0x01 };

unsigned char idata ID[12] = { 0x44, 0x44, 0x44, 0x44, 0x44, 0x44, 0x44, 0x44, 0x44, 0x44, 0x44, 0x44 };

unsigned char idata k1[12] = { 0x10, 0x10, 0x10, 0x10, 0x10, 0x10, 0x10, 0x10, 0x10, 0x10, 0x10, 0x10 };

unsigned char idata k2[12] = { 0x20, 0x20, 0x20, 0x20, 0x20, 0x20, 0x20, 0x20, 0x20, 0x20, 0x20, 0x20 };

Figure 13. Code: Master Side Test Data

```
unsigned char idata Pi[12] = { 0x32, 0x43, 0xF6, 0xA8, 0x88, 0x5A, 0x30, 0x8D,
0x31, 0x31, 0x98, 0xA2 };
unsigned char idata IDS[12] = { 0x01, 0x01, 0x01, 0x01, 0x01, 0x01, 0x01, 0x01,
0x01, 0x01, 0x01, 0x01 };
unsigned char idata ID[12] = { 0x44, 0x44, 0x44, 0x44, 0x44, 0x44, 0x44, 0x44,
0x44, 0x44, 0x44, 0x44 };
unsigned char idata k1[12] = { 0x10, 0x10, 0x10, 0x10, 0x10, 0x10, 0x10, 0x10,
0x10, 0x10, 0x10, 0x10 };
unsigned char idata k2[12] = { 0x20, 0x20, 0x20, 0x20, 0x20, 0x20, 0x20, 0x20,
0x20, 0x20, 0x20, 0x20 };
unsigned char idata n1[12] = { 0x22, 0x22, 0xFF, 0xFF, 0x22, 0x22, 0x22, 0x22,
0x22, 0x22, 0x22, 0x22 };
unsigned char idata n2[12] = { 0x23, 0x23, 0x00, 0x00, 0x23, 0x23, 0x23, 0x23,
0x23, 0x23, 0x23, 0x23 };
```

Figure 14. Code: Slave Side Test Data

```
unsigned char idata Pi[12] = { 0x32, 0x43, 0xF6, 0xA8, 0x88, 0x5A, 0x30, 0x8D,
0x31, 0x31, 0x98, 0xA2 };
unsigned char idata IDS[12] = { 0x01, 0x01, 0x01, 0x01, 0x01, 0x01, 0x01, 0x01,
0x01, 0x01, 0x01, 0x01 };
unsigned char idata ID[12] = { 0x44, 0x44, 0x44, 0x44, 0x44, 0x44, 0x44, 0x44,
0x44, 0x44, 0x44, 0x44 };
unsigned char idata k1[12] = { 0x10, 0x10, 0x10, 0x10, 0x10, 0x10, 0x10, 0x10,
0x10, 0x10, 0x10, 0x10 };
unsigned char idata k2[12] = { 0x20, 0x20, 0x20, 0x20, 0x20, 0x20, 0x20, 0x20,
0x20, 0x20, 0x20, 0x20 };
```

After the Gossamer round, the Master uses the modified key k1 to encrypt a message (temp array) and sends it to the Slave. After successful transmission, the Slave uses modified k1 to decrypt the message and displays it. The test was split into several stages to allow better readability.

Stage 1: Messages A and B creation (Master side - below).

$$A = ROT\big(\big(ROT\big(IDS + K1 + \pi + n1, K2\big) + K1, K1\big)$$

$$B = ROT\big(\big(ROT\big(IDS + K2 + \pi + n2, K1\big) + K2, K2\big)$$

Stage 2: N1 and N2 extraction from messages A and B (Slave side).

$$n1 = reversedA$$

$$n2 = reversedB$$

Stage 3: n3, k1next and k2next creation (Master side)

$$n3 = MIXBITS\big(n1, n2\big)$$

$$K1^* = ROT\big(ROT\big(n2 + K1 + \pi + n3, n2\big) + K2 \oplus n3, n1\big) \oplus n3$$

$$K2^* = ROT\big(ROT\big(n1 + K2 + \pi + n3, n1\big) + K1 + n3, n2\big) + n3$$

Figure 15. Gossamer messages A and B creation (Master)

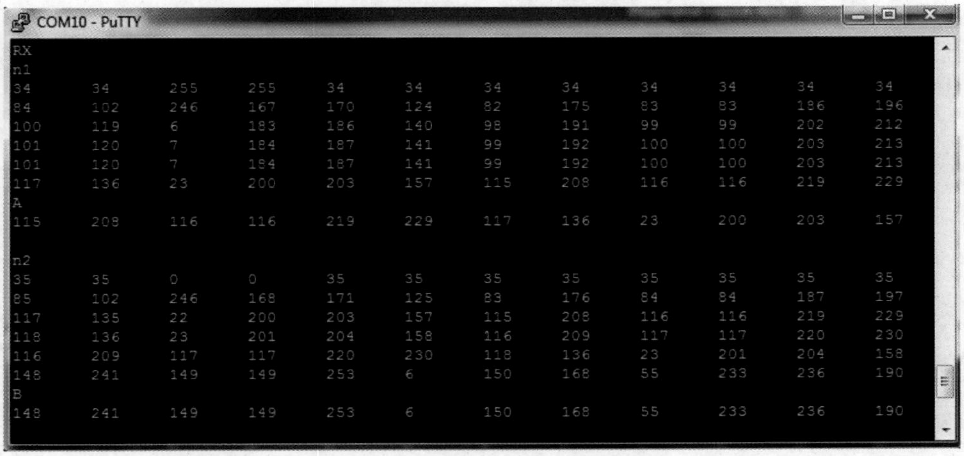

Figure 16. Gossamer n1 and n2 random numbers extraction (Slave)

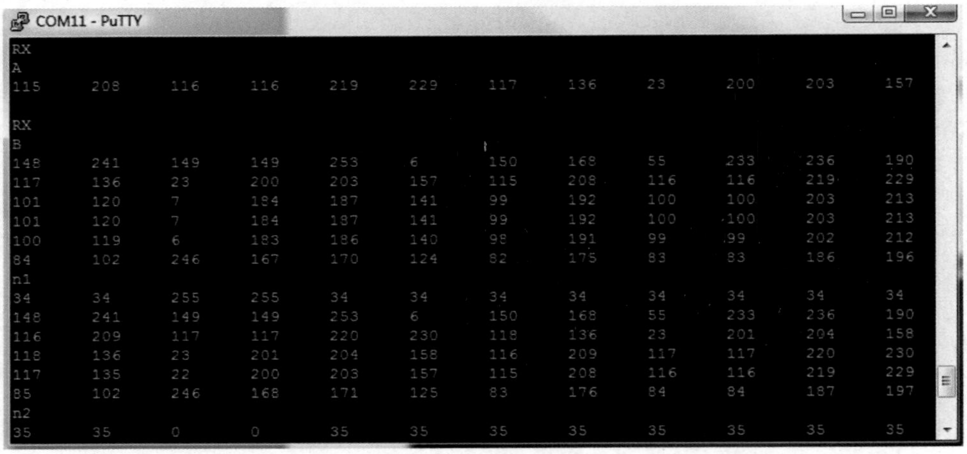

Stage 4: n3, k1next and k2next creation (Slave side)

$$n3 = MIXBITS\left(n1, n2\right)$$

$$K1^* = ROT\left(ROT\left(n2 + K1 + \pi + n3, n2\right) + K2 \oplus n3, n1\right) \oplus n3$$

$$K2^* = ROT\left(ROT\left(n1 + K2 + \pi + n3, n1\right) + K1 + n3, n2\right) + n3$$

Stage 5: Message C creation (Master Side)

$$n1^* = MIXBITS\left(n3, n2\right)$$

$$C = ROT\left(ROT\left(n3 + K1^* + \pi + n1^*, n3\right) + K2^* \oplus n1^*, n2\right) \oplus n1^*$$

Stage 6: Message C creation (Slave Side)

$$n1^* = MIXBITS\left(n3, n2\right)$$

$$C = ROT\left(ROT\left(n3 + K1^* + \pi + n1^*, n3\right) + K2^* \oplus n1^*, n2\right) \oplus n1^*$$

Stage 7: Message D creation (Master side)

$$D = ROT\left(ROT\left(n2 + K2^* + ID + n1^*, n2\right) + K1^* + n1^*, n3\right) + n1^*$$

Stage 8: Message D creation (Slave side)

$$D = ROT\left(ROT\left(n2 + K2^* + ID + n1^*, n2\right) + K1^* + n1^*, n3\right) + n1^*$$

Stage 9: IDS, k1 and k2 updating (Maer side)

$$n2^* = MIXBITS\left(n1^*, n3\right)$$

$$IDS = ROT\left(ROT\left(n1^* + K1^* + IDS + n2^*, n1^*\right) + K2^* \oplus n2^*, n3\right) \oplus n2^*$$

$$K1 = ROT\left(ROT\left(n3 + K2^* + \pi + n2^*, n3\right) + K1^* + n2^*, n1^*\right) + n2^*$$

$$K2 = ROT\left(ROT\left(IDS + K2^* + \pi + K1, IDS\right) + K1^* + K1, n2^*\right) + K1$$

Stage 10: IDS, k1 and k2 updating (Slave side)

$$n2^* = MIXBITS\left(n1^*, n3\right)$$

$$IDS_{old} = IDS$$

$$IDS_{next} = ROT\left(ROT\left(n1^* + K1^* + IDS + n2^*, n1^*\right) + K2^* \oplus n2^*, n3\right) \oplus n2^*$$

$$K1_{old} = K1$$

$$K1_{next} = ROT\left(ROT\left(n3 + K2^* + \pi + n2^*, n3\right) + K1^* + n2^*, n1^*\right) + n2^*$$

$$K2_{old} = K2$$

$$K2_{next} = ROT\left(ROT\left(IDS_{next} + K2^* + \pi + K1_{next}, IDS_{next}\right) + K1^* + K1_{next}, n2^*\right) + K1_{next}$$

Figure 17. Gossamer keys and IDS updating phase (Master)

Stage 11: SEA Encryption using k1 (Master side)
Stage 12: SEA Decryption using k1 (Slave side)

Long-Term Test

The goal here was to verify the proper functioning of the Gossamer Authentication Protocol and the SEA encryption/decryption algorithm using multiple values and multiple rounds. The test-Master and the test-Slave were pre-configured to loop indefinitely executing on both devices: mutual authentication between the test-Slave and the test-Master and updating values for the next round. Also on the master, it encrypts a 12-byte message using the SEA encryption algorithm (using the Gossamer key k1) and transmitting the payload to the test-Slave and on the slave, it receives the payload form the test-Master and decrypting it using the SEA decryption algorithm and the Gossamer key k1.

The test-Master used a delay function before transmitting messages over the radio to allow for better readability of the UART output. Both the test-Slave and the test-Master outputed informational messages to the UART during each loop iteration. The time to complete an iteration of the main loop in both programs was estimated at approximately 1.5 seconds. The test-Master and the test-Slave programs were left running for 7 days. It was estimated that both programs would execute approximately 403200 authentication and encryption/decryption rounds (see Figure 18 and Figure 19).

unsigned char idata Pi[12] = { 0x32, 0x43, 0xF6, 0xA8, 0x88, 0x5A, 0x30, 0x8D, 0x31, 0x31, 0x98, 0xA2 };

unsigned char idata IDS[12] = { 0x01, 0x01, 0x01, 0x01, 0x01, 0x01, 0x01, 0x01, 0x01, 0x01, 0x01, 0x01 };

unsigned char idata ID[12] = { 0x44, 0x44, 0x44, 0x44, 0x44, 0x44, 0x44, 0x44, 0x44, 0x44, 0x44, 0x44 };

unsigned char idata k1[12] = { 0x10, 0x10, 0x10, 0x10, 0x10, 0x10, 0x10, 0x10, 0x10, 0x10, 0x10, 0x10 };

unsigned char idata k2[12] = { 0x20, 0x20, 0x20, 0x20, 0x20, 0x20, 0x20, 0x20, 0x20, 0x20, 0x20, 0x20 };

unsigned char idata n1[12] = { 0x22, 0x22, 0x22, 0x22, 0x22, 0x22, 0x22, 0x22, 0x22, 0x22, 0x22, 0x22 };

unsigned char idata n2[12] = { 0x23, 0x23, 0x23, 0x23, 0x23, 0x23, 0x23, 0x23, 0x23, 0x23, 0x23, 0x23 };

unsigned char idata Pi[12]={ 0x32, 0x43, 0xF6, 0xA8, 0x88, 0x5A, 0x30, 0x8D, 0x31, 0x31, 0x98, 0xA2 };

unsigned char idata IDS[12]={ 0x01, 0x01, 0x01, 0x01, 0x01, 0x01, 0x01, 0x01, 0x01, 0x01, 0x01, 0x01 };

unsigned char idata ID[12]={ 0x44, 0x44, 0x44, 0x44, 0x44, 0x44, 0x44, 0x44, 0x44, 0x44, 0x44, 0x44 };

unsigned char idata k1[12]={ 0x10, 0x10, 0x10, 0x10, 0x10, 0x10, 0x10, 0x10, 0x10, 0x10, 0x10, 0x10 };

unsigned char idata k2[12]={ 0x20, 0x20, 0x20, 0x20, 0x20, 0x20, 0x20, 0x20, 0x20, 0x20, 0x20, 0x20 };

Figure 18. Code: Master Initial Values

```
unsigned char idata Pi[12] = { 0x32, 0x43, 0xF6, 0xA8, 0x88, 0x5A, 0x30, 0x8D, 0x31, 0x31, 0x98, 0xA2 };
unsigned char idata IDS[12] = { 0x01, 0x01, 0x01, 0x01, 0x01, 0x01, 0x01, 0x01, 0x01, 0x01, 0x01, 0x01 };
unsigned char idata ID[12] = { 0x44, 0x44, 0x44, 0x44, 0x44, 0x44, 0x44, 0x44, 0x44, 0x44, 0x44, 0x44 };
unsigned char idata k1[12] = { 0x10, 0x10, 0x10, 0x10, 0x10, 0x10, 0x10, 0x10, 0x10, 0x10, 0x10, 0x10 };
unsigned char idata k2[12] = { 0x20, 0x20, 0x20, 0x20, 0x20, 0x20, 0x20, 0x20, 0x20, 0x20, 0x20, 0x20 };
unsigned char idata n1[12] = { 0x22, 0x22, 0x22, 0x22, 0x22, 0x22, 0x22, 0x22, 0x22, 0x22, 0x22, 0x22 };
unsigned char idata n2[12] = { 0x23, 0x23, 0x23, 0x23, 0x23, 0x23, 0x23, 0x23, 0x23, 0x23, 0x23, 0x23 };
```

Figure 19. Code: Slave Initial Values

```
unsigned char idata Pi[12] = { 0x32, 0x43, 0xF6, 0xA8, 0x88, 0x5A, 0x30, 0x8D, 0x31, 0x31, 0x98, 0xA2 };
unsigned char idata IDS[12] = { 0x01, 0x01, 0x01, 0x01, 0x01, 0x01, 0x01, 0x01, 0x01, 0x01, 0x01, 0x01 };
unsigned char idata ID[12] = { 0x44, 0x44, 0x44, 0x44, 0x44, 0x44, 0x44, 0x44, 0x44, 0x44, 0x44, 0x44 };
unsigned char idata k1[12] = { 0x10, 0x10, 0x10, 0x10, 0x10, 0x10, 0x10, 0x10, 0x10, 0x10, 0x10, 0x10 };
unsigned char idata k2[12] = { 0x20, 0x20, 0x20, 0x20, 0x20, 0x20, 0x20, 0x20, 0x20, 0x20, 0x20, 0x20 };
```

After the Gossamer round, the Master uses the modified key k1 to encrypt a message (temp array) and send to the Slave. After successful transmission, the Slave will use modified k1 to decrypt the message and display it. Both the test-Master and the test-Slave were running continuously for 6 days and 23 hours and successfully executed approximately 400 000 mutual authentications and encryption/decryption rounds. The UART output was periodically monitored and no abnormalities were discovered.

RESULTS

The execution speed of different parts of the code was analyzed using an nRF9E5 timer interrupt set to 1 millisecond ticks and small timer handling functions. The timer was reset before entering a given block of code and the timer value was collected at the exit of the block. The full SEA (96, 8) encryption and decryption of a 12-byte block using 12-byte key and 93 rounds takes 27 milliseconds on an nRF9E5 microcontroller running at 16MHz. This gives an encryption/decryption throughput of 705 bytes per second. The full round of the Gossamer Protocol in the prototype program with no UART output (all PutString function calls removed) took 984 milliseconds on the Master side and 988 milliseconds on the Slave side. It must be noted that the Master uses a longDelay function which loops for 280ms before each transmission (TX) attempt. At this time, the Slave loops in the receiving mode (RX) waiting for messages. There are 3 TX attempts (messages A, B and C) so the total of 3*280ms can be subtracted from the total loop time on both the Master and the Slave side.

The full Gossamer loop time without the TX delay function for the master is 984ms - 3*280ms = 144ms and for the slave is 988ms - 3*280ms = 148ms. The Gossamer Protocol speed was also analyzed per major protocol stages. The message A and B creation were 2ms each (Master); message C creation was 65ms (Master and Slave); number n1 and n2 extraction: 2ms each (Slave); message D creation and verification: 3ms (Master); message D creation 2ms: (Slave) and keys and IDS update: 38ms (Master and Slave).

Additionally, the execution speed for each full round of the Gossamer Protocol (144 – 148ms) is relatively high (reflecting the limitations of nRF9E5 processing power). The simplicity of the underlying mathematical calculations would imply fast performance. In fact, the actual performance varies significantly from that expected. This may have adverse consequences on the efficiency of the communications protocol. Further code optimisation and/or native assembly code would reduce code space requirement and improve performance, but not by a magnitude large enough to justify the implementation of a software implementation of the Gossamer protocol on the reference platform. However, if another microcontroller without so strict memory limitations is used and the performance is regarded as satisfactory then the mechanism proposed can be considered for implementation. The SEA (96,8) implementation results were more promising than the Gossamer ones. As expected from an algorithm designed to be adapted easily to the native word size of the CPU, the code space footprint is very small (589 Bytes). Even when the RC51 libraries overhead is taken into consideration (552 Bytes), the total size of 1141 Bytes is just below 28% of the total code space available on the nRF9E5. SEA has not been proven to be insecure to date, thus it can be recommended for microcontroller implementations with associated low data throughput requirements. The code space requirement to implement Gossamer combined with the code space required by SEA is 3341 Bytes (2200 Bytes + 1141 Bytes) or 83% of available code space. The remainder of the code space is subsumed by simple radio functionality. Given the associated memory limitations, lack of hardware support for cryptographic primitives and the difficulty of implementing code banking with any degree of performance efficiency, the nRF9E5 cannot be recommended as a suitable platform on which to implement native authentication and encryption in security demanding wireless sensor networks. Low cost microcontroller alternatives, such as the Texas Instruments CC430 family of microcontrollers with an embedded UHF radio transceiver and hardware support for 128-bit AES encryption may be viable.

FUTURE WORK

The promising results of the SEA (96, 8) algorithm implementation (with respect to code size and no. of cycles required to complete the protocol) would suggest that there is room for further investigation in relation to key size and the associated security that this brings. It would be interesting to implement a (192, 8) version using a 24-byte key and block size. A comparative framework could then be drawn up to assess performance of both implementations.

In consequence of the significantly high code space overhead required by the software implementation of Gossamer, further study of authentication and the authentication protocols needs to emerge. The need for authentication protocols that can be implemented in terse code and negate all aspects of security breach remains a priority in the field of wireless sensor networks. There are additional implications for power consumption, battery life, signal strength and propagation distance that will have an influence on the evolution of both sensors and security protocols.

Implementation of the prototype on a larger scale (multiple sensors, single master and the back-end server) may significantly affect performance. Further research in this respect would identify performance-related issues and further test the suitability of the proposed solution for Infrastructure Wireless Sensor Networks.

Additionally, an approach that combines authentication, encryption and key exchange in a single protocol with shared keys of identical length may prove to be a useful line of academic enquiry.

CONCLUSION

Lightweight Authentication and Encryption protocols have emerged to fill the security void created by the transition from desktop to mobile environments. Fast processing and large memory has characterised desktop technologies. By contrast, mobile technologies are characterised by their small processing power and small memory. Authentication and encryption protocols designed for desktop technologies cannot be easily ported to mobile Resource Limited Devices (RLDs). The Gossamer and SEA protocols, are the most suitable of the family of ultra-lightweight security protocols for implementation on RLDs.

The algorithms are current, resistant to attacks and cryptanalysis and their design has been focused on providing solutions for resource limited devices. In addition, they can be implemented on an 8-bit platform. An augmented Gossamer protocol that incorporates elements of the SEA is presented as a possible solution to the implementation of security in networks of RLDs. A major goal of this work was to examine code space requirements of the augmented protocol's implementation (since memory is a critical resource). The target is to provide secure communications with protocols that subsume as little of the memory as possible of the RLD. Although Gossamer uses basic mathematical operations, which are easy to implement in hardware, the software implementation on an 8-bit CPU involves a great deal of code space overhead. The performance analysis shows that the total code space required by the Gossamer functions (~1700 Bytes) including the necessary RC51 libraries (552 Bytes) can be estimated at approximately 2200 Bytes, which is 55% of the code space available on the reference platform. The overhead mainly relates to operations on large numbers that have to be split into arrays with elements equal to the word size of the CPU. This leaves little room for the implementation of the radio protocol (hence the need for simplification) and zero room for ADC or other functionality.

REFERENCES

Abramson, N. 1970. The aloha system: Another alternative for computer communications. In *Proceedings of the November 17-19, 1970, fall joint computer conference*, 281–285.

Ahmed, E. G., Shaaban, E., & Hashem, M. (2010). *Lightweight Mutual Authentication Protocol for Low Cost RFID Tags. International Journal of Network Security & Its Application (IJNSA)*.

Akyildiz, I. F., Su, W., Sankarasubramaniam, Y., & Cayirci, E. (2002). Wireless sensor networks: A survey. *Computer Networks, 38*(4), 393–422. doi:10.1016/S1389-1286(01)00302-4

Andem, V. R. (2003). *A cryptanalysis of the tiny encryption algorithm*. Citeseer.

ARM Ltd. (2009a). *Keil C51 Compiler Basics*. Available at: http://www.esacademy.com/automation/docs/c51primer/c02.htm

ARM Ltd. (2009b). *LX51 User's Guide: Code Banking*. Available at: http://www.keil.com/support/man/docs/lx51/lx51_codebanking.htm

Bárász, M., Boros, B., Ligeti, P., Lója, K., & Nagy, D. (2007a). Breaking LMAP. *Proc. of RFIDSec, 7*. Available at: http://www.cs.elte.hu/~turul/pubs/lmap.pdf

Bárász, M., Boros, B., Ligeti, P., Lója, K., & Nagy, D. (2007b). Passive attack against the M2AP mutual authentication protocol for RFID tags. *Proc. of First International EURASIP Workshop on RFID Technology*. Available at: http://www.cs.elte.hu/~turul/pubs/mmap.pdf

Bogdanov, A., Knudsen, L. R., Leander, G., Paar, C., Poschmann, A., Robshaw, M. J., ... Vikkelsoe, C. (2007). PRESENT: An ultra-lightweight block cipher. *Lecture Notes in Computer Science, 4727*, 450–466. doi:10.1007/978-3-540-74735-2_31

Cadger, F., Curran, K., Santos, J., & Moffett, S. (2016). Location and mobility-aware routing for improving multimedia streaming performance in MANETs. *Wireless Personal Communications, 86*(3), 1653-1672. DOI:10.1007/s11277-015-3012-z

Cao, T., Bertino, E., & Lei, H. (2009). Security Analysis of the SASI Protocol. *IEEE Transactions on Dependable and Secure Computing*, 73–77.

Chien, H. (2007). SASI: A New Ultralightweight RFID Authentication Protocol Providing Strong Authentication and Strong Integrity. *IEEE Transactions on Dependable and Secure Computing, 4*(4), 337–340. doi:10.1109/TDSC.2007.70226

Chien, H., & Huang, C. W. (2007). Security of ultra-lightweight RFID authentication protocols and its improvements. *Operating Systems Review, 41*(4), 86. doi:10.1145/1278901.1278916

Chung, C., Hsieh, Y., Wang, Y., & Chang, C. (2016). Aware and smart member card: RFID and license plate recognition systems integrated applications at parking guidance in shopping mall. In *2016 Eighth international conference on advanced computational intelligence (ICACI)* (pp. 253–256). Academic Press.

Collotta, M., Pau, G., & Tirrito, S. (2015). A preliminary study to increase baggage tracking by using a RFID solution. In *Proceedings of the international conference on numerical analysis and applied mathematics 2014 (ICNAAM-2014)* (Vol. 1648). AIP Publishing. 10.1063/1.4912985

D'Arco, P., & De Santis, A. (2008). *From Weaknesses to Secret Disclosure in a Recent Ultra-Lightweight RFID Authentication Protocol*. Cryptology ePrint Archive. Retrieved from http://eprint.iacr.org/2008/470

Daemen, J., & Rijmen, V. (1999). *AES proposal*. Rijndael.

Doherty, J., Curran, K., & McKevitt, P. (2017). Streaming Audio Using MPEG–7 Audio Spectrum Envelope to Enable Self-similarity within Polyphonic Audio. *TELKOMNIKA (Telecommunication Computing Electronics and Control), 15*(1), 190-202. DOI: 10.12928/telkomnika.v15i1.4581

Eastlake, D., & Jones, P. (2001). *US secure hash algorithm 1 (SHA1)*. RFC 3174, September 2001.

Eisenbarth, T., Kumar, S., Paar, C., Poschmann, A., & Uhsadel, L. (2007). A survey of lightweight-cryptography implementations. *IEEE Design & Test of Computers, 24*(6), 522–533. doi:10.1109/MDT.2007.178

el Ruptor, M. (2007). *File:XXTEA.png - Wikipedia, the free encyclopedia*. Available at: http://en.wikipedia.org/wiki/File:XXTEA.png

EPCGlobal. (2008). *EPCglobal UHF Class 1 Gen 2*. Available at: http://www.epcglobalinc.org/standards/uhfc1g2

Federal Information Processing Standards. (1993). *FIPS 46-2 - (DES), Data Encryption Standard*. Available at: http://www.itl.nist.gov/fipspubs/fip46-2.htm

Ferry, E., O'Raw, J., & Curran, K. (2016). Security Evaluation of the OAuth 2.0 Framework. *Information & Computer Security, 23*(1), 73-101. doi: 10.1108/ICS-12-2013-0089

Harran, M., Farrelly, W., & Curran, K. (2017) A Method for Verifying Integrity & Authenticating Digital Media. *Applied Computing and Informatics, 13*(2), 34-40. DOI: 10.1016/j.aci.2017.05.006

Hartung, C., Balasalle, J., & Han, R. (2005). *Node compromise in sensor networks: The need for secure systems.* Department of Computer Science University of Colorado at Boulder. Available at: http://cite-seerx.ist.psu.edu/viewdoc/download?doi=10.1.1.134.8146&rep=rep1&type=pdf

Hegazy, A.E., Darwish, A.M., & El-Fouly, R. (2007). *Reducing μTESLA memory requirements.* Academic Press.

Hernandez-Castro, J. C., Estevez-Tapiador, J. M., Ribagorda-Garnacho, A., & Ramos-Alvarez, B. (2006). Wheedham: An automatically designed block cipher by means of genetic programming. *Proc. of CEC*, 192–199. 10.1109/CEC.2006.1688308

Hernandez-Castro, J. C., Tapiador, J. M., Peris-Lopez, P., & Quisquater, J. J. (2008). *Cryptanalysis of the SASI Ultralightweight RFID Authentication Protocol with Modular Rotations.* Arxiv preprint arXiv:0811.4257

HINT Project. (2010). *Research Project: HINT Project.* Letterkenny Institute of Technology.

Hong, S., Hong, D., Ko, Y., Chang, D., Lee, W., & Lee, S. (2004). Differential Cryptanalysis of TEA and XTEA. *Information Security and Cryptology-ICISC, 2003*, 402–417.

Jinwala, D.C., Patel, D.R. & Dasgupta, K.S. (2008). *Investigating and Analyzing the Light-weight ciphers for Wireless Sensor Networks.* Academic Press.

Juels, A. (2005). Strengthening EPC tags against cloning. *Proceedings of the 4th ACM workshop on Wireless security*, 76. Available at: http://citeseerx.ist.psu.edu/viewdoc/download?doi=10.1.1.68.6553&rep=rep1&type=pdf

Juels, A. (2006). RFID security and privacy: A research survey. *IEEE Journal on Selected Areas in Communications, 24*(2), 381–394. doi:10.1109/JSAC.2005.861395

Kamble, P., Kshirsagar, R. V., & Mankar, K. (2007). *Wireless Sensor Network Architecture.* Available at: http://www.ieee-spce.org/colloquium/proceedings/Communication_and_Networking/spit-1.pdf

Karlof, C., Sastry, N., & Wagner, D. (2004). TinySec: a link layer security architecture for wireless sensor networks. *Proceedings of the 2nd international conference on Embedded networked sensor systems*, 162–175. Available at: http://citeseerx.ist.psu.edu/viewdoc/download?doi=10.1.1.61.4930&rep=rep1&type=pdf

Kelsey, J., Schneier, B. & Wagner, D. (1997). Related-key cryptanalysis of 3-way, biham-des, cast, des-x, newdes, rc2, and tea. *Information and Communications Security*, 233–246.

Klimov, A., & Shamir, A. (2004). Cryptographic Applications of T-functions. *Lecture Notes in Computer Science, 3006*, 248–261. doi:10.1007/978-3-540-24654-1_18

Ko, Y., Hong, S., Lee, W., Lee, S., & Kang, J. S. (2004). Related key differential attacks on 27 rounds of XTEA and full-round GOST. Fast Software Encryption, 299–316. doi:10.1007/978-3-540-25937-4_19

Korba, A. A., Nafaa, M., & Ghanemi, S. (2016). Hybrid Intrusion Detection Framework for Ad hoc networks. *International Journal of Information Security and Privacy, 10*(4), 1–32. doi:10.4018/IJISP.2016100101

Ksiazak, P., Farrelly, W., & Curran, K. (2015). A Lightweight Authentication Protocol for Secure Communications between Resource-Limited Devices and Wireless Sensor Networks. *International Journal of Information Security and Privacy, 8*(4), 62-102. DOI: 10.4018/IJISP.2014100104

Kumawat, A., Sharma, A. K., & Kumawat, S. (2017). Identification of Cryptographic Vulnerability and Malware Detection in Android. *International Journal of Information Security and Privacy, 11*(3), 15–28. doi:10.4018/IJISP.2017070102

Lee, Y. C., Hsieh, Y. C., You, P. S., & Chen, T. C. (2009). A New Ultralightweight RFID Protocol with Mutual Authentication. *Information Engineering, 2009. ICIE'09. WASE International Conference on*, 58–61. 10.1109/ICIE.2009.24

Leong, K. S., Ng, M.L., & Engels, D.W. (2006). EPC Network Architecture. *Auto-ID Labs: EPC Network Architecture*. Available at: http://www.autoidlabs.org/uploads/media/AUTOIDLABS-WP-SWNET-012.pdf

Li, T., & Deng, R. (2007). Vulnerability analysis of EMAP-an efficient RFID mutual authentication protocol. *Proc. of ARes*, 7. Available at: http://citeseerx.ist.psu.edu/viewdoc/download?doi=10.1.1.63.6430&rep=rep1&type=pdf

Li, T., & Wang, G. (2007). Security analysis of two ultra-lightweight RFID authentication protocols. *International Federation for Information Processing, 232*, 109.

Liu, D., & Ning, P. (2004). Multilevel μTESLA: Broadcast authentication for distributed sensor networks. *ACM Transactions on Embedded Computing Systems, 3*(4), 800–836. doi:10.1145/1027794.1027800

Lu, J. (2009). Related-key rectangle attack on 36 rounds of the XTEA block cipher. *International Journal of Information Security, 8*(1), 1–11. doi:10.100710207-008-0059-9

McBrearty, S., Farrelly, W., & Curran, K. (2016). The Performance Cost of Preserving Data/Query Privacy Using Searchable Symmetric Encryption. *Security and Communication Networks, 9*(18), 5311–5332. doi:10.1002ec.1699

Menezes, A. J., Oorschot, P. C. V., & Vanstone, S. A. (1997). *Handbook of applied cryptography*. CRC Press.

Mollin, R. A. (2007). *An introduction to cryptography*. CRC Press.

Moon, D., Hwang, K., Lee, W., Lee, S., & Lim, J. (2002). Impossible differential cryptanalysis of reduced round XTEA and TEA. Fast Software Encryption, 117–121. doi:10.1007/3-540-45661-9_4

Needham, R.M. & Wheeler, D.J. (1997). *eXtended Tiny Encryption Algorithm*. Prentice Hall.

Ni, S. Y., Tseng, Y. C., Chen, Y. S., & Sheu, J. P. (1999). The broadcast storm problem in a mobile ad hoc network. *Proceedings of the 5th annual ACM/IEEE international conference on Mobile computing and networking*, 162. Available at: http://citeseerx.ist.psu.edu/viewdoc/download?doi=10.1.1.123.5000&rep=rep1&type=pdf

Nordic Semiconductors. (2009a). *Nordic Semiconductor - nRF905 Multiband Transceiver.* Available at: http://www.nordicsemi.com/index.cfm?obj=product&act=display&pro=83

Nordic Semiconductors. (2009b). *Nordic Semiconductor - nRF9E5 Multiband Transceiver/MCU/ADC.* Available at: http://www.nordicsemi.com/index.cfm?obj=product&act=display&pro=82

Ouafi, K., & Vaudenay, S. (2009). Smashing SQUASH-0. Advances in Cryptology - EUROCRYPT 2009, 300-312. doi:10.1007/978-3-642-01001-9_17

Patel, K. S., & Shah, J. S. (2016). Analysis of Existing Trust Based Routing Schemes Used in Wireless Network. *International Journal of Information Security and Privacy, 10*(2), 26–40. doi:10.4018/IJISP.2016040103

Peris-Lopez, P., Hernandez-Castro, J., Tapiador, J., & Ribagorda, A. (2009). Advances in Ultralightweight Cryptography for Low-Cost RFID Tags: Gossamer Protocol. Information Security Applications, 56–68.

Peris-Lopez, P., Hernandez-Castro, J. C., Estevez-Tapiador, J. M., & Ribagorda, A. (2006a). EMAP: An efficient mutual-authentication protocol for low-cost RFID tags. *Lecture Notes in Computer Science, 4277*, 352–361. doi:10.1007/11915034_59

Peris-Lopez, P., Hernandez-Castro, J. C., Estevez-Tapiador, J. M., & Ribagorda, A. (2006b). LMAP: A real lightweight mutual authentication protocol for low-cost RFID tags. *Workshop on RFID Security,* 12–14. Available at: http://citeseerx.ist.psu.edu/viewdoc/download?doi=10.1.1.110.2082&rep=rep1&type=pdf

Peris-Lopez, P., Hernandez-Castro, J. C., Estevez-Tapiador, J. M., & Ribagorda, A. (2006c). M^2AP: A Minimalist Mutual-Authentication Protocol for Low-Cost RFID Tags. *Lecture Notes in Computer Science, 4159*, 912–923. doi:10.1007/11833529_93

Peris-Lopez, P., Hernandez-Castro, J. C., Tapiador, J. M., van der Lubbe, J. C., Singh, M. K., Liang, G., . . . Kish, L. L. (2008). *Security Flaws in a Recent Ultralightweight RFID Protocol.* Arxiv preprint arXiv:0910.2115

Perrig, A., Canetti, R., Song, D., & Tygar, J. D. (2001). Efficient and secure source authentication for multicast. In *Network and Distributed System Security Symposium* (pp. 35–46). NDSS. Available at http://citeseerx.ist.psu.edu/viewdoc/download?doi=10.1.1.18.1680&rep=rep1&type=pdf

Perrig, A., Szewczyk, R., Tygar, J. D., Wen, V., & Culler, D. E. (2002). SPINS: Security protocols for sensor networks. *Wireless Networks, 8*(5), 521–534. doi:10.1023/A:1016598314198

Poschmann, A., Leander, G., Schramm, K., & Paar, C. (2007). New light-weight crypto algorithms for RFID. *Proceedings of The IEEE International Symposium on Circuits and Systems,* 1843–1846. Available at: http://citeseerx.ist.psu.edu/viewdoc/download?doi=10.1.1.80.1217&rep=rep1&type=pdf

Rabin, M.O. (1979). *Digitalized signatures and public-key functions as intractable as factorization.* MtT/LCS/TR-212.

Raisonance, S. A. S. (2010). *Raisonance, Corporate home page.* Available at: http://www.raisonance.com/

Ranasinghe, D. C., & Cole, P. H. (2008). *Networked RFID Systems and Lightweight Cryptography.* Springer Berlin Heidelberg. doi:10.1007/978-3-540-71641-9

Rinne, S., Eisenbarth, T., & Paar, C. (2007). *Performance analysis of contemporary light-weight block ciphers on 8-bit microcontrollers.* ECRYPT.

Rivest, R. L. (1995). The RC5 encryption algorithm. *Dr. Dobb's Journal of Software Tools for the Professional Programmer, 20*(1), 146–149.

Russell, M.D. (2004). *Tinyness: an overview of TEA and related ciphers.* Draft v0.3, 3.

Saarinen, M. J. (1998). *Cryptanalysis of Block Tea.* Unpublished manuscript.

Sarma, S. E. (2001). *Towards the five-cent tag.* Technical Report MIT-AUTOID-WH-006, MIT Auto ID Center. Available at: http://www.autoidlabs.org/uploads/media/mit-autoid-wh-006.pdf

Sarma, S. E., Weis, S. A., & Engels, D. W. (2003). RFID systems and security and privacy implications. *Lecture Notes in Computer Science, 2523,* 454–469. doi:10.1007/3-540-36400-5_33

Schneier, B. (1996). *Applied Cryptography: Protocols, Algorithms, and Source Code in C* (2nd ed.). Wiley.

Shamir, A. (2008). SQUASH – A New MAC with Provable Security Properties for Highly Constrained Devices Such as RFID Tags. Fast Software Encryption, 144-157. doi:10.1007/978-3-540-71039-4_9

Shen, J. (2016). A practical RFID grouping authentication protocol in multiple-tag arrangement with adequate security assurance. In *2016 18th international conference on advanced communication technology (ICACT).* IEEE.

Singh, S. K., Kumar, P., & Singh, J. P. (2017). Localization in Wireless Sensor Networks Using Soft Computing Approach. *International Journal of Information Security and Privacy, 11*(3), 42–53. doi:10.4018/IJISP.2017070104

Standaert, F., Piret, G., Gershenfeld, N., & Quisquater, J. (2006). SEA: A scalable encryption algorithm for small embedded applications. *Lecture Notes in Computer Science, 3928,* 222–236. doi:10.1007/11733447_16

Sun, H. M., Ting, W. C., & Wang, K. H. (2008). *On the security of chien's ultralightweight RFID authentication protocol.* Cryptology ePrint Archive, Report 2008/083. Available at: http://eprint.iacr.org/2008/083.pdf

Tanwar, S., & Kumar, A. (2017). A Proposed Scheme for Remedy of Man-In-The-Middle Attack on Certificate Authority. *International Journal of Information Security and Privacy, 11*(3), 1–14. doi:10.4018/IJISP.2017070101

Vance, P., Prasad, G., Harkin, J., & Curran, K. (2015). Designing a Compact Wireless Network based Device-free Passive Localisation System for Indoor Environments. *International Journal of Wireless Networks and Broadband Technologies, 4*(2), 28–43. doi:10.4018/IJWNBT.2015040103

Vault Information Services. (2009). *8052.com - The Online 8051/8052 Microcontroller Resource - 8052. com.* Available at: http://www.8052.com/

Wheeler, D., & Needham, R. (1994). TEA, a tiny encryption algorithm. Fast Software Encryption, 363–366.

Wheeler, D., & Needham, R. (1998). *XXTEA: Correction to XTEA. Technical report.* Computer Laboratory, University of Cambridge.

Wi-Fi Alliance. (2003). *Wi-Fi Protected Access: Strong, standards-based, interoperable security for today's Wi-Fi networks.* Author.

Yarrkov, E. (2010). *Cryptanalysis of XXTEA.* Available at: http://eprint.iacr.org/2010/254

Ye, W., Heidemann, J., & Estrin, D. (2002). An energy-efficient MAC protocol for wireless sensor networks. IEEE INFOCOM, 1567–1576.

Yu-Long, S., Qing-Qi, P.E.I., & Jian-Feng, M.A. (2007). *microTESLA: Broadcast Authentication Protocol for Multiple-Base-Station Sensor Networks.* Academic Press.

ENDNOTE

[1]   L denotes the length of one key or the IDS in bits. 96-bits in the case of the EPC RFID specifications.

Chapter 2
Trust–Based Analytical Models for Secure Wireless Sensor Networks

Aminu Bello Usman
Auckland University of Technology, New Zealand

Jairo Gutierrez
Auckland University of Technology, New Zealand

ABSTRACT

In this chapter, the authors hypothesize that in the design of a trust-based routing protocol, the exploration of the peers' routing attributes could significantly improve trust evaluation accuracy. In this regard, they study the properties of complex networks and their impact on trust and reputation propagation and evaluation. They start by illustrating the structural transitivity in the network and its approximation. They then proceed to present the theoretical and analytical relationship between trust and reputation model accuracy, average structural transitivity between peers, average shortest path between peers, and energy consumed by peers for trust and reputation propagation and evaluations. The experimental studies using simulation have further supported the results of the analytical study. In this chapter, the authors are paving a new angle of research on exploring the complex network properties impact on trust and reputation evaluation between wireless peers.

INTRODUCTION

The security in computing domain aim at guarding the information or protecting an information system through a range of security policies, strategies, security products, and cryptographic techniques (Pathan, 2016), and the goal of security in the network is to protect the information and systems' integrity, confidentiality and availability of data. However, in wireless Peer-to-Peer (P2P) networks this is a challenging goal. These networks have no central authority to perform the processes of authentication and verification of the registered peers in the network, and there are no central and high processing control points to perform the cryptographic computation and cryptographic key management that are required.

DOI: 10.4018/978-1-5225-5583-4.ch002

Under those circumstances, the decision-making ability of the peers can result on the adoption of a selfish behavior. For example, how can a peer know whether its communication partner is genuine or malicious? Can the request, content or message from any neighboring device be trusted? How can the peers perform self-organization processes to provide a secure network paradigm with a high quality of service? Obviously, to answer these questions, a distributed mechanism is needed to ensure a secure decentralized P2P network system.

Over the years, researchers have resorted to going back to the drawing board to borrow the concept of trust as an alternative strategy for addressing security problems in P2P networks (Boukerch, Xu, & El-Khatib, 2007). The idea behind trust and reputation models is for the peers to rate each other and then use the aggregated ratings to derive the trust scores, which can assist the peers in deciding whether to collaborate or not to collaborate in the future tasks (Bello, Liu, Bai, & Narayanan, 2015a). Many authors in the literature on trust and reputation in various fields show that the formation of effective cooperation, norms, and trust in the network largely depend on the type of actors, and relationships between the actors involved (Cho, Swami, & Chen, 2011). This is consistent with the suggestions proposed in (Chen & Cai, 2005) and indeed other relevant work, on the factors that influence efficient communication between the peers in P2P networks: 1) Consideration of the type of peers interaction such as: Human-to-human, Machine-to-machine, and Human-to-machine and 2) the behaviour of each peer in the network.

The study of trust and reputation was originally explored in sociology and other social sciences fields of study. Most the literature and the studies of trust in sociology pay more attention to exploring and debating on the natural factors that determine and influence trust including: relationship between actors, strong and weak ties between peers, structural properties which are fundamentals and natural attributes that can be used in predicting trust and reputation behaviour of the actors in the community. For a decade, the concept of trust and reputation became one of the dominant research topics in computer science, and information technology due to their significance to many related disciplines. Recently, due to the rapid development of complex and autonomous P2P networks, the concepts of trust, reputation and cooperation received enormous attention in the field of peer-to-peer (P2P) security. In addition, the concept of trust and reputation schemes was explored by different researchers due to the ability of trust and reputation to enable peers to cope with the uncertainty and uncontrollability caused by the free will of others' peers in the network.

Most of the literature and the studies on trust usually define the term based on their disciplines' discretion and views. For example, from the social psychological and sociological views, the work of (Lusher, Robins, Pattison, & Lomi, 2012) define trust as a unidirectional relation between trustor and a trustee expressing the firm belief of the trustor that the trustee will behave as expected with respect to a particular level of reliability within a specific context and at a particular time; further, the work defines trust as a social construct and it discusses the natural attributes of the relationship among social actors (group or individual), furthermore, (Grandison & Sloman, 2000) define trust as the subjective belief of someone in the character, ability, strength, reliability, honesty or truth of someone or something.

From the point of view of computing, one of the most cited definitions of trust is the work of (Al Ghamdi, Aseeri, & Ahmed, 2013) in which the authors distinguish between two main categories of trust namely: reliability trust and decision trust. The concept of reliability trust is mainly based on the probability that an actor can perform certain action either as a result of his capability, resources, location in the network, connectivity or its attributes while the concept of decision trust is based on the extent to which an actor is willing to defend the action or the decision of another actor with a feeling of relative security.

Obviously, as the concept of trust and reputation is being used in a wide range of disciplines, many definitions of trust will continue to emerge. In this work, we focus on trust that is explicitly exhibited by peers in a network to behave and provide a recommendation. We, therefore, adopted the definition of trust in (Jøsang, Ismail, & Boyd, 2007) as the extent to which one is willing to defend somebody in a given situation.

Reputation on the other hand, is based on the perception that a peer can build his reputation credentials through past actions, norms and behaviour in the network. The definition of reputation trust by (Jøsang et al., 2007) is one of the most frequently cited in the literature. The author defines reputation trust as a subjective expectation an actor can have about another actor's behaviour based on the previous history of their encounters. In this form of trust, the trust relationship is purely being established based on the aggregated reputation. The good behaviour increases the peers' trust level likewise the peers' reputation value will decrease relative to its miss-behaviour.

Basically, a reputation model in wireless routing protocol exhibit three main functions as follows:

- **Monitoring or Observation:** This is the process of observing the activities of the peers in the network.
- **Rating:** Based on the peers' observation, a peer can rate its neighbors or other peers depending on their track record and previous encounters for the recommendation or for trust decision purposes.
- **Response:** This is a decision based on the peers' rating value. The actions for the response include: rewarding well behaving peers and avoiding bad behaving peers by using rewards or demerit points for miss-behaving peers.

Many works in the reviewed literature presented different reputation trust models based on the aforementioned three reputation characteristics. For example, the work of (Fullam & Barber) analyse the basic types of trust models: experience-based trust models, and reputation-based trust models for determining whom to trust over the various systems using different transaction frequencies, reputation accuracies and trustee trustworthiness. The framework introduced a learning parameter to perform a weighting between reputation-based trust modeling and experience-based trust modeling. The author reported that, for effective trust modeling, the trustor should use the learning parameter for each potential trustee since the transaction frequency, accuracy of reputation, and trustworthiness characteristics may vary. The result of the work also demonstrated that the combination of experience and reputation-based models are better over a broad range of system characteristics.

TRUST EVALUATION AND CONNECTIVITY

Recently, the concept of network science has emerged as a new interdisciplinary field of study that allows scientists and engineers to analyse different network concepts and the connection among elements of the complex agent's system of large networks. In simple terms, a network is a collection of vertices or elements that are connected by links. In principle, such a high level of abstraction can be applied to any system of agents thereby providing a conceptual representation of interrelations between interacting agents or peers.

Some related studies, including (Hang & Singh, 2010), proposed a trust-based recommendation using topological attributes (vertex similarity between peers) based on the intuition that a good peer to seek a recommendation from, is a peer that is connected to many neighbouring peers. On the other hand, the study of trust and reputation models in routing protocols deals with the local and global routing behaviour of the peers. It is however, important to emphasize that the network approach also deals with mapping the interactions between peers, thus focusing on the local and global structure of the interactions within a system. Therefore, the detailed properties of each peer (local information of a peer), and network level (global information) can give substantial information about the behaviour of interacting peers for proper trust propagation and trust evaluations between peers in the network (Usman & Gutierrez, 2016).

On the same vein, this development may result in different forms of selfish behaviour and dynamic changes of a peer in the various forms of routing and handling communication tasks between the peers in the network. Although many researchers consider the P2P network architecture as a promising solution to the problems and limitations of client-server architectures, security remains one of the challenging problems to be addressed in emerging P2P WSNs. Therefore, a distributed alternative security solution is needed to tackle different security threats against the selfish behaviour of peers, masquerading behaviour and advanced persistent threats (i.e., using multiple attack vectors to pursue selfish behaviour) which are considered a result of poor self-defensive and poor cooperation between the peers in the network (Beck & Franke, 2009). The traditional security mechanisms (i.e., cryptography) cannot ensure a high degree of collaboration and self-policing for future WSNs. It is essential to look for an alternative solution to the limitations of cryptography techniques to promote cooperation and easy detection of malicious peers and malicious behaviour among autonomous WSN-based devices. However, the properties of self-cooperation, self-organization and self-control system of WSN does not come into existence automatically; they need to be enforced and managed so that the devices and the protocols of WSN-based devices can be prepared to overcome different problems associated with variable conditions, faulty peers and any strange or malicious behaviour from, both, inside and outside attacks. The three mechanisms recognized in the reported research on decision support and relevant to wireless sensor networks are trust, reputation and cooperation management.

The studies in this chapter collect the combined metrics of network performance, and trust evaluation in a style that focuses on principles that are likely to be valuable in trust-based routing protocol design. Furthermore, we believe that a fast and efficient trust-based routing algorithm could be realized using the presented performance matrix-based model.

We drive our inspiration from the "network thinking" paradigm which was recently adopted by many researchers as an analytic technique used to study the concepts of interacting agents in the contemporary view of complex networks including the work of (Falcone & Castelfranchi, 2012) (Falcone & Castelfranchi, 2009) and (Scott, 2017).

Related Work

The rapid development of complex and autonomous P2P networks, and the concepts of trust, reputation and cooperation received enormous attention in the field of peer-to-peer (P2P) networks (Shiakallis, Mavromoustakis, Mastorakis, Bourdena, & Pallis, 2015). The basic idea behind trust and reputation management in the P2P network is to let a peer rate each other and then use the aggregated ratings to derive trust scores, which can assist machines in making a trust decision. The concept of trust has been used in handling the problem of selfish behaviour, preventing false data injection attacks and in the process of making dynamic routing decisions (Airehrour, Gutierrez, & Ray, 2015). This is due to the ability of trust and reputation to enable peers to cope with the uncertainty and uncontrollability caused by the free will of other peers. On the other hand, the problem of forwarding packets in a non-cooperative ad-hoc P2P network has been widely studied. Many approaches and models for tackling the problem of selfish behaviour were proposed. A number of those models were based on game theory, since it is a known tool to model the cooperative behaviour of complex networks (Uysal, 2009). The proposed model in (Wang & Vassileva, 2003) defines the peers' reliability for providing the service as a measure of quantifying peers' trust worthiness, the model is based on the Bayesian network-based trust model for building a reputation in peer-to-peer networks. The work of (Sarkar & Datta, 2012) proposed a trust-based protocol for making energy-efficient routing decisions; the proposed protocol reduces packets' delays and routing overhead.

Trust and Reputation

With the recent exponential increase in WSN deployment (these networks are composed of many small resource-constrained devices and they operate autonomously) and the adoption of trust and reputation management as an alternative security strategy, the WSN-based devices are vulnerable to various security challenges such as fraud, malicious and selfish activities. This development brought the need to convert the WSN devices into self-cooperative and self-behaving peers in a network. However, many attacks to the trust and reputation systems, such as selfish peer attacks, Sybil attacks and bad recommendation attacks need to be addressed.

Furthermore, in P2P networks, trust can be derived from the neighbouring peers that have a direct relationship (direct trust) or have had an indirect (referral) experience with the target actors. For example, consider the diagram in Figure 1 below: the trust that peer i can derive about peer k (T_{ik}) depends on the level of trust that peer i have about peer j (T_{ij}). This can be understood since it is peer j that can recommend peer k to peer i. Thus, the trust of i on k relies on the trust of i on j. One can see that the trust level of i about k, T_{ik} can be explored using the concept of transitivity (topological clustering coefficient).

Subsequently, several topological algorithms can be applied to explore the peers' ranks and the roles for data transfer in the network using some topological concepts; such as average neighbour degree (Zhou & Hwang, 2007) in trust and reputation; average degree of connectivity in a distributed reputation, and trust management scheme for mobile peer-to-peer networks (Qureshi, Min, & Kouvatsos, 2012). To this end, several routing algorithms employed the concept of network structure to identify the most important peer or the shortest path for an efficient routing decision.

Trust-Based Protocols

To this date, various methods have been developed and introduced for quantifying peers' trustworthiness for routing decisions in P2P networks. For example, (Rezgui & Eltoweissy, 2007) proposed a trust aware routing protocol for SANETs, nonetheless, the model exploits past peers' routing behaviour and links' quality for determining the efficient paths with no concern about the peers' trust worthiness and peers' capability. (Dai, Jia, & Qin, 2009) uses the concept of fuzzy inference rules to improve the routing protocols with fuzzy dynamic programming in MANET.

Figure 1. Transitive Trust Path Illustration

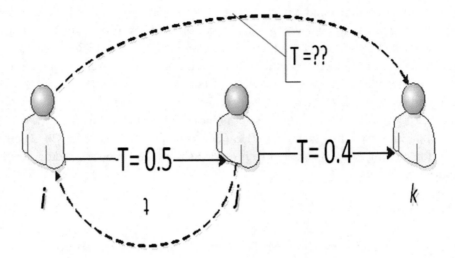

On the other hand, the problem of forwarding packets in a non-cooperative ad-hoc P2P network has been widely studied and reported in the literature. Many approaches and models for tackling the problem of selfish behaviour were proposed. A number of those models were based on game theory (Srivastava et al., 2005). Furthermore, in the proposed trust model of (Zahariadis, Leligou, Trakadas, & Voliotis, 2010), when the misbehaving peer is detected, the neighbouring peer can avoid the misbehaving peer in data forwarding or any other cooperative function. Nevertheless, the model only considers counting the systematic failure of the peers as a method for learning the peer's capability, not the peers routing attributes. In this type of model, the learning parameters can be faulty due to the dynamic change of peer's behaviour (good or bad). The work of (Maarouf, Baroudi, & Naseer, 2009) proposed a reputation system-based solution for trust-aware routing, which implements a new monitoring strategy called an efficient monitoring procedure. The model only considers the reputation values as a factor for a routing decision, which may not explicitly reveal the capacity of peers in handling routing tasks.

To sum it all, several trust-aware models based on energy-aware, and location-aware delay tolerant networks will continue to emerge. This indicate the need for a standard model that can holistically integrate any trust model and peers attributes in order to make efficient routing decisions. Our approach is not an attributes specific neither it is trust model specific. Our approach can be used in developing any trust-aware routing attributes while using any trust and reputation model.

TRANSITIVE CONNECTIVITY FOR TRUST PROPAGATION AND EVALUATION

Several trust and reputation models have been proposed around the idea that connectivity between peers has a significant effect and can influence trust propagation behaviour in P2P networks (Bello, Liu, Bai, & Narayanan, 2015b). Also, trust inference, which is one of the mechanisms for building a trust chain between peers, is a relation-driven phenomenon. Therefore, understanding a relationship that infers trust between peers who are directly or indirectly connected might be an important contribution in peer trust modeling and evaluation. Here, there are three main issues that need further exploration: the first issue is which category of the peers' relationship (connectivity) can facilitate effective trust evaluation between peers, and by extension, can enhance collaborative routing decisions in P2P wireless networks. The second issue is to investigate whether there is any correlation between the identified peer relationship (connectivity) and network performance metrics which is the essential consideration in the design of routing protocols. Third, routing selection algorithms should be introduced based on the identified peers' relationships or connectivity.

In this chapter, we attempt the first two questions with the study of structural transitivity for trust and reputation evaluation between wireless peers. We base our notion on the assumption that the trust and reputation evaluation between wireless peers is not merely a function of trust models, but also a network-wide activity in which the network structure matters (Bello et al., 2015a). We propose that the presence of a transitive relation anchor (transitive-chain) in a network of peers is more likely to promote an effective trust and reputation evaluation process. That is, when the peers are connected in a transitive form, they will be more likely to facilitate the trust recommendation or referral process, thus providing an effective trust evaluation system and further yielding good routing performance between the peers.

Additionally, we aim to obtain a derived metric that can quickly and intuitively give an indication of the relationship between structural transitivity, network performance in relationship trust and reputation evaluation. We derive the mathematical relationship between structural transitivity and average shortest paths, and average network efficiency.

Before defining transitivity in our network model, let us look at the concept of trust transitivity. Essentially, the properties of trust propagation on networks, based on a simple metric of trust transitivity, can be a requirement for the viability of global trust propagation in large systems (Liu, Wang, & Orgun, 2011). When a trust relationship between peers is transitive, the trust extends beyond the directly trusted and the trusting peer, to any other transitively trusted peer in the network. An illustration of the transitivity trust inference in the expression below can be understood as the essential elements of trust propagations. Which states: if $i \ T \ j \ \wedge \ j \ T \ k$ (meaning if peer i trusts peer j, and peer j trusts per k) then, there exist the possibility of j to refer $k \ to \ i$, so that peer i can trust peer k as well. For simplicity, this can be illustrated as follows:

$$\forall i, j \in N : iTj, jTK \therefore \exists iTK$$

Therefore, this can be understood, in a given wireless network, as:

$$G = (N, L) : i, j \in N, L \subseteq \{(i, j) : i, j \in N, i \neq j\}, \forall \{(i, j)\} \in L$$

where L represents the wireless connection between the peers.

Transitivity and Network Models

In particular, we are more interested in the proportion of transitive relations (that express a degree of balance in the network), which most theorists have proposed as an "equilibrium" or natural state toward network and structure formation that tends to efficiently promote trust and normative relationships between the actors in the network (Harary & Kommel, 1979).

Transitivity Coefficient Approximation

Arising from the theoretical foundation of transitivity, in this section, we present the transitivity coefficient approximation model.

Given a network $G = (N, L)$ consisting of peers $N = \{i, j, k\}$ and the set of communication links between the peers $L \subseteq \{(i, j)\} : i, j \in N, i \notin j$. Therefore, the transitivity coefficient between the peers in the network is given by the proportion of links between the peers within its neighbourhood divided by the maximum number of links that could exist between the peers.

If we denote the set of immediately connected neighbours or (clique members) of peer i as $n_i : n_i = \{j : \{(i, j)\} \in L, \{(j, i)\} \in L\} : \{(i, j)\}$ is district from $\{(j, i)\}$. For each peer $i \in N$, there are a possible number of distinct wireless interface connections $n_i (n_i - 1)$ that could exist among the peers within the neighbourhood of peer i. Therefore, we define the local transitive coefficient of peer i $\left(T_{coef(i)}\right)$, by the proportion of the exact interfaces between its neighbours divided by the number of interfaces that possibly could exist between them as presented in equation 1.

$$T_{coef(i)} = \frac{2\{| \{i, j\} : i, j \in N_i, \{i, j\} \in N |\}}{n_i(n_i - 1)} \tag{1}$$

Throughout this chapter, we are considering the undirected graph for network modelling; thus, to approximate the local and global transitivity in a given network, we use the clustering coefficient metrics to determine the degree of clustered peers. Here, we rely on the assumption that for undirected graphs, the weighted clustering coefficient is simply transitivity as inferred in (Landim, Fernandes, Mesquita, Collares, & Frota, 2010).

Depending on the strength of interdependency between network members, the clustering coefficient can reveal the transitivity level and interdependency between connected peers. Therefore, the average global clustering coefficient of the network can be estimated as the average transitivity coefficient of the network (Wohlgemuth, 2012).

$$av.Tra = \frac{1}{n}\sum_{i=1} T_{coef}(N) \tag{2}$$

Transitivity and Network Performance Analytical Modelling

Transitivity and Shortest Path Model

Let us first consider the distance among wireless peers in the network; and by distance here, we mean wireless distance between the peers based on peers' radio interface ranges. We therefore, consider the definition of the shortest path metric of the undirected, unweighted network, which we can be derived from equation 3 as follows.

$$A.SP(i->j) = \sum_{i,j \in N} \frac{dis(i->j)}{n(n-1)} \qquad (3)$$

i.e., the shortest path between p and q is the average shortest path between the two peers and n represents the number of hop counts between p1 and p2.

The transitivity characterizes the local cohesiveness of networks as well as the propensity to form clusters of interconnected peers (Watts & Strogatz, 1998). Therefore, one can deduce that the more the peers are clustered, the higher the cohesivity between the peers and the less effort it takes peers to spread aggregated trust (reputation) among peers, for trust evaluation (Falcone & Castelfranchi, 2012). In addition, we can define the closeness centrality of the peers in the network as follows:

$$CS(i) = \frac{n-1}{\sum_{i \notin j} dis(i->j)} \qquad (4)$$

where $dis(i->j)$ denotes the distance between i and peer j. From equation 4 and 2, we can deduce that a small average shortest path length between the peers yield a large structural transitivity coefficient between the peers in the network; therefore, the higher the average transitivity between the peers the higher the closeness centrality between the peers in the network.

Transitivity and Energy Model

Among others, energy consumption, data rate, and transfer time are parameters that are essential in trust-based routing protocol design. Therefore, it is important to discern a better understanding of energy efficient network operation for proper trust-based routing protocol design.

Compared to traditional security solutions (hard security solution), trust and reputation models are relatively better regarding energy overhead; however, the process of reputation aggregation, and evaluation of trust-based routing involves the transfer of a series of messages between wireless peers. Therefore, taking into account the energy model while designing trust and reputation model is essential. As presented in (You, Wang, Zhou, Dai, & Sun, 2010) the energy needed for two peers to communicate in a wireless network is a function of the distance between the source peer and the destination peer.

$$E(i->j) = dis(i,j)^{\alpha} + pow \qquad (5)$$

That is, the energy needed for two peers p and q to communicate depends on the distance between them and the processing power as indicated in equation 4.5 where α denotes the media attenuation coefficient factor and *pow* denotes the processing power. Thus, for the design of a trust-based routing protocol, the presented energy model can be understood in two ways. Firstly, if a peer is located at a nearby location of other peers, then it results in a reduction in the number of hops between the peers. Therefore, that condition can help in reducing the total energy and bandwidth consumption to forward messages and in minimizing the convergence of trust data (reputation). Secondly, the lower hops counted from the sources to the destination, can reduce message latency.

Network Efficiency Model

Some of the challenging aspects of designing trust-based routing protocols which work in a collaborative fashion, include network efficiency and peer energy depletion while trying to identify and establish communications with other peers in the network. Subsequently, the design of trust-based routing protocols is not limited to only one set of elements (peers) but includes an inter-relationship between the peers (i.e., links) and how efficiently the peers can communicate (exchange trust data or reputation). Furthermore, the ability of the network to resist structural attacks or structural vulnerability exploitations (failure of a networks' topological structure) depend on the efficiency and structural balance of the network (Williams & Musolesi, 2016); i.e. how the network of peers can resist the peers failure or links failure (Quattrociocchi, Caldarelli, & Scala, 2014).

Additionally, a good design principle of a trust-based routing protocol should take into consideration the characteristics of attacks such as Sybil attacks, blackhole attacks, wormhole attacks, etc. These types of attacks can cause a section of the network or some peers in the network to malfunction or to be converted into attacking peers. Therefore, understanding the nature of an efficient network structure that can withstand the presence of compromised peers or links in the network by using trust-based routing design is essential (Abusalah, Khokhar, & Guizani, 2008). Network efficiency is a measure of how efficiently peers can exchange information, which can be applied to both local and global scales in a network. Therefore, we define the network local efficiency as the inverse of the average shortest path (as described in equation 3) between the peers in the network.

$$E_{loc}(N_i) = \frac{1}{n} \sum_{i \in N} E(N_i) \tag{6}$$

where N_i is the local sub graph consisting only of a peer $i's$ immediate neighbours (peers in the same transmission range with peer i), but not peer i itself and $E_{loc}(N_i)$ is the local efficiency between i and j and $dis(i->j)$ is the shortest distance between the two peers. Therefore, the average network efficiency of the network can be defined as:

$$Eg = \frac{2}{n(n-1)} \sum_{i,j \in N}^{n} \frac{1}{dis(i->j)} \tag{7}$$

where n denotes the total number of peers in a network and $dis(i->j)$, denotes the length of the shortest path between a peer i and another peer j.

Transitivity and Network Performance Analytical Models

To put all the pieces together, we can analytically establish a relationship between the models we have introduced (transitivity, shortest path, energy and network efficiency) as follows:

- From the average transitivity model in equation 2; the closeness centrality in equation 4 and the average shortest path model from equation 3 it is not difficult to see that for any given network with a fixed number of links and nodes, the relationship between average transitivity and the shortest path between the peers is directly proportional. This is consistent with the findings in (Demetrescu & Italiano, 2006).

- From equation 7 above, we can see that the relationship between average network efficiency and average distance is related by inverse variation. In other words, as one becomes larger the other becomes smaller; i.e., the lower the shortest path (minimum distance between the peers in the network), the higher the efficiency of the network.

- Subsequently, from the energy model in equation 5, and the average shortest path equation in 3, we can observe a directly proportional relationship between energy and the average shortest path; i.e., the lower the average shortest path between the peers in the network, the lower the amount of energy needed for the peers for trust propagation, trust evaluation and message transfer between the peers.

- Therefore, we can analytically establish a relationship between structural transitivity and the energy model as inversely proportional and the relationship between average structural transitivity and the network efficiency model as directly proportional.

To determine the accuracy of our proposed model's implementation, we keep the density of the network fixed. We define network density as that portion of the connection that could potentially exist between two nodes regardless of whether or not it does. We calculate the average network density of the network g as the as the percentage of links present in the network with the following equation 8.

$$Av.D = \frac{L}{n(n-1)} \tag{8}$$

TRUST BASED MODEL

The Eigen Trust model is one of the most cited self-policing trust and reputation algorithms in P2P networks and it was developed to overcome the problem of peer to peer authentication. The algorithm is based on the transitive trust between the peers. The details of the algorithm can be shown below:

Each time peer i received a file from peer j, the local trust value $\left(C_{ij}\right)$ between peer i and peer j increases or decreases based on the authenticity or delivery of the file. i.e C_{ij} increases if the peer i received an authentic file from peer j and decreases otherwise. Therefore, sat (i; j): The local trust value between peer *i*, and *j* $\left(s_{i,j}\right)$ can be shown as:

$$S_{(i,j)} = sat(i,j) - unsat(i,j) \tag{9}$$

where $S_{(ij)}$ represents the number of satisfactory transactions (received) between peer i and peer j while $unsat(i, j)$ represents the number of unsatisfactory transactions (received) between peer i and peer j. The local trust value is normalized to overcome the under and over recommendation malicious attack with the value C_{ij}.

$$c_{ij} = \frac{\max(s_{ij}, 0)}{\sum_j \max(s_{ij}, 0)} \ \left\| \vec{c}_i \right\|_1 = 1, \ \ i.e. \ \sum_{j=1}^{N} c_{ij} = 1 \tag{10}$$

The local reputation vector can be computed as

$$\vec{c}_i = (c_{i1}, ..., c_{iN})^T, \ 0 \le c_{ij} \le 1$$

While the global reputation value can be computed as

$$t_{ik} = \sum_j c_{ij} c_{jk} \tag{11}$$

Peer i asks its friends about their opinions (trust value) on peer k. The computation continues in this manner depending on the size of the value of n. For a large value of n, the resultant trust vector of peer i can be represented below:

$$\vec{t}_i = (C^T)^n \vec{c}_i \tag{12}$$

If the trust adjacency matrix C is assumed to be a periodic and strongly connected, then the powers of the matrix C will converge to a stable value at some point. The resulting basic algorithm can be represented by algorithm 1 (Eigen Trust Algorithm) below:

for each peer i do{
query all peers $j \in A_i$ for $t_j^{(0)} = p_j$;
repeat
    compute $t_i^{(k+1)} = (1-a)(c_{1i} t_1^{(k)} + ... + c_{Ni} t_N^{(k)}) + a p_i$;
    send $c_{ij} t_i^{(k+1)}$ to all peers $j \in B_i$;
    compute $\delta = \left| t_i^{(k+1)} - t_i^{(k)} \right|$;
    wait for all peers $j \in A_i$ to return $c_{ji} t_j^{(k+1)}$
until $\delta < \varepsilon$;
}

While the distributed implementation of EigenTrust was proposed to overcome the problems of i) computation and storage of the global trust vector, and ii) central computation storage and message overhead. Unfortunately, the EigenTrust algorithm still faces some challenges in relation to exploring the peers' capability in the network.

SOLUTIONS AND RECOMMENDATIONS

To evaluate the presented analytical model, we adopted the Eigen Trust algorithm to simulate the transitivity model for efficient trust propagation in a given network of wireless devices. The Eigen Trust algorithm is a self-policing trust and reputation management model developed to overcome the peer-to-peer authentication problem. The model aims to assist the peer members of the network to choose the most reputable and trusted peers for routing decisions.

We used the TRMSim-WSN (Mármol & Pérez, 2009) simulator for the experiment. TRMSim-WSN is a Trust and Reputation Model Simulator for Wireless Sensor Networks. In the simulation studies, we consider a traditional WSN peer-to-peer based network, which comprises malicious nodes, benevolent nodes and relay nodes within the area of 100X100M2, with each node having a radio range of 10M. The nodes in the network send and receive data from their neighbouring node with equal traffic.

We have simulated the Eigen trust model, because it is one of the most widely known trust and reputation models. The model is developed in such a way that each peer in the network observes and takes notes about its interaction with the corresponding neighbours in the network. The local and global trust value of a peer can be computed when determining the reputation level of the peer. We generated six different random regular networks using NetworkX (Quattrociocchi, et al., 2014) a python graph package with the following settings: 50 nodes and 150 links which with each node having an average degree of six (6).

We then transferred the metrics to the TRMSim-WSN model for the modeling of trust and reputation behaviour and energy efficiency for the six generated network topologies as presented in Table 3 for six different scenarios so that the position of the links in the network will behave dynamically and take the reading of each simulation scenario.

We set up TRMSim-WSN with the parameters as shown in Table 1. We use equations 2 and 7 to compute the average transitivity coefficient of the network (av.Tra) and the average network efficiency using equation 7 for every simulation scenario as presented in Table 3.

From Table 3 above, we can see that while the density of the network topology is fixed with the value 0.122, the average transitivity changes with the corresponding change in the trust and reputation model accuracy. Also, it can be observed that an increase in the average transitivity causes a decrease in the average shortest path between the peers in the network.

Table 1. Simulation Variables

Model	NS	NE	% M	% C	PP		PW	ξ	ZP
Eigen Trust Model	50	10	70	15	0.3		5	0.1	0.2

Table 2. Definition of Terms of Table 1

NE	number of model execution
NS	number of sensors
%M	percentage of malicious peers
%C	percentage of client
W	simulation window size
ξ	epsilon
PP	pre-trusted peers percentage
ZP	zero probability

Table 3. Result of the Simulation

Variables	scenario 1	scenario 2	scenario 3	scenario 3	scenario 5	scenario 6
Av.Tra	0.068	0.076	0.080	0.084	0.092	0.100
Av.Spath	2.360	2.350	2.320	2.310	2.300	2.250
Av.D	0.122	0.122	0.122	0.122	0.122	0.122
Av.Acc.	78%	78%	81%	83%	85%	89%
Av.En	9.4X1016	6.9X1016	5.7X1016	4.2X1016	3.1X1016	1.1X1016

Table 4. Summary of Table 3

Av.Tra	Average Transitivity coefficient
Av.Spat	Average Shortest path
Av.D	Average Density
Av.Acc	average Accuracy of the model Implementation
Av.En	Average energy consume by each peer

Figure 2 presents the observed average transitivity coefficient and average trust and reputation model accuracy of the simulation. The average model accuracy is defined as the total possible accuracy of all the peers in the network to locate the corresponding benevolent peers in the network. This tells us that the more the peers are connected to a transitive anchor, the higher the accuracy of trust model implementation (trust propagation and trust evaluation).

Another interesting observation is with regards to the total amount of energy consumed by the peers during the simulation studies, from the graph of Figure 3, we can observe the results of the simulation study of the average transitivity coefficient vs energy. We observe that with an increase in the average transitivity coefficient, the amount of energy consumed by the peers reduced significantly. Thus, it requires the peers to spend less energy in the process of locating the behaving peer in the network.

Figure 2. Average Transitivity Coefficient VS Average Trust and Reputation Model Accuracy

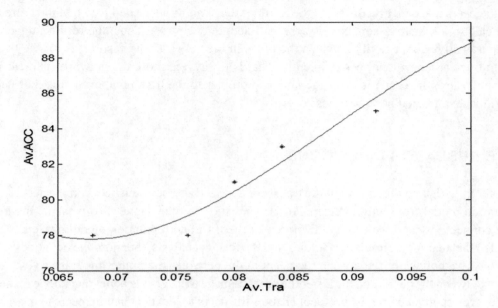

Figure 3. Average Transitivity Coefficient VS Average Energy Consumed by the peers

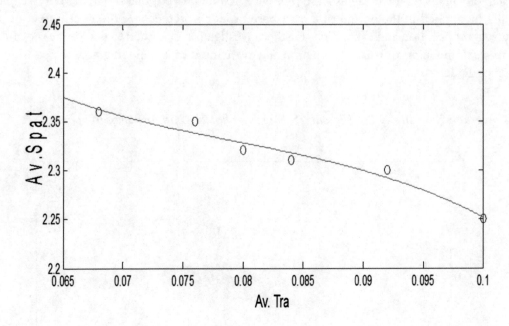

Also, Figure 4 shows the relationship between the average transitivity and the average shortest path between the peers respectively. Based on the result of the simulation we deduced that the more the peers are connected in a transitive connectivity, the path length decreases. Thus, the results suggest that the higher the transitive connectivity between the peers in the network, the easier it is for the peers in the network to trace a benevolent peer efficiently. That is to say, the more the network characterizes with a transitive closure, the easier it is for the nodes to propagate the trust data, evaluate other peers' trust levels and locate a trusted node with less energy.

FUTURE RESEARCH DIRECTIONS

This chapter investigated the impact of the transitive connectivity between peers on the accuracy of trust and reputation models' execution (Eigen Trust). The study in the chapter also presents the impacts of transitive connectivity and the energy efficiency of the trust and reputation model implementation. As illustrated in the analytical simulation studies and the results analysis, the more the network is characterized by transitive connectivity between the peers in the network, the higher the transitive connectivity coefficient between the peers, and the faster the peers manage to locate the benevolent node in the network with less energy spent because the protocol enables the peers to locate behaving peers using the shortest possible path. Based on the theoretical, analytical and simulation studies observed in this chapter, one can formulate the overall considerations of trust-based routing in P2P wireless networks. The findings of this chapter suggest that we can assume [but have not yet proved] that the transitivity-scaling factor can equally be applied in the design of a trust-based routing protocol for the intermittent network for efficient trust propagation and evaluation. Further investigation is needed to determine the effect of the transitivity-scaling factor for trust propagation and evaluation, especially in a network configuration of wireless mobile devices.

Figure 4. Average Transitivity Coefficient VS Average Shortest Path between the peers

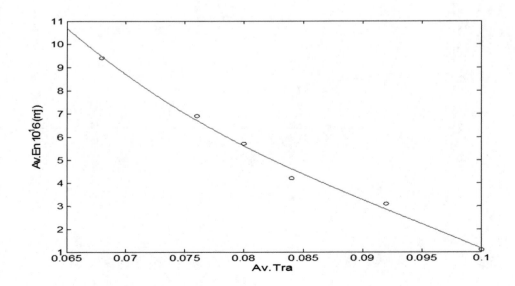

REFERENCES

Abusalah, L., Khokhar, A., & Guizani, M. (2008). A survey of secure mobile ad hoc routing protocols. *IEEE Communications Surveys and Tutorials*, *10*(4), 78–93. doi:10.1109/SURV.2008.080407

Airehrour, D., Gutierrez, J., & Ray, S. K. (2015). GradeTrust: A secure trust based routing protocol for MANETs. *IEEE Symposium conducted at the meeting of the Telecommunication Networks and Applications Conference (ITNAC), 2015 International.*

Al Ghamdi, A., Aseeri, M., & Ahmed, M. R. (2013). A Novel Trust and Reputation Model Based WSN Technology to Secure Border Surveillance. *International Journal of Future Computer and Communication*, *2*(3), 263–265. doi:10.7763/IJFCC.2013.V2.164

Beck, R., & Franke, J. (2009). Designing reputation and trust management systems. *E-Commerce Trends for Organizational Advancement: New Applications and Methods: New Applications and Methods*, 118.

Bello, A., Liu, W., Bai, Q., & Narayanan, A. (2015a). Exploring the Role of Structural Similarity in Securing Smart Metering Infrastructure. *Symposium conducted at the meeting of the Data Science and Data Intensive Systems (DSDIS), 2015 IEEE International Conference on Data Science and Data Intensive Systems (DSDIS).* 10.1109/DSDIS.2015.95

Bello, A., Liu, W., Bai, Q., & Narayanan, A. (2015b). Revealing the Role of Topological Transitivity in Efficient Trust and Reputation System in Smart Metering Network. *Symposium conducted at the meeting of the Data Science and Data Intensive Systems (DSDIS), 2015 IEEE International Conference on Data Science and Data Intensive Systems (DSDIS).* 10.1109/DSDIS.2015.114

Boukerch, A., Xu, L., & El-Khatib, K. (2007). Trust-based security for wireless ad hoc and sensor networks. *Computer Communications*, *30*(11), 2413–2427. doi:10.1016/j.comcom.2007.04.022

Chen, W., & Cai, S. (2005). Ad hoc peer-to-peer network architecture for vehicle safety communications. *IEEE Communications Magazine*, *43*(4), 100–107. doi:10.1109/MCOM.2005.1421912

Cho, J.-H., Swami, A., & Chen, R. (2011). A survey on trust management for mobile ad hoc networks. *IEEE Communications Surveys and Tutorials*, *13*(4), 562–583. doi:10.1109/SURV.2011.092110.00088

Dai, H., Jia, Z., & Qin, Z. (2009). Trust evaluation and dynamic routing decision based on fuzzy theory for manets. *Journal of Software*, *4*(10), 1091–1101. doi:10.4304/jsw.4.10.1091-1101

Demetrescu, C., & Italiano, G. F. (2006). Dynamic shortest paths and transitive closure: Algorithmic techniques and data structures. *Journal of Discrete Algorithms*, *4*(3), 353–383. doi:10.1016/j.jda.2005.12.003

Falcone, R., & Castelfranchi, C. (2009). Socio-cognitive model of trust. In *Encyclopedia of Information Science and Technology* (2nd ed.; pp. 3508–3512). IGI Global. doi:10.4018/978-1-60566-026-4.ch558

Falcone, R., & Castelfranchi, C. (2012). Trust and transitivity: how trust-transfer works. *Highlights on Practical Applications of Agents and Multi-Agent Systems*, 179-187.

Fullam, K., & Barber, K. (2007). *Dynamically learning sources of trust information: experience vs. reputation.* ACM. doi:10.1145/1329125.1329325

Grandison, T., & Sloman, M. (2000). A survey of trust in internet applications. *IEEE Communications Surveys and Tutorials, 3*(4), 2–16. doi:10.1109/COMST.2000.5340804

Hang, C.-W., & Singh, M. P. (2010). Trust-based recommendation based on graph similarity. *Proceedings of the 13th International Workshop on Trust in Agent Societies (TRUST).*

Harary, F., & Kommel, H. J. (1979). Matrix measures for transitivity and balance. *The Journal of Mathematical Sociology, 6*(2), 199–210. doi:10.1080/0022250X.1979.9989889

Jøsang, A., Ismail, R., & Boyd, C. (2007). A survey of trust and reputation systems for online service provision. *Decision Support Systems, 43*(2), 618–644. doi:10.1016/j.dss.2005.05.019

Landim, F. L. P., Fernandes, A. M., Mesquita, R. B., Collares, P. M. C., & Frota, M. A. (2010). Interpersonal network analysis: Application to the reality of a nursing team working in a hematology unit. *Saúde e Sociedade, 19*(4), 828–837. doi:10.1590/S0104-12902010000400010

Levin, D., Lee, Y., Valenta, L., Li, Z., Lai, V., Lumezanu, C., . . . Bhattacharjee, B. (2015). Alibi Routing. *Proceedings of the 2015 ACM Conference on Special Interest Group on Data Communication.*

Liu, G., Wang, Y., & Orgun, M. A. (2011). Trust Transitivity in Complex Social Networks. *Symposium conducted at the meeting of the AAAI.*

Lusher, D., Robins, G., Pattison, P. E., & Lomi, A. (2012). "Trust Me": Differences in expressed and perceived trust relations in an organization. *Social Networks, 34*(4), 410–424. doi:10.1016/j.socnet.2012.01.004

Maarouf, I., Baroudi, U., & Naseer, A. R. (2009). Efficient monitoring approach for reputation system-based trust-aware routing in wireless sensor networks. *IET Communications, 3*(5), 846–858. doi:10.1049/iet-com.2008.0324

Mármol, F. G., & Pérez, G. M. (2009). TRMSim-WSN, trust and reputation models simulator for wireless sensor networks. *Symposium conducted at the meeting of the Communications, 2009. ICC'09. IEEE International Conference on.*

Pathan, A.-S. K. (2016). *Security of self-organizing networks: MANET, WSN, WMN, VANET.* CRC Press.

Quattrociocchi, W., Caldarelli, G., & Scala, A. (2014). Self-healing networks: Redundancy and structure. *PLoS One, 9*(2), e87986. doi:10.1371/journal.pone.0087986 PMID:24533065

Qureshi, B., Min, G., & Kouvatsos, D. (2012). A distributed reputation and trust management scheme for mobile peer-to-peer networks. *Computer Communications, 35*(5), 608–618. doi:10.1016/j.comcom.2011.07.008

Rezgui, A., & Eltoweissy, M. (2007). TARP: A Trust-Aware Routing Protocol for Sensor-Actuator. *Networks Symposium conducted at the meeting of the Mobile Adhoc and Sensor Systems, 2007. MASS 2007. IEEE International Conference on.* doi:10.1109/MOBHOC.2007.4428674

Sarkar, S., & Datta, R. (2012). A trust based protocol for energy-efficient routing in self-organized manets. *IEEE Symposium conducted at the meeting of the India Conference (INDICON), 2012 Annual.*

Scott, J. (2017). Social network analysis. *Sage (Atlanta, Ga.).*

Shiakallis, O., Mavromoustakis, C. X., Mastorakis, G., Bourdena, A., & Pallis, E. (2015). Traffic-based S-MAC: A novel scheduling mechanism for optimized throughput in mobile peer-to-peer systems. *International Journal of Wireless Networks and Broadband Technologies*, *4*(1), 62–80. doi:10.4018/ ijwnbt.2015010105

Srivastava, V., Neel, J. O., MacKenzie, A. B., Menon, R., DaSilva, L. A., Hicks, J. E., ... Gilles, R. P. (2005). Using game theory to analyze wireless ad hoc networks. *IEEE Communications Surveys and Tutorials*, *7*(1-4), 46–56. doi:10.1109/COMST.2005.1593279

Usman, A. B., & Gutierrez, J. (2016). A Reliability-Based Trust Model for Efficient Collaborative Routing in Wireless Networks. *Proceedings of the 11th International Conference on Queueing Theory and Network Applications.*

Uysal, M. (2009). *Cooperative communications for improved wireless network transmission: Framework for virtual antenna array applications: Framework for virtual antenna array applications.* IGI Global.

Wang, Y., & Vassileva, J. (2003). Trust and reputation model in peer-to-peer networks. *Symposium conducted at the meeting of the Peer-to-Peer Computing, 2003 Proceedings. Third International Conference on.*

Watts, D., & Strogatz, S. (1998). Collective dynamics of small-world networks. *Nature*, *393*, 440–442. doi:10.1038/30918

Williams, M. J., & Musolesi, M. (2016). Spatio-temporal networks: Reachability, centrality and robustness. *Open Science*, *3*(6), 160196. PMID:27429776

Wohlgemuth, J. (2012). *Small World Properties of Facebook Group Networks.* University of Nebraska at Omaha.

You, C., Wang, T., Zhou, B., Dai, H., & Sun, B. (2010). A distributed energy-aware trust topology control algorithm for service-oriented wireless mesh networks. *Advances in Swarm Intelligence*, 276-282.

Zahariadis, T., Leligou, H. C., Trakadas, P., & Voliotis, S. (2010). Trust management in wireless sensor networks. *European Transactions on Telecommunications*, *21*(4), 386–395.

Zhou, R., & Hwang, K. (2007). Powertrust: A robust and scalable reputation system for trusted peer-to-peer computing. *IEEE Transactions on Parallel and Distributed Systems*, *18*(4), 460–473. doi:10.1109/ TPDS.2007.1021

Chapter 3
Semantically Secure Classifiers for Privacy Preserving Data Mining

Sumana M.
M. S. Ramaiah Institute of Technology, India

Hareesha K. S.
Manipal Institute of Technology, India

Sampath Kumar
Manipal Institute of Technology, India

ABSTRACT

Essential predictions are to be made by the parties distributed at multiple locations. However, in the process of building a model, perceptive data is not to be revealed. Maintaining the privacy of such data is a foremost concern. Earlier approaches developed for classification and prediction are proven not to be secure enough and the performance is affected. This chapter focuses on the secure construction of commonly used classifiers. The computations performed during model building are proved to be semantically secure. The homomorphism and probabilistic property of Paillier is used to perform secure product, mean, and variance calculations. The secure computations are performed without any intermediate data or the sensitive data at multiple sites being revealed. It is observed that the accuracy of the classifiers modeled is almost equivalent to the non-privacy preserving classifiers. Secure protocols require reduced computation time and communication cost. It is also proved that proposed privacy preserving classifiers perform significantly better than the base classifiers.

INTRODUCTION

Privacy preserving data mining is essential when useful trends, decisions or patterns are to be discovered from the sensitive data. However, this data could be distributed or centrally available. Mining on the distributed data allows miners to model multiple sites and deduce important conclusions. Let us consider

DOI: 10.4018/978-1-5225-5583-4.ch003

a situation where banks, credit card companies, tax collection agencies hold information about people within a locality. According to the Right to Financial Privacy Act, banks cannot reveal data about their customers to other companies or agencies. Similarly, Data Protection, Privacy and Law do not allow credit card companies to reveal any of their data. But useful inferences such as identifying fraud based on the tax collection, bank transactions and credit card details of an individual. Conclusions as to classify whether a person can be issued a loan, be provided with extra benefits or warned of a further loss or indicate whether the client can subscribe for a term deposit needs to be performed. The proposed privacy preserving classifiers creates classifier model from the data present at 3 different sites and enables any of these sites to make suitable decision. Similar situations can also be seen in hospital sector where hospitals hold the patient information including the type of treatment and its success. Doctors can obtain the private information of an individual and conclude on the type of treatment. Personal data of a patient could be present in bank datasets or insurance dataset where data cannot be revealed to the doctor.

Objectives of the Chapter

1. To build classifier models for the data vertically distributed at multiple sites.
2. To maintain the privacy of the sensitive data during mining and also use them for model building.
3. To construct efficient privacy preserving classifiers with improved performance.

BACKGROUND

The proposed approach allows to privately model classifiers based on the personal data maintained at insurance dataset and the hospital data for a large set of patients identified by name, age and locality without placing the data in a centralized site. As discussed in [(Agrawal & Aggarwal, 2001), (Yehuda & Benny, 2007), (Elisa, Dan, & Wei, 2008)], several approaches in Privacy Preserving data mining have evolved which can be broadly classified into perturbation, anonymization and cryptographic techniques. Perturbation involves transformations on the actual data before mining. This privacy preservation involves transfer of entire datasets as shown in (Jaideep, Hwanjo, & Xiaoqian, 2008) and (Hwanjo, Jaideep, & J, 2006) or partial datasets as mentioned in (Sun, Wei-Song, Biao, & Zhi-Jian, 2014) to single or multiple sites. A detailed survey on the needs and the various form of privacy preserving data mining can be found in (Lei, 2014). The key property of the randomization method is that the original records are not used after the conversion and data mining algorithms need to use the growing distributions of the perturbed data in order to perform the mining process. A symmetric perturbation approach and its reconstruction model that could be used for centralized association mining and classification is discussed in (Shipra, Jayant, & P, 2009).

(Agrawal & Srikant, 2000) Introduced the concept of perturbation in privacy preserving data mining were assorted algorithms are discussed to restructure distributions and learn a decision tree classifier from the perturbed data. Similar approaches of perturbation for privacy preserving association rule mining is conversed by (Rizvi & Haritsa, 2002) and (Zhang, Wang, & Zhao, 2004). (Latanya, 2002) And (Ashwin, Daniel, & Johannes, 2007) discusses anonymization techniques that can be used for privacy preserving data mining which involves two essential methods: generalization and suppression. (Arik, Assaf, & Ran, 2006) in their paper, confers the construction of a decision tree classifier using k-anonymity technique. Anonymization - Based Privacy preserving methods involves several attacks as seen in (Mielikainen,

2004). A privacy preserving distributed Naïve Bayes classifier for horizontally partitioned distributed data is proposed using k-anonymity constraints is mentioned in (Lambodar, 2013). (Elisa, Dan, & Wei, 2008) Clearly mentions that cryptographical approaches provide high level of data privacy compared to the randomization or anonymization approach of privacy preserving data mining.

The theoretical structure for all cryptographic protocols is Secure Multiparty Computation. Yao first developed a provably secure solution for the two-party comparison problem (Yao's Millionaire Protocol) (Yao, 1986). This approach to multiparty computations is discussed in (Goldreich, Micali, & Wigderson, 1987). However, the generic circuit evaluation technique does not work efficiently for large quantities of data. A detailed description of homomorphism is provided by (Benaloh, 1986). These homomorphic properties are used to perform secure computations in (Jaideep, Murat, & Clifton, Privacy-preserving Naïve Bayes classification, 2008), (Chen & Zhong, 2009) and (Yuan & Sheng, 2013). The additive and multiplicative homomorphic properties work well for our techniques. Privacy preserving protocols for back propagation and extreme learning machine for horizontally and vertically partitioned data using cryptography is discussed by Saeed and Ali in (Saeed, 2012). (Blum & Goldwasser, 1984), describes an efficient probabilistic public-key encryption that hides all partial information. This property enhances the privacy of our algorithm. [(Jaideep, Chris, Murat, & Scott, 2008) (Wenliang & Zhijun, 2002)] discusses the construction of decision trees from data partitioned between k sites with the site P_k holding the class attribute. However, the amount of communication and computations depends on the number of attributes, values of attribute and the complexity of the tree.

In (Jaideep, Murat, & Clifton, Privacy-preserving Naïve Bayes classification, 2008) a secure Naïve Bayesian Classifier is constructed on the data partitioned on multiple sites. This technique works on vertically partitioned data with attributes categorical or numeric in nature and the class label attribute maintained at a single site. Random secure sum protocol is used to compute the sum but this secure sum computation is not as secure as using homomorphic methods for secure sum calculation. However, a homomorphic semantically secure dot product protocol is applied for scalar product computation. On execution, it was observed that the computation time is comparatively high as the amount of communication between the parties is large for secure computations. Moreover, the random secure sum protocol used provides lesser security compared to the cryptographic methods.

Another protocol discussed in (Alka, 2013) briefs on a three layer Naïve Bayes Classifier for Vertically partitioned database which requires all the cooperating sites to have the class label attribute. In (Jiawei, 2013) the construction of a multi-party Neural Network learning algorithm on arbitrarily partitioned data with cloud is discussed. The ElGamal approach is used for secure computations. However ElGamal is not secure enough. Another interesting privacy preserving classifier (Chen & Zhong, 2009) models a back propagation neural network for vertically partitioned data using the probabilistic partial encryption /decryption property for secure computation of the activation function and product of two integers. On implementation, it is observed that the computation time and accuracy of the protocol largely depends on the number of attributes, number of epochs and number of hidden layers. This algorithm is modified to include the class attribute in a single site called as master site. As the number of hidden layers increase, the computation time almost doubles making this method of classification comparatively sluggish. It is obvious that as the number of sites increases the training time also increases drastically.

As mentioned in (Vaidya, 2008) SVM is an efficient classifier for classifying data. The results obtained by these classifiers provide better accuracy compared to other classifiers such as decision trees, Naïve Bayesian and Artificial Neural Networks. They are also lesser prone to data overfitting. The concept of Support vectors was introduced by (VN, 1998) followed by (Christianini N, 2000). The support vectors provide a compact representation of the trained model. A perturbation approach where data is locally perturbed by each of the parties using Gaussian distribution is used in [(Fung G, 2001), (Li Sin, 2014), (O. L. Mangasarian, 2008)]. The research article by (Haoran Li 2014) discusses the construction of a SVM classifier on horizontally distributed datasets using a perturbation based method.

OVERVIEW

Back Propagation Neural Network Learning

Back propagation (Jaiwei & Micheline, 2011) learns by iteratively processing a data set of training tuples, comparing the networks prediction for each tuple with the actual known target value. For each training tuple, the weights are modified so as to minimize the mean squared error between the networks prediction and the actual target value. Since the modification is made in the backwards direction, i.e. from the output layer, through the hidden layer this approach of learning the training dataset is called as back propagation. The ANN model building method is as shown below.

```
1. Initialize the weights in the network to small random numbers.
Each training tuple is processed by the following steps:
2. Propagate the inputs forward:
     For each of the input unit j,    O_j = I_j.
     For each hidden layer/ output layer unit j
       I_j = Σ_i w_ij * O_j
       O_j = 1/(1+e^-Ij)
3. Back propagate the error
     For each unit j in the output layer
       Err_j = O_j(1-O_j)(T_j-O_j); where T_j is the actual target value.
     For each unit j in the hidden layer
       Err_j = O_j(1-O_j) Σ_k Err_k w_jk;
     For each weight w_ij in network
         Δ w_ij = (ℓ) Err_j O_j ; // weight increment , where ℓ is the learning
rate.
         w_ij = w_ij +  Δ w_ij ;// weight update
```

Naive Bayesian Classification

Naïve Bayesian Classifier as seen in (Jaiwei & Micheline, 2011), uses the Bayes Theorem to train the instances in a dataset and classify new instances to the most probable target value. Each instance is identified by its N-attribute set and a class variable. Given a new instance X with N-attribute set, the posterior probability P (Class1/X), P (Class2/X) etc has to be computed for each of the class variable values based on the information available in the training data. If P (Class1/X)>=P (Class2/X)>=......>=P (Class/X) for N class values, then the new instance is classified to Class1or Class2…or ClassN accordingly.

This classifier estimates the class-conditional probability by assuming that the attributes are conditionally independent, given the class label y. The conditional independence can be obtained as follows:

$$P(X|Y=y) = \prod_{i=1}^{d} P(X_i|Y=y),$$ where each attribute set $X = \{X_1, X_2, \ldots, X_N\}$ consists of N attributes. Each of the N attributes can be categorical or numeric in nature.

Handling a Categorical Attribute

```
Input: p -> number of attribute values
C_xy -> represents number of instances having class x and attribute value y.
N_x - > represents number of instances that belong to class x
Output: P_xy -> represents the probability of an instance having class x and at-
tribute value y
For all class values y does
     {Compute N_x
      For every attribute value x
     {Compute C_xy
Calculate P_xy = C_xy/ N_x}}
```

Handling a Numeric Attribute

```
Input: x_jy -> value of instance j having class value y.
S_y -> represents the sum of instances having class value y
n_y -> represents number of instances having class value y
Output: Mean_y -> Mean of the values belonging to class y
Var_y -> Variance of class y
Stan_dev²_y -> Standard Deviation for class y
For all class values y do
```
$$\{\text{Compute } S_y = \sum_j x_{jy}$$
```
Compute n_y
Compute Mean_y = S_y/ n_y
Compute V_jy = (x_jy - Mean_y) ² for every instance j  that belongs to the class y
```
$$\text{Compute } Var_j \sum_j V_{jy}$$
```
Compute Stan_dev²_y = Var_j / (n_y-1)
}
```

Once the Variance and Standard Deviation is computed the probability for the numeric value provided in the test record for each of the class can be computed as follows:

P (given that (attribute_value = test_record_numeric_value)| Classy)

$$= 1 \frac{1}{\sqrt{2\text{Å}*\text{Stan}\_\text{dev}}} \exp\text{-} \frac{\left(\text{test}\_\text{record}\_\text{numeric}\_\text{value} - \text{Mean}\right)}{2 \text{ X Stan}\_\text{dev}\left(\text{of class y}\right)} y$$

On obtaining the Probabilities for each of the attributes with respect to each of the classes the class-conditional probabilities can be computed as follows:

For each of the class value I

Probability (test record having z attribute values I classI) = P(Attr1_valueIclassI) *P(Attr2_valueIclassI) *…….* P(Attrz_valueIclassI)

The test record belongs to the class has the maximum class-conditional probability.

SVM Classifier Methodology

SVM classifier searches for a hyperplane with the largest margin, which is known as the maximal margin classifier. For a binary classification problem consisting of N training examples, where each example is denoted by a tuple

(x_i, y_i) (i=1,2,……,N), where $x_i = (x_{i1}, x_{i2}, ………., x_{id})$, $x_{ij} = $ jth attribute of the ith tuple and $y_i \in \{1, -1\}$ which denotes the class label. The decision boundary of SVM classifier can be written in the form

wx + b =0, where w and b are parameters of the model.

Learning the SVM model can be formalized as the following constrained optimization problem:

$$\text{Min}_w \frac{\text{square}\| w \|}{2}$$

Subject to $y_i(w.x_i + b) >= 1$, i= 1,2,………..,N.

where square(x) = x^2

This objective function is quadratic and the constraints are linear for the parameters w and b, hence this is known as a convex optimization problem which can be solved using the Lagrange multiplier method. In order to proceed to the non-separable and non-linear cases it is useful to consider the dual problem. Rewriting the objective function that follows the constraints on the solutions results in a new objective function known as the Lagrangian for the optimization problem given as:

$$Lp = 0.5* \|w\|^2 - \sum_{i=1}^{N} \lambda_i \left(y_i \left(w.x_i + b \right) - 1 \right)$$ where λ_i are called the Lagrange multipliers.

Differentiating Lp with respect to w and b we obtain and set them to zero:

$$\frac{dLp}{dw} = 0 \text{ which gives } w = \sum_{i=1}^{N} \lambda_i y_i x_i$$

$$\frac{dLp}{db} = 0 \text{ to give } \sum_{i=1}^{N} \lambda_i y_i = 0.$$

Solving the above optimization problem is difficult because of the large number of parameters .i.e. w,b and λ_i. This problem is resolved by transforming the Lagrangian into a function of the Lagrange multipliers only, which leads to the dual formation of the optimization problem.

$$\text{Max } W(\lambda) = \sum_{i=1}^{N} \lambda_i - \frac{1}{2} \sum_{i=1}^{n} \sum_{j=1}^{n} \lambda_i \lambda_j y_i y_j K(x_i, x_j), 0 \leq \lambda_i \leq C, \forall i,$$

$$\sum_{i=1}^{n} y_i \lambda_i = 0$$

The Quadratic Programming (QP) problem can be solved using the extended SMO algorithm suggested by (S.S.Keerthi, 2002) which is an improvement over (Platt, 1998) to further improve the training time.

$K(x_i x_j)$ is the dot product function for linear classifiers. This computation is the only position where the training tuples would be referred. The values y_i and y_j are the class labels of the training tuples x_i and x_j.

The dot product function of tuples x_i and x_j, $K(x_i x_j) = (x_1 * x`_1) + (x_2 * x`_2) + (x_3 * x`_3) + \ldots\ldots +$ $(x_n * x`_n)$. Once the lagrange multipliers are obtained, a tuple with λ_i not equal to 0 are support vectors. These support vectors assist in computing the weights for each of the features and the final bias. In SVM the hyperplane is decided using support vectors which are essential training tuples and margins defined by support vectors.

Homomorphic Property

An important property of the (Paillier, 1999) assists in performing definite types of computations on the ciphertext and produce an encrypted result which when decrypted equates the outcome of an operation carried out on the plaintext. As Paillier is used to perform encryption and decryption of the data the notations used for encryption are E (value) and D (value) for decryption throughout this paper.

The two main homomorphic properties used are:

Homomorphic Addition

Let E (v_i) indicate the encryption of a plaintext v_i and D (v_i) indicate decryption of value v_i then,

D (E (v_1)*E (v_2)*E (v_3)*..........*E (v_n) mod nsquare) = $(v_1 + v_2 + v_3 + \ldots\ldots + v_n)$ mod n. In our case the values v_1, v_2, v_n are the locally computed values at each site.

Homomorphic Multiplication

Let $E(v_i)$ indicate the encryption of a plaintext v_i and $D(v_i)$ indicate decryption of value v_i then,

$D((((E(v_1)^{v2})^{v3})^{.......})^{vn})$ mod nsquare) $= (v_1 * v_2 * v_3 * .... * v_n)$ mod n. In our case the values v_1, v_2, v_n are the locally computed values at each site. This property is used to securely compute the product, mean and variance.

Secure Multiparty Computation

Secure multiparty computations enable parties to perform distributed computing tasks in a secure manner. The essential requirements on any secure computation protocol are privacy and correctness. The privacy requirement states that parties should learn their output and nothing else. The correctness requirement states that each party should receive its correct output. To incorporate this, the adversary must not be able to cause the result of the computation to diverge from the function that the parties have set out to compute. The basic building blocks or primitives of secure multiparty computations are oblivious transfer, oblivious polynomial evaluation and homomorphic encryption. A homomorphic encryption scheme is an encryption scheme which allocates certain operations to be carried out on the encrypted plaintext by applying an efficient operation to the corresponding ciphertext. In addition, most of encryption scheme which have this property are semantically secure.

PRIVACY PRESERVING HOMOMORPHIC CLASSIFIERS

Privacy Preserving Homomorphic Back Propagation Training on Vertically Partitioned Data (PPHANN)

A neural network structure includes input nodes, hidden and output nodes. At an instance the value in the input node is the value of the tuple. Since the data is vertically partitioned the input nodes are distributed at multiple sites. It is assumed that Party 1 (master site) decides on the number of hidden nodes. Only one output node is considered here. The number of hidden nodes is known to all the parties. Paillier's homomorphism property is used to securely compute the exponent of the product of the weights and the inputs for each of the hidden node (described in algorithm 2), in joint collaboration with all parties. The sigmoid function is computed from the obtained value by the master site. Master site proceeds to calculate the output based on the sigmoid value. As the target value is known party1 finds out the error in the weights of the output node and the hidden nodes. It then forwards this error values to each of the participating parties. All parties generate the updated weights for each of their inputs from the input values and the error values received. The process is repeated until terminating conditions. The final weights from each input to the hidden nodes are forwarded to the master site that further uses them to classify new test tuples. Algorithm 1 lists the steps. A flowchart is as shown in Figure 1.

Algorithm 1: Privacy-Preserving Distributed Algorithm for Back Propagation Training (PPHANN)

All the Collaborating Sites Normalize their attribute values to fall in the range 0.0 to 1.0.

```
1. Initialize all weights (w_ij, for i^th attribute and j^th hidden node)  to small
random numbers (b/w -0.1 to 0.1).
2. While the terminating condition is not satisfied
Repeat
```

For all the vertically partitioned training examples, with n attributes $\{x_1, x_2, \ldots x_n, t\}$ in Party1(main) where $1 =< n < m$ and remaining attributes $\{x_{n+1}, x_{n+2}, \ldots x_s\}$ in Party 2 $\{x_{s+1}, x_{s+2} \ldots, x_p\}$ in party3 and remaining attribute $\{x_{p+1}, x_{p+2}, \ldots, x_m)$ in party k , k indicates the number of collaborating parties and m are the total number of attributes in all these parties.

```
1. Propagate the inputs forward
1.1 for each hidden node h_j,
Party1 locally computes s_1 = (x_1*w_{1j}+x_2*w_{2j}+............+x_n*w_{nj}) and e^{-s1}
Remaining parties i=2 to k locally compute s_i = (x_{n+1}*w_{(n+1)j}+.....+x_s*w_{sj}) and e^{-si}
1.2 Party 1 to k use algorithm 2 (secure product), also shown in Figure 2 to
obtain
  e^{-s} = e^{-s1}* e^{-s2}*...*e^{-sk}.
1.3 For each of the hidden node h_j ,  Party 1 computes the sigmoid function  O_j
= 1/(1+ e^{-(S)}).
1.4 Party 1 initially assumes the weight (w_j) from each hidden node j to the
output node.
```

It further computes the net input $nvalue = \sum_{j=1}^{n} (w_j * O_j)$, output $O_o = 1/(1+e^{nvalue})$, where n is the number of hidden nodes and w_j is the weight from hidden node j to output node.

```
2.  Back propagate the error
2.1 As party 1 has the target attribute the error of the output node is com-
puted as
  Err_o = O_o*(1-O_o)*(T-O_o) where T is the value of the target attribute for the
training example.
2.2 To find error and update the weights from each input to hidden layer
For each unit j in the hidden layer,
Err_j = O_j(1-O_j) Err_o w_j    // w_j is the weight from hidden node h_j to Output
node.
```

Since the input of attribute i , I_i and weight from attribute i to hidden node j, w_{ij} is unknown the master site does the following operation

For each weight w_{ij} in network

The master site (party1) computes $Val_j = (\ell) \, Err_j$ where ℓ is the learning rate decided by the master site and broadcasts it to the cooperating sites.

Other sites compute $\Delta \, w_{ij} = Val_j * I_i$ where I_i is the value of the attribute i at site k. And also the updated weight $w_{ij} = w_{ij} + \Delta \, w_{ij}$. All sites move to the next tuple and repeats from step 1 until terminating condition (number of epochs). At the end of classification the weights from every tuple to every hidden node and the weight from the hidden nodes to the output node is obtained. Party 2 to k forward the weights of their attributes to the master site (i.e. party1).

To classify a new tuple with the attribute values $(y_1, y_2 \ldots y_n, y_{n+1}, \ldots, y_s, y_{s+1}, \ldots y_p, \ldots y_m)$

1. Party 1 for each hidden node j, performs $val_j = \sum_{i=1}^{m} y_i * w_{ij}$ where m is the total number of attributes in all parties.

2. Further output is computed as $O = \sum_{j=1}^{n} w_j * val_j$. If O is greater than 0.5 the class label value of the new tuple is taken as 1 otherwise class label value =0.

Algorithm 2: Secure Product Computation

Input: k parties have values $v_1, v_2 \ldots v_k$.
Output: Product $= v_1 * v_2 * \ldots * v_k$
1. Party 1 with v_1 generates the private and public keys.
2. Party 1 paillier encrypts $v_1 = \text{(int)}(v_1 * 100)$ {as only integer values can be encrypted) to obtain evalue= $E(v_1)$ and forwards it to neighboring party 2.
3. Party I = 2 to k update evalue = evalue.modpow((int)v_i* 100) and forward it to its neighbor.
4. Party k forwards evalue back to Party 1.
5. Party 1 now performs Product = D(evalue)/100 to get Product= $v_1 * v_2 * \ldots * v_k$ without knowing the values $v_2, v_3, \ldots, v_k$.

Privacy Preserving Homomorphic Naïve Bayesian Classifier on Vertically Partitioned Data (PPHNBC)

This classifier is built by a master site having the class label. It generates vectors holding Paillier encrypted values of 1's and 0's for each of its class label value, indicated by Y_Encrypt and N_Encrypt in the algorithm. Since Paillier encryption has the probabilistic property and is semantically secure as mentioned by (Ivan, Mads, & Jesper, September 2010), the result of encryption of every '1' or '0' results in a different encrypted value. These vectors are forwarded to each of the participating parties. Each of the parties on receiving the vectors multiplies only those vector (Y_Encrypt or N_Encrypt) values that have a particular categorical value. Hence each of the participating parties generate 2 values for each categorical value (i.e. from Y_Encrypt and N_Encrypt) vectors. This process is repeated for each of

Figure 1. Privacy Preserving Distributed Back propagation

Figure 2: Secure Product Computation

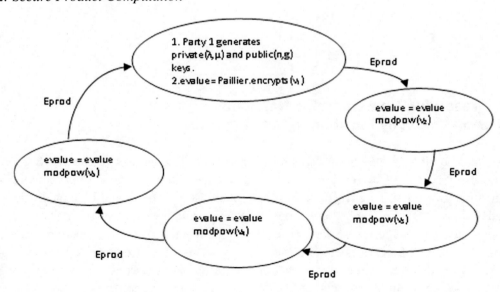

the categorical values. On receiving the encrypted products, decrypting them enables the master site is successfully computing the probability of occurrence of every categorical attribute value belonging to a class(Y or N) The flow diagram is shown in Figure 3 and a stepwise approach is discussed in Algorithm 3.

Algorithm 3: Privacy Preserving Homomorphic Naïve Bayesian Classifier for Categorical Attributes

```
// Handle categorical attributes present in other sites
Master Site (two class labels Yes and No)
1. for i= 1 to N //N is the number of tuples
if class label value = 'Yes'
{Y_Encrypt[i] = E(1);
N_Encrypt[i] = E(0);}
else
{Y_Encrypt[i] = E(0);
N_Encrypt[i] = E(1);}
Forward the vector Y_Encrypt and N_Encrypt to all the sites with the categori-
cal attribute.
2. Site k
Input: Y_Encrypt from master site
for j= 1 to M //M is the number of values of the categorical attribute
mul_result_k_V1[j]=1 // holds the multiplied result of the attribute V1 with
value j at site k for class value Yes.
mul_result_k_V2[j]=1 // holds the multiplied result of the attribute V1 with
value j at site k for class value No.
for i =1 to N // N is the number of tuples
if (value of the categorical attribute of tuple_i = j) then
{perform mul_result_k_V1[j] = mul_result_k_V1[j] * Y_Encrypt[i]
perform mul_result_k_V2[j] = mul_result_k_V2[j] * N_Encrypt[i]
}
forward mul_result_k_V1[j] and mul_result_k_V2[j] to master site.
3. Master Site
Input: mul_result_k_V1[j] and mul_result_k_v2[j] from site k for the value j
of a categorical attribute
Obtain Decrypt_mul_Y[j] = D(mul_result_k_V1[j]);
Obtain Decrypt_mul_N[j] = D(mul_result_k_V2[j]);
Probability of a categorical attribute having value j and belonging to class
Yes = Decrypt_mul_Y[j]/ no_tuples_Y, Where no_tuples_Y indicates the number of
tuples belonging to class Y.
Probability of a categorical attribute having value j and belonging to class
No= Decrypt_mul_N[j]/ no_tuples_N, Where no_tuples_N indicates the number of
tuples belonging to class N.
```

Figure 3. Flow Diagram of the Privacy Preserving Naïve Bayesian Classifier for categorical attribute

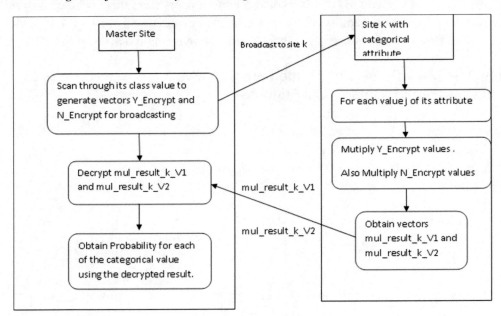

Handling numeric attribute values is a major challenge in construction of a Privacy Preserving Naïve Bayesian Classifier. To compute the mean for a class label Y, only those numeric values that belong to the class Y are added. But a site k (that is not a master site) is not aware of the class to which their numeric value belongs to; hence mean has to be securely computed. Computation of mean for a Naïve Bayes Classifier with respect to a class label value is shown as follows. For example:

mean (class_label = 'Yes') = sum_of_numeric_values$_k$/(number of tuples belonging to class = 'Yes')

Sum of all the values of a numeric attribute (denoted as numericvalue) belonging to a class belonging to a site could be calculated as follows:

$$\text{sum\_of\_numeric\_values}_k = \sum_{i=1}^{n} numericvalue * class\_value\left(given\ as\ 1\ or\ 0\right),\ \text{where}$$

class_value = 1 if the tuple i belongs to a class label (Yes) and 0 (for other than Yes) .

The sum_of_numeric_values$_k$ has to be computed securely as the class_value is not known to site k (that has the numeric value) but known only to master site. Hence the homomorphic property is used to perform this computation as follows

$$\text{sum\_of\_numeric\_values}_k = \prod_{i=1}^{n} \left(Y\_Encrypt\left[i\right] modulos\left(numericvalue\right)\right),$$ where Y_Encrypt array holds the paillier encrypted values of 1 and 0 when class value is Yes. Once the Master site gets the sum of all numeric values of an attribute in its encrypted form, it computes:

mean (class_label = 'Y') = Decrypt (sum_of_numeric_values$_k$) / (number of tuples belonging to class = 'Y')

To compute the variance (from the mean) the following principle is used.

Generally, a non secure computation of variance of n numbers is done as follows:

Variance = [(numericvalue$_1$-mean)^2+(numericvalue$_2$-mean)^2+...........+(numericvalue$_n$-mean)^2]/n

= [numericvalue$_1$^{2} + numericvalue$_2$^{2} +.....+ numericvalue$_n$^{2}]+ n*mean^2 – 2* mean *(numericvalue$_1$ + numericvalue$_2$+.............+numericvalue$_n$)]/n

But, for secure computation, the value of mean and n is known only to the master site, but site k(with the numeric attribute) only is aware of the remaining values numericvalue$_1$, numericvalue$_2$, ... numericvalue$_n$. Hence site k obtains:

$$\text{sum\_of\_numeric\_values}_k{}^2 = \prod_{i=1}^{n} \left(Y\_Encrypt\left[i\right] modulos\left(square\left(numericvalue_i\right)\right)\right)$$ and forwards to master site. Master site computes variance with respect to site k's attribute.

variance$_k$ = [decrypt (sum_of_numeric_values$_k$^{2}) + n * mean^2 – 2* mean * decrypt(sum_of_numeric_value$_k$)] / n, where n is the number of tuples belonging to a class .

The logic used here is (a-b)^2 = a^2+b^2 – 2*a*b where 'a' is the numeric value of a tuple at site k and 'b' is the mean at master site.

A detailed description of computing the mean and variance for numeric values available at participating sites is provided in algorithm 4.

Algorithm 4: Privacy Preserving Homomorphic Naïve Bayesian Classifier for Numeric Attributes (PPHNBC)

```
//Handle numeric attribute present at other sites
Master Site (two class labels Y and N)
1. For i= 1 to N //N is the number of tuples
if class label value = 'Yes'
{Y_Encrypt[i] = E(1);
N_Encrypt[i] = E(0);}
```

```
else
{Y_Encrypt[i] = E(0);
N_Encrypt[i] = E(1);}
```
Forward Paillier.nsquare, vectors Y_Encrypt and N_Encrypt to the remaining sites.
Paillier.nsquare is the square (p*q) where p and q are 2 large prime numbers.
2. Site p = 2 to k, for each of their numeric attribute
2a.Obtains Mean_Numerator_p_Y =

$$\prod_{i=1}^{n} Y\_Encrypt[i] \, modpow\left(numericval[i], Paillier.nsquare\right)$$

where numericval[i] is the numeric value of the attribute in tuple i in party p and Mean_Numerator_p_Y is the numerator of the mean at site p for class label 'Yes'
2b. Computes
variance_p_Y =

$$\prod_{i=1}^{n} Y\_Encrypt[i] \, modpow\left(square\left(numericval[i]\right), Paillier.nsquare\right)$$

variance_p_Y is the numerator part of the variance of at site p for class label 'Yes'
2c.Obtains Mean_Numerator_p_N =

$$\prod_{i=1}^{n} N\_Encrypt[i] \, modpow\left(numericval[i], Paillier.nsquare\right)$$

where numericval[i] is the numeric value of the attribute in tuple i.
Mean_Numerator_p_N is the numerator of the mean at site p for class label 'No'
2d.Computes
variance_p_N =

$$\prod_{i=1}^{n} N\_Encrypt[i] \, modpow\left(square\left(numericval[i]\right), Paillier.nsquare\right)$$

variance_p_Y is the numerator part of the variance of at site p for class label 'No'
2e. Forwards Mean_Numerator_p_Y, Mean_Numerator_p_N, variance_k_Y and variance_k_N to master site.
3. Master Site computes mean and variance of the numeric attribute r of site k

```
as follows
3a. Mean_r_k_Y = D(Mean_Numerator_p_Y)/ no_tuples_Y
Where no_tuples_Y indicates the number of tuples belonging to class Yes .
Mean_r_k_Y is the Mean for attribute 'r' present at site k for class value
'Yes'
3b. to compute variance_r_k_Y
i. Temp_val1 = 2* Mean_r_k_Y* D(Mean_Numerator_p_Y);
ii.variance_r_k_Y=(D(variance_p_Y)-Temp_val1+ no_tuples_Y*square(Mean_r_k_Y))/
no_tuples_Y.
3c. Mean_r_k_N = D(Mean_Numerator_p_N)/ no_tuples_N
Where no_tuples_N indicates the number of tuples belonging to class No.
3b. to compute variance_r_k_N
i. Temp_val2 = 2* Mean_r_k_N* D(Mean_Numerator_p_N);
ii.variance_r_k_N=(D(variance_p_N)-Temp_val2+no_tuples_N*square(Mean_r_k_N))/
no_tuples_N.
variance_r_k_Y and variance_r_k_N are the variance of the attribute 'r' pres-
ent at site k for class labels Yes and No
```

Once the variance and Standard Deviation= square root (variance) is computed the probability for the numeric value provided in the test record for each of the class i can be computed as follows:

```
P (given that (attribute_value = test_record_numeric_value)| Class_i)
```

$$= 1 \frac{1}{\sqrt{2\text{À}^*\text{Stan\_dev}}} \text{exp-} \frac{\left(\text{test\_record\_numeric\_value} - \text{Mean}\right)}{2 \text{ X Stan\_dev}\left(\text{of class y}\right)} y$$

On obtaining the Probabilities for each of the attributes with respect to each of the classes the class-conditional probabilities can be computed as follows:

For each of the class value I

Probability (test record having z attribute values | classI) = P (Attr1_value|classI) *P (Attr2_value|classI) *.......* P (Attrz_value|classI)

The test record belongs to the class has the maximum class-conditional probability.

Privacy Preserving Homomorphic Support Vector Machine Classification

Privacy Preserving Support Vector Machine classifier performs supervised learning on the data distributed at k sites. Each of the sites, 1 to k has a subset of features required for learning. Site k is called as the training party as it holds the class attribute as well as some of the features required for training. The number of tuples (T) used for model building is same for all the sites. Figure 4. shows the flow diagram of the PPHSVM modeling. Data preprocessing is performed on the datasets are conversion of categorical to numeric and handling missing values. The master party k that holds the class attribute initiates the classification process building by building a data matrix securely. It further uses the symmetric data matrix to generate lagrange multiplers . Once the weights and bias for all the attributes are computed they are forwarded to master party which can use these weights and biases to classify new tuples. The PPHSVM classification model generates the weights of all the attributes and the biases. Algorithm 5 shows the working of this privacy preserving classifier.

The privacy preserving linear SVM approach privately computes the dot product function, as shown in Figure 5. For secure computation, party k holding the class attribute, paillier encrypts its locally computed dot product value to obtain E(vk). It further transmits E(vk) and the public key to party 1 which performs E(vk)*E(v1) where v1 is the locally computed dot product value in party1.

This party passes the public key and the product to its neighboring party which repeats the process of evaluation (E(vk)*E(v1)*E(v2)) and forwards it to its neighbor and process repeats. The k-1 party on computing ((E(vk)*E(v1)*E(v2)*….*E(v(k-1))) forwards this result to the initiating party k. Party k decrypts the value to obtain the final dot product value from tuple x_i to x_j. Once the data matrix is obtained having the dot product values, support vectors are identified. Further these support vectors and class label at the master site are utilized to generate lagrange multipliers, weights and bias.

Algorithm 5: Privacy Preserving Homomorphic Linear Support Vector Machine Classification

Party k performs the following steps:

```
Step1
1.1 Generate the keys for Paillier encryption private keys (λ,μ)and public
keys(n,g)
1.2 Broadcast the public key to all the parties.
1.3 Obtains the dot product matrix of size (T*(T-1))/2 where T is the number
of tuples in each party.
k=0
```

Figure 4. Flow diagram of Privacy Preserving Linear SVM Classifiers

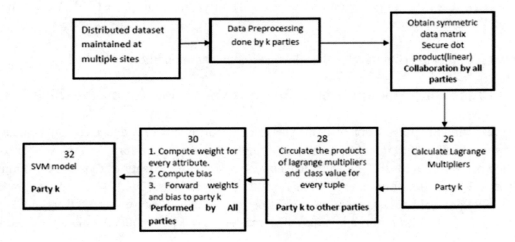

Figure 5. Secure multiparty computation of dot product from one tuple(x) to another tuple(x`)

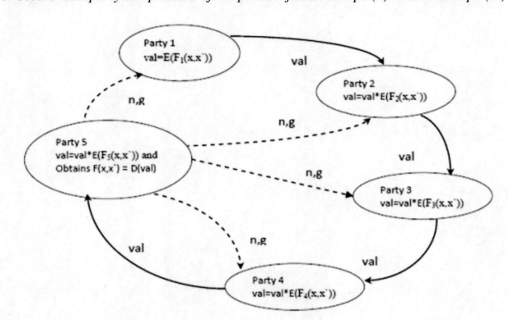

```
for i = 1 to T
for j = (i+1) to T
begin
compute sym_mat[k++]= f(xᵢ,xⱼ)  using Multiparty Secure Dot Product Protocol
(algorithm 6)
end
Step 2
```
With the vector sym_mat having $f(x_i,x_j)$ generate the symmetric data matrix as $f(x_i,x_j) = f(x_j,x_i)$. Using the data matrix, a class value vector Y, of size T, the lagranges multipliers vector λ for each of the tuples i is obtained using the Extended SMO convex quadratic programming algorithm.
Step 3
3.1 Locally compute the vector partial_prod(λY) as follows
for i=1 to T
partial_prodi= $\lambda_i Y_i$.
3.2 The vector partial_prod(λY) is broadcasted to remaining parties.

4.1 The remaining parties on receiving the partial_prod from master site compute the weight and bias for each of its attributes as follows
Party ℓ where ℓ = 1 to k-1
Receive the vector partial_prod(λY)
for i= 1 to p, p is the number of attributes in party ℓ

$$\text{weight}_i^\ell = \sum_{j=1}^{T} \left(x_{ij} * \text{partial\_prod}\left[j\right] \right),$$

where x_{ij} is the value of the attribute i for record j.
for h=1 to T

$$\text{compute bias}_h = 1 - \sum_{i=1}^{P} \left(\text{weight}_i^\ell * x_{ih} \right),$$

where x_{ih} is the value of the attribute i for record h.

$$\text{Bestbias}^\ell = \sum_{j=1}^{T} \text{bias}_j \, / \, T$$

4.2 Circulate the weight vector, weight$_i$' (that indicates weight of all the attributes) and the Bestbias' to party k.

Step 5
5.1 Party k also computes the weight and bias for each of its attributes as per step 4.1.

$$\text{Bestbias}^k = \sum_{j=1}^{T} \text{bias}_j \, / \, T$$

5.2 Party k receives the weight vector and Bestbias from all the parties.
5.3 The final_bias is computed as

$$\sum_{j=1}^{k} \text{Bestbias}_j \, / \, k$$

To classify a new tuple based on the learned SVM model
Given a tuple $x^T = (x_1, x_2, \ldots, x_n)$ with features $x_1, x_2, \ldots, x_n$

We obtain $\sum_{i=1}^{n} \text{weight}\left[i\right] * x_i$ + final_bias. Class value is decided based on the sign of the result. As party k has the weights of all attributes involved in the computation and bias the new tuple can be easily classified.

Multi Party Secure Computation of Dot Product

x and x` are tuples represented as features vectors.

The dot product $F(x,x`) = (x_{1*}x`_1) + (x_{2*}x`_2) + (x_{3*}x`_3) + \ldots\ldots + (x_{n*}x`_n)$, where $x_i$ and $x`_i$ are feature/attribute values of samples/tuples x and x` distributed at multiple sites. This function has to be computed in a distributed environment as the features/attributes are distributed at multiple sites. E(v) indicates encryption and D(v) indicates decryption.

Algorithm 6: Multiparty Secure Computation of Dot Product From Tuple x and x` Whose Attributes Are Distributed Across K Parties

Output: *Dot product for All The Distributed Attributes F(x,x`) from tuple x to x`*

Party k

1. Computes $Ex_k = (x_1*x`_1) + (x_2*x`_2) + (x_3*x`_3) + \ldots + (x_m*x`_m)$ for all its features (1 to m) except for the class label attribute.
2. It Paillier encrypts its value Ex_k to obtain $E(Ex_k)$ and forwards this to party 1.

Party 1

1. if Party 1, receives the encrypted value $E(Ex_k)$ and public key from party k
.
2. Computes $Ex_1 = (x_1*x`_1) + (x_2*x`_2) + (x_3*x`_3) + \ldots + (x_p*x`_p)$ for all its features (1 to p).
3. It then performs $Encrypt\_prod(x,x`) = E(Ex_k)*E(Ex_1) \bmod n^2$, and forwards this to its immediate next party i.e party 2.

Party I (I= 2 to k-1)

Party I receives the encrypted values from I-1 party.

1. Receives the value $Encrypt\_prod(x,x`)$ from its I-1th neighbor.
2. Computes $Ex_I = (x_1*x`_1) + (x_2*x`_2) + (x_3*x`_3) + \ldots + (x_q*x`_q))$ for all its features (1 to q).
3. It then updates $Encrypt\_prod(x,x`) = Encrypt\_prod(x,x`)*E(Ex_I) \bmod n^2$, and forwards this to its I+1th neighbor.

Party k-1 forwards its $Encrypt\_prod(x,x`)$ to party k. Party k obtains $F(x,x`)$ by decrypting $Encrypt\_prod(x,x`)$.

i.e. $F(x,x`) = D(Encrypt\_prod(x,x`))$.

Party k computes $F(x,x`)$ i.e the final dot product from tuple x to x` for all the features distributed from site 1 to site k using the logic,

$F(x,x`) = D(E(F_1(x,x`)) * E(F_2(x,x`)) * \ldots * E(F_k(x,x`)))) = F_1(x,x`) + F_2(x,x`) + \ldots + F_k(x,x`)$ by decrypting the Encrypt_prod(x,x`) i.e D(Encrypt_prod(x,x`)). It is important to note that the homomorphic property of Paillier is used to obtain the dot product of tuples x and x` with distributed features at multiple sites. To securely perform this computation, homomorphic property of Paillier is used. The whole process of dot product computation starts from party k which has the class attribute.

Figure 5 shows the working of the secure dot product computation. The master party k initiates the kernel function computation by forwarding the Encrypt_prod to its neighbor Party 1.

SECURITY ANALYSIS

The secure calculation of the sigmoid function using secure product protocol and the weight computation by each of the individual sites avoids interpretation of any data or intermediate results from the individual sites. This makes the privacy preserving ANN modeling highly secure as cryptanalysis is not possible. The only results revealed are the final weights of the attributes obtained on model building. The proposed approach provides better security when compared to the approach in (Chen & Zhong, 2009), where certain amount of inference on the data can be obtained, as encryption of a probable range of values is done.

The proposed privacy preserving Naïve Bayesian construction algorithm securely computes the probability for categorical attributes. Other cooperating sites cannot identify the number of tuples that belong to a particular class nor can the master site recognize the value of an attribute or the tuple containing the value. Similarly, for numeric attributes, mean and variance calculated is not revealed to any of the other cooperating parties. The homomorphic and the probabilistic property of Paillier's enable calculations to be performed without disclosing information making the proposed approach more secure to the baseline protocol.

The participating parties in privacy preserving homomorphic support vector machine classifier securely compute the dot product of every tuple to every other tuple without revealing the number of attributes and values of the attributes to each other. The process of modeling a privacy preserving version of SVM does not reveal information about any of the attributes. Encrypted values holding results of computations are transmitted between the sites hence making the model construction secure.

RESULT ANALYSIS

The above approaches have been implemented on data maintained at 3 sites for a set of individuals. The master site is a bank that holds age, job, marital, education, housing loan, personal loan, employment variation rate, consumer price index, consumer confidence index, and client has a term deposit with a class label attribute "profitable customers". The credit site consists a qualitative attribute Status of existing checking account, numerical Attribute Duration in month, a categorical attribute Credit history, purpose, Credit amount, Present employment years, Installment rate in percentage of disposable income, Age in years, Job, foreign worker. The third participating site is the tax collector site with attributes such as net operating loss from any business; business credit carryovers; minimum tax credit; capital losses; the basis of property; passive activity loss and credit carryover; and foreign tax credits.

The number of tuples in all the 3 sites is the similar and the datasets are built assuming that attributes age and name are known to all sites. For Privacy Preserving Homomorphic Back propagation classifier, categorical values are converted into their numeric forms and normalized to values from 0 to 1. However, for Privacy Preserving Homomorphic Naïve Bayes classifiers(PPHNBC), the values of the attributes are retained as they are with data preprocessing performed to handle missing values. As observed in Figure

6, the execution time of our approaches is faster compared to PPNBC (Vertically Partitioned) [(Jaideep, Chris, Murat, & Scott, 2008)] and PPANN [(Chen & Zhong, 2009)] methods.

Privacy Preserving Back propagation classifiers (PPANNB_VDD) are slower compared to Naïve Bayes owing to each tuple handled in each step and number of epochs considered. The number of epochs considered here are 1/10th of the actual dataset. The PPANN approach is sluggish as the quantity of encryptions performed in each epoch is large. For PPHSVMC, all the attributes maintained in multiple parties are numeric in nature with the binary class label having values 1 or -1. Hence an essential prerequisite to this approach involves conversion of categorical values to numeric. Whereas in PPANN (Zhong, 2011) too all the attributes are numeric in nature with the class label value 0 or 1. For PPNBC (J Vaidya., 2008) the attributes are either numeric or categorical in nature. The data preprocessing performed on this dataset is approximation of the missing values. Linear PPHSVMC classifier takes lesser execution time in model building compared to the other baseline privacy preserving classifiers .The number of sensitive attributes in each participating sites do not affect the computation time of the classifier. However, the number of tuples influences the computation.

The accuracy of the privacy preserving homomorphic Back Propagation algorithm and naïve Bayesian classifiers provide similar accuracy to their non privacy preserving version. As seen in Figure 7, the accuracy is better than the PPANN and PPNBC classifiers. The slight change is accuracy is due to the type conversions performed during encryption.

The accuracy of the privacy preserving homomorphic classifiers provides similar accuracy to their non privacy preserving version. The accuracy is better than the PPANN and PPNBC classifiers. There is a slight change in accuracy compared to the nonprivacy version. This is due to the type conversions of numeric values performed during encryption. For the sake of experiment, the bank dataset with 20 attributes is distributed at multiple parties to analyze the computation and accuracy of the models constructed. The total number of attributes and instances remains the same. Figure 8 indicates the accuracy measured. Accuracy largely depends on the amount of communications in the process of model building and conversions to the data performed. Hence, reduced communication between parties improves the accuracy of the model. It is also quite obvious from the result that the PPHSVM classifier is highly accurate and closer to the non-privacy version.

Figure 6. Computation time Comparison

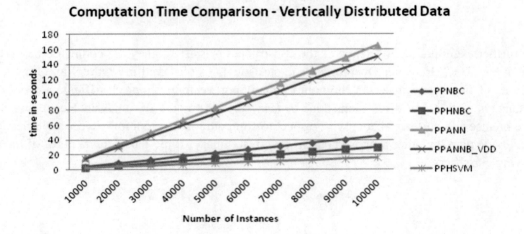

Figure 7. Accuracy Comparison

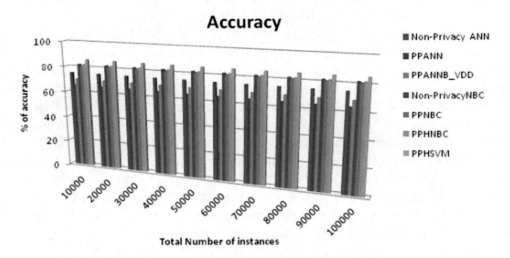

Figure 8. Accuracy with respect to number of participating sites

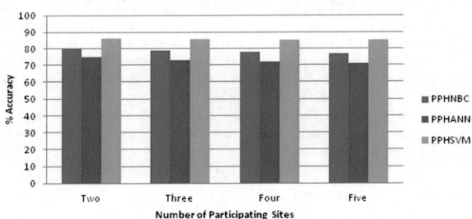

To further examine the efficiency of the constructed classifiers, they are compared based on their precision and ROC (Receiver Operating Characteristics). As observed in Figure 9 and Figure 10, the probability of the privacy preserving homomorphic support vector machine classifier to precisely predict an instance is high, as per discussions done by (Fawcett, 2006) on ROC analysis. Hence this classifier is more precise and performs better with respect to computation time complexity, communication time and accuracy, than the other proposed classifiers. In summary, Table 1 lists the features of the privacy preserving classifiers.

Figure 9. Comparison with respect to precision

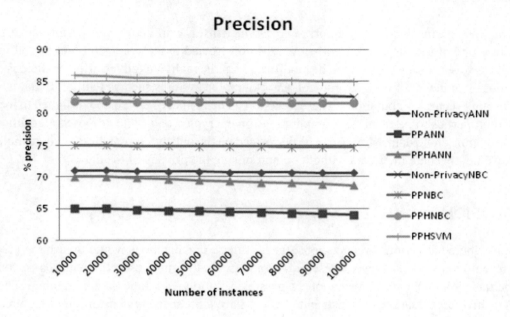

Figure 10. ROC Curve

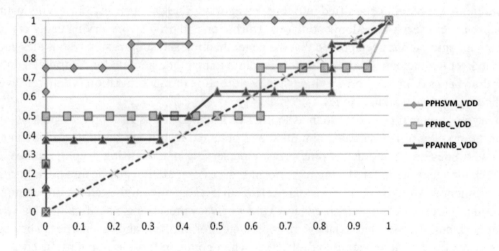

Table 1. Comparison of the classifiers

Privacy Preserving Naive Bayesian Classifier	Privacy Preserving Artificial Neural Networks	Privacy Preservation Support Vector Machines
Communication between parties is required to compute probability (for mean and variance) of each attribute. Hence the number of times that parties need to communicate depends largely on the number of attributes and values of the attribute	Communication between attributes is required for activation function computation and several product computations to calculate weight. These communications have to be performed for every epoch. Here too the number of communications is very large.	i. Communication is required only for secure dot product computation. ii. Communication to forward the lagrange multipliers. iii. Communication of final weights.

FUTURE SCOPE

The privacy preserving data mining algorithms presented in this work shows high performance. However, the future scope of the thesis is listed below. The constructed models are semi honest and follow the protocol. However, the algorithms can be modified to handle malicious adversaries. Malicious adversaries are those that deviate from the protocol. Cryptographic systems such as Paillier, ElGamal are used for performing secure computations. These systems can be further explored and designed to incorporate improved properties to perform fast computations on encrypted data. The proposed algorithms can be extended to mine cloud data. Mining can be performed on the outsourced databases, where multiple data owners efficiently share their data without compromising the privacy of the data.

CONCLUSION

Data is distributed at various organizations. Each of these organizations would breach the privacy rule if they reveal their data. However, these organizations want to mine essential patterns or conclusions based on their joint data and information. A possible solution is to mine data by retaining the privacy of the sensitive data. Data that is distributed could have similar features or different features. In data mining, classification models predict the categorical class based on the features. Clustering is another data mining technique used to group objects of similar nature. As per literature, privacy preserving data mining problems are broadly classified into three categories. They are privacy preserving using anonymization, privacy preserving randomization or perturbation and privacy preserving using cryptography. Under anonymization it has been proved that the generalization and suppression techniques used are not sufficient in keeping the data secure. Also this is found to be more suitable for centralized data. One of the major drawbacks of privacy preserving using perturbation or randomization is data retrieval and the tradeoff between privacy and accuracy.

When cryptographical protocols such as Paillier or Elgamal are used in privacy preserving it is assured that the privacy of the data is maintained and obtained results are accurate. Hence our research concentrated on designing and developing privacy preserving models using cryptographical methods. The major challenges encountered were to perform secure computation and design the algorithms with improved efficiency. An algorithm is considered efficient if it generates high accurcy, low communication cost, low computation cost and better precision. Under privacy preserving classification, Naive Bayesian models for horizontally distributed data were constructed for multiple and two parties. The constructed classifiers proved to be more secure and efficient when compared to the popularly used approaches. However, the features of the distributed data need not be same in all the participating parties. Hence, privacy preserving data mining on vertically distributed data were designed and developed. The privacy preserving homomorphic Naive Bayesian classifier performs computations to calculate probability, mean and variance for categorical and numeric attributes. In order to maintain data security only the relevant data are encrypted or communicated. As only one of the sites generates the public and private key, that site alone can decrypt to obtain the desired result.

In the privacy preserving Artificial Neural Networks using backpropagation, secure computations of product and the sigmoid function for two or multiple parties is performed. Here too the performance is better in comparison to the popularly used privacy preserving classifiers. However, the computation time, communication cost largely depends on the number of epochs. Hence the accuracy and computation time proved to be less compared to the other constructed classifier models. Privacy preserving versions of Support Vector Machine Classifier were constructed by performing secure dot product on the locally computed results. Computations were done only for the upper half of the distance matrix. The amount of communication in comparable to the earlier approaches is significantly less. Therefore, Privacy Preserving Support Vector Machine is more efficient than the other classifier with reduced computation time, increased accuracy and better precision.

REFERENCES

AC, Y. (1986). How to generate and exchange secrets. In *27th IEEE symposium on foundations of computer science*, (pp. 162–167). Los Alamitos, CA: IEEE Press.

Aggarwal, C., & Yu, P. S. (2008). A Survey of Randomization Methods for Privacy-Preserving Data Mining. *Advances in Database Systems, Springer, 34*, 137–156. doi:10.1007/978-0-387-70992-5_6

Agrawal, D., & Aggarwal, C. (2001). On the design and quantification of privacy preserving data mining algorithms. In *Twentieth ACM SIGACT-SIGMOD-SIGART Symposium on Principles of Database Systems* (pp. 247-255). Santa Barbara, CA: ACM. 10.1145/375551.375602

Agrawal, R., & Srikant, R. (2000). Privacy-preserving data mining. In *Proceedings of the 2000 ACM SIGMOD international conference on Management of data* (pp. 439-450). New York: ACM. 10.1145/342009.335438

Agrawal, R. S. (2000). *Privacy-preserving data mining. In 2000 ACM SIGMOD conference on management of data* (pp. 439–450). Dallas, TX: ACM.

Agrawal, S. (2006). FRAPP: A framework for high-accuracy privacy-preserving mining. Data Mining and Knowledge Discovery, 101-139.

Alka, G. R. (2013). Privacy Preserving Three-Layer Naive Bayes Classifier for Vertically Partitioned Databases. *Journal of Information and Computational Science*, 119–129.

Arik, F. S. A. (2006). k-Anonymous Decision Tree Induction. In Knowledge Discovery in Databases, PKDD (pp. 151-162). ACM.

Ashwin, M., Daniel, K., & Johannes, G. (2007). L-diversity: Privacy beyond k-anonymity. *ACM Transactions on Knowledge Discovery from Data*, 3.

Bansal, A., Chen, T., & Zhong, S. (2013). Privacy Preserving Back-Propagation Neural Network Learning over Arbitrarily Partitioned Data. *Neural Computing & Applications, 20*(1), 143–150. doi:10.100700521-010-0346-z

Benaloh, J. (1986). Lecture notes in computer science: Vol. 263. *Secret sharing homomorphisms: Keeping shares of a secret secret*. Berlin: Springer-Verlag.

Benjamin, C. M. F. W. (2010). Privacy-Preserving Data Publishing: A Survey of Recent Developments. ACM Computing Surveys, 42(4).

Bertino, E. L. (2008). A Survey of Quantification of Privacy Preserving Data Mining Algorithms. In Models and Algorithms. Springer.

Blum, M., & Goldwasser, S. (1984). An efficient probabilistic public-key encryption that hides all partial information. In R. Blakely (Ed.), *Advances in cryptology—Crypto 84 proceedings* (pp. 289–299). Berlin: Springer-Verlag.

Blum, M. G. S. (1984). An efficient probabilistic public-key encryption that hides all partial information. In R. Blakely (Ed.), *Advances in cryptology—Crypto 84 proceedings*. Berlin: Springer-Verlag.

Chen, T., & Zhong, S. (2009). Privacy-Preserving Backpropagation Neural Network Learning. *IEEE Transactions on Neural Networks, 20*(10), 1554–1564. doi:10.1109/TNN.2009.2026902 PMID:19709975

Christianini, N. S.-T. J. (2000). An introduction to support vector machines and other kernel-based learning methods. Cambridge University Press.

DuW. Z. Z. (2002). Building decision tree classifier on private data. In IEEE international conference on data mining workshop on privacy, security and data mining (pp. 1-8). Maebashi City, Japan: IEEE.

Elisa, B., Dan, L., & Wei, J. (2008). *Privacy-Preserving Data Mining*. Chicago: Springer US.

Evfimievski, A. S. R. (2002). Privacy preserving mining of association rules. In *Eighth ACM SIGKDD international conference on knowledge discovery and data mining* (pp. 217-228). Edmonton, Canada: ACM.

Fawcett. (2006). *Pattern recognition*. Academic Press.

Fung, G. M. O. (2001). Proximal support vector machine classifiers. In *Proceedings of the ACM SIGKDD international conference knowledge discovery and data mining* (pp. pp 77–86). ACM. 10.1145/502512.502527

Goldreich, O., & Micali, S., & Wigderson. (1987). A How to play any mental game—a completeness theorem for protocols with honest majority. *19th ACM symposium on the theory of Computing*, 218–229.

Hwanjo, Y., & Jaideep, V., & J, X. (2006). Privacy-Preserving SVM Classification on Vertically Partitioned Data. In *10th Pacific-Asia Conference, PAKDD 2006* (pp. 647-656). Singapore: Springer Berlin Heidelberg.

Ivan, D., Mads, J., & Jesper, B. N. (2010, September). A generalization of Paillier's public-key system with applications to electronic voting. *International Journal of Information Security*, 371–385.

Jaideep, V., Chris, C., Murat, K., & Scott, P. (2008). Privacy-Preserving Decision Trees over Vertically Partitioned Data. *ACM Transactions on Knowledge Discovery from Data*.

Jaideep, V., Hwanjo, Y., & Xiaoqian, J. (2008). Privacy-preserving SVM classification. *Knowledge and Information Systems*, 161–178.

Jaideep, V., Murat, K., & Clifton, C. (2008). Privacy-preserving Naïve Bayes classification. *The VLDB Journal — The International Journal on Very Large Data Bases*, 879-898.

Jaideep Vaidya, C. C. (2008). Privacy-Preserving Decision Trees over Vertically Partitioned Data. *ACM Transactions on Knowledge Discovery from Data*, 2(3), 14.

Jaiwei, H., & Micheline, K. (2011). *Data Mining –Concepts and Techniques*. Morgan Kaufmann.

JC, B. (1986). Secret sharing homomorphisms: Keeping shares of a secret secret. In Advances in cryptography—CRYPTO86 vol 263, Lecture notes in computer science (pp. 251–260). Berlin: Springer-Verlag.

Jiawei, Y. (2013). *Privacy Preserving Back-Propagation Neural Network Learning Made Practical with Cloud Computing. IEEE Transactions on Parallel and Distributes Systems*.

Keerthi, S. S. E. G. (2002). Convergence of a Generalized SMO Algorithm for SVM Classifier Design. Machine Learning, 351-360.

Lambodar, J. N. (2013). Privacy Preserving Distributed Data Mining with Evolutionary Computing. In *International Conference on Frontiers of Intelligent Computing: Theory and Applications* (pp. 259-267). Springer.

Latanya, S. (2002). k-ANONYMITY: A Model For Protecting Privacy. *International Journal of Uncertainty, Fuzziness and Knowledge-based Systems*, 557–570.

Lei, X. C. (2014). Information Security in Big Data: Privacy and Data Mining. *IEEE Access: Practical Innovations, Open Solutions*, 2, 1149–1174. doi:10.1109/ACCESS.2014.2362522

Li Sin, W.-S. M.-J. (2014). *A new privacy preserving proximal support vector machine for classification of vertically partitioned data. International Journal Machine Learning and Cybernetics*.

Machanavajjhala, A. (2007). L-diversity: Privacy beyond k-anonymity. *Journal of ACM Transactions on Knowledge Discovery from Data, 1*(1).

Mangasarian, O. L. E. W. (2008). Privacy-Preserving Classification of Vertically Partitioned Data via Random Kernels. ACM Transactions on Knowledge Discovery from Data, 2(3).

Mielikainen, T. (2004). Privacy Problems with Anonymized Transaction Databases. *7th International Conference, DS 2004* (pp. 219-229). Padova, Italy: Springer Berlin Heidelberg.

Oliveira, S. Z. O. (2003). Privacy preserving clustering by data transformation. *18th Brazilian symposium on databases*, 304–318.

P, P. (1999). Public key cryptosystems based on composite degree residuosity classes. In *Advances in Cryptology—Eurocrypt '99 proceedings, lecture notes in computer science* (vol. 1592, pp. 223–238). Berlin: Springer-Verlag.

Paillier, P. (1999). Public-Key Cryptosystems Based on Composite Degree Residuosity Classes. EU-ROCRYPT, 223–238.

Platt, J. C. (1998). *Fast Training of Support Vector Machines using Sequential Minimal Optimization.* Academic Press.

Portia, C. (2011). *Data mining and Neural Networks from Commercial Perspective.* Academic Press.

Raymond Chi-Wing Wong, J. L.-C. (2006). (α, k)-anonymity: an enhanced k-anonymity model for privacy preserving data publishing. In *12th ACM SIGKDD international conference on Knowledge discovery and data mining* (pp. 754-759). New York: ACM.

Rizvi, S., & Haritsa, J. (2002). Maintaining data privacy in association rule mining. In *28th Very Large Database Conference.* Hong Kong, China: Academic Press. 10.1016/B978-155860869-6/50066-4

Saeed, S. A. (2012). Privacy-preserving back-propagation and extreme learning machine algorithms. Data and Knowledge Engineering, 40-61.

Services, D. o. (2002). *Standard for privacy of individually identifiable health information.* Available: http://www.hhs.gov/ocr/ privacy/hipaa/administrative/privacyrule/privruletxt.txt

Shipra, A., & Jayant, R. H., & P, A. B. (2009). FRAPP: A framework for high-accuracy privacy-preserving mining. *Data Mining and Knowledge Discovery*, 101–139.

Sun, L., Wei-Song, M., Biao, Q., & Zhi-Jian, Z. (2014). A new privacy-preserving proximal support vector machine for classification of vertically partitioned data. *International Journal of Machine Learning and Cybernetics*, 109–118.

T, M. (2004). Privacy problems with anonymized transaction databases. In *7th international conference proceedings, Lecture notes in computer science* (vol. 3245, pp. 219–229). Berlin: Springer-Verlag.

Vaidya, J. M. K. (2008). Privacy Preserving Naïve Bayes Classification. The VLDB Journal, 879-898.

Vaidya, J. H. (2008). Privacy-preserving SVM classification. Knowledge and Information Systems, 14(2), 161-178.

VN, V. (1998). Statistical learning theory. New York: Wiley.

Wenliang, D., & Zhijun, Z. (2002). Building decision tree classifier on private data. *CRPIT '14 Proceedings of the IEEE international conference on Privacy, security and data mining* (vol. 14, pp. 1-8). ACM.

Yao, A. C.-C. (1986). How to generate and exchange secrets. In *Foundations of Computer Science, 1986., 27th Annual Symposium* (pp. 162 - 167). Toronto, Canada: IEEE.

Yehuda, L., & Benny, P. (2007). An Efficient Protocol for Secure Two-Party Computation in the Presence of Malicious Adversaries. In *26th Annual International Conference on the Theory and Applications of Cryptographic Techniques* (pp. 52-78). Barcelona, Spain: Springer Berlin Heidelberg.

Yuan, Z., & Sheng, Z. (2013). A privacy-preserving algorithm for distributed training of neural network ensembles. *Neural Computing & Applications*, 269–282.

Zhang, N. W. (2004). A new scheme on privacy-preserving association rule mining. In PKDD Proceedings of the 8th European Conference on Principles and Practice of Knowledge Discovery in Databases, Lecture Notes in Computer Science (vol. 3202, pp. 484-495). Academic Press, Pisa, Italy: Springer Berlin Heidelberg.

Zhong, S. Z. (2011). A Privacy-Preserving Algorithm for Distributed Training of Neural Network Ensembles. *Neural Computing & Applications*, *22*(1), 269–282.

Chapter 4
Building a Maturity Framework for Information Security Governance Through an Empirical Study in Organizations

Yassine Maleh
University Hassan I, Morocco

Mounia Zaydi
University Hassan I, Morocco

Abdelkbir Sahid
National School of Commerce and Management (ENCG), Morocco

Abdellah Ezzati
Faculty of Science and Technology (FST), Morocco

ABSTRACT

There is a dearth of academic research literature on the practices and commitments of information security governance in organizations. Despite the existence of referential and standards of the security governance, the research literature remains limited regarding the practices of organizations and, on the other hand, the lack of a strategy and practical model to follow in adopting an effective information security governance. This chapter aims to explore the engagement processes and the practices of organizations involved in a strategy of information security governance via a statistical and econometric analysis of data from a survey of 1000 participants (with a participation rate of 83.67%) from large and medium companies belonging to various industries. Based on the results of the survey regarding practices of information security management and governance, a practical maturity framework for the information security governance and management in organizations is presented.

DOI: 10.4018/978-1-5225-5583-4.ch004

INTRODUCTION

The threat to technology-based information assets is greater today than in the past. The evolution of technology has also reflected in the tools and methods used by those attempting to gain unauthorized access to the data or disrupt business processes (L. Goodhue & Straub, 1991). Attacks are inevitable, whatever the organization (IT Governance Institute, 2006). However, the degree of sophistication and persistence of these attacks depends on the attractiveness of this organization as a target (F. Rockart & D. Crescenzi, 1984), mainly regarding its role and assets. Today, the threats posed by some misguided individuals have been replaced by international organized criminal groups highly specialized or by foreign states that have the skills, personnel, and tools necessary to conduct secret and sophisticated cyber espionage attacks. These attacks are not only targeted at government entities. In recent years, several large companies have infiltrated, and their data have been "consulted" for several years without their knowledge. In fact, improving cyber security has emerged as one of the top IT priorities across all business lines. So, while companies (von Solms & van Niekerk, 2013) (Bowen, Chew, & Hash, 2007)

Areas such as the aerospace industry and strategic resources can be ideal targets for cyber espionage by nation-states, others managing financial assets or large-scale credit card information are equally attractive to international criminal groups (Posthumus & von Solms, 2004) (Humphreys, 2008).

These malicious actors no longer content themselves with thwarting the means of technical protection. Instead, they survey and exploit a variety of weaknesses detected in the targeted environment (Galliers & Leidner, 2014). These shortcomings are not only technological but also result from failures in protection procedures or gaps in vulnerability management practices. The best technology in the world, if misused will not provide an adequate defense against such threats (von Solms & van Niekerk, 2013).

Ensuring the information system IS security in a large organization is a real challenge (Sohrabi Safa, Von Solms, & Furnell, 2016). Only a good governance can reassure the general management, customers and partners, shareholders and ultimately the public at large (Mark Duffield, 2014).

The problem is that the security governance framework is designed to guide organizations in there IS security governance strategy, but does not define the practical framework for the engagement in this strategy.

To address these concerns, some practice repositories (ITIL, Cobit, CMMi, RiskIT) and international standards (ISO 27000 suite, ISO 15408) now include paragraphs on security governance. The first reports or articles in academic journals that evoke the governance of information security date back to the early 2000s.

The proposed referential and best practices designed to guide organizations in their IT security governance strategy. However, does not define the practical framework to implement or to measure the organization engagement in term of IS security governance.

In this paper, we will study the practices and commitments of organizations in IS security governance. A survey of 836 medium and large companies at the international level (USA, UK, France, Morocco, China, Russia, etc.) was set up to define the best practices of these organizations regarding information security governance and management. This study allowed us to propose a practical framework to evaluate the organization in their maturity state and to improve their level of IS security governance according to their needs and resources.

The chapter is structured as follows. Section 2 presents the previous work on information security governance proposed in the literature. Section 3 describes the survey carried out among 836 medium and large international companies and gave a faithful picture of their practices in IS security governance through statistical analysis. Then, we analyze and discusses the results of this research. Section 4 describes the proposed capability maturity framework for information security management and governance ISMGO. Section 5 discuss the results of the implementation of ISMGO through a practical use case. Finally, Section 6 presents the conclusion of this work, and section 7 gives some limitations and future directions.

THEORETICAL FRAMEWORK

Methodology

Our data are collected from large and medium companies on an international scale. There are several justifications for this choice. Governance first implemented by large firms, (Waddock & Graves, 1997) demonstrate that organizations with significant financial resources can invest more in strategic activities (Archibugi & Michie, 1995). Cohen (2006) states that organizations must consider the security dimension in their strategy when they are operating in a competitive environment, which is often the case for large enterprises. Moreover, SMEs has always shown an overall lack of security awareness (C. Mitchell, Marcella, & Baxter, 1999). They faced more serious problems than those encountered by large companies regarding security difficulties and a realistic assessment of the risks involved (Siponen & Willison, 2009) (L. Goodhue & Straub, 1991) (Peltier, 2013).

(Hong, Chi, Chao, & Tang, 2006) investigate the dominant factors for an organization to build an information security policy ISP, and whether an ISP may elevate an organization's security level in Taiwan. (De Haes & Van Grembergen, 2006) Interprets some important existing practices and models in the IT governance field and derives open research questions and some research suggestions from it. They form the basis of the pilot case research in Belgian organizations. (Lomas, 2010) argues that by integrating ISO 27001 the international information security standard in co-occurrence with the ISO 15489 document management standard, holistic information governance strategies will provide a responsive response to changes in UK context. (Bahl & Wali, 2014) examine, as a case, the perceptions of the ISP's (Service Provider) in India regarding information security governance and its impact on the security service quality. Ula, Ismail, and Sidek, (2011) propose an initial framework for governing the information security in the banking system. The framework classified into three levels: tactical level, strategic level, operational level and technical level. This proposed framework implemented in a banking environment. (Mohamed & Singh, 2012) propose a conceptual framework that examines information technology governance effectiveness, its determinants, and its impacts on private organizations. (Hung, Hwang and Liu, 2013) propose an ISG maturity model to search for relevant maturity characteristics of ISG. According to the information security assessment and maturity assessment tool, this study found that schools with a little maturity rate occupied 59.8%, 31.7% average and 8, 5%. With correlation analysis, this study concludes that 33 elements have a significant correlation with ISG maturity. With ANOVA, Post hoc scoping test, and ANOVA multiple comparative difference, this study finds that there are significant differences between the ISG maturity components. This study also finds that the maturity of schools is basic. They can improve their information security governance maturity according to this model. (Lunardi, Becker, Maçada & Dolci, 2014) attempt to study and measure the improvement in the financial performance of firms that have adopted an IT management and governance strategies through pre- and post-adoption measures. They found that the organizational activities of improved IT governance practices boost their performance compared to the control group, particularly about profitability. They also concluded that the impact of adopting an IT management and governance mechanisms on financial performance was more pronounced in the year following the adoption than in the year in which they took. (Adéle da Veiga & Martins, 2015) discuss through a case study of an international financial institution in which ISCA conducted at four intervals over a period of eight years in twelve countries. Multivariate and comparative analyses performed to determine whether the culture of information security has improved from one evaluation to another depending on the development actions implemented. One of the primary measures performed was training and awareness-raising on the critical dimensions identified by ISCA. The culture of information security has improved from one evaluation to another, with the most positive results in the fourth assessment. (Dhillon, Syed, & Pedron, 2016) use Hall's theory of cultural message flows (1959) to evaluate disturbances in the security culture following a merger. They conducted an exhaustive case study of a company in the telecom sector. The data were collected during the merger, allowing us to evaluate the changing structures in real time. The results of this analysis help researchers and practitioners to theorise on the formulation of security culture during a merger. On the practical side, decision-makers will find this analysis useful for engaging in strategic security planning. (Eroğlu & Çakmak, 2016) measure information systems regarding information security and risk. On the other hand, it also aims to describe the potential effects of evaluation techniques and tools for state organizations to manage their critical assets. The information systems of one of the major healthcare organizations in Turkey have evaluated through an international assessment tool adapted to Turkish specificities and conditions in certain parts of the legal regulations. The results obtained through an evaluation tool provide the current level of maturity of the organization and point out areas that should improve the security of information systems and essential components such as risks, processes, people, IT dependence and technology.

Data Collection and Demography

The target organizations belong to almost all sectors of activity: telecommunications and information technology, construction, transport, industry, commerce, services, and finance. This sectoral breakdown is in line with the International Standard Industrial Classification of All Economic Activities (Revision 4) Nations (2008) commonly used in community surveys.

The questionnaire was carried out in several stages. A first version has been developed to take into account the different theoretical assumptions. This first version has been tested with security managers and consultants. This pre-test allowed rephrasing certain questions to improve the comprehension of the questionnaire and to improve the quality of the given answers. In the end, the questionnaire consists of 45 questions divided into five topics: knowledge of the governance of information security and its strategic issues, its implementation conditions, its organization, its maturity level, and economic characteristics of the responding organizations. The questionnaire was written in the three most widely spoken languages in the organizations, namely English, French, and Spanish.

Data collection was conducted during the last quarter of 2016. It took place in two steps. Firstly,1000 questionnaires were transmitted by email to participants, using Google's facilities, giving 890 responses. 54 questionnaires were not considered mainly for confidentially reasons (65%), informal organization or outsourcing (20%), contact not interested (15%). Finally, 836 final questionnaires examined for data analysis. A response rate of 83.6%. Table 1 shows the demographics of participants in a concise form.

Table 1. Participants' demographics

Variables		Frequency	Percent
Gender	Male	480	57,42%
	Female	356	42,58%
Age (years)	21–30	185	22,13%
	31–40	290	34,69%
	41–50	240	28,71%
	51 and above	121	14,47%
Position	Top manager personnel	99	11,84%
	IT Manager/Risk Manager/Security Officer	266	31,82%
	Security Consultant/Engineer/Analyst	471	56,34%
Number of participants	Retail/wholesale	162	19,38%
	TelComs/IT	257	30,74%
	Financial Services	183	21,89%
	Education	95	11,36%
	Government	139	16,63%
Size of the Company (# of Employees)	Fewer than 500	263	31,46%
	500–999	227	27,15%
	1,000–4,999	155	18,54%
	5,000–10,000	118	14,11%
	More than 10,000	73	8,73%
Geography	North-America	116	13,88%
	Asia-Oceania	156	18,66%
	Europe/Middle-East/Africa	343	41,03%
	Central and South America	114	13,64%
	Global	107	12,80%
Evolution of Turnover and Revenue of the Company in $	Less than 1 million	216	25,84%
	million 1 million–5	243	29,07%
	6 million–10	166	19,86%
	10- 50	93	11,12%
	50-100	65	7,78%
	100-500	38	4,55%
	More than 500 million	15	1,79%

Survey Practices Results in Respondent Organizations

This section shows the detailed practices of organizations interviewed in the area of information security governance using descriptive statistics, thus answering our second research question.

IT Security Governance Knowledge

The survey reveals that 78% of organizations are familiar with practices of information security governance, mainly through the Internet, vocational training and technology watch. As shown in Figure 1, 75% of these organizations are involved in an approach to information security governance. 80% of organizations are aware of other organizations involved in information security governance, of which 34% are clients, 59% are suppliers, and 41% are competitors. Eighty of these organizations (78%) are involved in the governance of information security.

Conditions for Implementing Information Security Governance

Before embarking on an approach to information security governance. Practicing organizations took stock of actions already carried out internally (81%) as well as possible envisaged measures (87%), knowledge of standards and certifications (80%). Collected information from specialised security agencies and organisations (73%), evaluated of security budget and costs (75%) and reviewed actions by other organizations (39%). These results illustrated in Figure 2.

Figure 1. Involvement of organizations in governance approach to the security of the information system

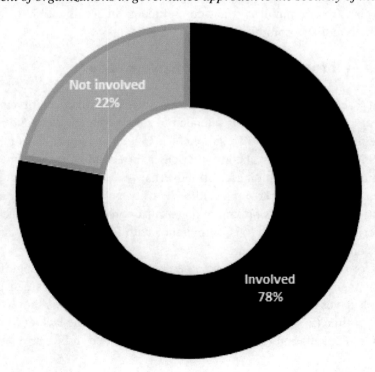

Figure 2. Key benefits of information security governance

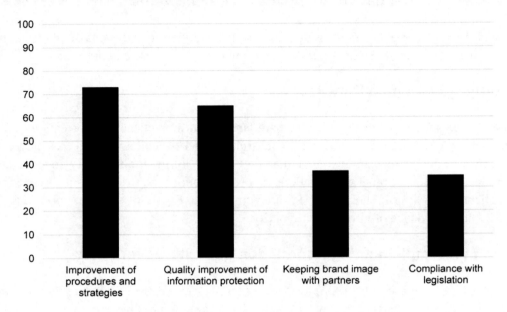

On average, 5 persons per organization assigned to the ISG process, including 2 managers, 2 members of the IT team, 1 external consultants. Almost one out of every two organizations (59%) has a budget dedicated to information security. The implementation of information security governance is described and valued by 38% of organizations in their activity report, by 27% on their website, by 63% in their internal documents (intranet, Procedures, IT charts), Nowhere for 23% of them. Similarly, 71% of the organizations have plans to communicate their commitments internally, 22% to the outside and 29% have not talked at all about these commitments.

Strategic Issues in Information Security Governance

In organizations that practice information security governance, its implementation is primarily the result of the need to satisfy customers (79%). It is intended to satisfy shareholders and management (48%), employees (40%), legislation in force (36%), suppliers (17%), local authorities or non-governmental organizations (12%). 95% of organizations believe they can gain a competitive advantage (very significant or significant benefits) from information security governance, and 75% are committed to the process. Among the benefits of an approach to information security governance, which are considered very important, organizations mainly focus on improving security procedures and strategies (73%). Quality improvement of information protection (65), compliance with legislation (35%), and Trust for partners (31%). These results are illustrated in Figure 2.

Conversely, 93% of organizations interviewed perceive difficulties (very significant or significant obstacles) in the implementation of information security governance, yet 74% are involved in the process. Examination of the obstacles considered very important by the organizations shows, in descending order of citation. The lack of time (27%), the lack of internal talent (24%), the lack of top management interest (19), the cost of implementation (17%). These results illustrated in Figure 3. Within organizations practising the governance of information security, the responsibility for this process is entrusted to an IS/IT (CIO) for 53% of them, a risk manager for 14% a chief executive officer (CEO) for 13%. A quality/compliance manager for 12%, and a CISO (Chief Information Security Officer) in only 8% of cases.

IT Security Governance Strategy and Metrics

According to the responding organizations, 70% of the organizations confirm that the definition of a strategy and policy plays the main role of adopting a governance approach to information security. Strategic alignment of security (68%), communication and training (63%), evaluation of performance by monitoring security indicators (73%), of value through optimization of security investments (75%). These results are illustrated in Figure 4.

Figure 3. Key obstacles to the implementation of information security governance

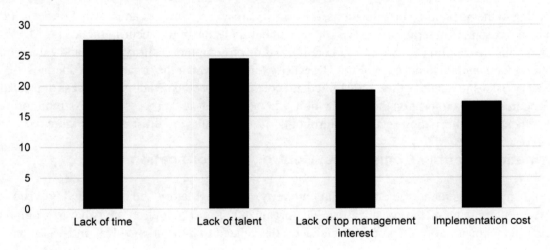

Figure 4. Information Security Governance: Strategy and Metrics

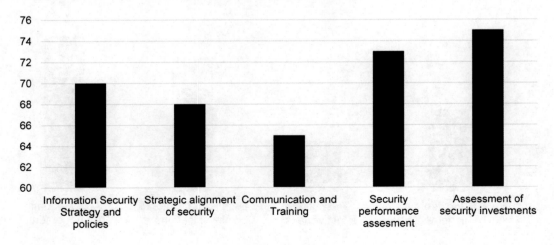

IT Service and Asset Security Management

Among the organizations practicing the governance of information security, 66% set measurable targets, such as reducing security incidents, reducing operational risk, implementing incidents management tools and procedures Security, etc. In terms of the definition of information security classes and data classification, 66% of the organizations take no interest in this axis. 78% of the organizations confirm the mastery of the technical architecture of their IS security, and 83% implement measures to manage their IT assets (servers, networks, storage devices, printers, and smartphones). 68% have a management and a return on investment concerning the hard and soft resources deployed for the security of the IS of the organization. 66% have access management tools and policies that enable them to identify and trace the various SI access operations, including granting, denying, and revoking access privileges. Figure 5 illustrates the results.

Vulnerability and Risk Management

According to the responding organizations, the priority areas (or values) of an information security governance approach is vulnerability and risk management. In terms of the security threats profile, 70% of organizations are adopting a process to gather information on computer security threats and vulnerabilities to better understand the landscape of the IT security threat in which the organization operates. 68% assess safety risks and quantify their probability and potential impact. 65% adopts a process of prioritizing risks according to its impact on the organization. 73% adopt tools and processes for risk monitoring and management and information security control options. The results are illustrated in Figure 6.

Information Security Compliance, Control, and Verification

To avoid any infringement of the intellectual property, legal, regulatory and contractual provisions and security requirements of the organization. The organization must adopt an approach to Compliance. Verification is focused on the processes and activities related to how an organization checks, and tests

Figure 5. IT Service and Asset Security Management Practices in Organisations

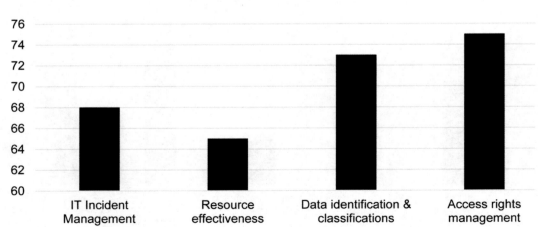

Figure 6. Vulnerability and Risk Management Practices in Organisations

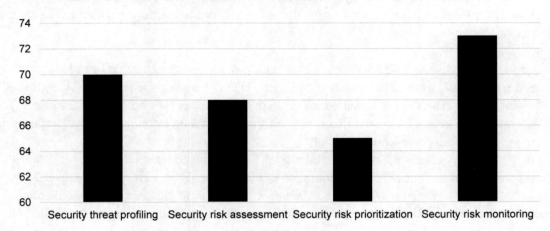

artifacts produced throughout software development. This typically includes quality assurance work such as testing, but it can also include other review and evaluation activities.

Among the organizations practicing the governance of information security, 80% adopted compliance repositories such as ISO 2700x and PCI DSS, 70% have conducted at least one IT security audit in the last 3 years. 60% have developed action plans, either current or future, within the framework of the governance of information security, such as the implementation of a business continuity plan, staff training, Network redundancy, data centralization, server virtualization, improved traceability, etc.

Organizational Maturity of Information Security Governance

In total, 51% of the organizations interviewed confirm that the governance of information security is indispensable 40% consider it necessary, 6% unhelpful and 3% useless. 87% of those surveyed perceive governance of information security as a significant value for the organization; 78% of these organizations

Figure 7. Security Compliance, control and verification practices in organizations

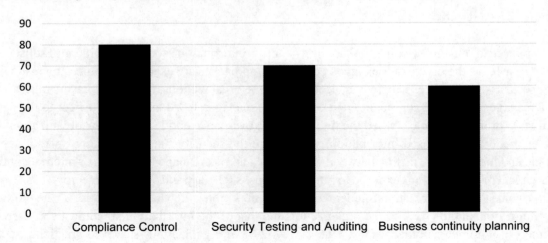

are engaged in an information security governance approach. By analyzing the maturity of organizations in the governance of information security according to a typology proposed by the (IT Governance Institute, 2006), it appears that:

- For 7% no procedure is applied. The organization does not recognise any need for information security. No obligation or liability is established. That corresponds to the basic level (level 0);
- 14% of procedures exist but remain disorganised. IT risks are assessed ad hoc per project. The organization recognises the need to secure its information resources but reactively. Responsibilities are informal. That corresponds to level 1;
- For 19% the procedures follow a defined model. IT risks are considered significant. Security policies are developed. The report is incomplete or inadequate. That corresponds to level 2;
- For 25% the procedures are formalised, documented and communicated by an organizational policy. The report remains focused on IT rather than on the organization. That corresponds to level 3;
- For 17% the procedures are monitored and measured. A senior manager provides the security function. Responsibilities are applied. The report is linked to the objectives of the organization. That corresponds to level 4;
- For 18%, procedures, safety technologies, and contingency plans are integrated into the organization's activity, optimized and automated. The report makes it possible to anticipate the risks. That corresponds to level 5.

These results are illustrated in Figure 8.

The projects portfolio of information security governance does not include any projects for 23% of organizations surveyed. Projects are envisaged for 43% of them (on average two projects per organization); Projects are in progress for 67% of the organizations (on average three projects per organization), and projects have closed during the last three years for 43% of them (on average four projects per organization). 87% of organizations that have embarked on an information security governance approach to report organizational changes: recruitment of external management profiles (31%). Changes in internal business for 59% (for example, changes in the technical profiles Specialization), implementation of specific training for 63%.

RESULTS AND DISCUSSION

The responses to our survey confirm that governance of information security is an integral subset of IS/IT governance, as the organizations involved in both approaches are exactly the same. The responsibility for security governance is attributed, according to the organizations, to various players ranging from the IT manager, risk manager, quality and compliance manager, RSSI or security officer to the general manager. Within the sample studied the link between governance and ISD concerns organizations with weak or moderately exposed information risks, where the security function is more operational than strategic and managerial. The link between governance and risk management, audit or internal control is rather typical of organizations exposed to information risks (tertiary and quaternary sectors). The linkage of governance to the organization's general management is preferred when information is the product of the organization, and the risk of the organization and that of the information are almost confused. It is also interesting to note another result of the survey: 29% of organizations surveyed practicing security

Figure 8. Information Security Maturity according to IT Governance Institute (2006)

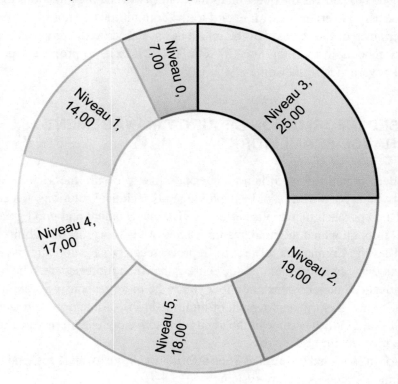

governance did not value this approach either internally or externally, and 34% have not communicated at all about their commitments. Evidence that the governance of information security is not necessarily considered an asset in the communication of the organization with its various stakeholders (or that the organization is in a sector of activity that does require No communication on the subject). Finally, the results of the survey lead us to wonder whether an important commitment of the organization to the approach of governance of the security of the information causes organizational changes. The empirical data collected show that sixty organizations (87%) already report organizational changes at level 2 of the previous typology; They are 100% at level 3. It would seem that these two events are correlated: the more important the organization's commitment to the governance of information security is, the more the organizational changes are generated (There is a link between organizational architecture and information security).

Given the results of the survey, it seemed interesting to test whether the perception of the stakes of the governance of the information security was the same or not, for the organizations actually involved in the process and for those n 'Having no practical experience. In view of the distinction made in the questionnaire with regard to the organizations involved in the governance of information security, we observe 100% similarity in the ranking of the first three profits by comparing the responses of each type of information security, Organization; The ranking then differs from only a few organizations (less than ten) for the following benefits. Regarding the perceived obstacles of the approach, we observe 100% of similarity on all the results of the classification. So the perceived strategic issues of information security governance are very similar, whether or not the organization is involved in this process.

Finally, we wished to address the question of the maturity of the organizations interviewed in terms of information security governance: with regard to the commitment or not of the organizations in the approach of governance of the security of the information. Based on the proposed empirical study and different maturity models in the literature (ISACA, ISO 2700x), we propose a practical IT security management and governance framework.

THE PROPOSED INFORMATION SECURITY MANAGEMENT AND GOVERNANCE FRAMEWORK

In the major modern organizations, it is no longer possible to ensure the security and governance of information assets on an ad hoc basis, or by deploying only technical solutions. Instead, these organizations need a holistic approach that applies effective risk management and good governance across the organization, and through which the fundamental values of visibility, accountability and responsibility are shared by all levels. Companies' efforts to improve security can motivate them to react and buy high-tech products that can make them more secure rather than more secure. The problem is that this proliferation of advanced attacks does not allow you to be more responsive. Taking a more proactive approach to security involves the deployment of multiple layers of integrated protection that stifle network violations. Table 2 indicates some of the trends of reactive organizations versus those that are more proactive or have more mature IT security:

The best approach is to make sure that your information security staff respond to new threats and your IT team member's process mature systems.

To responding to modern security challenges, organizations must continually apply effective risk management practices at all levels. Risks must be visible to senior management, who must play a fundamental role in accepting these risks or directing activities and allocating resources to reduce these risks to technically, commercially, legal, legislative and regulatory.

In this second part of this wok, we present an ISMGO capacity maturity framework focused on practitioners that integrate the technical, process and human dimensions. The framework is based on the fact that the pace and manner in which an organization can respond proactively to new and emerging security threats depends on the maturity of its ISMGO capacity. The fundamental pillars of the ISMGO must be fluid and responsive to the changing landscape of information security; By developing their capabilities to detect, assess and respond to new and emerging security threats, organizations can position themselves more proactively to efficiently and continuously secure information resources.

Table 2. Reactive\Proactive mature IT security

Reactive Organizations	Proactive Organizations
Low-level security	Multiple point solutions
Multi-layered security	Integrated security solution
Inefficient use of IT resources	Efficient use of IT resources and alignment of IT processes
Manual methods to quarantine threats	Automatic ways to isolate threats
IT Security manages all security processes	Security management processes are managed by IT operations, while IT security ensures surveillance and investigates threats.

Framework Overview

We propose a global maturity framework to achieve an effective information security management and governance approach, as shown in Figure 9. The path to security maturity requires a diversified range of layered endpoint protection, management and capabilities, all integrated and fully automated. The only practical and survivable defensive strategy are to move to a more mature security model that incorporate multiple layers of protective technology.

The ISMGO framework focuses on determining the capacity of an organization to direct oversee and monitor the actions and processes necessary to protect documented and digitised information and information systems and to ensure protection against access, unauthorized use, disclosure, disruption, alteration or destruction, and to guaranty confidentiality, integrity, availability, accessibility and usability of the data (Kenneally, Jim Curley, 2012). The framework extends the triad confidentiality, integrity and availability of commonly cited with accessibility and usability concepts. Concerning accessibility, a failure to support and understand how security can change work practices can impede how data and information are accessed, shared, and acted on in an increasingly dynamic, competitive environment. Similarly, usability is a one of a main key factor to engaging stakeholders in the business processes, independently of the availability of technology to support work practices, if the technology is difficult to interact and engage with, users might adopt other locally developed, less secure methods of access. The proposed Information Capability Maturity Framework is a comprehensive suite of proven management practices, assessment approaches and improvement strategies covering 5 governance capabilities, 21 objectives and 80 controls.

Figure 9. The Proposed Maturity Framework for Information Security Management and Governance in Organizations ITSMGO

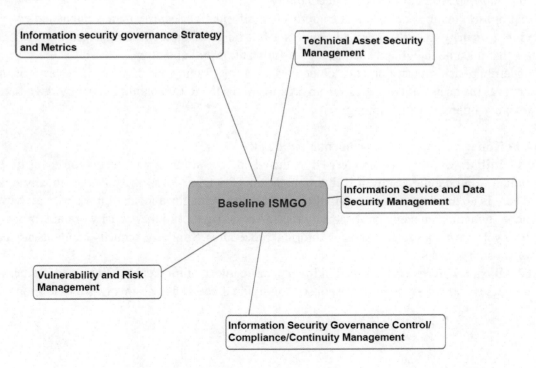

The ISMGO framework classifies the information security activities across the following five high-level function categories:

- Information security strategy and governance provide the oversight structures for supporting ISMGO; it implements information security strategy, policies, and controls; assigns. Define roles and responsibilities for ISMGO activities; provides communication and training; reports on ISMGO activities' effectiveness; and manages supplier security requirements; plans and tests the security of business continuity measures.
- Technical asset security management establishes a security architecture and implements measures to control IT component and physical infrastructure security.
- Information services, system and data management, provides security budgets, tools, and resources, and measures the resource efficiency of security investments. Defines data security classifications and provides guidance on managing access rights and data throughout its life cycle.
- Vulnerability and risk management to control profiles security threats and assesses priorities, handles, and monitors security-related risks.
- Information security compliance, control and verification.

As Table 3 shows, these high-level function categories are decomposed into 22 security practice objectives (SPOs).

Framework Maturity Profile

The bottom line on information security is that the threat environment of today is simply too dynamic. The only practical and survivable defence strategy are to move to a more mature security model that integrate multiple layers of protection technology.

We propose a mature and systematic approach to information security management and governance. Adopting a security maturity strategy requires a full range of protection, management and defensive features that must be integrated and capable of fully automated operation.

Concerning each security practice objectives SPO, the framework defines a five-level of maturity that serves as the basis for understanding an organization's ISMGO capability and provides a foundation for capability improvement planning.

Level 0 - None: No process or documentation in place.

Level 1 - Initial: Maturity is characterised by the ad hoc definition of an information security strategy, policies, and standards. Physical environment and IT component security are only locally addressed. There is no explicit consideration of budget requirements for information security activities, and no systematic management of security risks. Access rights and the security of data throughout its life cycle are managed at best using informal procedures. Similarly, security incidents are managed on an ad hoc basis.

Level 2 – Basic: Maturity reflects the linking of a basic information security strategy to business and IT strategies and risk appetite in response to individual needs. It also involves the development and

Table 3. The proposed ISMGO framework functions and security practices

Governance Functions	Security Practice Objective	Description
Information security governance Strategy and Metrics	Information Security Strategy and policies	Develop, communicate, and support the organization's information security objectives. Establish and maintain security policies and controls, taking into account relevant security standards, regulatory and legislative security requirements, and the organization's security goals.
	Strategic alignment of security	From risk analysis to the actual deployment of global policy, security must be aligned with the business priorities of the company while respecting regulatory and legal constraints
	Communication and Training	Disseminate security approaches, policies, and other relevant information to develop security awareness and skills.
	People Roles and responsibilities	Document and define the responsibilities and roles for the security of employees, contractors and users, by the organization's information security strategy
	Security performance assessment	Report on the efficiency of information security policies and activities, and the level of compliance with them.
	Assessment of security budget and investments	Provide Security related investment and budget criteria
Technical Asset Security Management	Security architecture	Build security measures into the design of IT solutions—for example, by defining coding protocols, depth of defence, the configuration of security features, and so on.
	IT component Security	Implement measures to protect all IT components, both physical and virtual, such as client computing devices, servers, networks, storage devices, printers, and smartphones.
	Physical infrastructure Security	Establish and maintain measures to safeguard the IT physical infrastructure from harm. Threats to be addressed include extremes of temperature, malicious intent, and utility supply disruptions.
Information Service/System/Data Security Management	Incident Management	Manage security-related incidents and near incidents. Develop and train incident response teams to identify and limit exposure, manage communications, and coordinate with regulatory bodies as appropriate.
	Ressource Effectiveness	Measure "value for money" from security investments; capture feedback from stakeholders on the effectiveness of security resource management.
	Data identification and Classifications	Define information security classes, and provide guidance on protection and access control appropriate to each level.
	Access Management	Manage user access rights to information throughout its life cycle, including granting, denying, and revoking access privileges.
	System Acquisition, Development, and Maintenance Security Policy	Ensure the management of security throughout the life cycle of Information Systems. Reduce risks related to exploiting technical vulnerabilities and applications.
Vulnerability and Risk Management	Security Threat profiling	Gather intelligence on IT security threats and vulnerabilities to better understand the IT security threat landscape within which the organization operates, including the actors, scenarios, and campaigns that might pose a threat.
	Security Risk Assessment	Identify exposures to security-related risks, and quantify their likelihood and potential impact.
	Security Risk Prioritization	Prioritize information security risks and risk-handling strategies based on residual risks and the organization's risk appetite.
	Security Monitoring	Manage the ongoing efficacy of information security risk-handling strategies and control options.
Information Security Governance Control/ Compliance/Continuity Management	Compliance Control	Identify applicable law, statutory and contractual obligations that might impact the organization. Establish security and compliance baseline and understand per-system risks.
	Security Testing and Auditing	Adopt solution for information security audit. Establish project audit practice. Derive test cases from known security requirements
	Business continuity planning	continuity management Business continuity planning Provide stakeholders throughout the organization with security advice to assist in the analysis of incidents and to ensure that data is secure before, during, and after the execution of the business continuity plan.

review of information security policies and standards, typically after major incidents. IT component and physical environment security guidelines are emerging. There is some consideration of security budget requirements within IT, and requirements for high-level security features are specified for major software and hardware purchases. A basic risk and vulnerability management process are established within IT according to the perceived risk. The access rights control and management depend on the solutions provided by the provider. Processes for managing the security of data throughout its life cycle are emerging. Major security incidents are tracked and recorded within IT.

Level 3 - Defined: Maturity reflects a detailed information security strategy that's regularly aligned to business and IT strategies and risk appetite across IT and some other business units.

Information security policies and standards are developed and revised based on a defined process and regular feedback. IT and some other business units have agreed-on IT component and physical environment security measures. IT budget processes acknowledge and provide for the most important information security budget requests in IT and some other business units. The security risk-management process is proactive and jointly shared with corporate collaboration. Access rights are granted based on a formal and audited authorization process. Detailed methods for managing data security throughout its life cycle are implemented. Security incidents are handled based on the urgency to restore services, as agreed on by IT and some other business units.

Level 4 - Managed: Maturity is characterized by regular, enterprise-wide improvement in the alignment of the information security strategy, policies, and standards with business and IT strategies and compliance requirements. IT component security measures on IT systems are implemented and tested enterprise-wide for threat detection and mitigation. Physical environment security is integrated with access controls and surveillance systems across the enterprise. Detailed security budget requirements are incorporated into enterprise-wide business planning and budgeting activities. A standardised security risk-management process is aligned with a firm risk-management process. Access rights are implemented and audited across the company. Data is adequately preserved throughout its life cycle, and data availability is effectively requirements. Recurring incidents are systematically addressed enterprise-wide through problem-management processes that are based on root cause analysis.

Level 5 – Optimized: Maturity reflects an information security strategy that is regularly aligned to business and IT strategies and risk appetite across the business ecosystem. Information security policies and standards are periodically reviewed and revised based on input from the business ecosystem. The management of IT component security is optimised across the security framework layers. Physical access and environmental controls are regularly improved. Security budget requirements are adjusted to provide adequate funding for current and future security purposes. The security risk-management process is agile and adaptable, and tools can be used to address the business ecosystem's requirements. The access rights control and management are dynamic and can effectively deal with the organizational restructuring of acquisitions and divestitures. Processes for managing data security throughout its life cycle are continuously improved. Automated incident prediction systems are in place, and security incidents are effectively managed.

USE CASE: APPLYING THE PROPOSED FRAMEWORK FOR IT SECURITY MANAGEMENT AND GOVERNANCE (ISMGO)

The pre-established questionnaire took into account the realities of the organization. At the end of this survey, and following a metric, we were able to evaluate the deviations from the norm and to assess the level of maturity regarding security concerning the different axes of our framework. The audit questionnaire consists of 100 questions divided into different objectives and control of the information security governance inspired by best practice guides ISO 27001 (Johnson, 2014) and OWASP (Deleersnyder et al., 2009) (See Appendix A). Each item is assigned a weighting coefficient on the effectiveness of the rule of the reference system to which the question relates regarding risk reduction. After the validation of the Questionnaire, the chosen answers were introduced in the software maturity framework that was used to allow the automation of the processing and to determine the maturity score. The treatment consists of calculating a weighted average of the scores obtained according to the chosen responses and the efficiency coefficient. The result is a numerical result (0 to 5 or expressed as a percentage) representing the level of security (maturity) of the audited IS.

Conducting Assessments

By measuring an organization based on defined security practices, a comprehensive picture of integrated security assurance activities is created. This type of evaluation is useful to understanding the extent of the security activities currently in place in an organization. Also, it allows the organization to use the maturity framework to create a future roadmap for continues improvement.

An important first step of the assessment is to define the assessment scope. An assessment can be carried out for a complete organization or selected business units. This scope should be agreed with the key stakeholders involved.

Scoring an organization using the evaluation spreadsheets is simple. After answering questions, assess the answer column to determine the score. Insurance programs may not always consist of activities that fall carefully over a limit between maturity levels.

An organization will receive credit for the different levels of work it has performed in practice. The score is fractional to two decimal places for each practice and one decimal for a response. Questions were also changed from Yes / No to five options related to maturity levels. Anyone who completed the assessment discussed whether to report a yes or no answer when it is honestly something in between.

The toolbox worksheet contains contextual answers for each question in the assessment. The formulas in the toolbox will average the answers to calculate the score for each practice, a loop average for each business function and an overall rating. The toolkit also features dashboard graphics that help to represent the current score and can help show program improvements when the answers to the questions change. An example of an evaluation calculation can be found in Appendix B.

Assessing Capability Maturity

The framework's assessment tool provides a granular and focused view of an organization's current maturity state for each SPO, desired or target maturity state for each SPO, and importance attributed to each SPO. These maturity and significance scores are primarily determined by an online survey undertaken by the organization's key IT and business stakeholders (See Appendix C1). The survey typically

Figure 10. Conducting assessment model

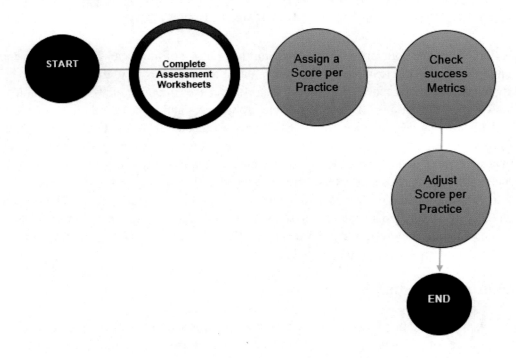

Figure 11. Assessment Score

takes each assessment participant 30–45 minutes to complete, and the data collected can be augmented by qualitative interview insights that focus on issues such as key information-security related business priorities, successes achieved, and initiatives taken or planned. The assessment provides valuable insight into the similarities and differences in how key stakeholders view both the importance and maturity of individual SPOs, as well as the overall vision for success. Figure 10 shows the results of an organization's ISMGO capability maturity assessment, outlining its current and target SPO maturity across all 22 SPOs. For each SPO, the maturity results are automatically generated by the proposed assessment tool, based on averaging the survey participants score across all questions about that SPO. Based on this average score achieved, the organization highlighted in figure 10 reflects a level 1.8 (initial) current maturity status for ISMGO overall, but it is less mature in some SPOs, such as security budgeting, resource effectiveness, security threat profiling, and security risk handling. Based on the average across all SPOs, its desired target ISMGO maturity state is maturity level 3.6 (intermediate).

Figure 12. The Proposed Information Security Management and Governance Assessment results

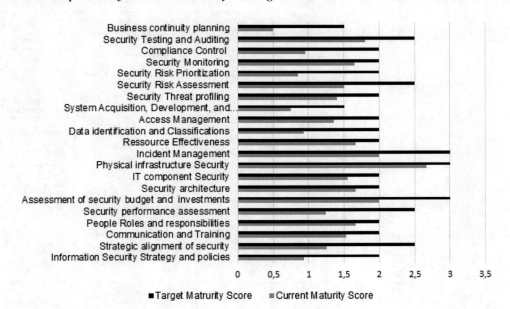

Developing Improvement Action Plans

The output from the framework's assessment supports understanding the actions necessary to drive improvement and enable the organization to transition from its current to target maturity state systematically. This is achieved by implementing a series of industry-validated practices that allow organizations to improve incrementally, and monitoring and tracking progress over time using a number of industry-validated metrics. Table 4 includes sample practices and metrics for the 5 SPOs highlighted for prioritised improvement. For each of these SPOs, the figure outlines the currently reported maturity and the practices required to transition to the next maturity state. Note that additional practices are available to support transitioning to the desired maturity state.

To reach the target maturity levels score, the organization adopted an action plan Plainfield over 3 phases in 2 years from 2016 to 2018 as shown in Table 5.

To reach the desired level of maturity. The organization implemented some programs during each phase of the rollout. The following initiatives were adopted for the first phase (Months 0-6):

- Construct a white paper of technical guidance for application security on the technologies used within the organization.
- Create a risk process and conduct high-level business risk assessments for application platforms and review the business risk.
- Prepare initial guidelines and technical standards for developers.
- Conduct short implementation reviews on application platforms that pose a significant risk to the organization.
- Develop test cases and use cases for projects and evaluate arguments against applications.
- Created a role in application security initiatives.

Table 4. Example practices and metrics to drive improvement in specific security practice blocks (CSPBs)

Governance Functions	Control Objective	Current Maturity Score	Target Maturity Score	Target Objectives to Increase Maturity Score	Metrics
Information security governance Strategy and Metrics	Information Security Strategy and policies	0,93	2	Develop basic information security strategies that consider IT and business strategies and risk appetite. Build and maintain technical guidelines	Existence and availability of security strategies that include business and IT strategies and risk appetite Number and percent of stakeholders aware of and using information security strategies
	Strategic alignment of security	1,25	2,5	Align the governance strategy of security with the organization's overall IS governance strategy.	Control objectives tied to specific strategic and business objectives.
	Communication and Training	1	2	Conduct technical security awareness training	Employee satisfaction surveys. % staff trained within the past year. % Analyst/management staff trained within the previous year.
	People Roles and responsibilities	1,67	2,8	A clear assignment of responsibilities for information security	System accounts-to-employees ratio. Security awareness level. Psychometrics.
	Security performance assessment	1,24	2,5	Develop a measurement dashboard and regular monitoring of the performance security if the body regarding availability, integrity, confidentiality and non-repudiation	A number of controls meeting defined control criteria/ objectives. % of controls that are ossified or redundant.
	Assessment of security budget and investments	2	3	Estimate overall business risk profile	IRR (Internal Rate of Return). The annual cost of information security controls. ROI (Return On Investment). ROSI (Return on Security Investment)
Technical Asset Security Management Information Service/ System/Data Security Management	Security architecture	1,67	2,4	Identify and promote security services and design patterns from architecture	% of project report, model, platform, and pattern usage feedback. % of project teams informed about appropriate security standards.
	IT component Security	1,55	2,4	Identify, inventory and classify all assets needed for information management. For each of them, a manager must be determined. It is responsible for enforcing the security policy for its assets.	Discrepancies between logical access location and physical location. A number of unacceptable physical risks on premises. % of IT devices not securely configured
	Physical infrastructure Security	2,67	3,5	Ensure the protection and availability of sensitive equipment. Ensure that only authorised persons have access to the buildings, technical premises and archives of the organization and that access is traced	Number IT assets without an owner. % of information assets not [correctly] classified

continued on following page

Table 4. Continued

Governance Functions	Control Objective	Current Maturity Score	Target Maturity Score	Target Objectives to Increase Maturity Score	Metrics
Information Service/ System/Data Security Management	Incident Management	2	3	Prioritize and manage security incidents based on the urgency to restore services. Identify indicators and establish security incidents Dashboards	A number of information security events and incidents, major and minor. IT security incidents cumulative cost to date. Non-financial impacts and effect of IT incidents.
	Ressource Effectiveness	1,5	2	Identify and classify data based on criticality, business risk, etc	% of data by degree of criticality.
	Data identification and Classifications	0,93	2	Establish a process to withdraw employee access rights if abused. Discourage sharing of credentials. Provide employees with access to a password-management package.	A Number of access rights audit exceptions. A Number of grant/revoke of access rights by the department.
	Access Management	1,35	2	Conduct basic intelligence gathering and create basic threat profiles.	% of inactive user accounts disabled by policy.
	System Acquisition, Development, and Maintenance Security Policy	0,75	1,5	Access control to applications/ programs source code. Restrictions on modifications to software Packages.	% of controls tested practically. % of technical security checks.
Vulnerability and Risk Management	Security Threat profiling	1,4	2	Create and conduct high-level risk assessments for application platforms and review business risk.	A number of unpatched vulnerabilities. IT security risk scores.
	Security Risk Assessment	1,5	2,5	Develop an application prioritisation approach that identifies "static" risks and "relative" risk of each application	A number of small, medium and high/ risks currently untreated/unresolved. Number of attacks
	Security Risk Prioritization	0,85	2	Implement Security Monitoring and Analytics tool to quickly detect, analyse and correct the widest range of threats to the organization's IT resources.	Application Availability Rates. IT Application Total Downtime. Average Response Time of IT components.
Information Security Governance Control/ Compliance/Continuity Management	Security Monitoring	1,65	2,2	Avoid violation of intellectual property, legal, regulatory, contractual and organizational security requirements.	Historical consequences of noncompliance. Status of compliance with internally mandated (corporate) information security requirements. Number or rate of security policy noncompliance infractions detected
	Compliance Control	0,95	2	Derive test cases from known security requirements Conduct audit and penetration testing on software releases	Number and severity of findings in audit reports, reviews, assessments etc.
	Security Testing and Auditing	1,8	2,5	Following a minor incident (failure of equipment), ensuring the IT back depending on business needs. Following a major incident impacting the whole of a machine room, ensure a continuity of computer activity of the sensitive goods in the shortest time and according to the needs of the trades	Disaster recovery test results. Business continuity plan for maintenance status

Table 5. Governance maturity assessment roadmap

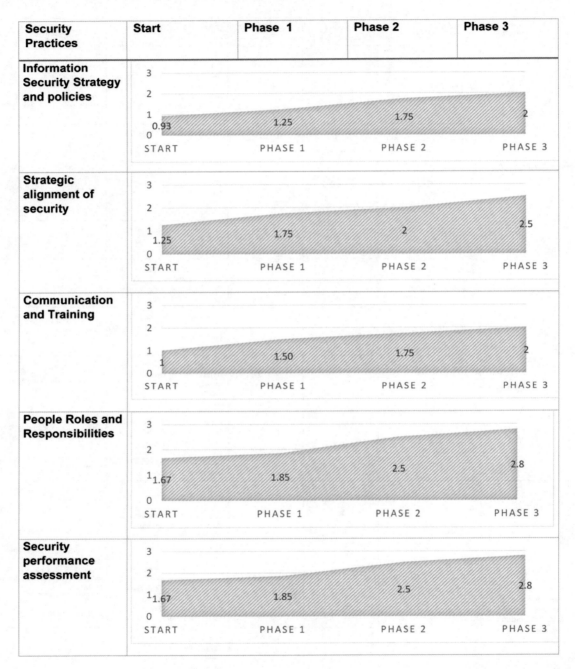

continued on following page

Table 5. Continued

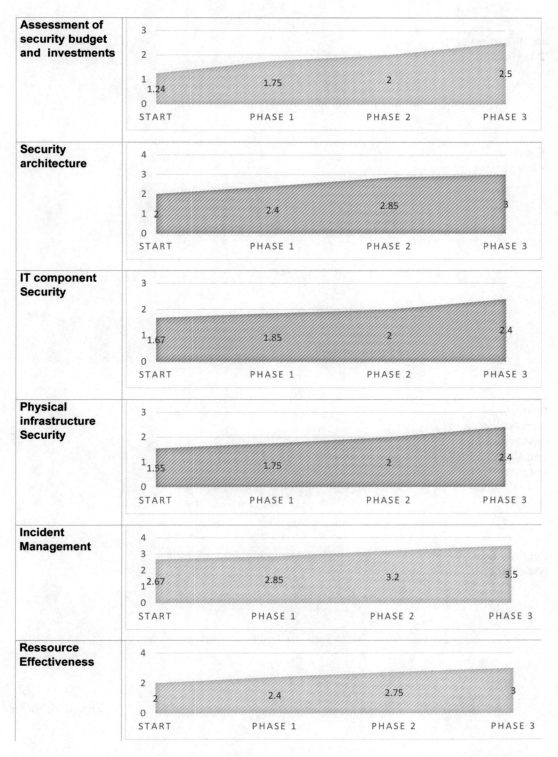

continued on following page

Table 5. Continued

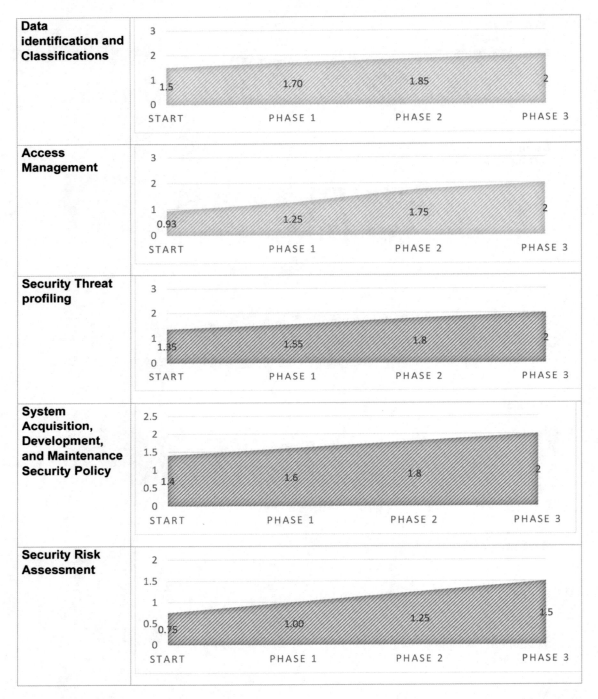

continued on following page

Table 5. Continued

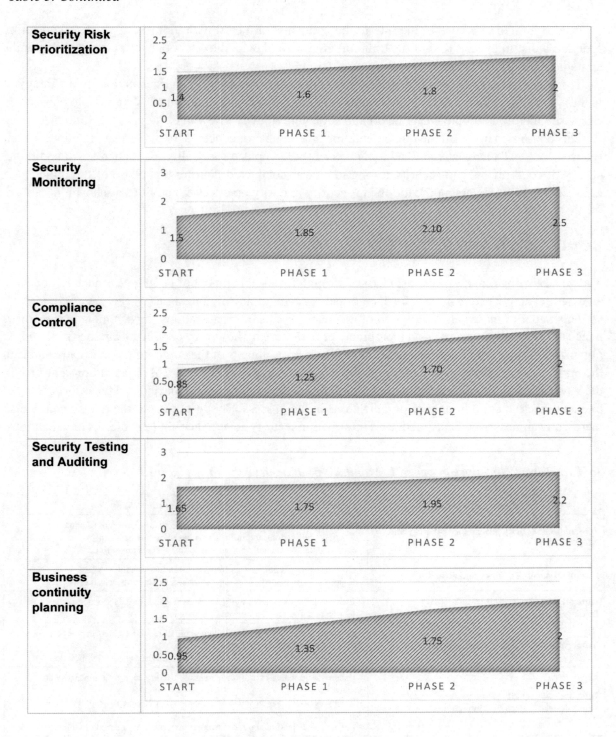

- Generated a strategic roadmap for the next phase of the security program.

Due to limited expertise in the intern, the company partnered with a third-party safety consulting group to assist in the creation of the training program and helped to elaborate a threat modelling and a strategic security road map.

The organization was aware that they had applications with vulnerabilities and no real strategy to identify existing vulnerabilities or resolve risks within a reasonable timeframe. A methodology based on risk assessment was adopted, and the organization undertook a review of existing application platforms.

This phase also included the implementation of a number of concepts for the IT team to improve their security tools. IT teams already had a number of tools in place for quality assessments. An additional survey of code review and security testing tools was conducted. During this phase of the project, the organization will implement the following security maturity practices & activities as shown in Table 6:

CONCLUSION AND FUTURE DIRECTIONS

Today, protecting ourselves against IT risks through the establishment of good governance has become an essential activity to maintain the operational capacity of any organization.

This paper proposes an exploration of the determinants of organizations' involvement in the governance of information security and their practices in this area. The survey conducted among five hundred organizations proposes a model consisting of seven determinants of the commitment of organizations in the information security governance process: it suggests that the knowledge of organizations engaged in the governance of security Information or promotion, the performance expected and the effort deployed to encourage the commitment of organizations in the process. The responses to the questionnaire also increase awareness of current practices of information security governance implemented by organizations.

Table 6. Target objectives of phase 1 (Months 0-6) to achieve the target maturity level

Governance Functions	Target Goals (Months 0-6)
Information security governance Strategy and Metrics	- Establish and maintain of assurance and protection program roadmap. - Classify applications and information based on business-risk - Ensure data owners and appropriate security levels are defined.
Technical Asset Security Management	- Derive security requirements from business functionality. - Ensure asset management system and process for hardware and software.
Information Service and Data Security Management	- Identify, inventory and classify all assets needed for data management. - Define and maintain appropriate security levels.
Vulnerability and Risk Management	- Ensure tha Standards are implemented on all machines, has current definitions and appropriate settings. - Ensure users are periodically informed of unit virus prevention policies.
Information Security Governance Control/ Compliance/Continuity Management	- Ensure documented control processes are used to ensure data integrity and accurate reporting. - Ensure periodic system self-assessments/risk assessments, and audits are performed. - Ensure identification and monitoring of external and internal compliance factors.

By this empirical study and the results of our survey, a framework for measuring the maturity of information security was proposed with the aim of providing a practical tool for measuring and improving governance of information security in the organization. ISMGO has been implemented in a medium organization to drive and improve ISMGOO maturity.

REFERENCES

Archibugi, D., & Michie, J. (1995). Technology and Innovation: An Introduction. *Cambridge Journal of Economics*, *19*. 10.1093/oxfordjournals.cje.a035298

Bowen, P., Chew, E., & Hash, J. (2007). *Information Security Guide For Government Executives Information Security Guide For Government Executives*. National Institute of Standards and Technology NIST. doi:10.6028/NIST.IR.7359

Cohen, F. (2006). *IT Security Governance Guidebook With Security Program Metrics*. Pennsauken, NJ: Auerbach Publishers Inc.

De Haes, S., & Van Grembergen, W. (2006). Information technology governance best practices in Belgian organisations. *Proceedings of the Annual Hawaii International Conference on System Sciences*, *8*. 10.1109/HICSS.2006.222

Deleersnyder, S., De Win, B., Glas, B., Arciniegas, F., Bartoldus, M., & Carter, J. (2009). *Glas, B. Software Assurance Maturity Model*.

Duffield, M. (2014). *Global governance and the new wars: The merging of development and security*, Z. B. Ltd.

Galliers, R. D., & Leidner, D. E. (2014). Strategic information management: challenges and strategies in managing information systems. *Information Strategy*, *625*. Retrieved from http://www.worldcat.org/isbn/0750656190

Goodhue, D., & Straub, D. (1991). Security concerns of system users: A study of perceptions of the adequacy of security. *Information & Management*, *20*. 10.1016/0378-7206(91)90024-V

Hong, K., Chi, Y., Chao, L. R., & Tang, J. (2006). An empirical study of information security policy on information security elevation in Taiwan. *Information Management & Computer Security*, *14*(2), 104–115. doi:10.1108/09685220610655861

Humphreys, E. (2008). Information security management standards: Compliance, governance and risk management. *Information Security Technical Report*, *13*(4), 247–255. doi:10.1016/j.istr.2008.10.010

IT Governance Institute. (2006). *Information Security Governance: Guidance for Boards of Directors and Executive Management Guidance for Boards of Directors and Executive Management*. Author.

Johnson, B. G. (2014). *Measuring ISO 27001 ISMS processes*. ISO.

Mitchell, R., Marcella, R., & Baxter, G. (1999). Corporate information security management. *New Library World* (Vol. 100). 10.1108/03074809910285888

Mohamed, N., & Singh, J. K. (2012). A conceptual framework for information technology governance effectiveness in private organizations. *Information Management & Computer Security, 20*(2), 88–106. doi:10.1108/09685221211235616

Nations, U. (2008). *International Standard Industrial Classification of All Economic Activities (Revision 4)*. New York: United Nations Publication.

Peltier, T. R. (2013). *Information Security Fundamentals* (2nd ed.). Taylor & Francis. doi:10.1201/b15573

Posthumus, S., & von Solms, R. (2004). A framework for the governance of information security. *Computers & Security, 23*(8), 638–646. doi:10.1016/j.cose.2004.10.006

Rockart, J., & Crescenzi, A. (1984). Engaging top management in information technology. *Sloan Management Review, 25*.

Siponen, M., & Willison, R. (2009). Information security management standards: Problems and solutions. *Information & Management, 46*(5), 267–270. doi:10.1016/j.im.2008.12.007

Sohrabi Safa, N., Von Solms, R., & Furnell, S. (2016). Information security policy compliance model in organizations. *Computers & Security, 56*, 1–13. doi:10.1016/j.cose.2015.10.006

Ula, M., Ismail, Z., & Sidek, Z. (2011). A Framework for the Governance of Information Security in Banking System. *Journal of Information Assurance & Cybersecurity, 23*(8), 1–12. doi:10.5171/2011.726196

von Solms, R., & van Niekerk, J. (2013). From information security to cyber security. *Computers & Security, 38*, 97–102. doi:10.1016/j.cose.2013.04.004

Waddock, S. A., & Graves, S. B. (1997). The Corporate Social Performance-Financial Performance Link. *Strategic Management Journal, 18*(4), 303–319. doi:

APPENDIX A

Table 7. Governance Maturity Assessment Roadmap

Security Governance Function	AB	Security Practices	Maturity Score	significance Score
Information security governance Strategy and Metrics	SM1	Information Security Strategy and policies	0,93	2
	SM2	Strategic alignement of security	1,25	2,5
	SM3	Communication and Training	1	2
	SM4	People Roles and responsibilities	1,67	2,8
	SM5	Security performance assessment	1,24	2,5
	SM6	Assessment of security budget and investments	2	3
Technical Asset Security Management	AS1	Security architecture	1,67	2,4
	AS2	IT component Security	1,55	2,4
	AS3	Physical infrastructure Security	2,67	3,5
Information Service and Data Security Management	SD1	Incident Management	2	3
	SD2	Ressource Effectiveness	1,5	2
	SD3	Data identification and Classifications	0,93	2
	SD4	Access Management	1,35	2
	SD5	System Acquisition, Development, and Maintenance Security Policy	0,75	1,5
Vulnerability and Risk Management	RM1	Security Threat profiling	1,4	2
	RM2	Security Risk Assessment	1,5	2,5
	RM3	Security Risk Prioritization	0,85	2
	RM4	Security Monitoring	1,65	2,2
Information Security Governance Control/ Compliance/Continuity Management	SC1	Compliance Control	0,95	2
	SC2	Security Testing and Auditing	1,8	2,5
	SC3	Business continuity planning	0,5	1,5

APPENDIX B

Table 8. Governance Maturity Assessment Interview (Sample)

Information security governance Strategy and Metrics		Current State	
Information Security Strategy and policies		**Answer**	**Rating**
SP1	Is there an information security policy and program in place?	Yes in ad-hoc basis	0,93
	Do the security rules specify a clear definition of tasks, specific roles affecting information security officers?	Yes a small percentage are/do	
	A plan ensures that the review is conducted in response to changes in the baseline of the initial assessment, such as major security incidents, new vulnerabilities, or changes to organizational or technical infrastructure?	Yes there is a standard set	
	Is there a formal contract containing, or referring to all security requirements to ensure compliance with the organization's security policies and standards?	Yes a small percentage are/do	
SP2	Management actively supports the organization's security policy through clear direction, demonstrated commitment, explicit function assignment, and recognition of information security responsibilities?	Yes at least half of them are/do	
	Are risk ratings used to adapt security and insurance required?	No	
	Does the organization know what's required based on risk ratings?	Yes at least half of them are/do	
Strategic alignment of security		**Answer**	**Rating**
SA1	Does the organization measure the contribution of IT security to its performance?	Yes a small percentage are/do	1,25
	Does the organization defined and managed the role of information security in the face of business and technological change?	Yes but on an ad-hoc basis	
SA2	Are there formal processes in place that emphasize strengthening the partnership relationships between IT Security and Business (e.g. cross-functional teams, training, risk sharing/recognition)?	Yes there is a standard set	
	What is the degree of IT control of security or business changes (implementation of new technology, business process, merger/ acquisition)?	Yes, a small percentage are/do	
SA3	What is the degree of perception of IT Security by the organization?	Yes, a small percentage are/do	
	Does the organization periodically use audits to collect and control compliance conformity?	Yes, localized to business areas	
Communication and Training		**Answer**	**Rating**
CT1	Have IT staff been given high-level security awareness training?	Yes we do it every few years	1
	Are system security items included with employee orientation?	Yes at least half of them are/do	
CT2	Are those involved and engaged in the IT process, given specific guidance and training on security roles and responsibilities?	Yes at least half of them are/do	
	Are users aware and equipped to comply with IS principles, policies and procedures	Yes a small percentage are/do	
CT3	Is ongoing security education of users planned and managed?	Yes teams write/run their own	
	There is any regular communication process with unit personnel (unit security newsletter/web page)	Yes a small percentage are/do	

continued on following page

Table 8. Continued

Information security governance Strategy and Metrics		Current State	
People Roles and responsibilities		**Answer**	**Rating**
PR1	Do the security rules specify a clear definition of tasks, specific roles affecting information security officers?	Yes we do it every few years	1,67
PR1	Are the roles and responsibilities for the safety of employees, contractors and third-party users defined and documented by the organization's information security policy?	Yes at least half of them are/do	1,67
PR2	Are users, IT Staff and providers gave roles and responsibilities for throughout the organisation?	Yes at least half of them are/do	1,67
PR2	Are information security responsibilities allocated to ensure accountability and responsibility for the implementation of IS initiatives?	Yes a small percentage are/do	1,67
PR3	Is security-related guidance centrally controlled and consistently distributed throughout the organization?	Yes teams write/run their own	1,67
PR3	Are responsibilities identified at the unit and at the division or enterprise level?	Yes we did it once	1,67
Security performance assessment		**Answer**	**Rating**
PA1	Are management oversight performed to ensure security measures in line with business requirements?	Yes we do it every few years	1,24
PA1	Does the organization use any tools or proprietary methods for conducting risk assessments and keeping the IT contingency plans up-to-date?	Yes at least half of them are/do	1,24
PA2	Has a risk assessment been conducted?	Yes at least half of them are/do	
PA2	Is there an overall coordination plan for implementation, including damage assessment, emergency response salvage, etc.?	Yes a small percentage are/do	
PA3	Are reports concerning risk assessments and risk mitigation measures produced regularly?	No	
PA3	Are standard reports concerning performance produced on a regular basis?	Yes we did it once	
Assessment of security budget and investments		**Answer**	**Rating**
BI1	Does Financial Management for IT Security provide information concerning forecasts of IT service delivery expenditure?	Yes we do it every few years	2
BI1	Does Financial Management of IT security offer information about the actual costs of providing services and resources against planned costs?	Yes at least half of them are/do	2
BI2	Does Financial Management for IT Security provide information concerning the performance of managing service costs against the financial target?	Yes at least half of them are/do	2
BI2	Does Financial Management for IT Security provide information concerning actions necessary to achieve financial targets?	Yes a small percentage are/do	2
BI3	Does Financial Management for IT Security provide information concerning the analysis of deviations from plans?	Yes teams write/run their own	2
BI3	Does Financial Management for IT Security provide information concerning the current charging policies & IT Accounting methods?	Yes we did it once	2

Section 2
Security and Privacy Management and Methods

Chapter 5

IT Security Risk Management Model for Handling IT–Related Security Incidents:
The Need for a New Escalation Approach

Gunnar Wahlgren
Stockholm University, Sweden

Stewart James Kowalski
Norwegian University of Science and Technology, Norway

ABSTRACT

Managing IT-related security incidents is an important issue facing many organizations in Sweden and around the world. To deal with this growing problem, the authors have used a design science approach to develop an artifact to measure different organizations' capabilities and maturity to handle IT-related security incidents. In this chapter, an escalation maturity model (artifact) is presented, which has been tested on several different Swedish organizations. The participating organizations come from both the private and public sectors, and all organizations handle critical infrastructure, which can be damaged if an IT-related security incident occurs. Organizations had the opportunity to evaluate the actual model itself and also to test the model by calculating the organization's escalation capability using a query package for self-assessment.

INTRODUCTION

The Swedish National Audit Office (2014) concluded that the overall capacity of government agencies in Sweden to handle the consequences that can arise from serious information security incidents are largely unknown. Overall risk evaluation is currently lacking, and instead there is uncertainty as to how strong the protection is and which incidents have taken place.

DOI: 10.4018/978-1-5225-5583-4.ch005

IT-related security incidents in the financial sector can, for example, have a cascading effect on other sectors in the economy. If bills cannot be paid, then both production and delivery slow down and in some cases stop completely. The Swedish Civil Contingencies Agency (2014) reported that in 2011, a major IT services provider in Sweden caused an IT-related security incident that had major operational disruptions among a number of government and private organizations in Sweden.

Managing IT-related security incidents is an important issue facing many organizations in Sweden and around the world. To manage the escalation of incidents, organizations need established crisis teams with reporting channels and related report management tools that can handle incidents that do not require immediate action. This chapter presents some ongoing research work to measure an organization's escalation capability of IT-related security incidents.

BACKGROUND AND RELATED WORKS

In this work, the term IT security risk is used to distinguish it from other business risks like investment risk, credit risk, market risk, and environmental risk. The National Institute of Standards and Technology (NIST) (2002) has proposed the following definition of risk: "Risk is a function of the likelihood of a given threat-source's exercising a particular potential vulnerability and the resulting impact of that adverse event on the organization" (p. 8). Given this definition, IT security risks are then defined as an adverse event affecting the IT systems of an organization.

All organizations today have some kind of information system (IS) based on information technology (IT). Organizations are exposed to different threats from both inside and outside. These threats can be avoided with the help of countermeasures of different kinds. However, it is difficult to justify spending effort on countermeasures for an IT system that has little business impact for the organization. To find the right mix of countermeasures to assist organizations, several IT security risk management methods and tools have been developed.

IT Security Risk Management

IT security risk management is a part of information security management, which in turn is related to IT security governance. Different standards have been established for management and governance. The International Organization for Standardization (ISO) (2013) has established a standard for information security management that represents one of the main documents in the area. The concept of IT security governance is described in *Guidance for Information Security Managers* (ITGI, 2008) and in the *Risk IT Framework* (ISACA, 2009).

The term IT risk management refers to approaches and methods that lead to cost-effective security solutions and countermeasures (ISO 27005, 2011a). This is done by measuring the security risk to IT systems and assuring adequate levels of protection. IT security risk management is a continuous process and consists of the following main steps:

- Risk monitoring
- Risk assessment and risk treatment
- Risk communication

The European Network and Information Security Agency (ENISA) (2005) published a survey of 13 risk management methods. The survey includes several methods but excluded general management-oriented methods like COBIT and Basel II and product or system security–oriented methods like Common Criteria. Examples of some well-known methods are presented later. Fenz, Heurix, Neubauer, and Pechstein (2014) outline current risk management approaches and an overview of problems and potential solutions.

Baskerville, Stucke, Kim, and Sainsbury (2013) have pointed out that a survey of risk management practices shows that most organizations do not use automated support for their risk management. Wahlgren (2004), in his study of large Swedish organizations, has come to a similar conclusion, and the tools used for risk analysis are rather simple; in only a very few cases is a more comprehensive tool used.

One interesting aspect is IT security risk management and compliance management. Compliance management is about conforming to stated requirements, like different predefined countermeasures. The disadvantage is that compliance is not risk oriented, that is, there is no valuation when it is cost-effective to have a specific countermeasure. During recent years, the practice of compliance management over risk management appears to have increased. This can be due to some extent to the passing of the Sarbanes-Oxley Act (SOX) in the United States, which requires companies listed on the stock exchange to report all material risks to regulatory agencies. To ensure that the reporting is correct, the companies need to prove that they are SOX compliant. Nilsson, Petkovski, and Räihä (2005) showed that SOX has had a great impact on Swedish companies, and the process of implementing SOX into Swedish companies has been an extensive project.

Multitier Organization-Wide Risk Management

NIST has introduced the framework of enterprise-wide risk management using three different levels (tiers) where one can look at the organization. This multitier concept is described in a number of publications from NIST (2010, 2011a, 2011b, 2011c).

Organizations can be modeled to have three different levels where IT security risk management decisions are made: top management (tier 1), middle management (tier 2), and operational staff (tier 3). The decision of top management is often strategic in nature, where middle management decisions are of a tactical nature. Staff, on the other hand, must deal with real IT security risk incidents and often must react directly to them.

The first tier looks at risks from an organizational perspective. Risk management activities at tier 1 directly affect activities on the other tiers by implementing a governance structure that is consistent with the strategic goals of the organization. Governance includes such things as determining risk tolerance. Risk tolerance is the level of risk that is acceptable to the organization. It is often influenced by the culture of the organization.

Tier 2 looks at risk from a mission/business processes perspective by designing and implementing processes that support business functions defined at tier 1. Important issues at tier 2 involve the enterprise architecture of which the information security architecture is an integral part. Another issue is risk response strategies, which could be placed into the following categories: acceptance, avoidance, mitigation, sharing, and transferring.

The information system perspective at tier 3 is guided by the risk-related decisions and activities at tier 1 and 2. Risk management activities at tier 3 are also integrated into the system development life cycle. At tier 3, risk-based decisions are made regarding the implementation, operation, and monitoring of organizational information systems.

A Combined Approach

We suggest that the ISO and NIST frameworks can be combined. The reason for this is that the authors' combined 70 years of work experience in IT security risk management has exposed them to all three level of organizations, and we have seen that each level uses their own individual risk monitoring, risk assessment/risk treatment, and risk communication. We have also observed that it is extremely important that communication between the different organizational levels is working (for example, regarding escalation routines) and that there are tools that can secure this. Figure 1 describes the combination of the ISO 27005 and NIST multitier framework and the basic steps that each organizational level must consider when dealing with a new incident.

IT Security Competence and Responsibility

An important aspect to consider in risk management and operation is the difference between competence, authority, and responsibility (CAR model) of the different organizational levels (Pigeau & McCann, 2002). The different levels use different terms and concepts depending on their authority, IT competence, and responsibility. Top management, for example, may have a great deal of authority but may lack the IT competence and language to communicate with individuals in IT operations. It is necessary to have a balance between the various organizational levels concerning competence, authority, and responsibility. Lock, Sommerville, and Storer (2009) present a graphics-based analytical technique for responsibility modeling within an organization. The technique is used to explore shortages in the responsibility structure between personnel.

Figure 1. Combination of ISO and NIST framework

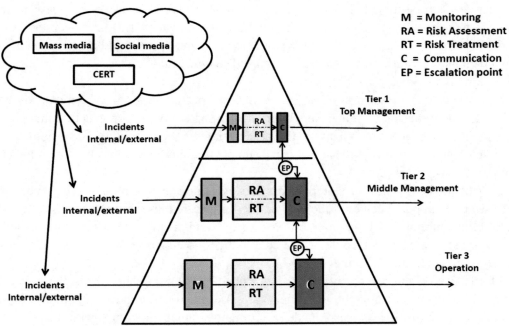

During the last years, responsibility for middle management has increased without an equal increase in authority. In many cases, the IT competence for middle management has decreased—for example, due to outsourcing of different kinds—and it is not unusual for middle management to be caught between top management and operations.

IT Security Risk Assessment and Risk Treatment

One of the main steps in IT security risk management is risk assessment and risk treatment, where different risks are compared against a risk level and, if necessary, new countermeasures are implemented. The result of risk assessment and risk treatment is an IT security risk model that represents how an organization handles threats to information assets with the help of various countermeasures. IT security risk assessment is discussed by ISO (2011a) and in the NIST *Guide for Conducting Risk Assessment* (2011a).

There are basically two ways to calculate risk: quantified or qualified approach. The quantitative approach uses the expected number of adverse events per year and the average cost for the occurrence of one event. The qualitative approach, on the other hand, uses a scale with, for example, three values: low, medium, or high. This scale is used to express both the expected number of events and the cost for one occurrence. As an alternative to the probability-based risk analysis described earlier, Baskerville et al. (2013) presents possibility-based risk analysis. Possibility theory is an extension of fuzzy set theory that considers both the possibility and the necessity of an event.

ENISA (2006) published a survey of 12 risk assessment tools. Most of the tools are connected to a specific method. Examples of methods and supporting tools are:

- CRAMM (UK)
  - CRAMM
- ISF methods for risk assessments and risk management (international)
  - IRAM, SARA, SPRINT
- IT-Grundschutz (Germany)
  - GSTOOL
- MAGERIT (Spain)
  - EAR/Pilar
- Octave (USA)
  - Octave Allegro

IT Security Risk Monitoring

The next main steps in IT security risk management is risk monitoring, which is described in several NIST publications like the *Guide for Applying Risk Management Framework to Federal Information System* where, for example, the monitoring strategy and selection of security controls are discussed (NIST, 2010). In NIST (2011c), Information Security Continuous Monitoring (ISCM) is described in more detail. Issues that are discussed include organization-wide ISCM and the role of automation. NIST has also developed a framework called CAESARS. An extension to that framework, an architecture view of continuous monitoring for an organization, is presented (NIST, 2012a).

To maintain an acceptable IT security risk level, IT security risk monitoring needs to be an ongoing process. NIST (2011c) defines information security–related continuous monitoring (CM) as "maintaining ongoing awareness of information security, vulnerabilities, and threats to support organizational risk management decisions" (p. VI). According to NIST (2012a), the data sources for CM include people, process, technology, and environment. Many CM implementations focus on technology, as it is easy to automate data collection. The people, process, and environment data sources cannot always be fully automated for data collection. In most cases, some human data collection effort is required.

Several methods can be used to collect data. Examples are surveys, standards-based methods, and tools, as well as sensors of different kinds. The methods could be both automated and manual, like automated methods/sensors. Data collection could be truly continual (always on) or continuous (collected periodically at some set interval).

The frequency of risk monitoring (automated or manual) depends on, among other things, the degree of changes in the organization's information systems, the potential impact of risks, and the degree to which the threat space is changing. The frequency could also be affected if automated or manual monitoring is used. By using automation, it is possible to monitor a greater number of security metrics, although it is not possible to fully automate all metrics; some metrics still need human analysis. NIST (2011c) describes 11 security automation domains that support CM. Examples include vulnerability management, assets management, network management, information management, configuration management, and event management.

IT Security Metrics

IT security risk monitoring uses different kinds of security metrics. Security metrics can be categorized by what they measure—for example, performance, outcomes, trends, and probabilities. These categories can be further broken down by the methods used to measure them. Methods can include maturity, benchmarking, and statistical analysis. Security metrics may also be classified according to how they are measured—for example, quality, throughput, frequency, and magnitude. Brotby (2006) proposes a taxonomy that defines 10 fundamental characteristics of metrics, which include the following:

- Objective/Subjective
- Quantitative/Qualitative
- Static/Dynamic
- Absolute/Relative
- Direct/Indirect

IT Security Risk Communication

The last main step in IT security risk management is risk communication. NIST (2011b) discusses risk response strategies like risk acceptance and risk mitigation in a multitier organization. Rasmussen (1997) has proposed a multilevel sociotechnical model that describes the organization's risks not only internally but also outside the organization—for example, communication to and from the government level. Figure 2, originally from Rasmussen, has been slightly modified. The model describes how it codes and decodes signals and communicates results between levels. The right side of the model describes "signals" from lower to upper levels in the form of different observations and reports. These "signals"

Figure 2. Multilevel model (adapted from Rasmussen 1997)

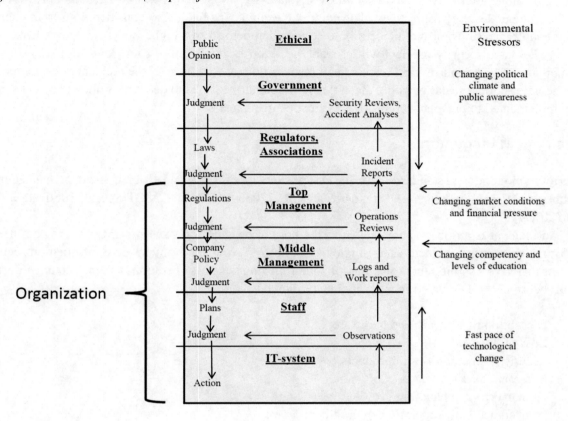

could lead to some kind of action at the upper level and/or could be sent to the next level. The model also shows environmental stressors that can affect the organization, from the fast pace of technological change to the changing political climate. The left side of the model describes different "signals" from one level to the level below, from public opinion to judgment on the government level, which then could become laws, to the next level, where laws will lead to different kinds of regulations. Regulations in turn will lead to company policy, etc.

Security Risk Escalation

In common language, the term escalation is used when different conflicts are sharpened and the conflict therefore is handled by a higher level in the organization or society (Kahn, 1986). The authors use the term in the sense that one seeks assistance, for example, guidance, decision, short term and long term resources etc. from a higher level when one cannot handle an incident. In both cases, this means that one also passes the responsibility to deal with an incident to a level above.

One of the most important aspects of IT security risk communication is the way risk escalation is handled and documented. When handling incidents, each level must consider if the incident would meet or exceed the acceptable risk level of the organization. There are three basic alternatives: it can accept the risk, it can try to mitigate the risk (risk treatment), or it can escalate the risk to the organizational level above. Another alternative is to transfer the risk to a third party, but this option is usually only available at the strategic level. Reasons to escalate could, for example, be budgetary considerations to implement new countermeasures, or the incident is so serious that help from a higher level is needed. Escalation of an IT-related security incident will probably lead to risk treatment of some kind. If a crisis occurs, the organization of course must respond and recover from any damage. If the incident does not require immediate action, escalation could mean that new countermeasures to deter, prevent, and detect should be implemented to prevent such incidents from occurring again.

Incident Management

Various guidelines and standards describe best practice for effective and efficient incident management. Examples of such guidelines and standards are ISO 27035 (2011b) and NIST Special Publication 800-61 (2012b).

An incident is an observable change to the normal behavior of a system. ISO (2011b) defines an information security incident as a "single or a series of unwanted or unexpected information security events that have a significant probability of compromising business operations and threatening information security." An IT-related security incident might be:

- Disruption in software and hardware
- Loss of data
- Security vulnerabilities in products
- External attacks
- Human errors in handling
- Interference in the operating environment
- External events

According to Brotby (2006) some of the questions one needs to ask when handling possible incidents are:

- Is it actually an incident?
- Is it a security incident?
- What immediate actions must be taken?
- Who must be notified?
- Is it a disaster?

The operational level (tier 3) handles many different types of incidents. Examples include the surveillance of IT systems, servers, and networks. Other examples are end users' error reports. Incidents at the next level, the middle management level (tier 2), include things that could influence the business processes that middle management is responsible for. At the top management level (tier 1) incidents that concern the core mission of the organization and that might affect risk tolerance are handled. Figure 3 shows how different security metrics are analyzed with the help of a risk assessment method, and depending on the outcome, it is determined if the incident should be accepted, resolved, or escalated.

Figure 3. Handling of an incident with the help of security metrics

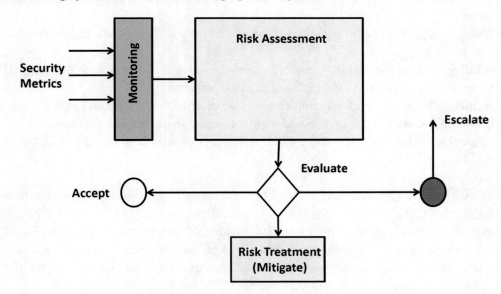

Maturity Models

Nolan (1973) was the first to present a descriptive stage theory concerning the planning, organizing, and controlling activities associated with managing the organization's computer resource. Nolan developed a model with different stages of growth-and several other researchers have been inspired by Nolan.

The capability maturity model (CMM) was first described by Humphrey, Edwards, LaCroix, Owens, and Schulz (1987), who used maturity models to assess the software engineering capability of contractors. The following are examples of the different process maturity levels that are used:

1. **Initial:** The initial environment has ill-defined procedures and controls, and the organization does not use modern tools and technologies. At level 1, the organization may have serious cost and schedule problems.
2. **Repeatable:** At level 2, the organization has generally learned to manage costs and schedules, and the process is now repeatable. The organization uses standard methods and practices for management.
3. **Defined:** At level 3, the process is well characterized and reasonably well understood. The organization has made a series of organizational and methodological improvements.
4. **Managed:** At level 4, the process is not only understood, but is quantified, measured, and reasonably well controlled. The organization typically bases its operating decisions on quantitative process data, and tools are used increasingly to control and manage the design process.
5. **Optimized:** At level 5, organizations have not only achieved a high degree of control over their process, they also have a major focus on improving and optimizing its operation.

The design principles of maturity models are discussed in ISO (2008), which defines organizational maturity as "an expression of the extent to which an organization consistently implements processes within a defined scope that contributes to the achievement of its business goals (current or projected)."

Solli-Sæther and Gottschalk (2010) discuss the modeling process for stage models, suggesting a five-step procedure.

Pöppelbuβ and Röglinger (2011) describe three design principles for maturity models:

- **Descriptive:** Where the maturity model is used as a diagnostic tool, and the assigned maturity levels can then be reported to internal and external stakeholders.
- **Prescriptive:** Where the maturity model serves a prescriptive purpose and indicates how to identify desirable maturity levels and provides guidelines on improvement measures.
- **Comparative:** Where the maturity model serves a comparative purpose and allows internal or external benchmarking.

Philips (2003) describes how to use a CMM to derive security requirements and how to use system security engineering CMM (SSE-CMM) as a useful foundation. Karokola (2012) describes how to integrate and e-government deployment maturity model with new maturity models concerning IT security.

ISACA (2009) presents how maturity models could be used to recognize on what maturity levels different processes are. This maturity model has been use as a basis for the authors' maturity model, which is discussed in more detail later in this chapter.

MAIN FOCUS OF THE CHAPTER

The authors have proposed a maturity model to be used by organizations and authorities to measure the capability to escalate IT-related security incidents both within and between organizations and authorities. The reason for choosing a maturity model as the basis is that escalation routines are a combination of processes and tools. The advantage to using a maturity model is that it makes it possible to obtain a measurable result to compare and consequently improve the organization's capabilities.

RESEARCH METHODOLOGY

The authors have chosen a design science approach to develop a concrete and an abstract artifacts. The abstract artifact is a process model to measure escalation maturity and the concrete artifact is a tool to collect and records this measurement. Design science research methodology consists of five steps (Vaishnavi & Kuechler, 2004). In the first step, information on the real-world problem is collected. The next step is a tentative design. In the third step an artifact is developed. In the fourth step the artifact is evaluated with the help of performance measures. In the last step, the design processes are completed and conclusions are drawn. These steps are iterated until the real-world situation is deemed to be improved.

The authors presented the research methodology and research plans at the Dewald Roode Information Security Research Workshop in Newcastle, UK (Wahlgren & Kowalski, 2014). The research is divided into three cycles. In the first cycle, version 1 of the maturity model was constructed to primarily be used in a cloud computing environment. The authors presented version 1 at the International Conference on Digital Information Processing, e-Business and Cloud Computing (DIPECC 2013) in Dubai, United Arab Emirates, and this version was then published in the IJEEI journal (Wahlgren & Kowalski, 2013). Version 1 of the model was then evaluated with the help of IT security specialists from both the private and public sector and from the academic world. The authors made some improvements based on the evaluation that the maturity model could be used not just in a cloud computing environment. In the second cycle, version 2 of the maturity model was tested on different organizations during 2015. In the first test, two of Sweden's largest banks used the model. In the second test a number of other Swedish organizations used the model. These two tests of version 2 of the model are described later in this chapter. In the third cycle the authors will construct version 3 of the model and then create test scenarios which are to a large extent based on IT-related security incidents that have been reported in Sweden and will then use these scenarios to establish the predictive ability of the maturity model.

DESCRIPTION OF THE ESCALATION MATURITY MODEL

Similar to ISACA's maturity model (2009), the authors' model consists of a matrix with different maturity levels as rows and different maturity attributes as columns, as shown in Figure 4. The authors have used the same five maturity levels as Humphrey et al. (1987) and have also, like ISACA, added a sixth level: "Nonexistent." Regarding the maturity attributes, the authors have used ISACA's maturity model as a starting point, but adapted the attributes around the management of IT-related security incidents.

The escalation maturity model has six different levels. Level 0, "Nonexistent," implies that different processes are not applied at all. Level 1, "Initial," is when the needs for measures have been identified and are initiated but the processes that are applied are ad hoc and are often disorganized. Level 2, "Repeatable," is when measures are established and implemented and the various processes follow a regular pattern. Level 3, "Defined," is when measures are defined, documented, and accepted within the organization. Level 4, "Managed," is when processes are monitored and routinely updated. Level 5, "Optimized," is when processes are continuously evaluated and improved using various performance measures tailored to the organization's goals.

There are also six different maturity attributes that are fairly obvious when one wants to assess an organization's escalation capability. The employees must have "Awareness" of IT-related security incidents. There must be a clear allocation of "Responsibilities" for IT-related security incidents within the organization. "Reporting" channels of IT-related security incidents must be clearly defined. "Polices and standards" must exist regarding when escalation of IT-related security incidents should take place.

Figure 4. Escalation maturity model

Attribute / Level	A Awareness	B Responsibility	C Reporting	D Policies and standards	E Knowledge and education	F Procedures and tools
0 Nonexistent						
1 Initial						
2 Repeatable						
3 Defined						
4 Managed						
5 Optimized						

"Knowledge" requirements for the different categories of employees of IT-related security incidents must be defined. There must be "Procedures and tools" for how escalation of IT-related security incidents should be managed. For a detailed description of the escalation maturity model, see the appendix.

The escalation maturity model also includes a query package to support self-evaluation. The idea is that after the organizations have responded to the questions in the query package, it shall be possible to determine the maturity level of the different maturity attributes. The number of questions in version 2 is 37. The answer to each question of the different maturity levels and attributes is "Yes" or "No." Here are examples of questions of the different attributes and to which maturity level each one belongs:

- Is there awareness among employees on various IT-related security incidents? (Attribute A, level 1)
- Is there awareness among employees about how different IT-related security incidents affect the organization? (Attribute A, level 2)
- Is there awareness among employees about what is required to counter IT-related security incidents? (Attribute A, level 3)
- Are the responsibilities of each employee regarding IT-related security incidents absolutely clear? (Attribute B, level 1)
- Has regular reporting on IT-related security incidents to the organization's management been defined, documented, and accepted? (Attribute C, level 3)
- Is there a continuous evaluation and improvement process for a number of years of both technical and business skills requirements and a training plan for the management of IT-related security and privacy incidents? (Attribute D, level 5)
- Have the knowledge requirements in the form of concrete training plans for employees regarding IT-related security incidents been established and implemented? (Attribute E, level 2)
- Is there a routine updating of procedures for the handling of IT-related security incidents? (Attribute F, level 4)

All the questions for a maturity attribute in one level must be satisfied before the next level can be obtained. It is important also to mention that the maturity level for various processes within one level also apply for the next level. To find the total maturity level, one needs take the maturity attribute that has the lowest value.

FIRST TEST OF THE ESCALATION MATURITY MODEL

In the first test, two of Sweden's largest banks used version 2 of the maturity model. The authors presented the result of the test at the HAISA conference in Frankfurt 2016 (Wahlgren, Fedotova, Musaeva, & Kowalski, 2016). In the first step of the test, the requirements of the various maturity attributes of the model were compared with the regulations set by the Swedish Financial Supervisory Authority (FSA) for the players in the financial sector. This was done by an interview with a representative from the FSA and by studying the FSA's regulatory codes (FSA, 2014a, 2014b). The interview was conducted with the operational risk manager during April 2015. The conclusion is that FSA's recommendations correspond well with the requirements of the various maturity attributes in the model. The difference is that with the model, the authors have introduced different levels, making it possible for an organization to conduct stepwise improvement of their processes.

In the next step, the authors tested the maturity model on two of Sweden's largest banks by conducting interviews with persons responsible for IT-related security incidents. Both interview subjects were from the tactical level (tier 2), and both interviews were conducted in April 2015. The banks show broadly similar patterns for the different maturity attributes, and all maturity attributes reach the maturity level "Optimized" except for one. The maturity attribute "Procedure and tools" only reaches the maturity level "Managed" because the procedures for managing IT-related security incidents are not fully automated.

Although these findings are from only two banks, these banks represent about 30 percent of the Swedish banking market (Swedish Bankers' Association, 2016). The representatives indicated that query package was relevant to evaluate the escalation process within the organization and that the maturity model for escalation capability of IT-related security incidents can be used to perform self-assessment in the banking sector in Sweden.

SECOND TEST OF THE ESCALATION MATURITY MODEL

Introduction

In the second test, the authors used version 2 of the maturity model on other Swedish organizations. The authors presented the result of second test at the WISP conference in Dublin in 2016 (Wahlgren & Kowalski, 2016). The starting point for the second test was a collaboration between the Swedish Civil Contingencies Agency (in Swedish: Myndigheten för Samhällsskydd och Beredskap, MSB), and the Department of Computer and Systems Sciences at Stockholm University. Four seminars were conducted during April 2015. The participating organizations were invited by the MSB.

Thirty-three persons representing an information security function from the different organizations attended the seminars. The seminar was divided into two parts. The first part was held by MSB. In the second part of the seminar the researcher from the university presented the maturity model as well as the query package that was related to the model. An evaluation form where the participants were able to evaluate the maturity model was also presented. After the end of the seminar copies of the query package for self-assessment and the evaluation form were distributed to the participants. The different organizations were expected to submit at least the evaluation form to the university in a prepaid envelope.

The person who answered the query package came from organizations with the following characteristics. Most organizations had more than 250 employees. All organizations had their own IT department. Most of the organizations had an IT support department. Most of the organizations had their own IT operations department. All the organizations handled critical infrastructure that can be damaged if an IT-related security incident occurs.

Result of the Evaluation Form

The organizations that responded were in the following sectors: trade and industry (7 out of 8), governmental agencies (4 out of 8), and county councils or municipalities (10 out of 17). Twenty-one organizations responded to the evaluation form. However, not all organizations answered each question in the evaluation form. This means that the rest of the answers to the other questions will vary depending on if the organization has chosen to answer the question or not. Following are some of the results from the evaluation form.

The maturity model includes six maturity levels (from "Nonexistent" to "Optimized"). Thirteen of the organizations answered that the number of maturity levels was okay. Six organizations thought that there should be fewer maturity levels. No organization thought there should be more maturity levels. The maturity model includes six maturity attributes (from "Awareness" to "Procedures and Tools"). Fifteen of the organizations answered that the number of maturity attributes was okay. Two organizations thought that there should be fewer maturity attributes. Two organizations thought there should be more maturity attributes. Fourteen of the organizations thought that no maturity attributes were missing. Two organizations thought that some maturity attributes were missing. An example of missing maturity attributes is "Follow-up of incidents."

Result of the Self-Assessment

Sixteen organizations submitted the query package. After a first review the answers from 10 organizations could be used. The results for most of the maturity attributes give a somewhat mixed picture. The most surprising results for the different maturity attributes were "Knowledge and education" as shown in Figure 5. A large number of organizations (8 of 10) do not understand the need for employees to have knowledge and training on IT-related security incidents. The implication of this is that these organizations have not identified the knowledge and training requirements for employees on IT-related security incidents and that education plans are not defined and documented.

Alignment Efforts

To get an idea of the extent of actions that each organization must perform to reach the next maturity level, the authors introduced the concept of alignment efforts. If an organization answered "No" to a question in the query package, this will lead to at least one action needing to be performed if the organization wishes to reach the next maturity level. The authors realize, of course, that the actions needed to meet the requirements that a question suggest can vary strongly, but still think that "alignment efforts" gives a good enough estimate of the amount of work that an organization must perform to reach the next maturity level. The authors define alignment efforts for a specific maturity level as the sum of the questions with the answer "No" to all of the maturity attributes of that maturity level, divided by the total number of questions for all maturity attributes of that level. Table 1 shows the alignment efforts (number of actions) that the organizations in the test must perform to reach the different maturity levels. Organization 3, for example, whose current total maturity level is "Nonexistent," must perform one action to reach the next total maturity level, "Initial." To reach the maturity level "Repeatable," the organization must perform two additional actions, and to reach the total maturity level "Defined," four additional actions, and so on.

Figure 5. Maturity levels for maturity attribute "Knowledge and education"

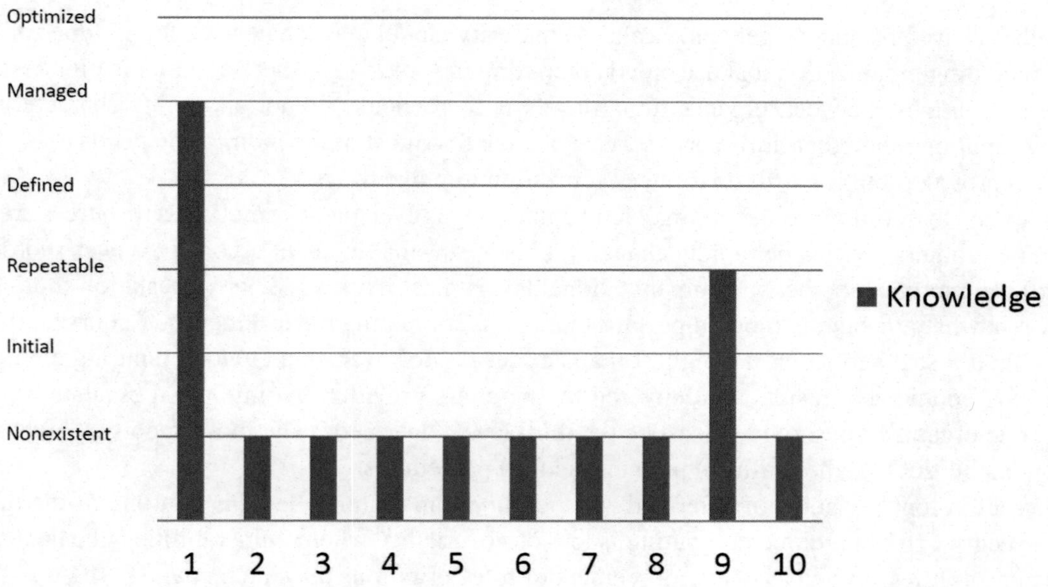

Table 1. Alignment efforts to reach the next maturity level

Org. nr.	Current total maturity level	Initiated	Repeatable	Defined	Managed	Optimized
Number of questions		7	7	7	9	7
1	Initiated	-	1/7	0/7	3/9	7/7
2	Nonexistent	1/7	1/7	2/7	2/9	2/7
3	Nonexistent	1/7	2/7	4/7	7/9	7/7
4	Nonexistent	5/7	7/7	7/7	9/9	7/7
5	Nonexistent	2/7	3/7	3/7	8/9	3/7
6	Nonexistent	4/7	5/7	7/7	7/9	7/7
7	Nonexistent	3/7	4/7	6/7	8/9	6/7
8	Nonexistent	1/7	1/7	3/7	5/9	4/7
9	Repeatable	-	-	2/7	4/9	4/7
10	Nonexistent	1/7	1/7	5/7	6/9	5/7

DISCUSSION

The authors have presented a general escalation maturity model that can be used for all types of organization including organization that use cloud computing in some form where communication (especially escalation routines) between organizational levels is of particular importance. The characteristics of cloud computing (and other third-party services) mean that most of the monitoring needs to be done by the cloud provider, but it is still up to the organization to judge the risk.

Compared to traditional outsourcing, cloud computing is even more complex, as resources are shared between customers and can be rapidly changed. This means that incident reporting is even more important and ccommunication between organizational levels must work, especially escalation routines. The question is what attribute is most important in a cloud computing environment. Of course, all organizations should strive to reach the highest maturity level. However, in a cloud computing environment where most monitoring results are delivered by the cloud provider, the minimum escalation maturity level for an organization should at least be the third level, "Defined." The most important attributes are (a) responsibilities together with (b) policies, and (c) procedures.

The reason for the choice of "Defined" as the minimum maturity level is that one of the most important security risks for cloud computing is loss of governance where vulnerabilities like unclear roles and responsibilities, as well as poor enforcement of role definitions play a vital part (ENISA, 2009). For an organization using cloud computing, it is necessary that escalation routines are clearly defined. For example, both technical and management roles need to be defined and job descriptions need to include risk response responsibilities, and technical and management policies need to be defined and documented.

FUTURE RESEARCH

In cycle 3, the authors are developing a PC-based tool to assist organizations in the self-assessment process. The tool will be based on version 3 of the model, where, among other things, some of the questions will be clarified. The tool will include a help function to assist organizations in the self-assessment process and will be used by organizations to enter answers to the questions in the query packet and then automatically calculate the total level of maturity, as well as the maturity level of the individual attributes. The tool will also calculate the alignment efforts and suggest what action the organization could take to achieve the desired level of maturity.

To verify the new maturity model and the PC-based tool, the authors will use the tool on some organizations both inside and outside Sweden. The authors will also use the tool to compare the level of maturity that different organizational levels (strategic, tactical, and operational) reach within the same organization.

The authors will create test scenarios that are to a large extent based on actual IT-related security incidents that have been reported in Sweden. The authors will select a number of organizations with different self-evaluated maturity levels. Then a security specialist from these organizations will describe how they will handle the test scenarios. The result will be judges by an independent observer. The results will then establish the predictive ability of the maturity model.

CONCLUSION

The most important contribution of the work is that it gives the organization the possibility to do self-evaluations and the possibility to follow up measurable results and conduct stepwise improvement. The escalation maturity model could, for example, be used by organizations to understand where shortcomings exist and help define targets and actions to overcome these shortcomings and could in some cases also be used for benchmarking.

REFERENCES

Baskerville, R., Stucke, C., Kim, J., & Sainsbury, R. (2013). The information security risk estimation engine. A tool for possibility based risk assessment. In Proceedings of 2013 IFIP 8.11/11.13 Dewald Roode Information Security Research Workshop. Niagara Falls, NY: IFIP.

Brotby, W. K. (2006). *Information security management metrics: A definitive guide to effective security monitoring and measurement.* Boca Raton, FL: Taylor & Francis Group.

ENISA - European Network and Information Security Agency. (2005). *Inventory of risk management/risk assessment methods.* Heraklion, Greece: European Union Agency for Network and Information Security.

ENISA - European Network and Information Security Agency. (2006). *Inventory of risk management/risk assessment tools.* Heraklion, Greece: European Union Agency for Network and Information Security.

ENISA - European Network and Information Security Agency. (2009). *Cloud computing: Benefits, risk and recommendation.* Heraklion, Greece: European Union Agency for Network and Information Security.

Fenz, S., Heurix, J., Neubauer, T., & Pechstein, F. (2014). Current challenges in information security risk management. *Information Management & Computer Security*, 22(5), 410–430. doi:10.1108/IMCS-07-2013-0053

FSA - Swedish Financial Supervisory Authority. (2014a). Regulations and general guidelines regarding governance, risk management and control at credit institutions. Stockholm, Sweden: Finansinspektionen.

FSA - Swedish Financial Supervisory Authority. (2014b). Regulations and general guidelines regarding governance, risk management of operational risks. Stockholm, Sweden: Finansinspektionen.

Humphrey, W., Edwards, R., LaCroix, G., Owens, M., & Schulz, H. (1987). *A method for assessing the software engineering capability of contractors (Technical Report, Software Engineering Institute, Carnegie Mellon University).* Springfield, VA: National Technical Information Services, U.S. Department of Commerce.

ISACA. (2009). *The risk IT framework.* Rolling Meadows, IL: ISACA.

ISO - International Organization for Standardization. (2008). *Information technology – process assessment; assessment of organizational maturity* (ISO/IEC Technical Report 15504-7). Geneva, Switzerland: ISO/IEC.

ISO - International Organization for Standardization. (2011a). *Information technology – Information security risk management (ISO/IEC 27005)*. Geneva, Switzerland: ISO/IEC.

ISO - International Organization for Standardization. (2011b). *Information technology – security techniques — information security incident management (ISO/IEC 27035)*. Geneva, Switzerland: ISO/IEC.

ISO - International Organization for Standardization. (2013). *Information technology –Information security management system Requirements. (ISO/IEC 27001)*. Geneva, Switzerland: ISO/IEC.

ITGI - IT Security Institute. (2008). *Guidance for information security managers*. Rolling Meadows, IL: IT Security Institute.

Kahn, H. (1986). *On escalation: Metaphors and scenarios*. Santa Barbara, CA: Praeger.

Karokola, G. (2012). *A framework for securing e-government services*. (Unpublished doctoral thesis). Department of Computer and System Sciences, Stockholm University, Sweden.

Lock, R., Sommerville, I., & Storer, T. (2009). *Responsibility modelling for risk analysis*. Retrieved June 2017 from http://archive.cs.st-andrews.ac.uk/STSE-Handbook/Papers/ResponsibilityModelling-forRiskAnalysis-Lock.pdf

Nilsson, G., Petkovski, P., & Räihä, T. (2005). *The implementation and the effects on Swedish companies* (Unpublished master's thesis). School of Business, Economics and Law, University of Gothenburg, Sweden.

NIST - National Institute of Standard and Technology. (2012b). *Computer Security Incident Handling Guide (NIST Special Publication 800-61 Revision 2)*. Gaithersburg, MD: U.S. Department of Commerce.

NIST - National Institute of Standards and Technology. (2002). *Risk management guide for information technology systems (NIST Special Publication 800-30)*. Gaithersburg, MD: U.S. Department of Commerce.

NIST - National Institute of Standards and Technology. (2010). *Guide for applying risk management framework to federal information systems (NIST Special Publication 800-37 Revision 1)*. Gaithersburg, MD: U.S. Department of Commerce.

NIST - National Institute of Standards and Technology. (2011a). *Guide for conducting risk assessment (NIST Special Publication 800-30 Revision 1)*. Gaithersburg, MD: U.S. Department of Commerce.

NIST - National Institute of Standards and Technology. (2011b). *Managing information security risk (NIST Special Publication 800-39)*. Gaithersburg, MD: U.S. Department of Commerce.

NIST - National Institute of Standards and Technology. (2011c). *Information security continuous monitoring (ISCM) for federal information system and organizations (NIST Special Publication 800-137)*. Gaithersburg, MD: U.S. Department of Commerce.

NIST - National Institute of Standards and Technology. (2012a). *CAESARS framework extension: An enterprise continuous monitoring reference model (NIST Interagency Report 7756 – Second Draft)*. Gaithersburg, MD: U.S. Department of Commerce.

Nolan, R. (1973). Managing the computer resource: A stage hypothesis. *Communications of the ACM*, *16*(7), 399–405. doi:10.1145/362280.362284

Philips, M. (2003). *Using a capability maturity model to derive security requirements*. Bethesda, MD: SANS Institute.

Pigeau, R., & McCann, C. (2002). Re-conceptualizing command and control. *Canadian Military Journal*, *3*(1), 53–64.

Pöppelbuß, J., & Röglinger, M. (2011). What makes a useful maturity model? A framework of general design principles for maturity models and its demonstration in business process management. In *Proceedings of the Nineteenth European Conference on Information Systems (ECIS 2011)*. Association for Information Systems Electronic Library (AISeL).

Rasmussen, J. (1997). Risk management in a dynamic society: A modeling problem. *Safety Science*, *27*(2), 183–213. doi:10.1016/S0925-7535(97)00052-0

Solli-Sæther, H., & Gottschalk, P. (2010). The modelling process for stage models. *Journal of Organizational Computing and Electronic*, *20*(3), 279–293. doi:10.1080/10919392.2010.494535

Swedish Bankers' Association. (2016). *Banks in Sweden*. Retrieved March 2016 from www.swedishbankers.se

Swedish Civil Contingencies Agency. (2014). *International case report on cyber security incidents – Reflections on three cyber incidents in the Netherlands, Germany and Sweden*. Stockholm, Sweden: Myndigheten för Samhällsskydd och Beredskap.

Swedish National Audit Office. (2014). Information security in the civil public administration. Stockholm, Sweden: Riksrevisionen.

Vaishnavi, V., & Kuechler, W. (2004). *Design research information systems*. Retrieved March 2016 from http://desrist.org/design-research-in-information-systems

Wahlgren, G. (2004). Use of risk analysis in large Swedish organizations. Department of Computer and System Sciences, University of Stockholm and Royal Institute of Technology Sweden, Report Series No. 06-019.

Wahlgren, G., Fedotova, A., Musaeva, A., & Kowalski, S. (2016). IT security incidents escalation in the Swedish financial sector: A maturity model study. In *Proceedings of the Tenth International Symposium on Human Aspects of Information Security & Assurance (HAISA 2016) Frankfurt, Germany*. (pp 45-55). Plymouth, UK: Plymouth University

Wahlgren, G., & Kowalski, S. (2013). IT security risk management model for cloud computing: A need for a new escalation approach. *International Journal of E-Entrepreneurship and Innovation*, *4*(4), 1–19. doi:10.4018/ijeei.2013100101

Wahlgren, G., & Kowalski, S. (2014). Evaluation of escalation maturity model for IT security risk management: A design science work in progress. Proceedings of 2014 IFIP 8.11/11.13 Dewald Roode Information Security Research Workshop.

Wahlgren, G., & Kowalski, S. (2016). A maturity model for measuring organizations escalation capability of IT-related security incidents in Sweden. In *Proceedings of the 11th Pre-ICIS Workshop on Information Security and Privacy*. Association for Information Systems Electronic Library (AISeL).

ADDITIONAL READING

Brewster, E., Griffiths, R., Lawes, A., & Sansbury, J. (2012). IT Service Management: A Guide for ITIL Foundation Exam Candidates, 2nd ed. BCS, The Chartered Institute for IT, United Kingdom.

ENISA - European Network and Information Security Agency. (2010). *Good Practice Guide for Incident Management*. Heraklion, Greece: European Union Agency for Network and Information Security.

ENISA - European Network and Information Security Agency. (2014). *Actionable Information for Security Incident response*. Heraklion, Greece: European Union Agency for Network and Information Security.

ENISA - European Network and Information Security Agency. (2015). *Security incidents indicators – measuring the impact of incidents affecting electronic communication*. Heraklion, Greece: European Union Agency for Network and Information Security.

ENISA - European Network and Information Security Agency. (2016). *The cost of incidents affecting CIIs – Systematic review of studies concerning the economic impact of cyber- security incidents on critical information infrastructures (CII)*. Heraklion, Greece: European Union Agency for Network and Information Security.

Grobauer, B., & Schreck, T. (2010). Towards incident handling in the cloud: Challenges and approaches. In *Proceedings of the 2010 ACM Workshop on Cloud Computing Security Workshop (CCSW '10) New York, NY, USA*. (pp. 77–86).

Hove, C., & Tårnes, M. (2013). *Information Security Incident Management – An Empirical Study of Current Practice*. (Unpublished master thesis.) Department of Telematics, Norwegian University of Science and Technology, Norway.

ISACA. (2009). *The Risk IT Practitioner Guide*. Rolling Meadows, IL: ISACA.

ISACA. (2012). *Incident Management and Response*. Rolling Meadows, IL: ISACA.

KEY TERMS AND DEFINITIONS

Escalation: Assistance from a higher organizational level when the current level cannot handle an incident.

Incident: An observable change to the normal behavior of a system.

Incident Management: The activities of an organization to identify, analyze, and correct organizational hazards.

IT Risk: The potential that a given threat will exploit vulnerabilities of an asset and thereby cause harm to the organization.

Maturity: A measurement of the ability of an organization to undertake continuous improvement in a particular discipline.

Maturity Model: A set of structured levels that describe how well an organization can reliably and sustainably produce required outcomes.

Organizational Levels: An organizational model that has three different levels: top management (tier 1), middle management (tier 2), and operational staff (tier 3).

Risk Management: Approaches and methods that lead to cost-effective security solutions.

APPENDIX

Table 2. Escalation maturity model part 1

Attribute Level	A. Awareness	B. Responsibility	C. Reporting
0. Nonexistent	The organization does not understand the need to make employees aware of IT-related security incidents.	The organization does not understand the need for accountability of IT-related security incidents.	The organization does not understand the need for reporting IT-related security incidents.
1. Initiated	Employees have some form of awareness of IT-related security incidents.	Employees have some support from management in terms of individual responsibility for IT-related security incidents, but it is not clear which responsibilities different employees have.	Reporting of IT-related security incidents to management has been identified and initiated.
2. Repeatable	Employees are aware of IT-related security incidents and how these may affect the operations.	The accountability for IT-related security incidents is established and implemented.	Regular reporting of IT-related security incidents to management has been established and implemented.
3. Defined	Employees have good knowledge of different defined and documented IT-related security incidents and of the requirements to counter these incidents.	The accountability for both the technical and administrative management of IT-related security incidents are defined, documented, and accepted by the organization.	Regular reporting of IT-related security incidents to management is defined, documented, and accepted by the organization.
4. Managed	Routine updates of awareness among employees of IT-related security incidents and how these may affect the orientation of the organization.	Routine updates of the responsibilities of both the technical and administrative management of IT-related security incidents. The organization has cooperation with external state agencies and organizations on IT-related security incidents.	Routine updates of reporting channels for the management of IT-related security incidents.
5. Optimized	Continuous evaluation and improvement for a number of years of awareness among employees of IT-related security incidents.	Continuous evaluation and improvement for a number of years of accountability for both the technical and administrative management of IT-related security incidents.	Continuous evaluation and improvement for a number of years of reporting channels for the management of IT-related security incidents.

Table 3. Escalation maturity model part 2

Attribute Level	D. Policies	E. Knowledge and education	F. Procedures
0. Nonexistent	The organization does not understand the need for policies regarding IT-related security incidents.	The organization does not understand the need for employees to have knowledge and training on IT-related security incidents.	The organization does not understand the need for procedures for management regarding IT-related security incidents.
1. Initiated	Policies for IT-related security incidents have been identified and initiated.	Knowledge requirements and training of employees on IT-related security incidents have been identified and initiated.	Procedures for managing IT-related security incidents have been identified and initiated.
2. Repeatable	Policies for IT-related security incidents are established and implemented.	Knowledge requirements and education plans for employees regarding IT-related security incidents have been established and implemented.	Procedures for managing IT-related security incidents are established and implemented.
3. Defined	Both technical and administrative policies for IT-related security incidents are defined, documented, and accepted by the organization.	Both the technical and administrative knowledge requirements for employees are defined and documented, and there is a formal education plan on IT-related security incidents.	Procedures for managing IT-related security incidents are defined, documented, and accepted by the organization.
4. Managed	Both technical and administrative policies for IT-related security incidents reflect the level of risk tolerance of the organization and are routinely updated.	Technical and managerial knowledge requirements and education plans for employees on IT-related security incidents are routinely updated.	Procedures for managing IT-related security incidents are automated and routinely updated.
5. Optimized	Continuous evaluation and improvement for a number of years of both technical and administrative policies for IT-related security incidents.	Continuous evaluation and improvement for a number of years of both technical and managerial skills requirements and education plans for employees on IT-related security incidents.	There is real-time monitoring of IT-related security incidents. Continuous evaluation and improvement for a number of years of procedures for managing IT-related security incidents.

Chapter 6
Security Visualization Extended Review Issues, Classifications, Validation Methods, Trends, Extensions

Ferda Özdemir Sönmez
Middle East Technical University, Turkey

Banu Günel
Middle East Technical University, Turkey

ABSTRACT

Security visualization has been an issue, and it continues to grow in many directions. In order to give sufficient security visualization designs, information both in many different aspects of visualization techniques and the security problems is required. More beneficial designs depend on decisions that include use cases covering security artifacts and business requirements of the organizations, correct and optimal use of data sources, and selection of proper display types. To be able to see the big picture, the designers should be aware of available data types, possible use cases and different styles of displays. In this chapter, these properties of a large set of earlier security visualization work have been depicted and classified using both textual and graphical ways. This work also contains information related to trending topics of the domain, ways of user interaction, evaluation, and validation techniques that are commonly used for the security visualization designs.

INTRODUCTION

The actions threatening information security have a variety of categories. For example, "web based attacks" is a name given to express a set of harmful activities targeting web-based information systems. The occurrence rates of these harmful events can be gathered from the numeric information provided by vendors of information security protection systems. Symantec programs blocked 190000, 464100 and 568700 "web-based attacks" in 2011, 2012 and 2013, respectively, showing a 23% increase between

DOI: 10.4018/978-1-5225-5583-4.ch006

2012 and 2013 (Symantec, 2014). This single example shows that there is a trend of increase in the occurrence of harmful events threatening information security. The number of actions is not increasing alone; indeed, the type of threats, their sophistication levels and impacts are also getting higher by time. This makes the field of information security very important. A single computing device without any network connections can still have security vulnerabilities. However, as the computing devices get connected to each other and to the Internet, the level of threats increases exponentially. These threats may be unintentional or intentional.

In order to detect and prevent these intentional or unintentional actions, systems such as intrusion detection, intrusion prevention and firewalls are commonly used in enterprises. The security analysts investigate the outputs of these systems either in real time or in a delayed manner. The main source of information provided by these systems is the log files. In order to warn against momentary or future events, some of the IDS systems or firewalls include some visual or audio alert systems.

Although the alternatives and capabilities of protection systems are getting better, there are problems with the usability of these systems. The main source of problems affecting the usability of these systems is the size of the data they process. The log files are often too large to be investigated manually. The frequency of alerts is often high which overwhelms the analysts. Each alert may not point out a correct situation. This results in omissions or ignorance in the long term. Numerous tools and programs are being used in order to overcome security vulnerabilities of the organizations. However, the outputs of these programs are rarely understood clearly.

Security visualization is the act of using information visualization techniques to ease the decision-making process for security analysts. It provides situational awareness. It offers new representations of security data to increase the comprehension and provide an efficient processing of the data. In general, there is a tendency to use the same type of display types for the same use cases, or the same type of display types for the data in similar formats. While this is the result of a consolidated learning in most cases, it may be useful to find alternative combinations of these use cases, display types and data attributes for novel security visualization designs.

To this end, while introducing the selected existing work in this chapter, these works are classified according to display types, use cases and data sources. The objective of this chapter is to classify the existing work which are similar to each other, and by doing so to find out gaps such as data types which are seldomly used for security visualization purposes. In this way, it is expected to find new ways of combining data coming from multiple sources and display types commonly used for some particular scenarios which may also be suitable for some other scenarios. This extended summary of security visualization designs may help researchers who want to solve security visualization problems by applying novel designs and those who investigate current status and trends in the security visualization domain.

The reviews written so far in the security visualization domain focus on a limited number of works. Survey results that depend on few designs can provide only an incomplete perspective of the domain information. In this chapter, the number of designs that are examined in detail is 79. This examination results in a detailed perspective of the security visualization domain. The contribution of this work to the existing literature can be summarized as follows:

- An extended summary of the existing work is given which may help novice researchers find out what has been done so far.

- The security visualization literature is classified according to use cases, display types and data sources to help researchers find out gaps and alternative combinations of data, display and usage scenarios.
- Notable features, interactivity and usability properties of the designs and their validation methods are depicted, and a short trend analysis of the security visualization domain is made.

The next section is the Background Section including the design issues, the common security visualization classification methods, and the methodology of the review study describing the overall procedure taken through the study including the scope definition. This section is followed by the main section, Extended Review of the Selected Studies, including the classified findings, and validation methods of security visualization studies. The next section is the Future Research Directions Section. Finally, there is the Conclusion Section.

BACKGROUND

Security Visualization

Due to the increase of data in information technologies, visualization has become a popular technique for analyzing, and communicating the big data. Using visualization in the security domain is a relatively new research area. The first published work appeared in 2004. The major reason for the emergence of security visualization is the necessity of analyzing the huge size of security related data in a timely manner. Security visualizations enable human assessment of large size log files efficiently, which results in timely and improved decision making.

Marty (Marty, 2009) described the benefits of security visualization as being able to answer questions, posing new questions, allowing exploration and discovery, supporting decisions, communicating information, increasing efficiency, and inspiring the researchers. Security visualization designs may have different purposes such as summarizing the data, simulating past incidents, allowing pattern discovery, detection of malicious activities, anomalies, misconfigurations, and outliers. Security visualization may provide multiple views of the same data simultaneously or it may visualize different data in the same view.

Basic elements of visualization are data type, which can be categorical, ordinal, interval and ratio, the color, size, orientation, and shape of the graph, position, length and space allocated by the data on the graph and the use and purpose of chart axes (Marty, 2009). Types of displays vary from simple line charts to 3-D gamification and/or simulation displays. A list of alternative display types is shown in Table 1.

Choosing the right display type depends on the maximum number of data values, the number of data dimensions, data types and use-cases. Designing security visualizations needs expertise on security, data analyses techniques and visualization techniques. In order to make a contribution to the existing work, one should gain expertise in both security and visualization techniques. The majority of the journals concerning security visualization and conference papers visualize network traffic data. However, there are also other designs which visualizes other types of data.

Table 1. Types of displays

Category	Display Types
Simple 2-D Charts	Line Cart, Bar Chart, Pie Chart
Simple 3-D Charts	3-D Line Chart, 3-D Bar Chart, 3-D Pie Chart
Stacked Charts	Stacked Pie Chart, Stacked Bar Chart, Stacked Line Chart
Histograms	Histogram Chart
Box-Plots	Box-Plot
Matrixes	2-D Matrix, 3-D Matrix
Scatter Plots	2-D Scatter Plot, 3-D Scatter Plot
Parallel Coordinate Views	2-D Parallel Coordinates, 3-D Parallel Coordinates
Link Graphs	2-D Node Link Graph, 3-D Node Link Graph
Maps	Geographic Map, Globe View
Treemaps	2-D Treemap, 3-D Treemap
Advanced Views	Animation, Gamification, Simulation Views

Design Issues

There are numerous survey articles which depict the design issues of security visualization. Langton and Newey (2010) listed the design challenges and requirements of security visualizations as scaling for the size and dimensionality of cyber security datasets, displaying both historical and real-time data, addressing different data types, designing new human interaction techniques and improving them.

Harrison and Lu (2012) evaluated several state-of-the-art approaches such as Clique (Best, Hafen, Olsen, & Pike, 2011) and Clockview (Kintzel, Fuchs, & Mansmann, 2011) ending with a conclusion that existing tools solve many of the design problems; however, there is still a need for the improvement stating that while some visualization designs are scalable for a high volume of data, such as histograms, they are not scalable for a high number of dimensions. Other tools are better for high dimensions such as parallel coordinates. Security analysis techniques mentioned in network traffic analysis section require the analysis of information coming from a combination of data sources such as firewalls and IDSs to get meaningful results. Most of the existing security visualization tools, however, visualize data coming from a single source. Harrison and Lu also state that the existing security visualization studies lack risk awareness and management and analysis reporting. Another important issue identified by Harrison and Lu is that some of the attack types such as worms and persistent threats are still not detectable by the existing visualization systems. Another way of identifying the design issues isthe bottom up approach. Luse (2009) defined the necessary components of a network security visualization tool as overview, zoom, filter, details-on-demand, relate, history, extract and primary notification. Luse examined the architectures of several visualization frameworks such as Tudumi (Takada & Koike, 2002), TNV (Goodall, Lutters, Rheingans, & Komlodi, 2005), NVisionIP (Lakkaraju, Yurcik, & Lee, 2004), Visual (Lee, Tros, Gibbs, Beyah, & Copeland, 2005) and IDSRainstorms (Abdullah, Lee, Conti, Copeland, & Stasko, 2005) by checking the existence of particular components in each framework. The necessary component sets can be enlarged by considering the new technological achievements.

Common Security Visualization Classification Methods

The majority of the taxonomies made so far for visualization tools or prototypes use three major types of categories. The input data driven type of categorization puts the visualization techniques using the same type of log files into the the same group. The second method, use-case driven, categorizes the security visualization designs according to usage scenarios, and the third method takes the categories of graphical approaches as the categorization criteria. There are also some sub-categorization systems which may be based on techniques such as being signature-driven or not and being real time or not..

All three major categorization systems are beneficial in their unique ways. The first method enables to find out and compare various types of visualizations for the same data types, such as traffic data, firewall log data, operating system data, and network structure data. For example, a traffic data may be displayed using a link graph or parallel coordinates graph, or firewall log data may be represented using a simple histogram chart or a complex graph showing more attributes.

The second method focuses on details of use cases better. Some survey articles in the security visualization research area depict possible use-cases of visualization for information security. Shiravi et al. (2012) classified the existing security visualization systems based on use case scenarios. The first group of use cases is the host-server monitoring which intends to monitor the current state of the hosts and the servers in a network. The second group of use cases is internal hosts with external IP numbers. The third group of use cases depends on port activity monitoring which aims to detect abnormal activity on ports to detect trojans, worms, and viruses which in general show abnormal patterns in port activities. The fourth group of use cases is the monitoring of attack patterns. The visualization systems in this group aims to visualize not only a snapshot of an attack but the behavior of the attack over a time period. The fifth group of use cases focuses on routing behaviors aiming to understand border gateway routing evolution in time.

The third method is useful to learn about and evaluate the technical diversity in security visualization techniques. Zhang et al. (2012) made a classification of security visualization techniques based on display types. The categories foreseen by the authors are text-based visualization which include works using geolocation such as the work by StoneGate Management Center (Geolocation Map, 3), wireless network tools such as IntraVue (Conti & Abdullah, 2004), Wi-Viz (McPherson, Ma, Krystosk, Bartoletti, & Christensen, 2004) and WVis (Bogen, Dampier, & Carver, 2007), parallel visualization techniques such as PicViz (Tricaud, 2008), Rumint (McRee, 2008) and Visual Firewall (Lee, Tros, Gibbs, Beyah, & Copeland, 2005), hierarchical visualization techniques such as Treemaps (Johnson & Shneiderman, 1991), three-dimensional visualization techniques such as INetVis (McRee, 2008), Flamingo (Oberheide, Goff, & Karir, 2006), Mineset (Brunk, Kelly, & Kohavi, 1997) and other visualization techniques which do not fall into any categories such as a border gateway protocol (BGP) based design (Teoh, Ma, Wu, & Zhao, 2002).

The classifications of general information visualization techniques are different from the security visualization techniques. The first type of classification is made based on the complexity of the model, which is calculated as the number of the dimensions of the data. The second type of categorization is made to make a differentiation between infographics studies and data visualization studies. The graphic generation methods are compared according to the amount of algorithmic work and the amount of manual drawings, the amount of aesthetic work, the capability of running for different data, and the quality of the data used. The third type of categorization is based on the purpose of the visualization, which may be exploration, explanation, and a combination of both, hybrid. Information visualization categorization attributes are also examined throughout the study.

Methodology of the Review Study

This study aims to synthesize the existing knowledge in the domain of security visualization through the review of existing literature. This research has two principle parts. The first part concentrates on reviewing the literature with keywords, which critically affects the quality of any review study. The second part includes investigating the selected literature. The methodology used during the preparation of this chapter is explained through the description of the tasks carried out, as in the following order:

The Identification of Research Questions

The main concern of the authors at the start of this review study was to find out the parameters of the preparation of novel security visualization designs. Therefore, a preliminary literature research was done in the security visualization domain to find out the attributes affecting the overall structure and purpose of the design. After the preliminary research, the authors were curious about whether a systematic method of alternative display types, alternative data sources, and alternative security visualization usage scenarios are related to each other, and whether these choices changed over time. As a result of this rigorous work, new associations of these alternatives can be made, such as making a new association of a display type with a use case or associating a data source with a use case, which were not done before.

After the initial curiosity about the parameters of security visualization designs, some secondary research questions arose which are: "What type of user interactions exist?", "In what ways can these interactions be improved?", "Which type of interactions are more beneficial for some display types?", "Are the level and ways of evaluation and validation of existing designs adequate?" "In what ways can these evaluation and validation methods be improved?" during the evaluation of the selected work.

Conducting the Search

Web of Science database was used as the main source of the review. The details of query results were as follows:

1. **keyword** = «Security Visualization», # of results = 96.
2. **keyword**= «Network Traffic Visualization» # of results = 21.
3. **keyword** = Security Visualization (without quotation marks), # of results = 936.

Selection of Earlier Work

The query results were stored in three Excel files containing title, authors, and abstract of the studies. The lists were examined according to their relevance to the study and their correspondence to the research questions. The works on implementation architectures were not included in this study, but reserved for future work. Similarly, although authors benefited from earlier review work, these were not included in the final set of studies. The articles which introduce the design and/or implementation of a new security visualization work are selected. Numerical details related to the selection results are as follows:

1. 21 of the results were eliminated from the first group.
2. 1 of the results was eliminated from the second group.
3. 263 of the results were eliminated from the third group directly due to their irrelevance to the "security visualization" topic. The rest of the works were examined manually in the order of relevance until the content of articles was comphrensive enough to be included in the study for a correct perspective of the domain.

The overall result set included a total of 79 tool and prototype designs.

Investigation of the Selected Studies

Investigation was divided into steps which have various focus points as listed below. This part of the research included returning to previous steps multiple times as the new findings required re-examination, re-classification or clarification of the earlier findings. The focus points of these steps are explained below.

1. Investigate display types used in the selected work
    a. Classify the display types and associate each selected study to a display type
    b. Examine display properties
        i.   Point out the designs providing properties which do not commonly exist in other designs
        ii. Point out designs having higher usability level and/or looking more appealing
        iii. Point out designs having lower usability levels
2. Find out the data sets used in the selected work (While data sets are explicit in some earlier works, in others they were not.)
    a. Point out data sets used independently from other information
    b. Point out data sets which are combined with other information
    c. Point out the attributes used most often in displays
    d. Point out dataset which are not used often in the existing designs
    e. Point out the attributes used most often in displays
    f. Point out data attributes which are not used often in existing designs
3. Find out the objectives of the visualization designs
    a. Point out and name the use cases of the design
    b. Categorize the resulting use-cases based on their usability for enterprises
4. Mix the information gathered in the previous steps for comparison of designs with each other and to provide a solid domain knowledge
    a. Give the example works using similar display types
    b. Give the example of works which have similar objectives
    c. Give the examples of works which use the same type of data

Discussion of the Selected Studies: In this part, whenever possible, recurring design properties were discussed along with missing points and subsequent design issues. Analysis results and the changes of design decisions over time were also included in this part of the study.

EXTENDED REVIEW OF THE SELECTED STUDIES

Issues, Controversies, Problems

Existing review studies focus on relatively small set of designs which result in a limited perspective of the area. Majority of the reviews also make the comparison of designs based on only one categorization item. However, examining the existing designs with multiple perspectives is necessary to understand current status of the domain. Examination of a larger set based on multiple criteria will provide better guidance to security visualization researchers.

The design issues introduced in the Background Section of this chapter point out common security visualization design problems. This provides an upper level identification of the design issues without details. Hence, to fill this gap, an extended review of the domain is provided with details in this section to improve the upper level design issues mentioned so far. Additionally, further investigation of sets of existing designs prepared for some usage scenarios and having some particular display or data source attributes provided in this section, can be used as starting points during the creation of similar novel designs.

Examination Results

In this part of the chapter, the findings are classified under five sub-sections. Some particular designs are related only to one sub-section, such as having interesting display designs or noteworthy interaction features. However, the majority of the designs are related to more than one sub-section. There are also some designs which are related to all of the five categories. The findings which are not associated with the prior categories are included in the Other Notes Section.

Findings Related to Use Cases

In this part, while considering the use cases of the earlier visualization designs, notable results, the designs more suitable for enterprises/institutions are pointed out. Table 2 provides a summary classifying the use-cases identified during this study. The findings display that network traffic visualization is the most frequently studied use case. Visualization of the end-to-end traffic between internal hosts and external IP's, such as TNV (Goodall, Lutters, Rheingans, & Komlodi, 2005), Visual (Ball, Fink, & North, 2004), Visflowconnect (Yin, Yurcik, Treaster, Li, & Lakkaraju, 2004), port activity monitoring, such as Spinning Cube of Potential Doom (Lau, 2004), Existence plots (Janies, 2008), PortViz (McPherson, Ma, Krystosk, Bartoletti, & Christensen, 2004), network anomaly detection, such as Tri Linear visualization (Whitaker & Erbacher, 2011), monitoring of attack patterns such as P3D (Nunnally, et al., 2013), Rumint (Conti G., et al., 2006), Krasser et al. (2005), Girardin (1999), visualizing web browsing activities of a host, such as Hviz (Gugelmann, Gasser, Ager, & Lenders, 2015), visualization of large-scale network data for planning and monitoring, such as Histomap (Mansmann F., Keim, North, Rexroad, & Sheleheda, 2007) are various types of network traffic visualization use cases.

The type of use cases which aim to detect alarm situations are, generally, grouped under the title "Monitoring of attack patterns" in the literature. Although network traffic data is also taken as data source for some designs, such as Abdullah et al. (2005) and Netbytes Viewer (Taylor, Brooks, & McHugh, 2008) to detect network intrusions, intrusion detection and/or prevention system data is used more in this group to classify true and false alarms Some designs are prepared for specific intrusion detection tools such

Table 2. Groupings of use-cases

Among the enterprises: Use-Cases Which Focus on Network Traffic Visualization			
Visualization of end to end traffic: *e.g. TNV, Visual, Visflowconnect*	Port Activity Monitoring: *e.g. Spinning cube of potential doom, Existence plots, PortViz*	Network anomaly detection: *e.g. Tri Linear Visualization*	Monitoring of attack patterns of network traffic: *e.g. P3D, Rumint, Krasser et al.*
Visualizing web browser activities: *e.g. HVIZ*	Visualization of large-scale network data for monitoring and planning purposes: *e.g. Histomap*	Intrusion detection using traffic data: *e.g. Abdullah et al., Netbytes viewer*	Monitoring of attack patterns using IDS data: *e.g. Snortview, IP-Matrix, Vizalert, IDTk*
Inside the Enterprises: Use-Cases Which Are More Applicable to Enterprises/Institutions			
Firewall configuration visualization: *e.g. PolicyVis*	Firewall log visualization: *e.g. Visual Firewall by Lee et al., Vafle*	Network topology visualization for network planning and thrust relationships: *e.g. TrustVis, Mansman et al., SecureScope*	Visualization of application(s), service(s) and host(s) interaction: *e.g. Tudumi, Enavis, Nagios*
Visualization of hosts and network level vulnerability scanner results: *e.g. NV*	Application vulnerability level visualization: *e.g. Goodal et al, Dang and Dang, Alsaleh et al.*	Visualization of filesharings: *e.g. Rode et al., Tri and Dang*	Various type of network traffic visualization use-cases
Beyond the Enterprises: Use-Cases Which Focus on Network Routing and DNS Protocols			
Visualization of BGP update messages: *e.g. Teoh et al., BGP Eye*	Visualization of BGP events (not updates): *e.g. Teoh et al., Teoh et al.*	Visualization of AS route changes and routing behaviours: *e.g. Teoh et al., Tamp, LinkRank, Elisha, BGPlay*	Visualization of DNS queries: *e.g. SEO et al.*
Other: Other Use-Cases Focusing Mostly on Attack Types			
Web attack scenarios in space and time coordinate systems: *e.g. Dang and Dang*	Visualization of Sybil attacks: *e.g. Lu et al.*	Visualization of Botnets: *e.g. Dorothy project*	Visualization of malware: *e.g. Nataraj et al.*

as Snortview (Koike & Ohno, 2004) which visualizes Snort IDS alarms. Other examples visualizing IDS data are IP Matrix (Koike, Ohno, & Koizumi, 2005), Vizalert (Livnat, Agutter, Moon, Erbacher, & Foresti, 2005) and IDtk (Komlodi, Rheingans, Ayachit, Goodall, & Joshi, 2005).

In addition to the network traffic and alarm situations monitoring related use cases listed above, there are also some use cases which seem to be applicable to improve enterprise security. Use-cases related to firewall utilization are in this group. These are use cases related either to firewall configuration or log monitoring. For example, firewall configuration visualization is focused on in PolicyVis (Tran, Al-Shaer, & Boutaba) aiming to help the investigation of complicated firewall rules. Besides investigating configuration rules, visualization finds other use cases for itself in using the firewall data. Visual Firewall by Lee et al. (2005) focuses on visualizing firewall reactions to network traffic and Vafle (Ghoniem, Shurkhovetskyy, Bahey, & Otjacques, 2014) focuses on firewall log visualization.

Another group of use-cases which are applicable to the enterprises include host/network topology visualization. Network topology visualization is used for network planning and trust relationship management in TrustVis (Peng, Chen, & Peng, 2012) aiming to visualize trust and to help identifying attacks in an organization. Visualizing the application - host interaction is a use case which combines the hosts' topology, the hosts' location and network traffic data in a way such as in Mansman et al. (2008) and Securescope (Ferebee & Dasgupta, 2008).

Visualization of applications, services and hosts interaction is also beneficial for the enterprises. Visualization of network access and log-in information of a group of users to a server is studied in Tudumi (Takada & Koike, 2002) which is also similar in that sense. A visualization study which focuses on enterprise security visualization is Enavis (Liao, Blaich, Striegel, & Thain, 2008). In this study, the association between users and applications in an enterprise network is given in a link graph which consists of hosts, users, and applications. The aim of this work is to answer the question of "who does what in an enterprise network". The system is based on agent scripts deployed on hosts and servers which call Unix commands periodically. A subtype of monitoring hosts and services is the availability monitoring. Nagios Core (Josephsen, 2007) checks the availability of hosts and services and differentiates the unreachable or down machines and services. Nagios (Josephsen, 2007) uses multiple sets of command calls such as Ping, HTTP, SSH and MYSQL to collect data from different points. The designs based on periodical control of some information, such as this, include parameter settings. For example, as check and recheck interval, the maximum number of checks and a period for each check are among these parameters.

Vulnerability analysis scans visualization is also another category of visualization, which targets enterprise security. A design by Harrison et al. named NV (Harrison, Spahn, Iannacone, Downing, & Goodall, 2012), takes Nessus Vulnerability Scanner data, and visualizes the data using a combination of treemaps and bar charts. This model illustrates the level of vulnerability for each workstation in an enterprise. There are other ways of visualizing vulnerability levels. Specially designed vulnerability scanners search for application vulnerabilities using a number of code files. Visualization of outputs of such programs forms another visualization use case group. This type of visualization may be used to search for and make an analysis of enterprise application vulnerabilities. An example of this group of visualization designs is provided by Goodall et al. (2010).

Visualization becomes beneficial for evaluators as it facilitates collaboration during application security level examinations. A study for web application vulnerability visualization was made by Dang and Dang (2014). This design enables communication among vulnerability evaluators over visualization software. Another example of application level visualization focuses on PHP based web applications. This application visualizes security logs aiming to support security analysts for decision making during ongoing web server attacks (Alsaleh et al.) (Alsaleh, Alarifi, Alqahtani, & Al-Salman, 2015).

Monitoring the file sharings both with the insiders and/or with the external parties has high importance in terms of enterprise security. Visualization of file sharings among users is studied by Rode at al. (2006). This design provides additional features such as monitoring all the users' history who worked on the files before, providing list of the files which have not been shared at all yet. Another design which focuses on visualization of file sharings is by Tri and Dang (2009). This design focuses on file events instead of user actions.

There are some use cases which are more related to the data beyond the interior of the enterprises to the Internet. Border gateway protocol is responsible to make the Internet routings between AS's on the Internet. It does not include any features related to the diagnosis of the routing decisions. Visualization is used to analyse and detect the anomalies in Internet routing protocols. Visualization of AS route changes' and routing behaviours' are studied in Teoh et al. (2002), Tamp (Wong, Jacobson, & Alaettinoglu, 2005), LinkRank (Lad, Massey, & Zhang, 2006), Elisha (Teoh, et al., 2003), and BGPlay (Colitti, Di Battista, Mariani, Patrignani, & Pizzonia, 2005). Visualization of BGP update messages is studied by Teoh et al. (2004) (Teoh, Ma, Wu, & Jankun-Kelly, 2004). Visualization of BGP events (not BGP updates) is also studied by Teoh et al. (2006) in BGP Eye. Use cases which visualize DNS queries are also in this group of use-cases. DNS queries data can be counted as more related to data beyond the entrprises to the Internet. An example of visualization of DNS queries is provided by Seo et al. (2014).

While there are designs which aim to detect multiple types of attacks, there are other visualization designs which focus on a particular type of attack. An example use-case which focuses on a single attack type is the work by Lu et al. (Lu, Wang, Dnyate, & Hu, 2011) aiming to visualize the network topology in order to detect Sybill attacks. Another example is the Dorothy project (Cremonini & Riccardi, 2009) which visualizes the botnets using honeynet analysis results. The study by Seo et al. (2014) also visualizes the botnet traffic. Another visualization study by Nataraj et al. (2011) makes a the malware visualization. The study by. Seo et al. (2014) uses DNS queries to detect botnets. Dorothy (Cremonini & Riccardi, 2009) project focuses on botnet detection based on a totally different approach. The researchers installed a honey-net and found out the hosts with some specific malwares installed through IRC channels. They used the resulting information to find out the zombie and C&C machines using some particular metrics. Visualization of malwares is a type of visualization which is commonly used for the classification purposes. This use case has its own unique features different from other security visualization designs. In this type of designs, the binary of malwares are converted to 8-bit vectors, and these vectors are converted to grayscale images. Various part of images correspond to different sections of the binaries. Thus, malwares which belong to the same family have similar images.

The use-cases focusing on visualization of attack scenarios form another group of use-cases. Visualizing web attack scenarios in space and time coordinate systems is an interesting study by Dang and Dang (2014), who offer that in order to understand intrusion detection attacks, it is important to understand the cause and effect relationships. Therefore, Dang and Dang (2014), developed a prototype which visualizes attack scenarios. This visualization system is based on exploiting the links between pages of web applications and does not require the predefinition of cause and effect relationships (Dang & Dang, 2014).

Findings Related to Data Sources

One way of calculating the complexity of visualization designs is to identify the number of dimensions of the visualized data. While identifying the dimensions in this chapter, the following difficulties have been encountered.

- Although the majority of the designs describe the data sources, many of them do not explicitly identify all the data attributes.
- Some particular designs are able to visualize multiple types of data sources each having different number of attributes.
- The number of dimensions also changes due to the parameter selection of the users for some designs.

So, instead of defining attributes and dimensions, a categorization based on data sources is made. Examining the data sources of the visualization works results in the following findings.

In Figure 1, the distribution of selection of data sources for security visualization designs over years is demonstrated. While the majority of the security visualization studies focus on visualization of network traffic data such as TNV (Goodall, Lutters, Rheingans, & Komlodi, 2005), Visual (Ball, Fink, & North, 2004), Visflowconnect (Yin, Yurcik, Treaster, Li, & Lakkaraju, 2004), Spinning Cube of Potential Doom (Lau, 2004), Existence plots (Janies, 2008), PortViz (McPherson, Ma, Krystosk, Bartoletti,

& Christensen, 2004), Tri Linear visualization (Whitaker & Erbacher, 2011), P3D (Nunnally, et al., 2013), Rumint (Conti G., et al., 2006), Krasser et al. (2005), Girardin (1999), Hviz (Gugelmann, Gasser, Ager, & Lenders, 2015), and Histomap (Mansmann F., Keim, North, Rexroad, & Sheleheda, 2007) and visualization of IDS data such as Snortview (Koike & Ohno, 2004), IP Matrix (Koike, Ohno, & Koizumi, 2005), Vizalert (Livnat, Agutter, Moon, Erbacher, & Foresti, 2005), IDtk (Komlodi, Rheingans, Ayachit, Goodall, & Joshi, 2005), IDS Rainstorm (Abdullah, Lee, Conti, Copeland, & Stasko, 2005), Avisa (Shiravi, Shiravi, & Ghorbani, 2010) and Avisa2 (Shiravi, Shiravi, & Ghorbani, 2012), there are others, which work on disparate data types or combinations of them. There are many alternative data sources such as firewall data (Lee, Tros, Gibbs, Beyah, & Copeland, 2005), network topology data (Peng, Chen, & Peng, 2012), application code data (Goodall, Radwan, & Halseth, 2010), event classification data (Zhao, Zhou, & Shi, 2012), web site topology data (Dang & Dang, 2014), file sharing data (Tri & Dang, 2009), and vulnerability scanner data (Nunnally, Uluagac, Copeland, & Beyah, 2012), and NV (Harrison, Spahn, Iannacone, Downing, & Goodall, 2012).

The reason of selecting a specific data source or a group of datasources for a visualization study case can sometimes be easily predicted but not always. Vulnerability scanner data is used to visualize vulnerability levels of a group of hosts. This data is combined with IDS data, firewall log data, key logger data and network traffic analyser data in 3DSVat (Nunnally, Uluagac, Copeland, & Beyah, 2012) aiming to allow quick response in case of vulnerability level increase for a host. In order to incorporate application vulnerability levels, software codes are used as the visualization data source. An example is from Goodall et al. (2010). Social interaction data of members of a network is used to visualize the trust in an environment in Trustvis (Peng, Chen, & Peng, 2012).

When going one step further from internal network activities and server calls, alternative sources of data visualization become available. Such a data source is DNS log files. Lai et al. (2015) used DNS log files in a large campus network to find out tendencies of the web users. Internet routing protocol data is one source of data used to detect BGP routing anomalies and for planning large-scale networking decisions. Ren et al. (2006) used DNS query data gathered from a diverse set of caching servers in order to provide situational awareness for system administrators.

The majority of the designs use only one type of data such as netflow data or IDS data, but there are also some designs which use multiple data sources. NetSecRadar (Zhao, Zhou, & Shi, 2012) uses netflows, firewall data and host health status data. Netvis (Kan, Hu, Wang, Wang, & Huang, 2010) uses IDS data together with a huge department and user management data. Visual Firewall (Lee, Tros, Gibbs, Beyah, & Copeland, 2005) uses Firewall data along with IDS data. Dang and Dang (2014) uses web site hierarchical structure data along with multiple web site vulnerability scan results. Tamp (Wong, Jacobson, & Alaettinoglu, 2005) combines BGP routing data with IGP data, network traffic data and internet routing policies.

When protocol distribution of studies using network traffic data is examined, it is seen that TCP traffic data is the main source for the majority of network traffic visualization systems. TCP protocol data is used as the main and/or only source for these systems, such as Security Quad and Cube (Chang & Jeong, 2011), Abdullah et al. (2005). InetVis (Riel & Irwin, 2006) extends this by including ICMP and UDP protocols.

While the majority of the network traffic visualizers do not attempt to isolate the data in terms of traffic types, HTTP(S) traffic aggregation and visualization, Hviz (Gugelmann, Gasser, Ager, & Lenders, 2015), designed by Gugelmann et al. is an interesting example since it distils HTTP traffic from overall

Figure 1. Distribution of selection of data sources for visualization designs over years

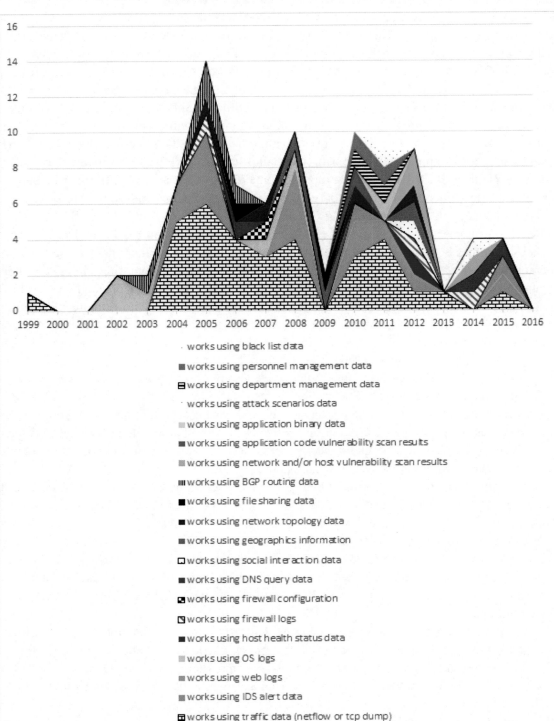

- works using black list data
- works using personnel management data
- works using department management data
- works using attack scenarios data
- works using application binary data
- works using application code vulnerability scan results
- works using network and/or host vulnerability scan results
- works using BGP routing data
- works using file sharing data
- works using network topology data
- works using geographics information
- works using social interaction data
- works using DNS query data
- works using firewall configuration
- works using firewall logs
- works using host health status data
- works using OS logs
- works using web logs
- works using IDS alert data
- works using traffic data (netflow or tcp dump)

traffic data to visualize the web browsing activities of the users. It may be a good idea to make designs for other traffic types, such as streaming data traffic and/or bit torrent data traffic.

Since the log files are occasionally big, it is always necessary to find a way to reduce the data size. Another way of reducing the data is using only some part of the data, such as Abdullah et al. (2005). Abdullah et al. (2005) uses only the packet header part of the data to show port activity and eliminate the rest of the data.

Many of the visualization studies focus on generic data formats. However, visualization of data sources should not have to be generic. There are visualization systems which visualize the data belonging to in-house applications. For example, Impromptu (Rode, et al., 2006) visualize the data of a file sharing application developed as a test bed for the visualization system.

Visualization of log files of middleware servers is valuable in terms of security. However, most of the server applications/types are not given enough importance in security visualization domain. Web server log data is used by Alsaleh et al. (2015) along with attack logs as a part of dashboard visualization. Ballora and Hall (2010) visualize the web log data along with sonification technique. This design aims to help intrusion detection activities and may handle both delayed and real time data. Other alternatives of server log files, such as application server logs, proxy server logs, mail server logs may be the source of novel security visualization designs.

Operating system logs are also valuable in terms of security. However, using system logs belonging to single or multiple hosts and/or servers is rare. Tudumi (Takada & Koike, 2002) uses Sys log file to gather network access to a server, Wtmp log-file to gather user log ins and log outs to the server and Sulog log file to gather user substitution messages.

Independent of the data source, most frequently visualized attributes are time, source IP, source port, destination IP, destination port and classification of the event, such as alert type. Including other TCP fields such as RST, FIN, ACK, SYN as in P3D (Nunnally, et al., 2013) may allow a better understanding and increase the detection of attack patterns (scenarios) either manually or automatically.

Findings Related to Display Types

Examining the display types of the visualization works results in the following findings. Although each of the selected visualization design provides one or more graphics illustrating either the actual picture of the designed software display or graphical illustration of the presented design, it is difficult to capture the repeatedly used visualization attributes looking at those graphics. The complexity of the provided images from earlier work is variant. Some of the graphics accommodated more than one display property which increased the difficulty of capturing the useful display properties. There are also other difficulties about using the graphics from earlier work, such as copyrighting issues. Due to the listed difficulties, as a contribution to the area, a graphical library consisting of 51 images is prepared by using the hand drawing method. The hand driven figures are converted to computerized images using Adobe Illustrator software. These graphical library is demonstrated in for parts in Figure 2, Figure 3, Figure 4, and Figure 5.

Having a set of security visualization illustrations may serve many purposes. The motivation for creating these graphics set include using them during requirement analysis for capturing security visualization requirements,during the design of novel work, during all phases of security visualization studies to improve the communication of display properties, and for educational purposes.

The findings and contributions concerning the various types of display elements are as follows: Each of the illustrations in the graphics set corresponds to captured simplified property(ies) commonly used in security visualization designs. Some of the previous visualization designsdepend on simple graphical charts, like pie chart or histogram, Figure 2 (1,2,3,4). For example, Abdullah et al. (2005) uses histograms to visualize the network traffic. Specifically, they visualize the aggregated port activities and demonstrate that time-dependent aggregated histogram charts can capture worm traffic and botnet activity. Line charts are used for web usage trend analysis in a campus network (Lai, Zhou, Ma, Wu, & Chen, 2015). In Net IQ Manager tool (Ferebee & Dasgupta, 2008) histograms are used to visualize the number of events for each host as a part of security trend analysis. Although, these charts look simple, the visualization designs in this group are highly comprehensible. These type of designs mostly focus on only some part of the data which results in clear understandability.

Parallel axis views allow visualization of multi-dimensional data where hosts are shown as nodes and flow of them are shown between vertical parallel axes, Figure 2 (5), Rumint (Conti & Abdullah, 2004), Visflowconnect (Yin, Yurcik, Treaster, Li, & Lakkaraju, 2004), IDSRainStorm (Abdullah, Lee, Conti, Copeland, & Stasko, 2005), Krasser et al. (2005). It is possible to visualize the end to end flow between external world and internal hosts by using three parallel axes together for external hosts, internal hosts and external hosts respectively. This enables flow direction visualization, Figure 2 (6). In general, the x-axis is reserved for time dimension in parallel axis views. Some additional display features are included in some designs for different purposes. For example, colored lines, Figure 2 (10) are used pointing out interactions coming to or going out from specific ports to help users "recognize and diagnose the problems" (Nielsen, 1995). Animation of network flow data over time is used to find out trends and detect anomalies Visflowconnect (Yin, Yurcik, Treaster, Li, & Lakkaraju, 2004). Rumint (McRee, 2008) uses parallel axis view to visualize a massive amount of network traffic data. This design allows selection of visualized attributes as text rainstorms for each axis which would "help recognize and diagnose" (Nielsen, 1995) of some specific type of attacks. Krasser et al. (2005) uses both 2-D and 3-D parallel coordinate plots in combination with time varying scatter plots to monitor large-scale network traffic. The effective use of labelling, fading, scaling and animation are also investigated in these designs in order to improve the visualization quality of large-scale network traffic, Figure 2 (7). Unlike other parallel coordinate systems, Krasser et al. (2005) show the protocol type by using coloring and the packet length by using vertical lines at the end of parallel axis connecting lines, Figure 2 (8), in the same view. Displaying these additional attributes minimize the "requirement of remembering" during navigation among multiple views and increase the overall "recognition" (Nielsen, 1995).

IDSRainstorm (Abdullah, Lee, Conti, Copeland, & Stasko, 2005) is an advanced parallel axis view based design which includes several parallel axes representing IP address groups. Horizontal dividers exist in this design to isolate departments, Figure 2 (9). IDSRainstorm (Abdullah, Lee, Conti, Copeland, & Stasko, 2005) takes its name from its rainstorm like display. The area between axes is reserved for time varying number of IDS alarms generated for each IP for a time frame. Incorporating multiple axes in a display in this way allows visualization of IDS alarms in large networks.

Some of the designs use glyphs as a less important attribute of the visualization. For some other designs the overall design is based on the use of glyphs.For example, Clockview (Kintzel, Fuchs, & Mansmann, 2011), Erbacher et al. (2002), and, Erbacher (2003). The latter group may also have their own glyph designs instead of using standard shapes. For example, in Clockview (Kintzel, Fuchs, & Mansmann, 2011), clockview shaped circular glyph design divided into 24 parts is used to indicate the hourly traffic rate for each host in a matrix shaped display. This resulted in 24 times fewer number of cells for the total number of hosts. Erbacher et al. (2002) use a set of arrow designs which represent various network behaviors for intrusion and misuse detection purposes.

Figure 2. Graphical illustrations of simplified display properties- Part 1

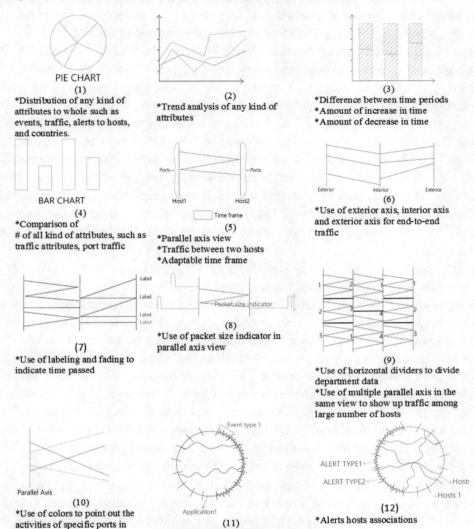

Radial (circular) design is another display type which is popularly used in the earlier works in various manners and for different purposes. Radial structures are, in general, proper to answer questions involving three terms, where, what and when. Addition of other visual elements such as information stacks improve such designs by allowing reaching to details such as Avisa (Shiravi, Shiravi, & Ghorbani, 2010) and Avisa2 (Shiravi, Shiravi, & Ghorbani, 2011). Vizalert (Livnat, Agutter, Moon, Erbacher, & Foresti, 2005) is an IDS data visualization system having a radial shape, Figure 2, Figure 3 (11,12,13,14). It gives answers to questions what, where, when and how by placing the location of the alert on the map, the time on the concentric circles and the type of the alert to the angle of the circle. It allows multiple views simultaneously such as displaying alerts based on snort groups in one radial view and displaying alerts based on snort classifications in another view. Erbacher et al. (2005) uses radial display to present IDS data. The concentric rings in this design map to time units. As the time passes the intensity of the rings gets smaller to reduce the impact of older records. This design is also capable of animating the data and allows selection of various display parameters including the number of the rings.

Real-Time Visualization System for Network Security, NetsecRadar (Zhao, Zhou, & Shi, 2012) allows real-time visualization of intrusion detection alerts. The designers of NetsecRadar manages to visualize the hosts, alert type, and the histogram of attacks in one circular chart design The colored arcs in this design show network security event types, the bars drawn on each arc show the number of events for each event type in the sampling time period, the colored nodes in the center of the graph show the servers or workstations in the selected corporate network, and the curves drawn between the central points and the arcs indicate the source and destination addresses of the selected security events, Figure 3 (13). Radial Traffic Analyzer (Keim, Mansmann, Schneidewind, & Schreck, 2006) uses a radial design for the monitoring of the current state of hosts and servers. In this design, each radial ring is mapped to one traffic attribute assigned by the user, Figure 3 (17). The relatively more important attributes are selected to be displayed in the inner rings. The hosts share the angle parts based on their amount of traffic for that specific attribute.

Impromptu (Rode, et al., 2006) uses a radial display to visualize file sharings. The angles of the radial are shared by the users which are also assigned different colors, Figure 3 (16). The file icons belonging to any user have the same color with the user. As a file is shared more and more it gets closer to the center of the radial display. The files which are not shared at all, stay at the outer part of the radial shape. The file icon blinks with the color of the user who is actively working on itself. As the users get involved with the file in time, a ring is formed around the file icon having the users' color. This property allows identifying the users' history over the files. The angle parts of the users are marked by user characterization signs which correspond to unknown user, wireless user and wired user aiming to find out suspicious user activity. The thickness of the edges for each angle part corresponds to the level of user activity for that angle. This design "matches the system with the real world" (Nielsen, 1995). Thus, itis easy to understand. Being able to show user history also increases "recognition of activity". This design is aesthetically in well shape and seems to be effortless to use for even novice users. Tri and Dang (2009) uses a radial shape to visualize file sharings in a local area network, Figure 3 (15). This model does not include the user point of view. Instead, file events are included on an adjacent page to remove the need for checking them from the event viewer. Their approach minimizes the user's memory load by making events visible in the same page. The visualization is extended by human readable explanations which appear on top of the design to reduce the learning curve of the users of the design.

Lu et al. (Lu, Zhang, Huang, & Fu, 2010) proposes concentric–circle display as an improvement to parallel coordinates in CCScanViewer, Figure 3 (20), (Lu, Zhang, Huang, & Fu, 2010) (Zhang, et al., 2009). Lu et al. uses CCScanViewer to demonstrate various types of network scans and DDOS attacks. Their use of circular view is different than the rest of the circular designs. They use concentric circles analogous to x, y, z axis from a 3D scatterplot.

Cylindrical coordinates security visualization, CCSVis (Seo, Lee, & Han, 2014) is a design based on cylindrical coordinates visualizing DNS queries. Cylindrical coordinates allow monitoring of multiple subjects, such as multiple hosts, multiple DNS servers simultaneously in one graph, Figure 3(21), without totally overlapping the data by means of having multiple center points along the center line of the cylinder. This type of visualization allows also catching the interactions of multiple hosts with some exterior callers simultaneously.

Figure 3. Graphical illustrations of simplified display properties – Part 2

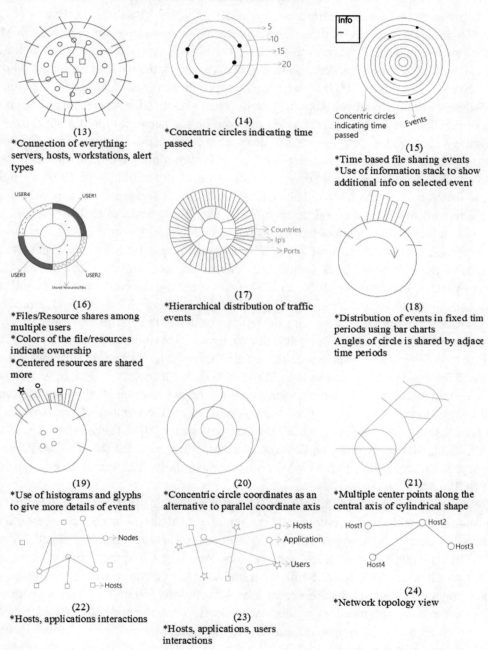

(13)
*Connection of everything: servers, hosts, workstations, alert types

(14)
*Concentric circles indicating time passed

Concentric circles indicating time passed

(15)
*Time based file sharing events
*Use of information stack to show additional info on selected event

(16)
*Files/Resource shares among multiple users
*Colors of the file/resources indicate ownership
*Centered resources are shared more

(17)
*Hierarchical distribution of traffic events

(18)
*Distribution of events in fixed tim periods using bar charts
Angles of circle is shared by adjace time periods

(19)
*Use of histograms and glyphs to give more details of events

(20)
*Concentric circle coordinates as an alternative to parallel coordinate axis

(21)
*Multiple center points along the central axis of cylindrical shape

(22)
*Hosts, applications interactions

(23)
*Hosts, applications, users interactions

(24)
*Network topology view

Another group of visualization is based on node-link diagrams. An example of this category is by Mansman et al. (2008). Mansman et al. uses link analysis in which some particular applications are visualized as nodes. The behavior of hosts is visualized by showing their interaction with the nodes using a force directed graph, Figure 4 (30). Hviz (Gugelmann, Gasser, Ager, & Lenders, 2015) is another example, which visualizes the web browsing activities by illustrating the visited web pages as nodes and links between them as links. Enterprise Network Activities Visualization, Enavis (Liao, Blaich, Striegel, & Thain, 2008) focuses on the enterprise security data and have similarities with Mansman et al. Both designs use node-link diagram to visualize the hosts, users and applications in an enterprise, Figure 3 (23), aiming to show connections among them to answer the basic question of "who does what on where". Nagios (Josephsen, 2007) uses a node link type of design to visualize the topology, Figure 3 (24), and determine the availability of topology items. Trust visualisation service for online communities, TrustVis (Peng, Chen, & Peng, 2012) is a design based on the network topology visualization. In this system, Figure 4 (27), nodes are the users and links are the interactions among them. This design aims visualization of trust management in a network. TrustVis allows unique profile drawings for each user rather than having a female and a male user type icon. Availability of unique profile drawings increases usability and users' recognition level and decreases "recall". It also ends up with a more aesthetic design compared to having single type of user icon for every user. Dang and Dang (2014) visualizes the web site topology in a hierarchical manner using the node-link diagram, Figure 4 (28). Lai et al. (2015) uses a node-link graph to visualize the most active IP addresses in three DNS servers, Figure 4 (26), and to point out most popular domain names, Figure 4 (29), in two adjacent graphs. Visualizing Packet-Process Correlation, Portall (Fink, Muessig, & North, 2005) visualized the selected set of client and server hosts as the nodes in a node-link type of display, Figure 3 (22). The hierarchies between the processes of the hosts are also shown in the same view. This design can visualize the end-to-end traffic in process level for a small number of processes, (around 40), due to display size limitations.

Node link type designs are suitable to represent all kinds of internet routing activities among devices and systems. Threshold and Merge Prefixes, Tamp (Wong, Jacobson, & Alaettinoglu, 2005) combines node-link diagrams with the animation to simulate the internet routings. Colors are used to represent packet pathways, Figure 4(32). Size of the links get thicker as the number of prefixes using any link increases. This tool is designed to diagnose the internet routing algorithms either in real time or using historical data. BGPlay (Colitti, Di Battista, Mariani, Patrignani, & Pizzonia, 2005), and Linkrank (Lad, Massey, & Zhang, 2006), Figure 4(33) are other examples which use node link type of displays to present BGP data.

BGP Routing Visualization, BGPlay (Colitti, Di Battista, Mariani, Patrignani, & Pizzonia, 2005) does not only visualize the paths among autonomous systems, AS's, it also points out changed and unchanged paths in a time frame. In this design dashed lines are used to show the unchanged paths, Figure 4(30). Information Visualization System for Monitoring and Auditing Computer Logs, Tudumi (Takada & Koike, 2002) extends an ordinary node-link diagram by including concentric disks, Figure 4 (31). The nodes which stay on the bottom disk represent user substitutions and nodes which stay on upper disks represent access to hosts and user log-in information. Positioning the nodes on concentric disks results in more compact appearance compared to arbitrarily laying out the nodes on display space. Network Intrusion Visualization Application, Niva (Nyarko, Capers, Scott, & Ladeji-Osias, 2002), which is a 3-D node link based intrusion detection visualization system allows the user to navigate within the dataset with the haptics integration. Haptics integration results with the ability of touching and manipulating the computer generated objects. Thus, this sense of touch improves experiences of users.

Matrixes, grids or x-y (-z) plots are commonly used in the security visualization domain. Existence Plots (Janies, 2008) uses two x-y diagrams together to visualize the inbound and outbound port activity, Figure 4 (35). In this design, y axis is reserved for logarithmic scale of either 2^{16} inbound or outbound ports and x axis is reserved for the time dimension.

Figure 4. Graphical illustrations of simplified display properties – Part 3

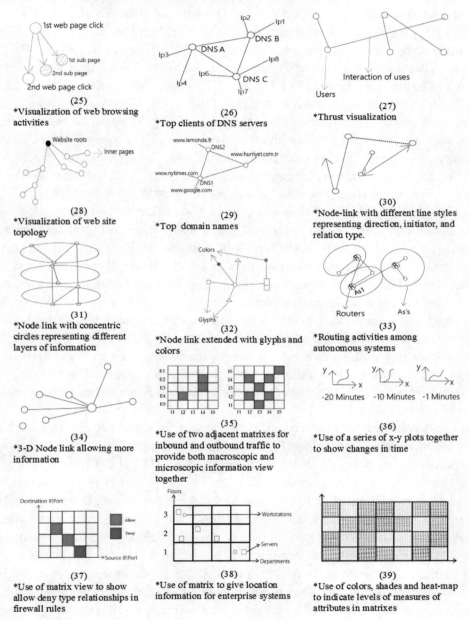

Use of logarithmic scale reduces the required space for the large range of port values. Correlation Layers for Information Query and Exploration, Clique (Best, Hafen, Olsen, & Pike, 2011) visualizes the time-aggregated network traffic data using an x-y axis plot. It is assumed that the variance of counts around mean should be constant over time. However, as the number of traffic increases this assumption does not hold. So, the designers visualize square root of the aggregated values instead of aggregated values to reduce this effect for large values.

Sybil attack results due to malicious hosts which act as other hosts by impersonating their identities or using other fake identities. Lu et al. (2011) uses 2D matrixes to visualize the Sybil attacks, Figure 5 (41). Generally, this type of attack is demonstrated by topology diagrams. Lu et al. (2011) visualize time variant network topology and detect patterns which point to Sybil attacks in their work. PolicyVis (Tran, Al-Shaer, & Boutaba) uses the x-y axes to visualize the complicated allow/deny type rules of firewalls through the use of an easily readable design, Figure 4 (37). In general, matrix type of displays uses color of matrix cells which indicate the severity or number of the events. The x-y axes are commonly used for time-port, time–IP, source IP-destination IP, port-IP respectively. Some of the matrix designs use additional lines to connect the matrix cells with other matrix cells, Time-based Network Visualizer, TNV (Goodall, Lutters, Rheingans, & Komlodi, 2005) or with other display elements, Figure 5(44), Visual Information Security Utility for Administration Live, Visual (Ball, Fink, & North, 2004).

Securescope (Ferebee & Dasgupta, 2008) is another design which has a matrix type display. In this design, a matrix like 2-D grid is used visualizing the location of the hosts using the department names and the flooring number of the building, Figure 4 (38). Such a design is useful for enterprise network management purposes. Similar to TNV, the hosts which stay in the 2-D matrix are connected to nodes reserved for different communication protocols through lines. The size of the protocol nodes shows the amount of network traffic for that protocol. As the number of hosts or events increases, these type of designs combining node-link and matrixes become complicated. If there are the additional connecting lines between matrix cells the understandability would even decrease due to the overlapping lines. Visual analytics of firewall log events, Vafle (Ghoniem, Shurkhovetskyy, Bahey, & Otjacques, 2014) adopts a 2D matrix display including custom heatmap view, magic lens interaction, clustering, multi-level navigation, and on demand details techniques, which increase its usability, Figure 4 (39). The authors also think that it is mandatory to use vertical and horizontal scrollbars in these matrix, or grid type of displays as in the Vafle case.

2D and 3D scatterplot designs allow visualization of relatively higher size of data, because data points consume less space in these display types, Figure 5 (41). For example, Xiao et al. (2006) uses 2-D scatter plots to visualize network traffic attributes. Security Quad and Cube (Chang & Jeong, 2011) uses a cube structure to visualize network anomalies Figure 5 (42). The attributes used in this visualization are source IP and port and destination IP and port. Netbytes viewer (Taylor, Brooks, & McHugh, 2008) uses a 3-D impulse graph, which is similar to 3-D scatterplots using the port, time, and bytes attributes.

Tool for Port-Based Detection of Security Events, Portvis (McPherson, Ma, Krystosk, Bartoletti, & Christensen, 2004) uses scatterplots to visualize port activity. It breaks the port number into two- byte x-y location on the plot. Compared to Abdullah et al. (2005)'s simple histogram based port activity monitoring design, these scatter plots require much more effort for data preparation and understanding phases. Independent of the designs, as the amount of the data increases the readability of these matrixes decreases generally. However, when reinforced with pattern evaluation and detection methods, as in the Lu et al. (2011), such 2-D, 3-D matrix type of displays become more appropriate for automatic and manual detection of attacks.

Intrusion Detection and Analysis Using Histographs, IDGraphs (Ren, Gao, Li, Chen, & Watson, 2005) is a design which has a scatter plot like display aiming to detect network intrusions using traffic data. Most of the scatterplot and matrix like designs use IP's and/or ports as second dimension in addition to the time dimension. IDGraphs uses a different approach. It uses the ratio of number of SYN/ number of SYN-ACK as a second dimension to detect attacks such as TCP SYN flooding, worm outbreaks, and

Figure 5. Graphical illustrations of simplified display properties –Part 4

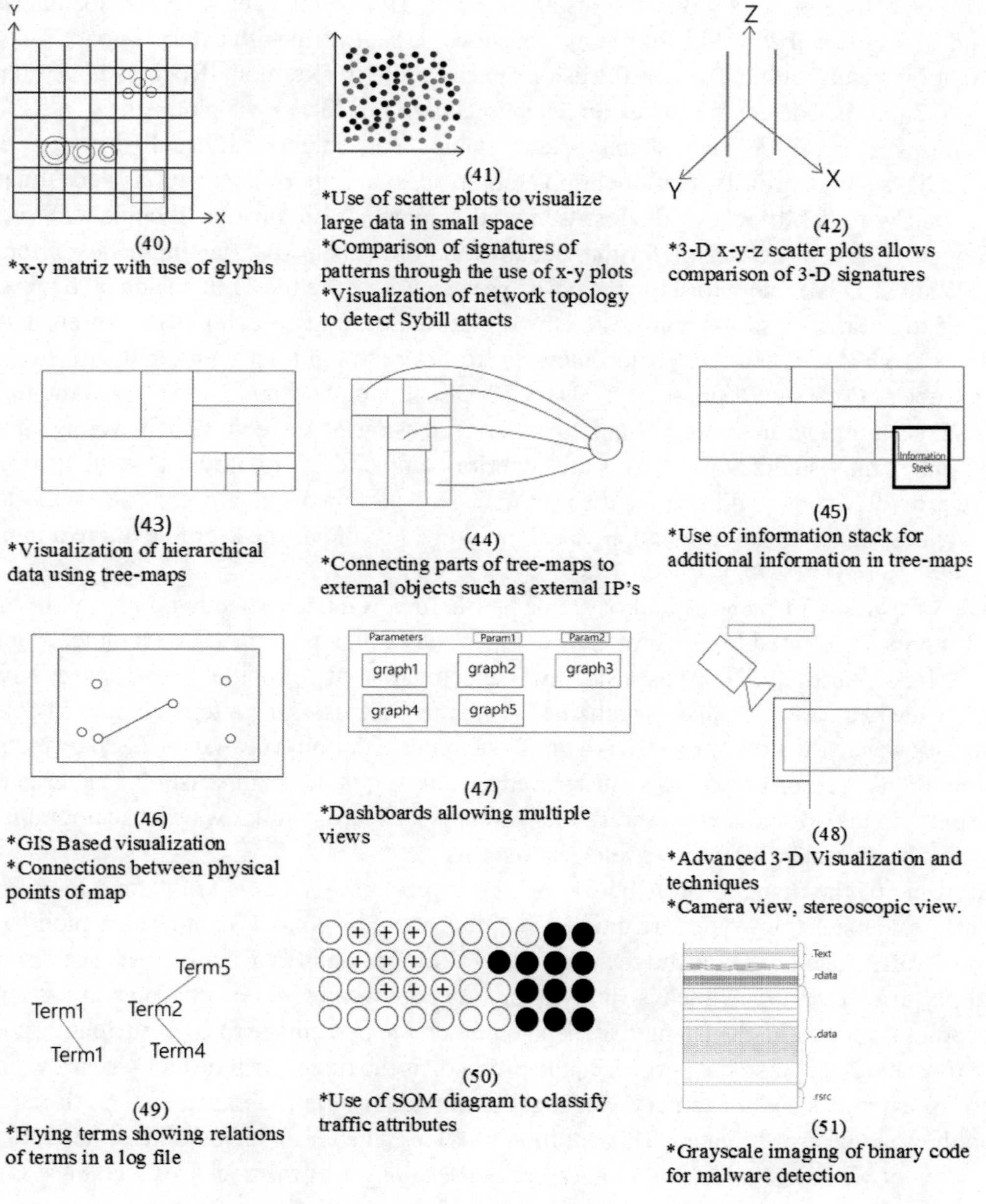

(40)
*x-y matriz with use of glyphs

(41)
*Use of scatter plots to visualize
large data in small space
*Comparison of signatures of
patterns through the use of x-y plots
*Visualization of network topology
to detect Sybill attacts

(42)
*3-D x-y-z scatter plots allows
comparison of 3-D signatures

(43)
*Visualization of hierarchical
data using tree-maps

(44)
*Connecting parts of tree-maps to
external objects such as external IP's

(45)
*Use of information stack for
additional information in tree-maps

(46)
*GIS Based visualization
*Connections between physical
points of map

(47)
*Dashboards allowing multiple
views

Parameters | Param1 | Param2
graph1 | graph2 | graph3
graph4 | graph5

(48)
*Advanced 3-D Visualization and
techniques
*Camera view, stereoscopic view.

Term5
Term1   Term2
Term1   Term4

(49)
*Flying terms showing relations
of terms in a log file

(50)
*Use of SOM diagram to classify
traffic attributes

.Text
.rdata
.data
.rsrc

(51)
*Grayscale imaging of binary code
for malware detection

port scanning. It is based on histograph technique including the brightness level of the cell based on the value of the data.

Although the data format is identical for both internal network traffic and network traffic with external nodes, two adjacent matrixes are used to visualize the IP traffic between internal hosts and external IP's in IPMatrix (Koike, Ohno, & Koizumi, 2005). It was necessary to find an approach which uses the display space effectively to show the 32 bit IP address information for a large dataset. Taking every bit individually would be complicated and unreadable. The information identifying the traffic differs for both traffic type. Therefore, x,y dimensions are selected as 3rd 8 bits, and 4th 8 bits for internal traffic matrix and 1st 8 bits, and 2nd 8 bits for the matrix showing the traffic with external hosts.

Information Visualization Tool for Intrusion Detection, IDtk (Komlodi, Rheingans, Ayachit, Goodall, & Joshi, 2005) is a design for intrusion detection based on a 3-D x,y,z plot using glyphs. It extends 3D capabilities by including size, shape, opacity, labels, and colors and visualizing more than three data attributes, such as priority, classification, source IP, source port, destination IP, destination port, and protocol, Figure 5 (40). Network Host-Centered Anomaly Visualization Technique, Svision (Onut & Ghorbani, 2007) is a 3-D design for the visualization of hosts to find out anomalies in their uses of services. While 2-D is enough to show the hosts' service usage, the third dimension is required to show the level of real traffic load for that host. This design uses only two colors to represent internal and external hosts, but it uses changing color intensity from dark to light representing the time of activities. Spinning Cube of Potential Doom (Lau, 2004) is a 3-D scatter plot design, Figure 5 (42),monitoring port activity. 3-D scatter plots are more difficult to understand using 2-D screens due to overlaying problems. 3-D full immersion visualization systems are superior compared to ordinary 3-D visualization systems since they provide virtual reality where the user may get better involved with the data. Ballora and Hall (2010) provides on a 3-D full immersion visualization which allows the user to explore a huge amount of data, Figure 5 (48).

Visual comparison of patterns and/or signatures is important for detecting any kind of anomalies. Various features are offered to users for easy comparison of data patterns. For example, Muelder et al. (Muelder, Ma, & Bartoletti, 2005) uses side by side comparison by providing view spaces having same size side by side in the same display visualizing 2-D scatter plot views of patterns, Figure 5 (41). Muelder et al. also uses wavelet scalogram which is a graphical representation type of data based on mathematical conversions. This type of graphs have sharper edges causing better comparison of patterns compared to scatterplot graphs. Muelder et al. shows that similar scans have similar wavelet scalograms, and dissimilar scans have totally different wavelet scalograms.

While some of the displays or visualization styles repeatedly emerge with some modifications in various works, some display types are unique and, thus, more original. Use of ternary plots to visualize the network traffic data is an innovative approach by Whitaker and Erbacher (2011). The ternary plot is a general purpose graph type which is suitable for data composed of three attributes. It has a triangular shape. A point is plotted on the triangular shape based on the percentage of each attribute value. Whitaker and Erbacher (2011) take the port, size, and protocol as the three attributes for ternary visualization. They further extends standard ternary visualization by adding the time attribute. As time passes, the points on the triangle are animated. This addition provides a better understanding of network events.

Some type of visualization of malicious activity uses images of the codes, executables or execution log files as the display elements. Grayscale imaging of binaries is displayed to detect malwares in Nataraj et al. (2011), Figure 5 (51). The aim of this type of display is to enable a visual classification of software programs based because malware programs have similarities with each other in terms of their binary structure which reflects their software architectures and implementations, and in terms of their execution log files which reflect the results of executed statements.

Treemap displays are commonly used to visualize hierarchical data, Figure 5 (43)(44)(45). Network Security Management Visualization Tool based on treemap, Netvis (Kan, Hu, Wang, Wang, & Huang, 2010) has a 2D treemap display that detects abnormal patterns in a network while supporting network management activities. NFlowViz (Fischer, Mansmann, Keim, Pietzko, & Waldvogel, 2008) visualizes the network traffic similar to Visual (Ball, Fink, & North, 2004), but unlike it, it uses treemap cells instead of matrix cells to represent hosts. Thus, it can show groups of hosts having same prefixes and the amount of network traffic for each host in the same view. HNmaps (Mansmann F., Keim, North, Rexroad, & Sheleheda, 2007) is an interactive treemap design which focuses on visualization of hosts' interaction with various AS's. This tool can visualize traffic of coming from any kind of hierarchical network structure, such as country-wise traffic including the ASs or a campus network including departments. In this designs, treemap cells are connected to other treemap cells via colored lines indicating the amount of network traffic. Using different tones of same color indicates the amount of traffic, however, ends up with a complicated graphic. But, choosing totally random line colors ends up with less information, loosing the traffic amount information, but simply with a more readable graph. Histomap (Mansmann F., Keim, North, Rexroad, & Sheleheda, 2007) uses large scale network traffic data among multiple AS's to visualize continentwise network traffic. The number of IP's assigned to each country is represented by the size of treemap cells and the number of incoming traffic to each cell is represented by the cell color. Using the treemap display type this way, with large datasets, ends up with a visualization model which may be used for monitoring and network planning rather than detecting threats, and anomalies. While, the designs which visualize internet routing protocol data, adopt a node-link type of display in general, Experimental Visual Anomaly Detection, Elisha (Teoh, et al., 2003) has a totally different approach. It uses a quad tree approach, similar to treemap diagrams, dividing the display space according to IP address prefixes, and setting the size of the cells as the number of IP's reserved for that specific cell. It shows the internet routings by drawing lines between the cells. It is known that as the number of nodes increases, node link type of diagrams have scalability problems. The designers of Elisha (Teoh, et al., 2003) claim that one of the important benefits of their design is its scalability. Designs which aim to detect the anomalies in the Internet routing protocols are based on the fact that user may detect the abnormal patterns by eye as the changes in the paths do not occur often. Since node link based designs better represent real life situations of this type of data, and are more user friendly, they would have definetely much more shorter learning curves compared to Elisha (Teoh, et al., 2003). Treemaps are also used to visualize the vulnerability results. Nessus network level vulnerability results are visualized by NV (Harrison, Spahn, Iannacone, Downing, & Goodall, 2012), and application level (application code level) vulnerability results are visualized by Goodall et al. (2010). In the former case, workstation groups are taken as the higher level hierarchy elements and host IP's as the lower level hierarchy elements. Size and color of the cells are available to associate with attributes, such as number, and level of vulnerabilities. In the latter case, vulnerability categories, such as input validation, encapsulation, encryption, and suspicious code are taken as the treemap top level hierarchy elements and application files are taken as the lower level hierarchy elements. The colors of the treemap cells indicate the severity of the vulnerabilities. The sizes of the cells indicate the number of vulnerabilities for the selected category.

Another group of visualization provide a set of views simultaneously in dashboard format, Figure 5 (47). An example of this type of design is Visual Monitoring of Network and System Security Sensors, Synema (Bousquet, Clemente, & Lalande, 2011) visualized data from a distributed set of sensors such as Snort sensor, and SELinux sensor and encloses different types of visualizers for various types of sensors. Another example is from Alsaleh et al. (2015) visualizes of an open source IDS (PhpIDS), and web server log data in various display types including attacker aggregation, bar view, attack frequency view, IP aggregation, parallel coordinates, radial multiple source view, ring view, scatter plot, radial IP, treemap, treeview, and radial view. In terms of flexibility and efficiency of use (Nielsen, 1995), Synema (Bousquet, Clemente, & Lalande, 2011) has exceptional features. It provides the capability of creation of new frames as user requests in the display window, allowing simultaneous view of data coming from different sensors simultaneously. Visual Firewall (Lee, Tros, Gibbs, Beyah, & Copeland, 2005) design is also a dashboard like design which is capable of displaying real-time traffic data, visual signatures, statistics information, and IDS alarms.

Another group of visualization designs is based on GIS displays. Li et al. (2012), uses geographic information systems, network topology graphs, bar charts, pie charts, dashboards, attack patterns to provide an overall view for situational security (Teoh, Ranjan, Nucci, & Chuah, 2006). Dorothy project (Cremonini & Riccardi, 2009) uses Google Maps to visualize the locations of command and control, C&C, hosts, and satellites, Figure 5 (46). Specifically, for some particular cases in which seeing the end-to-end traffic or global view using maps is more appropriate in terms of matching with the real world situations (Nielsen, 1995).

There are designs which use more advanced graphical models. Parallel 3D Coordinate Visualization, P3D is a design (Nunnally, et al., 2013) using stereoscopic 3D parallel visualization for network scans. Stereoscopic visualization models are superior compared to 2D and 3D models. 3D Stereoscopic Vulnerability Assessment Tool for Network Security, 3DSVAT (Nunnally, Uluagac, Copeland, & Beyah, 2012) is another stereoscopic design illustrating vulnerabilities of a group of nodes simultaneously in one display, Figure 5 (48). In this view, each host is represented by a cube. The pink, orange, and yellow regions represent host groups having different levels of vulnerabilities. The scatter plots show the highest CVE group number, such as level 3, level 5, which is assigned to each host group. The textures of the cubes represent various operating systems. Severity scores calculated for each host are shown using bar graphs. The hosts which stay in the stereoscopic region have the highest severity scores pointing out the vulnerabilities that may result in most severe actions. The design aims to provide a full perspective of vulnerabilities of the hosts in a network to the network managers.

There are some visualization designs which do not belong to these display type categories. For example, Flying Terms is one of them used in Ren et al.'s (2006) DNS traffic visualization design, Figure 5 (49). Flying Terms indicate the quantity of the traffic for each DNS query. It is a word cloud like text visualization technique which uses an x-y plot type background, capable of showing the change in queries in time. Ren et al. (2006) also adapted Chernoff Face Glyphs which are capable of showing 10 attributes in a 2D face display as part of a passive monitoring system. A series of glyphs is shown in this display type. If a face is quite different from previous faces, then it is a sign that an abnormal event may occur in the network.

Using various graphical filters over 2D or 3D visualization models to better represent abnormalities is being examined by some researchers (Alsaleh, Barrera, & Van Oorschot, 2008). In addition to improving the visual display, there are some techniques which rely on other senses. An interesting design related to network monitoring uses human aural, and visual pattern recognition ability simultaneously for higher rates of intrusion detection (Ballora & Hall, 2010).

The majority of display types require a prior knowledge on the data, such as the number of records, the number of dimensions etc. Girardin (1999) uses a totally different visualization system based on self-organizing map (SOM) diagrams which do not require prior knowledge of the data, Figure 5 (50). In this design, numerous attributes including time, packet size, flags, IPs, and ports are visualized in a rectangular shaped SOM diagram. The part of traffic data which point out some abnormal activities, such as high packet sizes, unacknowledged SYN requests, TCP connections which did not complete three hand shake communication protocol are grouped in the SOM diagram. Following this initial visualization, the user should investigate the details of the suspicious parts of the SOM to detect abnormal traffic activities.

Figure 6. Distribution of display types of security visualization designs over years

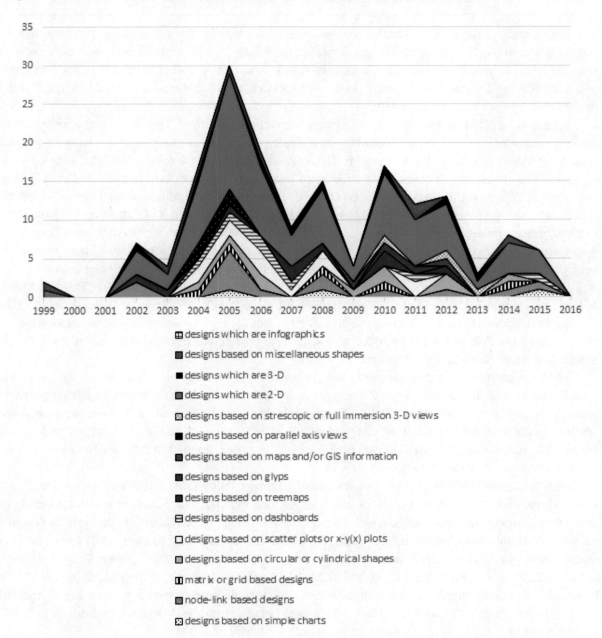

designs which are infographics

designs based on miscellaneous shapes

designs which are 3-D

designs which are 2-D

designs based on strescopic or full immersion 3-D views

designs based on parallel axis views

designs based on maps and/or GIS information

designs based on glyps

designs based on treemaps

designs based on dashboards

designs based on scatter plots or x-y(x) plots

designs based on circular or cylindrical shapes

matrix or grid based designs

node-link based designs

designs based on simple charts

Since security visualization designs have to be used, in general, both frequently and for long periods of time during the monitoring and analyses tasks, being visually appealing (Nielsen, 1995) would eventually enhance the usability of these designs. Among many other alternatives, Impromptu (Rode, et al., 2006), CCSVis (Seo, Lee, & Han, 2014), and Vafle (Ghoniem, Shurkhovetskyy, Bahey, & Otjacques, 2014) stand out in this respect.

Findings Related to User Interaction

The interactivity of the selected studies is investigated theoretically rather than using experimental approach due to the difficulty of reaching an executable version to many of the designs. Few examples selected for this review study lack user interaction features, such as Abdullah et al. (2005), Security Quad and Cube (Chang & Jeong, 2011), and Dorothy Project (Cremonini & Riccardi, 2009). The interactivity of the other designs has various levels.

There may be different aims of the user system interactions, Figure 7. The first group of interactions act in getting user inputs. The most popular ways of interactions in this group enable selections of some aspects of visualizations by the users, as in NetsecRadar (Zhao, Zhou, & Shi, 2012). It is possible to select the time frame, or so called time window of the data in most of designs, such as Tamp (Wong, Jacobson, & Alaettinoglu, 2005), and Inetvis (Riel & Irwin, 2006). In addition to time period, some designs which show discrete time intervals or which are based on aggregation of data over time, allow the users to change the time scale of the designs, such as in Inetvis (Riel & Irwin, 2006). Independent of the display type, majority of the designs, such as Alsaleh et al. (2015), allow selection of other parameters being continents, countries, sets of IP's, and ports, and alert types. Similar to parameter selection, 2-D or 3-D axis based designs may allow definition of purposes for axes, such as PolicyViz (Tran, Al-Shaer, & Boutaba), Rumint (Conti G., et al., 2006), and NIVA (Nyarko, Capers, Scott, & Ladeji-Osias, 2002). Parameter selection is a way of filtering the display data. Doing this more interactively, such as via mouse clicks is also possible, which is included as a feature in Radial Traffic Analyzer (Keim, Mansmann, Schneidewind, & Schreck, 2006) design.

Generally, security visualization tools are designed to be used by advanced users. Adapting the visualization according to the viewers' expertise level is an extraordinary interaction design property which is proposed by Wong et al. (2010). This model takes users' expertise level on network security, and adapts the security visualization views accordingly. In this model, as the user's expertise level increases, the number of attributes shown on the display increases, animation features are included, and level of interactivity also increases.

The second group of interactions focuses on helping the user by providing better navigation. Since security visualization requires display of large sets of data in small space, navigation and zooming in and out are among the most necessary user interactions, which are provided for the users in designs, such as, IDSRainStorm (Abdullah, Lee, Conti, Copeland, & Stasko, 2005), Krasser et al. (2005), PortVis (McPherson, Ma, Krystosk, Bartoletti, & Christensen, 2004), Vizalert (Livnat, Agutter, Moon, Erbacher, & Foresti, 2005), Tri and Dang (2009), and 3DSVAT (Nunnally, Uluagac, Copeland, & Beyah, 2012). In addition to other common interaction techniques, such as parameter selection, zooming in and out and navigation, both 2-D and 3-D scatter plot designs benefit from the drill down and drill up kind of user interactions, such as in NVisionIP (Lakkaraju, Yurcik, & Lee, 2004).

The third group of interactions aims improving the analists' experiences by allowing searching or saving the data. While monitoring of attack patterns, IDGraphs (Ren, Gao, Li, Chen, & Watson, 2005) allows searching for similar traces in the overall data once a trace subset of network data is selected by the user through highlighting. This incommon type of interaction which is called interactive query enables identifying distributed or recurring type of attacks, such as recurring traces from single or multiple sources. Sometimes interpretation of user findings using security visualization solutions may take time or may require further efforts such as comparison with other diagrams or recall of other data. Capability of saving discoveries and reusing those findings for later discoveries is a feature which may decrease these type of difficulties increasing the overall usability of visualization designs. Such a property is offered by Xiao et al. (2006) allowing save of network patterns which are visualized using scatter plot diagrams.

Interactions focusing on giving feedback to the users form the fourth group. Some designs which encapsulate multiple display types allow users to select the display type, as in, Alsaleh et al. (2015). Some patterns of data would be more obvious in some displays. This interactivity feature provides the user the ability to use various display types for the same data. Majority of the node-link type of designs allow selection and replacement of nodes and links for better view, such as Mansman et al. (2008). Another interactivity related to giving feedback is not based on user actions, but is based on automatically highlighting some display elements. Examples to this type of interaction include blinking the file icons in the assigned color of the shared user in a file sharing application, as in Impromptu (Rode, et al., 2006) or highlighting an autonomous system (AS) as the number of network activity passes a threshold value in a network routing monitoring application as in Bgp Eye (Teoh, Ranjan, Nucci, & Chuah, 2006). Some of the designs combine interactivity with the animation by animating a part of the data in time, Avisa (Shiravi, Shiravi, & Ghorbani, 2010), Tamp (Wong, Jacobson, & Alaettinoglu, 2005), and Erbacher et al. (2005).

Enabling a summary view of the data upon user request is a specific type of user interaction useful in some designs, such as IDGraphs (Ren, Gao, Li, Chen, & Watson, 2005). Tooltips is also used to display full label of information in case of displaying data in small segments of display area, such as in Radial Traffic Analyzer (Keim, Mansmann, Schneidewind, & Schreck, 2006). This design also offers popup menu based displaying of detailed information for a segment, which is accessible upon user request. Including human readable explanations of the discovered patterns also is an uncommon way of interaction with the user. This approach increases the understandability of the models, such as in (Tri & Dang, 2009), and reduce the learning curve of the users.

Other Notes

In this part there are review results related to encapsulation of classification or statistical analysis methods as part of visualization systems. The majority of the works, visualize the already classified data. However, some of the studies classify the data as a part of its workflow. For example, Security quad and cube (Chang & Jeong, 2011) makes a classification of patterns. When the number of hosts involved in the network traffic exceeds a limit, prioritization and selection of hosts is needed for effective visualization.

Figure 7. Types of user interactions found in security visualization designs

⬇ USER INPUT	🔍 NAVIGATE	💡 ANALYSIS	♻ GIVE FEEDBACK
•Selection of time frame/frequency •Selection of time scale •Selection of other parameters (continent, IP, port..) •Selection via mouse clicks on display area •Selection of purposes of display elements (such as axes) •Selection of expertise level	•Zooming in •Zooming out •Navigation •Drilling down and up	•Search similar traces •Save patterns	•Selection of display type •Movement and replacement of nodes for better view •Highlighting display elements (blinking, changing color) •Enable animation of data •Summary view upon user request •Tooltips upon user request •Human readable explanations of patterns

Both Avisa (Shiravi, Shiravi, & Ghorbani, 2010) and Avisa2 (Shiravi, Shiravi, & Ghorbani, 2012) use heuristic host selection algorithms to make a prioritization among hosts. Based on this prioritization, the hosts which would actively be displayed on the view are selected. Lu et al. (2010) efficiently evaluates and classifies the host topology signatures to detect Sybil attacks.

Use of statistical value displays or information stacks is an important property which affects the usability of the overall design, because users are more used to interpret numerical results, rather than visual displays. Thus, including statistical numerical attributes as a part of visualization system, elevates its understandability. As mentioned earlier, Avisa2 (Shiravi, Shiravi, & Ghorbani, 2012) is better in terms of readability due to the existence of information stack having graphics showing number of alerts for each alert type and their change over time.

Although Treemap display type is flexible in terms of the amount of data displayed and number of the hierarchies among them, it requires an information stack or detail window to explain what happens in some specific parts of the treemap as in Netvis (Kan, Hu, Wang, Wang, & Huang, 2010). In Dang and Dang's (2014), statistical outputs from multiple web site vulnerability scanners are at the heart of the visualization design. This main source of data for visualization is used in combination with hierarchical web site structure data by assigning pages as nodes and connections between them as links. Portall (Fink, Muessig, & North, 2005) is another design which includes the use of information stacks and popups for better understanding of network traffic between nodes of processes.

IDGraphs (Ren, Gao, Li, Chen, & Watson, 2005) includes a specific correlation analysis view based on the correlations of netflows within each other in a time frame. Positively and negatively correlated flows are shown in green and red colors. This type of display is useful to detect recurring or simultaneous patterns targeting multiple hosts or originating from multiple sources, in general, generated data from multiple points in a network.

NFlowviz (Fischer, Mansmann, Keim, Pietzko, & Waldvogel, 2008) provides an overall statistics of traffic data in addition to the treemap display of network traffic. One more interesting property of NFlowviz (Fischer, Mansmann, Keim, Pietzko, & Waldvogel, 2008) is, it allows making detailed analyses of hosts by enabling the use of popular query tools, such as, Whois, as a part of visualization solution. Thus, users do not have to leave the visualization tool to make further analysis of the hosts using these external query tools.

Correlation layers of information query and exploration is used in Clique (Best, Hafen, Olsen, & Pike, 2011). This is also a design based on highly usage of statistical calculations. This design finds out count of particular network traffic events in meaningful groupings, such as enterprise wise, department wise and protocol wise. Aggregation is made for 1 minute of intervals and the resulting values are defined as summary signals which are visualized instead of raw network data.

Validation of Security Visualization Studies

Nearly every selected study includes a section for the presentation of design evaluation results. However, there is no systematic approach which may be taken as a standard for the validation of security visualization designs. This issue also makes it difficult to make a comparison of these designs. Every design selected for this chapter includes an implementation of the design either at prototype level or at product level. These prototypes and products are used to demonstrate several types of attacks for majority of the designs. Naturally, each specific design is more powerful for demonstrating some type of scenarios or attacks and less powerful for some others. This issue results in the inclusion of around three to five different types of scenario demonstrations for each paper.

The data sources used for validation purposes for the selected studies are randomly generated data as in PolicyViz (Tran, Al-Shaer, & Boutaba), known data sets such as DARPA 99 (Laboratory, 1998-1999), as in Vafle (Ghoniem, Shurkhovetskyy, Bahey, & Otjacques, 2014), and Svision (Onut & Ghorbani, 2007), data collected from laboratory conditions as in Vizalert (Livnat, Agutter, Moon, Erbacher, & Foresti, 2005), and data collected from the real world environments as in Security Quad and Cube (Chang & Jeong, 2011), and Whitaker and Erbacher (2011). The laboratory generated data may include experimental attacks using various attack tools as in Security Quad and Cube (Chang & Jeong, 2011). Figure 8 illustrates a taxonomy of the validation data used for selected articles referenced in this text. As mentioned earlier, every design is more successful or more focused to visualize some group of scenarios. The success of the validation also depends on the demonstration data size, data quality, and data expressiveness. Unfortunately, this information is lacking for the majority of the designs.

Although all of the designs aim to visualize some types of attack patterns, anomalies and misuses as part of their validation efforts, they have various approaches. The first group of validation approach is based on making experiments on the data for visualization purposes, commonly named as experimental validation. The second group of validation approach follows a predefined scenario steps to achieve expected patterns commonly named as case study. The third group of validation approach is more systematic including a predefined set of attack tools and attack scenarios or vulnerabilities, and examines the results of combinations of them which may be named as a survey type validation. Although use of known data

Figure 8. Validation data sources

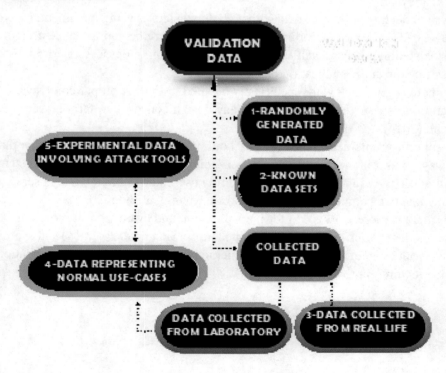

sets enable visualization of attack patterns in a more extended manner due to the prior knowledge of attack data, the selected designs are either based on case studies or experiments.

Another issue related to the validation of the designs is the validation subjects. With few exceptions, most of the selected studies lack clear description of validation subjects, such as students, experts and their expertise level on information security issues.

FUTURE RESEARCH DIRECTIONS

The security visualization domain is in its early stages yet, thus there are numerous new study subjects. In this part of the chapter, some of the trends gathered through the examination of the literature work, which do not directly aim to produce novel designs but would improve the designs in some ways will be explained. The trending topics which are presented in this section forms a limited set of trends which may not include some of the studies and approches since the security domain is evolving in many directions simultaneously and continuously.

Finding out novel designs is the continuing topic in the security visualization domain. There are also the design constraints mentioned in previous sections. Primary topics of the trending studies are related to improving or solving those design constraints.

As the size of the data and number of dimensions increase, the readability of the diagrams becomes an important issue in visualization systems. Dimension reduction methods are one of the top trending topics in security visualization domain. For example, in Avisa (Shiravi, Shiravi, & Ghorbani, 2010) and Avisa2 (Shiravi, Shiravi, & Ghorbani, 2012) heuristic methods are used to reduce the number of hosts shown in the display.

Another way of dealing with large data with high dimensions is using incremental ways (Zhang, Liu, Nepal, & Chen, 2013), which is a trending topic itself. This incrementation can be used in earlier phases of the data visualization process, such as during data collection, preprocessing or in later phases, such as during classification and visualization phases.

Although, there is not much work specifically devoted to finding proper color schemes for security data visualization, this issue has been part of many design concerns so far, one sample work is from Mittelstädt et al. (2014).

Improvement of user interaction methods is a continuous trending topic. There are manys researchs on improved ways of user interaction. Including reasoning to user interactions, such as semantic interaction is one of them. This requires sensing and capturing user interaction, inferring user models, adaptive interaction, and adaptive computation (Endert, North, Chang, & Zhou, 2014).

In general, there is more work to do for the validation, and evaluation of the security visualization designs. This includes the definition of evaluation metrics (Staheli, et al., 2014) and evaluation methods for the models. Evaluation of human computer interaction ways for security visualization designs also is an area which require improvement in itself.

CONCLUSION

While researchers studying for the information security domain may have a better understanding of the attack tools, and platforms, ordinary system administrators and security analysts may not have same level of knowledge about what types of tools and platforms attackers use. Knowledge on attack types may result in expectations of predefined shapes in visualization displays, and may facilitate detection of patterns in the visualization designs. However, the designs should also be understandable without this knowledge for the users in the second group.

However, security visualization designs should not depend on the assumption that users of the systems already have such kind of knowledge. This requires use of easily recognizable patterns, properly identification of all partitions of display shapes, and purposes of them by the users. Improving human computer interaction ways for all kinds of designs, reducing the complexity of the designs whenever applicable, decreasing the size of the data by proper filtering methods, and decreasing the number of data dimensions for the simplicity of the designs are also necessary for increased usability.

Some visualization properties are used repeatedly in the same way for more than one design. This repetition of some features is identical to each other in some designs, but there are some exceptions that use the same visualization attributes differently. Distance from a reference point is used to represent time past for an event repeatedly in designs. For example, distance from the radial center point is used in radial designs to represent different time periods, and distance from axis zero point is used as time passed for one axis of x-y-z charts. Color is most often used either to make a distinction between internal and external hosts, protocol types or to represent severity of the events. In some rare samples fading color or color intensity is used to represent the time past from a starting point in time. Another example of using a visual property in a different way than from usual is done by glyphs. Although, glyphs are most often used to point out the severity of events, they have been used to identify different groups of hosts and servers in some works.

There is much to say about the use of glyps in security visualization designs. Use of glyphs puts into understandability of the designs. For example, the difficulty of showing the same data in a regular shaped matrix cells or cells filled with different shaped glyphs indicating various types of attributes is nearly equal. However, the second one would have much more meaning to the user.

As the visualization system offers its own set of glyph designs, instead of using generic shapes like point, square, triangle, or star, it may describe more complicated situations, such as series of actions which take place in network traffic. This property looks like the main advantage of using design specific glyphs.

As the number of data dimension increase the designs become more complex. Instead of visualizing all the dimensions in the same graph, visualizing graphs for different set of dimensions simultaneously is useful for dimension reduction. For some particular attack types, in order to understand the actual event which takes place within a time frame it is necessary to visualize a long period of time. Under such conditions, repeating the graph for subsequent small time periods would be useful and would result in better understandability specifically for 2-D, 3-D scatter plot type of visualizations.

One other issue related to the display types is the number of designs using advanced visualization techniques, such as animation or simulation. These types of displays are quite few. In the future, there should be more designs using these advanced interactivity and display features.

The existing visualization works commonly depend on data coming from a system and/or network analysis or monitoring tools. This results in a limited perspective of system monitoring results, because although there are quite large alternative data sources for security visualization systems few of them are commonly used in existing designs. The number of works which collect its own data using command sets, such as operating system commands, network commands, and database commands is restricted. The reason for this seems to be that such designs require more effort for the data collection and consolidation phases. Specifically, if the design is related to multiple hosts and/or servers, then the data collection would require implementation of multiple sort of agents which collect data from multiple points. An IDS system would automatically do this, but in order to use other commands these agents should be implemented as a part of the solution. These types of designs may also require the use of multiple sources of data simultaneously, which happens to be more complicated to interpret and visualize. Although difficult, such efforts may end up with novel designs with better usability levels.

Another issue related to data sources is the difficulties of using multiple sources at a time. These difficulties include different cardinalities, different time frames, normalized data versus unnormalized data, and different coding systems. Working to overcome these difficulties, especially in the case of using large data sets is a research topic in itself.

There is also the selection of visualized attibutes arguments related to the data topic. The set of visualized attributes in the existing designs is not large. Although there are a few designs which use conceived metrics, the majority of the designs visualize common networking attributes. In this domain, there is a requirement of well understood set of metrics. These metrics would help in seizing network events and trends and in diminishing the visualized data size and dimensions resulting in better visualization designs.

The validation parts of the existing work are not satisfactory. New validation methods are required, which give more idea on the level of the design constraints of the designs. Also, the existing evaluation system does not enable to make any comparison between security visualization designs. There is a need for a framework which would help to define the design properties of the visualization system and enable evaluation and validation of the works. As a part of this framework a set of security visualization evaluation metrics should also be defined.

This work mainly focuses on display types, use cases and data sources of security visualization designs. There are some other categorization methods which are used in information visualization and/or security visualization domains and are not mentioned here. The way of handling anomalies is one type of categorization attribute used in the security visualization domain, such as being signature based or being anomaly based. Some particular data and use cases are more appropriate to be signature based designs than others. Since a detailed analysis has been made on data types and use cases, no additional classification is done based on being signature or anomaly based.

Another classification method used in the information visualization domain is the level of interactivity of the designs. Although interactive properties of the designs are studied and noted throughout the study, only notable interactive features and a classification of them are included in this chapter. Assignment of an interactivity level for each selected design would require more experimental ways and platforms and is beyond the scope of this review study.

Considering the information visualization categorization attributes, as mentioned earlier the level of complexity is not determined throughout the study, because although the data sources are defined, the exact data attributes are not explicitly referenced in the majority of the selected designs.

There are some visualization categorization attributes, which are not specific to the security visualization domain. In the information visualization domain, one evaluation criteria makes a distinction between an infographics study and a visualization study. In terms of this evaluation criteria, all the works included in this review study are visualization studies. Another information visualization categorization attribute is the purpose of the visualization designs, which may be exploratory, explanatory or hybrid. All the works included in this review study are either exploratory or hybrid studies.

No review results are found on efficiency and performance of the selected designs. It is difficult to make any comments related to the performance and efficiency of the designs due to two reasons. First reason is, this review is not based on an experimental approach. Therefore, actual trial and testing of this large set of designs is not possible. The main resource is the textual explanations and graphical definitions of design and display structures provided by the articles. Although the majority of the works are supported with case studies, the articles lack enough performance and efficiency related information. Second reason is, standardization of the data, such as number of data points, length of time definitions is not exist for the diverse set of designs which are required in order to make a comparison of the performances, and efficiencies of the models. Yet, the usability of the works is discussed to some extent by thoroughly investigating the graphical images and corresponding data and design sections.

REFERENCES

Abdullah, K., Lee, C., Conti, G., & Copeland, J. A. (2005). Visualizing network data for intrusion detection. In *Proceedings from the Sixth Annual IEEE SMC Informational Assurance Workshop* (pp. 100-108). West Point, NY: IEEE. 10.1109/IAW.2005.1495940

Abdullah, K., Lee, C., Conti, G., Copeland, J. A., & Stasko, J. (2005). Ids rainstorm: Visualizing ids alarms. In *Proceedings of the IEEE Workshops on Visualization for Computer Security* (p. 1). Washington, DC: IEEE Computer Society.

Alsaleh, M., Alarifi, A., Alqahtani, A., & Al-Salman, A. (2015). Visualizing web server attacks: Patterns in PHPIDS logs. *Security and Communication Networks*, 8(11), 1991–2003. doi:10.1002ec.1147

Alsaleh, M., Barrera, D., & Van Oorschot, P. C. (2008). Improving security visualization with exposure map filtering. In *Annual Computer Security Applications Conference* (pp. 205-214). IEEE. 10.1109/ACSAC.2008.16

Ball, R., Fink, G. A., & North, C. (2004). Home-centric visualization of network traffic for security administration. In *Proceedings of the 2004 ACM workshop on Visualization and Data Mining for Computer Security* (pp. 55-64). ACM. 10.1145/1029208.1029217

Ballora, M., & Hall, D. L. (2010). Do you see what I hear: experiments in multi-channel sound and 3D visualization for network monitoring? Proceedings: Vol. 7709. *Cyber Security, Situation Management, and Impact Assessment II; and Visual Analytics for Homeland Defense and Security II.* Orlando, FL: SPIE.

Best, D. M., Hafen, R. P., Olsen, B. K., & Pike, W. A. (2011). Atypical behavior identification in large-scale network traffic. In *IEEE Symposium on Large Data Analysis and Visualization* (pp. 15-22). IEEE. 10.1109/LDAV.2011.6092312

Bogen, A. C., Dampier, D. A., & Carver, J. C. (2007). Support for computer forensics examination planning with domain: a report of one experiment trial. In *40th. Annual Hawaii International Conference on System Sciences* (pp. 267b-267b). IEEE. 10.1109/HICSS.2007.505

Bousquet, A., Clemente, P., & Lalande, J. F. (2011). SYNEMA: Visual monitoring of network and system security sensors. In *Proceedings of the International Conference on Security and Cryptography* (pp. 375-378). IEEE.

Brunk, C., Kelly, J., & Kohavi, R. (1997). MineSet: An Integrated System for Data Mining. In *Proceedings of the Fourth International Conference on Knowledge Discovery and Data Mining* (pp. 135-138). Academic Press.

Chang, B. H., & Jeong, C. Y. (2011). An efficient network atack visualization using security quad and cube. *Electronics and Telecommunications Research Institute Journal*, 33(5), 770–779.

Colitti, L., Di Battista, G., Mariani, F., Patrignani, M., & Pizzonia, M. (2005). Visualizing Interdomain Routing with BGPlay. *Journal of Graph Algorithms and Applications*, 9(1), 117–148. doi:10.7155/jgaa.00102

Conti, G., & Abdullah, K. (2004). Passive visual fingerprinting of network attack tools. In *Proceedings of the 2004 ACM workshop on Visualization and data mining for computer security* (pp. 45-54). ACM. 10.1145/1029208.1029216

Conti, G., Abdullah, K., Grizzard, J., Stasko, J., Copeland, J. A., Ahamad, M., ... Lee, C. (2006). Countering Security Analyst and Network Administrator Overload Through Alert and Packet Visualization. *IEEE Computer Graphics and Applications*, 26(2), 60–70. doi:10.1109/MCG.2006.30 PMID:16548461

Cremonini, M., & Riccardi, M. (2009). The Dorothy Project: An Open Botnet Analysis Framework for Automatic Tracking and Activity Visualization. In *Proceedings of the 3rd European Conference on Computer Network Defense* (pp. 52-54). Milano, Italy: Academic Press. 10.1109/EC2ND.2009.15

Dang, T. T., & Dang, T. K. (2014). An Extensible Framework for Web Application Vulnerabilities Visualization and Analysis. In *Future Data and Security Engineering* (pp. 86–96). Basel, Switzerland: Springer. doi:10.1007/978-3-319-12778-1_7

Dang, T. T., & Dang, T. K. (2014). Visualizing Web Attack Scenarios in Space and Time Coordinate Systems. *Transactions on Large-Scale Data and Knowledge Centered Systems*, 1-14.

Endert, A., North, C., Chang, R., & Zhou, M. (2014). Toward usable interactive analytics: Coupling cognition and computation. In *Proceedings of the ACM SIGKDD Workshop on Interactive Data Exploration and Analytics* (pp. 52-56). New York: ACM.

Erbacher, R. F. (2003). Intrusion behavior detection through visualization. *IEEE International Conference on Systems, Man and Cybernetics*, 3, 2507-2513.

Erbacher, R. F., Christensen, K., & Sundberg, A. (2005). Designing visualization capabilities for ids challenges. In *IEEE Workshop on Visualization for Computer Security* (pp. 121-127). Minneapolis, MN: IEEE.

Erbacher, R. F., Walker, K. L., & Frincke, D. A. (2002). Intrusion and misuse detection in large-scale systems. *IEEE Computer Graphics and Applications*, 22(1), 38–47. doi:10.1109/38.974517

Ferebee, D., & Dasgupta, D. (2008). Security Visualization Survey. In *Proceedings of the 12th Colloquium for Information Systems Security Education* (pp. 119-126). Dallas, TX: CISSE.

Fink, G. A., Muessig, P., & North, C. (2005). Visual correlation of host processes and network traffic. In *IEEE Workshop on Visualization for Computer Security* (pp. 11-19). IEEE.

Fischer, F., Mansmann, F., Keim, D. A., Pietzko, S., & Waldvogel, M. (2008). Large-scale network monitoring for visual analysis of attacks. In *Visualization for Computer Security* (pp. 111–118). Berlin: Springer. doi:10.1007/978-3-540-85933-8_11

Geolocation Map. (2009). *SecViz- Security Visualization*. Retrieved May 2016, 19, from http://secviz. org/content/geolocation-map

Ghoniem, M., Shurkhovetskyy, G., Bahey, A., & Otjacques, B. (2014). VAFLE: visual analytics of firewall log events. Proceedings: Vol. 9017. *Visualization and Data Analysis 2014. 9017* (p. 901704). San Francisco, CA: International Society for Optics and Photonics. doi:10.1117/12.2037790

Girardin, L. (1999). An Eye on Network Intruder-Administrator Shootouts. *Workshop on Intrusion Detection and Network Monitoring*, 19-28.

Goodall, J. R., Lutters, W. G., Rheingans, W. G., & Komlodi, A. (2005). Preserving the big picture: Visual network traffic analysis with tnv. In *IEEE Workshop on InVisualization for Computer Security* (pp. 47-54). IEEE. 10.1109/VIZSEC.2005.1532065

Goodall, J. R., Radwan, H., & Halseth, L. (2010). Visual Analysis of Code Security. In *Proceedings of the Seventh International Symposium on Visualization for Cyber Security* (pp. 46-51). New York, NY: ACM. 10.1145/1850795.1850800

Gugelmann, D., Gasser, F., Ager, B., & Lenders, V. (2015). Hviz: HTTP(S) traffic aggregation and visualization for network forensics. In *Proceedings of the Second Annual DFRWS Europe*. Dublin, Ireland: Elsevier. 10.1016/j.diin.2015.01.005

Harrison, L., & Lu, A. (2012). The future of security visualization: Lessons from network visualization. *Network*, *26*(6), 6–11.

Harrison, L., Spahn, R., Iannacone, M., Downing, & Goodall, J. R. (2012). NV: Nessus vulnerability visualization for the web. In *Proceedings of the Ninth International Symposium on Visualization for Cyber Security* (pp. 25-32). Seattle, WA: ACM. 10.1145/2379690.2379694

Janies, J. (2008). Existence plots: A low-resolution time series for port behavior analysis. *Visualization for Computer Security*, 161-18.

Johnson, B., & Shneiderman, B. (1991). Tree-maps: A space-filling approach to the visualization of hierarchical information structures. In *IEEE Conference on Visualization Proceedings* (pp. 284-291). San Diego, CA: IEEE. 10.1109/VISUAL.1991.175815

Josephsen, D. (2007). *Building a monitoring infrastructure with Nagios*. Upper Saddle River, NJ: Prentice Hall.

Kan, Z., Hu, C., Wang, Z., Wang, G., & Huang, X. (2010). NetVis: A network security management visualization tool based on treemap. In *2010 2nd International Conference on Advanced Computer Control*. Shenyang, China: IEEE.

Keim, D. A., Mansmann, F., Schneidewind, J., & Schreck, T. (2006). Monitoring network traffic with radial traffic analyzer. In *IEEE Symposium On Visual Analytics Science And Technology* (pp. 123-128). Baltimore, MD: IEEE. 10.1109/VAST.2006.261438

Kintzel, C., Fuchs, J., & Mansmann, F. (2011). Monitoring large ip spaces with clockview. In *Proceedings of the 8th international symposium on visualization for cyber security* (p. 2). Pittsburgh, PA: ACM.

Koike, H., & Ohno, K. (2004). SnortView: visualization system of snort logs. In *Proceedings of the 2004 ACM workshop on Visualization and data mining for computer security* (pp. 143-147). Washington, DC: ACM.

Koike, H., Ohno, K., & Koizumi, K. (2005). Visualizing cyber attacks using IP matrix. In *IEEE Workshop on Visualization for Computer Security* (pp. 91-98). Minneapolis, MN: IEEE.

Komlodi, A., Rheingans, P., Ayachit, U., Goodall, J. R., & Joshi, A. (2005). A user-centered look at glyph-based security visualization. In *IEEE Workshop on Visualization for Computer Security* (pp. 21-28). Minneapolis, MN: IEEE.

Krasser, S., Conti, G., Grizzard, J., Gribschaw, J., & Owen, H. (2005). Real-time and forensic network data analysis using animated and coordinated visualization. *Proceedings from the Sixth Annual IEEE SMC Information Assurance Workshop*, 42-49. 10.1109/IAW.2005.1495932

Laboratory, M. L. (1998-1999). *Darpha Intrusion Detection Data Sets*. Lincoln: Author.

Lad, M., Massey, D., & Zhang, L. (2006). Visualizing internet routing changes. *IEEE Transactions on Visualization and Computer Graphics, 12*(6), 1450–1460. doi:10.1109/TVCG.2006.108 PMID:17073368

Lai, Q., Zhou, C., Ma, H., Wu, Z., & Chen, S. (2015). Visualizing and characterizing DNS lookup behaviors via log-mining. *Neurocomputing, 169*, 100–109. doi:10.1016/j.neucom.2014.09.099

Lakkaraju, K., Yurcik, W., & Lee, A. J. (2004). NVisionIP: netflow visualizations of system state for security situational awareness. In *Proceedings of the 2004 ACM workshop on Visualization and data mining for computer security* (pp. 65-72). Washington, DC: ACM. 10.1145/1029208.1029219

Langton, J. T., & Newey, B. (2010, April). Evaluation of current visualization tools for cyber security. In *SPIE Defense, Security, and Sensing*. International Society for Optics and Photonics.

Lau, S. (2004). The Spinning Cube of Potential Doom. *Communications of the ACM - Wireless Sensor Networks, 47*(6), 25-26.

Lee, C. P., Tros, J., Gibbs, N., Beyah, R., & Copeland, J. A. (2005). Visual firewall: real-time network security monitor. In *IEEE Workshop on Visualization for Computer Security* (pp. 129-136). IEEE.

Li, X., Wang, Q., Yang, L., & Luo, X. (2012). The research on network security visualization key technology. In *Fourth International Conference on Multimedia Information Networking and Security* (pp. 983-988). Nanjing, China: IEEE. 10.1109/MINES.2012.236

Liao, Q., Blaich, A., Striegel, A., & Thain, D. (2008). ENAVis: Enterprise Network Activities Visualization. In *Proceedings of the 22nd conference on Large installation system administration conference* (pp. 59-74). San Diego, CA: Usenix.

Livnat, Y., Agutter, J., Moon, S., Erbacher, R. F., & Foresti, S. (2005). A visualization paradigm for network intrusion detection. In *Proceedings from the Sixth Annual IEEE SMC Information Assurance Workshop* (pp. 92-99). West Point, NY: IEEE. 10.1109/IAW.2005.1495939

Lu, A., Wang, W., Dnyate, A., & Hu, X. (2011). Sybil Attack Detection through Global Topology Pattern Visualization. *Information Visualization*, *10*(1), 32–46. doi:10.1057/ivs.2010.1

Lu, L. F., Zhang, J. W., Huang, M. L., & Fu, L. (2010). A new concentric-circle visualization of multi-dimensional data and its application in network security. *Journal of Visual Languages and Computing*, *21*(4), 194–208. doi:10.1016/j.jvlc.2010.05.002

Luse, A. (2009). *Exploring utilization of visualization for computer and network security*. Ames, IA: Iowa State University.

Mansman, F., Meier, L., & Keim, D. A. (2008). Visualization of Host Behavior for Network Security. In *Proceedings of the Workshop on Visualization for Computer Security* (pp. 187-202). Berlin: Springer. 10.1007/978-3-540-78243-8_13

Mansmann, F., Keim, D. A., North, S. C., Rexroad, B., & Sheleheda, D. (2007). Visual Analysis of Network Traffic for Resource Planning, Interactive Monitoring, and Interpretation of Security Threats. *IEEE Transactions on Visualization and Computer Graphics*, *13*(6), 1105–1112. doi:10.1109/TVCG.2007.70522 PMID:17968053

Marty, R. (2009). *Applied security visualization*. Addison Wesley Professional.

McPherson, J., Ma, K. L., Krystosk, P., Bartoletti, T., & Christensen, M. (2004). Portvis: a tool for port-based detection of security events. In *Proceedings of the 2004 ACM workshop on Visualization and data mining for computer security* (pp. 73-81). Washington, DC: ACM. 10.1145/1029208.1029220

McRee, R. (2008). Security Visualization: What you don't see can hurt you. Information Systems Security Association, 38-41.

Mittelstädt, S., Stoffel, A., & Keim, D. A. (2014). Methods for Compensating Contrast Effects in Information Visualization. *Computer Graphics Forum*, *33*(3), 231–240. doi:10.1111/cgf.12379

Muelder, C., Ma, K.-L., & Bartoletti, T. (2005). Interactive Visualization for Network and Port Scan Detection. In *International Workshop on Recent Advances in Intrusion Detection* (pp. 265-283). Seattle, WA: Springer Berlin Heidelberg.

Nataraj, L., Karthikeyan, S., Jacob, G., & Manjunath, B. S. (2011). Malware images: visualization ad automatic classification. In *Proceedings of the 8th international symposium on visualization for cyber security* (p. 4). Pittsburgh, PA: ACM.

Nielsen, J. (1995). *10 usability heuristics for user interface design*. Fremont, CA: Nielsen Norman Group.

Nunnally, T., Chi, P., Abdullah, K., Uluagac, A. S., Copeland, J. A., & Beyah, R. (2013). P3D: a parallel 3D coordinate visualization for advanced network scans. In *2013 IEEE International Conference on Communications* (pp. 2052-2057). London: IEEE.

Nunnally, T., Uluagac, A. S., Copeland, J. A., & Beyah, R. (2012). 3DSVAT: a 3D stereoscopic vulnerability assessment tool for network security. In *2012 IEEE 37th Conference on Local Computer Networks* (pp. 111-118). Clearwater, FL: IEEE.

Nyarko, K., Capers, T., Scott, C., & Ladeji-Osias, K. (2002). Network intrusion visualization with NIVA, an intrusion detection visual analyzer with haptic integration. In *10th Symposium on Haptic Interfaces for Virtual Environment and Teleoperator Systems* (pp. 277-284). Orlando, FL: IEEE. 10.1109/HAPTIC.2002.998969

Oberheide, J., Goff, M., & Karir, M. (2006). Flamingo: Visualizing internet traffic. In *10th. IEEE/IFIP Network Operations and Management Symposium* (pp. 150-161). Vancouver, Canada: IEEE.

Onut, I. V., & Ghorbani, A. A. (2007). Svision: A novel visual netwok-anomaly identification technique. *Computers & Security*, *26*(3), 201–212. doi:10.1016/j.cose.2006.10.001

Peng, D., Chen, W., & Peng, Q. (2012). TrustVis: Visualizing Trust towards Attack Identification in Distributed Computing Environments. *Security and Communication Networks*, *6*(12), 1445–1459. doi:10.1002ec.521

Ren, P., Gao, Y., Li, Z., Chen, Y., & Watson, B. (2005). IDGraphs: intrusion detection and analysis using histograms. In *IEEE Workshop on Visualization for Computer Security* (pp. 39-46). Minneapolis, MN: IEEE.

Ren, P., Kristoff, J., & Gooch, B. (2006). Visualizing DNS traffic. In *Proceedings of the 3rd international wrkshop on Visualization for computer security* (pp. 23-30). Alexandria, VA: ACM.

Riel, J.-P., & Irwin, B. (2006). InetVis, a visual tool for network telescope traffic analysis. In *Proceedings of the 4th international conference on Computer graphics, virtual reality, visualisation and interaction in Africa* (pp. 85-89). Cape Town, South Africa: ACM.

Rode, J., Johansson, C., DiGioia, P., Filho, R. S., Nies, K., Nguyen, D. H., ... Redmiles, D. (2006). Seeing Further: Extending Visualization as a Basis for Usable Security. In *Proceedings of the second symposium on Usable privacy and security* (pp. 145-155). New York: ACM. 10.1145/1143120.1143138

Seo, I., Lee, H., & Han, S. C. (2014). Cylindrical Coordinates Security Visualization for multiple domain and control botnet detection. *Computers & Security*, *46*, 141–153. doi:10.1016/j.cose.2014.07.007

Shiravi, H., Shiravi, A., & Ghorbani, A. A. (2010). IDS alert visualization and monitoring through heuristic host selection. *Information and Communications Security*, 445-458.

Shiravi, H., Shiravi, A., & Ghorbani, A. A. (2011). Situational assessment of intrusion alerts: A multi attack scenario evaluation. *Information and Communications Security*, 399-413.

Shiravi, H., Shiravi, A., & Ghorbani, A. A. (2012). *A survey of visualization systems for network security*. Academic Press.

Staheli, D., Yu, T., Crouser, J. R., Damodaran, S., Nam, K., O'Gwynn, D., ... Harrison, L. (2014). Visualization Evaluation for Cyber Security: Trends and Future Directions. In *Proceedings of the Eleventh Workshop on Visualization for Cyber Security* (pp. 49-56). New York: ACM. 10.1145/2671491.2671492

Symantec. (2014). *Symantec Internet Security Threat Report 2014*. Retrieved April 5, 2016, from http://www.symantec.com/content/en/us/enterprise/other_resources/b-istr_main_report_v19_21291018.en-us.pdf

Takada, T., & Koike, H. (2002). Tudumi: Information visualization system for monitoring and auditing computer logs. In *Sixth International Conference on Information Visualization* (pp. 570-576). London, UK: IEEE. 10.1109/IV.2002.1028831

Taylor, T., Brooks, S., & McHugh, J. (2008). NetBytes viewer: An entity-based netflow visualization utility for identifying intrusive behavior. In *Proceedings of the Workshop on Visualization for Computer Security* (pp. 101-114). Berlin: Springer. 10.1007/978-3-540-78243-8_7

Teoh, S. T., Ma, K. L., Wu, S. F., & Jankun-Kelly, T. J. (2004). Detecting flaws and intruders with visual data analysis. *IEEE Computer Graphics and Applications*, *24*(5), 27–35. doi:10.1109/MCG.2004.26 PMID:15628098

Teoh, S. T., Ma, K. L., Wu, S. F., Mankin, A., Massey, D., Zhao, X., . . . Bush, R. (2003). ELISHA: A Visual-Based Anomaly Detection System for the BGP Routing Protocol. *IFIP/IEEE DistributedSystems: Operations and Management*, 155-168.

Teoh, S. T., Ma, K. L., Wu, S. F., & Zhao, X. (2002). Case study: Interactive visualization for internet security. In *Proceedings of the conference on Visualization'02* (pp. 505-508). Boston: IEEE Computer Society.

Teoh, S. T., Ranjan, S., Nucci, A., & Chuah, C. N. (2006). BGP eye: a new visualization tool for real-time detection and analysis of BGP anomalies. In *Proceedings of the 3rd international workshop on Visualization for computer security* (pp. 81-90). Alexandria, VA: ACM. 10.1145/1179576.1179593

Teoh, S. T., Zhang, K., Tseng, S. M., Ma, K. L., & Wu, S. F. (2004). Combining visual and automated data mining for near-real time anomaly detection and analysis in BGP. In *Proceedings of the 2004 ACM workshop on Visualization and data mining for computer security* (pp. 35-44). Washington, DC: ACM. 10.1145/1029208.1029215

Tran, T., Al-Shaer, E., & Boutaba, R. (n.d.). PolicyVis: Firewall Security Policy Visualization and Inspection. *21st Large Installation System Administration Conference*, *7*, 1-16.

Tri, D. T., & Dang, T. K. (2009). Security Visualization For Peer-To-Peer Resource. *International Journal on Computer Science and Engineering*, *1*(2), 47–55.

Tricaud, S. (2008). Picviz: Finding a needle in a Haystack. In *Proceedings of the First USENIX conference on Analysis of system logs* (pp. 3-3). Berkeley, CA: USENIX Association.

Whitaker, R. B., & Erbacher, R. F. (2011). A tri-linear visualization for network anomaly detection. In *SPIE Proceedings of Visualization and Data Analysis 2011*. San Francisco, CA: The Society for Imaging Science and Technology.

Wong, D. H., Chai, K. S., Ramadass, S., & Vavasseur, N. (2010). Expert-Aware Approach: A New Approach to Improve Network Security Visualization Tool. In *Second International Conference on Computational Intelligence, Communication Systems and Networks* (pp. 227-231). Liverpool, UK: IEEE. 10.1109/CICSyN.2010.64

Wong, T., Jacobson, V., & Alaettinoglu, C. (2005). Internet routing anomaly detection and visualization. In *Proceedings of International Conference on Dependable Systems and Networks* (pp. 172-181). Yokohama, Japan: IEEE.

Xiao, L., Gerth, J., & Hanrahan, P. (2006). Enhancing visual analysis of network traffic using a knowledge representation. In *IEEE Symposium On Visual Analytics Science And Technology* (pp. 107-114). Palo Alto, CA: IEEE. 10.1109/VAST.2006.261436

Yin, X., Yurcik, W., Treaster, M., Li, Y., & Lakkaraju, K. (2004). VisFlowConnect: netflow visualizations of link relationships for security situational awareness. In *Proceedings of the 2004 ACM Workshop on Visualization and Data Mining for Computer Security* (pp. 26-34). Washington, DC: ACM. 10.1145/1029208.1029214

Zhang, J., Wen, Y., Nguyen, Q. V., Lu, L., Huang, M., Yang, J., & Sun, J. (2009). Multi-dimensional Data Visualization using Concentric Coordinates. *Visual Information Communication*, 95-118.

Zhang, X., Liu, C., Nepal, S., & Chen, J. (2013). An efficient quasi-identifier index based approach for privacy preservation over incremental data sets on cloud. *Journal of Computer and System Sciences*, 79(5), 542–555. doi:10.1016/j.jcss.2012.11.008

Zhang, Y., Xiao, Y., Chen, M., Zhang, J., & Deng, H. (2012). A survey of security visualization for computer network logs. *Security and Communication Networks*, 5(4), 404–421. doi:10.1002ec.324

Zhao, Y., Zhou, F., & Shi, R. (2012). NetSecRadar: A real-time visualization system for network security: VAST 2012 Mini Challenge Award: Honorable mention for interesting use of radial visualization technique. In *IEEE Conference on Visual Analytics Science and Technology* (pp. 281-282). Seattle, WA: IEEE. 10.1109/VAST.2012.6400516

ADDITIONAL READING

Collins, M. (2017). *Network Security Through Data Analysis: From Data to Action*. Sebastopol, California: O'Reilly Media, Inc.

Conti, G. (2007). *Security data visualization: graphical techniques for network analysis*. San Francisco, California: No Starch Press.

Edward, T. R. (2001). *The visual display of quantitative information*. Cheshire, Connecticut: Connecticut Graphics Press.

Few, S. (2012). *Show Me the Numbers: Designing Tables and Graphs to Enlighten*. Burlingame, California: Analytics Press.

Jacobs, J., & Rudis, B. (2014). *Data-Driven Security: Analysis, Visualization and Dashboards*. Indianapolis, Indiana: John Wiley & Sons.

Kirk, A. (2016). *Data Visualization A Handbook for Data Driven Design*. London: Sage Publications.

Knaflic, C. (2015). *Storytelling with data: A data visualization guide for business professionals*. Hoboken, New Jersey: John Wiley & Sons. doi:10.1002/9781119055259

Yau, N. (2013). *Data points: Visualization that means something*. Indianapolis, Indiana: John Wiley & Sons.

KEY TERMS AND DEFINITIONS

Attack-Type: Type of actions that target altering, stealing, disabling, destroying, unauthorized accessing to, and unauthorized using of an asset.

Data Collection: It is the process of gathering data from a variety of relevant sources in an established systematic fashion for analysis purposes.

Display Type: A computer-generated pictorial representation type of data that may also be interactive.

Information Visualization: It is the computer-supported, visual representation of data in a meaningful way to help people understand and analyze the data.

Intrusion Detection: It is a type of security management system designed to automatically alert the administrators if an action targeting to compromise the information system occurs.

Network Traffic: Amount of data that is sent from or received by a computer or a network.

Security Data Source: Computer-generated data used for information security protective and detective purposes.

Security Visualization: It is an information visualization category that focuses on security data and use cases.

Use Case: It is a list of events and actions among systems and users in a specific environment and for a specific goal.

APPENDIX 1

In this part, the selected data source attributes, and corresponding studies are presented in Table 3, and Table 4.

Table 3. Attributes related to data sources- Part 1

Attribute Name	Attribute Value	Sample Work
# of works using traffic data (netflow or tcp dump)	33	Abdullah et al. (2005), Security Quad and Cube (Chang & Jeong, 2011), Mansman et al. (2008), NetsecRadar (Zhao, Zhou, & Shi, 2012), Whitaker and Erbacher (2011), P3D (Nunnally, et al., 2013), CCScanViewer (Lu, Zhang, Huang, & Fu, 2010), Lu et al. (2010), Hviz (Gugelmann, Gasser, Ager, & Lenders, 2015), Enavis (Liao, Blaich, Striegel, & Thain, 2008), Wong et al. (2010), Clique (Best, Hafen, Olsen, & Pike, 2011), NVisionIP (Lakkaraju, Yurcik, & Lee, 2004), Visflowconnect (Yin, Yurcik, Treaster, Li, & Lakkaraju, 2004), Rumint (Conti & Abdullah, 2004), Krasser et al. (2005), HNmaps (Mansmann F., Keim, North, Rexroad, & Sheleheda, 2007), Histomap (Mansmann F., Keim, North, Rexroad, & Sheleheda, 2007), Visual (Ball, Fink, & North, 2004), TNV (Goodall, Lutters, Rheingans, & Komlodi, 2005), PortVis (McPherson, Ma, Krystosk, Bartoletti, & Christensen, 2004), Girardin (1999), IDGraphs (Ren, Gao, Li, Chen, & Watson, 2005), Inetvis (Riel & Irwin, 2006), Muelder et al. (2005), Existence plots (Janies, 2008), Xiao et al. (2006), NFlowviz (Fischer, Mansmann, Keim, Pietzko, & Waldvogel, 2008), Svision (Onut & Ghorbani, 2007), Clockview (Kintzel, Fuchs, & Mansmann, 2011), Portall (Fink, Muessig, & North, 2005), Hone (Fink, Muessig, & North, 2005), Radial Traffic Analyzer (Keim, Mansmann, Schneidewind, & Schreck, 2006)
# of works using IDS alert data	16	Avisa (Shiravi, Shiravi, & Ghorbani, 2010), Avisa2 (Shiravi, Shiravi, & Ghorbani, 2012), Mansman et al. (2008), Netvis (Kan, Hu, Wang, Wang, & Huang, 2010), Alsaleh et al. (2015), Synema (Bousquet, Clemente, & Lalande, 2011), IDSRainStorm (Abdullah, Lee, Conti, Copeland, & Stasko, 2005), Securescope (Ferebee & Dasgupta, 2008), Net IQ Manager tool (Ferebee & Dasgupta, 2008), Snortview (Koike & Ohno, 2004), IPMatrix (Koike, Ohno, & Koizumi, 2005), Vizalert (Livnat, Agutter, Moon, Erbacher, & Foresti, 2005), IDtk (Komlodi, Rheingans, Ayachit, Goodall, & Joshi, 2005), Spinning Cube of Potential Doom (Lau, 2004), NIVA (Nyarko, Capers, Scott, & Ladeji-Osias, 2002), NFlowviz (Fischer, Mansmann, Keim, Pietzko, & Waldvogel, 2008)
# of works using web logs	2	Ballora and Hall (2010), Alsaleh et al. (2015)
# of works using OS logs	5	Net IQ Manager tool (Ferebee & Dasgupta, 2008), Tudumi (Takada & Koike, 2002), Erbacher et al. (2002), Erbacher (2003), Nagios (Josephsen, 2007)
# of works using host health status data	1	NetsecRadar (Zhao, Zhou, & Shi, 2012)
# of works using firewall logs	3	NetsecRadar (Zhao, Zhou, & Shi, 2012), Vafle (Ghoniem, Shurkhovetskyy, Bahey, & Otjacques, 2014), Visual Firewall (Lee, Tros, Gibbs, Beyah, & Copeland, 2005)
# of works using firewall configuration	1	PolicyViz (Tran, Al-Shaer, & Boutaba)
# of works using DNS query data	3	CCSVis (Seo, Lee, & Han, 2014), Lai et al. (2015), Ren et al. (2006)
# of works using social interaction data	1	TrustVis (Peng, Chen, & Peng, 2012)

Table 4. Attributes related to data sources- Part 2

Attribute Name	Attibute Value	Sample Work
# of works using geographics information	3	Li et al. (2012), Dorothy project (Cremonini & Riccardi, 2009), Securescope (Ferebee & Dasgupta, 2008)
# of works using network topology data	4	Lu et al. (2010), Li et al. (2012), Vizalert (Livnat, Agutter, Moon, Erbacher, & Foresti, 2005), Nagios (Josephsen, 2007)
# of works using file sharing data	2	Impromptu (Rode, et al., 2006), Tri and Dang (2009)
# of works using BGP routing data	4	Tamp (Wong, Jacobson, & Alaettinoglu, 2005), LinkRank (Lad, Massey, & Zhang, 2006), BGPlay (Colitti, Di Battista, Mariani, Patrignani, & Pizzonia, 2005), Elisha (Teoh, et al., 2003)
# of works using network and/or host vulnerability scan results	3	NV (Harrison, Spahn, Iannacone, Downing, & Goodall, 2012), Dang and Dang (2014), 3DSVAT (Nunnally, Uluagac, Copeland, & Beyah, 2012)
# of works using application code vulnerability scan results	1	Goodall et al. (2010)
# of works using application binary data	1	Nataraj et al. (2011)
# of works using attack scenarios data	1	Dang and Dang (2014)
# of works using black list data	1	Clockview (Kintzel, Fuchs, & Mansmann, 2011)
# of works using department management data	3	Netvis (Kan, Hu, Wang, Wang, & Huang, 2010), Synema (Bousquet, Clemente, & Lalande, 2011)
# of works using personnel management data	2	Netvis (Kan, Hu, Wang, Wang, & Huang, 2010), Synema (Bousquet, Clemente, & Lalande, 2011)

APPENDIX 2

In this part, the selected display type attributes, and corresponding studies are presented in Table 5, and Table 6.

Table 5. Attributes related to display types- Part 1

Attribute Name	Attribute Value	Sample Work
# of designs based on simple charts	3	Abdullah et al. (2005), Net IQ Manager tool (Ferebee & Dasgupta, 2008), Lai et al. (2015)
# of node-link based designs	14	Mansman et al. (2008), Hviz (Gugelmann, Gasser, Ager, & Lenders, 2015), Enavis (Liao, Blaich, Striegel, & Thain, 2008), TrustVis (Peng, Chen, & Peng, 2012), NIVA (Nyarko, Capers, Scott, & Ladeji-Osias, 2002), Portall (Fink, Muessig, & North, 2005), Dang and Dang (2014), LinkRank (Lad, Massey, & Zhang, 2006), Hone (Fink, Muessig, & North, 2005), BGPlay (Colitti, Di Battista, Mariani, Patrignani, & Pizzonia, 2005), Tudumi (Takada & Koike, 2002), Wong et al. (2010), Krasser et al. (2005), Tamp (Wong, Jacobson, & Alaettinoglu, 2005)
# of matrix or grid based designs	5	Lu et al. (2010), Vafle (Ghoniem, Shurkhovetskyy, Bahey, & Otjacques, 2014), Securescope (Ferebee & Dasgupta, 2008), IPMatrix (Koike, Ohno, & Koizumi, 2005), Teoh et al. (2004)
# of designs based on circular or cylindrical shapes	10	Avisa (Shiravi, Shiravi, & Ghorbani, 2010), Avisa2 (Shiravi, Shiravi, & Ghorbani, 2012), NetsecRadar (Zhao, Zhou, & Shi, 2012), CCScanViewer (Lu, Zhang, Huang, & Fu, 2010), CCSVis (Seo, Lee, & Han, 2014), Vizalert (Livnat, Agutter, Moon, Erbacher, & Foresti, 2005), Impromptu (Rode, et al., 2006), Radial Traffic Analyzer (Keim, Mansmann, Schneidewind, & Schreck, 2006), Teoh et al. (2004), Tri and Dang (2009)
# of designs based on scatter plots or x-y(x) plots	12	Security Quad and Cube (Chang & Jeong, 2011), PolicyViz (Tran, Al-Shaer, & Boutaba), Spinning Cube of Potential Doom (Lau, 2004), Netbytes Viewer (Taylor, Brooks, & McHugh, 2008), PortVis (McPherson, Ma, Krystosk, Bartoletti, & Christensen, 2004), Muelder et al. (2005), IDGraphs (Ren, Gao, Li, Chen, & Watson, 2005), IDtk (Komlodi, Rheingans, Ayachit, Goodall, & Joshi, 2005), Existence plots (Janies, 2008), Inetvis (Riel & Irwin, 2006), Svision (Onut & Ghorbani, 2007), Xiao et al. (Xiao, Gerth, & Hanrahan, 2006), Clique (Best, Hafen, Olsen, & Pike, 2011)
# of designs based on dashboards	7	Alsaleh et al. (2015), Synema (Bousquet, Clemente, & Lalande, 2011), Ren et al. (2006), BGP Eye (Teoh, Ranjan, Nucci, & Chuah, 2006), Visual Firewall (Lee, Tros, Gibbs, Beyah, & Copeland, 2005), NVisionIP (Lakkaraju, Yurcik, & Lee, 2004), Nagios (Josephsen, 2007)
# of designs based on treemaps	6	Netvis (Kan, Hu, Wang, Wang, & Huang, 2010), NV (Harrison, Spahn, Iannacone, Downing, & Goodall, 2012), HNmaps (Mansmann F., Keim, North, Rexroad, & Sheleheda, 2007), Histomap (Mansmann F., Keim, North, Rexroad, & Sheleheda, 2007), NFlowviz (Fischer, Mansmann, Keim, Pietzko, & Waldvogel, 2008), Goodall et al. (2010)
# of designs based on glyps	5	Ballora and Hall (2010), IDtk (Komlodi, Rheingans, Ayachit, Goodall, & Joshi, 2005), Clockview (Kintzel, Fuchs, & Mansmann, 2011), Erbacher et al. (2002), Erbacher (2003)
# of designs based on maps and/or GIS information	2	Li et al. (2012), Dorothy project (Cremonini & Riccardi, 2009)
# of designs based on parallel axis views	4	Rumint (Conti & Abdullah, 2004), Visflowconnect (Yin, Yurcik, Treaster, Li, & Lakkaraju, 2004), IDSRainStorm (Abdullah, Lee, Conti, Copeland, & Stasko, 2005), Krasser et al. (2005)

Table 6. Attributes related to display types- Part 2

Attribute Name	Attribute Value	Sample Work
# of designs based on strescopic or full immersion 3-D views	3	Ballora and Hall (2010), P3D (Nunnally, et al., 2013), 3DSVAT (Nunnally, Uluagac, Copeland, & Beyah, 2012)
# of designs which are 2-D	71	All the designs except listed in # of designs which are 3-D listing
# of designs which are 3-D	8	Ballora and Hall (2010), P3D (Nunnally, et al., 2013), 3DSVAT (Nunnally, Uluagac, Copeland, & Beyah, 2012), Netbytes Viewer (Taylor, Brooks, & McHugh, 2008), NIVA (Nyarko, Capers, Scott, & Ladeji-Osias, 2002), Svision (Onut & Ghorbani, 2007), Inetvis (Riel & Irwin, 2006), Spinning Cube of Potential Doom (Lau, 2004)
# of designs based on miscellaneous shapes	8	Whitaker and Erbacher (2011), Nataraj et al. (2011), Dang and Dang(2014), Girardin (1999), TNV (Goodall, Lutters, Rheingans, & Komlodi, 2005), Elisha (Teoh, et al., 2003), Ren et al. (2006), Teoh et al. (2004)
# of designs which are infographics	0	-

Section 3
E–Health Security Management and Methodologies

Chapter 7
Compliance of Electronic Health Record Applications With HIPAA Security and Privacy Requirements

Maryam Farhadi
Kennesaw State University, USA

Hisham Haddad
Kennesaw State University, USA

Hossain Shahriar
Kennesaw State University, USA

ABSTRACT

Electronic health record (EHR) applications are digital versions of paper-based patients health information. EHR applications are increasingly being adopted in many countries. They have resulted in improved quality in healthcare, convenient access to histories of patient medication and clinic visits, easier follow up of patient treatment plans, and precise medical decision-making process by doctors. EHR applications are guided by measures of the Health Insurance Portability and Accountability Act (HIPAA) to ensure confidentiality, integrity, and availability. However, there have been reported breaches of protected health identifier (PHI) data stored by EHR applications. In many reported breaches, improper use of EHRs has resulted in disclosure of patient's protected health information. The goal of this chapter is to (1) provide an overview of HIPAA security and privacy requirements; (2) summarize recent literature works related to complying with HIPAA security and privacy requirements; (3) map some of the existing vulnerabilities with HIPAA security rules.

DOI: 10.4018/978-1-5225-5583-4.ch007

BACKGROUND

In 2009, the American Reinvestment & Recovery Act (ARRA) was enacted with the aim to modernize Health Information Technology in USA. Notably, Health Information Technology for Economic and Clinical Health (HITECH) Act founded the concept of meaningful usage having five pillars. One of the pillars is to ensure adequate privacy and security protection of personal health information ("Center For Disease Control and Prevention," 2007). The HITECH act provided incentives to health care providers to adopt Electronic Health Record (EHR) applications. The act mandated all healthcare providers to adopt EHRs when dealing with patient data by 2015. Otherwise, there are penalties for not complying. As of today, most hospitals, clinics, and affiliates have adopted Electronic Health Record (EHR) applications ("HITECH Act Summary," 2009).

Health Insurance Portability and Accountability Act (HIPAA) was established in 1996 (later revised in 2013) to establish specific privacy and security requirements for safeguarding health information. The information is created or received by various covered entities such as health care providers, health plan providers or insurance companies, employers, and health care clearing houses ("What is Protected Health Information," n.d.). Healthcare professionals and covered entities (e.g., insurance companies, business associates such as laboratories) collect, store and transmit data while providing healthcare related services to patients ("Health Professional," n.d.). Over the lifetime of a person, healthcare data is being collected in the form of electronic records (*The Importance of Data in Healthcare*, n.d.).

HIPAA identifies a set of personally identifiable information as Protected Health Information (PHI). Some examples of PHI include names, social security numbers, medical record numbers, addresses, dates (birth date, admission date, discharge date, date of death), phone and fax numbers, e-mails, health plan beneficiary information, certification/license numbers, vehicle identifiers or license plate numbers, device identifiers and serial numbers, names of relatives, biometrics (fingers and voice prints), and full face photographic images or any comparable images ("Examples of PHI Identifiers Health information :," n.d.).

As health care application becomes more and more evidence-based, storing health data is becoming more important. Weak health data protection may lead to identity theft, obtain medical care at the expense of others, order expensive drugs for resale, and claim of fraudulent insurance (*The Importance of Data in Healthcare*, n.d.). Moreover, health care data hacks may threaten patient's health due to the change of patient's medical history. For example, if health records do not contain a correct listing of allergies, the patient could suffer serious consequences or death due to wrong prescription (Smith et al., 2010).

Compare to banks and financial institutions, patients' data has less protection. Banks are mostly equipped with two-factor authentication while healthcare applications are not. Two-factor authentication is an extra protection which includes not only username and password, but also some unique information that only the user has, such as a physical token. Furthermore, unlike bank accounts that can be locked and changed for protection, it is completely impossible to get back the compromised and disclosed health data (Oliynyk, 2016; *What is 2FA? An extra layer of security that is known as multi factor authentication*, n.d.).

In 2017, Emory Healthcare's appointment system was hacked compromising almost 80,000 patients PHI information such as names, birth dates, internal medical record and appointment information. The appointment related information was stored into local databases unencrypted, which opened the door for hackers to obtain plain text information. According to a report (Arndt, 2017), this incident is the largest breach in 2017 across USA. The HIPAA Meaningful Usage act requires that any data security breaches affecting 500 or more patients be reported to public through US Health and Human Service Office for Civil Rights' Breach Portal and the affected healthcare provider must take appropriate steps within a certain time limit, otherwise, faces further penalties. Thus, PHI leakage not only brings reputation problem for health care providers, but also affects patient's privacy and well-being.

The prevalence of health care data (PHI) security breach can be observed both inside and outside USA. According to 2016 Data Breach Investigations Report (DBIR), there were 115 cases of data breach in North America during 2015. It included 32% privilege misuse, 22% miscellaneous errors, 19% stolen assets, 7% point of sale, 3% cyber-espionage, 3% crimeware, 3% web applications, and 11% other incidents. Healthcare is among the top industries vulnerable to physical theft and loss, miscellaneous errors, insider and privilege misuse, and everything else. Physical theft and loss is any occurrence where information or a device containing information is missing. Miscellaneous errors occur when accidental actions weaken a security attribute. Insider threats and privilege misuses refer to all unapproved or malicious use (Verizon, 2016).

According to Verizon survey report, some of the reported healthcare data breaches in 2015 were as follows: In February, Anthem, a Blue Cross health insurance member-company, reported a data breach where 80 million patients were affected. In March, Premera, another Blue Cross member, reported a data breach affecting 11million people. In both cases, ThreatConnect ("ThreatConnect, Security Operations and Analytics Platform," n.d.) announced that Chinese threat Actor "Deep Panda" was probably the attacker. Partners HealthCare, CareFirst Blue Cross and Blue Shield, MetroHealth and Bellvue Hospital reported breaches in April of 2015. In June of the same year, US Office of Personnel Management (OPM) reported mega-breaches for health insurance. The US Department of Health and Human Services reported a breach in August 2015 (Verizon, 2016).

Digital version of electronic health data improved the quality of care due to easier follow-ups, lowering cost of patient care, enabling data track over time, and making more precise medical decisions. Three types of health records are defined: (1) *Electronic Medical Records* (EMRs) refer to digital version of paper-based clinical data. The clinical data, gathered by clinicians, include information that enables the clinicians to make better medical decisions; (2) *Electronic Health Records* (EHRs) provide a more comprehensive view of the patient's overall well-being. It contains information collected by all clinicians engaged in the patient's healthcare. Therefore, information in EHRs can be shared among all involved providers; and (3) *Personal Health Records* (PHRs) are EHRs that can be controlled and accessed by the patients ("What are the differences between electronic medical records, electronic health records, and personal health records?," 2015, "What is an electronic health record (EHR)?," n.d.).

In order to maintain better healthcare, individuals must ensure that their personal health information is private and secure. Otherwise, if patients do not feel that their information remains confidential, they may not want to disclose their health information to the healthcare provider, which could endanger the patient's life. Moreover, when a security breach occurs, it may lead to financial harm for the healthcare provider or the patient alike (HealthIT.gov, 2013).

In this chapter, we first discuss HIPAA security and privacy requirements. Then, we review literature works related to comply with HIPAA security and privacy requirements. In particular, we look at literature works for compliance with HIPAA requirements using four different perspectives: *security vulnerability in EHR, access control, privacy and monitoring,* and *the gaps between HIPAA requirements and breach notification.* We also map some of the existing vulnerabilities with HIPAA security rules.

HIPAA SECURITY REQUIREMENTS

Although EHRs resulted in better care, concerns of security and privacy breach always exist among digital formats. HIPAA (Health Insurance Portability and Accountability Act) was established in 1996 to protect health care coverage for individuals with lower income ("HIPAA Background," 2010). It also provides federal protections for patient health information (HealthIT.gov, 2013) by specifying measures to ensure EHR confidentiality, integrity, and availability (Bowers, 2001). Table 1 shows a set of HIPAA security requirements which are divided into three types: Administrative, Physical, and Technical.

The first column of the table refers to applicable sections of HIPAA law on security requirements. For example, Section 164.312 specifies all technical safeguards that covered entity must comply with. These include implementing access control through unique user identification, emergency access to PHI procedure, automatic logoff after a time of inactivity, encrypt and decrypt PHI, audit the access and usage of PHI, detection of improper access and alteration of PHI, verification of the integrity of received PHI electronically, and authentication (verify that an individual seeking access to PHI is recognized based on provided credential information) ("Legal Information Institute," 1992). The second column provides a high-level requirement to ensure safeguards. The requirement can be referring to other guidelines. For example, in the second row, under Administrative Safeguards, the National Institute of Standards and Technology (NIST Special Publication 800-30[1]) need to be looked at. The third column (status) refers whether a safeguard is required or addressable. The required rules are mandatory for all EHR applications, whereas addressable means optional features.

The safeguards status is required and therefore must be implemented. Not implementing these requirements leads fines and penalties ("HIPAA Background," 2010). Few requirements are marked as addressable, which should be implemented in EHR so that PHI remains secured. We will focus on issues related to Technical Safeguards. If technical safeguards are complied with in an implemented EHR, then it enables not only meeting some of the other types of safeguards (*e.g.*, providing tools and applications to check and monitor administrative security policies), but also can prevent unwanted incidents (due to not complying physical safeguards). For example, if a laptop having an EHR application gets lost or stolen, it would be very difficult to hack PHI data if authentication mechanism is established and encryption of data is applied into databases.

IMPLEMENTATION VULNERABILITIES

Since EHR applications are traditional web applications implemented using various languages (e.g., PHP, JSP) and deployed with databases (e.g., MySQL, MSSQL, Oracle) in well-known servers (e.g., Apache), they may be vulnerable in the implementation. Attackers may exploit the vulnerabilities by providing malicious inputs and compromising the data processed and stored by EHR applications. A number of literature works have explored the magnitude of vulnerabilities present in popular and open source EHRs and checked whether EHR implementations are complying with HIPAA related acts.

For example, (Smith et al., 2010) empirically evaluated the ability of the Certification Commission of Healthcare IT (CCHIT) to identify a range of vulnerability types. CCHIT focuses on required functional capabilities in EHR applications, such as ambulatory (with prefix AM), ambulatory interoperability (IO-AM), and security (SC).

Table 1. HIPAA Security Checklist

Security Rule Reference	SAFEGUARD	STATUS
Administrative Safeguards		
164.308(a)(1)(i)	Security Management Process: Implement policies and procedures to prevent, detect, contain, and correct security violations.	
164.308(a)(1)(ii)(A)	Have a Risk Analysis completed based on NIST Guidelines.	REQUIRED
164.308(a)(1)(ii)(B)	Complete Risk Management process based on NIST Guidelines.	REQUIRED
164.308(a)(1)(ii)(C)	Have formal sanctions or policies against employees who fail to comply with security policies and procedures.	REQUIRED
164.308(a)(1)(ii)(D)	Implement procedures to regularly review records of activities such as audit logs, access reports, and security incident tracking.	REQUIRED
164.308(a)(2)	Assigned Security Responsibility: Identify the security official who is responsible for the development and implementation of the policies and procedures required by this subpart for the entity.	REQUIRED
164.308(a)(3)(i)	Workforce Security: Implement policies and procedures to ensure that all members of its workforce have appropriate access to EPHI, as provided under paragraph (a)(4) of this section, and to prevent those workforce members who do not have access under paragraph (a)(4) of this section from obtaining access to electronic protected health information (EPHI).	
164.308(a)(3)(ii)(A)	Implement procedures for the authorization and/or supervision of employees who work with EPHI or in locations where it might be accessed.	ADDRESSABLE
164.308(a)(3)(ii)(B)	Implement procedures to determine that access of employees to EPHI is appropriate.	ADDRESSABLE
164.308(a)(3)(ii)(C)	Implement procedures for terminating access to EPHI when an employee leaves you organization or as required by paragraph (a)(3)(ii)(B) of this section.	ADDRESSABLE
164.308(a)(4)(i)	Information Access Management: Implement policies and procedures for authorizing access to EPHI that are consistent with the applicable requirements of subpart E of this part.	
164.308(a)(4)(ii)(A)	For clearinghouses, implemented policies and procedures to protect EPHI from the larger organization.	ADDRESSABLE
164.308(a)(4)(ii)(B)	Implement policies and procedures for granting access to EPHI, for example, through access to a workstation, transaction, program, or process.	ADDRESSABLE
164.308(a)(4)(ii)(C)	Implement policies and procedures that are based upon your access authorization policies, established, document, review, and modify a user's right of access to a workstation, transaction, program, or process.	ADDRESSABLE
164.308(a)(5)(i)	Security Awareness and Training: Implement a security awareness and training program for all members of its workforce (including management).	
164.308(a)(5)(ii)(A)	Provide periodic information security reminders.	ADDRESSABLE
164.308(a)(5)(ii)(B)	Develop policies and procedures for guarding against, detecting, and reporting malicious software.	ADDRESSABLE
164.308(a)(5)(ii)(C)	Develop procedures for monitoring login attempts and reporting discrepancies.	ADDRESSABLE
164.308(a)(5)(ii)(D)	Develop procedures for creating, changing, and safeguarding passwords.	ADDRESSABLE
164.308(a)(6)(i)	Security Incident Procedures: Implement policies and procedures to address security incidents.	
164.308(a)(6)(ii)	Develop procedures to identify and respond to suspected or know security incidents; mitigate to the extent practicable, harmful effects of known security incidents; and document incidents and their outcomes.	REQUIRED

continued on following page

Table 1. Continued

Security Rule Reference	SAFEGUARD	STATUS
164.308(a)(7)(i)	Contingency Plan: Establish (and implement as needed) policies and procedures for responding to an emergency or other occurrence (for example, fire, vandalism, system failure, and natural disaster) that damages systems that contain EPHI.	
164.308(a)(7)(ii)(A)	Establish and implement procedures to create and maintain retrievable exact copies of EPHI.	REQUIRED
164.308(a)(7)(ii)(B)	Establish (and implement as needed) procedures to restore any loss of EPHI data that is stored electronically.	REQUIRED
164.308(a)(7)(ii)(C)	Establish (and implement as needed) procedures to enable continuation of critical business processes and for protection of EPHI while operating in the emergency mode.	REQUIRED
164.308(a)(7)(ii)(D)	Implement procedures for periodic testing and revision of contingency plans.	ADDRESSABLE
164.308(a)(7)(ii)(E)	Assess the relative criticality of specific applications and data in support of other contingency plan components.	ADDRESSABLE
164.308(a)(8)	Establish a plan for periodic technical and nontechnical evaluation, based initially upon the standards implemented under this rule and subsequently, in response to environmental or operational changes affecting the security of EPHI that establishes the extent to which an entity's security policies and procedures meet the requirements of this subpart.	REQUIRED
164.308(b)(1)	Business Associate Contracts and Other Arrangements: A covered entity, in accordance with Sec. 164.306, may permit a business associate to create, receive, maintain, or transmit EPHI on the covered entity's behalf only of the covered entity obtains satisfactory assurances, in accordance with Sec. 164.314(a) that the business associate appropriately safeguard the information.	
164.308(b)(4)	Establish written contracts or other arrangements with your trading partners that documents satisfactory assurances required by paragraph (b)(1) of this section that meets the applicable requirements of Sec. 164.314(a).	REQUIRED
Physical Safeguards		
164.310(a)(1)	Facility Access Controls: Implement policies and procedures to limit physical access to its electronic information systems and the facility or facilities in which they are housed, while ensuring that properly authorized access is allowed.	
164.310(a)(2)(i)	Establish (and implement as needed) procedures that allow facility access in support of restoration of lost data under the disaster recovery plan and emergency mode operations plan in the event of an emergency.	ADDRESSABLE
164.310(a)(2)(ii)	Implement policies and procedures to safeguard the facility and the equipment therein from unauthorized physical access, tampering, and theft.	ADDRESSABLE
164.310(a)(2)(iii)	Implement procedures to control and validate a person's access to facilities based on their role or function, including visitor control, and control of access to software programs for testing and revision.	ADDRESSABLE
164.310(a)(2)(iv)	Implement policies and procedures to document repairs and modifications to the physical components of a facility, which are related to security (for example, hardware, walls, doors, and locks).	ADDRESSABLE
164.310(b)	Implement policies and procedures that specify the proper functions to be performed, the manner in which those functions are to be performed, and the physical attributes of the surroundings of a specific workstation or class of workstation that can access EPHI.	REQUIRED
164.310(c)	Implement physical safeguards for all workstations that access EPHI to restrict access to authorized users.	REQUIRED

continued on following page

Table 1. Continued

Security Rule Reference	SAFEGUARD	STATUS
164.310(d)(1)	Device and Media Controls: Implement policies and procedures that govern the receipt and removal of hardware and electronic media that contain EPHI into and out of a facility, and the movement of these items within the facility.	
164.310(d)(2)(i)	Implement policies and procedures to address final disposition of EPHI, and/or hardware or electronic media on which it is stored.	REQUIRED
164.310(d)(2)(ii)	Implement procedures for removal of EPHI from electronic media before the media are available for reuse.	REQUIRED
164.310(d)(2)(iii)	Maintain a record of the movements of hardware and electronic media and the person responsible for its movement.	ADDRESSABLE
164.310(d)(2)(iv)	Create a retrievable, exact copy of EPHI, when needed, before movement of equipment.	ADDRESSABLE
Technical Safeguard		
164.312(a)(1)	Access Controls: Implement technical policies and procedures for electronic information systems that maintain EPHI to allow access only to those persons or software programs that have been granted access rights as specified in Sec. 164.308(a)(4).	
164.312(a)(2)(i)	Assign a unique name and/or number for identifying and tracking user identity.	REQUIRED
164.312(a)(2)(ii)	Establish (and implement as needed) procedures for obtaining necessary EPHI during and emergency.	REQUIRED
164.312(a)(2)(iii)	Implement procedures that terminate an electronic session after a predetermined time of inactivity.	ADDRESSABLE
164.312(a)(2)(iv)	Implement a mechanism to encrypt and decrypt EPHI.	ADDRESSABLE
164.312(b)	Implement Audit Controls, hardware, software, and/or procedural mechanisms that record and examine activity in information systems that contain or use EPHI.	REQUIRED
164.312(c)(1)	Integrity: Implement policies and procedures to protect EPHI from improper alteration or destruction.	
164.312(c)(2)	Implement electronic mechanisms to corroborate that EPHI has not been altered or destroyed in an unauthorized manner.	ADDRESSABLE
164.312(d)	Implement Person or Entity Authentication procedures to verify that a person or entity seeking access EPHI is the one claimed.	REQUIRED
164.312(e)(1)	Transmission Security: Implement technical security measures to guard against unauthorized access to EPHI that is being transmitted over an electronic communications network.	
164.312(e)(2)(i)	Implement security measures to ensure that electronically transmitted EPHI is not improperly modified without detection until disposed of.	ADDRESSABLE
164.312(e)(2)(ii)	Implement a mechanism to encrypt EPHI whenever deemed appropriate.	ADDRESSABLE

In a prior study, the authors discussed more than 400 vulnerabilities they discovered using automated security testing tools in OpenEMR ("What is an electronic health record (EHR)?," n.d.). In their current work, they tried to observe the consequences of the vulnerabilities rather than finding all vulnerabilities of a particular type. The authors exploited a range of common vulnerabilities in code-level and design-level in EHR applications. Code-level refers to implementation bugs and design-level refers to design flaws. Some of the consequences of these exploits were denial of service, users' login information exposure, and editing health records by any users.

A team of instructed attackers was created to target the two EHR applications: OpenEMR and ProprietaryMed. The attackers' focus was on misuse cases of the CCHIT criteria not the overall security of the applications. Misuse cases are defined as actions that are not allowed in the system and can help developers to think like an attacker. The test attack environment included OpenEMR and ProprietaryMed applications, hacking scripts with additional server, and the researchers' computer with WebScarab and Firebug. WebScarab - which is a Java-based application- was used as a proxy to execute testing attacks and record any traffic between the computers and the test servers. Firebug was used as JavaScript debugger to monitor the attacks. Firebug is a web development plug-in integrates with Firefox and enable users to edit HTML, JavaScript, and Cascading Style Sheets. Firebug is also able to executes any script live. Therefore, the researchers did not need an additional webpage for storing attacks.

In implementation bug situations, the following problems occurred while none of them had previously been exposed by CCHIT test script: SQL injection, cross-site scripting, session hijacking, phishing, PDF exploits, denial of service (file uploads), and authorization failure. Table 2 shows the misuse case(s) of vulnerabilities that has not been addressed by CCHIT.

Results show that CCHIT certification process has two failures: First, when an application meets the security requirements, CCHIT test scripts do not test the application for implementation bugs. Second, some security items about patient's health records are not considered at all. It has been suggested that misuse cases are added to the manual test script to simulate the attacks. Moreover, the test scripts can be more comprehensive by launching various attacks on the host application. The manual test scripts should also include the most current list of threats.

Austin and Williams (2011) discussed insufficient vulnerability discovery techniques from EHR applications. Four discovery techniques were applied to EHR applications to understand when to use each type of discovery techniques. The evaluated EHR applications were OpenEMR and Tolven eCHR.

Table 2. List of vulnerabilities missing in CCHIT criteria

Implementation Bugs	
Vulnerability	**Misuse Case(s)**
SQL injection	Attacker obtains every user's username and password.
Cross-Site Scripting	Attacker causes a denial of service by rendering the home page to be blank for all future users. Attacker injects scripts that execute additional malicious code.
Session Hijacking	Attacker spoofs another user's identity. Attacker obtains unauthorized access to the system.
Phishing	Attacker obtains the victim's username and password.
PDF Exploits	Attacker executes applications on the client's computer. Attacker executes embedded applications.
Denial of Service: File Uploads	Attacker renders the web server slow or unresponsive.
Authorization Failure	Attacker creates a new user account with any access privileges the attacker desires.
Design Flaws	
Repudiation	Attacker modifies data in an untraceable fashion thus making fraud an unperceivable event to the EHR.
Lack of Authorization Control	Attacker views patient's confidential health records and personal identification information.

The techniques were systematic and exploratory manual penetration, automated penetration, and static analysis. Penetration testing looks at the security of an application from a user perspective and examines the functionality of an application. In manual penetration testing, no automated tools are used. Exploratory manual penetration is testing an application based on tester's prior experience and it has no test plan. Systematic penetration testing is a test based on a predefined test plan. Automated penetration testing uses automated tools to speed up the process of scanning. Static analysis testing examines the code without executing the program. It can be examination of the source code, the machine code, or the object code. The authors first collected the vulnerabilities detected by each technique, then classified vulnerabilities based on being true or false positive (False positive: mistakenly label code as contain fault. True positive: when faults are correctly identified). The techniques that generated false positives were static analysis and automated penetration testing. The developers need to manually examine each potential false report to recognize if they are false positives. Table 3 shows the true and false positive vulnerabilities identified by these two techniques.

Some of the detected vulnerabilities were SQL injection, cross-site scripting, system information leak, hidden fields, path manipulation, dangerous function, no HTTP Only attribute, dangerous file inclusion, file upload abuse, and header manipulation. The authors classified vulnerabilities as either implementation bugs or design flaws. They empirically proved that no single technique is sufficient for discovering every type of vulnerability and also there is almost no vulnerabilities that can be detected by several techniques. Results showed that systematic manual penetration is more efficient than exploratory manual penetration in terms of detecting vulnerabilities. Systematic manual penetration was effective at finding design flaws. Static analysis detected the largest number of vulnerabilities. Automated penetration was the fastest technique, while static analysis, systematic penetration, and manual penetration were ranked in the next order respectively.

It is suggested that in case of time constraint, automated penetration is used to detect implementation bugs, and systematic manual penetration for discovering design flaws. The study has the following limitations: The selected tools for representing static analysis and automated penetration is not a representative of other tools. The authors used just one tool for measuring each detection technique, while other tools might detect other types of vulnerabilities. The examined EHR applications are not representative of all other software. The classification of errors (true positive and false positive) were time consuming and error prone. Human errors can cause vulnerabilities to be neglected.

Table 3. True and false positive vulnerabilities detected by static analysis and automated penetration testing

Static Analysis			
EHR Application	True Positive	False Positive	False Positive Rate
Tovlen eCHR	50	2265	98%
OpenEMR	1321	3715	74%
Automated Penetration			
Tovlen eCHR	22	15	40%
OpenEMR	710	25	3%

ACCESS CONTROL IN EHR

In EHR applications, access control is one of the necessary security requirements in terms of protecting patient information from being compromised (Helms & Williams, 2011). Below is some of the studies that has been done in this area.

Helms and Williams (2011) claimed that there has been little effort to evaluate access control vulnerabilities in EHR applications. Four EHR applications were evaluated based on 25 criteria related to access control. The evaluated EHRs were OpenEMR, OpenMRS, iTrust, and Tolven. The criteria were retrieved from HIPAA, Certification Commission for Health Information Technology (CCHIT) Criteria, National Institute for Standards and Technology (NIST) Meaningful Use, and NIST Flat role-based access control (RBAC). CCHIT criteria was met by iTrust but other applications were configuration dependent. OpenEMR and openMRS are able to create super user roles which make them be target of insider attack. Among all evaluated applications, none of them addressed access control during the emergency time. Moreover, the EHR applications failed to allow creating roles with separation of duty. Separation of duty prevents a task to be done by just a single user. In addition, none of the certification criteria covered the implementation standards.

Oladimeji, Chung, Jung, and Kim (2011) discussed that traditional access controls are not insufficient in ubiquitous applications. They proposed a goal-oriented and policy-driven framework to mitigate the security and privacy risks of ubiquitous applications in healthcare domain. The framework captures application's security and privacy requirements and decreases the threats against those requirements. In the proposed framework, these items are modeled: (1) security and privacy objectives, (2) threats against those objectives, (3) mitigation strategies in the form of safeguards or countermeasures. The paper uses emergency response scenario to show the efficiency of the framework.

It is mentioned that issues such as untimely arrival of ambulance is a real problem that could happened as a result of verbal misinformation, GPS misleading, or imprecise policies guiding. Introducing some automated mediation may lead to significant improvement. The eHealth security and privacy issues are described in 4 categories: confidentiality, privacy, integrity, and availability. The authors mentioned that there are no universal solutions to these issues that fit all ubicomp applications. Therefore, each ubicomp application needs context-sensitive evaluation of what threats need to be addressed.

The authors proposed the framework based on this idea that ubicomp security and privacy are context-sensitive problems, and need to be addressed not only in infrastructure level but application level. In the proposed framework, each step leads to creation of a visual model that is used as a security and privacy requirement. These models can be used as semantically rich means of communication among requirements analysts, architects, developers and other stakeholders. The framework consisted of context definition, sensitivity characterization, risk and tradeoff analysis, and purpose-driven policy analysis.

- **Context Definition:** To establish a context for an application, there should be a specific *definition* of what security and privacy really mean in the application. To create the context, the authors used a semantics non-functional requirement (NFR) framework. In the framework, NFRs are modeled as *softgoals* to be *satisfied* or *denied*.
- **Sensitivity Characterization:** Protecting health data as Electronic Health Record (EHR) is a high-level protection and it's too restrictive. Therefore, for sensitive context evaluation, the authors classified data into hierarchical structure and assigned a security and privacy requirement to each level. Thus, instead of defining data as EHR, data was classified as health information (HI),

protected health information (PHI), highly sensitive health information (HSHI), sensitive personal information (SPI), and personally identifiable information (PII).

The work of (Tuikka et al., 2016)is based on systematic literature review of previous studies about patients' involvement in EHR applications. Based on this paper, patients' opinion has not been properly considered in EHR development. It is suggested that ethical values be considered in designing EHRs, and patients' access to all their records and even able to add some information to them. The paper concluded that the best representatives for the patients' needs are the patients themselves not the organizations or advocates.

In 2016, (Tuikka et al., 2016) discussed the delegation of access in EHR applications and proposed an Information Accountability Framework (IAF) to balance the requirements of both healthcare professionals and patients in EHR applications. In the framework, patients have explicit control over who access and use their information and set usage policies. The IAF framework ensures that the right information is available to the right person at the right time. To operationalize the framework, it needs to provide for a diverse range of users and use cases. For example, the requirements for delegation of access to another user on your behalf.

PRIVACY AND MONITORING OF HER ACTIVITIES

Privacy protections apply to patient's "individually identifiable health information" ("Protecting Your Privacy & Security, Your Health Information Privacy," n.d.). As medical records are digitized, patient privacy becomes a more challenging issue (Kam, 2012). A number of studies have discussed the patient privacy and the required monitoring over patient records.

In order to improve accountability of EHR applications, (Mashima & Ahamad, 2012) presented a patient centric monitoring system that monitors all the updates and usage of health information stored in EHR/PHR repository. The proposed system uses cryptographic primitives, and allows patients to have control over their health record accessibility. However, in this system the monitoring agent is assumed trusted.

King & Williams (2014) discussed that in EHR applications, viewing protected data is often not monitored. Therefore, unauthorized views of PHIs remain undetected. They proposed a set of principles that should be considered during developing logging mechanisms. They monitored the current state of logging mechanisms to capture and prove user's activities in the application. The authors supplemented the expected results of existing functional black- box test cases to include log output. They used an existing black-box test suite provided by the National Institute of Standards and Technology (NIST). They selected 10 certification criteria from the NIST black-box testing including demographics, medication list, medication allergy list, etc. The authors executed the 30 test cases on EHR applications. 67.8% of applicable executed test cases failed. Four of failed cases was related to viewing of critical data, showing that users may view protected information without being captured.

In order to meet HIPAA's privacy requirements, (Reinsmidt, Schwab, & Yang, 2016) proposed an approach that provides a secure connected mobile system in a mobile cloud environment. The connection between mobile systems takes place using authentication and encryption. The protocol execution includes encryption, decryption, and key generation time. After a mobile device opens a socket with the listening server, the server responds with its public part of the DH exchange. The mobile device hashes the results with SHA-256 to calculate the symmetric encryption/decryption key. This key is used in the advanced encryption standard (AES).

Kingsford, Zhang, Ayeh, and MaryMargaret, (2017) proposed a mathematical framework to improve the preservation of patient's privacy in EMR applications during the collection of patient health data for analysis. The authors used an identity based encryption (IBE) protocol. In the proposed framework, patient's identity is delinked from the health data before submitting to health workers for analysis. Health data is encrypted before submitting. The administrator then decrypts the submitted data. Patient's identity is delinked from submitted data in this stage. The administrator checks that only the health data (not the identity of the patient) is sent to health worker for analysis. Therefore, the identity of the patient will not be disclosed and PU's privacy is preserved.

GAP BETWEEN HIPAA REQUIREMENTS AND BREACK NOTIFICATION

Gaps between security policies and real breaches always exist in healthcare. Policies are often stated in an ambiguous manner (Kamsties, 2005; Popescu, Rugaber, Medvidovic, & Berry, 2008). Therefore, in reality not all the breaches are addressed by policies. Below is a study about measuring the breach coverage percentage by HIPAA security policies.

Kafali, Jones, Petruso, Williams, and Singh, (2017) proposed a semantic reasoning framework to identify gaps between HIPAA policy and security breaches. They revealed that only 65% of security breaches are covered by HIPAA policy rules. Moreover, HIPAA security policy is more successful in covering malicious misuse than accidental misuse.

Table 4 shows mapping of some detected vulnerabilities in EHRs to HIPAA rules that have been violated.

CONCLUSION

Electronic Health Record is a digital version of paper-based patient's health information. EHR applications are increasingly being implemented in many countries. They have resulted in better healthcare, lower costs, easier follow ups, and more precise medical decisions. EHR applications are guided by

Table 4. Mapping of detected vulnerabilities in EHRs to HIPAA rules.

Name	HIPAA Security Rule Reference
SQL Injection	164.312(a)(1), 164.312(a)(2)(i)
Cross-site scripting	164.312(c)(1), 164.312(c)(2)
Session Hijacking	164.312(a)(1), 164.312(a)(2)(i)
Phishing	164.312(a)(1), 164.312(a)(2)(i)
PDF Exploits	164.312(e)(1)
Denial of Service: File Uploads	164.312(e)(1)
Authorization Failure	164.312(a)(1), 164.312(a)(2)(i), 164.312(b)

measures of HIPAA to ensure confidentiality, integrity, and security. However, concerns of security breach always exist in digital formats. In many reported breaches, improper use of EHRs has resulted in disclosure of patient's protected health information. Therefore, more awareness in existing EHRs capability of protecting patient's healthcare data is needed.

In this chapter, we have provided an overview of HIPAA and HITECH acts which is driving today's EHR applications adoption by healthcare facilities, clinics, hospitals, and insurance affiliates. We elaborate some recent research efforts that strive to examine the compliance of current EHR applications with HIPAA through various perspectives. These include security vulnerability in EHR, access control, privacy and monitoring, and the gaps between HIPAA requirements and breach notification. We also provide a mapping of some vulnerabilities in implementation and design that may affect the technical HIPAA security and privacy requirements. The findings will provide guidance to practitioners on the limitations of existing HER applications and developers for patching vulnerabilities to comply with HIPAA security and privacy requirements.

REFERENCES

Arndt, R. Z. (2017). *Emory Healthcare cyberattack affects 80,000 patient records*. Retrieved from http://www.modernhealthcare.com/article/20170302/NEWS/170309983/emory-healthcare-cyberattack-affects-80000-patient-records

Austin, A., & Williams, L. (2011). One Technique is Not Enough: A Comparison of Vulnerability Discovery Techniques. *2011 International Symposium on Empirical Software Engineering and Measurement*, 97–106. 10.1109/ESEM.2011.18

Bowers, D. (2001). The Health Insurance Portability and Accountability Act: Is it really all that bad? *Proceedings - Baylor University. Medical Center, 14*(4), 347–348. Retrieved from http://www.pubmedcentral.nih.gov/articlerender.fcgi?artid=1305898&tool=pmcentrez&rendertype=abstract PMID:16369644

Center For Disease Control and Prevention. (2007). Retrieved from https://www.cdc.gov/ehrmeaningfuluse/introduction.html

Examples of PHI Identifiers Health information. (n.d.). Retrieved from http://www.irb.emory.edu/documents/phi_identifiers.pdf

HealthIT.gov. (2013). *Guide to Privacy and Security of Health Information*. Author.

Helms, E., & Williams, L. (2011). Evaluating access control of open source electronic health record systems. *Proceeding of the 3rd Workshop on Software Engineering in Health Care - SEHC '11*, 63. 10.1145/1987993.1988006

HIPAA Background. (2010). Retrieved from http://hipaa.bsd.uchicago.edu/background.html

HITECH Act Summary. (2009). Retrieved from http://www.hipaasurvivalguide.com/hitech-act-summary.php%09

Kafali, O., Jones, J., Petruso, M., Williams, L., & Singh, M. P. (2017). How Good Is a Security Policy against Real Breaches? A HIPAA Case Study. *Proceedings - 2017 IEEE/ACM 39th International Conference on Software Engineering, ICSE 2017*, 530–540. 10.1109/ICSE.2017.55

Kam, R. (2012). *Top 3 issues facing patient privacy*. Retrieved from http://www.healthcareitnews.com/news/top-3-issues-facing-patient-privacy

Kamsties, E. (2005). Understanding ambiguity in requirements engineering. *Engineering and Managing Software Requirements*, 245–266. 10.1007/3-540-28244-0_11

King, J., & Williams, L. (2014). Log Your CRUD: Design Principles for Software Logging Mechanisms. *Proceedings of the 2014 Symposium and Bootcamp on the Science of Security*, 5:1--5:10. 10.1145/2600176.2600183

Kingsford, K. M., Zhang, F., Ayeh, M. D. N., & MaryMargaret, A. (2017). A Mathematical Model for a Hybrid System Framework for Privacy Preservation of Patient Health Records. *2017 IEEE 41st Annual Computer Software and Applications Conference (COMPSAC)*, 119–124. 10.1109/COMPSAC.2017.21

Legal Information Institute. (1992). Retrieved from https://www.law.cornell.edu/cfr/text/45/164.308

Mashima, D., & Ahamad, M. (2012). Enhancing accountability of electronic health record usage via patient-centric monitoring. *Proceedings of the 2nd ACM SIGHIT International Health Informatics Symposium*, 409–418. 10.1145/2110363.2110410

Oladimeji, E. a., Chung, L., Jung, H. T., & Kim, J. (2011). Managing security and privacy in ubiquitous eHealth information interchange. *Proceedings of the 5th International Confernece on Ubiquitous Information Management and Communication - ICUIMC '11*, 1. 10.1145/1968613.1968645

Oliynyk, M. (2016). *Why is healthcare data security so important?* Retrieved from https://www.protectimus.com/blog/why-is-healthcare-data-security-so-important/

Popescu, D., Rugaber, S., Medvidovic, N., & Berry, D. M. (2008). Reducing ambiguities in requirements specifications via automatically created object-oriented models. Lecture Notes in Computer Science), 5320, 103–124. doi:10.1007/978-3-540-89778-1_10

Protecting Your Privacy & Security, Your Health Information Privacy. (n.d.). Retrieved from https://www.healthit.gov/patients-families/your-health-information-privacy

Reinsmidt, E., Schwab, D., & Yang, L. (2016). Securing a Connected Mobile System for Healthcare. *Proceedings of IEEE International Symposium on High Assurance Systems Engineering*, 19–22. 10.1109/HASE.2016.53

Smith, B., Austin, A., Brown, M., King, J. T., Lankford, J., Meneely, A., & Williams, L. (2010). Challenges for protecting the privacy of health information. *Proceedings of the Second Annual Workshop on Security and Privacy in Medical and Home-Care Systems - SPIMACS '10*, 1. 10.1145/1866914.1866916

ThreatConnect. (n.d.). *Security Operations and Analytics Platform. Author*.

Tuikka, A.-M., Rantanen, M. M., Heimo, O. I., Koskinen, J., Sachdeva, N., & Kimppa, K. K. (2016). Where is patient in EHR project? *ACM SIGCAS Computers and Society*, 45(3), 73–78. doi:10.1145/2874239.2874250

Verizon. (2016). 2016 Data Breach Investigations Report. *Verizon Business Journal*, (1), 1–65. 10.1017/ CBO9781107415324.004

What are the differences between electronic medical records, electronic health records, and personal health records? (2015). Retrieved from https://www.healthit.gov/providers-professionals/faqs/what-are-differences-between-electronic-medical-records-electronic

What is 2FA? An extra layer of security that is known as multi factor authentication. (n.d.). Retrieved from https://www.securenvoy.com/two-factor-authentication/what-is-2fa.shtm

What is an electronic health record (EHR)? (n.d.). Retrieved from https://www.healthit.gov/providers-professionals/faqs/what-electronic-health-record-ehr

What is Protected Health Information. (n.d.). Retrieved from https://www.truevault.com/protected-health-information.html

ENDNOTE

[1]   http://nvlpubs.nist.gov/nistpubs/Legacy/SP/nistspecialpublication800-30r1.pdf

Chapter 8
Standards and Guides for Implementing Security and Privacy for Health Information Technology

Francis E. Akowuah
Syracuse University, USA

Jonathan Land
The University of Tennessee at Chattanooga, USA

Xiaohong Yuan
North Carolina A&T State University, USA

Li Yang
The University of Tennessee at Chattanooga, USA

Jinsheng Xu
North Carolina A&T State University, USA

Hong Wang
North Carolina A&T State University, USA

ABSTRACT

In this chapter, the authors survey security standards and guides applicable to healthcare industry including control objective for information and related technologies (COBIT), ISO/IEC 27001:2005 (which has been revised by ISO/IEC 27001:2013), ISO/IEC 27002:2005 (which has been revised by ISO/IEC 27002:2013), ISO 27799:2008 (which has been revised by ISO 27799:2016), ISO 17090:2008 (which has been revised by ISO 17090:2015), ISO/TS 25237:2008, HITRUST common security framework (CSF), NIST Special Publication 800-53, NIST SP 1800, NIST SP 1800-8, and building code for medical device software security. This survey informs the audience of currently available standards that can guide the implementation of information security programs in healthcare organizations, and provides a starting point for IT management in healthcare organizations to select a standard suitable for their organizations.

DOI: 10.4018/978-1-5225-5583-4.ch008

INTRODUCTION

National Institute of Standards and Technology (NIST) defines Health Information System (HIS) as a discrete set of information resources organized expressly for the collection, processing, maintenance, use, sharing, dissemination, or disposition of health information (NIST, 2009). Usually, HIS is made up of one central main hospital information system, which covers basic Enterprise Resource Planning (ERP)-like functionality, such as patient registration, billing, documentation, inventory, and other functions required at the corporate level. Also, ancillary systems such as laboratory, pharmacy and x-ray components may be included or connected. Administrative personnel and clinicians (physicians and nurses) use or access HIS by workstations and mobile devices running several applications to view or collect medical and/or administrative information (Luethi & Knolmayer, 2009).

Health information systems improve the quality of healthcare delivery by increasing the timeliness and accuracy of records and administrative information. The information maintained by these systems is often faced with security threats from a wide range of sources including computer-assisted fraud, espionage, sabotage, vandalism, fire or flood. Security incidents such as computer hacking, malicious code and denial of service attacks have not only become common but also increasingly sophisticated. Organizations, especially healthcare organizations, should devote adequate resources to ensure the protection of their information assets. Many governments demand certain security requirements from healthcare organizations and custodians of personal health information by enacting laws and other regulations (Akowuah, Yuan, Xu, & Wang, 2012). These security requirements levied on healthcare organizations can be achieved by implementing one or more information security standards.

Standards help to ensure an adequate level of security is attained, resources are used efficiently and the best security practices are adopted (HKSAR, 2008). Standard is defined as a document that provides requirements, specifications, guidelines or characteristics that can be used consistently to ensure that materials, products, processes and services are fit for their purpose (ISO, 2013). Information security standards specify security controls that help organizations to attain acceptable level of security. "Security controls are the management, operational, and technical safeguards or countermeasures employed within an organizational information system to protect the confidentiality, integrity, and availability of the system and its information" (NIST, 2009). In this paper, we survey current security standards applicable to the healthcare industry. For each standard, a brief description of the standard, the background and challenges in applying the standard are discussed. This survey informs the audience currently available standards that can guide the implementation of information security programs in healthcare organizations, and provides a starting point for IT management in healthcare organizations to select a standard suitable for their organizations.

We describe the standards that are generic in nature first and move on to standards that are geared toward the healthcare industry. The standards and guides are summarized in Table 1 including COBIT, ISO/IEC 27001:2005, ISO/IEC 27002:2005, ISO 27799:2008, ISO 17090:2008, ISO/TS 25237:2008, HITRUST Common Security Framework (CSF), NIST Special Publication 800-53, NIST SP 1800, NIST SP 1800-8, and Building Code for Medical Device Software Security. The applicability of these standards, and issues related to the implementation of a security standard are also discussed.

Table 1. Security and Privacy Standards and Guides in Health Information Technology

Standards/Guides	Organization	Websites
Control OBjective for Information and related Technologies (COBIT)	Information System Audit and Control Association (ISACA)	https://www.isaca.org/
ISO/IEC 27001:2005 (has been revised by ISO/IEC 27001:2013) Information technology -- Security techniques -- Information security management systems -- Requirements	International Organization for Standardization	www.iso.org
ISO/IEC 27002:2005 (has been revised by ISO/IEC 27002:2013) Information technology -- Security techniques -- Code of practice for information security management	International Organization for Standardization	www.iso.org
ISO 27799:2008 (has been revised by ISO 27799:2016) Health informatics -- Information security management in health using ISO/IEC 27002	International Organization for Standardization	www.iso.org
ISO 17090:2008 (has been revised by ISO 17090:2015) Health informatics – Public Key Infrastructure	International Organization for Standardization	www.iso.org
ISO/TS 25237:2008 Preview Health informatics -- Pseudonymization	International Organization for Standardization	www.iso.org
HITRUST Common Security Framework (CSF)	the HITRUST Alliance	https://hitrustalliance.net
NIST Special Publication 800-53 Security and Privacy Controls for Information Systems and Organizations	US National Institute of Standards and Technology	www.nist.gov
NIST SP 1800 Securing Electronic Health Records on Mobile Devices	US National Institute of Standards and Technology	www.nist.gov
NIST SP 1800-8 Securing Wireless Infusion Pumps In Healthcare Delivery Organizations	US National Institute of Standards and Technology	www.nist.gov
Building Code for Medical Device Software Security	The Institute of Electrical and Electronics Engineers (IEEE)	www.ieee.org

CONTROL OBJECTIVE FOR INFORMATION AND RELATED TECHNOLOGIES (COBIT)

Background of COBIT

Information System Audit and Control Association (ISACA) is an international organization formed in 1969 by individuals who realized the "need for a centralized source of information and guidance in the growing field of auditing controls for computer systems." It currently boasts of more than 100,000 members in over 180 countries and members hold diverse professional IT-related positions. (ISACA, 2012)

When members in the financial audit community faced challenges with automated systems, ISACA designed Control and OBbjective for Information and related Technologies (COBIT) to guide their work in the IT environment. Although it was initially designed as a framework to carry out IT audit assignments, COBIT later became a framework for control and management tasks by the year 2000 (van Grembergen & de Haes, 2009). COBIT is the end-product of strong cooperation among business and

IT experts coupled with years of research. It "provides an authoritative, international set of generally accepted IT practices for business managers and auditors" (Pathak, 2005). Due to its worldwide use, COBIT has been translated into a number of languages such as French, German, Japanese, Korean, Spanish, Italian, Hungarian, Russian, Portuguese etc.

The management and governance of enterprise information is a complex undertaking. While there is the need to protect the confidentiality and integrity of the information, at the same time, the information must be made available to authorized users. COBIT eases this complexity by providing relevant guidance on developing and managing information systems.

Over the years, ISACA has released versions of COBIT with COBIT 5 being the latest at the time of writing. The first version COBIT 1, released in 1996, was mainly an audit framework. COBIT 2, released in 1998 added control objectives. In 2000, management guidelines were added to release COBIT 3. With the release of COBIT 4, the framework became an IT governance framework. It was expanded in 2007 and released as COBIT 4.1. April 2012 saw the release of COBIT 5. It offers a comprehensive IT governance and management framework "so that IT can deliver more value to the business" (Parker, 2012). ISACA released *COBIT 5 for Information Security* in June 2012 at the INSIGHT 2012 Conference.

Structure of COBIT

This section briefly discusses COBIT 5 in general and narrows down to *COBIT for Information Security*.

COBIT 5 builds on previous versions of COBIT, VAL IT and RISK IT. VAL IT is a governance framework that can be used to create business value from IT investments. RISK IT provides an end-to-end, comprehensive view of all risks related to the use of IT and a similarly thorough treatment of risk management, from the tone and culture at the top, to operational issues. VAL IT and RISK IT are both products of ISACA. (ISACA, 2012)

COBIT 5 helps enterprises to create value. Value creation is "realizing benefits at an optimal resource cost while optimizing risk" (ISACA, 2012). COBIT 5 consists of five principles and seven enablers that are useful for organizations of all sizes and types. ISACA defines enablers as anything that can help to achieve the objectives of the enterprise. The five principles of COBIT 5 include:

- **Meeting Stakeholder Needs:** Enterprises strive to create value for their stakeholders by optimizing risk and use of resources while achieving benefits. COBIT 5 enumerates processes and enablers that help enterprises to create value through the use of information technology.
- **Covering the Enterprise End-to-End:** COBIT 5 not only focuses on the IT function but also covers all functions and processes in an enterprise. Information and related technologies are handled as an asset that needs to be dealt with just like any other asset by everyone in the enterprise. IT-related governance and management enablers are also considered to be enterprise-wide thus including everyone and everything.
- **Applying a Single Integrated Framework:** A number of standards and best practices exist to offer guidance on subset of IT activities. COBIT aligns with relevant standards and frameworks at a high level to provide an overarching governance and management framework for enterprise IT.
- **Enabling a Holistic Approach:** To achieve an effective and efficient IT governance and management, a holistic approach is required by taking into consideration a number of interacting components. COBIT 5 helps to implement a comprehensive governance and management system for enterprise IT.

- **Separating Governance From Management:** Governance and management are two distinct disciplines that have different types of activities, organizational structure requirements and purposes. COBIT 5 thus makes explicit distinction between governance and management. According to COBIT, governance ensures that stakeholder needs, conditions and options are evaluated to determine balanced, agreed-on enterprise objectives to be achieved; setting direction through prioritization and decision making; and monitoring performance and compliance against agreed-on direction and objectives. Usually governance is the responsibility of the board of directors under the leadership of the chairperson. Management plans, builds, runs and monitors activities in alignment with the direction set by the governance body to achieve the enterprise objectives. Executive management bears this responsibility under the leadership of the Chief Executive Officer (CEO).

The seven enablers include:

- Principles, Policies and Frameworks
- Processes
- Organisational Structures
- Culture, Ethics and Behaviour
- Information
- Services, Infrastructure and Applications
- People, Skills and Competencies

In summary, "COBIT 5 brings together the five principles that allow the enterprise to build an effective governance and management framework based on a holistic set of seven enablers that optimises information and technology investment and use for the benefit of stakeholders".

COBIT for Information Security is the second of the published COBIT 5 professional guides (Olzak, 2013). According to Greg Grocholski, international president of ISACA, the guide was produced "in response to the heavy demand for security guidance that integrates other major frameworks and standards". It extends COBIT 5 by explaining each component from information security perspective. Thus, it provides security professionals with the requisite knowledge to develop, implement and maintain information security in the business policies, processes and structures of an enterprise. In other words, the guidelines help to manage security appropriately thereby keeping risks at acceptable levels. COBIT 5 for Information Security guide has three major sections:

- Information Security
- Using COBIT 5 Enablers for Implementing Information Security in Practice
- Adapting COBIT 5 for Information Security to the Enterprise Environment

COBIT's guidelines are generic in nature and quite difficult to apply to a particular organization without substantial expert knowledge (Morimoto, 2009). Although the release of COBIT for Information Security has deepened the understanding of the guidelines for information security, it is still not tailored to any particular type of organization.

ISO/IEC 27001:2005 (Has Been Revised by ISO/IEC 27001:2013)

ISO/IEC 27001:2005 is a certification standard that posits the requirements for "establishing, implementing, operating, monitoring, reviewing, maintaining and improving a documented Information Security Management System (ISMS) within the context of the organization's overall business risks" (ISO, 2013). ISMS is defined as a systematic approach to managing sensitive enterprise information so that it remains secure by the use of processes, IT systems and people.

The international standard is not tailored to any specific industry, thus, a wide range of organizations may seek certification of their Information Security Management System (ISMS). Over 7,300 organizations worldwide have already been certified compliant with ISO/IEC 27001 or equivalent national variants. Even though certification is not compulsory, it is increasingly being demanded by some business partnerships. In terms of marketing, the certificate gives assurance to business partners of the status of the organization with regards to information security without the necessity of conducting their own security reviews (ISECT, 2012). Getting certified under ISO/IEC 27001 is a means of providing assurance that "the organization has not only implemented a system for the management of information security, but also maintains and continuously improves the system". (SRI, 2012)

Suitable uses of the standard include the following (ISO, 2013):

- Use within organizations to formulate security requirements and objectives;
- Use within organizations as a way to ensure that security risks are cost effectively managed;
- Use within organizations to ensure compliance with laws and regulations;
- Use within an organization as a process framework for the implementation and management of controls to ensure that the specific security objectives of an organization are met;
- Definition of new information security management processes;
- Identification and clarification of existing information security management processes;
- Use by the management of organizations to determine the status of information security management activities;
- Use by the internal and external auditors of organizations to determine the degree of compliance with the policies, directives and standards adopted by an organization;
- Use by organizations to provide relevant information about information security policies, directives, standards and procedures to trading partners and other organizations with whom they interact for operational or commercial reasons;
- Implementation of business-enabling information security;
- Use by organizations to provide relevant information about information security to customers.

Background of ISO/IEC 27001:2005

Entitled *Information technology — Security techniques — Information security management systems – Requirements* was born as BS 7799 Part 2 in 1999. BS 7799 was written by the United Kingdom Government's Department of Trade and Industry (DTI). British Standards Institution (BSI) revised BS 7799 in 2002 and was adopted by ISO/IEC in 2005. Like other ISO 2700 series standards, ISO/IEC 27001:2005 is currently undergoing revision. (ISECT, 2012)

Structure of ISO/IEC 27001:2005

The 34-page document is structured into nine sections and has three appendices. Highlight of each section is described below:

- **Introduction:** Asserts the standard uses a process approach.
- **Scope:** It specifies generic ISMS requirements suitable for organizations of any type, size or nature.
- **Normative References:** The standard recommends the essential use of ISO/IEC 27002:2005
- **Terms and Definitions:** A brief, formalized glossary
- **Information Security Management System:** The details of the standard, based on the Plan-Do-Check-Act cycle where Plan = define requirements, assess risks, decide which controls are applicable; Do = implement and operate the ISMS; Check = monitor and review the ISMS; Act = maintain and continuously improve the ISMS. Also specifies certain specific documents that are required and must be controlled, and states that records must be generated and controlled to prove the operation of the ISMS (e.g. certification audit purposes).
- **Management Responsibility:** Management must demonstrate their commitment to the ISMS, principally by allocating adequate resources to implement and operate it.
- **Internal ISMS Audits:** The organization must conduct periodic internal audits to ensure the ISMS incorporates adequate controls which operate effectively.
- **Management Review of the ISMS:** Management must review the suitability, adequacy and effectiveness of the ISMS at least once a year, assessing opportunities for improvement and the need for changes.
- **ISMS Improvements:** The organization must continually improve the ISMS by assessing and where necessary making changes to ensure its suitability and effectiveness, addressing nonconformance (noncompliance) and where possible preventing recurrent issues.
- **Annex A:** Control objectives and controls - little more in fact than a list of titles of the control sections in ISO/IEC 27002, down to the second level of numbering (e.g. 9.1, 9.2), 133 in total.
- **Annex B:** OECD principles and this International Standard - a table briefly showing which parts of this standard satisfy 7 key principles laid out in the OECD Guidelines for the Security of Information Systems and Networks.
- **Annex C:** Correspondence between ISO 9001:2000, ISO 14001:2004 and this International Standard - the standard shares the same basic structure of other management systems standards, meaning that an organization which implements any one should be familiar with concepts such as PDCA, records and audits.

ISO/IEC 27002:2005 (Has Been Revised by ISO/IEC 27002:2013)

ISO/IEC 27002:2005 is another generic standard that can be applied to health information systems to ensure security. It establishes general principles and guidelines for effective initialization, implementation, maintenance and improvement of information security management. The objectives outlined therein provide general guidance on the commonly accepted goals of information security management. Thus any organization seeking to adopt a comprehensive information security management program or improve its existing information security practices can use the standard. The ISO standard asserts that information can be protected using a wide variety of controls. Such controls include hardware and software functions, procedures, policies, processes and organizational structures. Organizations including healthcare organizations, must develop, implement, monitor, evaluate and improve these types of security controls. (PRGL, 2011).

Background of ISO/IEC 27002:2005

ISO/IEC 27002 2005 is entitled *Information technology - Security techniques - Code of practice for information security management*. It is published by the International Organization for Standardization (ISO) and International Electrotechnical Commission (IEC).

ISO/IEC 27002:2005 was developed from BS7799, a British standard that was published in the 1990s. ISO/IEC adopted this standard as ISO/IEC 17799:2000 in December 2000. In June 2005, the standard was revised and officially published as ISO/ IEC 17799:2005. On July 1, 2007, it was renumbered ISO/ IEC 27002:2005 to align with the other ISO/IEC 27000-series standards (PRGL, 2011).

On the other hand, ISO/IEC 27002:2005 has been revised by ISO/IEC 27002:2013 (ISO/IEC, 2013).

Structure of ISO/IEC 27002:2005

The thirty-nine main security categories of the standard are specified under eleven security control clauses. Each main security category contains one control objective stating what is to be achieved. In addition, one or more controls are specified to help achieve the control objective. The standard also has one introductory clause that discusses risk assessment and treatment. The control clauses include:

1. Risk assessment and treatment
2. Security policy
3. Organization of information security
4. Asset management
5. Human resources security
6. Physical and environmental security
7. Communications and operations management
8. Access control
9. Information systems acquisition, development and maintenance
10. Information security incident management
11. Business continuity management
12. Compliance

Although ISO/IEC recommends a complete consideration of the practices, organizations do not have to implement every recommended security practice stated therein. The important thing is to know what works best for the unique information security risks and requirements. (ISECT, 2012)

Like COBIT, ISO/IEC 27002:2005 is generic in nature and thus can be applied in several areas. It has to be fine-tuned to suit an organization's need.

ISO 27799:2008 (Has Been Revised by ISO 27799:2016)

As noted above, ISO/IEC 27002:2005 provide security guidelines to a wide range of organizations. The ISO technical committee TC215 responsible for health informatics published ISO 27799:2008 to tailor the use of ISO/IEC 27002 to the healthcare industry. In other words, it specifies guidelines that help to interpret and implement ISO/IEC 27002 in health informatics perspective. Specifically, it addresses the special information security management needs of the health sector and its unique operating environments. Thus, the standard defines detailed controls for the management of health information security. Healthcare organization as well as other organizations that handle personal health information that implements ISO 27799, stands a good chance of ensuring the minimum security level that is germane to their organization's circumstance.

ISO 27799 applies to all facets of health information which includes (ISO, 2013) (ISECT, 2012):

- The form it takes: words, numbers, video, sound recording, medical images
- The means of storage: printed paper, written paper, electronic storage
- The means of transmission: by hand, fax, post, computer network

Background of ISO 27799:2008

ISO 27799:2008 is entitled *Health informatics -- Information security management in health using ISO/IEC 27002*

It was indicated in ISO/IEC 27002:2005 that "not all the controls described will be relevant to every situation, nor can they take account of local environmental or technological constraints, or be present in a form that suits every potential user in an organization." By 2003, the need was recognized for a practical guide for information security management in healthcare. Work of creating this guideline fell on ISO Technical Committee on health informatics (ISO/TC 215) and began in autumn of 2003 (Fraser, 2006). The 58-page document has been available as of 12th June 2008 (ISO, 2013)

The ISO Technical Committee 215-Health Informatics develops standards related to healthcare information and has published more than 30 standards, specifications and reports. The standards relates to data models, communications for medical devices, terminologies, security health cards among others. The committee also works to support eight other working groups of ISO. Its first meeting was held in 1998 (Fraser, 2006).

Structure of ISO 27799:2008

The content sections are (ISO27000, 2007) (RedCard Security, 2008):

- Scope
- Normative References
- Terms and definitions
- Abbreviated terms
- Health information security (Goals; Security within information governance; Health information to be protected; Threats and vulnerabilities)

- Practical action plan for implementing ISO/IEC 27002 (Taxonomy; Management commitment; Establishing, operating, maintaining and improving an ISMS; Planning; Doing; Checking, Auditing)
- Healthcare implications of ISO/IEC 27002 (Information security policy; Organization; Asset management; HR; Physical; Communications; Access; Acquisition; Incident Management; BCM; Compliance)
- **Annex A:** Threats to health information security
- **Annex B:** Tasks and related documents of the Information Security Management System
- **Annex C:** Potential benefits and required attributes of support tools
- **Annex D:** Related standards

ISO 17090:2008 ISO 17090:2008 (Has Been Revised by ISO 17090:2015)

ISO17090 is another healthcare-specific standard for the secure exchange of healthcare information on the internet. Digital certificate technology is one solution to providing appropriate protection for data conveyed across the internet in a cost-effective way. The technology uses public key cryptography to protect information in transit and digital certificates to confirm the identity of the person or the device that sent the information.

ISO 17090 titled *Health Informatics: Public Key Infrastructure* is a three-part standard that defines how digital certificates can be used to provide security services in the healthcare industry. Certain requirements need to be addressed in order to successfully implement digital certificates in the protection data exchange within an organization, between organizations and across jurisdictional boundaries. These requirements are described by ISO 17090 and they include technical, operational and policy requirements.

The first part, ISO 17090-1:2008 describes the basic concepts underlying the use of digital certificates in healthcare. Also, it provides interoperability scheme in establishing a digital certificate-enabled secure communication of health information. The informative general overview provided shall be beneficial to senior administrators. The second part, ISO 17090-2:2008, on the other hand shall be helpful to technical implementation teams as it contains detailed technical information. The certificate profiles required to exchange healthcare information are stipulated in this part. Uses of digital certificates in the health industry are well elaborated as well. ISO 17090-3:2008, the third part, provides guidelines for certificate management issues involved in deploying digital certificates in healthcare. *Business analysts and administrative implementation teams will find a detailed policy framework and administrative requirements to support implementation in Part 3* (ISO, 2013).

Background of ISO 17090:2008

Released in February 2008, ISO 17090 was developed by ISO's Technical Committee (TC) 217. TC 217 is tasked with the standardization of health information and communication, thereby, allowing for compatibility and interoperability between independent systems. It has several working groups that work on different aspects of Electronic Health Record (EHR) such as messaging and communication, privacy and security, data structure, devices among other. This standard is a product of the working group WG4. ISO 17090:2008 replaces ISO/TS 17090:2002

Part 4 of the document is currently under development. It is titled *Public key infrastructure --Digital Signatures for healthcare documents.* (ISO, 2013)

Structure of ISO 17090:2008

ISO 17090-1:2008 is a 36-page document consisting of nine main sections. The first four sections are introductory as it defines the scope, normative references, terms and definitions, and abbreviations used in the document. The other section provides overview of digital certificates in healthcare context as well as the requirement for security in healthcare applications. Sections 7 and 8 discuss public key cryptography and deployment of digital certificates respectively. Last section describes interoperability requirements. ISO 17090-1:2008 has been revised by ISO 17090-1:2013. (ISO, 2013)

Moreover, with 27 pages, ISO 17090-2:2008 is made up of seven sections. Sections one through four provide introduction as in Part 1. Healthcare CPs and general certificate requirements are the main highlights of sections five and six. Last section gives the use of certificate extensions. (ISO, 2013)

Furthermore, ISO 17090-3:2008 is also a 36-page document with eight sections. Like Part 1, the first four sections are introductory. Requirements for digital certificate policy management in a healthcare context are provided in the fifth section. Section 6 describes the structure of healthcare CPs and healthcare CPSs. The following section stipulates the minimum requirements for a healthcare CP. Lastly, the model PKI disclosure statement is provided. (ISO, 2013)

ISO/TS 25237:2008

One standard that deals with the privacy of health information is ISO/TS 25237:2008. It has the title Health informatics – Pseudonymization. It details principles and requirements for privacy protection by the use of pseudonymization services for the protection of personal health information in databases (ISO, 2013). Pseudonymization is a method "where identification data is transformed and then replaced by a specifier that cannot be associated with the identification data without knowing a certain secret" (Neubauer & Heurix, 2011). It brings about the removal of an association with a data subject. By this method, data is linked with patient only under specified and controlled circumstances.

The standard defines the basic concept of pseudonymization as well as gives an overview of the various use cases of both reversible and irreversible pseudonymization. Specified in the standard are the policy framework and minimal requirements for trustworthy practice and controlled re-identification. The basic methodologies for pseudonymization are defined in addition to guidelines to risk assessment for re-identification. (ISO, 2013)

Moreover, ISO/TS 25237:2008 can be used by implementers of pseudonymization as a general guide whiles also serving quality assurance purposes. In an indirect way, the standard helps users to determine their trust in the services provided. (ISO, 2013)

Background of ISO/TS 25237:2008

Like previous standard discussed, ISO/TS 25237:2008 is a product ISO/TC Technical Committee 215. It was released in March 2009 (ISO, 2013)

Structure of ISO/TS 25237:2008

The 57-page standard document consists of nine main sections. As peculiar to ISO standard documents, the first four sections are for introductory purposes thus, it describes the scope, normative references, terms and definitions, and symbols. The fifth section discusses the requirements for the privacy protection of identities in healthcare. Methods and implementation of the pseudonymization process are described in the sixth section. Like previous section, section7 describes the methods and implementation of re-identification process. Specification of interoperability of interfaces, and the policy framework for operation of pseudonymization services are stipulated in sections 8 and 9 respectively.

HITRUST COMMON SECURITY FRAMEWORK (CSF)

Like ISO 27799:2008 standard, HITRUST Common Security Framework is not generic in nature but tailored to the healthcare industry. It is a certifiable framework that is useful to organizations of all sizes that create, access, store or exchange personal health and financial information. Healthcare organizations are required to comply with a number of regulations and standards such as HIPAA, HITECH, COBIT, NIST among others. CSF strives to harmonize, leverage and cross-reference these existing standards and regulations helping to avoid the introduction of redundancy and ambiguity into the industry. The framework thus helps organizations to easily understand their compliance status across a wide range of authoritative sources and standards (HITRUST, 2012).

Background of CSF

Common Security Framework is a product of Health Information Trust Alliance (HITRUST) in collaboration with healthcare, business, technology and information security leaders. Released in March 2009, CSF became the first IT security framework developed specifically for healthcare information.

Structure of CSF

The two components that comprise CSF are described below:

Information Security Control Specifications Manual

It is best-practice-based specification that provides prescriptive implementation guidance. It entails recommended security governance practices and security control practices to ensure the effective and efficient management of information security. The manual specifies thirteen security control categories, 42 control objectives and 135 control specifications. Control categories are:

1. Information Security Management Program
2. Access Control
3. Human Resources Security
4. Risk Management
5. Security Policy

6.   Organization of Information Security
7.   Compliance
8.   Asset Management
9.   Physical and Environmental Security
10. Communications and Operations Management
11. Information Systems Acquisition, Development and Maintenance
12. Information Security Incident Management
13. Business Continuity Management

Under circumstances that CSF requirements are difficult or impractical to implement, CSF supports "a concept of approved Alternate Controls as a risk mitigation or compensation strategy for a system control failure".

Standards and Regulations Mapping

This component provides reconciliation of the framework to common and different aspects of generally adopted standards and regulations. As indicated above, CSF cross-references and leverages regulations and standards that pertain to healthcare. Each control specification is mapped to implementation requirement thereby helping one to understand how HITRUST CSF aligns with other standards. This simplifies compliance efforts of the organization. Certainly, there are gaps that are not addressed by other requirements. The mapping process identifies these gaps which are then covered by CSF (HITRUST, 2012)

CSF can only be accessed by subscribing to HITRUST Central, the managed online community for healthcare information security professionals. Standard subscriptions at no charge are available to individuals from qualifying organizations as defined by HITRUST. The online, interactive version of the CSF, authoritative sources and the CSF Assurance Kit are available only through a paid subscription (HITRUST, 2012).

NIST SPECIAL PUBLICATION 800-53

The National Institute of Standards and Technology (NIST) develops and issues Special Publications (SP) as recommendation and guideline documents. The purpose of SP 800-53 is *to provide guidelines for selecting and specifying security controls for information systems supporting the executive agencies of the federal government...* (NIST, 2009). The document further indicates that state, local, and tribal governments, as well as private sector organizations may use guidelines as deemed applicable. Thus healthcare organizations can also implement the guidelines for protection of their sensitive information.

Background of NIST SP 800-53

NIST Special Publication 800-53 is entitled *Security and Privacy Controls for Federal Information Systems and Organizations.* NIST established the Special Publication 800 series in 1990. These series publish documents of general interest to the computer security community. They report on Information Technology Laboratory's research, guidelines, and outreach efforts in computer security, and its collaborative activities with industry, government, and academic organizations.

Structure of NIST SP 800-53

There are two revisions of the publication. SP 800-53 Revision 3 was released in August 2009 and SP 800-53 Revision 4 was released in February 2012 and finalized in April 2013.

SP 800-53 Rev 4 comprises three chapters and supporting appendices. The first chapter introduces the standard by providing the background and purpose, applicability, target audience, relationship to other security control publications and organizational responsibilities. Chapter Two describes the fundamental concepts associated with security control selection and specification including: multitiered risk management; security control structure, baselines and designations; external service providers; assurance and trustworthiness. Chapter Three describes the process of selecting and specifying security controls for an information system including: (1) selecting security control baselines; (2) tailoring baseline security controls; (3) creating overlays; (4) documenting the control selection process; (5) new development and legacy systems.

NIST SPECIAL PUBLICATION 1800-1

Similar to the entry mentioned above (NIST SP 800-53), NIST SP 1800-1 is a part of NIST's Special Publications (SP) series. The purpose of the document is to be a "standards-based reference design" that *provides users with information they need to replicate this approach to securing electronic health records transferred among mobile devices* (NIST, 2015). In terms of intended audience and content covered, the guidelines of NIST SP 1800-1 are far-reaching in scope, which makes the document applicable to a broad range of individuals implementing IT security standards. For instance, regarding mobile processing and transmitting of patient data, the publication not only raises awareness to the vulnerabilities of mobile computing within health care systems, but it also explains step-by-step network configurations in order to make health care systems more secure, or EHRs less susceptible to exploitation. In other words, depending on one's technical skillset in heath care contexts, the guide can be used in different ways.

Background of NIST SP 1800-1

NIST Special Publication 1800-1 entitled, *Securing Electronic Health Records on Mobile Devices* was released in July 2015. The work was produced though NIST's National Cybersecurity Center of Excellence (NCCoE) by a consortium of team members from organizations, such Intel, Cisco, MITRE, Medtech Enginuity, Symantec, IBM, and RSA. Three primary factors motivated the publication: First, NIST conducted a risk assessment within healthcare contexts, and members of the health care industry made it clear that the topic deserved further attention (NIST, 2015). Second, at the 2012 Health and Human Services Mobile Devices Roundtable, collaborators raised awareness that mobile devices were being used by providers for transferring health care information without having privacy and security safeguards in place prior to use. The third factor was the 41-page, *Fifth Annual Benchmark Study on Privacy and Security of Healthcare Data*, which was produced by the Ponemon Institute in May 2015. Among other insights, the study found that over the span of a five-year period, the number of cyber attacks on information systems and devices rose by 125% (NIST, 2015). Moreover, the study indicated that in 2013 inadequate preparedness to safeguard patient health records from being stolen (leading to medical identity theft) or altered cost health organizations $12 billion a year (NIST, 2015).

In addition, NIST SP 800-124 entitled, *Guidelines for Managing the Security of Mobile Devices* and NIST SP 800-30, also inform the background content for NIST SP 1800-1. NIST SP 800-124 defined what should be considered a mobile device, such as smart phones and tablets, based on certain technical characteristics, and NIST SP 800-30 presented a risk assessment methodology. Specifically, NIST 1800-1a builds on NIST SP 800-124, focusing on tablets and cell phones, and NIST SP 1800-1e applies the risk assessment methodology found in NIST SP 800-30.

Structure of NIST SP 1800-1

NIST SP 1800-1 is divided into five volumes (lettered a-e). The following is a list of the volumes, along with a cursory summary of the content (NIST, 2015).

- **NIST SP 1800-1a:** Executive Summary
  - Presents a summary of the challenges within health care contexts, which use mobile computing for handling patient data
  - Emphasizes the relevance of a standards-based approach to cyber-security to better protect patient's privacy and an organization's network
  - Mainly relevant for chief security and technology officers and health care organization leaders
- NIST SP 1800-1b
  - Maps security characteristics to NIST's best practices and standards, and to Security Rules of HIPAA, and other organization's standards
  - Provides a comprehensive architecture that focuses on security controls
  - Facilitates ease of use through automated configuration of security controls
  - Brings awareness to the need of different types of implementation (outsourced or in-house)
  - Focuses on risk assessment considering how the following threats may result in loss of confidentiality, loss of integrity, or loss of availability
  - Mainly to provide guidance for implementers and security engineers
- **NIST SP 1800-1c:** How-To Guides
  - Introduces a hypothetical scenario of primary care physicians using mobile devices
  - Presents all products employed in reference design
  - Shows how the products influence the example solution
  - Mainly relevant for IT professionals
- NIST SP 1800-1d
  - Presents a complete list of security standards that were used to create the architecture
  - Lists best practices
  - Mainly relevant for IT professionals
- NIST SP 1800-1e
  - Shows step-by-step what happens when a cyber-attack is attempted in order to access electronic health records
  - Presents risk assessment methodology
    - Table driven method
    - Attack/fault-tree assessment method
  - Gives results of an independent test on the reference design presented in the guide
  - Mainly relevant for IT professionals

NIST SPECIAL PUBLICATION 1800-8

Similar to the entries mentioned above (NIST SP 800-53 and NIST SP 1800-1), NIST SP 1800-8 is a part of NIST's Special Publications (SP) series. The purpose of the guide is to explain various security vulnerabilities within external infusion pumps in healthcare delivery organizations (HDO), and to provide IT professionals and engineers with standards to safeguard them against vulnerabilities.

Infusion pumps were once "standalone instruments" (NIST, 2017), meaning that they were not part of wireless networks and/or intricate systems. With advancements in medical technology, however, these devices became wirelessly connected to various sources in health care networks and systems; thus, contributing to the Internet of Things (IoT), or more specifically, what NIST refers to as the Internet of Medical Things (IoMT), where medical devices increasingly have the capacity to communicate with other devices and networks via the internet (NIST, 2017). While the increased interconnectedness of infusion pumps increases the functionality, and therefore, the efficiency of patient care, the drawback is that this leaves them more susceptible to risks, such as unauthorized access from malicious attacks, resulting in loss of patient data and healthcare services, health information breaches, and also significant monetary repercussions due to loss of public confidence to safeguard patient data. For these reasons, some of the main goals of NIST SP 1800-8 are the following (NIST, 2017):

- To configure and deploy wireless infusion pumps to mitigate cybersecurity vulnerabilities
- Avoid the consequences of operations risks, such as device interference and loss of patient data
- Develop a layered security strategy in order to safeguard against a single point failure
- Show HDOs how cybsersecurity standards and best practices can be contextually applied

Background of NIST SP 1800-8

The NIST Special Publication 1800-8 entitled, *Securing Wireless Infusion Pumps in Healthcare Delivery Organizations* was released in May 2017. Initially, The National Cybersecurity Center of Excellence (NCCoE) at NIST formed a questionnaire-based risk assessment of infusion pumps. The assessment focused on the vulnerabilities of the devices within HDOs. After the assessment results, NCCoE created example implementations as to how health organizations could apply a standard-based approach in order to mitigate risks involved with the devices. In addition, the study integrates the insight and technological expertise of collaborators from various companies and technological vendors such as Braun, Baxter Healthcare Corporation, Becton, DigiCert, Hospira Inc., Clearwater Compliance, Cisco, Intercede, MDISS, Ramparts, Smiths Medical, MITRE Corporation, TDi Technologies, Symantec Corporation, and PFP Cybersecurity (NIST, 2017).

Structure of NIST SP 1800-8

NIST Special Publication 1800-8A-C is comprised of three lettered volumes (Volume A: Executive Summary, Volume B: Approach, Architecture, and Security Characteristics, and Volume C: How-To Guides). The following is a short description and/or summary of the main topics within each volume (NIST, 2017).

- **Volume A:** Executive Summary
  - ○ Introduces HDO challenges in securing the wireless infusion pumps
  - ○ Presents the example solution created at the NCCoE
  - ○ Discusses the advantages of implementing NCCoE's solution
- **Volume B:** Approach, Architecture, and Security Characteristics (this volume is divided into nine sections)
  - ○ **Section 1:** Introduces the specific issues found by NCCoE, gives a detailed analysis of their approach in terms of the architecture and security characteristics used to arrive at a solution, discusses how the solution answers the challenges (along with its advantages), lists the project's collaborators, and gives direction in terms of how to respond to the findings of the project
  - ○ **Section 2:** How to Use This Guide discusses how program managers, business decision makers, information technology (IT) professionals, and biomedical engineers can utilize the content
  - ○ **Section 3:** Presents a comprehensive scope of the project, describes the underlying security platform assumptions, introduces risk assessment guidelines, and various components in which collaborators contributed to implement platform development
  - ○ **Section 4:** Risk Assessment and Mitigation discusses the various risks found and presents solutions in order to lower these vulnerabilities
  - ○ **Section 5:** Architecture explains various scenarios of security platforms, including the different cybersecurity components
  - ○ **Section 6:** Life Cycle Cybersecurity Issues discusses topics in cybersecurity life-cycle, such as procurement, maintenance, and end of life
  - ○ **Section 7:** Security Characteristics Analysis describes the different techniques used to implement risk assessments on wireless infusion pumps
  - ○ **Section 8:** Functional Evaluation summarizes the test sequences used to show the different security platform services, etc.
  - ○ **Section 9:** Future Build Considerations is an overview of other application options that NIST might focus on to find further solutions to securing wireless infusion pumps
- **Volume C:** How-to Guides
  - ○ A step-by-step guide for IT professionals who want to follow the example solution found in the document
  - ○ A guide to replicating the various aspects of the build that was created in the NCCoE lab (i.e., installation, configuration, and integration instructions)
  - ○ Other topics: core network, identity services, Symantec endpoint protection and intrusion detection, risk assessment tools

BUILDING CODE FOR MEDICAL DEVICE SOFTWARE SECURITY (IEEE CYBER-SECURITY)

The Institute of Electrical and Electronics Engineers (IEEE) is a professional and global computing membership organization that was formed in the early 1960s as an integration of the American Institute of Electrical Engineers and the Institute of Radio Engineers. In 2014, the IEEE Computer Society launched the IEEE CyberSecurity Initiative for the main purposes of (a) providing accessible online content for issues related to cyber-security, (b) helping students and educators to better understand cyber-security concepts/issues, and (c) giving advanced technical insight of Security and Privacy designs for professionals (IEEE CyberSecurity, 2014). The IEEE produces many effective and relevant collaborative works that serve as technical guidelines for creating secure systems.

The purpose of the report, *Building Code for Medical Device Software Security* (BCMDSS) is to serve as a starting point for *building code for software security that will reduce the vulnerability of their systems to malicious attacks* (Haigh & Landwehr, 2014). This commitment is based on the metaphor that just as "building codes" are needed in order mitigate vulnerabilities of physical buildings, the same concept can be applied to medical device software. That is, just as a building being constructed must have proper thought put into it (design and implementation) so as to stand against elements that may eventually put that infrastructure at risk; similarly, technical guidelines and stronger code elements are necessary to provide the same sort of stability to software systems. In regard to BCMDSS, the risk could take the form of releasing sensitive information, or causing a device to be altered from its specified purpose, etc. Since the majority of cyber-security vulnerabilities are often associated with implementation errors, instead of design errors, the report particularly focuses on code elements introduced in the implementation phase (Haigh & Landwehr, 2014).

BCMDSS does not assume technical infallibility. The authors make it clear that the report is a "beginning" to the discussion, and they encourage readers to extend and/or strengthen the insights found within their respective technical context (Haigh & Landwehr, 2014). The work does, however, give expert advice as to the purpose and requirements of specific elements that will strengthen software systems in a constructive way.

Background of Building Code for Medical Device Software Security (IEEE Cyber-Security)

BCMDSS was released in November 2014. The publication was not an isolated effort. The code elements/guidelines were the result of 40 volunteers with various backgrounds (cybersecurity, programming languages, software engineering, medical device development, medical device standards, and medical device regulation), who first collaborated online, and then met for two days (co-sponsored by the IEEE Cybersecurity Initiative and the National Science Foundation) of workshops in New Orleans, Louisiana to consider various standards of a proper building code. After the workshop, a mature set of elements was organized into a draft, "Draft Building Code for Medical Device Software Security," which resulted in the report (Haigh & Landwehr, 2014).

Structure of Building Code for Medical Device Software Security (IEEE Cyber-Security)

The structure of the publication is relatively straightforward. The individual elements or guidelines are organized into 10 categories (A-I and X). Those that are more design focused (FGHI, X) are mentioned, but left empty. Those that are more implementation oriented are expounded upon, and are further divided into four subsections, which provide a clear description of each element. The four subsections of each element are guided by the following questions (Note: In BCMDSS, these questions are answered in relation to each code element [Haigh & Landwehr, 2014]):

- **Description:** What is the meaning and purpose of this element?
- **Vulnerabilities Addressed:** What vulnerability types will be reduced if this element is implemented properly?
- **Developer Resources Required:** What resources will the individual or organization developing the software/device require to satisfy this element?
- **Evaluator Resources Required:** What is required for a third party to assess whether the device satisfies this element?

The specific code elements, along with suggestions/topics sub-headings of the article, are listed below (A-I, X [Haigh & Landwehr, 2014]):

- (A) Elements intended to avoid/detect/remove specific types of vulnerabilities at the implementation stage
    - Use memory safe languages
    - Language sub-setting
    - Use of secure coding sections
    - Automated memory safety error mitigation and compiler-enforced buffer overflow elimination
    - Automated thread safety analysis
    - Automated analysis of programs (source/binary) for critical properties
    - Modification condition decision coverage
    - Operational use case identification and removal of unused functions
- (B) Elements intended to assure proper use of cryptography
    - Accredited cryptographic algorithms and implementation
    - Secure random numbers
- (C) Elements intended to assure software/firmware provenance and integrity, but not to remove code flaws
    - Digitally signed firmware and provenance (supply chain)
    - Software/firmware update validation
    - Whitelisting
    - Least operating system privilege
    - Anti-tampering of hardcoded secrets/keys/data within medical device software
- (D) Elements intended to impede attacker analysis or exploitation but not necessarily remove flaws
    - Non-executable data pages
    - Full recognition of inputs before processing
    - Least operating system privilege
    - Anti-tampering of hardcoded secrets/keys/data within medical device software
- (E) Elements intended to enable detection/attribution of attack
    - Security event logging
- (F) Elements intended to assist in safe degradation of function during an attack
    - Design consideration
- (G) Elements intended to assist in restoration of function after attack
    - Design consideration
- (H) Elements intended to support maintenance of operational software without loss of integrity
    - Design consideration

- (I) Elements intended to support privacy requirements
  - Design consideration
- (X) Desired characteristics of the building code, for example, standard names use, building code maintenance over time, and scope
  - No proposed standards at this time

DISCUSSION

Though COBIT is one of the most popular frameworks used by publicly traded companies in the US to comply with Sarbanes-Oxley Act, the purpose is for IT management and compliance. It helps strengthen the security of healthcare systems, but security is not the main goal of COBIT. This standard may not be suitable to small healthcare organizations who want to improve the security of their system.

ISO/IEC 27002:2005 can be applied to organization of any size concerned with the information security of their systems. A healthcare organization can use this standard as a guide to manage their information security program. Healthcare organizations can seek certification for their Information Security Management System to be compliant with ISO/IEC 270001: 2005.

Although NIST Special publication 800-53 is mainly used by Federal government, it could be used by healthcare organization as a reference in implementing their systems.

ISO 27799:2008 is a companion to the ISO/IEC 27002, which is specifically targeted to healthcare information systems. Therefore, we suggest healthcare organizations of all sizes study and adopt this standard.

Rather than being a new standard, HITRUST's CSF is a combination of existing standards with industrial experience. The access to the standard is limited to the members of HITRUST. Healthcare organizations with budget can get education on healthcare information security from HITRUST and have their systems certified.

The above standards can be used to address the management aspect of information security in a healthcare organization. ISO 17090:2008 and ISO/TS 25237:2008, however, address some specific technical issues in healthcare IT. ISO 17090:2008 provides guidance on implementing secure exchange of healthcare information using digital certificate technology, while ISO/TS 25237:2008 provides guidance on privacy protection of personal health information through pseudonymization.

The security standards or frameworks described in this paper are some of the commonly used ones. There are other related standards. ISO 31000:2009 is a standard that can be used to ensure a comprehensive coverage of risk-related issues. ISO/TS 13606-4:2009 provides a methodology that specifies the privileges necessary to access EHR data, and addresses the unique EHR communications requirements. It also represents and communicates EHR-specific information that informs an access decision. General security requirements applicable to EHR communications are referred and *points at technical solutions and standards that specify details on services meeting these security needs* (ISO, 2013). Further, for long term archival of electronic health records, ISO/TS 21547:2010 defines basic principles needed for its secure preservation in any format. With regards to remote maintenance services (RMS) for health information systems, ISO/TR 11633-1:2009 gives it the relevant focus and depicts an example of carrying out a risk analysis with the aim of protecting the information system and the personal health data in a safe and efficient manner. The part 2 of the standard, ISO/TR 11633-2:2009 shows an example of selected and applied controls for RMS security. ISO/PRF TS 14441, titled Health informatics -- Security and privacy requirements of EHR systems for use in conformity assessment is a new standard currently under development. As its name suggests, it will address security and privacy needs of EHR.

Regardless of the standard(s) selected, a concerted effort from top management down to end-users is requisite for the successful implementation of the security controls specified. Various risk analysis must be conducted to ensure that the guidelines are relevant to, applicable to and practical for healthcare business and operational practices. It is recommended that organizations perform

a 'gap analysis' to identify the current security controls within the organization, the potential problems and issues, the costs and benefits, the operational impact, and the proposed recommendations before applying any chosen Standards (HKSAR, 2008).

Implementation should follow only after the completion of a gap analysis with the support of the management in tow. The selection of security controls should be based on factors such as organization's criteria for risk acceptance, risk treatment options as well as the general risk management approach. Of course, the selection decision should also be in compliance to all relevant national and international legislation and regulations.

Training and user awareness programs should also be conducted. This ensures that all employees understand the benefits and impacts before the deployment of new security policies and guidelines. Failure to do this usually results in user complaints after implementation. A balance of functional requirements, security requirements and user requirements signifies a successful implementation of information security standard(s) (HKSAR, 2008)

Lastly, cooperation at all levels of an organization is indispensable to the successful implementation of security standards. As a fact, security is something that all parties should be involved in. It should not be seen as the sole responsibility of the IT department or a package that senior management must provide. Rather, *senior management, information security practitioners, IT professionals and users all have a role to play in securing the assets of an organization* (HKSAR, 2008). Everyone's involvement creates a very safe environment.

CONCLUSION

This paper provides an overview of security standards applicable to health information systems. It describes the following standards: COBIT, ISO/IEC 27001:2005, ISO/IEC 27002:2005, ISO/IEC 27001:2005, ISO 27799:2008, ISO 17090:2008, ISO/TS 25237:2008, HITRUST Common Security Framework (CSF), NIST Special Publication 800-53, NIST SP 1800, NIST SP 1800-8, and Building Code for Medical Device Software Security.. This survey provides a starting point for IT management in healthcare organizations to select a standard suitable for their organization for managing or improving their information security programs.

Though COBIT, ISO/IEC 27002:2005, ISO/IEC 27001:2005, and NIST Special Publication 800-53 can be used as a guide or reference to manage the information security program of health care organizations, they are not tailored for healthcare organizations. ISO 27799:2008 is specifically targeted to healthcare information systems. Therefore, we suggest healthcare organizations of all sizes study and adopt this standard. HITRUST's CSF is a combination of existing standards with industrial experience.

The access to the standard is limited to the members of HITRUST. Healthcare organizations with budget can get education on healthcare information security from HITRUST and have their systems certified.

ISO 17090:2008 and ISO/TS 25237:2008 address some specific technical issues in healthcare IT including implementing secure exchange of healthcare information using digital certificate technology, and privacy protection of personal health information through pseudonymization. The "Building Code for Medical Device Software Security (BCMDSS)" aims to reduce the vulnerability in software in medical devices from malicious attacks. NIST 1800-1 was developed to secure electronic health records on mobile devices. NIST 1800-8 provides guidance on how to secure wireless infusion pumps as one of Internet of Medical Things.

REFERENCES

Akowuah, F., Yuan, X., Xu, J., & Wang, H. (2012). An Overview of Laws and Standards for Health Information Security and Privacy. In *Security & Management International Conference* (pp. 403-408). Las Vegas, NV: CSREA Press.

Boehmer, W. (2009). Cost-Benefit Trade-Off Analysis of an ISMS Based on ISO 27001. In *International Conference on Availability, Reliability and Security (ARES '09)* (pp. 392- 399). Fukuoka: CPS. 10.1109/ARES.2009.128

Fraser, R. (2006, June 6). *Canada Health Infoway*. Academic Press.

Haigh, T., & Landwehr, C. (2014). *Building Code for Medical Device Software Security*. Retrieved October 10, 2017, from IEEE Cybersecurity: https://www.computer.org/cms/CYBSI/docs/BCMDSS.pdf

Health Infoway Website. (n.d.). Retrieved from http://sl.infoway-inforoute.ca/downloads/Ross_Fraser_-_ISO_27799.pdf

HITRUST. (2012, March). Retrieved from Health Information Trust Alliance: http://www.hitrustalliance.net/csf/

HKSAR. (2008, February). *An Overview of Information Security Standards*. Retrieved September 17, 2012, from Info Sec Website: http://www.infosec.gov.hk/english/technical/files/overview.pdf

IEEE CyberSecurity. (2014). *About*. Retrieved October 10, 2017, from IEEE Cybersecurity: https://cybersecurity.ieee.org/about/

ISO27000. (2007). *ISO 27000 Standards*. Retrieved September 16, 2012, from The ISO 27000 Directory Website: http://www.27000.org/iso-27799.htm

ISACA. (2012). Retrieved July 03, 2012, from ISACA Website: http://www.isaca.org

ISECT. (2012). *ISO 27001 Security*. Retrieved September 2012, from ISO 27001 Security: http://www.iso27001security.com/html/27002.html#HistoryOfISO17799

ISO. (2013). *Home: Standards*. Retrieved March 24, 2013, from ISO Website: http://www.iso.org/iso/home/standards.htm

ISO/IEC. (2013). *ISO/IEC 27002:2013*. Retrieved March 24, 2014 from http://www.iso.org/iso/home/store/catalogue_ics/catalogue_detail_ics.htm?csnumber=54533

Luethi, M., & Knolmayer, G. F. (2009). Security in Health Information Systems: An Exploratory Comparison of U.S. and Swiss Hospitals. In *42nd Hawaii International Conference on System Sciences* (pp. 1-10). Waikoloa, HI: CPS.

Morimoto, S. (2009). Application of COBIT to Security Management in Information Systems Development. *Fourth International Conference on Frontier of Computer Science and Technology*, 625-630. 10.1109/FCST.2009.38

NIST. (2009, August). *NIST Special Publication 800-53*. Retrieved September 16, 2012, from National Institute of Standards and Technology: http://csrc.nist.gov/publications/nistpubs/800-53-Rev3/sp800-53-rev3-final.pdf

NIST. (2015, July). *NIST Special Publication 1800-1*. Retrieved October 7, 2017, from National Institute of Standards and Technology: https://nccoe.nist.gov/projects/use-cases/health-it/ehr-on-mobile-devices

NIST. (2017, May). *NIST Special Publication 1800-8*. Retrieved October 10, 2017, from National Institute of Standards and Technology: https://nccoe.nist.gov/sites/default/files/library/sp1800/hit-infusion-pump-nist-sp1800-8-draft.pdf

Olzak, T. (2013, September). *COBIT 5 for Information Security: The Underlying Principles*. Retrieved March 23, 2014, from TechRepublic: http://www.techrepublic.com/blog/it-security/cobit-5-for-information-security-the-underlying-principles/

Parker, J. (2012, March). Retrieved July 3, 2012, from Enfocus Solutions Inc.: http://blog.enfocussolutions.com/Powering_Requirements_Success/bid/131740/COBIT-5-is-Coming

Pathak, J. (2005). Information Technology Governance and COBIT. In J. Pathak (Ed.), Information Technology Auditing: An Evolving Agenda (pp. 151-156). Springer Berlin Heidelberg.

PRGL. (2011, December 22). Retrieved March 4, 2012, from Praxiom Research Group Limited: http://www.praxiom.com/iso-17799-intro.htm

RedCard Security. (2008). *ISO 27799:2008*. Retrieved September 16, 2012, from RedCard Security Website: http://www.redcardsecurity.com/pages/resources_files/ISO27799-2008.pdf

Slater, D. (2004, January 4). *Numbers: ITIL, COBIT and More: Who Uses What?* Retrieved March 23, 2014 from http://www.csoonline.com/article/216935/numbers-itil-cobit-and-more-who-uses-what-

Van Grembergen, W., & De Haes, S. (2009). COBIT as a Framework for Enterprise Governance of IT. In *Enterprise Governance of Information Technology* (pp. 137–164). Springer US. doi:10.1007/978-0-387-84882-2_5

Chapter 9
A Semiotic Examination of the Security Policy Lifecycle

Michael Lapke
University of Mary Washington, USA

ABSTRACT

Major security breaches continue to plague organizations decades after best practices, standards, and technical safeguards have become commonplace. This worrying trend clearly demonstrates that information systems security remains a significant issue within organizations. As policy forms the basis for practice, a major contributor to this ongoing security problem is a faulty security policy lifecycle. This can lead to an insufficient or worse, a failed policy. This chapter is aimed at understanding the lifecycle by analyzing the meanings that are attributed to policy formulation and implementation by the stakeholders involved in the process. A case study was carried out and a "snapshot in time" of the lifecycle of IS security policy lifecycle at the organization revealed that a disconnect is evident in the security policy lifecycle.

INTRODUCTION

Information Systems (IS) security issues continue to pose significant cost and damage to organizations. Cybercrime costs more than $7.35 million per U.S. organization in 2017, (Ponemon, 2017). This is a 5% increase from 2016 despite a 25% increase in organizational investment in information security in the same time period. As a result, system security is an ongoing concern for organizations and their stakeholders. The increased investment did decrease the amount of the days to identify the data breach from an average of 201 in 2016 to 191 days in 2017 (Ponemon, 2017). Also, the average days to contain the data breach from decreased from 70 to 66 days. The fact remains that malicious attacks have been continuing to escalate, as can be seen from the increased cybercrime costs.

In recent years, there have been a plethora of widely publicized security breaches. Security breaches at Equifax, Target, and Anthem in 2017, 2015, and 2014 affected billions of consumers. Information including names, social security numbers, birth dates, driver's licenses, and addresses were all stolen. The author of this chapter was directly affected by each and every one of these incidents. The incidents were all widely reported and had a dramatic impact on the respective organizations' stock value and earnings.

DOI: 10.4018/978-1-5225-5583-4.ch009

What is driving continued cybercrime is primarily a market economy deep in the black market. Products such as the personal information described above are sold in bulk to identity thieves who use this information to open lines of credit. Credit card information stolen from websites are sold for $10-$20 each (SecureWorks, 2017). Criminals lock down systems with Ransomware and demand large sums to unlock data for organizations. Mobile malware is a significant threat and will continue to grow, with information theft and spying capabilities becoming widely available (SecureWorks, 2017). Most alarmingly, the perceived gap between criminality and nation-states, in terms of both actors and capabilities, will continue to shrink (SecureWorks, 2017).

We argue that a significant contributor to the issue of internal and external IS Security breaches within organizations is a disconnect between IS Security policy formulation and IS security policy implementation. This disconnect leads to a failure of IS Security policy. This detachment manifests in several ways. For instance, a stakeholder may have intended an IS Security policy to be implemented a particular way but written it to imply a different intent. Another instantiation of the disconnect is when the intent is inferred to mean something different by a stakeholder. In practical terms, one such scenario would manifest itself in terms of a policy board creating vague policy that does not explicitly address the pertinent issues. Another instantiation of a scenario would be seen by a user interpreting a "robust" password policy to mean that they should keep track of their changing passwords via a list taped to their monitor.

Given the complexity of organizations, at a technological and social level, it is not reasonable to think there could a simple solution. Organizations have attempted to deal with this in a continuously evolving manner. The first of the three generations of security development described by Baskerville (1993) is the checklist methodology. The complexity is seen in this first and simplest of the generations. While the simplest of the three, the methodology was still a multifarious venture including unwieldy specifications that were hard to read, understand, and maintain (Baskerville, 1993). There were a variety of lists, some approaching 1,000 potentially subjective and vague items. Despite their seemingly thorough nature, Baskerville (1993) describes a major weakness of checklists in that they oversimplify the security considerations that arise in more complex information systems. Dhillon and Backhouse (2000) term this oversimplification as atheoretical.

More critical to the policy issue is the fourth generation of security development described by Siponen (2001); behavior and responsibility. Responsibility, defined as:

The relationship between two agents regarding a specific state of affairs, such that the holder of the responsibility is responsible to the giver of the responsibility, the responsibility principal (Siponen, M, 2001, pg. 129)

is implied in the very existence of a IS Security Policy. The concept of responsibility in IS security was originally discussed by Backhouse and Dhillon (1996). A policy informs a user of their responsibilities regarding an Information System's use. Assuring a proper line of communication between the makers of the policy and the users of the policy is essential or said responsibility may never be properly understood or properly articulated.

BACKGROUND

Business policy has been conceptualized as a form of strategic management (Mintzberg, H, Lampel, Quinn, & Goshal, 2003). Two perspectives make up the way in which strategy is made: deliberate formulation and emergent formation (Mintzberg, Henry, 1983). The classical approach advocated by Quinn is the approach to strategy grounded in the military strategy used for thousands of years. This type of strategy advocates the use of deliberate plans to win battles and wars. Noted historical figures in the area of military strategy, such as Sun Tzu, Napoleon, Lenin, and Machiavelli have contributed to advancing the classical strategy to its modern form. Mintzberg (2003) stepped away from this rigid approach to business strategy and policy by advocating an emergent approach. In this, an organization's realized strategy is a combination of the organizations deliberate strategy with the evolving emergent strategy. This emergent strategy is identified by a stream of actions which can represent a pattern.

These two perspectives of strategic management can be used to investigate the research behind IS security policy. One stream is grounded in the classical approach while the other in the emergent approach. The following section will utilize each of these perspectives in examining the literature behind IS security policy.

From the classical, planned strategic perspective, research has aimed to provide information security professionals and top management a framework through which useable security strategy and policy for applications can be created and maintained in line with the standard information technology life cycle (Rees, Subhajyoti, & Spafford, 2003). This framework was cyclical in nature and consisted of four stages, plan, access, operate, and deliver. At the theoretical level, Glasgow and Macewen (1992) created a formal framework for specifying security policies. This framework, called Security Logic, defines what a subject knows, what information a subject has permission to know, and what information a subject is obligated to know. The paper presented this via a logical approach based on modal logic formalism (Glasgow & Macewen, 1992).

Continuing with the classical perspective, Kühnhauser (1999) expounded on how to rationally plan out multi-policy system. These are defined as systems that support a multitude of independent security domains in which an individual IS Security Policy is enforced on the applications. Kühnhauser performed a logical analysis to introduce a formal model of policy groups. Research has also examined the issue of multi-policy systems by investigating the emerging "digital government" (Joshi, Ghafoor, & E, 2001). A sequence of solutions to the issues of multi-domain environments are presented including ad hoc approaches, formal approaches, model-based methods, agent-based methods, architectural methods, and the database federation approach (Joshi et al., 2001). Policy enforcement however does not highly correlate with policy effectiveness (Knapp, et al, 2007).

The classical perspective has also witnessed a call for a security meta-policy (Baskerville & Siponen, 2002). It is noted that existing IS Security Policy approaches do not pay much attention to policy formulation itself. In other words, the actual creation of the policy is done in an ad hoc manner. Calling for a meta-policy implies that the way to the best strategy or policy is through concise rational planning.

On the emergent side of the strategic paradigm, researchers have examined how problems are dealt with after the creation of an IS security policy. It has been noted that 52% of all logistical and physical security breaches arose from the activities of personnel within the organization (Willison, 2002). Research has sought to determine the most optimal control method to handle these breaches (Willison, 2002). IS Security Policy formally defines security requirements, outline the main security objectives, and allocate responsibilities. To maximize the probability of compliance, the enlightenment of staff to their responsibilities as outlined in the IS Security Policy is one potential solution (Willison, 2002). An actor's behavior can help a manager justify the information security policy so that it gains wider acceptance or government can educate the public on how to avoid computer malware (Sommestad, et al, 2015). Or, it may help a security officer formulate new policy that best fits the organization.

Also from the emergent perspective, there has been a call for the improvement of audit management technology to allow administrators to configure the software to reflect the security needs of an organization as defined in the IS Security Policy (Ahmad & Ruighavar, 2003). This demonstrates a dynamic approach to the policy in that it can be reactive to how an audit trail affects an Information System. Changing the configuration from the status quo bottom-up approach to a policy-centric top-down approach would help the configuration more closely match an organization's security goals (Ahmad & Ruighavar, 2003).

While not explicitly approaching the issue from an emergent perspective, Coyne and Kluksdahl's (1994) examination of a failed IS Security Policy implementation demonstrates an analysis from an emergent perspective. The implication resides in how the implementers could have adapted to how the actual scenario was different from the rational plan. They found that compliance-based approaches are more prone to failure than risk-based approaches. A de-facto compliance-based policy led to the reaction of all security related matters being adversarial in nature (Coyne & Kluksdahl, 1994).

While all of this research provides for insight into the issue of IS Security Policy, it does not explore how to analyze stakeholder interpretations of such policy. This emergent perspective is critical in the development of optimal IS security policy. It is hoped that the analysis provided in this paper will give an opportunity for researchers to shed light into this phenomenon. A theoretical basis for such an analysis is presented in the following section.

THEORETICAL FOUNDATION

Given the exploratory nature of this study and the fact that stakeholder interpretations are being extrapolated, a theory that focuses on "meaning" is most appropriate. Semantic theory is the essence of analyzing the meaning of information (Katz, 1970; Stamper, 1973). With semantic theory, a researcher can understand the meanings attributed to the item of study by the stakeholders. Semantic Theory has been used in IS literature (Backhouse, James, 2000; Dhillon, Gurpreet, 2007; Fitzgerald, 1998).

Semantic theory is a subset of semiotic theory. According to Anderson (Anderson, 1990), semiotics is the science of sign systems including linguistics, as well as the study of all other sign systems. Semiotics also includes the general principles that underlie all sign systems. It is thus more comprehensive than linguistics; much more, because there is a semiotic dimension to practically every human artifact (Anderson, 1990). This makes the semiotic approach quite appropriate to investigating Information Systems. Several IS researchers have utilized the semiotic approach (Anderson, 1990; Backhouse, James, 1992; Dhillon, G & May, 2006; Liebenau & Backhouse, 1990; Ulrich, 2001).

As seen in Table 1, Stamper (1973) presents a framework for semiotics that breaks down information into four different "levels." These are empirics, syntactics, semantics and pragmatics. They represent a spectrum of information that moves from the natural world to the social. Semantics is representative of the meanings of signs. The semantic sense of what meaning is will be discussed in the following five paragraphs. Stamper provides a concise and elegantly simple semantic model, as part of his overall semiotic model, that one can use to build a framework in which all dimensions of meaning can be explained.

Table 1. Semiotic Model (Stamper, 1973)

Signification		Mode of	
		Denotative	Affective
Intention of	Descriptive	designations, facts, evidence, forecasts	appraisals, value judgments
	Prescriptive	instructions, plans, policies, orders	inducements, coercion, threats, rewards

The four dimensions of meaning in the semantic sense described are denotative descriptions, affective descriptions, denotative prescriptions, and affective prescriptions. Denotative descriptions are simply a statement of something that exists. These are signs that *must be justified by showing their relationships with things which can be observed by anyone* (Stamper, 1973, p. 75). This indicates a low level of subjectivity. Morris (1970) also describes this by stating that designative signs help gather relevant information regarding the nature of the environment in which the organism operates. Further demonstrating the objectivity of it, denotative descriptions are described as *easy with a physical object, difficult with a statement about a past event* (Stamper, 1973, pg 75).

The second semantic element, affective descriptions are those that are more based on subjective feelings and human values. These are described as value judgments: reports on staff, estimates of the relative difficulties of jobs (Stamper, 1973). The key, distinguishing characteristic of affective information is that which refers to individual human feelings. Credence is led to this subset of semantic theory by acknowledging that *only by reference to the human organism and its power of appraisal can we justify designating a supposed pattern of data as a thing* (Stamper, 1973, pg 75).

A new area is uncovered in the next semantic element, denotative prescriptions. The first two dealt with how a sign is described. This element and the next one differ from descriptions in that they are directive. They are *an order, a rule or a recommendation that will denote the objects to which the prescribed action must be related* (Stamper, 1973, pg 77). Prescriptive signs guide the actor's behavior according to the ways in which the organism must act upon the environment in order to satisfy its need (Morris, 1970).

The final semantic element, affective prescriptions, takes the directive approach and mixes the human element. In essence, words may have the superficial appearance of a command or law (Stamper, 1973). The key is that their prescriptive standing is only justifiable in so far as they arouse expectations about the consequences of obeying or disobeying them. The human element however is not only indicative of those that prescribe but also those who are prescribed upon. Whatever sanctions can be applied largely depends upon the permission of those to whom they are supposed to apply.

The study of semantics essentially reduces to the examination of meaning. By looking at the concrete ways in which an object or artifact is described, the subjective way an object or artifact is described, the concrete way rules about that object or artifact exist, and the subjective interpretation of those rules, one can get a clear semantic understanding of that given object or artifact. The dimensions of semantics outlined in this section are condensed into a framework that can be used for future research on IS security policy formulation. This semantic framework is presented in Table 2, in the appendix.

METHODOLOGY

This research was conducted via an interpretive case study in the Information Technology Department of a large state University in the southeastern portion of the United States. The interpretive tradition perceives that the knowledge of reality is a social construction by human actors (Walsham, 1993). In contrast to the assumptions of positivist science, this knowledge of reality applies equally to researchers and leads to the perception that there is no objective reality which can be discovered by researchers (Walsham, 1993). This perspective is also described whereby "interpretive research provides in depth insights into social, cultural and historical contexts within which particular events and actions are described and interpreted as grounded in the authentic experiences of the people studied" (Howcroft & Trauth, 2005, pg 33).

Approximately 45 employees worked for the department under study. Of these, 20 participated in the interviews. The subjects that did participate were the stakeholders involved in the formulation and implementation of the IS Security Policy. They included the Chief Information Officer, Security Officer, and a group of operational level employees who were members of a Security Planning Team (SPT). The members of SPT included systems analysts, web developers, a database administrator, two school administrators, and three faculty members. The employees within the department who did not participate in the study included those that were not stakeholders in the IS Security policy formulation and implementation process.

The interviews were grounded by the previously discussed conceptual framework. Though the interview questions were grounded in the theoretical framework, they were conducted in a semi-structured manner. Many IS researchers have utilized semi-structured interviewing techniques such as Earl (1993), Orlikowski (1993), Reich and Benbasat (2000), and Wilson and Howcroft (2002). The semi-structured nature of the interview questions helped facilitate affective aspects. As discussed in the framework, affective aspects refer to subjective value judgments. Immediately after each of the interviews, the investigator debriefed. This process of immediate "debriefing" helped clarify the researcher's interpretations and deepen his level of understanding (Walsham, 1993).

Besides gathering data, the interviews served as subject recruitment opportunities. The process of building the network of interviewees was done in a "referral" manner. This means that the interviewees themselves will point the researcher to the next best contacts in which to continue the interview process. The point of saturation (Walsham, 1993) became apparent when the same names began to appear. It was at this point that the totality of who the stakeholders were that were involved in the IS Security policy process became clear.

Once the interview process was complete, the data was interpreted by the researcher (Walsham, 1993). This process involved a systematic analysis and categorization of the data by emergent themes that the researcher identified. These themes were not known a priori but emerged as the data was categorized by thematic principles. These thematic principles, which included such topics as security awareness, deterrence, and resistance, emerged in part from existing themes in the security literature and by the data gathered in the course of the study. The result of this process is explored in the Discussion section.

CASE STUDY

The case study took place at the University over the course of a one year period. The number of students at the University totaled more than 30,000 at the time of the study. There were over 3000 faculty members and 18,000 staff members. Though this was a very large site, the context of the study was limited to a relatively small IT department in the university. This limitation was due to the study examining the process of IS Security policy formulation and implementation. It was only these select subjects that had a hand in that process. The extended time required for the study was a result of difficult access to the subjects as well as multiple visits to subjects. The security officer was interviewed four times and the CIO was interviewed three times. During the course of the study, both the CIO and security officer were removed from their positions and new employees replaced them. This required yet more follow up interviews.

Initially, the recruitment strategy involved fostering a growing communicative network starting with a single participant. This participant is a known associate or "insider" (Walsham, 1993). With her technical position in the University and involvement in the SPT, she was in a situation where she knew individuals who were most directly tied to the process of IS Security Policy formulation. This network of participants became saturated towards the end of the study. By the end of the study, the total number of participants totaled 20 subjects. This group of subjects represented approximately 50% of the people within the IT department at the University.

DENOTATIVE DESCRIPTIONS

The first semantic element, as discussed in the semantic theory section, is denotative descriptions. Given the concrete nature of this element, in that it is simply a statement of something that exists, it was relatively straightforward to devise areas of exploration concerning policy. Regarding policy formulation, questions included the following: How secure is the system in question? What are the current known vulnerabilities of the system? How many and what kinds of security incidents have occurred with the current system? On the policy implementation side, the questions were as straightforward in content but actually more difficult to answer. These included the following: Is the IS Security Policy in place easily accessible by the users and IS staff? Is the IS security policy required reading for all the users of the system? Are the IS Security Policy procedures actually followed by the IS users?

A member of the Security Planning Team, an operating systems analyst, was vague in his answer regarding the level of security of the system. Specifically, he stated that:

It's as secure as it can be in our University environment. We don't want to lock everything down but we don't want to be attacked either.

This strongly speaks towards a lack of control over the control itself as described by Baskerville and Siponen (2002) The perspective was substantiated by the view of an administrative member of the university's IS security policy advisory board. She stated that *the labs are set up by a staff of students with limited technical skills*. This interpretation was reinforced by a number of relatively serious incidents described by the interviewee. The security officer explained how users of the system continuously violate policy by downloading copyrighted material (particularly music) through the University network. University servers are routinely hacked by outside entities. The security officer cited another example, where users disregard policy by opening executable attachments to email. The consequences to the University network were catastrophic at times due to the inevitable viruses and worms that are ahead of the virus definitions of the virus scanners. On the implementation side, the Chief Information Officer (CIO) and some of the lower level network administrators provided pertinent information. It was quite surprising that none of the administrators were even aware that a specific IS Security Policy even existed. The CIO stated that:

We could probably make [the policy] more visible. If an IT administrator wanted to find, they wouldn't have much of a problem but most users wouldn't know where to start.

What further intensifies the issue is that the policy is in fact required reading by all users of the system. When an account is created, a user has to certify (by placing an 'x' in a box next to a statement saying they read the policy) that they have read the IS Security Policy. If the relatively savvy and experienced network administrators ignored this, it is pretty clear that the average user would as well. This lack of awareness (Schultz, 2004; Straub & Welke, 1998; Trompeter & Eloff, 2001; Willison, 2002) can significantly lead to an increase in a system's risk to attack.

AFFECTIVE DESCRIPTIONS

Affective descriptions make up the second semantic element. This deals with issues that are more based on subjective feelings and human values. Regarding policy formulation, the following types of questions would need to be addressed: What is the current sentiment among the IS staff about the level of security with the IS? Do the IS users feel that the current level of security is acceptable? How much of a burden do the IS users feel the current security measures cause? Because policy tends to be a behind-the-scenes issue with many users, gauging emotional reactions is slightly more difficult. None-the-less, the areas identified included determining whether the IS security policy was written in simple language that most (non-technical) users could easily understand and whether the procedures detailed in the IS security policy are ridiculed or readily accepted by the IS users.

The unique environment of the organization, in that it is a state University, affected this area of the semantic analysis. According to the CIO, the sentiment of staff towards the IS security policy "depends on which staff you talk to." A faculty member of the security planning team stated that, in her department:

The users are content and aware of the policy but in other departments, people either don't seem like they know about security concerns or don't care about them.

The relationship between decentralized organizations and decentralized IS services is discussed in the literature (Olson & Chervaney, 1980). It seems though that this attitude reverses quite quickly when additional security measures are suggested. Prior in the paper, an example of poor security was presented via users opening and distributing executable email attachments. Given the lag of virus definitions to keep up with the incredibly fast distribution of new viruses, this practice often caused disastrous results. The security officer, with the consent of the policy committee, decided to formulate a policy which would ban all zipped and executable attachments. According to him:

The email attachment policy was met with tons of negative feedback and endless arguing [by the general user population].

It wasn't until a particularly powerful worm wreaked havoc to the University system that everyone began to agree this would be a good idea. The CIO summed up the feelings of users towards security measures by explaining that:

There is a universal response to security measures: You're making my job harder. We had a situation where we blocked ports for computers that had a web server set up but had not registered the server with us. We had a ton of faculty explode with protest. What is ironic was that ended up making my job harder.

This phenomenon of resistance to IS Security Policy implementation has not been thoroughly explored in security literature. Some issues with resistance to IS Security Policy, including user acceptance towards authentication (Furnell, Dowland, Illingworth, & Reynolds, 2000) and implementation of E-Medical records (Huston, 2001) have been examined. The area appears fertile ground for future research though.

DENOTATIVE PRESCRIPTIONS

The next major area of semantic analysis takes a step away from descriptions and moves towards prescriptions. The first classification of prescriptions, denotative, is an order, a rule or a recommendation that will denote the objects to which the prescribed action must be related. This is addressed in policy formulation by determining how the current IS Security Policy handles data security issues (confidentiality, data integrity, and availability) and how it handles socially related security issues. These were first described by as responsibility, integrity, trust, and ethicality (Backhouse, J & Dhillon, 1996). These areas address the soft issues of security that had been ignored for technical issues prior to this work. For policy implementation, it should be determined if IS users are aware of the specific security policies in terms of socially related and technically oriented security (Dhillon, G & Backhouse, 2000).

Examination of the IS Security Policy artifact reveals that it does have extensive guidelines regarding technical security. For example, it is quite detailed describing which ports should be shut and which ones should be open on servers, which applications should be restricted, and blocking executable attachments in emails to name a few. It also discusses many socially related security issues. For example, it states *Accounts and passwords may not be shared with, or used by, other persons within or outside the University*. Most of the language is vague though regarding social issues. The areas of responsibility, integrity, trust, and ethicality (Dhillon & Backhouse, 2000) are not addressed. Examples of this vague language include "Respect for the rights of others is fundamental to ethical behavior," "Actions that impede, impair or otherwise interfere with the activities of others are prohibited," and "the University may require users to limit or refrain from specific uses."

This vagueness is damaging because it fails to account for the fourth generation of security development (Siponen, M, 2001). This is detrimental because it fails to account for the social dimensions of IS security described by Dhillon and Backhouse (2001). On the implementation side, the CIO stated that users are *probably not consciously aware of most of the specific issues*. This is reinforced by interviews with network administrators. None of them were actively aware of an IS security policy, much less of the details of such a policy. They demonstrated that there is an acute need for creating and heightening socio-ethical information security awareness.

AFFECTIVE PRESCRIPTIONS

The final part of the semantic analysis, affective prescriptions, deals with the consequences of obeying or disobeying the prescriptions discovered in the previous portion. On the policy formulation side, this can be answered by determining if the consequences for non-conformation to the IS Security Policy included in said policy and if the consequences are included, are they judged to be a sufficient deterrent? Regarding policy implementation, it should be established if any personnel that have broken IS Security Policy actually were punished. Also, if they have been punished, are any of them repeat-offenders?

The policy artifact does include references to consequences but only regarding severe digressions. For example, the policy states that:

actions that threaten or cause harm to other individuals are violations of both [University] policies and of [state] and federal law. Such actions may be prosecuted through both the University judicial process and, independently, in state or federal court.

This is a scenario that is probably outside of the realm of typical IS security concerns but needs to be addressed, none-the-less. It also states that:

violations of copyright, licenses, personal privacy, or publishing obscene materials or child pornography may result in civil or criminal legal actions as well as University disciplinary actions.

Again, the consequences are either vague or outsourced to an agency that has clearly defined methods for consequences (i.e. the legal system). Going back to the copyright infringement issue, the way the University deals with this is by first shutting down the network connection and then counseling the student. Once the counseling is complete, the network connection is reestablished. A student can commit this digression over and over and receive the same minimal consequence every time. The security officer stated:

What can we do? We're really at a loss with how to deal with problems. It's not like the bulk of the users work for the organization. Anyway, they are the ones who will be sued by the copyright owner so that should be deterrent enough.

This blasé attitude is dangerous in that it completely misses the point in providing disincentives against non-compliance and the compound effect of these sanctions on others from a lack of compliance (Straub, 1990). The literature indicates that strong deterrence factors decrease insider's abuse (Lee, Lee, & yoo, 2003).

The interviews and document reviews conducted over the course of this case study shed considerable light on the policy formulation and implementation at this particular organization. Granted, it is a unique scenario, but it is indicative of the problems faced by organizations formulating and implementing policy. Ensuring users are aware of, read, and actually follow IS Security Policy is a challenging task. Coming up with good and effective policy is critical though. This is discussed in the following section.

DISCUSSION AND FUTURE TRENDS

In the analysis of the case study data, five emergent themes were identified. These themes clearly had a significant impact on the hypothesized disconnect between IS Security Policy formulation and IS Security Policy implementation. The denotative descriptions phase of semantic analysis revealed the organization had a lack of control over the control itself. The term control is being used interchangeably with policy and the lack of control demonstrated that a deliberate and concise control mechanism is necessary. Baskerville and Siponen. (2002) describe this deliberate control mechanism as a meta-policy, or that which defines who is responsible for making policies, and when such policymaking should take place. Three imperatives are defined that a meta-policy needs in order to be effective. These include suppleness, political simplicity, and being criterion-oriented (Baskerville & Siponen, 2002). The suppleness describes the ability for a quick reaction to changing environments or organizational realities. Political simplicity can aid suppleness. This is described by defining the political goal of organizational meta-policy as maximizing *policy compliance without totally outlawing non-compliance where situations warrant* (Baskerville & Siponen, 2002, p. 8). The final imperative, criterion-oriented, is described as having the policy makers have an explicit focus on the priorities of the organization. Enacting a meta-policy as described by Baskerville and Siponen (2002) could alleviate the ambiguity demonstrated by the makers of the IS Security Policy at this particular organization.

The most frequently occurring theme appeared during the investigation of the denotative description, affective description, and denotative prescription areas of semantic analysis. This was the issue of lack of awareness of the IS Security Policy. This is not a problem unique to this organization as the literature indicates that only one third of organizations provided any form of security awareness training (Willison, 2002). Furthermore:

unless the policy is brought to life through education and awareness programs, then all the work undertaken to create a policy will ultimately have been a waste of time. (Willison, 2002)

Trompeter and Eloff (2001) describe the acute need for creating and heightening socio-ethical information security awareness. This can be best done through the education and awareness programs described by Willison (2002). Of course, if such a program is not already in place, it is not likely an organization will immediately be willing to spend the resources to begin one without a concrete reason. It has been noted that *nothing in the practice of information security produces as much return on investment (ROI) as security training and awareness* (Schultz, 2004, pg 1). Schultz (2004) treats this with a healthy amount of skepticism but calls on the research community to examine the issue further. Given their perception as non-critical, training programs are quite vulnerable and having solid evidence to support their critical nature would help bolster their significance. This paper echoes the call of Schultz (2004) to see many more papers on topics related to security training and awareness. This is especially true given that the semantic analysis found this area to be the most pervasive of all the emergent themes.

Resistance to new security measures was the third emergent theme identified. As was previously stated, there is little security literature that explores this phenomenon. The issue has been touched on by Siponen (2000) who stated that resistance may arise from a person seeing certain actions as totally wrong or deficient. Furthermore, he found that if guidelines (which typically take the form of policy) are so weighty and obligatory that they lead to prescriptive states, they can cause greater risks in the form of resistance. Huston (2001) studied security issues with the implementation of E-Medical records. IS Security Policy was not at issue but Huston did find that resistance to security devices was apparent. Though vague, a starting point for dealing with resistance was stated as *eliciting the feelings of users concerning their activities and interactions may allow the change agent to positively address areas of resistance*. (Huston, 2001, pg 94). Although a lot of work has been done in the area of resistance to change (Baronas & Louis, 1988; Karahana, Straub, & Chervany, 1999; Markus, 1983; Orlikowski, 1993), there is little work that directly examines how an organization's members might resist IS Security Policy implementation.

A lack of specific and well defined socio-organizational controls was the fourth emergent theme identified. This is a still emerging area in the field of security, spearheaded by Dhillon and Backhouse (2000) and integrated into the overall structure of the development of security by Siponen (2001). Four socio-organizational principles are identified by Dhillon and Backhouse (2001). These are responsibility, integrity, trust, and ethicality. Responsibility is defined as:

not just carrying the can for when something has gone wrong in the past (accountability—for attributing blame) but refers also to handling the development of events in the future in a particular sphere. (Dhillon, G & Backhouse, 2000, pg 127)

Integrity, or the steadfast adherence to a strict moral code, can be strengthened informally secure arrangements. Trust for and within the members of an organization encompasses personal confidentiality and is reinforced by face to face contact. Ethicality, as it relates to informal norms and behavior, is introduced by the very culture of the organization. Using each of these four areas, a policy formulator can drill down and determine specific issues that can be and should be addressed by a given organization. The ad hoc, reactionary, and vague measures present in the artifact studied for this research show no such analysis.

The final emergent theme identified was the absence of an effective deterrent. The fact that college students continuously downloaded copyrighted material (Chiang & ASsane, 2007) demonstrates that the consequences to their actions did not preclude the students from carrying out those actions. Straub (1990) describes two sub-constructs to deterrence: certainty of sanction and severity of sanction. Both of these sub-constructs are called into question in this scenario. Not only are the majority of users unaware of the policy (removing any certainty of sanction unless they are repeat offenders) but when they are sanctioned, the punishment is nominal. It is reasonable to assume that if students were expelled from the University or even just lost network connectivity permanently, the copyright violation policy abuse would drop dramatically. Effective *IS deterrents result in reduced incidence of computer abuse* (Straub, 1990, p. 21). Given his findings, Straub (1990) calls for detailed IS Security Policy, the enlightenment and education of users to the policy, and effective technical controls.

CONCLUSION

The purpose of this study was to establish that a disconnect between IS Security Policy formulation and implementation exists. The problem that arises from this situation is an ineffective IS Security Policy and thus a vulnerable system. In order to examine the phenomena, we created a semantic framework which was based on Semantic Theory (Katz, 1970). This framework guided our collection of data and gave a structure for analyzing the data.

The "snapshot in time" of the lifecycle of IS Security Policy at the organization under study demonstrated that a disconnect is evident between IS Security Policy formulation and implementation. Not only were most users unaware of the existence of a IS Security Policy, but the makers of the policy were not aware of this ignorance. They did not have an opportunity to be a part of the process evolving and developing this document into an optimized form. There also was no guidance available for the formulation policy itself. Some security measures were met with stiff resistance from the user base. Socio-organizational controls were vague and ill described in the policy artifact. Finally, the sanctions to non-compliance tended to be so underwhelming that the consequence became irrelevant. The result of all of this is that you have an organization that has a chaotic and unordered security environment. The IS Security Policy artifact is far from a connecting entity between the two sides that should interact with it. The plethora of security incidents cited by the interviewees could be contained and controlled if this disconnect could be minimized.

Further research is needed to determine situation within more controlled environments, such as commercial or private organizations. Being a state educational entity may have distorted the results to a degree and having additional, more diverse data would validate the framework to a greater level. Also, this study focused on the relatively small subset of those most directly involved in policy. A quantitative examination of a wide base of users might shed some additional light on policy implementation.

REFERENCES

Ahmad, A., & Ruighavar, A. (2003). *Improved Event Logging for security and Forensics: developing audit management infrastructure requirements*. Paper presented at the Security Conference.

Anderson, P. (1990). A Theory of Computer Semiotics: Semiotic Approaches to Construction and Assessment of Computer Systems. *Computational Linguistics*, *18*(4), 555–562.

Backhouse, J. (1992). *The use of semantic analysis in the development of information systems*. London: London School of Economics.

Backhouse, J. (2000). *Searching for Meaning – Performatives and Obligations in Public Key Infrastructures*. Paper presented at the International Workshop on the Language-Action Perspective on Communication Modelling.

Backhouse, J., & Dhillon, G. (1996). Structures of Responsibility and Security of Information Systems. *European Journal of Information Systems*, *5*(1), 2–9. doi:10.1057/ejis.1996.7

Baronas, A., & Louis, M. (1988). Restoring a Sense of Control During Implementation: How User Involvement Leads to System Acceptance. *Management Information Systems Quarterly, 12*(1), 329–336. doi:10.2307/248811

Baskerville, R. (1993). Information Systems Security Design Methods: Implications for Information Systems Development. *ACM Computing Surveys, 35*(4), 375–414. doi:10.1145/162124.162127

Baskerville, R., & Siponen, M. (2002). An information security meta-policy for emergent organizations. *Logistics Information Management, 15*(5/6), 337–346. doi:10.1108/09576050210447019

Chiang, E., & Assane, D. (2007). Determinants of Music Copyright Violations on the University Campus. *Journal of Cultural Economics, 31*(3), 187–204. doi:10.100710824-007-9042-y

Coyne, J., & Kluksdahl, N. (1994). *"Mainstreaming" Automated Information Systems Security Engineering (A Case Study in Security Run Amok).* Paper presented at the ACM Conference.

Dhillon, G. (2007). *Principles of Information Systems Security: Text and Cases.* Hoboken, NJ: John Wiley & Sons.

Dhillon, G., & Backhouse, J. (2000). Information System Security Management in the New Millennium. *Communications of the ACM, 43*(7), 125–128. doi:10.1145/341852.341877

Dhillon, G., & Backhouse, J. (2001). Current Directions in IS Security Research: Towards Socio-Organizational Perspectives. *Information Systems Journal, 11*(2), 127–153. doi:10.1046/j.1365-2575.2001.00099.x

Dhillon, G., & May, J. (2006). Interpreting Security in Human-Computer Interactions: A Semiotic Analysis. In P. Zhang & D. Galletta (Eds.), *Human-Computer Interaction and Management Information Systems: Foundations.* Armonk, NY: M.E. Sharp.

Earl, M. (1993). Experiences in Strategic Information Systems Planning. *Management Information Systems Quarterly, 17*(1), 1–24. doi:10.2307/249507

Fitzgerald, B. (1998). An empirical investigation into the adoption of systems development methodologies. *Information & Management, 34*(6), 317–328. doi:10.1016/S0378-7206(98)00072-X

Furnell, S., Dowland, P., Illingworth, H., & Reynolds, P. (2000). Authentication and Supervision: A Survey of User Attitudes. *Computers & Security, 19*(6), 529–539. doi:10.1016/S0167-4048(00)06027-2

George, R. (2013). How Cybercriminals Choose Their Targets and Tactics. *Information Week.*

Glasgow, J., Macewen, G., & Panangaden, P. (1992). A Logic for Reasoning about Security. *ACM Transactions on Computer Systems, 10*(3), 226–264. doi:10.1145/146937.146940

Howcroft & Trauth. (2005). *Handbook of Critical Information Systems Research.* Northampton, UK: Edward Elgar Publishing, Inc.

Huston, T. (2001). Security Issues for Implementation of E-Medical Records. *Communications of the ACM, 44*(9), 89–94. doi:10.1145/383694.383712

Joshi, J., Ghafoor, A., Aref, W. G., & Spafford, E. H. (2001). Digital Government Security Infrastructure Design Challenges. *Computer, 34*(2), 66–72. doi:10.1109/2.901169

Karahana, E., Straub, D., & Chervany, N. (1999). Information Technology Adoption Across Time: A Cross-Sectional Comparison of Pre-Adoption and Post-Adoption Beliefs. *Management Information Systems Quarterly, 23*(2), 183–213. doi:10.2307/249751

Katz, J. (1970). *Semantic Theory*. New York: Harper and Row.

Knapp, K., Marshall, T., Rainer, R. Jr, & Ford, N. (2007). Information Security Effectiveness: Conceptualization and Validation of a Theory. *International Journal of Information Security and Privacy, 1*(2), 37–60. doi:10.4018/jisp.2007040103

Kühnhauser, W. (1999). Policy Groups. *Computers & Security, 18*(4), 351–363. doi:10.1016/S0167-4048(99)80081-9

Lee, S., Lee, S.-G., & Yoo, S. (2003). An integrative model of computer abuse based on social control and general deterrence theories. *Information & Management, 41*(6), 707–718. doi:10.1016/j.im.2003.08.008

Liebenau, J., & Backhouse, J. (1990). *Understanding Information: An Introduction*. London: Macmillan. doi:10.1007/978-1-349-11948-6

Markus, M. (1983). Power, Politics, and MIS Implementation. *Communications of the ACM, 26*(6), 430–444. doi:10.1145/358141.358148

Mintzberg, H. (1983). *Structures in Fives: Designing Effective Organizations*. Englewood Cliffs, NJ: Prentice Hall.

Mintzberg, H., Lampel, J., Quinn, J., & Goshal, S. (2003). *The Strategy Process*. Prentice Hall.

Morris, C. (1970). *Foundations of the Unity Of Science: Toward an International Encyclopedia of Unified Science*. Chicago: University of Chicago Press.

Olson, M., & Chervaney, N. (1980). The Relationship between Organizational Characteristics and the Structure of the Information Services Function. *Management Information Systems Quarterly, 4*(2), 57–68. doi:10.2307/249337

Orlikowski, W. (1993). CASE Tools as Organizational Change: Investigating Incremental and Radical Changes in Systems Development. *Management Information Systems Quarterly, 17*(3), 309–340. doi:10.2307/249774

Ponemon, L. (2017). *2017 Cost of Data Breach Study*. IBM Security and Ponemon Institute LLC.

Purkait, S. (2012). Phishing Counter Measures and Their Effectiveness - Literature Review. *Information Management & Computer Security, 20*(5), 382–420. doi:10.1108/09685221211286548

Rees, J., Subhajyoti, S., & Spafford, E. (2003). PFIRES: A Policy Framework for Information Security. *Communications of the ACM, 46*(7), 101–106. doi:10.1145/792704.792706

Reich, B., & Benbasat, I. (2000). Factors that influence the social dimension of alignment between business and information technology objectives. *Management Information Systems Quarterly, 24*(1), 81–113. doi:10.2307/3250980

Richardson, R. (2008). *2008 CSI Computer Crime & Security Survey*. Computer Security Institute.

Schultz, E. (2004). The case for one-time credentials. *Computers & Security, 23*(6), 441–442. doi:10.1016/j.cose.2004.08.001

SecureWorks. (2017). *State of Cybercrime: Exposing the threats, techniques and markets that fuel the economy of cybercriminals*. Atlanta, GA: SecureWorks.

Siponen, M. (2000). A conceptual foundation for organizational information security awareness. *Information Management & Computer Security, 8*(1), 31–41. doi:10.1108/09685220010371394

Siponen, M. (2001). An analysis of the traditional IS security approaches: Implications for research and practice. *Information Management & Computer Security, 8*(1), 31. doi:10.1108/09685220010371394

Sommestad, T., Karlzén, H., & Hallberg, J. (2015). A Meta-Analysis of Studies on Protection Motivation Theory and Information Security Behaviour. *International Journal of Information Security and Privacy, 9*(1), 26–46. doi:10.4018/IJISP.2015010102

Stamper, R. (1973). *Information in Business and Administrative Systems*. New York: Halstead Press.

Straub, D. Jr. (1990). Effective IS Security: An Empirical Study. *Information Systems Research, 1*(3), 255–276. doi:10.1287/isre.1.3.255

Straub, D., & Welke, R. (1998). Coping with Systems Risk: Security Planning Models for Management Decision Making. *Management Information Systems Quarterly, 22*(4), 441–469. doi:10.2307/249551

Trompeter, C., & Eloff, J. (2001). A Framework for the Implementation of Socio-ethical Controls in Information Security. *Computers & Security, 20*(5), 384–391. doi:10.1016/S0167-4048(01)00507-7

Ulrich, W. (2001). A Philosophical Staircase for Information Systems Definition, Design, and Development. *Journal of Information Technology Theory and Application, 3*, 55–84.

Walsham, G. (1993). *Interpreting Information Systems in Organizations*. Chichester, UK: Wiley.

Willison, R. (2002). *Opportunities for Computer Abuse: Assessing a Crime Specific Approach in the Case of Barings Bank* (Unpublished Dissertation). London School of Economics, London, UK.

Wilson, M., & Howcroft, D. (2002). Re-conceptualising failure: Social shaping meets IS research. *European Journal of Information Systems, 11*(4), 236–250. doi:10.1057/palgrave.ejis.3000437

APPENDIX

Table 2. Conceptual Framework for Semantic Analysis

Semantic Element	Description and seminal works	Semantic Issues in IS Security Policy Formulation	Semantic Issues in IS Security Policy Implementation
Denotative Descriptions • Designation • Facts • Evidence • Forecasts	This semantic element is simply a statement of something that exists. (Stamper, 1973) The nature of the environment in which the organism operates."" (Morris, 1970).	What are the known current vulnerabilities of the system in question? How technically secure is the IS in its current state? How physically (and socially) secure is the IS in its current state? How many and what kind of security incidents have occurred with the current system?	Is the security policy in place easily accessible by the users and IS staff? Is the security policy required reading for all the users of the system? Are the security policy procedures actually followed by the IS users?
Affective Descriptions • Appraisals • Value • judgments	Value judgments: reports on staff, estimates of the relative difficulties of jobs. (Stamper, 1973) How the actor can transfer his choice of an impulse-satisfying object from the consummation phase to the orientation phase. (Morris 1970)	What is the current sentiment among the IS staff about the level of security with the IS? Do the IS users feel that the current level of security is acceptable? How much of a burden do the IS users feel the current security measures cause?	Is the security policy written in simple language that most (non-technical) users could easily understand? Are the procedures detailed in the security policy ridiculed or readily accepted by the IS users (i.e. regular password changing is rarely followed)?
Denotative Prescriptives • Instructions • Plans • Policies • orders	An order, a rule or a recommendation that will denote the objects to which the prescribed action must be related. (Stamper, 1973) Guide the actor's behavior according to the ways in which the organism must act upon the environment in order to satisfy its need. (Morris, 1970).	How does the current security policy handle non-compliance? Are the consequences for non-conformation to the security policy included in said policy?	Are IS users aware of the specific security policies in terms technical security? Are IS users aware of the specific security policies in terms of social security?
Affective Prescriptives • Inducements • Coercion • Threats • rewards	"Words may have the superficial appearance of a command or law but their prescriptive standing is only justifiable in so far as they arouse expectations about the consequences of obeying or disobeying them." (Stamper, 1973)	If the consequences are included, are they judged to be a sufficient deterrent? How much of a burden is security policy enforcement?	Have any personnel that have broken security policy actually been punished? If they have been punished, are any of them repeat-offenders?

Section 4
Intrusion Detection Systems

Chapter 10
Intrusion Detection Systems Alerts Reduction:
New Approach for Forensics Readiness

Aymen Akremi
Umm Al-Qura University, Saudi Arabia

Hassen Sallay
Umm Al-Qura University, Saudi Arabia

Mohsen Rouached
Sultan Qaboos University, Oman

ABSTRACT

Investigators search usually for any kind of events related directly to an investigation case to both limit the search space and propose new hypotheses about the suspect. Intrusion detection system (IDS) provide relevant information to the forensics experts since it detects the attacks and gathers automatically several pertinent features of the network in the attack moment. Thus, IDS should be very effective in term of detection accuracy of new unknown attacks signatures, and without generating huge number of false alerts in high speed networks. This tradeoff between keeping high detection accuracy without generating false alerts is today a big challenge. As an effort to deal with false alerts generation, the authors propose new intrusion alert classifier, named Alert Miner (AM), to classify efficiently in near real-time the intrusion alerts in HSN. AM uses an outlier detection technique based on an adaptive deduced association rules set to classify the alerts automatically and without human assistance.

INTRODUCTION

With the growth of digital world, malicious viruses or generally digital attacks are in continuous spreading using different methods and techniques making their detection very hard especially for unknown attacks which are malicious threat that their signature and updating security provisions databases or exploited vulnerability are not determined yet . Therefore, the compromised systems are seriously damaged. Vul-

DOI: 10.4018/978-1-5225-5583-4.ch010

nerabilities may occur due to several factors such as human breaking of security policies which in turn may be exploited by malicious threats. The anomaly based intrusion detection systems are known by their high accuracy of unknown attacks detection since each new network behavior is considered as an attack. This feature makes anomaly-based intrusion detection systems largely used by organization and governments to protect from digital attacks and specially unknown attacks.

However, the use of data gathered from IDS for forensics purposes has initiated several discussions (Sommer, 1998; Stephenson, 2000; Yuil, 1999). The challenge is how much the IDS can meet and respect legal requirements in terms of integrity and original data preservation when collecting evidence during ongoing attacks. Although IDSs are not designed to collect and protect the integrity of the type of information required to conduct law enforcement investigation (Sommer, 1998), Yuil et al (Yuil, 1999) claimed that the IDSs are able to collect enough information during an ongoing attack to profile the attacker. The IDS may help detecting attacks in an early stage and therefore giving the opportunity to improve the readiness of the forensics system. Also, it links attack to events and gives a profound understanding of the attack type and targeted component which facilitates the suggestion of hypothesis about the suspect and help locate in advance the files and logs to be analyzed. The proposed digital forensics framework for SOA should include a smart log manager system allowing the collection, integration, reduction, and manipulation of the gathered logs from different components and security tools as IDS. However, IDS are known by their tremendous amount of the security alerts due to the high speed alert generation throughput and sensitivity to new network behavior which make the forensics management of intrusion detection alerts both compute and memory intensive. Obviously, the high level rate of wrong alerts reduces the performance and efficiency of IDS which minimizes its capability to prevent attacks and make the alert analysis tasks very difficult and time consuming.

In this chapter, we focus on the design and the implementation of an efficient IDS alert classifier that helps investigators to analyze the gathered data in real or near real time and improve the live forensics readiness to be used by the log management system under the log reduction and manipulation. More specifically, we propose Alert Miner; a classifier using a new alert classification algorithm based on a frequent pattern outlier detection data mining approach. The rest of this chapter is organized as follows: section 2 presents related work to IDS alert classification, section 3 shows the IDS alert processing model and the main data mining techniques used in the network specification extraction and classification improvement and section 4 presents the algorithm description. Section 5 shows the results of our implementation and our performance study. Finally, in section 6, we conclude the chapter by discussing the proposed approach, and proposing some future works.

RELATED WORK

Digital security attacks are being more sophisticated, unpredictable and frequent. Their danger is becoming more serious with the emergence of High-Speed Networks like Infiniband and Gigabit-Ethernet. New serious management problems mainly related to real time constraints, scalability, efficiency and portability raise key challenges to Intrusion Detection Systems successful deployment until now. More specifically the tremendous amount of security alerts due to the high speed alert generation throughput make the management of intrusion detection process both compute and memory intensive. Obviously the high level rate of wrong alerts degrades performance and efficiency of IDS which reduce its capability to prevent attacks and make the alert analysis tasks very difficult. Intensive research efforts have been proposed in the literature to address these challenges but few of them have been dedicated to forensics purposes in high speed network context. Since data mining techniques have the capacity to handle large amount of data (traffic, alert file logs, etc...) in short time (P. U.Fayyad, 1996), it was and still being used by many researchers to extract properties from huge IDS alerts logs. These extracted properties and information from file logs are used within appropriate techniques to predict and classify new coming alerts.

The approaches that have been proposed to identify and reduce IDS alerts using data mining techniques can be divided into three categories:

Methods Based on Classification

Vaarandi (2010) and Vaarandi (2009) propose a data mining method for distinguishing important network IDS alerts from frequently occurring false positives and events of low importance. Knowledge is mined from IDS logs and processed in order to build an alert classifier. The classifier is then used in real-time environment for distinguishing important IDS alerts called "interesting" from frequently occurring false positives and events of low importance named "routine"(Vaarandi, 2010) discovered that only 10 prolific signatures trigger over than 95% of alerts. Similar results were yielded by (J. D. Viinikka, H.Mé,L. Lehikoinen,A.Tarvainen,M, 2009)and(J. D. Viinikka, H.Mé,L.Séguier,R.Tarvainen,M, 2006). Moreover, according to (Vaarandi, 2010)and (J. D. Viinikka, H.Mé,L. Lehikoinen,A.Tarvainen,M, 2009) the signatures that trigger alerts frequently over long periods of time are relatively small and produce most of these alerts with vast majority of them being either false positive or alerts that correspond to normal behaviors. Pietraszek (2004) propose another classifier. It firstly generates training examples based on the analyst's feedback. Then, these data are used by machine learning techniques to initially build and subsequently update the classifier. Finally, the classifier is used to process new alerts. The above methods can classify alerts automatically. They have unfortunately three main drawbacks namely (1) the fact that they are based on training data which collection is labor intensive, (2) that they are error prone and, (3) they do not support high speed networks.

Authors in Bhuyan, Bhattacharyya, and Kalita (2014) surveys anomaly based detection methods, systems and tools. They conclude that a normal model must be learned using feature from several resources (system, security provision, network tools) to surround all possible paths may be used by the attacker. Also, they recommend the use of combination of supervised (based on signatures and predefined rules) and unsupervised (outlier and clusters based) to accurately build normal behavior and reduce false positives. A dynamic update of normal model should be maintained without decreasing the detection performance in the case of over model training. In (Grill, Pevný, and Rehak (2017) authors uses Local Adaptive Multivariate Smoothing (LAMS) to smooth the output of anomaly detectors by replacing the anomaly detector's output on a network event with an aggregate of its output on all similar network events observed previously. The paper Shittu, Healing, Ghanea-Hercock, Bloomfield, and Rajarajan (2015) uses post correlation methods to reduce false positive alerts. It consists on the use of new metric for prioritising alerts based on anomalous behavior, a new method for applying clustering on correlated alerts, and an improved data structure for representing robust attack patterns. They achieve 97% of false positive alert reduction. However, this approach requires hard training of attack patterns which in turn Bayes approach are used to corrolate alerts due to its simple training and without predfined knowledge (Goeschel, 2016; Ramaki, Khosravi-Farmad, & Bafghi, 2015). Also, clustering algorithms are used with fuzzy C mean algorithm, to identify false alerts, to reduce invalid alerts and to purify alerts for a better analysis (Liang, Taihui, Nannan, & Jiejun, 2015). Genetic algorithms are also used in classifying

IDS alerts and reducing flase positive alerts but still complains from the large training time(Narsingyani & Kale, 2015). Paper Meng, Li, and Kwok (2015) uses k-nearest-neighbor clusterin approach to filter unwanted IDS alerts based on experts knowldge.

Methods Based on Root Causes Analysis

Driven by fact that small number of root causes generally accounts for over then 90% of all alerts (K.Julish, 2001)and most of these root causes are related to configuration issues which triggers false positive alerts. K.Julish (2001) proposed a semi-automatic clustering method to identify and resolve the root causes of false positive alerts. The identification of root causes is handled by clustering and grouping similar alerts and assuming that these alerts have the same root causes. Then, in a second step, summarizing each alert cluster into single generalized alert in order to simplify the identification of root causes. But, this method builds generalized hierachy for each attribute which is not easy and depends on the experience of domain experts and collecting enough background knowledge. Also this method supports only off-line process. In Cotroneo, Paudice, and Pecchia (2016) authors use weighing approach of relevant alert attributes to determine the root causes of false alerts. Then, they adopt a clustering approach to classify alerts based on the alert attributes weights which enable a minimum human intervention and improve the alert tagging automation.

Methods Based on the Assumption That Frequent Alert Sequences Are Likely Resulted From Normal Behavior (Xiao, 2010)

Xiao (2010) describes a new data mining method for reducing IDS false positive alerts. They designed a frequent pattern outlier detection method aiming to identify true alerts from the false positives ones based on the alert attribute frequency. Then, it determines the threshold of true alerts after extracting all frequent alert patterns. Besides, it classifies new coming alerts into false positive or true ones based on the predefined threshold. (J. D. Viinikka, H.Mé,L.Séguier,R.Tarvainen,M, 2006) filters IDS alerts by monitoring alert flow. It models regularities in alert flow with classical time series methods. After removing the periodic components, slowly changed trend and random noise from time series, the reaming is regarded as true alerts. (Clifton, 2000) adopts the assumption that *normal operation often produces traffic that matches likely attack signatures resulting in false alerts*. Based on the above assumption, they proposed to use generalized frequent episodes as a data mining technique in order to identify the frequent sequences of alerts from IDS file logs. When the frequent sequences of alerts having the same destination are found, they will be presented to users in order to determine whether they are false positive or not. This method enables the construction of custom site-specific filters aiming to improve the selectivity of IDS. The above methods, except (Xiao, 2010) are based on modeling false positives by frequent or periodic alert sequences. It is effective in the environment where normal behavior normal change. However, it often mistakes the new normal behavior or infrequent ones for true alerts. This assumption is also used by (Cotroneo et al., 2016) to create weight for frequent alerts and classify them using clustering approach.

ALERT PROCESSING MODEL AND TECHNIQUES

In the purpose to avoid the loss of data when classifying and filtering IDS alerts using our new approach, we present the following model (see Figure 1) which consists essentially on the storage of all generated alerts and only forward true positive alerts to the forensics investigator in real-time. This model is integrated in the reduction component under the log management system.

Thus, we preserve all generated alerts and avoid the loss of misclassified true alerts and keeping high live forensics readiness. Also, the forensics investigator can verify the false classified alerts when required. The alert miner classifier consists on the use of an adaptive outlier detection algorithm based on automatic network specification for identifying relevant alerts. This method uses two main data mining techniques which are:

- **Feature Selection of Relevant Alert Attributes:** For Intrusion Detection Systems, ranking the relevance of features is a problem of significant interest, since the elimination of irrelevant or useless inputs leads to a simplification of the problem and may allow faster and more accurate detection. This is especially critical for the construction of efficient real-time IDS able to comply with the constraints of high speed networks. We applied a heuristic for variable selection (HVS) technique which is a neural network based feature selection on a sample of alerts from the used dataset Kyoto 2006+ including 24 attributes for each alert. Then, we select the best five discriminative attributes having the best impact on the alert classification. Using only five attributes instead of 24 may significantly reduce the classification processing time and therefore keep up with the HSN.

Figure 1. NIDS alerts processing model

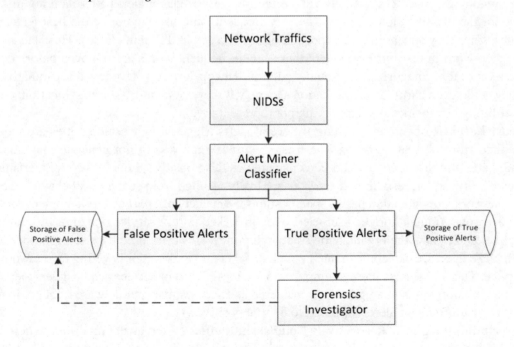

- **Association Rules for Adaptive Network Specification Extraction:** Association rules is first introduced in Agrawal (1993) for extracting interesting correlations, frequent patterns, associations or casual structures among sets of items in the transaction databases or other data repositories. Association rule mining is to find out association rules that satisfy the predefined minimum support and confidence from a given database. These parameters determine the interestingness of such rules. In our outlier detection method, we benefit from the efficiency of association rules to depict suspicious and trust regularities and relations mined form historical detected alerts. Then we adopt these rules as network specification used for the score calculation of new coming alerts. We update the specification files continuously by new rules each time we receive new alerts. The introduction of association rules in our method reduces the tedious task of human research of network specifications. Also, it resolves the problem of specification dependence to networks and automatically locates strong relations and determines the relevant network specifications.

ALERT MINER CLASSIFIER

Classification Criteria

While *Alert Pattern frequency* is a good classification criterion for several data mining application fields it is not discriminative enough to capture correctly all the true positive alerts or at least minimize the alert misclassification to its minimal level. For that purpose we propose that an alert pattern will be selected according to three following criteria:

- **Frequency Degree (Respectively Infrequency):** Very frequent alert pattern are not discriminative for the classification process. The very frequent patterns may not be the best feature candidates, since they appear in a large portion of the data set, in different classes. This is analogous to the stop word in text retrieval where those highly frequent words are removed before document retrieval or text categorization. Equally pattern that appear rarely have low discriminative power. They could even harm the classification accuracy if they are included for classification, due to the over fitting effect since the features are not representative.
- **Trust Level (Respectively Untrust):** Several alerts triggered by trusted entities are most likely resulted from normal behavior. The trusted entities supposed to not generate malicious traffic and therefore these alerts should be considered as false positive. Equally several alerts targeting locked ports and access-limited services are likely resulted from suspicious behavior. Generally, any network's organization has its specifications. Some network port or services are not accessible for everyone. If unauthorized user tries to log in locked port or service one time we can conclude that he didn't know the organization's network policy. However, if he tries several times to log in to a locked port we can confirm that he is an attacker and looking for breaking the network port or service. The IDS detects these attempts to log in locked port or services and triggers alerts. These alerts are not frequent enough to be considered as false positives but they are frequent in the context of just infrequent alerts supposed to be true positives.
- **Discrimination Level (Respectively Nondiscrimination):** Alert attributes differ in their discriminative weight according to their presence in both false and true positive alerts or just in one of them. One time an attribute appears in both sets, it means that it is not a discriminant element to

distinguish between the two sets. While, the attribute can significantly determine the alert set if it belongs only to one set all the time.

Algorithm Design

Based on the aforementioned refinements/assumptions, we propose our Alert Miner outlier detection algorithm. Mainly, the algorithm contains four phases which are initialization, learning, online and update.

Algorithm 1: Alert Miner Outlier Detection Algorithm (Main)

Phase 1: Initialization
1: Construct LDataSet (Learning data set), TDataSet (Test data set)
2: Select relevant alert attributes using feature selection method (HVS)
3: Generate frequent/infrequent item sets from learning data (FI)
4: RT(Right truncate for ignoring negligible itemset greater then RT),LT(Left truncate for ignoring negligible
itemset less then LT)
5: Fix Minsupp(Minimum support), C (Confidence)
6: Fix Lsize(Local size), Gsize(Global size),P(Percentage of true positive alerts)
Phase 2: Learning phase
7: Generate rules of suspicious activities from learning data
8: Compute the frequent based weight (FW), Trust rule based weight (TRW), and Suspicious rules based weight (SRW)
9: Compute the traffic behavior (TB) //Based on the frequency of the received alerts
10: Calculate the frequent based threshold (FT), Trust rule based threshold (TRT),
 Suspicious rule based threshold (SRT)
Phase 3: Online phase
11: Saving each new coming alerts (A) and increment the number of alerts AN
12: Compute the alert frequent based score (AFS)
13: **If** AFS < FT&&TB is normal **Then**
14:    Compute the suspicious alert rule based score (SAS)
15:    **If** SAS ≤SRT **Then**
16:     TAG(A)←TP
17:    **Else**
18:     TAG(A)←FP
19:    **End If**
20: **End If**
21: **If** AFS ≥ FT&&TB is normal **Then**
22:    Compute the alert trust rule based score (ATS)
23:    **If** ATS ≤ TRT Then
24:     TAG(A)←FP

```
25:   Else
26:     TAG(A)←TP
27:   End If
28: End If
29: If AFS ≤ FT&&TB is attack Then
30:     Compute the alert trust rule based score (ATS)
31:   If ATS ≤ TRT Then
32:      TAG(A)←FP
33:   Else
34:      TAG(A)←TP
35:   End If
36: End If
37: If AFS ≥ FT&&TB is attack Then
38:     Compute the suspicious alert rule based score (SAS)
39:   If SAS ≥ SRT Then
40:     TAG(A)←TP
41:   Else
42:     TAG(A)←FP
43:   End If
44: End If
Phase 4: Update phase
45: If AN % Lsize== 0 Then
46:    We update only the feature set locally
47: Else
48: If AN % Gsize == 0&&TB is changed Then
49:    We update the feature set & the association rules & the alert attributes
weights & the threshold
50: End IfInitialization Phase
```

In this phase we:

- Collect n alerts randomly from the dataset in order to construct the learning dataset. The rest of the dataset will be considered as the testing dataset.
- Select relevant alert attributes using feature selection techniques HVS (Heuristic for Variable Selection)(Yacoub, 1997).
- Run FP-Growth algorithm on the learning dataset to produce a set of all possible itemsets with their supports.
- Related to the frequency degree criterion, (R. Chirkova, 2007)proves that the minsupport values near 0 and 1 are not highly discriminative to determine frequent itemsets enabling efficient data classification. By ignoring the itemsets with minsupport values near 0 or 1, not only we improve the learning and the update process speed but also we reduce the feature set to only more discriminative patterns which enables high classification efficiency. Furthermore this filtering step will

systematically filter frequent attacks such as denial of service attack if their frequency is greater than a specific threshold in specific time period.

- After truncating the very frequent (minsupport near to 1) and the very infrequent (minsupport near to 0) we get our set of all remaining itemsets. Finally in this phase we fix some parameters required in the other phases.

Learning Phase

- Generate rules of suspicious/normal activities from learning data to find out association rules that satisfy the predefined minimum support and confidence from a given database. These parameters determine the interestingness of such rules. In our detection method, we benefit from the efficiency of association rules to depict from small labeled alerts suspicious and trust relations between networks attributes and then we use these rules on the classification of new coming alerts. The introduction of association rules in our method reduces the human research of network specifications tasks. Also, it resolves the problem of specification dependence to networks and automatically locates strong relations and determines the network specifications.

- Compute the discriminative weight(or frequent based weight): we compute for each frequent pattern X its discriminative level by calculating the discriminative weight for each of its attributes. Then, the weight of X is set to the largest weight of all attributes it contains. For each attribute we trace its values presence in false and true positive alerts. If an attribute value appears in both sets, it means that this attribute value is not discriminant element to distinguish between the two sets. While, when the attribute value belongs only to one set all the time its discrimination is significant. To compute the global weight W_i for each attribute, we start by classifying all alerts used for the training phase into two classes; true positives and false positives. Secondly, for each attributes i, all frequent values of it were found, and the total number (recorded as S_i) of frequent values that appeared in both false positives and true ones was calculated. After that, the weight of attribute$_i$ (i.e. weight$_i$) is calculated according to Formula 1:

$$Wi = 1 - \frac{Si}{Ti} \tag{1}$$

where T_i is the total number of frequent values of the attribute.

Finally, we repeat the above steps for several times, and we set the weight of each attribute to the mean of the results we got in each round.

- **Compute Rules Based Weights:** Based on the extracted rules, we compute the weight W_i of each attribute as shown in the following formula:

$$Wi = 1 - \frac{\sum ACi}{Ti * RFi * TA} \tag{2}$$

where AC_i is the confidence value of the rule containing the attribute value i, T_i is the frequency of the attribute value i in the learning data set, RF_i is the frequency of the attribute value i in rules specification file, and TA is the total number of the alerts in the learning data set. This weight gives more impact to the attributes having more confidence to be true alerts or false ones.

- Computing the traffic behavior (*TB*) based on the frequency of the received alerts in order to know whether the frequent alerts are true or false. If this indicator shows a traffic with majority of true alerts, the alert miner classifier assigns for the alerts with high scores (more frequent) true label whereas the remaining alerts (with low scores) false label.
- Set the frequent based, suspicious and trust rule based thresholds (resp *FT*, *SRT*, *TRT*): this step starts as shown in the algorithm 2 by computing for each alert a score followed by ordering them ascendenly or descendenly depending to the traffic behavior *TB*. Then, we select the first *p%* as candidate true or false alerts. The threshold of true positive or false positive alerts is set to the largest or smallest alert score from the selected set of alerts.

Algorithm 2: Compute Threshold

```
1: Function ComputeThreshold(P,CD,FS,WeightSet)
2: Alertscore← 0
3: For each alert a ∈ CD Do
4:     For each itemset X ∈ FS Do
5:         If a contains X Then
6:             Alertscore ← Alertscore + weightSet(X) * support
7:         End If
8:     End For
9: End For
10: Order CD (scored alerts) ascendly or descendly based on the
traffic behavior
11: Return Threshold ← Alertscore ( nb(CD)*P/100 ) //Set the threshold on the
Pᵗʰ alert Alertscore form CD
12: End Function Online Phase
```

The main work in this phase is calculating the score for each new coming alert, and then comparing this score with the convenient threshold, so as to determine it is true or false. Besides, the feature set is updated continually in order to keep its accuracy. Detailed process in this phrase is presented as follows:

It begins by filtering each new coming Alert. When a new alert come, it is firstly put into the alert cache, then its score is calculated based on the feature set by CalculateAlertScore(see Algorithm 3) If the score is not bigger than the threshold in the case of normal traffic behavior for example, this alert is regarded as true and is recommended to users, otherwise it is discarded.

Algorithm 3: Alert Score Computing

```
1: Function CalculateAlertScore(P,alert,FS,WeightSet)
2: Alertscore←0
```

```
3: For each itemset X ∈ FS Do
4:    If alert contains X Then
5:        Alertscore ← Alertscore + weightSet(X)*support
6:    End If
7: End For
8: Return FPscore
9: End Function
```

Update Phase

In this phase we update the feature set of frequent, infrequent alerts,and the rule set and we check the traffic behavior. As soon as the account of alerts in cache(new received alerts) is equal to n, a frequent itemset and association rules data mining techniques are executed on these alerts. After checking the traffic behavior, we add the rules and the new itemsets to the convenient sets. As to the patterns that the feature set already has, we only need to update the support, i.e., their supports in feature set are set to the mean of the new support and the old one. Finally, we store all alerts in cache into alert database, and then we clear up the cache (see Algorithm 4). We should mention that with the coming of new alerts, the threshold calculated based on the early feature set will become inaccurate gradually. Moreover, although the feature set is updated continually, some global patterns are still possibly missed. So it is necessary to mine the whole alert databases so as to adjust the threshold and the support of frequent patterns. This process can be done at comparatively long intervals. And in order to avoid affecting the real-time filtering, it had better be executed in background off-line.

Algorithm 4: Update

```
1: Procedure ParametersUpdate (P,LD,MinSupport,FS,WeightSet,Flag)
2: IFS ← FP-Growth(LD,MinSupport) //generating frequent itemsets
3: For X ∈ IFS Do
4:    If FS contains X Then // If feature set exist
5:        Support(FS(X)) ← (Support(IFS(X) + (SupportFS(X)/2) //Updating their
support
6:    Else // if itemset not existing
7:        FS← FS U (Cotroneo et al., 2016) //Adding the new itemset to the Fea-
ture set
8:    End If
9: End For
10: If Flag =="Global" Then
11:    ComputeThreshold (P,LD,FS,WeightSet) //Updating the threshold
12: End If
13: End Procedure
```

VALIDATION

Learning and Update Modes

For this work, we opt to two kind of update categories performed on three kinds of learning mode:

- **Accurate Learning (AL):** Is based on data labeled by the network monitor/analyst specialist used only on global updates.
- **Predictive learning (PL):** Is based on a data labeled by our outlier alert classifier.
- **Feature set learning (FL):** Only feature set of frequent/infrequent patterns are updated in order to detect any new alerts types. This mode doesn't need labeled dataset.

The update process active learning involves two types:

- **Local Update (L):** Is an incremental process performed after each short period. The classification decision will depend incrementally on the previous labeled data.
- **Global Update (G):** Is performed after long intervals. We mine in this step the whole alert database and we adjust consequently the feature set, association rules, alert attribute weights, and the threshold.

Description of Different Learning Scenarios

Based on the learning modes, update categories, and active learning types we present five strategies as follows:

- **A1 (FLL-NGL):** We update only the feature set with local update (No global learning update).
- **A2 (NLL-AGL):** We use accurate learning with global update only (No local learning update).
- **A3 (FLL-AGL):** We use feature set update with local learning and accurate learning with global update.
- **A4 (NLL-NGL):** We only learn the model and we did not launch any local or global updates.
- **A5 (PLL-AGL):** We use predictive learning update on local update and accurate learning on global update only.

Dataset: Kyoto 2006+

The Kyoto 2006+ (Song, 2011)is an evaluation dataset of network detection mechanism obtained from diverse honeypots from November 2006 to August 2009. This dataset capture the real network traffic without any human alteration or deletion. It encompasses the recent trends of network attacks distinguished from normal traffic via the use of honeypots. It consists of 24 statistical features where 14 conventional features are extracted from KDDCUP'99 dataset, and 10 additional features are added that may enable to investigate more effectively what kind of attacks happened in the networks.

The Kyoto dataset is labeled; the label indicates whether the session was attack or not; in the original database, there was three labels: '1' (normal session), '-1' (known attack), and '-2' (unknown attack).

Nevertheless, since the unknown attacks in the database are extremely rare (0.7%), we attributed a same label for known and unknown attacks, so that the problem becomes a binary classification.

Experiments Metrics

We introduce in this section the measures used in our experiments. We define the true positive (TP), false positive (FP), true negative(TN), false negative (FN) as follows:

- **TP:** A true positive alert classified as true positive.
- **FP:** A false positive alert classified as true positive.
- **TN:** A false positive alert classified as false positive.
- **FN:** A true positive alert classified as false positive.

In order to study the performance of our different alert classification algorithms, we compute the following measures: Sensitivity ([T P=(T P +F N)]), Fall-out ([F P=(F P +T N)]), Accuracy ([(T P +T N)=(T P +F N+F P +T N)]), Specificity ([T N=(F P + T N)]), Precision ([T P=(T P + F P)]), Negative predictive value ([T N=(T N + F N)]), False discovery rate ([F P=(F P + T P)]), Matthews correlation coefficient, F measure, online learning processing time.

Algorithm Parameters Tuning

We tuned the different algorithm parameters as Learning rate, Threshold percentage (P), Min-support, Min-confidence, Global update, and local update in the purpose to find the best configuration giving best accuracy.

Where:

- **Min-Support:** This parameter defines the minimal value of minimal support for the generation of frequent/infrequent feature set. All patterns with support equal or greater than the fixed min-support are frequent features while patterns with support less than the fixed min support are infrequent features. Small min-support will bring more frequent patterns and consequently reduce the infrequent patterns. In the case of normal traffic behavior, setting small min-support will increase the possibility of mining patterns belongs to frequent attacks.
- **Min-Confidence:** Used with association rules algorithm for the definition of the rules interestingness.
- **Threshold Percentage (P):** Denotes the proportion of candidate true or false alerts in the whole dataset. It is used in both learning phase and online phase (when launching global update)
- **Global Update:** Determines the number of new coming alerts to launch global updates.
- **Local Update:** Determines the number of new coming alerts to launch local updates
- **Learning Rate:** Is the percentage of alerts used on off-line mode to learn the model.

The Figures 2, 3, and 4 represent respectively the impact of the learning rate, min-support, and the parameter (p) on the accuracy for the FLL-AGL strategy for example. We notice that using 10% from the data set as initial learning data, 20% as min-support for the generation of frequent patterns, and 50% as value of the parameter (p) gives the best accuracy.

Figure 2. Impact of the learning rate in the accuracy for the FLLAGL

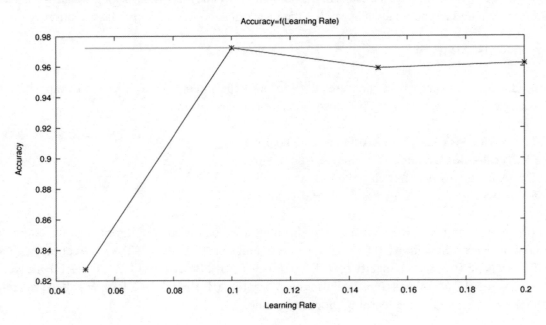

Figure 3. Impact of the Min-support in the accuracy for the FLLAGL

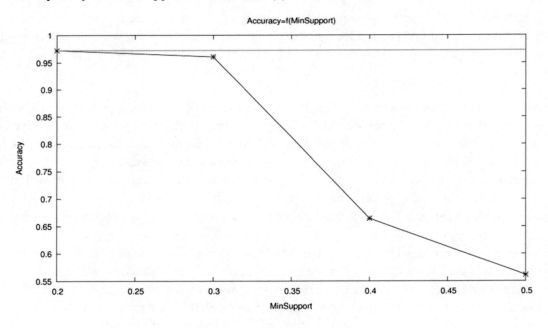

Figure 4. Impact of the parameter (P) in the accuracy for the FLL-AGL strategy

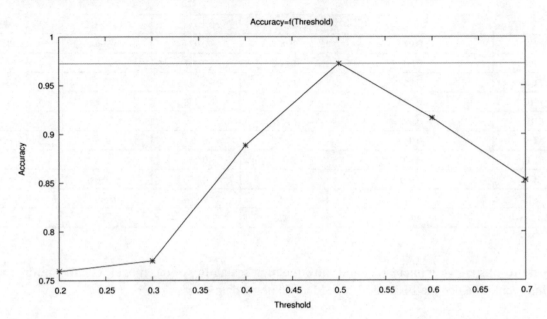

Then we set the following range values parameters vector depicted in Table 1 as best configuration in general for the different strategies.

Results and Analysis

The Table 2 depicts the different results obtained using the parameters in Table 1. According to this table, we can see that all strategies except PLL-AGL perform slightly similarity for all metrics. We notice that NLL-AGL has the best accuracy followed by FLL-AGL while FLL-NGL has the minimum execution time and slightly diminution in the accuracy. These results are expected and explained by the traffic behavior slightly changement in each periodic local update (the NLL-AGL has better accuracy than FLL-AGL).Also, a slightly traffic behavior changement in each global update (the FLL-NGL has an accuracy very proche to FLL-AGL).

Table 1. Algorithm configuration

Parameters	Values
Min-support	20%
Min-confidence	90%
Threshold percentage (P)	40-50%
Global update	1000 alerts
Local update	100 alerts
Learning rate	10-20%

Table 2. Different results of the different learning/update modes

	FLL-AGL	FLL-NGL	NLL-AGL	NLL-NGL	PLL-AGL
ACC	0.972	0.967	0.974	0.966	0.920
FPR	0.007	0.002	0.001	0	0.114
TPR	0.953	0.938	0.952	0.936	0.952
TNR	0.992	0.997	0.998	1	0.885
PPV	0.992	0.997	0.998	1	0.898
NPV	0.952	0.938	0.951	0.936	0.946
FDR	0.007	0.002	0.001	0	0.101
MCC	0.945	0.936	0.950	0.936	0.841
F1	0.972	0.967	0.974	0.966	0.924
Time(ms)	113073	1878	93307	1353	78465

These results are very interesting and show the high scalability of our model with the minimum human intervention since the FLL doesn't need any labeled data.

Execution Time Improvement Based on the Traffic Behavior

Based on the previous results in Table 2, we observe that the periodic accurate global update takes considerable time which is not required when the network traffic keeps the same behavior and therefore only the local feature set update is sufficient. So, in order to reduce the processing time and match the real time constraints, we launch before each global update a verification test applied on the alerts stored in the buffer. If the traffic is slightly modified, we keep the actual configuration and skip the global update. Otherwise, we launch a global update. The Figure 5 and 6 shows the impact of the test verification on the execution time and the accuracy represented by FLL-AAGL and PLL-AAGL strategies.

We notice the improvement of the accuracy with controlled global update explained by the over fitting of the feature set and rules which modifies consequently the alerts attributes weights.

To evaluate the performance of our classifier for different strategies, we have used also the ROC analysis as shown in Figure 7. According to this figure, we can conclude that all strategies perform similarly.

CONCLUSION

We developed a new algorithm based on Outlier Detection method to identify sequences of alerts that are likely result from normal behavior or match some extracted rules from the traffic historic enabling the construction of filters to eliminate those alerts. Alert Miner (AM) would be an interesting collection tool for the forensics readiness and investigation process. The inclusion of association rules for the analysis of the traffic and the identification of dangerous network connections automatically and in real time. This data mining method extracts automatically strong regularities between the received alerts and identifies interesting rules between them.

Figure 5. Execution time of the different strategies

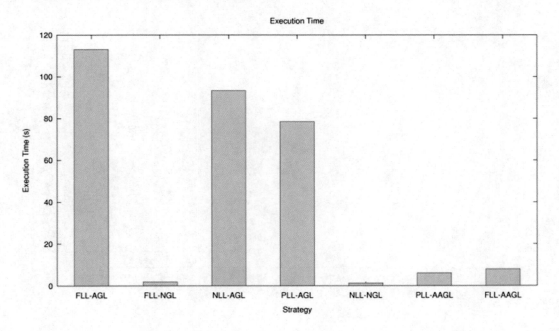

Figure 6. Accuracy of the different strategies

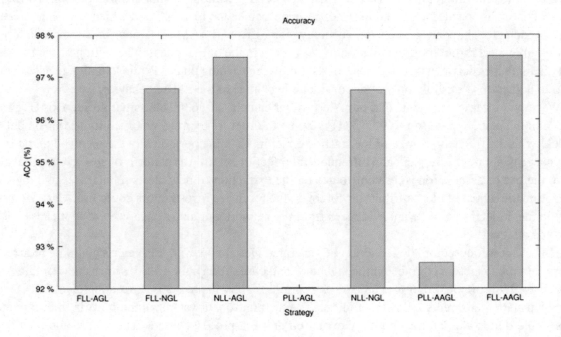

Figure 7. Roc curve for all different strategies

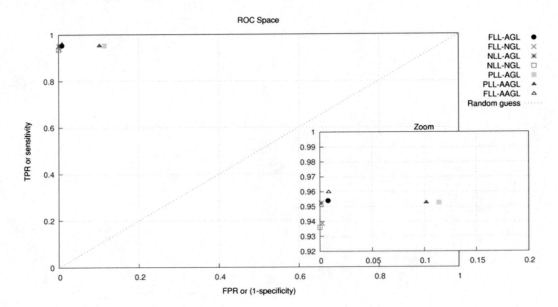

The use of association rules enables the automatic adaptivity to the network behavior changes and therefore adjusting automatically the alert attributes weights without any human intervention. The importance of association rules is proved in the experiments since the FLL-AGL in which we use association rules in each global update gives better accuracy than FLL-NGL. AM classifies almost immediately the new coming alert through the calculation of alert score in the online phase. The setting of the threshold that distinguishes between true and false alerts is built on learning phase. While in online phase we don't need to adjust this threshold only after considerable change in the traffic behavior.

We shows after experiments that our Alert Miner can classify 6300 alerts within seconds (Figure 5) with a high accuracy rate (up to 97.5%) (Figure 6) In order to keep the adaptability of our model and to deal with the frequent change of the traffic behavior, we mine periodically the received alerts in the purpose to generate the frequent and infrequent alert feature set used as patterns of attack or normal alert. Also, the use of association rules contributes on the extraction of new alerts regularities and therefore the automatic adjust of alert attributes. Moreover, the forensics investigators could use Alert Miner not only in the collection of relevant evidences from the network but also to analyze the root causes of the detected attacks.

This chapter focused on the reduction of generated alerts; however, false alerts could be reduced by improving the detection engine and the signature database. Today, the world witness new unknown attacks wave (Jim Finkle, 2016, December; phys.org, 2017; Symantec, 2017; Varadharajan, 2014) using unknown malicious threats and vulnerabilities. The surround of all system vulnerability is, approximately, impossible due to the large technology evolution and big processed data. The use of anomaly based IDS will be very effective since any abnormal behavior whatever malicious or benign (the latter is false positive), known or unknown is alerted. However, anomaly based IDS techniques suffer from both the high generation of false positive alerts since any abnormal behavior even benign activity is considered as attack and the non-effective automatic technique to model the normal behavior which is responsible for non-detection of attacks and overwhelming the administrator by false alerts. We believe that future work on this research area must focus on the accurate automatic modeling of normal system or network normal behavior (Varadharajan, 2014) to detect unknown attacks and avoid false positive alerts in the same time.

ACKNOWLEDGMENT

This chapter is a partial result of a research project granted by King Abdul Aziz City for Sciences and Technology (KACST), Riyadh, Kingdom of Saudi Arabia, under grant number 11-INF1787-08.

REFERENCES

Agrawal, T. I. s., & Swami, A. (1993). Mining association rules between sets of items in large databases. *SIGMOD Rec., 22*(2). 10.1145/170035.170072

Bhuyan, M. H., Bhattacharyya, D. K., & Kalita, J. K. (2014). Network Anomaly Detection: Methods, Systems and Tools. *IEEE Communications Surveys and Tutorials, 16*(1), 303–336. doi:10.1109/SURV.2013.052213.00046

Chirkova, R. A. D., Ozsu, M. T., & Sellis, T. K. (Eds.). (2007). *Proceedings of the 23rd International Conference on Data Engineering.* Istanbul, Turkey: Academic Press.

Clifton, G. (2000). Developing custom intrusion detection filters using data mining. *21st Century Military Communications Conference Proceedings.* 10.1109/MILCOM.2000.904991

Cotroneo, D., Paudice, A., & Pecchia, A. (2016). Automated root cause identification of security alerts: Evaluation in a SaaS Cloud. *Future Generation Computer Systems, 56*(Supplement C), 375–387. doi:10.1016/j.future.2015.09.009

Fayyad, P. U. G. P.-s. (1996). *Knowledge discovery and data mining: Towards a unifying framework.* AAAI Press.

Goeschel, K. (2016). *Reducing false positives in intrusion detection systems using data-mining techniques utilizing support vector machines, decision trees, and naive Bayes for off-line analysis.* Paper presented at the SoutheastCon 2016.

Grill, M., Pevný, T., & Rehak, M. (2017). Reducing false positives of network anomaly detection by local adaptive multivariate smoothing. *Journal of Computer and System Sciences, 83*(1), 43–57. doi:10.1016/j.jcss.2016.03.007

Jim Finkle, T. F. a. J. W. (2016, December). *Cyber saudi-shamoon-targets.* Academic Press.

Julish, K. (2001). *Mining alarm clustering to improve alarm handling efficiency.* Paper presented at the Computer Security Applications Conference.

Liang, H., Taihui, L., Nannan, X., & Jiejun, H. (2015). *False positive elimination in intrusion detection based on clustering.* Paper presented at the 2015 12th International Conference on Fuzzy Systems and Knowledge Discovery (FSKD).

Meng, W., Li, W., & Kwok, L.-F. (2015). Design of intelligent KNN-based alarm filter using knowledge-based alert verification in intrusion detection. *Security and Communication Networks, 8*(18), 3883–3895. doi:10.1002ec.1307

Narsingyani, D., & Kale, O. (2015). *Optimizing false positive in anomaly based intrusion detection using Genetic algorithm.* Paper presented at the 2015 IEEE 3rd International Conference on MOOCs, Innovation and Technology in Education (MITE).

Ramaki, A. A., Khosravi-Farmad, M., & Bafghi, A. G. (2015). *Real time alert correlation and prediction using Bayesian networks.* Paper presented at the 2015 12th International Iranian Society of Cryptology Conference on Information Security and Cryptology (ISCISC).

Shittu, R., Healing, A., Ghanea-Hercock, R., Bloomfield, R., & Rajarajan, M. (2015). Intrusion alert prioritisation and attack detection using post-correlation analysis. *Computers & Security, 50,* 1–15. doi:10.1016/j.cose.2014.12.003

Sommer, P. (1998). Intrusion detection systems as evidence. *Proceedings of the RAID 98 Conference.*

Song, H. T., Okabe, Y., Eto, M., Inoue, D., & Nakao, K. (2011). Statistical analysis of honeypot data and building of kyoto 2006+ dataset for nids evaluation. *Proceedings of the First Workshop on Building Analysis Datasets and Gathering Experience Returns for Security.* 10.1145/1978672.1978676

Stephenson, P. (2000). The application of intrusion detection systems in a forensic environment. *Proceedings of the RAID 2000 Conference.*

Symantec. (2017). *Ransom.Wannacry. Security Response.* Author.

Vaarandi, R. (2009). Real-time classification of ids alerts with data mining techniques. *Proceedings of the 2009 IEEE MILCOM Conference.* 10.1109/MILCOM.2009.5379762

Vaarandi, R. (2010). Network ids alert classification with frequent itemset mining and data clustering. *Proceedings of the 2010 IEEE Conference on Network and Service Management.* 10.1109/CNSM.2010.5691262

Varadharajan, B. M. V. (2014). *Design and Analysis of Security Attacks against Critical Smart Grid Infrastructures.* Paper presented at the 19th International Conference on Engineering of Complex Computer Systems, Tianjin.

Viinikka, J. D., Mé, L., Lehikoinen, A., & Tarvainen, M. (2009). Processing intrusion detection alert aggregates with time series modeling. *Information Fusion Journal,* 312–324.

Viinikka, J. D. H., Mé, L., Séguier, R., & Tarvainen, M. (2006). *Time series modeling for ids alert management.* Paper presented at the ACM Symposium on Information Computer and Communications Security. 10.1145/1128817.1128835

Xiao, F. J., S. (2010). A novel data mining-based method for alert reduction and analysis. *Journal of Networks.*

Yacoub, M. B. Y. (1997). *Hvs: A heuristic for variable selection in multilayer artificial neural network classifier.* Paper presented at the International Conference on Artificial Neural Networks and Intelligent Engineering.

Yuil, J. F. S. (1999). *Intrusion detection for an ongoing attack.* Paper presented at the International Workshop on Recent Advances in Intrusion Detection RAID 99.

Chapter 11
Visualization Technique for Intrusion Detection

Mohamed Cheikh
Constantine 2 University, Algeria

Salima Hacini
Constantine 2 University, Algeria

Zizette Boufaida
Constantine 2 University, Algeria

ABSTRACT

Intrusion detection system (IDS) plays a vital and crucial role in a computer security. However, they suffer from a number of problems such as low detection of DoS (denial-of-service)/DDoS (distributed denial-of-service) attacks with a high rate of false alarms. In this chapter, a new technique for detecting DoS attacks is proposed; it detects DOS attacks using a set of classifiers and visualizes them in real time. This technique is based on the collection of network parameter values (data packets), which are automatically represented by simple geometric graphs in order to highlight relevant elements. Two implementations for this technique are performed. The first is based on the Euclidian distance while the second is based on KNN algorithm. The effectiveness of the proposed technique has been proven through a simulation of network traffic drawn from the 10% KDD and a comparison with other classification techniques for intrusion detection.

INTRODUCTION

Intrusion Detection Systems (IDSs) were introduced by Anderson (Anderson.J,1980). Denning (Denning.D,1987) designed then an intrusion detection model which marked a real impetus of the field. IDSs are essential complements to the preventive security mechanisms provided for computing systems and networks. They are used in the monitoring control process for the detection of potential intrusions and infections (Zanero, 2004).

DOI: 10.4018/978-1-5225-5583-4.ch011

IDS is based on two basic approaches, the behavioral approach and the scenario approach. The scenario approach, often called misuse detection approach defines the user actions that constitute abuse. It uses rules defined to encode and detect known intrusions. The behavioral approach, on its side, can detect unknown intrusions, and does not require any prior knowledge of intrusions (Boudaoud.K,2000). This approach is based on the fact that an intruder does not behave the same way as a regular user. Contrary to the user, who has a normal behavior, the intruder has an abnormal behavior. Thus, all intrusive activities are necessarily abnormal (Sundaram.A,2000).

Classification techniques in IDS intended to classify network traffic into two classes: "normal" and "intrusion". Classification requires learning. The accuracy of this learning provides lower false positive rate and false negative rate (Maxime DUMAS,2011).

Among the techniques commonly used for classification in IDS, we find the ANN, SVM and often the K-means and others (see section 2).

This chapter presents a new technique for classifying DoS attacks based on a visual representation of the network traffic. This representation is based on simple geometric forms and has two objectives:

1. Find models of DoS attacks and in particular be able to distinguish between them and the normal traffic. These models are later used in the classifiers. Seven models were identified to recognize six types of DoS attacks (Neptune, Smurf, Teardrop, Land, Pack, Pod) to which is added the normal case.
2. Improve the detection rate, which presents a great challenge for IDS.

The effectiveness of this technique has been proved through simulation of network traffic drawn from the 10% KDD. The proposed technique treats DoS attacks. However, it can also be applied to other types of attacks with the integration of their geometric forms in the detection system.

The remaining of this chapter is organized as follows: Section 2 presents some works dealing with the classification in IDS, Section 3 describes the proposed detection technique. Finally, Section 4 concludes the chapter and suggests some perspectives.

RELATED WORK

There are several techniques used for classification in IDS, the most frequently are ANN, SVM and K-means as well as others.

The k-means classifier, originally an algorithm for pattern recognition that has proven its effectiveness against the text processing (Yang Y,1997) represents a simple and popular classification that uses statistics properties (Kaplantzis.S & N. Mani,2006). It allows the partition of a collection of objects into K classes (K is a number set by the user). In the context of intrusion detection, there are generally two groups (classes), one for attack and another for normal cases. The classification is then performed by taking each individual point in a test set and associating it with the nearest class. At the end, each point is assigned to a class "attack" or "normal." Most distance measures used in this category of classification algorithms are Euclidean and Manhattan distances.

Neural networks are also used for ANN classification in IDS (Kevin L et al,1990), (Herve Debar et al,1992), (Jake Ryan et al,1998), (James Cannady,1998), (B. Subba, 2016). In the work of Fox et al. (Kevin L et al,1990), the authors propose the use of artificial neural networks to detect intrusions. The input network is actually a collection of URLs elements that often appear together to refine the recognition of simultaneous occurrence of different elements. (Herve Debar et al,1992) Proposed to learn the next commands predict using the history of previous commands of the user. In this case, a window offset **w** recent orders is used. The predicted command of the user is compared with the current command of the user and each deviation is shown as an intrusion. The size of the window **w** plays an important role, because if **w** is too small, there will be many false positives and it is too attacks will not be detected (Fady HAMOUI,2007).

The neural network intrusion detector NNID (Neural Network Intrusion Detector) (Jake Ryan et al,1998) identifies intrusions based on the distribution of commands used by a user. This approach is based on three phases. Firstly, the training data are derived from audit files for each user. A vector represents the distribution of the execution of a command for each user. In the second phase, the neural network is trained to identify the user based on these vectors control distribution. In the last phase, the network identifies the user for each new vector control distribution. If it identifies a user as different from the current user, an intrusion is reported.

In this context, the neuron networks are also proving effective in the case of noisy data (Fady HAMOUI,2007). However, the main problem with this approach lies in the training of neural networks where the training phase requires a very large amount of data and also an important time.

The technique of SVM (Support Vector Machines) has been used in (Srinivas Mukkamala et al,2003) (Kim, D.S,2003). This technique belongs to the class of supervised learning, developed in 1998 by Vapnik (Vapnik.V.N,1998). SVM learning is machines that project the vector drive space properties labeling each vector by its class. SVM classify the data by determining a set of support vectors, which are members of the inputs of the learning set which generates a surface in space hyper property. This type of approach has proven they can be a good solution for intrusion detection because of their speed (Fady HAMOUI,2007).

An interesting comparative study of Kaplantzis and Mani (Kaplantzis.S & N. Mani, 2006) on the three classification techniques (K-Means, ANN, SVM) for intrusion detection showed that the SVM is learning in the shortest amount of time with acceptable accuracy while the ANN provides high accuracy through long hours of learning.

Other classification techniques were used in Cohen.W. W,(1995), Wenke Lee et al,(1999), Giordana.A et al, (1995), Chittur.A, (2001), Chris Sinclair et al,(1999), Dickerson.J.E. and Dickerson.J.A, (2000), and Lue.J, (1999). They are based on the generation of inductive rules, genetic algorithms, fuzzy logic, etc.

We begin with the RIPPER system (Cohen.W. W,1995) which uses the "generation of inductive rules" classification (Wenke Lee et al,1999; Wenke Lee & Salvatore Stolfol,1998; Wenke Lee & Salvatore Stolfol, 2000; Wenke Lee et al,2000). It is effective to classify cases in the normal category and in various cases of intrusions (n-ary classification). RIPPER has two characteristics (Saneifar. H,1999):

- Generated rules are easy to understand.
- Possibility to generate multiple sets of rules.

REGAL (Giordana.A et al,1995) is another system using IDS classification techniques based on genetic algorithms (Filippo Neri,2000). It looks like approaches based on inductive rules but the author does not clarify the effectiveness of the approach (Saneifar. H,1999). Generally, this approach which uses the concept of natural selection is applied to a population of potential solutions to a difficult problem (which is not the optimal solution) to find an approximate solution in a reasonable time. In the case of

IDS, the initial population can be basic detection rules. Through the genetic algorithm, other rules that cover the best case of abnormal flows are generated.

The decision tree is also used as a classification technique in Chittur's work (Chittur.A,2001). Each node of the tree represents an attribute in the data set. Attributes are weighted and the final decision on the type of connection depends on the weight of attributes. By traversing the tree from the root to the leaves, there are decision rules (consisting of attributes and values present on the corresponding nodes) that enable classification of new instances.

In Chris Sinclair et al (1999), the authors convert attributes of network connections in the form of a gene sequence. Each connection is compared to all chromosomes. If there is no match, the connection is labeled as an anomaly.

In Dickerson.J.E. and Dickerson.J.A (2000), a combination of fuzzy logic and classification has been proposed to address portions of the data to be classified into two categories: "general" and "intrusion". This approach is effective in detecting intrusions type SCAN: the network is scanned to determine the architecture and to discover vulnerabilities. A user connects to multiple hosts sequentially for a short time. Because the classification is done on portions connected temporally, this approach has good results for detecting scans. The disadvantage is the difficult task of generating rules and definition of a good constraint (Time-Window) to determine the portions.

Lue (Lue.J,1999) developed the work of Wenke Lee et al,(1999), Wenke Lee and Salvatore Stolfol,(1998) by adding the concept of fuzzy logic. Its work scored more flexible. According to him, the intrusion detection is a natural application of fuzzy logic for determining an absolute given that a connection is an intrusion or not is not possible, but with fuzzy logic, we can give the probability of an intrusion.

Despite the development marked by the application of these techniques known as classification, many problems still arise. Many researches have inspired works based on neural networks. While they may be effective in the context of detection and provide better accuracy, they have a major shortcoming; it is not possible to know the reasons for the output algorithm. In other words, the end user does not have a clear definition of what characterizes an attack of non-attack. Moreover, the high rate of false alarms remains the black point of IDS. Fortunately, it is possible to limit the scope of most of the problems mentioned above using some visualization techniques. Latter is to represent graphically complex sets of information in order to highlight relevant elements (Maxime DUMAS,2011).

THE PROPOSED DETECTION TECHNIQUE

The proposed detection technique is based on a visual representation of network traffic after normalization of some parameters in the KDD. This representation aims to find visual models of DoS attacks and be able to distinguish between them and normal traffic. These models are subsequently used in the classifiers for intrusion detection. Seven models were identified to recognize six types of DoS attacks (Neptune, Smurf, Teardrop, Land, Pack, Pod) to which is added the normal case.

We can therefore consider the problem of intrusion detection as a pattern recognition problem. Thus, the classification is not made on the basis of parameters often complex, but rather on the basis of forms from a geometric transformation.

The Visualization

The Choice of Visualization Parameters

We focus in this work the application of our technique on DoS attacks. The choice of parameters based KDD derives from several tests and some work (Kayacık.H. G et al, 2005;Aikaterini M et al,2005), which cover both better visual classification of attacks and a small number of parameters. For this, the 41 KDD parameters are taken and a representation of the parameters as geometric forms is applied. The used parameters are those that give a better discrimination of forms. Our study has highlighted ten parameters (*Cf.* Table 1).

The transformation of collected values for these parameters has highlighted seven geometric forms leading to the classification of the six attacks (Smurf, Neptune, Teardrop, Land, Back, Pod) and the normal case.

The Representation Graph

Our technique is based on a graphical representation of the attacks which performs a transformation of parameters values by using the polar system. Each parameter value is well represented by polar coordinates, which are the radial coordinate r and the angular coordinate θ. Thereafter, each packet is represented by all ten descriptors di(i= 1, .. 10) corresponding to the ten parameters of detection. For example, a normal packet is represented as follows:

Normal Packet $=\{$d1$(1,0)$, d2$(0, \frac{\pi}{5})$, d3$(0, \frac{2\pi}{5})$, d4$(1, \frac{3\pi}{5})$, d5$(1, \frac{4\pi}{5}$., d6$(0, \pi)$, d7$(0, \frac{6\pi}{5})$, d8$(0, \frac{7\pi}{5})$, d9$(0, \frac{8\pi}{5})$, d10$(0, \frac{9\pi}{5})\}$. The result of this transformation is similar to a radar graph. Figure 1 shows the geometric form of a normal packet.

Table 1. Detection parameters

	Parameters	**Description**
1	Pr(1)	duration
2	Pr(23)	Count
3	Pr(24)	srv count
4	Pr(13)	compromised
5	Pr(25)	serror rate
6	Pr(26)	srv serror rate
7	Pr(29)	same srv rate
8	Pr(34)	dst host same srv rate
9	Pr(38)	dst host serror rate
10	Pr(39)	dst host srv serror rate

Figure 1. Representation of a normal packet

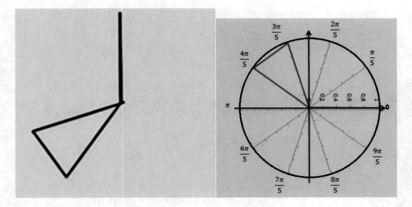

Practically, if we take all normal packets, the graph keeps the same pace with some insignificant changes (form remains invariant in space). This experiment was repeated using packet DoS attacks taken from 10% KDD. Each type of attack (Smurf, Neptune, Teardrop, Land, Back, Pod) has its own geometric form (see Figure 2) (for better visualization, the forms are displayed with a rotation of 90 °).

It can be noted from Figures 2 and 3 that the detection of DoS attacks will be greatly simplified through representation by means of the simple geometric forms.

Classification of Packets

For the packets classification we used two techniques, the first one is based on Euclidean distance, and the second one is at the base of Kppv algorithm.

Minimum Distance Classification

Pattern recognition (Kumar.S & Spafford.E. G,1995) is to encode the signatures of known intrusions into forms that can be recognized in the audit data in the model, based on the notion of event. In our case, we used the calculation of the Euclidean distance between the vector form of the unknown object (new packet) and the vector form of the reference object (the attack model / Normal). To determine the form vector of the reference object, we used a mean vector of a set of vectors according to the following formula:

$$Mj = \frac{1}{Nj} \sum_{X \in \omega j} Xj \qquad j = 1, 2, 3, \ldots, W \tag{1}$$

where Nj is the number of form vectors in the class ωj, and Mj the reference vector. We distinguish seven classes: $\omega 1, \omega 2, \omega 3, \omega 4, \omega 5, \omega 6, \omega 7$ and each class of attack is evaluated by ten descriptors (d1, d2, d3, d4, d5, d6, d7, d8, d9, d10) where each descriptor represents a detection parameter characterized by two arguments: r (module) and θ (angle) (we use only the argument r to calculate the Euclidean distance).

Figure 2. Forms representing DoS Attacks

	Form	Type
1		Back
3		Land
3		Teardrop
4		Neptune
5		Pod
6		Smurf

For example, the Smurf attack shown in Figure 3 represents a model (reference vector) graphic of Smurf Attack, taken randomly from a sample of 1000 Smurf packets.

Thus, at each occurrence of new packet, the Euclidean distance between the vector form of the unknown packet and the reference vector of Smurf attack (Smurf attack model) is estimated:

IF the Euclidian distance is minimal **Then** This packet denotes a Smurf attack

ELSE this packet is not a Smurf attack.

Similar processing is applied to other DoS attacks and also to normal packet.

Detection System Architecture

The intrusion detection system proposed is applicable to network traffic, so the parameters observed concern the detection during the routed packets in the network. They were, in this case, taken from KDD10%. A set of classifiers is used to distribute the task of detection. Seven classifiers are adopted to detect DOS attacks and normal packets. Each classifier is identified by a reference vector (model) created during the learning phase. Thus, with each occurrence of a new packet, each classifier computes

Figure 3. Form of the Smurf attack

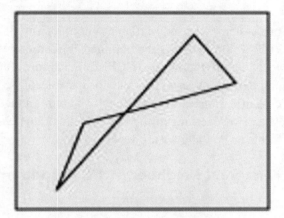

the Euclidean distance between the input vector (parameters of packet) and the reference model. The results of these classifiers are subsequently used in the overall decision algorithm. The classifier that has the minimal distance value is the one whose class corresponds to the final decision. Figure 4 shows the overall architecture of the proposed detection system.

The task of the detection system is divided into three steps. The first relates to learning phase and deals with the creation of reference models associated to each attack. The second step is to manage the task of partial decision made by each classifier on the analyzed packet. Finally, the third step generates the final decision on basis of the collection of classifiers results, this decision is based on the minimum distance. In parallel with these operations, the task of visualization is performed to recognize DoS attacks by simple geometric forms. In addition, it offers the possibility of intervening in the detection system to correct any detection anomalies in the system.

Figure 4. The detection System architecture

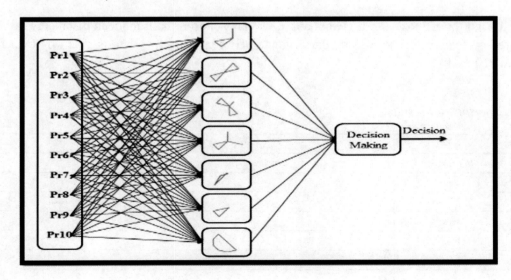

Experimentation

To test the effectiveness of our system, we used Matlab as a tool for simulation of network traffic from the 10% KDD base. Table 2 (*Cf.* Table 2) shows the obtained simulation results.

We will calculate the correct classification rate (CCR) for each form (attack). For this we will randomly take samples of each type of attack as well as the normal case of packets.

We note that the Correct Classification Rate is excellent for Neptune attack, good for Smurf, Teardrop, Back, Land and normal packets. However, regarding the Pod attack, the CCR is a bit low compared to the other attacks, since the forms of Pod attacks are very varied.

Classification by the K-Nearest Neighbor (KNN) Algorithm

KNN Algorithm

The KNN algorithm is among the simplest artificial learning algorithms. In a classification context of a new observation x, the basic idea is to vote nearest neighbors of this observation. The class of x is determined as a function of the majority class among the k closest neighbors of the observation x. The KNN method is therefore a neighborhood-based, non-parametric method; This meaning that the algorithm allows for a classification without making assumptions about the function $y = f(x1, x2, ... xp)$ which connects the dependent variable to the independent variables (MATHIEU-DUPAS, 2010).

The k-neighrest neighbors algorithm is an intuitive algorithm, easily parameterized to handle a classification problem with any number of labels. The principle of the algorithm is particularly simple: for each new point x we start by determining the set of its k-nearest neighbors among the learning points that we denote by Vk (x) (of course we must choose $1 \leq k \leq n$ to make sense). The class which is assigned to the new point x is then the majority class in the set Vk (x). An illustration of the method is given in Figure 5 for the case of three classes (Anne Sabourin, 2015).

The Distance

In order to find the K closest to a given datum, we have chosen the Euclidean distance. Let two data represented by two vectors xi and xj, the distance between these two data is given by (MATHIEU-DUPAS, 2010):

Table 2. Experimental results

	Type	Correct Classification Rate %
01	**Normal**	**97%**
02	Smurf	99.8%
03	TearDrop	99.8%
04	Back	96.6%
05	Pod	68.6%
06	Land	90.5%
07	Neptune	100%

Figure 5. Example of the k-nearest neighbor's method for parameter values k = 5 and k = 11 (Anne Sabourin, 2015)

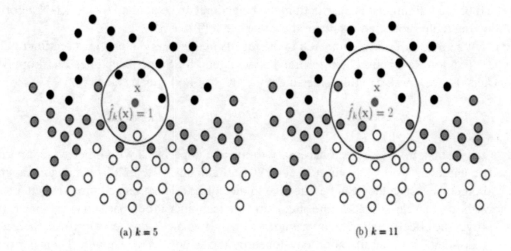

$$d(x_i, x_j) = \sqrt{\sum_{k=1}^{d} (x_{ik} - x_{jk})^2}$$

(2)

Implementation

It involves implementing in the JAVA language the algorithm of the K-nearest neighbors to predict the classes of new data (Packets) from learning data labeled (the attack/normal model (see Section 3.2 .1)).

These are the same learning data as in the previous section, but this time we take the models (attacks / normal) (see Figure 6) as an image.

Figure 6. Images show the attack patterns

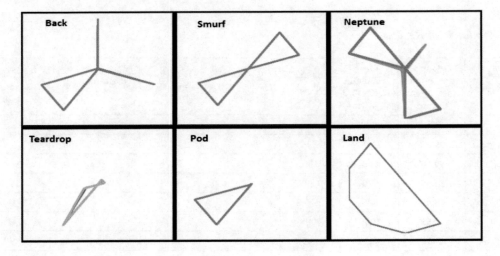

By the following we applied the different binarization and projection steps (vertical and horizontal), to obtain the global vector of the image.

At the end of the training data construction, the detection can be applied by the KNN algorithm.

The following table shows the results of the experiment (Table 3).

There is not a great difference compared to the results obtained in the previous section (3.2.1). The Correct Classification Rate is excellent for Land attack, good for Smurf, Neptune, Teardrop, Back and normal packets. However, also in this experiment the CCR of Pod attack is low.

Validation

To validate the results, it was deemed necessary to make comparisons with other works; particularly those based on neural networks (Naoum.R.S et al, 2012;Sammany.M et al,2007; Chaivat Jirapummin et al,2002) and others, because they can be effective in the context detection and provide better accuracy. Table 4 shows the correct classification rate outcome of our technique in comparison with other techniques.

Table 4 proves the effectiveness of our technique with the two methods used. However, there are many algorithms and methods of classification developed by the scientific community. Their performances are evaluated on the datasets indexed (such as KDD'99). Applied to the same set of data, some methods

Table 3. Experimental results

	Type	Correct Classification Rate %
01	Normal	95.5%
02	Smurf	99.9%
03	Tear drop	94%
04	Back	97%
05	Pod	64%
06	Land	100%
07	Neptune	98.3%

Table 4. Comparison Results

	Type	Our Technique (Minimum Distance)	Our Technique (KNN algorithm	(Jiang.S, Song.X, 2006)	(Gunes Kayacik.H, 2006)	ERBP (Naoum.R.S, 2012)	(Sammany.M, 2007)	(Chaivat Jirapummin, 2002)
01	Normal	**97%**	95.5%			84.3%	96.3%	-
02	Smurf	**99.8%**	99.9%	99.96%	99.9%	-	-	-
03	TearDrop	**99.8%**	94%	26%	16.7%	-	-	-
04	Back	**96.6%**	97%	0.32%	50%	-	-	-
05	Pod	**68.6%**	64%	3.79%	6.9%	-	-	-
06	Land	**90.5%**	100%	100%	100%	-	-	-
07	Neptune	**100%**	98.3%	99.99%	96.4%	-	92.4%	99.7%

provide good results, that is to say, the results are conform to our expectations of good classification such a good packet classification between different types of attack and the normal case, while others provide results generally less efficient. However, a less efficient method results can highlight links that have not been seen by the most effective (Maxime DUMAS,2011) and also can provide more efficient results against some types of attacks. The basic idea is that the information provided by the different classifiers or different methods are complementary, and therefore the combination of different classification methods such as ANN, SVM, minimum distance, and others can increase their effectiveness and their accuracy. (Projet Pari, 2013) One classification is performed based on the results of methods with different viewpoints: all decisions of individual classifiers are used to obtain a consensus decision. (Yang Y,1997) The challenge is how to improve the overall performance by combining the advantages and without keeping disadvantages.

CONCLUSION

In this chapter, we present a new technique for intrusion detection, that can detect, classify and visualize attacks in real time. Packets related to traffic represented by our graphs as images with simple geometric forms, to find models of visual DoS attacks and be able to distinguish between them and the normal traffic. These models are used in classifiers for intrusion detection.

So we can consider the problem of intrusion detection as a pattern recognition problem where the classification is not made on the basis of often complex arithmetic parameters, but rather on the basis of forms derived from a geometric transformation.

Finally, simulation results with KDD10% illustrate the effectiveness of this technique with a high rate of correct classification. To improve the detection rate, the combination of different classification methods using a Multi-Agents System is considered. Its aim is to obtain a consensus classification that can improve the detection rate and reduce the false alarm rate.

REFERENCES

Aikaterini, M., & Christos, D. (2005). Detecting Denial of Service Attacks Using Emergent Self-Organizing Maps. *2005 IEEE International Symposium on Signal Processing and Information Technology.*

Anderson, J. (1980). *Computer security threat monitoring and surveillance.* Academic Press.

Anne Sabourin, J. S. (2015). *Méthodes des k-plus proches voisins.* Paris: Travaux Pratiques, Telecom Paristech.

Boudaoud, K. (2000). *Détection d'intrusions: Une nouvelle approche par systèmes multi-agents* (Thèse de doctorat). l'école Polytechnique Fédérale de Lausanne.

Cannady, J. (1998). Articial neural networks for misuse detection. *Proceedings of the 1998 National Information Systems Security Conference (NISSC'98),* 443-456.

Chittur, A. (2001). *Model generation for an intrusion detection system using genetic algorithms* (PhD thesis). Ossining High School in cooperation with Columbia Univ.

Cohen, W. W. (1995). Fast effective rule induction. In *Machine Learning: the 12th International Conference*. Morgan Kaufmann. 10.1016/B978-1-55860-377-6.50023-2

Debar, H., Becker, M., & Siboni, D. (1992). A neural network component for an intrusion detection system. In *SP '92: Proceedings of the 1992 IEEE Symposium on Security and Privacy*. IEEE Computer Society. 10.1109/RISP.1992.213257

Denning, D. (1987). An intrusion-detection model. *IEEE Transactions on Software Engineering, 13*, 222–232.

Dickerson, J. E., & Dickerson, J. A. (2000). Fuzzy network proling for intrusion detection. In *Proc. of NAFIPS 19th International Conference of the North American Fuzzy Information Processing Society* (pp. 301-306). North American Fuzzy Information Processing Society (NAFIPS).

Dumas, M. (2011). *Alertwheel: Visualisation radiale de graphes bipartis appliquée aux systèmes de détection d'intrusions sur des réseaux informatiques*. Mémoire de l'école de technologie supérieure, université du Québec.

Fady, H. (2007). *Détection de fraudes et Extraction de Connaissances* (Master's thesis). Montpellier 2 Univ.

Fox, Henning, Reed, & Simonian. (1990). A neural network approach towards intrusion detection. *Proceedings of the 13th national computer security conference*, 125-34.

Giordana, A., Neri, F., & Saitta, L. (1995). Search-intensive concept induction. *Evolutionary Computation, 3*(4), 375-416.

Jiang, S., Song, X., Wang, H., Han, J.-J., & Li, Q.-H. (2006). A clustering-based method for unsupervised intrusion detections. *Pattern Recognition Letters, 27*(7), 802–810. doi:10.1016/j.patrec.2005.11.007

Jirapummin, C., Wattanapongsakorn, N., & Kanthamanon, P. (2002). Hybrid neural networks for intrusion detection system. *2002 International Technical Conference on Circuits/Systems,Computers and Communications (ITC-CSCC 2002)*, 928–931.

Kaplantzis, S., & Mani, N. (2006). A study on classification techniques for network intrusion detection. *IASTED Conference on Networks and Communication Systems (NCS 2006)*.

Kayacik, G. (2006). A hierarchal SOM-based intrusion detection system. *Engineering Applications of Artificial Intelligence*. doi:10.1016/j.engappai.2006.09.005

Kayacık, H. G., Zincir-Heywood, A. N., & Heywood, M. I. (2005). Selecting Features for Intrusion Detection: A Feature Relevance Analysis on KDD 99 Intrusion Detection Datasets. *Third Annual Conference on Privacy, Security and Trust*.

Kim, D. S., & Park, J. S. (2003). Lecture Notes in Computer Science: Vol. 2662. *Network-based Intrusion Detection with Support Vector Machines*. Berlin: Springer-Verlag. doi:10.1007/978-3-540-45235-5_73

Kumar, S., & Spafford, E. G. (1995). *A Software Architecture to support Misuse Intrusion Detection*. Technical Report CSD-TR-95-009, Purdue University.

Lee, W., Stolfo, S. J., & Mok, K. W. (1999). A data mining framework for building intrusion detection models. *IEEE Symposium on Security and Privacy*, 120-132.

Lee, W., & Stolfo, S. (1998). Data mining approaches for intrusion detection. *Proceedings of the 7th USENIX Security Symposium.*

Lee, W., & Stolfo, S. J. (2000). A framework for constructing features and models for intrusion detection systems. *Information and System Security*, *3*(4), 227261.

Lee, W., Stolfo, S. J., & Mok, K. W. (2000). Adaptive intrusion detection, a data mining approach. *Artificial Intelligence Review*, *14*(6), 533567. doi:10.1023/A:1006624031083

Lue, J. (1999). *Integrating fuzzy logic with data mining methods for intrusion detection* (Master's thesis). Mississippi State Univ.

Mathieu-Dupas, E. (2010). *Algorithme des K plus proches voisins pondérés (WKNN) et Application en diagnostic.* Montpellier: SysDiag, Unité Mixte de Recherche CNRS-BIO-RAD.

Mukkamala, Sung, & Abraham. (2003). *Intrusion detection using ensemble of soft computing paradigms.* Academic Press.

Naoum, R.S.. Abdula Abid, N., & Namh Al-Sultani, Z. (2012). An Enhanced Resilient Backpropagation Artificial Neural Network for Intrusion Detection System. *International Journal of Computer Science and Network Security, 12*(3).

Neri, F. (2000). Comparing local search with respect to genetic evolution to detect in-trusion in computer networks. In *Proceedings of the 2000 Congress on Evolutionary Computation CEC00* (pp. 238-243). IEEE Press.

Pari, P. (2011-2013). *Classification consensuelle.* Retrieved from http://pari.ai.univ-paris8.fr/?author=1

Ryan, J., Lin, M.-J., & Miikkulainen, R. (1998). Intrusion detection with neural networks. In M. I. Jordan, M. J. Kearns, & S. A. Solla (Eds.), Advances in Neural Information Processing Systems: Vol. 10. *The MIT Press.*

Sammany, M., Sharawi, M., El-Beltagy, M., & Saroit, I. (2007). Artificial Neural Networks Architecture for Intrusion Detection Systems and Classification of Attacks. *Fifth international conference- INFO 2007.*

Saneifar, H. (2008). *Clustering de motifs séquentiels Application à la détection d'intrusions* (Master's thesis). Montpellier 2 Univ.

Sinclair, C., Pierce, L., & Matzner, S. (1999). An application of machine learning to network intrusion detection. In *ACSAC '99: Proceedings of the 15th Annual Computer Security Applications Conference.* Washington, DC: IEEE Computer Society. 10.1109/CSAC.1999.816048

Subba, B., Biswas, S., & Karmakar, S. (2016). A Neural Network based system for Intrusion Detection and attack classification. In *Communication (NCC), 2016 Twenty Second National Conference on* (pp. 1-6). IEEE.

Sundaram, A. (1996). An Introduction to Intrusion Detection. Technical Report, Purdue University.

Vapnik, V. N. (1998). *Statistical learning theory. Adaptive and learning systems for signal processing, communications, and control.* New York: Wiley.

Yang, Y. (1997). *An evaluation of statistical approach to text categorization.* Rapport interne Technichal Report CMU-CS-97-127, Carnegie Mellon University.

Zanero, S. (2004). Behavioural intrusion detection. In *Proceedings of the 19th ISCIS Symposium* (pp. 657-666). Springer-Verlag.

Chapter 12
False Alarm Reduction:
A Profiling Mechanism and New Research Directions

Salima Hacini
Constantine 2 University, Algeria

Zahia Guessoum
Pierre et Marie Curie University, France

Mohamed Cheikh
Constantine 2 University, Algeria

ABSTRACT

Intrusion detection systems (IDSs) are commonly used to detect attacks on computer networks. These tools analyze incoming and outgoing traffic for suspicious anomalies or activities. Unfortunately, these generate a significant amount of noise complexifying greatly the analysis of the data. This chapter addresses the problem of false alarms in IDSs. Its first purpose is to improve their accuracy by detecting real attacks and by reducing the number of unnecessary alerts. To do so, this intrusion detection mechanism enhances the accuracy of anomaly intrusion detection systems using a set of agents to ensure the detection and the adaptation of normal profile to support the legitimate changes that occur over time and are the cause of many false alarms. Besides this, as a perspective of this work, this chapter opens up new research directions by listing the different requirements of an IDS and proposing solutions to achieve them.

INTRODUCTION

Intrusion Detection Systems (IDSs) are essential complements to the preventive security mechanisms provided for computing systems and networks. They are used in the monitoring control process for the detection of potential intrusions and infections (Zanero, 2004).

DOI: 10.4018/978-1-5225-5583-4.ch012

The IDS research community has developed two categories of solutions: misuse detection and anomaly detection (Axelsson, 2000). The misuse detection defines, in a specific way, the user actions which constitute an abuse. Rules are therefore deduced for the detection of known intrusions. These rules are thus effective at detecting known intrusion attempts. However, they fail to recognize novel attacks (Wang, 2004). Anomaly detection (sometimes referred to as behaviour based) overcomes this limitation of misuse detection by focusing on normal behaviour, rather than attacks. For example, a heuristic analysis enables the generation of an alarm when the number of sessions bound for a given port exceeds a threshold in a preset time interval. This technique can be applied to both human users and software applications or services.

In spite of the noticeable development based on the anomaly techniques, the problem of the high rate of false alarms remains an open issue (Pokrywka, 2008; Khosravifar & Bentahar, 2008; Ohta et al., 2008; Jyothsna et al., 2011; Shruti et al., 2012). False alarms are indeed the main cause of alarm overload. Many recent researches report that false alarms still represent a consequent subset of the overall number of alarms (Nadiammai et al., 2011; Singh & Gupta, 2012) and several works have shown that the inspection of thousands of alarms per day is infeasible, especially if 99% of them are false positives (Perdisci et al., 2006). In fact, false alarms and timely identification of new attacks are among the biggest challenges to the effective use of IDSs. Thus, the success of anomaly detection systems relies on the development of detection approaches that improve the detection of attacks without misclassifying legitimate behaviour.

The implementation of anomaly-based detection systems requires the setting up of two phases: the training phase which allows the build of normal profile and the detection phase which enables the detection of all the activities that are out of the so-built normal profile. However, it is not possible to observe, during the training phase, all potential legitimate behaviours and the IDSs have to deal with dynamic changes and evolution of legitimate behaviour to adapt their diagnosis. So, based on the fact that Anomaly intrusion detection is used to find unknown attacks by using the concept of profiling normal behaviors and that significant false alarm may be caused because it is difficult to obtain complete normal behaviors (Jyothsna, Rama Prasad & Munivara Prasad, 2011), the normal profile must be adaptive. To do so, this chapter introduces a new Agent-based Adaptive Intrusion Detection mechanism (named AIDA). The latter relies on adaptation of the normal profile during the detection stage to minimize the number of false alarms and thus, enhances the accuracy of anomaly Intrusion Detection.

Moreover, to reduce the complexity of the current attacks, the proposed approach distributes their detection on a set of entities which cooperate to effectively detect the attacks and to adapt the normal profile when new legitimate activities appear. These entities are designed and implemented by agents; agents are the most suitable solution to the resolution of the problem of network intrusion detection (Boudaoud, 2000; Kannadiga & Zulkernine, 2005; Khosravifar & Bentahar, 2008; Zubair, 2012).

The proposed mechanism is used to study the network traffic and the malformed packets detection.

The remainder of this chapter is organized as follows. Section 2 provides some work related to the problem of false alarms in intrusion detection. Section 3 gives an overview of AIDA and presents the associated agent-based architecture. Section 4 describes the adaptation process provided by AIDA. Section 5 defines the roles of the participating entities. Section 6 illustrates, through an example, the influence of the adaptation on the rate of false alarms. Section 7 is conducting a study on the required properties for a good IDS, the origins of errors generating false positives or false negatives and proposes research directions that could make improvements by providing it with these properties. Finally, Section 8 concludes the chapter.

LITERATURE REVIEW

The problem of false alarms has become a major concern in the use of IDSs (Luo & Xia, 2014). Garcı́a-Teodoro et al. (2009) highlight that it is one of the most significant challenges in the area to be dealt with for the wide scale deployment of anomaly-based intrusion detectors. The vast imbalance between actual and generated false alarms has undoubtedly undermined the performance of IDS (Chyssler et al., 2004). The number of undesirable false alarms generated by commercial IDSs in a site can reach thousands per day. Even worse, when security officers receive huge amount of false alarms everyday and treat them as a norm, they may oversee the importance of incoming alerts when real attacks occur (Julisch, 2000). For that reason, the main challenge of IDS development is now no longer focusing only upon its capability in correctly identifying real attacks, but also on its ability to reduce the false alarms. Indeed, several methodologies were introduced to deal with the problem of false alarms (Axelsson, 2000; Kumar, Hanumanthappa, & Suresh Kumar, 2011).

The paper in (Qassim et al., 2014) puts forward a new approach for intrusion detection and prevention systems based on risk analysis to reduce false alarm rates in IDPS by implementing fuzzy logic-risk analysis technique for analyzing the generated alarms. The fuzzy logic-risk analysis technique will calculate the significance and the impact severeness of each detected activity. This way, the system will be able to better determine whether an activity is classified as an attack attempt or a normal behavior.

The research in (Jabez & Muthukumar, 2015) work proposed a new approach called outlier detection where, the anomaly dataset is measured by the Neighborhood Outlier Factor (NOF).

Here, trained model consists of big datasets with distributed storage environment for improving the performance of Intrusion Detection system. The experimental results proved that the proposed approach identifies the anomalies very effectively than any other approaches.

Data mining technologies have been largely employed and they have shown their capabilities to reduce more than one half of false alarms (Pietraszek & Tanner, 2005; Manganaris et al., 2000; Julisch, 2001; Nor Badrul & Hasimi, 2008). For example, Law and Kwok (2004) proposed an approach where the false alarms are let being issued as they are, and then detect any abnormal pattern from them using data mining techniques. In their study, KNN classifier is used to classify new data points into normal or abnormal being based on the Euclidean distances. However, the data mining approaches for intrusion detection tend to produce a large number of rules that increase the complexity of the system (Deepa & Kavitha, 2012).

More recently, a study in (Duquea & bin Omar, 2015) proposes machine learning and the k-means data mining algorithm to develop an IDS model with higher efficiency and lower false using the NSL-KDD data set.

Several projects have tried to solve the problem of false alarms by employing various other methods such as Chronicles Formalism in order to justify alarm relationships (Morin & Debar, 2003), reconfiguring IDS to produce less false alerts (Abimbola et al., 2006), trying to spot abnormalities through Exponentially Weighted Moving Average control charts (Viinikka & Debar, 2004), connecting to the Honeypot system for a more close investigation (Khosravifar & Bentahar, 2008), or proposing an efficient hybrid Intrusion Detection learning model based on modified K-means and the C4.5 Decision Tree Classifier (Al-Yaseen et al., 2015).This model has the accuracy rate at 90.22% and detection rate at 83.94%.

Moreover, there exist some interesting works in adaptive intrusion detection supported by expert system technology. Neural networks and fuzzy logic are largely used to deal with the intrusion detection issue. The work of Alshammari (Alshammari et al., 2007) is a good example for this category. The proposed approach requires some training on labelled alerts in order to be able to reduce false alarms. We mention also, as example, the work of Cordella who proposes a serial multi-stage classification system for facing the problem of intrusion detection in computer networks (Cordella et al., 2004). The whole decision process is organized into successive stages, each one using a set of features tailored for recognizing a specific attack category. In case of uncertainty, information related to a possible attack is only logged for further processing, without raising an alert for the system manager. This permits to reduce the number of false alarms. More recently, the DTPAIDS (Elfeshawy & Faragallah, 2013) tackled the false positive problem by employing adaptation strategy using RBF neural network to improve reactively the global performance of the proposed DTPAIDS and also maintains them at a high level.

The majority of the research systems that do support some form of adaptation focuses primarily on the issue of learning or discovering patterns or states that are indicative of intrusive behaviour (Carb´o et al., 2003; Cheung et al., 1999; Orfila et al., 2005; Qasim Ali et al., 2013; Ragsdale et al., 2000). These systems show an obvious need for profile updating which is a difficult and time-consuming task.

Each of the considered adaptive agent-based intrusion detection systems supports a specific aspect of the adaptation. We present the adaptation specificity of three of them:

The Adaptive Hierarchical Agent based Intrusion Detection System (AHA! IDS) provides detection adaptation in three specific areas (Ragsdale et al., 2000): (1) by adjusting the amount of system resources devoted to the task of detecting intrusive activities, (2) by dynamically invoking new combinations of low-level detection agents in response to changing circumstances, (3) by adjusting the confidence metric that it associates with the low-level detection agents.

The Adaptive Agent based Intrusion Response System (AAIRS) provides response adaptation by weighting those responses that have been successful in the past over those techniques that have not been as successful (Ragsdale et al., 2000).

Corba et al. (Carb´o et al., 2003) proposed a system of agents that make prediction over the presence of intrusions. Some of the agents act as predictors and suggest if there is an intrusion or not. An assessment agent asks them for a prediction and weights them according to the previous level of success, and afterwards, makes a binary decision based on such weighted references. Finally, the manager agent communicates the results to the assessor agent. The manager agent knows if there was an intrusion or not because the experiment is done under a training environment.

The proposed adaptation solutions are useful and improve the performance of IDS. However, the improvement is not significant; the rate of false alarms is still high. So, the problem of avoiding false alarms remains an open issue.

In fact, Intrusion Detection System researchers have tended to build systems that are hard to manage and are applicable only on specific systems. Recently, Singh and Gupta (Singh & Gupta, 2012) highlighted regarding to their comparative results that the researches in developing intrusion detection systems still need to consider some aspects and make some efforts to, for instance, reduce the rate of false alarms.

A NEW ADAPTIVE DETECTION MECHANISM

The anomaly approach does not require any preliminary knowledge on the intrusions (Zanero & Savaresi, 2004). It establishes a use profile based on a normal behaviour. Any deviation from the established profile is viewed as abnormal. This approach is often performed into two classical phases: a training phase and a detection phase.

- **The Training Phase:** The user behaviour is observed in the absence of attacks, and the system of detection learns the normal behaviour and thus creates the normal profile.
- **The Detection Phase:** The system observes the user activities and compares them with the normal profile. An alarm is then generated when the trace of audit does not match the profile.

Several works (see for instance Elshoush & Osman, 2011) show that the detection of all the intrusions is impossible. In fact, the normal profile cannot be provided by the designer before runtime or built in a training phase. The so built profile and associated behaviour may evolve when running the detection phase. It is therefore crucial to adapt the user profile when needed to consider new legitimate activities and so avoid considering them as attacks. Indeed, our approach is based on three phases: 1) The training phase, 2) The detection phase, 3) The adaptation phase which is executed when needed.

The adaptation phase focuses primarily on the issue of discovering the information that is indicative of non intrusive behaviour and thus allows preventing false alarms.

This section emphasizes the impact of the update of the legitimate activities on the false alarms reduction, and then describes the architecture of AIDA.

A NEW AGENT-BASED ARCHITECTURE

Many techniques have been developed to adapt the profile. Neuronal (Verdenius & van Someren, 1997) and inductive learning (Mitaim & Kosko, 1998) are examples of these adaptation techniques. However, these solutions are "black box solutions". So, the dynamics of new information system and networks requires new architecture and mechanisms. Multi-agent systems have thus emerged as a new software solution. Multi-agent systems represent a new and promising generation of computing systems, and they are considered as one of the most recent developments in Intrusion Detection. They can monitor an environment and diagnose alerts or start intervention action. Moreover, the goal of a diagnosis system is to supervise and diagnose a system while adapting to the evolution of its environment. The adaptation of the diagnostic entities which specify or enrich their own model, when possible, to dynamically follow the system is thus an important feature. Therefore, the use of agents is very interesting since they offer adaptation feature: agents can decide to adapt their behaviour to their environment (Pro-activeness). So, we propose an agent-based approach (named AIDA) where the key idea is to involve many small co-operating and hierarchically organised agents.

We consider, in this chapter, the network traffic (packets) where a legitimate packet is characterized by various parameters. These parameters are analysed according to their normality or abnormality and then the user profile is adapted accordingly. So, we introduce a hierarchical multi-agent architecture (*Cf.* Figure 1) to represent the functionalities of the three levels: detection level, adaptation level and decisional level.

The first level includes several Artifacts of Detection (AD_i, i=1, n) that act as sensors to observe the different parameters (Pr_i, i=1, n) describing a packet. The role of each AD_i is limited to the supervision of the associated parameter Pr_i. Therefore, at a given time, each AD_i deals with the capture of a value V_i related to a specified parameter Pr_i and acquired from the same packet. Moreover, each AD_i encapsulates a KB_i (Knowledge Base) which reflects a part of the legitimate behaviour. Each KB_i defines the legitimate values of the observed parameter. In fact, each AD_i carries out two main functions: The perception and the deliberation.

The perception of the environment and the interaction with AA (Adaptation Agent) provide the result of deliberation, or get the adaptation request.

The deliberation process is used to capture the value V_i of parameter and to check the validity of V_i according to KB_i. It provides dA_i (1 or 0) that denotes the decision of AD_i regarding the value V_i and indicates if the parameter value in a specific packet is normal or abnormal. If $(dA_1, dA_2, \ldots, dA_n) = (1,1,\ldots,1)$ then the checked packet is normal.

The second level uses an Adaptation Agent (AA) which interacts with n ADs and uses their decisions $(dA_1, dA_2 \ldots dA_n)$ to check whether the adaptation is needed or not. Indeed, the normal profile, created during the training phase, must be adapted to the various parameters values emanating from a legitimate user. The KBs are thus enriched with new legitimate values after each adaptation operation.

The third level uses a Global Decision Agent (GDA) that is responsible for the total decision-making related to the release of an alarm. This crucial decision is based on the ADs decisions. Algorithm1 (*Cf.* Figure 4) gives more details on GDA behaviour.

ADAPTIVE INTRUSION DETECTION

In AIDA, the adaptation corresponds to the enrichment of legitimate activities by adding new legal ones. As the cause of false alarm is often an unknown legitimate activity, the adaptation phase intends to reduce its rate. This section describes the three phases of AIDA.

The Training Phase

This phase is based on a commonly used statistical approach for the generation of a normal-behaviour model. This generation task is distributed among the ADs. Each AD_i realizes statistical measures to

Figure 1. AIDA architecture

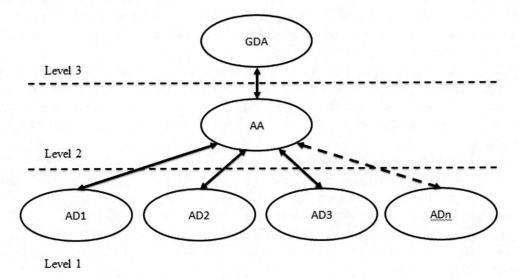

model the observed parameter Pr_i according to the normal profile of a packet. During this phase, each AD_i builds in accordance with the observed parameter (*Cf.* Table 1):

- A list of the normal values in the case of an unquantifiable parameter such as the list of legitimate network services: telnet, ftp, etc.
- An interval in the case of a quantifiable parameter, such as the duration of connection: [0,31].

This modelling leads to the construction of its KB_i.

The Detection Phase

The detection phase is based on the various decisions of ADs (*Cf.* Figure 2) to obtain a global decision which leads to the release or to the obstruction of an alarm. To achieve this global decision, the GDA has to carry out the following computations:

After receiving the primarily decisions values (dA_1, dA_2...dA_n) of ADs that are sent by AA, GDA computes the global decision value D using the following formula:

$$D = \frac{\sum_{i=1}^{n} dA_i}{n}$$

An interval [a, d] representing a space of decision (a=0, d=1) is considered. Note that the use of a bad threshold can result in a bad detection, whereas an interval of ambiguity can handle the various disturbances which can occur during intrusion detection (*Cf.* Figure 3). Thus, instead of classifying each activity as normal or anomalous, AIDA adds the 'ambiguous' qualifier to deal with unexpected situations.

The [a, d] space is subdivided into three intervals: [a, b[, [b, c] and]c, d] that represent respectively an anomalous behaviour and releases an alarm, an ambiguous behaviour and a normal behaviour . An example of these values can be: a=0, b= 0.4, c= 0.6, d=1. Note that only b and c values could be modified by the security officer according to the security strategy.

GDA determines the interval which includes D (*Cf.* Figure 4). There are three possible cases:

In the second case, the number of ADs which decide that a packet is normal is very close or equal to the number of ADs deciding that this same packet is abnormal. The decision of GDA depends then on the Negative Weight (NW) of each AD. It takes into account the decisions of ADs which have lower NWs. The NWs are calculated by the AA in the following way:

Table 1. Example of observed parameters

Artifact of Decision	Parameter	Representation
AD1	Duration of connection	Interval
AD2	Number count of connections towards the same host in the 2 last seconds	Interval
AD3	Number of connections Srv count towards the same service in the 2 last seconds	Interval
AD4	Protocol type (tcp, udp, etc.)	List
AD5	Network Service (telnet, ftp, etc.)	List

Figure 2. AIDA detection phase

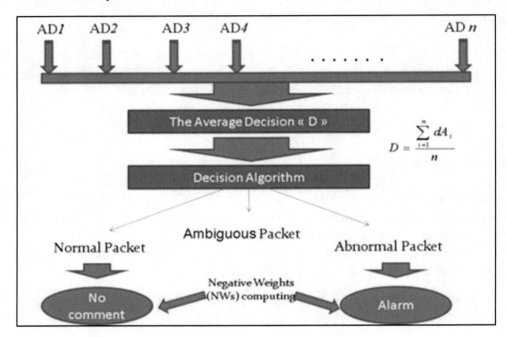

Figure 3. Benefit of an interval decision use in AIDA mechanism

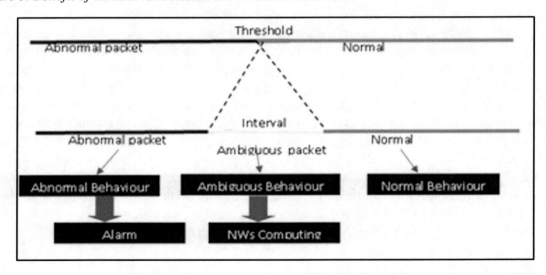

A new factor A_n is introduced. It represents the number of operations of adaptation carried out by each AD (initially $A_n = 0$ for all ADs). Whenever an AD_i executes an operation of adaptation, its An_i is incremented. The NWi of an AD_i is then calculated. Thus, NW_i represents a weight calculated using Equation 4 and assigned to AD_i. It is called Negative Weight since its value and the reliability of AD_i are inversely proportional. Moreover, more NW_i is large, less the associated AD_i is trustworthy:

Figure 4. The GDA life cycle

Algorithm 1 : The GDA life Cycle
Input: ADs decisions concerning the parameters values emanating from the same packet
Output: possible alarm release

1. Read the AD decisions
2. Calculate D

$$D = \frac{\sum_{i=1}^{n} dA_i}{n}$$

3. Determine the interval which includes D. Three cases can occur:
   3.1 $D \in [a, b[$: represents an anomalous behaviour and generates an alarm.
   3.2 $D \in]c, d]$: represents a normal behavior.
   3.3 $D \in [b, c]$: represents an ambiguous behavior.

$$\text{If} \left(\frac{\sum NW_i(for(dAi=1))}{m^2} \right) < \left(\frac{\sum NW_i(for(dAi=0))}{p^2} \right) \text{Then}$$

Normal behavior
else
Abnormal behavior (alarm generation)

These NWs give the advantage of the decision emanating from ADs having carried out few updates of their KB. This means that these artifacts encapsulate a good profile and they are thus more trustworthy.

The Adaptation of the ADs Knowledge Bases

The adaptation of the ADs knowledge bases is achieved during the detection phase. It is carried out according to this assumption:

If the number of ADs, deciding that a packet is normal, is equal to or higher than K (K represents a threshold of majority) and lower strictly than n, a request for adaptation is sent by AA to ADs which decided that this same packet is abnormal.

After the recovery of the request for adaptation, the concerned ADs update their KBs. For this purpose, ADs employ a technique to validate the new values of the normal profile. An Adaptation List (ALi) is associated with each AD_i. This list is initially empty. Then, when an adaptation request for a new acquired value V is sent by AA, AD_i checks if the number of occurrences of V in the list AL_i is equal to or higher than an integer number R_i related to AD_i, representing a factor of confidence on a Pr_i. The new value V is then added to KB_i and removed from AL_i. Otherwise, if this number is lower than R_i, AD_i adds V to AL_i. Moreover, if an AD_i carries out an operation of adaptation, it must imperatively send a message to AA to confirm the adaptation (*Cf.* Figure 5).

Figure 5. The AD task

```
Algorithm 2 : The AD Task
Input : Value V of the observed parameter P
Output : associated decision dA (0 or 1)

    1.  Acquire a value V;
    2.  Verify the validity of V and provide decision on V to AA;
    3.  If (request for adaptation on V) then
        Begin
            If (number of occurrences of V in AL_i ≥ Ri ) then
            Begin
                Add V to its KB;
                Remove V from AL_i;
                Confirm that the adaptation was carried out
            End
            Else  Add V to AL_i
        End
```

The factor of confidence R is used to prevent the flatting of anomalies. Its value can be different for each AD_i and the attacker cannot easily predict the set of R_i values. In the other hand, more the value of R_i increases more the adaptability of the related parameter becomes slow. So, when one wishes to be prudent, the value of each R_i must be large enough.

Adaptation of KBs is achieved by:

- A modification of an interval of decision such as a duration length interval:

Let [Vi,Vs] be the interval of decision, and V a new value to be added:

If $(V \geq Vs)$ then $Vs \leftarrow V$

If $(V < Vi)$ then $Vi \leftarrow V$

- An addition of new values to a list of decisions such as the list of legitimate network services.

AGENT BEHAVIOUR

The AIDA mechanism employs three kinds of entities: GDA, AA and multiple ADs. Their tasks are carried out at various levels of the detection process. This section emphasizes the role of each entity.

Each Artifact of Detection (AD) is associated to one observed parameter. After this initialization, the training phase is started and the KB of each AD is generated.

By the end of the training phase, the intrusion detection task begins. With each occurrence of a packet, each AD acquires a parameter value V and provides a partial decision which indicates the validity or not of the observed parameter value on the observed packet. The AD activities are described by Algorithm 2 (*Cf.* Figure 5).

The second step of the detection mechanism is performed by the Adaptation Agent (AA). Algorithm 3 (*Cf.* Figure 6) describes the AA behaviour and shows the way to solve ambiguity.

In parallel with the adaptation operation, the Global Decision Agent (GDA) decides if the analysed packet is normal or not. It carries out its task according to Algorithm1 where m (respectively p) represents the number of ADs that claim that the examined packet is normal (abnormal).

IMPLEMENTATION AND EXPERIMENTS

To validate AIDA, a prototype is implemented using JADE (Java Agent DEvelopment framework) platform which is a software framework for multi-agent systems in Java. We run our experiments on a Pentium(R) 4 CPU 3.00 GHz - RAM 448 MB- Disk 80 Go - Windows Xp sp2.

KDD 99 intrusion detection dataset is used to evaluate AIDA (Kayacık et al., 2005).

The aim of our experiments is to prove the effect of the adaptation and the Negative Weights on the False Alarms Probability (FAP), and to verify the preservation of the Probability of detection (Pdet) quality.

Figure 6. The AA life cycle

Algorithm 3 : The AA life cycle

Input: ADs decisions concerning the parameters values emanating from the same packet

Output: ADs decisions and a possible adaptation request

1. The AA receives the decisions from all ADs;
2. L ← the number of ADs deciding that a packet is normal;
   If (K < L) and (L< n) **Then**
   The AA provides an adaptation request to each AD, which decides that this same packet is abnormal;
3. **For** (each AD_i having carried out an adaptation of its KB_i) **Do**

$$An_i \leftarrow An_i + 1$$

4. **For** (i=1 to n) **Do**

$$NW_i \leftarrow \frac{An_i}{\sum_{j=1}^{n} An_j}$$

5. Go to 1.

But before discussing the realized experiments and the obtained results, the first sub-section illustrates the detection and adaptation by providing, through an example, the various steps that are used to manage a packet.

Example

We consider, in this example, three instances of packet (*Cf.* Table 2). Three situations are presented: how a packet is examined, how the adaptation can be applied and how the ambiguity is resolved. We use five ADs and assume the following assumptions:

n=5 (number of ADs)

[a,b[= [0,0.4[(abnormal packet), [b,c]=[0.4,0.6] (ambiguous packet) and]c,d]=]0.6,1] (normal packet)

each AD_i has carried out, in the past, a number A_i of operations of adaptation as follows: $(A_1,A_2,A_3,A_4,A_5)=(0,2,1,3,2)$
a Negative Weight value NWi is associated to each AD_i: $(NW_1,NW_2,NW_3,NW_4, NW_5)=(0,0.25,0.12,0.37,0.25)$
each ADi has a Factor of confidence R_i: $(R_1,R_2,R_3,R_4,R_5)=(4,5,2,3,2)$, and the threshold of majority is fixed at K=3
We suppose that a training phase has been fulfilled with a sufficient number of packets and has allowed to build the ADs' Knowledge Bases (KBs) as follows:

KB_1: [0,0]
KB_2: [1,31]
KB_3: [1,50]
KB_4: {tcp}
KB_5:{http}

After the training phase, the detection phase starts with the arrival of the first packet (*Cf.* Table 2). As stated above, with each occurrence of a packet, each AD_i (according to its KB_i and the observed parameter) acquires a value V which allows a partial decision on the packet.

The examination of the first packet (*Cf.* Figure 7) generates the following decisions from the ADs: $(dA_1,dA_2,dA_3,dA_4,dA_5)=(1,1,1,1,0) \Rightarrow$ according to formula 3, D is computed: D= 0,8 $\in$]0.6,1] so the packet is evaluated as normal and since K=3, AA sends an adaptation request to AD_5 because the col-

Table 2. Example of received packets

	Duration	Count	Srv count	Protocol	Service
First packet	0	10	15	tcp	telnet
Second packet	0	25	40	tcp	telnet
Third packet	0	25	40	udp	Domain_u

Figure 7. Example of a packet analysis

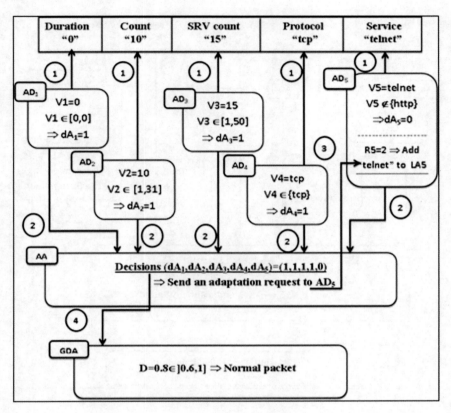

lected value "telnet" does not belong to its KB. Given that its factor of confidence R_5 is equal to 2, AD_5 does not adapt but adds the value "telnet" to its list LA_5 so LA5={telnet}. The GDA examines D value and decides that this packet is normal.

The inspection of the second packet (*Cf.* Figure 8) generates the next decisions: $(dA_1,dA_2,dA_3,dA_4, dA_5)$=(1,1,1,1,0) $\Rightarrow$ D=0,8 $\in$]0.6,1] so the packet is also evaluated as normal and since K=3, AA sends an adaptation request to AD_5 because the collected value "telnet" does not belongs to its KB. Given that the factor of confidence R_5 is equal to 2 and LA5={telnet, telnet}, AD_5 adapts. So, KB_5 is enriched with the new legitimate value (KB_5= {http, telnet}) and the number A_5 of its operations of adaptation is incremented and becomes equal to 3. According to formula 4, NW_5 is calculated (NW_5=0.33). Based on D value, the GDA decides that this packet is normal.

The inspection of the third packet (*Cf.* Figure 6) generates the following decisions: $(dA_1,dA_2,dA_3,d A_4,dA_5)$=(1,1,1,0,0) $\Rightarrow$ D=0,6 $\in$ [0.4,0.6] so the packet is evaluated as ambiguous. In this case, GDA must calculate the NWs of all ADs to make a decision. Theses NWs give the advantage to the decision emanating from ADs that carried out few updates to theirs KBs (they are seen as more reliable). In this case the computations give the following result:

$(NW_1+NW_2+NW_3)/3$=0,12 < $(NW_4+NW_5)/2$=0,35 $\Rightarrow$ the ambiguous packet becomes normal.

Figure 8. Example of an adaptation

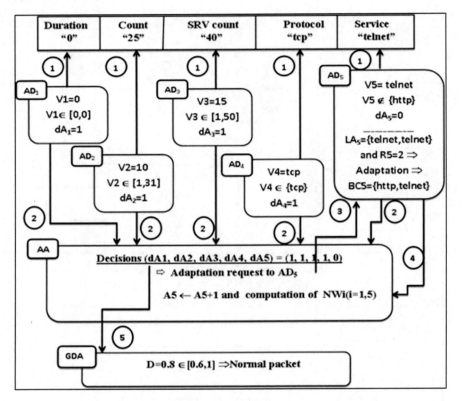

The Impact of the Adaptation and the Negative Weights on FAP Value

To evaluate the effect of the adaptation on FAP, series of experiments are performed. The observed parameters are mainly picked among the "traffic" features (time-based) and the intrinsic features (Stolfo et al., 2000; Tavallaee et al., 2009) which can be used for general-purpose traffic analysis.

In our experiments, we opt to detect Smurf attack which is a type of DOS attacks. So, to distinguish normal connections from Smurf attacks a set of meaningful features is required. For these experiments, we use five parameters which are revealed to be sufficient to detect Smurf attacks. Thus, we consider five ADs:

AD_1 controls the duration of connection
AD_2 verifies the number Count of connections towards the same host during the 2 last seconds
AD_3 deals with the number of connections Srv count towards the same service during the 2 last seconds
AD_4 observes the Protocol type (tcp, udp, etc)
AD_5 controls the called network Service (telnet, ftp, etc).

Besides the duration connection parameter which is a normal traffic feature, all the others parameters are employed in a DoS type Smurf attack detection (Kayacık et al., 2005).

Figure 9. Example of an ambiguity resolution

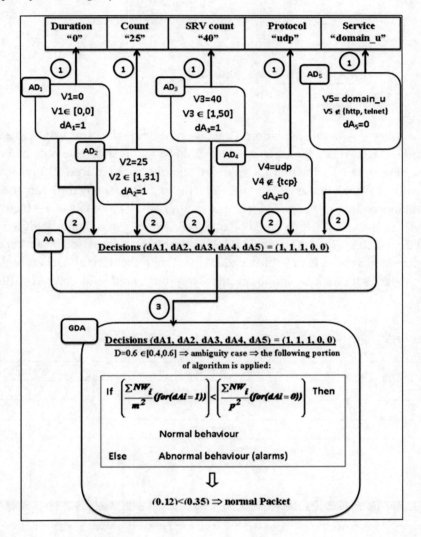

The training is based on a sample of the 10% of KDD. The normal packets are used for the construction of KBs related to ADs.

We consider that the training phase was held in a healthy environment and the contents of the knowledge bases are considered by the detection phase as trustworthy.

This first series of experiments allows examining the performances of AIDA mechanism by evaluating FAP without and with adaptation. We use 1400 legitimate packets. These packets were chosen randomly. The parameters specific to AIDA mechanism were fixed:

n=5

K=4

a=0, b=0.75, c=0.75, d=1 (i.e. a threshold equal to 0.75).

FAP is evaluated as follows:

$$FAP = \frac{Number \ of \ packets \ declared \ as \ abnormal}{Total \ number \ of \ packets}$$

First, FAP is evaluated without adaptation. Then, we proceed in the same way (same parameters) but with the adaptation of KBs related to different ADs. Table 3 summarizes the obtained results.

From the two results, we notice that the FAP has clearly been reduced (0.11 with the adaptation instead of 0.24 without the adaptation). Consequently, the results given by the adaptation are improved.

For a better understanding of the effect of the adaptation, measurements of FAP are taken each 200 packets. Figure 10 shows that FAP (without adaptation) decreases gradually with the increase of the number of packets until the value 1000, where FAP is significantly decreased by an important rise. This means that the detection system is not able to adapt itself with the normal packets included in the test base. However, the test with the adaptation reveals a continuous reduction of FAP with the number of

Table 3. FAP results

	Without Adaptation	With Adaptation
Normal packets	1059	1246
Abnormal packets	341	154
FAP	0.24357143	0.11

Figure 10. The effect of the adaptation

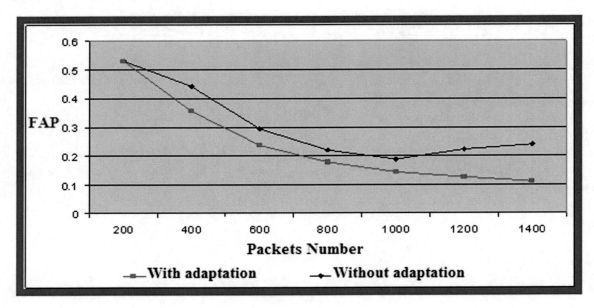

the used packets. Thus, AIDA adapts itself perfectly with normal packets not initially included in the training base. In its two first rows, Table 4 provides a comparison between the KBs of ADs before and after this test. It is noticed that there is an adaptation of the KBs of AD_1 and AD_5; and this explains the previous results.

The reduction of the FAP (with adaptation) has also a relationship with the choice of the value of factor K. This choice has an impact on the PDet. To note these effects, an experiment is carried out. The value of K is now equal to 3. After the phase of test, all KBs are adapted as shown in the last row of Table 4. The results of the test are shown in Figure 11.

Note that the evaluation of FAP for (K=3) provides a significant reduction, by the 1/10 compared to FAP for (K=4); what corresponds to a considerable improvement of FAP.

To understand this enhancement, FAP measures are taken each 200 packets. We observe a very significant reduction of the FAP for (K=3) with the increase of the packets number (*Cf.* Figure 11). We underline that the value of the threshold of majority K depends on the number of ADs and on the degree of exposure of the environment. So, when the environment is insecure, the K value must be great and vice versa. Note that when the value of K is low, the speed of the adaptation becomes higher. The reason is that the generation of adaptation requests becomes more frequent.

We must bear in mind that the increase of the FAP does not induce a reduction of the PDet. For this purpose, we choose (k=3) and we test the effect on the PDet. We opt for a DoS type Smurf attack which is a denial-of service attack that floods a target system via spoofed broadcast ping messages to flood a target system.

To evaluate PDet, a base of 1000 packets is used. The 1000 packets are taken randomly. The probability of detection is calculated as follows:

$$PDet = \frac{Number\ of\ packets\ declared\ as\ abnormal}{Total\ number\ of\ packets}$$

The results have shown that the change having occurred on K (K=3, K=4) does not influence the value of PDet since it tends, in both cases, towards 1.

Table 4. Comparison between contents of KBs before and after the test

	After the Training and Before the Test					After the Test				
	AD1	AD2	AD3	AD4	AD5	AD1	AD2	AD3	AD4	AD5
Without adaptation	[0,0]	[1,31]	[1,50]	{tcp}	{http}	[0,0]	[1,31]	[1,50]	{tcp}	{http}
With adaptation (k=2)	[0,0]	[1,31]	[1,50]	{tcp}	{http}	[0,30]	[1,31]	[1,50]	{tcp}	{http, smtp, finger, auth, ftp_data, telnet, ftp, other}
With adaptation (k=3)	[0,0]	[1,31]	[1,50]	{tcp}	{http}	[1,63]	[1,74]	[1,74]	{tcp, udp, icmp}	{http, domain_u, ntp_u, ecr_i, smtp, finger, auth, ftp, ftp_data, telnet}

Figure 11. The effect of the factor K on FAP (k=3)

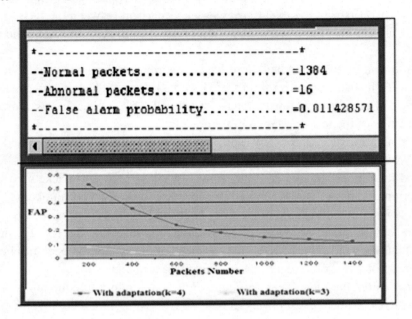

The Effect of the Negative Weights on FAP

In all the previous tests, a threshold has been fixed to 0.75. However, AIDA mechanism works on the basis of an interval of decision rather than on a threshold of decision. The interval is divided into three sub-intervals [a, b[, [b, c[and [c, d]. In order to explain the effect of the intervals chosen previously, the packets of the test base are classified according to the three intervals which are fixed as follows:

a=0, b=0.4, c=0.6, d=1 ⇒ [0,0.4[, [0.4,0.6] and]0.6,1]

K=3

It is noticed that the errors of classification caused by decision given on the basis of threshold are caught up in the mechanism using intervals of decision since the badly classified packets are converted into ambiguous packets. This ambiguity is solved by the use of the NWs. The obtained results are provided by Table 5.

It is observed that AIDA mechanism adjusted the decision of 16 packets and FAP is equal to 0.0042 instead of 0.011. Note that the use of NWs improves significantly FAP. Figure 12 shows the impact of the use of the Negative Weights on the decision making. A noticeable enhancement of FAP is observed, and thus the use of the NWs effectively improves the performance of AIDA mechanism.

The factor of confidence R_i is also considered as a significant factor in the evolution of the continuous training task. For all the previous tests, the value of R_i is equal to 1 for all ADs (note that this value can be different for each AD). Table 6 gives the resultants when $R_i = 0$.

Table 5. The ambiguity solved by the use of the NWs

	Classification	NWs Reasoning
Normal packets	1384	1394
Abnormal packets	0	6
Ambiguous packets	16	0
FAP	0.011	0.004285714

Figure 12. The benefit of the use of the NWs on the decision-making

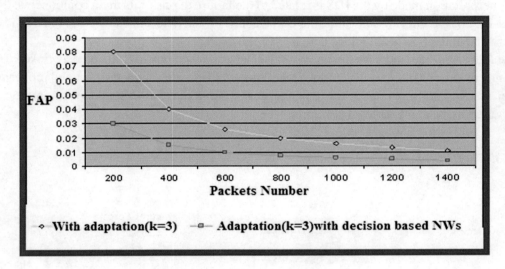

When R=0 we notice a reduction of the number of ambiguous packets. Therefore the total number of correctly detected packets becomes 1398; what leads to a diminution in the FAP. But, if the value of R_i is 2, the FAP value will increase (*Cf*. Table 6). Thus the value of the factor Ri should be judiciously fixed.

FUTURE RESEARCH DIRECTIONS

Intrusion detection systems are becoming increasingly an integral part of any security policy and researchers continue to explore new approaches to optimize detection, particularly in terms of accuracy and response speed (Manoranjan et al., 2016).

Table 6. FAP with R=0 or R=2 (for all ADs)

	R=0	After reasoning (R=0)	R=2	After reasoning (R=2)
Normal Packets	1391	1398	1375	1382
Abnormal Packets	0	2	0	18
Ambiguous Packets	9	0	25	0
FAP	0.0014285714		0.012857143	

The knowledge gained through this work has opened several opportunities for improving intrusion detection operation. These outcomes resulted from a three-stage study:

- Discovery of the origins of detection errors generating false positives or false negatives;
- Enumeration of properties and characteristics required for a good IDS;
- Highlighting the ways in which an IDS can be provided with these properties.

Origins of Intrusion Detection Errors

The misinterpretation made by the IDS is related to the failure of one of its main components: the sensor that takes care of the information gathering or the analyzer that determines whether the traffic contains characteristic elements of a malicious activity (*Cf.* Figure 13).

These failures, which increase the rates of false negatives and positive, are closely linked to internal factors and / or external factors. The external factors result from the characteristics and properties of the computer system and in particular those of the sensor while internal factors depend on the analytical approach used at the analyzer level (*Cf.* Figure 14).

Figure 13. The IDS components

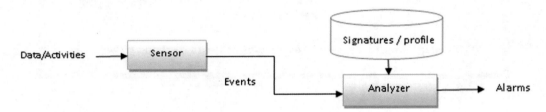

Figure 14. The Origin of positive or negative false alarms

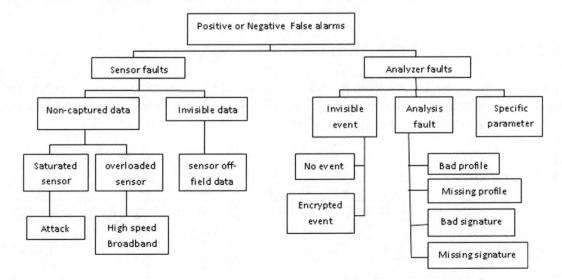

Sensor

The cause of a sensor error can be mainly due to one of two factors: invisible data or non-captured data. Data is invisible if it is outside the scope of the IDS. Data is not captured because of the sensor overload that cannot support the rate at which data flows or because of sensor saturation by malicious traffic.

In addition, several factors, related to external criteria that depend on the environment to be secured, increase false negative and positive rates and can therefore influence the reliability and relevance of the sensor component. These criteria are essentially the traffic flow and the location of the IDS.

The continuous increase of network speeds poses new challenges for security systems, particularly IDSs. A short inter-arrival delay between the packets forces the IDS to pass packets without inspecting them while these packets may contain attacks; which increases the rate of false negatives. In the same context, these missing packets may contain important information such as initializing or closing a connection. Loss of these packets increases the rate of false positives since the IDS expects to receive accurate information while this information has not been captured or analyzed. Thus the reliability of detection of an IDS is inversely proportional to the flow rate (the rate of false negatives depends on the flow rate). Its reliability can even after a certain threshold collapse completely (Jiang et al., 2005; Kim & Lee, 2007).

The location of the IDS system can also have undesirable consequences on the relevance and reliability of the IDS since it can after a certain threshold collapses completely (Morin, 2004).

Analyzer

A false positive or negative can occur due to an analysis error, an unseen event or specific parameters. An analysis error is associated to internal factors of the analyzer, whereas the invisibility of the event and the existence of specific parameters are rather related to external factors which are summed up in the absence of taking into account the properties of the environment to be secured at the analysis level.

For the behavioral approach, a model of normal behavior of the monitored system is previously constructed. During monitoring, the current behavior of the system is measured; any significant deviation of the current behavior from the reference behavior gives rise to an alert. This approach covers two distinct problems: the definition of the reference profile on the one hand and the specification of the criteria used to evaluate the observed behavior with respect to this profile in the other hand.

The false negatives are due, for example, to an attack scenario that took place during the training phase and thus integrated the legitimate profile. While false positives may be due to a training phase that has not been able to detect all legitimate activities for some reason (short duration, slow period, evolution, etc.). On the other hand, an attacker can slowly modify his activities in order to achieve non-intrusive behavior that will be gradually assimilated by the IDS; which will generate a false negative.

The detection carried out via the misuse approach depends on the existence and relevance of the IDS database signatures. In the case where the signature is absent, the IDS cannot detect this attack; which generates a false negative. Therefore, it is necessary to perform an active update of the attack signature database.

In the case where the signature is present, it must still satisfy two criteria:

- It must be accurate to avoid generating false positives.
- It must be generic enough to detect different variants of the same attack and thus avoid false negatives.

In addition, an IDS is unable to analyze encrypted traffic. Therefore, if an attacker has succeeded in compromising an encryption system, it will be very easy for him to encrypt his attack without the IDS detecting it.

Required Properties and Characteristics

A good intrusion detection system must be characterized by a number of properties:

- **Effectiveness:** This term specifies that the IDS must not only be able to detect the most complex attack scenarios when they arise in audit trails but also be able to do so in real time;
- **Relevance:** This propriety refers to the ability to issue an alert only in the event of a violation of the security policy. IDSs are relevant in the absence of false positives.
- **Reliability:** This term refers to the ability of IDS to deliver an alert for any violation of the security policy. IDSs are reliable in the absence of false negatives.
- **Fault Tolerance:** It is the property that enables a system to continue operating properly in the event of the failure of (or one or more faults within) some of its components.
- **Adaptability:** The IDS must be able to adapt to changes in the system and user behaviors over time and must be able to detect new attacks as it must be able to integrate new legitimate activities.

Towards a Good IDS

By exploring the possible ways of endowing an IDS with the previously mentioned properties, a number of solutions have emerged, such as visualization for rapid attack management, use of classifiers for better detection accuracy, the use of consensual algorithms as well as the multi-agent paradigm for fault tolerance and reliability (*Cf.* Table 7).

Knowing that an experienced professional analyst can handle on average 230 alerts per hour when in reality the number of alarms generated is significantly higher; the benefit provided by the visualization in the field of intrusion detection becomes clear. Moreover, several researchers have used visualization to improve detection (Cheikh et al., 2014).

Visualisation, from a security point of view, consists in generating an image based on the data contained in the computer log entries. It is particularly interesting when the number of elements to be analyzed is very important. It is therefore very suitable for the analysis of alarms generated by IDS.

Chabot (2009) proposes four classic cases where visualization is particularly interesting:

- To analyze and understand large datasets;
- To analyze and understand complex datasets;
- To discover and understand new visual paradigms;
- To discover and understand hidden elements in the data.

One quickly notices that the data processed by security analysts meet all of these situations. Indeed, the main challenge for security analysts is to make sense of the plethora of data generated by network traffic. It is important that the response to an attack occurs as quickly as possible (real time) to reduce its impact and to avoid the critical resources being reached. The visualization by the simplicity of presentation of the data in the form of images or graphs constitutes an invaluable aid for the analyst who is often overwhelmed by the volume of the information presented in the logs.

On the other hand, numerous works have shown that the combination of classifiers clearly improves the performance of the intrusion detection system with respect to each of the classifiers taken individually. The work of Giacinto et al (Perdisci, 2006; Giacinto, 2008) attest this. They use three categories of attributes associated respectively with a different group of classifiers. The final decision is obtained through a vote exploiting the merger of the outputs of these three groups.

A second work (Giacinto et al. 2005) constructs a NIDS based on the behavioral detection approach using several classifiers. These can detect different types of attacks. Another work (Nguyen, 2008) proposes a model based on three complementary classifiers, JRip for detection of Dos and Probe attacks, DecisionTable for that of U2R and OneR for R2L. The results of this model give a detection rate of 99.27% for the Probe class, 99.88% for the DoS, 99.96% for R2R, 99.97% for R2L, and 99.27% for the Normal class.

These aggregation methods showed an improvement over methods using a single classifier. They benefit from the strengths of each of the classifiers used individually to achieve a better end result. However, they also have some disadvantages such as:

- These combination systems are less efficient for detecting certain categories of attacks such as U2R, R2L, etc.
- The central analyzer is a point of vulnerability. If an intruder manages to break down, the entire network is left unprotected.
- The problem of the accuracy of the information provided by the classifiers and the confidence that can be given to each of them;
- These problems can be supported by the use of consensual algorithms (Kuncheva, 2004) that could identify malicious nodes. It should be noted that the consensus decision is probably a major problem especially in an asynchronous system with failures.
- Moreover, since intrusion detection and agent technology proved to offer several potential advantages, there has been a great tendency for using agents to build optimal, adaptive and comprehensive intrusion detection systems to fit security requirements (Mechtri et al., 2016). The consensus problem arises naturally in a number of multi-agent systems and consensus algorithms have been widely exploited in distributed computing for two decades. They were originally intended to withstand blunt failures, but were then adapted to withstand Byzantine breakdowns. This is the case, for example, with the Paxos algorithm.

To improve intrusion detection, the consensual classification seems attractive since it allows the generation of a single decision based on the results obtained from various detection methods having different points of view.

Thus, as a perspective, it would be interesting to propose an agent-based model for a consensual classification to improve detection while guaranteeing robustness under a distributed architecture supported by the Paxos algorithm (Kuncheva, 2004) which represents a family of protocols to find consensus in a distributed system.

Table 7. IDS's proprieties and suggested solutions

Propriétés	Characteristics	Directions
Adaptability	It must be able to adapt to system changes and user behaviors over time and must be able to detect new attacks and integrate new legitimate activities	Integrate adaptability techniques
	It must be able to be reused in different environments with a minimum of adaptation effort.	Reconfiguration
	It must resist subversion. The IDS must be able to control itself and detect if it has been modified by an attacker.	Use of the concept of reflexivity which offers the possibility of reasoning and acting on oneself
Reliability	It must be reliable and always be able to make a decision (attack or not attack). suppress",	Use of decision Algorithms (e.g. the vote) To exploit classifiers for the simultaneous use of several detection approaches.
	It must be able to provide a "minimum crisis service", ie if some components of the IDS cease to function, the other components must not be affected by this state of degradation.	Use of multi-agent systems (if an agent fails, other agents ensure continuity of detection) to detect and recover faults
Fault Tolerance	It must be able to recover its initial functional state after a crash (due to voluntary or involuntary activity)	Use of consensual algorithms Use of multi-agent systems
Effectiveness and relevance	It must provide efficient detection	Joint use of several detection approaches in order to benefit from their assets in the detection of specific attacks
	It must be able to operate in real time and not be saturated by the number of collected information. It must be able to process a large amount of data without being overloaded, in order to highlight important events on the network and assist analysts in their work. It must rapidly extract useful information in order to react quickly to a proved intrusion.	Take Advantage of Visualization

CONCLUSION

Almost of anomaly detection approaches require an update of normal profile which evolves over time. The discrepancy between the initial legitimate profile and the current system behaviour generates a large number of false alarms and the Intrusion Detection System becomes more and more unusable.

To amend this, we introduced a new adaptive intrusion detection mechanism to deal with the reduction of the false alarms rate. This mechanism is based on a multi-agent system (named AIDA). The agents allow not only the detection of intrusions but also the adaptation of the profile of a normal behaviour.

In this work, adaptation focuses primarily on the issue of discovering the information that is indicative of nonintrusive behaviour and thus prevents false alarms. AIDA is characterized by the fact that each parameter is observed in an isolated way. This parameter is initially defined by a set of values which can be enriched by new legitimate values as the adaptation takes place. This solution offers several benefits:

- Each AD becomes over time an expert since it monitors only one parameter. The number of false positive decreases, the accuracy increases and the detection becomes more reliable.

- Each parameter in the packet can have a different factor of confidence R. What complicates the task of the attacker if he wishes to insert new values in an underhand way in order to attack without being detected.
- The configuration of a set of ADs according to the type and the number of observed parameters make the proposed mechanism more open and flexible while it can combine different behaviours, and offers a high degree of accuracy to the intrusion detection mechanism. Moreover, it solves the problem of ambiguity among the decisions emitted by different ADs using the Negative Weights attributed to each AD.
- The proposed detection mechanism is simple and efficient.

Indeed, two techniques were used to reduce the probability of false alarms and to preserve the detection rate. The first technique concerns the KBs adaptation and the second one resolves the decision ambiguity using NWs. The two techniques were evaluated via the KDD 99, a largely used test basis. The experiments demonstrate that AIDA mechanism improves the detection of the real intrusions with a significant decrease of the false alarms rate. Moreover, the use of the factor of confidence R makes the intruders' task more complex. The mechanism employs the anomaly detection technique, and can be applied to either host-based or network-based IDSs, because it aims at optimizing the results derived from an anomaly-based IDS, by reducing its false alarms.

Following this work, the acquired knowledge has been used to think about improving the efficiency of IDS. So, to enhance detection and avoid false alarms, a three-stage study has been developed. These steps include studying the origin of false alarms, listing the proprieties required by IDS and finally prospect the approaches, techniques or paradigms to achieve them.

REFERENCES

Abimbola, A. A., Munoz, J. M., & Buchanan, W. J. (2007). Investigating false positive reduction in http via procedure analysis. In ICNS '06: proceedings of the international conference on networking and services (pp. 87–93). Washington, DC: IEEE Computer Society.

Al-Yaseen, W. L., Othman, Z. A., & Nazri, M. Z. (2015). *Hybrid Modified K-Means with C4.5 for Intrusion Detection Systems in Multiagent Systems* (Vol. 2015). The Scientific World Journal.

Alshammari, R., Sonamthiang, S., Teimouri, M., & Riordan, D. (2007). Using neuro-fuzzy approach to reduce false positive alerts. In *CNSR '07: proceedings of the fifth annual conference on communication networks and services research* (pp. 345-349). Washington, DC: IEEE Computer Society.

Axelsson, S. (2000). The Base-Rate Fallacy and the Difficulty of Intrusion Detection. *ACM Transactions on Information and System Security*, *3*(3), 186–205. doi:10.1145/357830.357849

Badrul, N. A., & Hasimi, S. (2008). Identifying false alarm for network intrusion detection system using data mining and decision tree. In *DNCOCO'08: Proceedings of the 7th conference on Data networks, communications, computers* (pp. 22-28). Bucharest, Romania: World Scientific and Engineering Academy and Society (WSEAS).

Barford, P., Jha, S., & Yegneswara, V. (2004). Fusion and Filtering in Distributed Intrusion Detection Systems. *The 42nd Annual Allerton Conference on Communication, Control and Computing.*

Bass, T. (2000). Intrusion detection systems and multisensor data fusion. *Communications of the ACM, 43*(4), 99–105. doi:10.1145/332051.332079

Boudaoud, K. (2000). *Détection d'intrusions: Une nouvelle approche par systèmes multi-agents* (PhD thesis). Ecole Polytechnique Fédérale de Lausanne.

Carb'o, J., Orfila, A., & Ribagorda, A. (2003). Adaptive Agents Applied to Intrusion Detection. LNAI 2691, 445–453. doi:10.1007/3-540-45023-8_43

Chabot, C. (2009, March/April). Demystifying Visual Analytics. *IEEE Computer Graphics and Applications, 29*(2), 84–87. doi:10.1109/MCG.2009.23 PMID:19462638

Cheikh, M., Hacini, S., & Boufaida, Z. (2014). Classification of DOS Attacks Using Visualization Technique. *International Journal of Information Security and Privacy, 8*(2), 19–32. doi:10.4018/IJISP.2014040102

Cheung, S., Crawford, R., Dilger, M., Frank, J., Hoagland, J., Levitt, K. N., . . . Zerkle, D. (1999). The Design of GrIDS: A Graph-Based Intrusion Detection System. CSE-99-2.

Chyssler, T., Burschka, S., Semling, M., Lingvall, T., & Burbeck, K. (2004). Alarm Reduction and Correlation in Intrusion Detection Systems. *Proceedings of Detection of Intrusions and Malware & Vulnerability Assessment, GI SIG SIDAR Workshop (DIMVA 2004).*

Cordella, L. P., Limongiello, A., & Sansone, C. (2004). Network intrusion detection by a multi-stage classification system. *Lecture Notes in Computer Science, 3077*, 324–333. doi:10.1007/978-3-540-25966-4_32

Deepa, A. J., & Kavitha, V. (2012). A comprehensive survey on approaches to intrusion detection system. *Procedia Engineering, 38*, 2063–2069. doi:10.1016/j.proeng.2012.06.248

Duquea, S. (2015). Nizam bin Omar, M. (2015). Using Data Mining Algorithms for Developing a Model for Intrusion Detection System (IDS). *Procedia Computer Science, 6*, 46–51. doi:10.1016/j.procs.2015.09.145

Elfeshawy, N. A., & Faragallah, O. S. (2013). Divided two-part adaptive intrusion detection system. *Wireless Netw, 19*, 301-321.

Elshoush, H. T., & Osman, I. M. (2011). Alert correlation in collaborative intelligent intrusion detection systems - A survey. *Applied Soft Computing, 11*(7), 4349–4365. doi:10.1016/j.asoc.2010.12.004

Forrest, S., Hofmeyr, S. A., & Somayaji, A. (1997). Computer immunology. *Communications of the ACM, 40*(10), 88–96. doi:10.1145/262793.262811

Garcı'a-Teodoro, P., Dı'az-Verdejo, J., Macia'-Ferna'ndez, G., & Va'zquez, E. (2009). Anomaly-based network intrusion detection: Techniques, systems and challenges. *Computers & Security, 28*(1-2), 18–28. doi:10.1016/j.cose.2008.08.003

Giacinto, G., Perdidci, R., & Roli, R. (2005). Network Intrusion Detection by Combining One-class Classifiers. *International Conference on Image Analysis and Processing, ICIAP*, 58-65. 10.1007/11553595_7

Giacinto, G., Perdisci, R. M., Del Rio, M., & Roli, F. (2008). Intrusion detection in computer networks by a modular ensemble of one-class classifiers. *Inf. Fusion, 9*(1), 69–82.

Hacini, S., Guessoum, Z., & Cheikh, M. (2013). False Alarm Reduction Using Adaptive Agent-Based Profiling. *International Journal of Information Security and Privacy, 7*(4), 53–74. doi:10.4018/ijisp.2013100105

Hooper, E. (2006). An intelligent detection and response strategy to false positives and network attacks. *Proc. fourth IEEE International Workshop on Information Assurance IWIA*, 12-31. 10.1109/IWIA.2006.4

Jabez, J., & Muthukumar, B. (2015). Intrusion Detection System (IDS): Anomaly Detection using Outlier Detection Approach. *Procedia Computer Science, 48*, 338–346. doi:10.1016/j.procs.2015.04.191

Jiang, W., Song, H., & Dai, Y. (2005). Real-time intrusion detection for high-speed networks. *Computers & Security*.

Julisch, K. (2000). Dealing with False Positives in Intrusion Detection. *3rd Intl. Workshop on the Recent Advances in Intrusion Detection*.

Julisch, K. (2001). Mining Alarm Clusters to Improve Alarm Handling Efficiency. *Proceedings of the 17th Annual Conference on Computer Security Application*, 12-21. 10.1109/ACSAC.2001.991517

Jyothsna, V., Rama Prasad, V. V., & Munivara Prasad, K. (2011). A Review of Anomaly based *Intrusion Detection Systems. International Journal of Computers and Applications, 28*(7), 26–35. doi:10.5120/3399-4730

Kannadiga, P., & Zulkernine, M. (2005). DIDMA: A Distributed Intrusion Detection System Using Mobile Agents. *First ACIS International Workshop on Self-Assembling Wireless Networks (SNPD/SAWN'05)*, 12-21. 10.1109/SNPD-SAWN.2005.31

Kayacık, H. G., Zincir-Heywood, A. N., & Heywood, M. I. (2005). Selecting Features for Intrusion Detection: A Feature Relevance Analysis on KDD 99 Intrusion Detection Datasets. *Proceeding of the Third Annual Conference on Privacy, Security and Trust PST2005*, 3-8.

Khosravifar, B., & Bentahar, J. (2008). An Experience Improving Intrusion Detection Systems False Alarm Ratio by Using Honeypot. *22nd International Conference on Advanced Information Networking and Application: AINA 2008*, 997-1004. 10.1109/AINA.2008.44

Kim, S., & Lee, J. (2007). A system architecture for high-speed deep packet inspection in signature-based network intrusion prevention. *Journal of Systems Architecture, 53*(5-6), 310–320. doi:10.1016/j.sysarc.2006.10.005

Kumar, M., Hanumanthappa, M., & Suresh Kumar, T. V. (2011). Intrusion Detection System - False Positive Alert Reduction Technique. *ACEEE International Journal of Network Security, 2*(3), 37–40.

Kuncheva, L. I. (2004). Combining Pattern Classifiers: Methods and Algorithms. John Wiley & Sons.

Law, K., & Kwok, L. F. (2004). IDS False Alarm Filtering Using KNN Classifier. LNCS, 3325, 114-121.

Luo, B., & Xia, J. (2014). A novel intrusion detection system based on feature generation with visualization strategy. *Expert Systems with Applications*, *41*(9), 4139–4147. doi:10.1016/j.eswa.2013.12.048

Manganaris, S., Christensen, M., Zerkle, D., & Hermiz, K. (2000). A data mining analysis of RTID alarms. *Computer Networks*, *34*(4), 571–577. doi:10.1016/S1389-1286(00)00138-9

Manoranjan, P., Nayak, C. K., & Pradhan, S. D. K. (2016). Intrusion Detection System (IDS) and Their Types. *Network Security Attacks and Countermeasures*, 228–244.

Mechtri, L., Tolba, F. D., & Ghanemi, S. (2016). Agents for Intrusion Detection in MANET: A Survey and Analysis. In W. Awad, E. El-Alfy, & Y. Al-Bastaki (Eds.), *Improving Information Security Practices through Computational Intelligence* (pp. 126–147). Hershey, PA: IGI Global; doi:10.4018/978-1-4666-9426-2.ch006

Mitaim, S., & Kosko, B. (1998). Neural Fuzzy Agents for Profile Learning and Adaptive Object Matching. *Presence (Cambridge, Mass.)*, *7*(6), 617–637. doi:10.1162/105474698565965

Morin, B. (2004). *Corrélation d'alertes issues d'outils de détection d'intrusions avec prise en compte d'informations sur le système surveille* (PhD thesis). Institut National des Sciences Appliquées de Rennes, France.

Morin, B., & Debar, H. (2003). Correlation of intrusion symptoms: an application of chronicles. *Proceedings of the 6th international conference on Recent Advances in Intrusion Detection (RAID'03)*, 94-112. 10.1007/978-3-540-45248-5_6

Nadiammai, G. V., Krishnaveni, S., & Hemalatha, M. (2011). A Comprehensive Analysis and study in Intrusion Detection System using Data Mining Techniques. *International Journal of Computers and Applications*, *35*(8), 51–56.

Nguyen, H. A., & Choi, D. (2008). Application of Data Mining to Network Intrusion Detection: Classifier Selection Model Challenges for Next Generation Network Operations and Service Management Lecture Notes. *Computer Science*, *5297*, 399–408.

Ohta, S., Kurebayashi, R., & Kobayashi, K. (2008). Minimizing False Positives of a Decision Tree Classifier for Intrusion Detection on the Internet. *Journal of Network and Systems Management*, *16*(4), 399–419. doi:10.100710922-008-9102-4

Orfila, A., Carb'o, J., & Ribagorda, A. (2005). Intrusion Detection Effectiveness Improvement by a Multiagent System. *International Journal of Computer Science & Applications*, *2*(1), 1–6.

Perdisci, R., Giacinto, G., & Roli, F. (2006). Alarm clustering for intrusion detection systems in computer networks. *Engineering Applications of Artificial Intelligence*, *19*(4), 429–438. doi:10.1016/j.engappai.2006.01.003

Pietraszek, T., & Tanner, A. (2005). Data mining and machine learning– towards reducing false positives in intrusion detection'. *Information Security Technical Report, 10*(3), 169–183. doi:10.1016/j.istr.2005.07.001

Pokrywka, R. (2008). Reducing False Alarm Rate in Anomaly Detection with Layered Filtering. LNCS, 5101, 396-404.

Qasim Ali, M., Al-Shaer, E., Khan, H., & Khayam, S. A. (2013). Automated Anomaly Detector Adaptation using Adaptive Threshold Tuning. *ACM Transactions on Information and System Security, 15*(4), 1–30. doi:10.1145/2445566.2445569

Qassim, Q., Patel, A., & Mohd-Zin, A. (2014, September). Strategy to Reduce False Alarms in Intrusion Detection and Prevention Systems. *The International Arab Journal of Information Technology, 11*(5).

Ragsdale, D., Carver, C., Humphries, J., & Pooch, U. (2000). Adaptation techniques for intrusion detection and intrusion response system. *SMC 2000 Conference Proceedings 2000 IEEE International Conference on Systems, Man, and Cybernetics Evolving to Systems Humans Organizations and their Complex Interactions*, 2344-2349.

Shruti, G., Umang, S., Reddy, B. V. R., & Hoda, M. N. (2012). Analytical Study of Existing Methodologies of IDS for False Alarm Rate - A Survey and Taxonomy. *International Journal of Emerging Technology and Advanced Engineering, 2*(4), 393–399.

Singh, U., & Gupta, S. (2012). Incorporation of IDS in Real World Applications. *Journal of Emerging Trends in Computing and Information Sciences, 3*(1), 15–20.

Stolfo, J., Wei, F., Lee, W., Prodromidis, A., & Chan, P. K. (2000). Mining with Application to Fraud and Intrusion Detection: Results from the JAM Project. *Proceedings of DARPA Information Survivability Conference and Exposition*, 130-144.

Tavallaee, M., Bagheri, E., Lu, W., & Ghorbani, A. A. (2009). A Detailed Analysis of the KDD CUP 99 Data Set. *Proceedings of 2009 IEEE Symposium on Computational Intelligence in Security and Defense Applications (CISDA 2009)*, 53-58. 10.1109/CISDA.2009.5356528

Verdenius, F., & van Someren, M. W. (1997). Applications of inductive learning techniques: a survey in the Netherlands. *Journal of AI Communications, 10*(1), 3-20.

Viinikka, J., & Debar, H. (2004). Monitoring IDS background noise using EWMA control charts and alert information. LNCS, 3224, 166-187.

Wang, K., & Stolfo, S. J. (2004). Anomalous Payload-Based Network Intrusion Detection. LNCS, 3224, 203-222.

Yuan, Y., & Guanzhong, D. (2007). An Intrusion Detection Expert System with Fact-Base. *Asian Journal of Information Technology, 6*(5), 614–617.

Zanero, S. (2004). Behavioural Intrusion Detection. *Proceedings of the 19th ISCIS Symposium*, 657-666.

Zanero, S., & Savaresi, S. M. (2004). Unsupervised Learning Techniques for an Intrusion Detection System. *Proceedings of the ACM Symposium on Applied Computing, ACM SAC*, 412-419. 10.1145/967900.967988

Zubair, A. B. (2012). Multi-agent systems for protecting critical infrastructures: A survey. *Journal of Network and Computer Applications*, *35*(3), 1151–1161. doi:10.1016/j.jnca.2012.01.006

Section 5
Cyber Security and Malware

Chapter 13
Internet Crime and Anti–Fraud Activism:
A Hands–On Approach

Andreas Zingerle
Woosong University, South Korea

Linda Kronman
Woosong University, South Korea

ABSTRACT

Scambaiting is a form of vigilantism that targets internet scammers who try to trick people into advance fee payments. In the past, victims were mainly contacted by bulk emails; now the widespread use of social networking services has made it easier for scammers to contact potential victims – those who seek various online opportunities in the form of sales and rentals, dating, booking holidays, or seeking for jobs. Scambaiters are online information communities specializing in identifying, documenting, and reporting activities of scammers. By following scambaiting forums, it was possible to categorize different scambaiting subgroups with various strategies and tools. These were tested in hands-on sessions during creative workshops in order to gain a wider understanding of the scope of existing internet scams as well as exploring counter strategies to prevent internet crime. The aim of the workshops was to recognize and develop diverse forms of anti-scam activism.

INTRODUCTION

Cybercrime and online fraud are a growing phenomenon in computer-mediated communications. In 2015 the Internet Complaint Center (IC3) registered over 288,000 complaints; 127,145 reporting a loss on an average of $3,718 (FBI, 2015). In the past, victims were mainly contacted by 'unsolicited bulk emails': now, the widespread use of social networking services, messenger apps and heavy increase of ransomware malware has increased the possibilities for scammers to contact potential victims and infect multiple devices at once. (Bregant, and Bregant, 2014) (Edwards et al., 2017) Scambaiting arose as a counterattack to scams carried out by vigilante online communities who investigate scam emails and

DOI: 10.4018/978-1-5225-5583-4.ch013

implement several social engineering techniques to document, report or warn potential victims. (Atkins, 2013) Scambaiters are persons who reply to scam emails, being fully aware that emails are written by scammers, tricking them into believing that you are a potential victim. This means that scambaiters turn tables and lure the scammers into incredible story-plots, always giving scammers the feeling that they will get a lot of money. (Smallridge et al., 2016) Every scambaiter has their own personal motivation to justify their actions. Tuovinen et al. (2007) illustrate three possible motives: community service (social activism), status elevation and revenge. In workshops the authors emphasized the role of community service by documenting and sharing scambaiter plots, wasting time of scammers and exploiting their resources as well as raising awareness about online fraud. Scambaiting is often portrayed as a practice of humiliating the other. Lisa Nakamura (2014) argues that some of the scammers' photos resemble a 'parody of Christian baptism', whereas others remind her of 'something you have seen from Abu Ghraib', but she also points out that 'images are put out of context' and that they 'rely on users who understand the conditions under which they were created'. Still her conclusion is that the 'main purpose of scambaiting is to humiliate the other'. Often, correspondences are also hard to grasp or make no sense when put out of context since it is never clear what was communicated beforehand over email in order to receive for example a requested photo or a specific document. Dara Byrne (2013) oversimplifies that 'scambaiters are racists' and 'scambaiting tactics have never proved to be useful in crime prevention'. The author's intention is not to deny that there are subcultures within the scambaiting culture that are humiliating and show racist tendencies. Whereas prior research heavily emphasizes scambaiters motivated by status elevation and revenge, the author's interest is in understanding other sub-groups that see themselves as netizens who have a duty to provide a service to the internet community.

Over the recent years, the authors formed the 'KairUs Art+Research' (n.d.) collective and followed different vigilante communities who fight against online fraud and implemented their strategies in artistic case studies and workshops. The authors created two different workshop formats:

1. A general workshop called 'Revisiting the spam folder', where participants received an introduction into spam, scam and online vigilantism with hands-on exercises for beginning a dialog with scammers and developing story worlds using easy access online anonymization tools.
2. The 'Credible fiction – deceptive realities' workshop that builds upon artistic research conducted for the 'Megacorp.[1]'(n.d.) artwork and provided participants with a hands-on approach to collect open source intelligence about fraudulent online businesses.

The following paragraphs will take a closer look on two workshop models, different anti-fraud activist groups, and presents hands-on examples that participants were conducting during workshops.

The Workshop Models

The 'Revisiting the spam folder' workshop offered participants both a theoretical and practical introduction to narratives in fraud attempts and fictional story worlds created by scammers and scambaiters. The group sought to understand different sides of online fraud and through creative storytelling reflected on issues like online privacy, virtual representation and trust within networks. Through a 'Scam-the-Scammer Kit' (Figure 1) participants learned to create fictional online characters and infiltrated a scammers story world to observe and interrupt their workflow. Each group explored how persuasive narratives are set-up, how characters are designed and how dialog is exchanged to build trust between the acting parties. By using social media, various content generators and other tools to orchestrate internet fiction, workshop participants created entrance points to a story world and started spreading traces of information in different channels, to raise awareness about online scams and to raise issues of trust betwixt and between real and virtual. The workshop provided a base to discuss if components of scambaiting culture can be used in terms of community service in form of creative activism. Participants learned how story worlds are build, how characters are designed and dialog exchanged to build trust between actors.

Workshops were planned in two modules: a 'theoretical introduction' and 'hands-on' exercises. By introducing several scambaiting subgroups participants got to know different scam formats and strategies to unveil, disrupt and document the criminal attempts. In hands-on excercises participants had a chance to try out the introduced tactics.

THE THEORETICAL MODULE

This part introduced participants to the history of real life scamming, starting off from early 16th century where face-to-face persuasion known as 'Spanish prisoner scheme' or 'Pig in a poke' were widely used to trick victims. Over centuries basic schemes have been adapted to new ways of communication: letters, telegraph, fax, phone or Internet. A global boost happened in the 80's with growing use of emails, enabling scammers to contact a large number of people fast and very cost efficiently. Participants discussed their encounters with online scams and shared strategies they knew to report or adjust spam filters. For describing different scam types the authors designed quartet cards (Figure 2) that were created as part of the artistic installation 'Re: Dakar Arts Festival' (KairUs, 2011). The cards follow the design of classic quartet cards that were originally developed for educational purposes. In a playful way, the cards raised awareness about various scam types, provided background information and offered further links to communities who fight against and report criminals. Scambait forums, investigative researchers or law enforcement all have their own methods for categorizing scams. Therefore, a challenge was to design eight categories, with four cards in every category and each card revealing a scam type, while still keeping it short and fun. Some of the cards are linked to online sources, giving yet another layer to dig deeper into the world of scamming.

After establishing a collective understanding of what scams were investigated how the world of fraud has been reflected on in different genres – ranging from pop culture to contemporary art. The authors introduced latest artistic projects and research including related artistic works such as 'Spamming back' by Christoph Schwarz, 'spam-scamscam' by Dean Cameron and Victor Isaac and 'The Scammer and scambaiter issue' by Mishka Henner. Looking at related artistic reflections on spam and scams, the authors presented artistic performances and visualizations of the phenomena.

In his work 'Spamming back' Christoph Schwarz (n.d.) plays the role of a young gallery owner, who discovers internet scammers as a new avant-garde art movement. He interprets received scam mails as part of artists' portfolios and starts selling them in his gallery. After each purchase, a polaroid photo of Schwartz and the collector is taken and immediately sent to the con-artist via email. Using the same types of promises as spammers do, he offers his services as a leading gallery in Austria, while trying to trick scammers into a contract of advanced payment at the same time. Confronting the spammers with their own strategy is the eponymous principle behind the artwork.

Figure 1. 'Scam-the-scammer kit'

Dean Cameron and Victor Isaac are performance artists, who perform a duologue on stage in their theatre performance 'Spam- scamscam' (n.d.), which is taken from the actual email correspondence with a scammer, documenting a hilarious relationship as it descends into a 'miasma of misunderstanding, desperation, and deception'. This example illustrates well how complex storyworlds emerge from dialogs between a scammer and a scambaiter.

Mishka Henner picks up issues of the scambaiting topic in his artworks: For the photograph 'The Skammerz Ishu' he corresponded for a month with a scammer and directed him to pose with a Barack Obama mask (Vice, 2013). The photo and the background story were featured in the VICE magazine UK. In a second work, 'Scambaiters' (2014), he exhibited hand-drawn sign boards and trophy images of posing scammers taken from the 419Eater forum. Both works emphasize the humiliating side of some scambaiters and do not represent the tedious work that a lot of anti-scam activists perform against online criminals.

Figure 2. Scam quartet cards

The three works introduce the main characters; the scammer, the victim and the scambaiter, and provide a base to further discuss questions such as:

- How do scammers justify their actions?
- What makes victims reply on the most ridiculous spams?
- What motivates scambaiters?
- What tools do scambaiters use to gain the trust of scammers?
- What different strategies do scambaiters use?

The discussions were initiated through various exercises depending on the length of the workshops.

Several videos portray the scammers, victims and the scambaiting culture and its terminology and draw parallels to role playing and computer gaming culture. The authors bring up for discussion themes of trust: face-to-face vs. online, physical being vs. self-representation or real vs. the virtual. With this introduction to the world of scams, the organizers wanted the participants to try out strategies used by different scambaiting groups. In the following paragraphs the authors present scambaiting and anti-fraud activist groups, outline their main strategies and give examples how their methods were explored in the workshops.

THE PRACTICAL MODULE

The practical part of the 'Revisiting the spam folder' workshop started out by introducing the participants to a specially designed 'Scam-the-Scammer Kit' (Figure 1), a collection of tips for secure and ethical scambaiting, instructions how to start a non-traceable design of a new online identity, tools to quickly design a credible character and a story world around the bait by using transmedia storytelling methods, social media and various content generators. The participants were guided to perform a scambait either through a pre-established online narrative or through several tasks and 'missions' that allow one to design an own character within a virtual story world. The participants crafted first reply-mails to scammers and depending of the time-frame of the workshop it was also possible to receive answers from criminals. By replying to a scammers email participants started to collect background information in order to report and alert others about the scam on different web-forums. To support their warning reports, they collected evidence in form of background information or documents that were provided by the scammer.

The following paragraphs introduce different subgroups of scambaiters and their creative methods and easy to use tools that were tested out during the workshops. These subgroups include:

1. 'Scam Alerters', a group who report scam emails to warning platforms.
2. 'Trophy Hunters', a group who contact scammers in order to collect evidence that the scammer believes the scambaiters stories.
3. 'Website reporters', who host the world's largest database of fraudulent websites.
4. 'Romance scam seekers' who report fraudulent profiles on SNS and online dating platforms.
5. 'Inbox Divers', who gain access to scammers email inbox to monitor and report criminal activities.

Scam Alerters

'Alerters' identify and report online scams to increase general awareness of internet scams. They warn individuals and groups who are vulnerable to scams, providing detailed and reliable information. Furthermore, they supervise victims to protect them against follow-up scam attacks. Several websites and forums provide information for potential victims; romancescam.com spotlights particular issues like online dating scams, whereas others like scamvictimsunited.com provide support for fraud victims. By taking a closer look at scamwarners.com, ones can see that members of 419eater.com initiated it to document unsolicited emails and fraudulent offerings. The forum serves as a platform to authenticate and discuss received emails. As a result, other potential victims are informed about new scam types and warned against email proposals that are just 'too good to be true'. For victims who have already fallen for a scam, this platform provides a section with FAQs and further advice.

Workshop Exercises: Identity Creator Tools and Online Searches

Each scam narrative needs actors who engage in wild stories about stereotypical corrupt politicians and large sums of money, funds that you can claim as a next-of-kin. To show the workshop participants how scam identities are created, they were introduced to different online name generators. An 'Identity creator' (n.d.) lets you create a virtual persona within a couple of mouse clicks. By choosing parameters like gender, age, name set, and country, it is possible to create quite a plausible fake identity. It also provides random street addresses and background information like birthday, occupation, blood type, weight and height. These basic traits help when character's personality, physical appearance or soft skills are further defined. With the generated identity they were able to reply to certain emails and start collecting informations that can be posted on warning platforms.

In a second exercise the authors reversed the objective of the task, this time diving into participants spam-folders, identifying different characters and perform an online search to find background information of involved participants. Participants found several online warning platforms that focus on raising awareness on online scams and document fraudulent email accounts and phone numbers.

The Trophy Hunters

Trophy Hunters' are scambaiters who reply to scam emails, tricking internet scammers into believing they are a potential victim. These type of scambaiters aim for so called 'trophies'. A trophy - something that scambaiters acquired from scammers - can be of physical or virtual nature. It functions as proof of a scammer believing story-plots and serves as an evidence of additional work or expenses that were caused while following terms of the scambaiter. A trophy can vary depending on actual goals of the scambaiter: it can be some kind of documentation like a photo, recorded audio or video, a filled out form, a fake bank check, sometimes even hand crafted objects (Berry, 2006). A trophy can also be acquired when a scambaiter manages to lure a scammer into fulfilling a time consuming and tedious task to interrupt the scammer's workflow. There are many different examples of trophies, ranging from humiliating photographs to documents that show scammer's wasted time, unveil their working practice or help to identify criminals who run the scam.

Workshop Exercise: Fake Forms

When businesses operate on an international level, administrative barriers can easily get in the way. This is a tactic often used by scammers and scambaiters for their own reasons. To appear professional and gather sensitive data, scammers use forms that victims have to fill out in order to proceed with business. Forms are taken from real companies or mimic businesses like banks, shipping traders or state institutions. Most famous bogus certificates are: 'Anti-Drug clearance form', 'Anti-Terrorist certificate' and 'Anti-Money laundering certificate'. (Figure 3) The certificates are supposedly issued by the United Nations, the International Court of Justice or by the local government in the country where business takes place. Scammers often use these certificates to request another money transfer. Scambaiters use simple forms to either waste scammers time by filling out long documents or to gain more information about scammers identities. They collect these forms as a proof that scammers believe narratives of the scambaiter. During the workshop participants were handed printouts of several forms to check which ones are real and which ones are fake. Fake forms were further discussed in which story-plots they can be used and if they would be more beneficial for scammers or scambaiters.

Workshop Exercise: Calling a Scammer

Besides filled out forms also audio recording of a more personal communication with a scammer can serve as a trophy. During an exhibition of 'Let's talk business', a scam-related artwork of the 'KairUs Art+Research' collective, several scam emails that include phone numbers were presented to the public and phone numbers that criminals used to get in direct contact were called. Once connected to a criminal, visitors were able to ask questions regarding the business proposal and discussed which further steps are necessary to continue the business. Whole conversations were recorded and considered a trophy, proofing that visitors were bold enough to talk with an online scammer. In discussions after the exercise this experience helped participants to understand that there is a real person behind the scam, something that often remains unnoticed in text based correspondence.

Figure 3. Fake 'Anti-Drug clearance form' and 'Anti-Terrorist certificate'

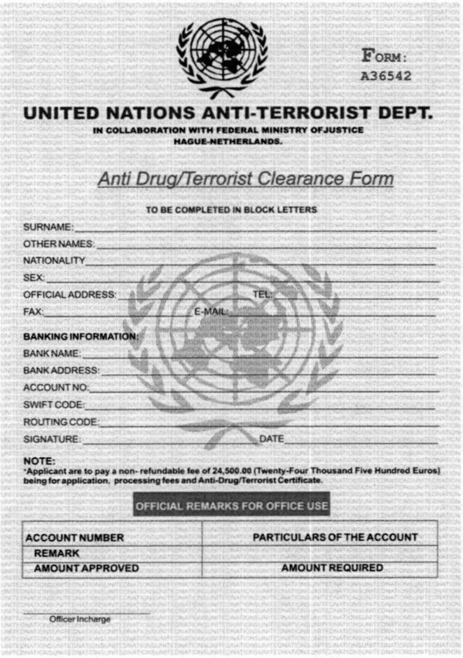

FORM:
A36542

UNITED NATIONS ANTI-TERRORIST DEPT.
IN COLLABORATION WITH FEDERAL MINISTRY OFJUSTICE
HAGUE-NETHERLANDS.

Anti Drug/Terrorist Clearance Form

TO BE COMPLETED IN BLOCK LETTERS

SURNAME:
OTHER NAMES:
NATIONALITY
SEX:
OFFICIAL ADDRESS: TEL:
FAX: E-MAIL:

BANKING INFORMATION:
BANK NAME:
BANK ADDRESS:
ACCOUNT NO:
SWIFT CODE:
ROUTING CODE:
SIGNATURE: DATE

NOTE:
*Applicant are to pay a non- refundable fee of 24,500.00 (Twenty-Four Thousand Five Hundred Euros) being for application, processing fees and Anti-Drug/Terrorist Certificate.

OFFICIAL REMARKS FOR OFFICE USE

ACCOUNT NUMBER	PARTICULARS OF THE ACCOUNT
REMARK	
AMOUNT APPROVED	AMOUNT REQUIRED

Officer Incharge

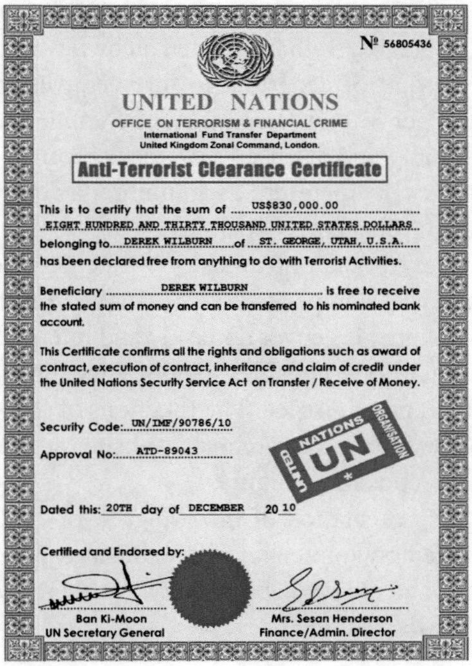

№ 56805436

UNITED NATIONS
OFFICE ON TERRORISM & FINANCIAL CRIME
International Fund Transfer Department
United Kingdom Zonal Command, London.

Anti-Terrorist Clearance Certificate

This is to certify that the sum of US$830,000.00 EIGHT HUNDRED AND THIRTY THOUSAND UNITED STATES DOLLARS belonging to DEREK WILBURN of ST. GEORGE, UTAH, U.S.A. has been declared free from anything to do with Terrorist Activities.

Beneficiary DEREK WILBURN is free to receive the stated sum of money and can be transferred to his nominated bank account.

This Certificate confirms all the rights and obligations such as award of contract, execution of contract, inheritance and claim of credit under the United Nations Security Service Act on Transfer / Receive of Money.

Security Code: UN/IMF/90786/10

Approval No: ATD-89043

UNITED NATIONS ORGANISATION UN

Dated this: 20TH day of DECEMBER 20 10

Certified and Endorsed by:

Ban Ki-Moon
UN Secretary General

Mrs. Sesan Henderson
Finance/Admin. Director

Website Reporters

To appear professional and to increase their trustworthiness, scammers often run fake websites on Top Level Domains (TLDs) as part of their scams. These websites mimic real businesses – online shops, banks, charity organizations, religious groups or IT companies. (Tambe Ebot, 2017) 'Website Reporters' identify these websites for instance by linking DNS entries to scammer databases. They then document any illegal activities and report their findings to hosting providers to get the websites removed or banned. The largest Internet community dedicated to stopping these activities is called 'Artist against 419' (AA419), which hosts one of the world's largest databases of fraudulent websites. Once a fake website is registered, AA419 informs the hosting provider of the site, giving detailed evidence of illegal activities and requesting the site to be shut down for violation of terms of business. In 2003, the group started using custom software like 'Muguito' or 'Lad Vampire' to organize virtual Flash Mobs. The programs repeatedly downloaded images from fraudulent websites until the bandwidth limit was exceeded. This action can be considered as 'bandwidth hogging' rather than a 'Distributed Denial-of-service' attack (DDoS), since a DDoS attack targets a whole server and not just a single website. The group provoked lots of discussions and controversy with these illegal virtual Flash Mobs, but itself saw this as a valid way to take action against hosting providers that did not react to their requests to take down a fraudulent website. According to their website, the group stopped organizing virtual Flash Mobs and discontinued the development of those particular software programs after September 14th, 2007. In the same year, AA419 teamed up with the London Area Metropolitan Police fraud alert unit. They also continued maintaining good relationships with many hosting providers, who now use the AA419 database to locate illegal sites and delete them from their servers. (Espiner, 2007)

Workshop 'Credible Fictions: Deceptive Realities'

For this subcategory authors created an own workshop in which the artwork 'Megacorp.' by the authors served as a point of departure to further investigate Internet activism, fake websites and how 'open source intelligence tools' (osint) can be applied to unveil these fraudulent businesses. Companies exist only virtually and are used by cyber criminals for phishing attacks or to support scam stories. The 'Megacorp.' exists therefore as an umbrella company for subsidiary companies that are 100% dummy corporations. 'Megacorp.' operates on a global scale and is constantly growing with firms represented in almost every branch of industry. Strategic objectives according to the 'Megacorp.' Mission statement is to: "offer complete services from one source which can serve the entire market". Accordingly subsidiary companies cover domestic and international export, real estate agents, insurance companies, law firms, security companies, banks, educational institutions, hospitals, online commerce, economic communities and ministries. The functions of 'Megacorp.' are presented in the form of an interim report and company visuals. The archived websites are locally available allowing visitors to explore the current fake website repository (Figure 4).

After the presentation of the 'Megacorp.' collection of fraudulent websites the authors proceeded to an exercise how to recognize fake businesses online. A checklist of osint-tools was presented to the participants, and evidence of fraud was gathered and discussed.

The checklist included:

- General look & feel of a website:
  - Are photos squeezed to fit in certain places?
  - Are logos pixelated or badly manipulated to fit into an image?

Figure 4. The 'Megacorp.' business conglomerate artwork

- ○ Are domain names spelled correctly?
- ○ Are contact emails same as the domain name or is it a free-to-use webmail service?
- Check freely accessible meta-data like:
- ○ Trade registry number,
- ○ VAT number or the
- ○ Company address and telephone number.
- A 'whois-lookup' on targeted domains can unveil when a domain was registered, most recently updated and how long this registration is valid.
- An online plagiarism checker helped to find clones of websites.
- Using a reverse 'IP-address lookup tool' it is possible to gain more insight about all different websites and domains hosted on that IP-address. Often scammers run several websites at once and it is just easier, cheaper and more convenient to host them under the same provider. This way, it is often possible to observe working methods of a group of scammers who operate several websites at once.

By applying these tools and working through a checklist, participants analyzed a website, raised the suspicion that the website is not legit and collected background information to report the suspicion to the hosting provider. Through a form the participants reported their suspicion of the fraudulent website on the AA419 forum and added it to their database. After that, it was possible to file a 'Terms of Service (TOS) and Acceptable Use Policy (AUP) Violation' report to the hosting provider, asking the abuse team to investigate the website in question with a request to take it offline as soon as possible.

Romance Scam Seekers

People use 'Social Networking Sites' (SNS) to keep in touch with family and friends or find new partners to extend their private and business networks. Some use SNS, chat rooms or special 'Online Dating' websites to develop a personal, romantic, or sexual relationship with like-minded people. Scammers use these sites to set up their fake profiles, often targeting single men and women who are willing to pay them money. These profiles often use photos taken from modeling or social networking sites, making the photographed people as much victims as the people who take them as legit. This sort of online relationship can be a very intense experience, since scammers will try to get in touch with victims on a daily basis by using multiple media channels (Email, Chat, VoIP, etc.), as well as sending physical evidence to acknowledge their deepest love. Blinded by love, victims pay upfront for translation fees, medical bills or visa fees. (Warner, 2011) 'Romance scam seekers' are fully aware that scammers contact victims with the intention of tricking them into making fraudulent payments. They pretend to be flattered by the scammers' attentions and give impressions that they can be trusted easily. These scambaiters then document the scammers' practices and post their findings on victim warning forums like scamdigger.com or compile stories for booklets like 'Hello Sweaty' or guides like 'The Scam Survivors' Handbook' to warn potential victims (Cambaiter, 2012). They also try to track down people whose photos are used in scams and block scammers from creating more fake profiles on dating websites. In the case of romance scams it is important to understand that dating cultures are diverse, and each individual asking or providing financial help is not necessarily a scammer. As Jenna Burrell (2012) describes in her book 'The invisible Users', Africans in general face prejudices because of West African scammers when trying to contact strangers online. Several West African countries are blacklisted, and access to Online Dating, Internet Banking or Auction Sites are blocked. Denied access to information and services based on geographical location reveals unequal and undemocratic sides of the Internet.

Workshop Exercise: Exif-Data and Reverse Image Search Engines

Scammers often send images to prove their authenticity to victims. Images that come in the .jpg or .tiff format carry metadata that is stored as 'Exchangeable image file format' data (short Exif-data). When taking a photo, metadata like date, time, camera settings (e.g. camera model, aperture, shutter speed, focal length, metering mode, ISO speed), GPS location information and an image- thumbnail is saved and embedded within the image file itself. This is mostly done by default without camera owner's notice. This Exif-data is also saved in wav-audio files.

By introducing different exif-data viewers participants were able to analyze whether a photo was edited or where and when it was taken. This can often help to prove authenticity of a person or a story. Another tool to test authenticity of images is to use 'reverse image search' engines that specify finding matching images rather than finding content according to keywords, metadata or watermarks. When an image is submitted, a digital fingerprint is created that is compared to every other indexed image. Different engines and plugins vary in their accuracy, from finding similar images to exact matches including those that have been cropped, modified or resized. This way it is easily possible to analyze an image and check if the same or similar images are posted on other blogs and websites.

Inbox Divers

'Inbox Divers' are social engineers (Mann, 2010) who log into the scammers email account and warn potential victims or report ongoing criminal activities. (Krebs, 2013) Browsing through an email Inbox gives a very personal insight into working methods of a scammer. Scammers often use email inboxes to store additional information, like other account passwords, documents they use to gain victims trust, email-drafts unveiling their scamming practice or chat-conversations with fellow gang members. A scambaiter has been collecting email accounts and potential passwords of scammers and provides them to his fellow anti-scam activists. Group members then log into the scammers email account to monitor the criminals practices, warn victims and file reports.

Workshop Exercise: Analyzing a Scammers Inbox

During a workshop participants were handed out login details of a scammers email account. They were also suggested a checklist to follow while analyzing the Inbox:

1. Lookout for potential victims who are in regular contact with the scammer and believe the stories of the scammer, or even worse, are ready to pay money. These victims should be warned and are advised to stop any correspondence with the scammer.
2. Once all potential victims are warned the inbox is scanned for credit card numbers or bank account information. Account details are further reported to bank officials or credit card fraud departments

who monitor accounts. For this the scambaiter forwards a copy of scammers email including the account holder's name, bank name and address, account number, IBAN and BIC code.

3. Email accounts are often used to store email scripts, harvested email addresses, fake documents (passport templates, fake identification cards, Anti- terrorism and Drug clearance Certificates) or photos that scammers use as material to tell their stories.

These photos and documents get clearly labeled as 'FAKE' or 'used by scammers' and published on anti-fraud websites. By doing so participants were using the same forums as the 'Scam Alerters' do. In group discussions participants presented their findings and together discussed where to publish gathered information and how to proceed with infiltrated accounts.

CONCLUSION

This chapter presented individual or community-driven scambaiting and anti-fraud activists strategies that were explored in workshops for taking action against internet criminals. Lots of time and effort is invested by these groups in documenting and sharing methods of scammers to warn other internet users. 'Scam Alerters' post scam emails and give tips to victims on how to avoid further scamming schemes. Some 'Trophy Hunters' use humiliating methods like asking the scammer to send embarrassing photos, while others try to document their practice by asking for official documents, or waste the scammers time by giving them long and tedious jobs to accomplish. 'Romance scam seekers' track down scammers on online dating platforms and post findings on victim warning forums. To prove the authenticity of photographs they use reverse image search engines or analyze the images metadata. 'Website reporters' compile a register of fake web-sites and cooperate with hosting providers to get websites shut down. 'Inbox Divers' infiltrate scammers email accounts to warn victims and document organized scamming activities. Between 2013 and 2015 the authors organized more than ten workshops varying from a lecture series held at the Department of Web Sciences, University of Art and Design Linz (Austria), to full-day or half-day workshops at conferences and festivals. Shorter workshops (2-3 hours) were better suited to give an overview over different scam methods and discuss ethical issues when being in contact with Internet scammers. In longer workshops tools were presented in more detail and people had time to actively work on storytelling and corresponded with scammers. Looking at scam phenomenons from the perspectives of scammers, scambaiters, anti-fraud activists and victims enabled discussions on topics such as data security, digital divide self-representation on the web. By introducing tactics and tools that scammers and scambaiters use in their communication demystified the communities and offered a new and engaging approach to deal with them. In the workshops it was also proven that scambaiters are a far more diverse group than media as well as previous literature or artworks have been portraying them. The exercises and tools tested by the participants were found useful in recognizing fake and fraud among our daily digital stream of information. Further experimental investigations into the scambaiting subcultures are needed to determine what tools are used by groups such as 'bank guards' or 'safari agents'. (Kronman, & Zingerle, 2013) Whereas online fraud can't be totally prevented this type of workshops can be seen as an important addition to any netizens media competence skills.

REFERENCES

Atkins, B., & Huang, W. (2013). A Study of Social Engineering in Online Frauds. *Open Journal of Social Sciences*, *1*(03), 23–32. doi:10.4236/jss.2013.13004

Bregant, J., & Bregant, R. (2014). Cybercrime and Computer Crime. The Encyclopedia of Criminology and Criminal Justice.

Burrell, J. (2012). *Invisible Users: Youth in the Internet Cafes of Urban Ghana.* MIT Press. doi:10.7551/mitpress/9780262017367.001.0001

Edwards, M., Peersman, C., & Rashid, A. (2017). Scamming the scammers: towards automatic detection of persuasion in advance fee frauds. In *Proceedings of the 26th International Conference on World Wide Web Companion* (pp. 1291-1299). International World Wide Web Conferences Steering Committee.

FakeNameGenerator. (n.d.). Retrieved from: http://www.fakenamegenerator.com/

FBI. (2015). *2015 Internet crime report.* Federal Bureau of Investigation. US Department of Justice. Retrieved from: https://pdf.ic3.gov/2015_IC3Report.pdf

Henner, M. (2014). Scambaiters. *G-L.* Retrieved from: http://zkm.de/event/2015/09/globale-infosphare/g-l#mischka-henner

KairUs. (2011). RE: Dakar arts festival. *KairUs Art+Research.* Retrieved from: http://kairus.org/re-dakar-arts-festival-2011/

KairUs Art+Research. (n.d.). Retrieved from: http://kairus.org/

Krebs, B. (2013). *The Value of a Hacked Email Account.* Available: http://krebsonsecurity.com/2013/06/the-value-of-a-hacked-email-account/

Kronman, L., & Zingerle, A. (2013). Humiliating Entertainment or Social Activism? Analyzing Scambaiting Strategies against Online Advance Fee Fraud. In *Cyberworlds (CW), 2013 International Conference on.* IEEE.

Mann, I. (2010). *Hacking the human: Social engineering techniques and security countermeasures.* Gower Publishing, Ltd.

MegaCorp. (n.d.). *KairUs Art+Research.* Retrieved from: http://megacorp.kairus.org

Nakamura, L. (2014). 'I WILL DO EVERYthing That Am Asked': Scambaiting, Digital Show-Space, and the Racial Violence of Social Media. *Journal of Visual Culture*, 258–273.

Schwarz, C. (n.d.). *Spamming back.* Retrieved from: http://www.christophschwarz.net

Smallridge, J., Wagner, P., & Crowl, J. N. (2016). Understanding cyber-vigilantism: A conceptual framework. *Journal of Theoretical & Philosophical Criminology*, *8*(1), 57.

Spamscamscam. (n.d.). *Urgent & confidential.* Retrieved from: http://www.spamscamscam.com/

Tambe Ebot, A. C. (2017). Explaining two forms of Internet crime from two perspectives: toward stage theories for phishing and Internet scamming. *Jyväskylä Studies in Computing, 259*.

Vice. (2013). Welcome to the skammerz ishu. *Vice*. Retrieved from: https://www.vice.com/en_us/article/kwp8zz/welcome-to-the-skammerz-ishu

Warner, J. (2011). Understanding cyber-crime in Ghana: A view from below. *The International Journal of Cyber Criminology, 5*, 736–749.

ADDITIONAL READING

Atta-Asamoah, A. (2009). Understanding the West African cybercrime process. *African Security Studies, 18*(4), 105–114. doi:10.1080/10246029.2009.9627562

Blythe, M., Petrie, H., & Clark, J. A. F for fake: four studies on how we fall for phish (pp. 3469–3478). Presented at the *Proceedings of the 2011 annual conference on Human factors in computing systems*. 2011. 10.1145/1978942.1979459

Brunton, F. (2012). *Spam: a shadow history of the Internet*. MIT Press.

Rogers, M. (2003). The role of criminal profiling in the computer forensics process. *Computers & Security, 22*(4), 292–298. doi:10.1016/S0167-4048(03)00405-X

KEY TERMS AND DEFINITIONS

Digital Storytelling: Digital storytelling describes the practice of everyday people who use digital tools such as social media, blogs, podcasts, video sharing, or email messages to tell stories. These stories can include digital narratives such as web-based stories, interactive stories, hypertexts, and narrative computer games. Many people use elaborate non-traditional story forms, such as nonlinear and interactive narratives.

Nigerian 419-Scam: 419-scam is a form of advance fee fraud that mainly uses telephone and email as a communication medium. The number 419 refers to the section of the Nigerian Criminal Code dealing with fraud, but is not limited to fraud schemes originating from Nigeria. 419-scam or "four-one-niner" became a common term for all advance fee fraud scams that are carried out over the internet, no matter whether they originate from Nigeria or from a different country.

Open Source Intelligence: Open source intelligence (osint) strategies refer to intelligence that has been derived from publicly available sources both on- and offline. It includes a wide variety of information and sources such as traditional media (radio, newspaper, tv, advertisement), web-based communities (social networking sites, wikis, blogs), publicly available government reports, company advertisement, gray and white papers, or observation and reporting. The term *open source* is not related to *open source software*.

Phishing: An attempt to get sensible information such as bank details, username and password combinations, insurance details, or credit card numbers for malicious reasons. Phishing is typically carried out in email communication by masquerading a trustworthy company and copying their corporate identity.

Scambaiting/Scambaiters/Anti-Fraud Activists: Scambaiting arose as a form of counter movement to the massive unsolicited bulk mailing of spam and scam mails. It is considered a form of online vigilantism and encompasses forms of online anti-fraud activism in order to waste the time and resources of the scammers, collectively gather information that will be of use to authorities, and publicly expose the scammer. In this thesis, the author uses both the terms *scambaiter* and *anti-fraud activist*. The term *scambaiters* refers to a very diverse group of online vigilantes, whereas *anti-fraud activist* refers to persons who take action motivated by a certain sense civic duty.

ENDNOTE

[1]   "Megacorp" is a corporate conglomerate inspired by its equally powerful counterparts in science fiction. The artwork is based on a collection of fake websites scraped from internet. These companies exist only virtually and are used by cyber criminals for phishing attacks or to support scam stories.

Chapter 14
Metamorphic Malware Detection Using Minimal Opcode Statistical Patterns

Mahmood Fazlali
Shahid Beheshti University, Iran

Peyman Khodamoradi
Aryanpour School of Culture and Education, Iran

ABSTRACT

High-speed and accurate malware detection for metamorphic malware are two goals in antiviruses. To reach beyond this issue, this chapter presents a new malware detection method that can be summarized as follows: (1) Input file is disassembled and classified to obtain the minimal opcode pattern as feature vectors; (2) a forward feature selection method (i.e., maximum relevancy and minimum redundancy) is applied to remove the redundant as well as irrelevant features; and (3) the process ends by classification through using decision tree. The results indicate the proposed method can effectively detect metamorphic malware in terms of speed, efficiency, and accuracy.

INTRODUCTION

The enterprise network security is currently under highly volatile conditions, and the security landscape gets darker when mixing up internet environments with the rate of the increasing and improved malicious software (malware) (Fernandes et al. 2014). The huge amount of files on the net makes the efficient and effective investigation of particular files as a challenging activity through common methods like static and signature-based approaches. The signature based approach is a well-known malware detection type that is utilized by antivirus developer (Aycock, 2006). A signature is a string of bits that specifically appear in the structure of malware.since malware programmers are aware of signature-based approaches, they invented new techniques to prevent detections techniques (Lin & Stamp, 2011; Szor, 2005) like polymorphism and metamorphosis aim at complicating the detection process via reconstructing the malware programs without destructing their functions (Mathur & Hiranwal, 2013).

DOI: 10.4018/978-1-5225-5583-4.ch014

Metamorphic malware (Chouchane & Lakhotia, 2006) is one of the most serious threatening types of malware, which generates new code structures after each infection, while no destruction happens in their functions. This continuous mutation causes difficulty in detecting the malware. Besides, the number of emerging worms and Trojans that utilize this technique is rising (Anderson et al. 2011). Some examples of these malicious functions are the destruction of data, information theft and assuming ownership of computer resources. Also, money is another major trend in developing malwares (Plonk, A., & Carblanc, 2008).

Metamorphic malwares emerged as a new generation of polymorphic malware. A polymorphic malware encrypts its instruction codes and alters the decryption code section by generating a new decryption procedure after each infection. This mechanism creates different morphs of a virus (Szor, 2005). The main limitation of polymorphic malwares is derived from their unpacked code section. Although they have an encrypted code section, their unpacked code is constant and it must be loaded into the memory to perform the functions. Therefore, an approach for detecting polymorphic malware is to wait for the virus to start decryption. Then, compare the signature of the program with the dictionary of signatures. On the other hand, metamorphic malware has no decryption procedure, since they directly alter the body of codes (Schiffman, 2010; You and Yim, 2010).

There are two classes for present methods of metamorphic malware detection: dynamic analysis and static analysis approaches (Konstantinou, E., & Wolthusen, 2008). Dynamic analysis executes the suspicious code and observes its behavior. The suspicious code may contain an infected code section. A vivid problem is the execution environment; in the sense that running the malicious code might diffuse the infection from the analyst machine. On the other hand, execution of code on a dedicated machine has overhead (Bayer et al. 2006). Static analysis is prior to dynamic approach if malicious code is detectable through features analysis or pattern recognition. In addition, when detecting the threatening code needs uncommon execution situations, the static analysis might eventuate to a better performance. On the other side, static analysis techniques are dependent on the source of the code; so they will fail if the code is not available (Daoud, Jebril, & Zaqaibeh, 2008).

So far, detection methods are accompanied by different problems: They have a better performance against the known viruses. The database of viruses needs to be updated continually; otherwise, their efficiency will be decreased. Updating the database is a time-consuming process (Daoud, Jebril, & Zaqaibeh 2008). In recent years, anti-virus producers have been forced to use semantic features for fighting against metamorphic malware complexity. The important issue in using semantic method is the need of an imposing number of basic functions. Analyzing and producing semantic signature needs more time. Also, semantic methods are not possible in dynamic scanners (Karnik, A., Goswami, S., & Guha 2007).

Although the detector is intelligent enough for careful detection of malware, it is not acceptable to use a method that needs so much time for analyzing and detecting the mutant version of a malware. In contrary, the syntactic signature strategies need records of signatures update continually. Thus, for storing a trusted database, some experts have to take the time to extract the digital signatures and update the database with the most trustable signatures (Bonfante et al. 2007). Nevertheless, all efforts may fail because of metamorphic technique. To overcome these problems, data mining methods/ machine learning (Witten, I. H., Frank, 1999) have been introduced. The main idea is to use a classified supervised machine, which considers the known samples of malware and non-destructive programs as a training set. A set of features in the training files is used to build the classification model to demonstrate these two classes (malware and non-destructive)

Data mining and machine learning methods are based on this hypothesis: malware has certain specifications, which do not exist in non-destructive programs. For example, the authors of the malware may use some of the production tools to write and interpret their codes, so the produced malware with these tools has certain common specifications, which are known for tools, interpreter and the programming environment. So it is expected to detect malware with a reasonable accuracy by using machine-learning methods. Of course, the function of this method is related to the feature set in classification.

On the other hand, due to the exponential increase of the new malwares, it is necessary to reduce the set of used opcodes as features so that this approach is effective and acceptable in the real world. In the previous articles (Fazlali, M., Khodamoradi, P., Mardukhi, F., Nosrati, M., & Dehshibi 2016; Khodamoradi et al. 2015), we introduced a concentrated approach for detecting metamorphic malware by using opcodes. Three sets of the opcode (features) were made and tested. The main idea is that the anomalies created by the techniques of obfuscation can provide a good knowledge for detecting malware. Now, we are going to develop our research by using a smaller feature set to accelerate the malware detection besides achieving high accuracy of detection.

In this chapter, a new method for recognition and classification of executable files is presented which has less real-time processing in comparison to the previous works. It aims at two general goals: first, a metamorphic malware detection method with the least number of features (repeated opcodes) is proposed. Second, an empirical study is performed to evaluate the proposed method. Due to that, six machine learning algorithms are utilized for creating the classifiers.

We assessed and compared five sets of a feature of opcodes. The results indicate that the proposed feature set here can obtain better real-time processing besides having comparable accuracy in comparison to previous works and commercial antiviruses.

Rest of the chapter is organized as follows: in the second section, a brief overview of related works is presented. The third section is dedicated to the primary definitions and describing the obfuscation techniques. Proposed method with the complete architecture of the pack is presented in the fourth section. The fifth section talks about experimental results of the proposed method besides comparison to commercial antiviruses. Finally, conclusions are argued as the sixth section.

BACKGROUND

Various techniques for metamorphic malware detection have been proposed in the literature. Many of these techniques are based on the statistical features analysis of metamorphic engines of malware. The most important research on opcodes was done by Bilar (Bilar, 2007). Bilar studied different the types of opcodes including the most usable and rare samples. He demonstrated that the frequency of rare opcodes in malware files and healthy files is different from the commonly used opcodes, and reached significant results. He showed the ability of opcodes as a feature to detect malware. Therefore, he analyzed the statistics of opcode abilities and used the high reliability to determine the maliciousness of each executable file. He proved that opcodes can be used as a strong representative for executable files.

In Milgo (2009), Milgo proposed two methods for relating each variant with its engine. In his approach, N-gram Frequency Vector (NFV) of opcodes is considered as a feature vector. Then, a 2-gram frequency vector is used for classification of variants according to their proximity to average NFV of known variants. In Chouchane, Walenstein, and Lakhotia (2007), authors stated that statistical features which are obtained from code analysis of different variants of a virus could be considered as the signature of that virus family. They introduced a classifier for detecting the variants of this family of viruses. A probability-based engine is utilized for anticipating the distribution of metamorphic format of other variants. Then, these distributions are used to define statistical features of the engine. This way, the classifier can decide that the input file is a malware family member or not.

Abou-Assaleh et al. (2004) used N-gram model to extract the features and select the L most frequent ones. Also, a nearest adjacent method is utilized for classification. In a research by Moskovitch et al. (2009), N-gram model is utilized on a greater scale (Abou-Assaleh et al., 2004). They continued their study in Moskovitch et al. (2009) with feature extraction via N-gram model. They proposed that appearance of scarce assembly codes could be a good metric for detecting malicious programs. In this study, three feature selection strategies are investigated in detail including document frequency, fisher score and the information obtaining rate. They proved that with the distribution of 15% of malware in the sample, 99% accuracy could be achieved.

In a study by Schultz et al. (2001) Extraction of non-coded strings was proposed. Due to it, Ripper, Rule-based, Naïve Bayes and Multi naïve Bayes algorithms were investigated and it was indicated that all of these algorithms had better performances in comparison to signature-based approach. In Dolev, S., and Tzachar (2008), the transformation of binary codes to assembly and extraction of codes as the features is proposed. Kolter and Maloof (2004) utilized information obtaining a method for feature selection and structural classification of malicious codes. They focused on the structural problem caused by the unfair tendency of the algorithm to the features with most diversity. Classifiers that were investigated include *KNN*, Naïve Bayes, *TFIDF* and *SVM*; where the last three classifiers had a better performance.

Igor Santos et al. (2013) are the pioneers of malware detection based on opcodes. They proposed different malware detection methods based on techniques of opcode sequences. For example, their first study is a concentrated approach to detect the vague malware by using iteration number of opcode sequence frequency to build a representation of executable files. To do this, they disassembled the executable files. Then they built a profile of opcodes by using this assembly file which includes a list of opcodes and computed the relationship of each opcode with the current cases in both datasets based on their iteration numbers (for example the infected files dataset and healthy files dataset) (Peng, Long, & Ding 2005). Finally, they used the Weighted Term Frequency (WTF) (Igor Santos et al., 2011) to make a vector of sufficient features for executable files. They used this feature vector to detect the types of vague malware. Finally, they computed the cosines similarities between both feature vectors (for example feature vector of new sample and feature vector of malware variables).

In the next study, Santos et al. proposed a new method of feature extraction based on opcodes sequences (Peng, Long, & Ding 2005) and some of the machine learning classifiers were trained by using the extracted features. As we know, machine learning based on classification requires many samples for each conceptual class and try to diagnose (such as malware or safe). It is difficult to obtain date value as a real value. Thus, Santos et al. have offered some methods to overcome this limitation in their next researches methods such as group classification (Igor Santos, Laorden, & Bringas 2009), single-class learning (I. Santos et al., 2011) and semi-supervised learning (Igor Santos et al., 2011).

Runwal, Low, and Stamp (2012) proposed a new method based on opcodes to detect unknown and metamorphic malware based on measuring the similarities of a simple graph. They derived opcodes from both files (malware & safe). The number of each pair of opcodes has appeared respectively, and a graph of opcodes has been built based on their numbers. After this, it can anticipate the maliciousness of a new executable file by computing the similarity of the obtained graph of both executable files and finally the file will belong to the class with the most similarities.

Shabtai et al. (2012) attempted to detect the unknown malicious codes by using classification techniques on opcode patterns. They created a set of safe and malicious executable data for Windows operating system. After disassembling the executable files, they computed Term Frequency (TF) and Inverse Document Frequency (IDT), which represent the feature of each file. Finally, they used some classic classification techniques such as Support Vector Machine (SVM), Logistic Regression (LR), Artificial Neural Networks (ANN) etc. to investigate the feature selection method.

Although these researchers indicate the importance of metamorphic malware detection, their effectiveness still needs to be improved. Therefore, in (Fazlali, M., Khodamoradi, P., Mardukhi, F., Nosrati, M., & Dehshibi 2016; Khodamoradi et al. 2015) we proposed a new technique for detecting unknown malware based on counting the assembly instructions. However, in that method, speed was not considered as a challenging issue. Due to the online extraction of statistics from assembly codes, we have to accelerate the method while maintaining high accuracy. In this article, we consider fewer numbers of features to overcome this overhead.

BASIC DEFINITIONS AND CONCEPTS

In order to escape detection, metamorphic malware changes its code and signature patterns after each iteration. This is done through obfuscation techniques for creating a new generation of the code, without destruction in malware functions. To do this, the malware must be able to disintegrate and change when it propagates. A metamorphic malware's main body never appears in the memory. This is due to the lack of decryption and compression processes. It causes detection to be much more difficult for malware scanners (You & Yim, 2010).

Metamorphic malware has a metamorphic engine, which aims to obfuscate the code. The body of a metamorphic malware consists of two parts: metamorphic engine and malicious code (Kaushal, Swadas, & Prajapati 2012).

A set of techniques for generating multiple variants of code, with identical functions but different morphs is called Obfuscation. It is difficult to understand that the ripped program is equal to the original program (Shankarapani et al. 2011; Vinod, P., Jaipur, R., Laxmi, V., & Gaur 2009):

Common Obfuscation Techniques

Garbage code appending is a simple method for adding some futile instructions to the main program, to change the morph of the program without altering its functions (You & Yim, 2010). Instructions like "SUB ax 0", "MOV ax, ax," NOP and XCHG are some of its examples (Kaushal, Swadas, & Prajapati, 2012). Renaming the registers is another simple method for changing a malware from generation to generation, while the main functions remain intact (You & Yim, 2010). Another technique is randomly changing the order of sub-routines that makes the code of malware obfuscated. For N sub-routines in the program code, there are $N!$ Permutations to generate the new program code. For instance, "Win32/Ghost" has 10 sub-routines, so it is capable of creating $10!$ orders of sub-routines, and consequently 3628800 various malwares (You & Yim, 2010).

Unconditional jump (*jmp*) is used as the backbone of code-reordering technique to obfuscate the code. This technique maintains the function of the code, although it creates several morphs of the code by reordering the code parts. The number of added *jmp* instructions depends on the reordered code parts

(Shabtai et al. 2012). By substitution of equivalent instructions as another technique, malware substitutes some of the instructions with equivalent alternatives. For example, both "xor eax, eax" and "sub eax, eax" change the value of the register to zero (Kaushal, Swadas, & Prajapati, 2012). Malware is able to substitute these instructions using a library of equivalent instructions (You & Yim, 2010).

THE PROPOSED METHOD

The basis of this research is the ability to investigate operational codes (opcodes) to detect malware. Researcher in (Fazlali, M., Khodamoradi, P., Mardukhi, F., Nosrati, M., & Dehshibi, 2016) showed opcodes can detect a significant difference between a safe program and a malware and that rare opcodes can anticipate better than common opcodes. Operators in machine instruction can be removed and opcodes can explain the difference between a safe program and a malware automatically. Thus, our approach only uses the opcodes, and operators are removed from the instruction. We used a set of 227 opcodes and make assembly of five set of opcode features. Then, they were tested by classification algorithm of the decision tree. We seek to find the most relevant opcode to detect malware, increase the speed and effectiveness and preserve the high accuracy rate.

The proposed method includes a static detection procedure. This method was built to detect metamorphic malware and to understand whether a program is infected by a metamorphic malware or not. This method is affected by code obfuscation techniques and considers the whole program as the input file. This means the method does not concentrate on detection of a part of the code that is related to malware. Therefore, it can analyze the whole program and after that, certain interferences can be done. Of course, the proposed method can be considered a heuristic method because it can make false positives in optimum condition. For example, analysis of a program, which is written incorrectly without optimization, may cause a False Positive (*FP*). Our method works on disassembled executable files and exclusively works on the assembly code. In our experiments, we use the 8086 assembly instruction.

The proposed method considers that there are common features among the generated morphs of a metamorphic engine. It considers extracted statistics from analysis of different morphs of malware as a signature, which can be utilized to detect the malware. Statistics based approaches opened a new way for malware detection in recent years. Statistical approaches investigate different generations of variants, through executing the malware several times. Due to it, basic version of malware is executed. It generates the next variant, which is an input for investigation. Execution of series of variants provides several inputs. Since these variants are generated by a similar engine, they are obfuscated similarly. These resemblances are not vividly detectable, but they can be revealed by statistics. Statistical analysis of a generation of metamorphic malware leads to the development of a process for creating an automatic signature for that class of malware.

A complete list of statistics includes the size of the file, runtime size of the file, metrics of garbage codes, special opcodes measurement, compression, etc. It is not essential to grab all these statistics from all the variants of malware. It leads to developing a classifier for detecting malware based on a specific number of statistics. It needs to set a threshold for each class of malwares. A complete list of statistics joined with the threshold lets the classifier detect the metamorphic malware.

The proposed method includes the statistics of opcodes, which their thresholds are obtained through the algorithms of the decision tree; so, it may differ relying on various algorithms. Outputs of these algorithms (which are the thresholds) assist in making a distinction between malware and healthy files. An instance of utilizing thresholds is elaborated in "System evaluation" at section 5.

The proposed model of malware detection is described as follows. Detection is based on the common executable codes of malware. Techniques such as garbage codes, reordering and renaming are utilized by the malware, where they can be detected by investigation of their side effects. Our model is based on the optimization. A healthy compiled code differs from the code of a malware. The healthy code is generated by the compiler, so it is optimized. Malware is also generated by a compiler, so it is optimized for the first generation. But, the next generations are created by the previous generations, not through a compiler. So, they are not as optimized as the first generation. Consequently, analysis of a metamorphic engine lets us extract the statistical features and train a classifier for detecting variants of malware. Indirectly we aim to probe the optimization of a program to make a decision if it is a malware or not. It is practically possible through extracting the statistics of opcodes. In following sub-sections, details of the proposed method are explained.

Steps of the Proposed Method

Our method is applicable to disassemble executable files. The detection and classification are performed in three steps:

Step 1: In this step, a disassembled file is generated from the original files (including both malware and healthy ones). A disassembler converts the codes of the executable file to assembly codes, unlike the compiler. It should be noted that disassembler is independent of the source programming language. The main advantage of disassembling is to provide an overview of the whole code. In this step, all the executable files (malware and healthy) are disassembled by "IDA Pro Disassembler", and the assembly codes are stored.

Step 2: Disassembled codes contain futile contents like comments, labels, empty lines, etc. Futile codes that cause a problem in counting must be omitted. We have created *AFP* tool for preprocessing and removing the futile codes. Next, our tool, titled *OSE*, calculates the frequency of opcodes. *OSE* is the base of this method. It statistically analyzes the disassembled codes and stores the results in an Excel file. Table 1 shows an example of statistics of the sample file. The output of this step is the base of the decision in the next step.

Step 3: Five feature sets are selected from the output of the previous step, and each of them is sent to a machine learning classifier which can determine whether a code is a malware or not. The specific classifier can detect the metamorphic malware from non-malware programs, and this is performed by considering a specific threshold to each opcode set.

Table 1. An example of OSE obtained statistics

Class	cmp	Dec	jmp	jnz	jz	mov	push	xor
Test_AFP.asm	2	1	1	1	1	1	1	1

System Architecture

Traditional trends for malware detection are designed according to heuristic and signature-based approaches. They are not able to detect metamorphic malware, so it was essential to develop new innovations for detection. Current study supposed that statistical metrics could be utilized for detecting such malware. Although the malware has different morphs, all the morphs are generated by a single engine. Consequently, it is possible to find similar statistical patterns among them. The proposed method is going to show that statistics is an appropriate tool for detecting similar patterns and features of malware variants.

The general focus of this study is to investigate the portable executable files; because most of the virus attacks are performed through such files. Figure 1 shows the details of the proposed method in four distinct components: disassembler, preprocessor, feature extractor and classifier. The main part of the method is feature extraction. As soon as the features were extracted, the classifier would be trained and tested.

Features Extraction

Classification of malicious code can be done based on generated features. On the other hand, a higher number of features results in an increase in the algorithm's execution time. Feature selection is one of the most used techniques in pre-processing of machine learning, data-mining and image processing to overcome this problem. Our goal is to accelerate the malware detector by removing extraneous features, besides maintaining the quality of other parameters such as accuracy. Feature extraction is an important part of a malware detector. In this way, we consider the frequency of opcodes in an executable code as

Figure 1. Details of the proposed method

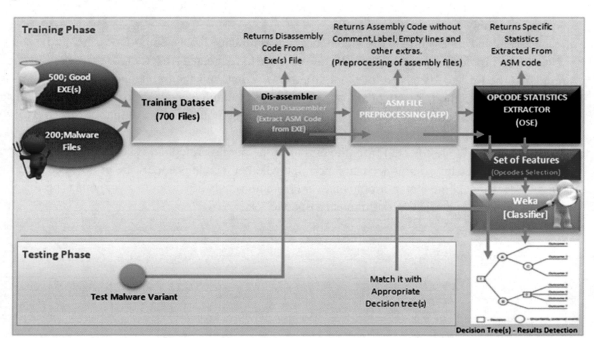

a feature. In particular, an assembly code contains a set of instructions and each instruction includes two tuples *opcode and a list of parameters*. Since the opcode is our feature and the significant part, we remove parameters and assume that a program is composed only of opcodes. Therefore, in our experiments, we will analyze the opcodes. In our research, we examined a total of 227 assembly opcodes as our primary features (Khodamoradi et al., 2015). Opcodes are mostly retrieved from and.

Generally increasing the number of features increases the dimensions of the problem. Therefore, finding the minimum and the most influential number of features has been one of the major challenges in data mining. The same challenge in our research is to find the most effective opcodes (features) to reduce the computational load in malware detection. We extracted five feature sets from 227 assembly opcodes. The first one includes all 227 opcodes. The second set includes all opcodes except those that have zero frequency. The third set includes 20 opcodes that have the most occurrences in five classes of malware and healthy files. According to research conducted by (Bilar, 2007), only 14 opcodes of Intel instruction set have the largest repetition in executable files. Therefore, we have considered these 14 opcodes as our fourth feature set. The fifth feature set includes 13 features, which includes 12 features from opcodes with the most frequent and a feature from 32 conditional and unconditional jump instructions. Table 2 shows the opcodes used in feature sets 3, 4 and 5.

Table 2. Instructions with the maximal frequencies

20 Features	14 Features(Bilar)	13 Features
MOV	MOV	MOV
PUSH	PUSH	PUSH
CALL	CALL	CALL
POP	POP	POP
CMP	CMP	CMP
JZ	JZ	-------
LEA ‹	LEA	LEA
TEST	TEST	TEST
JMP	JMP	-------
ADD	ADD	ADD
JNZ	JNZ	-------
RETN	RETN	RETN
XOR	XOR	XOR
AND	AND	AND
SUB		SUB
OR		All JUMPs
DEC		
INT		
INC		
NOP		

The reason behind creating a number of the feature sets is: disregarding low repetitions opcodes in executing codes and focusing on high repetitions opcodes to reduce the time complexity.

EXPERIMENTAL RESULTS

Training Datasets

Generally, the number of healthy datasets in a system is more than malicious ones. Therefore, training data sets include five distinct classes of executable files. The first class includes 500 healthy files that are gathered from different versions of Microsoft Windows directory and applications in Program files. The second class is constructed from 50 samples of viruses that are generated by Next Generation Virus Creation Kit "*NGVCK*" which is one of the most famous tools for creating metamorphic malwares. The third class involves 50 samples of viruses that are created by Virus Creation Lab "*VCL*." The fourth class contains 50 samples, which were created using Mass Code Generator "*MPCGEN*," and, finally, the fifth class includes 50 samples of Second Generation virus generator "*G2*". All of the mentioned tools have been successful in creating metamorphic malware. These tools provide a toolkit that allows the code to change its morph in every execution using obfuscation techniques. It should be noted that no destruction would happen in their functions during obfuscation. Therefore, the new morph has the same function as the previous generation, but with a different signature. All the mentioned tools are available at VXHeavens website.

Implementation

To evaluate the proposed method we implemented it in "Mathworks Matlab R2015a". Also, programming language Python 2.7.9 was utilized to implement our tools, and Weka (Garner 2007) was employed for different classification algorithms. Implementation platform includes Intel Core i7 4710HQ processor (8-core with clocking rate 2.50GHz), 8GB RAM and Windows 7 Ultimate 64-Bit.

System Evaluation

In this section, we are going to answer the question "How efficient is the proposed method for detecting metamorphic malware?" The testing set consists of 130 executable files including 50 healthy files and 20 samples per each *NGVCK, G2, VCL* and *MPCGEN* classes.

Training data sets are used in Weka in order to train the classifier. Six classification algorithms were utilized for assessing the system. They are: *j48* (Quinlan 2014), *j48graft, LADTREE, RANDOMFOR-EST* (Breiman, 2001; Kam, 1995), *NBTREE*, and *REPTREE*. These algorithms create decision trees so that every decision node applies some conditions on one of the attributes. Terminal nodes appear in the predicted class. A path from the root of the tree to the terminal node passes from a set of decisions (each attribute must be less/greater than a specified threshold) to get to the predicated class (Hall, M., I. Witten, 2011; Quinlan, 1986).

Algorithms of decision trees are utilized to calculate and set the thresholds. Inspection of outputs of these algorithms leads to obtaining thresholds for detection of each family of malwares. Thresholds make the distinction between malware and healthy files. For example, according to the appearance frequencies of opcodes "retn" and "push" in the file, if the frequency of opcode "retn" is less than or equal to 3 and the frequency of opcode "push" is greater than 20, then the file is anticipated to be a member of *G2* malware. In this way, the signature of each family of malware can be specified by rules of decision trees.

To evaluate the proposed method we have considered parameters "*FPR* (False Positive Rate), *TPR* (True Positive Rate), Receiver Operating Characteristic (*ROC*) Area, Accuracy, Precision, Recall, Learning Time, and Testing Time and the time of Real-Time processing. The results based on each parameter are explained underneath.

Time of Real-Time Processing

Most of the antiviruses run in real time manner. Therefore, it is important to have acceptable real-time processing overhead for each malware detector algorithm. In this way, we measure the time of real-time processing which is composed of:

- **Pre-Processing Time:** Measuring the required time for the pre-processing of assembly files via *AFP*.
- **Time of Opcode (Feature) Extraction:** Measuring the time of opcode extraction for each feature set via *OSE*.

Figure 2 illustrates the required time for pre-processing of assembly files via *AFP*. As you can see in the figure, the large executable files require more pre-processing time. For the maximum size in our dataset, pre-processing time is 1500 *ms, which* is acceptable and of course can be improved by more parallelization techniques in future works.

Figure 3 shows the feature extraction time for all feature sets. This step extracts opcodes via *OSE* by using the pre-processing file. The feature set with 227 opcodes needs the average extraction time of 96.25 *ms*. For the second feature set with 120 opcodes, the average extraction time is 41.11 *ms*. For the third feature set with 20 opcodes, the average extraction time is 11.97 *ms*. This means that, based on our assumption; we can reduce the extraction time by decreasing the number of features.

Figure 2. Pre-processing time of assembly files via AFP

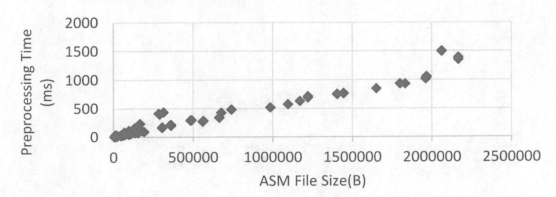

We can conclude that the required extraction time is related to the number of features (opcode) and size of the files. For the fourth feature set with 14 opcodes, the average extraction time is 9.58 *ms* and for the fifth feature set with 13 features (12 opcodes and set of 32, jump assembly), the average extraction time is 25.87 *ms*. Here the average extraction time increases for 13 features. This is because we considered all the jump instructions. Here we used 12 opcodes in five-set and a set of opcodes including all jump assembly, which is 44 opcodes in total (12 opcodes with the highest frequency and 32 jump assembly). So using 14 features is more acceptable whenever we need to reduce the time of real-time processing.

Due to the fact the duration of real-time processing is the summation of preprocessing and feature extraction time, we can conclude that it is decreased by reducing the number of features and using the feature sets with 13 features and 14 opcodes is better than the other feature sets.

TPR, FPR, and ROC

Since one of our goals is to minimize *FPR*, we have compared decision tree algorithms based on *TPR* and *FPR*. The results in Table 3 show that J48 algorithm has the maximum *TPR* and the minimum *FPR* for all feature sets. Also, the results in Table 3 indicate that for the feature set of 227 opcodes in all algorithms *TPR* is 1 and *FPR* is 0. This is the same for 120 feature set except in *REPTREE* algorithm, however; *TPR* and *FPR* are still acceptable. By decreasing the size of the feature set to 20 (the second set), four algorithms *LADTree, NBTree, RANDOMFOREST*, and *REPTREE* no longer have the maximum *TPR* and Minimum *FPR*. Then again, *TPR* and *FPR* are near 1 and 0 for these algorithms. By employing 14 features although *J48graft* has *TPR* equal to 0.971 and *FPR* equal to 0.005, *LADTree, NBTree* and *RANDOMFOREST* have the maximum *TPR* and the minimum *FPR*. This demonstrates the correctness of our selection of 14 features for our feature set. The results in the table indicate that for the last and minimum size feature set (13 feature set) we have reached *TPR* equal to 1 and *FPR* equal to 0 for all algorithms except for *REPTREE* algorithm. This is the same as employing 120 feature set.

The low rate of *FPR* for the feature sets with a minimum number of opcodes indicates that the proposed method has a low-risk rate in considering a malware as a safe software besides acceptable real-time processing.

Figure 3. Feature extraction time for five sets of features via OSE

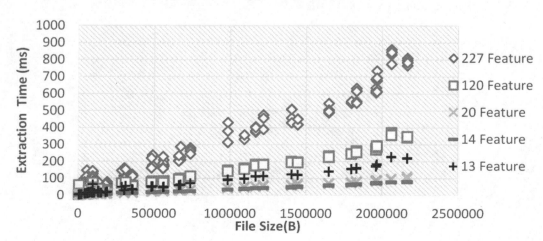

Table 3. Results of TPR, FPR and ROC AREA with 6 classification algorithms and 5 sets of features

ROC AREA	FPR	TPR	Num of Opcodes (Features)	Classification Algorithm
1	0	1	227	
1	0	1	120	
1	0	1	20	J48
1	0	1	14	
1	0	1	13	
1	0	1	227	
1	0	1	120	
1	0	1	20	J48graft
0.983	0.005	0.971	14	
1	0	1	13	
1	0	1	227	
1	0	1	120	
1	0.003	0.987	20	LADTree
1	0	1	14	
1	0	1	13	
1	0	1	227	
1	0	1	120	
1	0.002	0.987	20	NBTree
1	0	1	14	
1	0	1	13	
1	0	1	227	
1	0	1	120	
1	0.006	0.974	20	RANDOMFOREST
1	0	1	14	
1	0	1	13	
1	0	1	227	
0.988	0.009	0.985	120	
0.984	0.006	0.974	20	REPTREE
0.998	0.001	0.985	14	
0.998	0.001	0.985	13	

Analysis of Table 4 indicates that the proposed method can classify four metamorphic malware and healthy files. Many decision tree algorithms in the table, reach a value of 1 for the area of *ROC*, especially for the feature sets with 13 features (12 opcodes + all Jumps) and 14 opcodes. This indicates that this method works correctly because the area of *ROC* that equals 1 identifies a correct classifier. This is another factor that suggests that our method has high accuracy especially for the minimal number of feature sets. A conclusion that is worth mentioning is that our method can correctly classify a metamorphic malware.

Accuracy, Precision, and Recall

Accuracy is calculated using equation: *(TPR+TNR) / (TPR+TNR+FPR+FNR)*. *The accuracy* of the proposed method, which is tested on different benchmarks, is illustrated in Figure 4. For the feature set of 227 opcodes, all of the decision tree algorithms achieved 100% *accuracy*. For the feature set of 120 opcodes and 13 features, all algorithms except *REPTREE* algorithm achieved 100% *accuracy*. Here *REPTREE* gained the *accuracy* of 98.52%. For the feature set of 20 opcodes *J48* and *J48graft* algorithms achieved 100% *accuracy*. While *LADTREE* and *NBTREE* had an *accuracy* of 98.71% and *REPTREE* and *RANDOMFOREST* had an *accuracy* of 97.43%. For the feature sets of 14 opcodes, the obtained *accuracy* is in the range of 97.05% to 100%. The best results were taken from algorithms *j48*, *LADTREE*, *NBTREE*, and *RANDOMFOREST* with 100% *accuracy*; while *j48graft* with an *accuracy* of 97.05% and *REPTREE* with an *accuracy* of 98.52% were weaker than their same opponents.

Totally, the best results were obtained by *J48*, which resulted in 100% *accuracy*. This classifier has a long history in text categorization and good performance in this area. Almost every classifier resulted in more than 97% in terms of *accuracy*. However, *REPTREE* did the worst in comparison to its counterparts.

Precision and *Recall* values of all the classification algorithms with separated properties are shown in Figure 5. *Precision* and *Recall* metrics are two of the most recognized parameters. *Precision* is the total amount of classified and connected evidence divided by total evidence. *Precision* demonstrates the true percentage of the set of proposals, and *Recall* is the division of the amount of total classified and connected observations by the total observations. *Precision* and *Recall* values are equal to 1 for all the algorithms in the feature set of 227 opcodes.

This is the same for the value of *Precision* for the feature set of 120 opcodes. Only for *REPTREE* algorithm of class *G2* it is equal to 0.96 and the value of *Recall* for the Non-Malware class is equal to 0.93 and in the other algorithms, values of *Precision* and *Recall* are equal to 1. For the feature set of 20 opcodes, *Precision* is from 0.92 to 1 while *Recall* is from 0.84 to 1.

Figure 4. Accuracy of classifiers algorithms

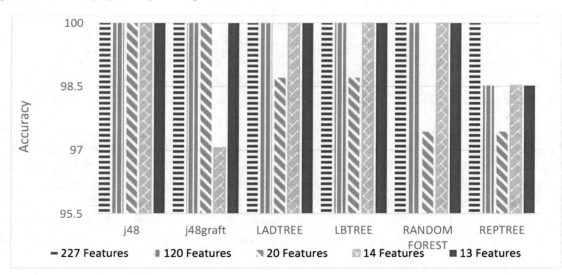

For the feature set of 14 opcodes, *Precision* is equal to 1 for all classification algorithms except in non-Malware class of algorithm *J48graft* that is equal to 0.83, and in the *VCL32* class of algorithm *REPTREE* which is equal to 0.85. Also, *Recall* is equal to 1 except in algorithms *J48graft* and class *VCL32* that is equal to 0.66. Also for the algorithm *REPTREE* and class *Ngvck*, *Recall* is equal to 0.95, and for the other algorithms, it is equal to 1.

Considering the feature set of 13 features, only in class *VCL32* of algorithm J48graft *Precision* is 0.95, and in class *VCL32* of algorithm *REPTREE*, it is 0.85 while in other algorithms *Precision* is equal to 1. *Recall* parameter for this feature set is equal to 1 except for the Non-Malware class of J48graft algorithm which is equal to 0.92 and Non-Malware class of J48graft algorithm that is equal to 0.92. Also, it is the same for the class *Ngvck* of algorithms *REPTREE* which *Recall* is equal to 0.95. These results indicate that we have acceptable *Precision* and *Recall* rates for the minimum number of feature sets.

Required Time for Classification

In order to obtain the processing overload of the proposed method, we have to measure the training time and the test time:

- **Training Time:** The time to create different classification algorithms. This time is offline and does not affect the real-time processing. However, it should be acceptable for various numbers of input benchmarks.
- **Test Time:** The time to evaluate test features on the input benchmark. This time is online and affects the real-time processing.

Figure 6 and Table 4 show the training time and test time of decision tree algorithms for each of the feature sets.

For the first feature set with 227 opcodes, *LADTree* algorithm with 1.84 seconds of training time and 1.65 seconds of testing time is the slowest in terms of training time. In addition, *J48* algorithm with 0.14 seconds of training time and 0.00 of testing time is the fastest. For the second feature set with 120 opcodes, *LADTree* is the slowest in terms of training time with 0.85 seconds of training time and 0.77 seconds of testing time. And algorithm *J48* with a training time of 0.12 and testing time of 0.00 seconds is the fastest.

For the third feature set with 20 opcodes, *NBTree* with a training time of 0.27 and test time of 0.03 seconds is the slowest of all and *LADTree* with a test time of 0.77 has the slowest test time. And *J48* algorithm with a training time of 0.01 and test time of 0.00 is the fastest of all.

For the fourth feature set with 14 opcodes, *NBTree* with a training time of 0.19 seconds and test time of 0.03 seconds is the slowest and *LADTree* with a test time of 0.14 seconds has the slowest test time. *J48* with a training time of 0.01 seconds and test time of 0.00 is the fastest of all.

For the fifth feature set with 13 opcodes, *NBTree* with a training time of 0.18 seconds and test time of 0.03 seconds is the slowest and *LADTree* with a test time of 0.13 seconds has the slowest test time. *J48* with a training time of 0.01 seconds and test time of 0.00 seconds is the fastest of all.

The times of the third and fourth feature sets are lower than the times of the first and the second feature sets. This is because the number of features is less than the others, and this is based on our assumption. Also, we found out that *J48* is the fastest algorithm and *NBTree* is the slowest one of all the studied algorithms.

Figure 5. Precision and Recall parameters of five feature sets for six classification algorithms running on malware and healthy benchmark files

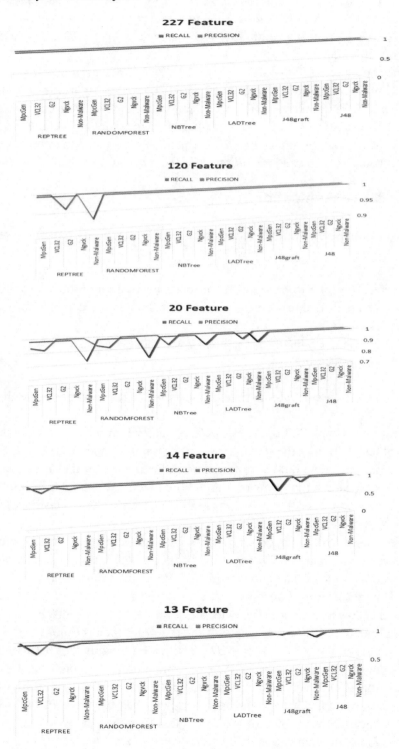

Figure 6. Training time and testing time of six algorithms, six categories for each five feature set.

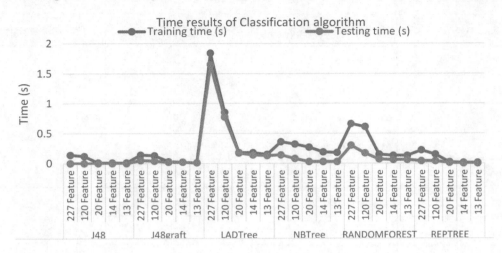

According to the previous results, we showed that the feature sets of 20 feature, 14 feature and 13 feature set with fewer features could obtain high detection rates and have less computational overload.

Comparison With Other Antivirus Software

One of the problems in malware research is that no general dataset exists for the researchers to test their algorithms and prove their hypothesis. On the other hand, malwares are dangerous files and cannot be accessed easily, so only the research and educational centers access them. Researchers often use mathematical equations to prove their works, or they test their dataset by popular anti-virus software's to compare their works. We did the same in our research. The proposed methodology was compared with leading anti-virus software available in the market. 20 sample files of each malware family were chosen and were scanned using commercial anti-viruses. Anti-virus software with update date November 28, 2015, was tested on 80 files of the test set.

Table 5 shows the results of scanning files using anti-viruses and, the proposed method. In this table, *N* means not detecting any malware by the antivirus. For example, Avira can detect all *NGVCK* malware files and *VCL32* malware files. However, it cannot detect 6 *G2* malware files and 7 *Mpcgen* malware files. Other anti-viruses behave the same; however, the proposed method can effectively detect all virus files.

Obtained results, validated our theory stating that developing a recognizer for metamorphic malware is possible due to the statistics of opcodes. Decision tree classifiers gained a high performance in classifying metamorphic malware. However, there are observations that need to be made about the usage of this method. First, overload of processing the method highly depends on the number of opcodes. In our experiments, we analyzed that the number of opcodes effect on the overload of processing the method. Secondly, our method of recognition only benefits from opcodes and ignores operands in machine code instructions. Thirdly, due to the static nature of the presented method, this method cannot overcome destructive software packs. Static recognition methods are only able to overcome destructive software packs using the signature of Packers.

Table 4. Time results of the classification algorithm

Testing Time (s)	Training Time (s)	Num of Opcodes (Features)	Classification Algorithm
0.00 ± 0.00	0.14 ± 0.05	227	
0.00 ± 0.00	0.12 ± 0.03	120	
0.00 ± 0.00	0.01 ± 0.00	20	*J48*
0.00 ± 0.00	0.01 ± 0.00	14	
0.00 ± 0.00	0.01 ± 0.00	13	
0.05 ± 0.01	0.14 ± 0.06	227	
0.04 ± 0.02	0.13 ± 0.03	120	
0.02 ± 0.01	0.03 ± 0.01	20	*J48graft*
0.02 ± 0.01	0.02 ± 0.01	14	
0.01 ± 0.01	0.01 ± 0.01	13	
1.65 ± 1.60	1.84 ± 1.71	227	
0.77 ± 0.76	0.85 ± 0.81	120	
0.17 ± 0.16	0.18 ± 0.17	20	*LADTree*
0.14 ± 0.13	0.18 ± 0.15	14	
0.13 ± 0.12	0.15 ± 0.13	13	
0.14 ± 0.3	0.36 ± 0.16	227	
0.08 ± 0.07	0.32 ± 0.14	120	
0.03 ± 0.04	0.27 ± 0.11	20	*NBTree*
0.03 ± 0.02	0.19 ± 0.17	14	
0.03 ± 0.02	0.18 ± 0.17	13	
0.3 ± 0.2	0.66 ± 0.22	227	
0.17 ± 0.16	0.61 ± 0.22	120	
0.07 ± 0.05	0.15 ± 0.13	20	*RANDOMFOREST*
0.06 ± 0.05	0.13 ± 0.12	14	
0.06 ± 0.05	0.13 ± 0.12	13	

continued on following page

Table 4. Continued

Testing Time (s)	Training Time (s)	Num of Opcodes (Features)	Classification Algorithm
0.04 ± 0.03	0.22 ± 0.05	227	
0.04 ± 0.02	0.15 ± 0.02	120	
0.01 ± 0.01	0.02 ± 0.01	20	*REPTREE*
0.00 ± 0.00	0.01 ± 0.00	14	
0.00 ± 0.00	0.01 ± 0.00	13	

Table 5. Comparison with antivirus products on the market

Antivirus	Ngvck	G2	VCL32	Mpcgen
AntiVir (Avira)	20	14	20	13
Avast	7	N	N	N
AVG	2	20	20	20
BitDefender	4	N	20	20
ESET NOD32	N	20	10	N
G Data	4	N	20	20
Kaspersky	N	20	20	20
McAfee	7	N	17	6
Microsoft Security Essentials	N	N	15	20
Panda Security	N	20	20	19
Proposed Methodology	**20**	**20**	**20**	**20**
Quick Heal Antivirus	N	N	13	12
Symantec Norton Antivirus	9	20	20	19
Trend Micro	N	N	20	20

CONCLUSION

In this article, we presented a new technique for detecting metamorphic malware. The significant advantage of the research is utilizing statistics of opcode frequency, which do not need the signature of malware, and, malware can be detected in anti-virus engine. Despite its simplicity, results indicate the trustworthiness and accuracy of the presented method for detecting the metamorphic malware. Furthermore, it does not need to run the code so it can simply be implemented in any antimalware. To evaluate the performance of the opcode statistical method, five feature sets were used above. After that, all of the five feature sets were tested in the same conditions and using different classifications. We deducted that recognition based on statistics can turn into a useful tool for recognizing metamorphic malware.

All the four groups of metamorphic malwares such as *NGVCK*‹*G2* ‹*MPCGEN* and *VCL* were detected using this method. Six decision trees were made based on statistics for each feature set that can act as signatures of malware variables. We also used Weka tool as a classifier for creating decision trees based on experimental data.

With producing different feature sets with effective features, considering their low number of characteristics, the number of features, used memory, computational complication and required time for creating the model was reduced significantly. Results related to the accuracy of different classifications imply that the first and second feature sets, despite classifying the samples with more details, are not specifically better than third to fifth feature sets. Statistically based malware detection method is based on analysis of assembly instructions. The proposed method has low complexity and can be simply implemented. The accuracy of this method depends on the quality of disassembler. Increase in the quality of disassembler increases the Accuracy of the whole performance. In addition, the accuracy of the proposed method relies on the accuracy of statistics. Statistics should be unique. Development of statistic creator modules for detecting new automatic statistics can be a good candidate for research. Malware creators use various techniques that cause difficulty in disassembling these programs. Hence, researchers should develop better disassemblers for performing acceptable researches. For the last notion, the speed of malware detection will be improved using this technique.

REFERENCES

Abou-Assaleh, T., Cercone, N., Keselj, V., & Sweidan, R. (2004). N-Gram-Based Detection of New Malicious Code. *Proceedings of the 28th Annual International Computer Software and Applications Conference*, 2(1).

Anderson, B. (2011). Graph-Based Malware Detection Using Dynamic Analysis. *Journal in Computer Virology*, 7(4), 247–258.

Aycock, J. (2006). *Computer Viruses and Malware*. Springer Science & Business Media.

Bayer, U., Moser, A., Kruegel, C., & Kirda, E. (2006). Dynamic Analysis of Malicious Code. *Journal in Computer Virology*, 2(1), 67–77. doi:10.100711416-006-0012-2

Bilar, D. (2007). Opcodes as Predictor for Malware. *International Journal of Electronic Security and Digital Forensics*, 1(2), 156. doi:10.1504/IJESDF.2007.016865

Bonfante, G. (2007). *Control Flow Graphs as Malware Signatures To Cite This Version: Control Flow Graphs as Malware Signatures*. Academic Press.

Breiman, L. (2001). Random Forests. *Machine Learning*, 1–33.

Chouchane, M. R., & Lakhotia, A. (2006). Using Engine Signature to Detect Metamorphic Malware. *Proceedings of the 4th ACM workshop on Recurring malcode - WORM '06*, 73. 10.1145/1179542.1179558

Chouchane, M. R., Walenstein, A., & Lakhotia, A. (2007). Statistical Signatures for Fast Filtering of Instruction-Substituting Metamorphic Malware. *Proceedings of the 2007 ACM workshop on Recurring malcode - WORM '07*, 31. 10.1145/1314389.1314397

Daoud, E. A., Jebril, I., & Zaqaibeh, B. (2008). Computer Virus Strategies and Detection Methods. *International Journal Open Problems Computer and Mathematics, 1*(2), 122–129.

Dolev, S., & Tzachar, N. (2008). *Malware Signature Builder and Detection for Executable Code*. Academic Press.

Fazlali, M., Khodamoradi, P., Mardukhi, F., Nosrati, M., & Dehshibi, M. M. (2016). Metamorphic Malware Detection Using Opcode Frequency Rate and Decision Tree. *International Journal of Information Security and Privacy, 10*(3), 67–86. doi:10.4018/IJISP.2016070105

Fernandes, D. A. B., Soares, L. F. B., Gomes, J. V., Freire, M. M., & Inácio, P. R. M. (2014). Security Issues in Cloud Environments: A Survey. *International Journal of Information Security, 13*(2), 113–170. doi:10.100710207-013-0208-7

Garner, S. R. W. (2007). *The Waikato Environment for Knowledge Analysis*. Waikato ML Group.

Hall, M., Witten, I., & Frank, E. (2011). *Data Mining: Practical Machine Learning Tools and Techniques*. Kaufmann.

Kam, H. T. (1995). Random Decision Forest. *3rd Int'l Conf. on Document Analysis and Recognition*, 14–18.

Karnik, A., Goswami, S., & Guha, R. (2007). Detecting Obfuscated Viruses Using Cosine Similarity Analysis. *Modelling & Simulation, 2007. AMS'07. First Asia International Conference on IEEE*, 165–70. 10.1109/AMS.2007.31

Kaushal, K., Swadas, P., & Prajapati, N. (2012). Metamorphic Malware Detection Using Statistical Analysis. *International Journal of Soft Computing and Engineering, 2*(3), 49–53.

Khodamoradi, P., Fazlali, M., Mardukhi, F., & Nosrati, M. (2015). Heuristic Metamorphic Malware Detection Based on Statistics of Assembly Instructions Using Classification Algorithms. *2015 18th CSI International Symposium on Computer Architecture and Digital Systems (CADS)*. 10.1109/CADS.2015.7377792

Kolter, J. Z., & Maloof, M. A. (2004). Learning to Detect Malicious Executables in the Wild. *Proceedings of the 2004 ACM SIGKDD international conference on Knowledge discovery and data mining - KDD '04*, 470. 10.1145/1014052.1014105

Konstantinou, E., & Wolthusen, S. (2008). Metamorphic Virus: Analysis and Detection. Royal Holloway University of London.

Lin, Da, & Stamp. (2011). Hunting for Undetectable Metamorphic Viruses. *Journal in Computer Virology, 7*(3), 201–14.

Mathur, K., & Hiranwal, S. (2013). A Survey on Techniques in Detection and Analyzing Malware Executables. *International Journal of Advanced Research in Computer Science and Software Engineering, 3*(4), 422–428.

Milgo, E. C. (2009). *Statistical Tools for Linking Engine-Generated Malware to Its Engine*. Columbus State University.

Moskovitch, R., Stopel, D., Feher, C., Nissim, N., Japkowicz, N., & Elovici, Y. (2009). Unknown Malcode Detection and the Imbalance Problem. *Journal in Computer Virology, 5*(4), 295–308. doi:10.100711416-009-0122-8

Peng, H., Long, F., & Ding, C. (2005). Feature Selection Based on Mutual Information: Criteria of Max-Dependency, Max-Relevance, and Min-Redundancy. *IEEE Transactions on Pattern Analysis and Machine Intelligence, 27*(8), 1226–1238. doi:10.1109/TPAMI.2005.159 PMID:16119262

Plonk, A., & Carblanc, A. (2008). *Malicious Software (Malware): A Security Threat to the Internet Economy*. Academic Press.

Quinlan, J. R. (1986). Induction of Decision Trees. *Machine Learning, 1*(1), 81–106. doi:10.1007/BF00116251

Quinlan, J. R. (2014). *C4. 5: Programs for Machine Learning*. Elsevier.

Runwal, N., Low, R. M., & Stamp, M. (2012). Opcode Graph Similarity and Metamorphic Detection. *Journal in Computer Virology, 8*(1–2), 37–52. doi:10.100711416-012-0160-5

Santo, I. (2013). Idea: Opcode-Sequence-Based Malware Detection. *Information Sciences*.

Santos, & Laorden, & Bringas. (2009, January). Collective Classification for Unknown Malware Detection. *Learning*.

Santos, I. (2011). Opcode-Sequence-Based Semi-Supervised Unknown Malware Detection. Lecture Notes in Computer Science, 6694, 50–57. doi:10.1007/978-3-642-21323-6_7

Santos, I., Brezo, F., Sanz, B., Laorden, C., & Bringas, P. G. (2011). Using Opcode Sequences in Single-Class Learning to Detect Unknown Malware. *IET Information Security, 5*(4), 220. doi:10.1049/iet-ifs.2010.0180

Schiffman, M. (2010). *A Brief History of Malware Obfuscation: Part 2 of 2*. Cisco Blog.

Schultz, M. G., Eskin, E., Zadok, E., & Stolfo, S. J. (2001). Data Mining Methods for Detection of New Malicious Executables. *Proceedings of the 2001 IEEE Symposium on Security and Privacy*, 38–49. 10.1109/SECPRI.2001.924286

Shabtai, A., Moskovitch, R., Feher, C., Dolev, S., & Elovici, Y. (2012). Detecting Unknown Malicious Code by Applying Classification Techniques on OpCode Patterns. *Security Informatics, 1*(1), 1. doi:10.1186/2190-8532-1-1

Shankarapani, M. K., Ramamoorthy, S., Movva, R. S., & Mukkamala, S. (2011). Malware Detection Using Assembly and API Call Sequences. *Journal in Computer Virology, 7*(2), 107–119. doi:10.100711416-010-0141-5

Szor, P. (2005). *The Art of Computer Virus Research and Defense*. Pearson Education.

Vinod, P., Jaipur, R., Laxmi, V., & Gaur, M. (2009). Survey on Malware Detection Methods. *Proceedings of the 3rd Hackers' Workshop on Computer and Internet Security (IITKHACK'09)*, 74–79.

Witten, I. H., & Frank, E. (1999). *Data Mining: Practical Machine Learning Tools and Techniques with Java Implementations*. Academic Press.

You, I., & Yim, K. (2010). Malware Obfuscation Techniques: A Brief Survey. *Proceedings - 2010 International Conference on Broadband, Wireless Computing Communication and Applications*, 297–300. 10.1109/BWCCA.2010.85

Chapter 15
Classification of Web–Service–Based Attacks and Mitigation Techniques

Hossain Shahriar
Kennesaw State University, USA

Victor Clincy
Kennesaw State University, USA

William Bond
Kennesaw State University, USA

ABSTRACT

Web services are being widely used for business integration. Understanding what these web services are and how they work is important. Attacks on these web services are a major concern and can expose an organizations' valuable resources. This chapter performs a survey describing web service attacks. The authors provide a taxonomy of web service vulnerabilities and explain how they can be exploited. This chapter discusses some of the approaches that make up best practices and some that are in the development phase. They also discuss some common approaches to address the vulnerabilities. This chapter discusses some of the approaches to be using in planning and securing web services. Securing web services is a very important part of a cybersecurity plan.

INTRODUCTION

Web services are increasingly becoming a strategic vehicle for the exchange of data and content distribution for companies and corporations (large and small). It is a vital component of online stores. Within web services, the Simple Object Access Protocol (SOAP) XML-based messages are used to transmit data between the consumer and the provider over the network. This is done using the http or https protocols. These interactions take place when the consumer (client) sends a SOAP message request to the provider (server) (Vieira, Antunes, Vieira, & Madeira, 2009).

DOI: 10.4018/978-1-5225-5583-4.ch015

There are existing attacks on web services and many mitigation approaches. However, there is little effort in providing a taxonomy of attack types and mitigation approaches. In this paper, we do an extensive survey of web service-based attacks and mitigation approaches.

This paper is organized as follows: Section 2 discusses SOAP and RESTFul web services. Section 3 describes a number of common attacks on web services. Section 4 discusses common tools and approaches from the literature that mitigate web service attacks. Section 5 discusses best practices to mitigate against web service attacks. Section 6 highlights the limitation of the approaches. Finally, Section 7 concludes the paper.

SOAP AND RESTFUL WEB SERVICES

In this section, we introduce the two common types of web services: SOAP (Section 2.1) and RESTFul (Section 2.2).

SOAP

The Simple Object Access Protocol (SOAP) is used in the exchange of XML-based messages between the client and the server, these messages are sent over the network using http or https protocols. In the interactions between a consumer (client) and a provider (server), the client sends a request SOAP message to the server. The server processes the request and sends a message back to the client with the results of the request.

XML is widely used standard in web services for integration and data exchange. There is a big problem with XML as it is not very secure and have been many vulnerabilities uncovered. Web services using XML provides many opportunities for attacks such as Denial of Service attacks or XML Injection attacks. Systems that utilize XML are vulnerable to those types of attacks.

Web Services are widely based on XML Protocols (Tiwari & Singh, 2011). There are three main elements of web services that use XML:

- Simple Object Access Protocol (SOAP). SOAP is a W3C standard for exchanging XML based messages over computer networks. SOAP uses HTTP/HTTPS, it is important for application development as it allows Internet Communications between two or more programs. SOAP is platform independent, agnostic, flexible and general-purpose XML Protocol (Jan, Nguyen, & Briand, 2015; Tiwari & Singh, 2011).
- Web Service Description Language (WDSL) is a language used to define web services and describe how to access them. The various operations required to access the web services are defined in the WSDL language along with the parameter information (Jan, S., Nguyen, C. D., & Briand, LJ, 2015; Tiwari & Singh, 2011).
- Universal Description, Discovery and Integration (UDDI) specification is for publishing and locating information about web services. It also defines the information framework that enables service providers to describe and classify their organization, services and the technical details about the interfaces of the web services that they want to expose for use.

Service composition is a promising solution for many businesses. Using Service Compositions an organization can connect their applications, databases and systems to provide a single point service to the consumers. Service composition is an aggregation of other atomic and composite web services. These web services interact with each other in accordance to a process model. For example, a travel website that allows you to book an airline flight, as well as book a hotel room, rental car and other services such as travel insurance, or car service (Tiwari & Singh, 2011). Example of Service composition is shown in Figure 1. A new customer is created and in turn calls other services such as validating the customer, Updating the customer database and Generating and billing the account. Generate Bill Account in turn calls the New Bill Account creation service which calls to the credit card number validation service and the Card limit validation service.

RESTFul

REpresentational State Transfer (REST) is a stateless client-server architecture in which the web services are viewed as resources and can be identified by their URLs. In this case, URLs are exposed for the public to perform create, read, update and delete (CRUD) operations on data. REST creates a one-to-one mapping of the CRUD operations to the HTTP methods. To create a resource on the server a developer will use the POST method. To retrieve a resource a developer will use the GET method. To update a resource a developer will use the PUT method. To delete a resource a developer will use the DELETE method. REST does contain an inherent design flaw that can allow HTTP methods to be used for unintended purposes. A GET method usually identifies one resource only to be retrieved, but, some web API's use HTTP's GET to trigger something transactional such as adding records to a database. See example below.

GET /adduser?name=William HTTP/1.1

Figure 1. Example of service composition (Tiwari & Singh, 2011)

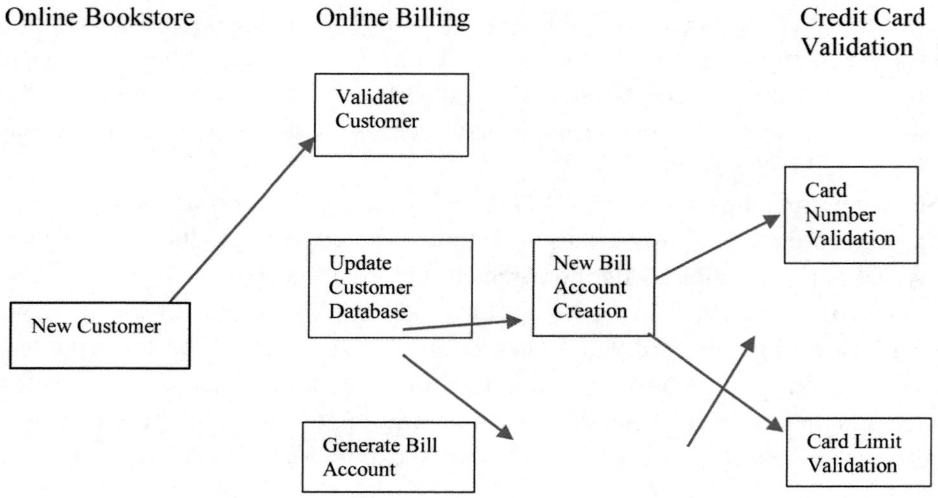

Web Service Composition BPEL

Businesses such as travel websites require web services composition, using web services composition they can connect their applications, databases and system together to provide the customer a single point of connection. These applications, and services operate together in accordance to a given business process model. This aggregates multiple services together on one page or a single point of service. This could be hotel booking, car rental, and airline booking together on a travel website.

Business Process Execution Language is a well-known specification for the composition of web services. BPEL provides mechanisms for calling existing web services. BPEL uses XML based language to define enterprise business processes. BPEL provides the language for defining the execution order of web service calls. BPEL allows for asynchronous communication with the client. The messages from BPEL are used to invoke remote services and orchestrate execution.

TYPES OF ATTACKS ON WEB SERVICES

In web services, there are several attacks that are directly related to the way that the web service code is structured (Jan, Nguyen, & Briand, 2016; Ye, 2008). These vulnerabilities include SQL Injection and XPath Injection (Vieira et al., 2009). These types of injection attacks take advantage of improper coded applications to change SQL commands that are sent to the database or tamper with XPath queries used to access parts of an XML Document.

Injection Attacks

SQL Injection

It is possible "to alter the construction of backend SQL statements. An attacker can read or modify database data and, in some cases, execute database administration operations or commands in the system.

XPath Injection

It is possible to modify an XPath query to *be parsed in a way differing from the programmer's intention* (Gruschka & Luttenberger, 2006). Attackers may gain access to information in XML documents (Jan et al., 2016). An Example of an XPath Injection Attack is seen in Figure 2. If this code is used an XPath expression is injected, an attacker providing these values as a user name: ' or 1=1 or ''='' can cause the semantics of the original XPath to change and it will always return the first account number in the XML document. The query, in this case, will be: string(//user[name/text()='' or 1=1 or ''='' and password/text()='foobar']/account/text()) This is similar to: string(//user/account/text()) Therefore it will yield the first instance of //user/account/text(). The attacker would be logged in without providing a valid user name or password (Tiwari & Singh, 2011).

XML Injections attacks are carried out by injecting pieces of XML code with malicious intent into user inputs to produce harmful XML messages. When a system receives a malicious XML message, the system may crash resulting in denial of services or may be compromised by allow an attacker to attack other systems or subsequent components that process those XML messages (Jan et al., 2016).

Figure 2. Example of an XPath attack

```
XmlDocument XmlDoc = new XmlDocument();
XmlDoc.Load("…");

XPathNavigator nav = XmlDoc.CreateNavigator();
XPathExpression expr =
Nav.Compile('string(//user[name/text()='"+TextBox1.Text
and password/text()'"+TextBox2.Text+
"']/account/text())");

String account=Conver.ToString(nav.Evaluate (expr))
If (account==""){
            //name+password is not found in the XML Document-
            //login failed.
} else {
            //login found -> Login Suceeded.
            //Proceed into the application.
}
```

SOAP action overriding: SOAP messages can give birth to new types of attacks called SOAPAction Spoofing. Since XML processing is not needed for the use of HTTP header, therefore the SOAPAction field in HTTP header is used as a service operation identification which enables man in middle attack. (Gruschka & Luttenberger, 2006) have demonstrated SOAPAction spoofing. They have shown that attackers can bypass SOAP of HTTP filters by merely changing the SOAP actions. One class of SOAPAction Spoofing can be executed by a man-in-the middle attacker who tries to invoke an operation different from the one specified inside the SOAP body. The other class of SOAPAction spoofing attacks can be executed by the Web Service client and tries to bypass an HTTP Gateway. Determining the operation by the SOAP body content could be a good countermeasure for this kind of attack (Liu Qiang, Liu Li, & Wang Chunlei, 2014). Figure 3 Shows Example of SOAPSpoofing. It demonstrates a SOAP message. This SOAP message will return Student's name if the envelope's action is invoked, but if the HTTP header's action overrides the envelope, the student's roles will be disclosed.

Privilege Escalation

Arbitrary Code Execution

This attack makes it possible to manipulate the application inputs to cause or trigger server-side execution of arbitrary code (Jan et al., 2016). This type of attack uses a known vulnerability to execute malicious code on the server machine that could result in privilege escalation. This is generally performed using some software that allows the execution of machine code and allows the attacker to inject shellcode and run arbitrary code on the remote computer.

Parameter Tampering

Web parameter tampering attacks are executed by an attacker manipulating the parameters exchanged between the client and the server to modify application data. These parameters include such informa-

Figure 3. Example of SOAPSpoofing

```
POST/DEMO.asmx HTTP/1.1
...
SOAPAction:"getStudentRoles"
<Envelope>
<Body>
<getStudentName>

<StudentID>432</StudentID>
</getStudentName>
</Body>
</Envelope>
```

tion as user credentials (usernames, passwords and permissions) or price and quantity of products. Web Services get information and variables from a SOAP messages. This information is generally transmitted to the server through cookies, hidden form fields or URL Query Strings. These parameters are used to increase application functionality and control. An attacker performing an attack such as a man-in-the-middle attack attempts to modify SOAP parameters, URL parameters and Query string. Form field manipulation is another way of achieving tampering, data can also be tampered with as it is passing thru a network. Session Management and Session Replay can also be used in Parameter tampering attacks (Tiwari & Singh, 2011).

Disclosure Attacks

Username/Password Disclosure

The web service response contains information related to usernames and/or passwords. An attacker can use this information to get access to a user's private data (Jan et al., 2016).

Server Path Disclosure

The response contains a fully qualified path name to the root of the server storage system. An attacker can use this info to discover the server file system structure and devise other security attacks (Jan et al., 2016). This vulnerability can allow the attacker to devise an attack that allows him to steal the configuration files of the web application or operating system. If a filepath is outside of the webroot folder is in the Path Disclosure, after successfully compromising the server, attackers know where to look for sensitive information. If a user's name is in the path, an attacker could brute force the user's password and gain control of the server.

Denial of Service Attacks

Buffer Overflow

It is possible to manipulate the inputs in ways that can cause a buffer overflow problem, this includes overwriting parts of the memory (Jan et al., 2016). During a buffer overflow attack, it creates a denial of service or, in more extreme cases can *alter application flow and force unintended actions* (Gruschka & Luttenberger, 2006).

Resource Exhaustion Attack

These attacks are intended to consume resources which provide services. Most important DoS attack in case of web services are coercive parsing and oversized payload. In these cases, attackers exploit the resource and time-consuming characteristics of XML parsing. 'Coercive Paring Attack' exploits the legacy of XML-enabled components in the existing operational infrastructure. Main objective of these types of attacks is either to overwhelm the processing capabilities of the system or install malicious mobile code. Since XML is verbose by nature and therefore 'Oversized Payload Attack' employ very long or deeply nested XML structures in attack. Figure 4 shows an example of 'Oversized Payload' in this case the Item hello is repeated many times over until the message reaches a very large size. DOM model based parsers are very susceptible to Oversized Payload attack as it needs to model the entire document in memory prior to parsing (Tiwari & Singh, 2011).

Figure 4. Oversized payload attack

```
<Envelope>
<Body>
<getLength>
<item>hello</item>
<item>hello</item>
<item>hello</item>
...
</getLength>
</Body>
</Envelope>
```

Oversized Cryptography

Here attacker relies on including huge amount of encrypted or digitally signed fragments in messages (Patel, Mohandas, & Pais, 2010). In this case server need to perform huge XML parsing, decryption and signature validation tasks which causes tremendous effect on the server performance. Another form of oversized cryptography is one in which each encrypted key is used to encrypt another key in a chained encrypted key structure. Countermeasure to this attach can be done by imposing restrictions on usages of WS Security elements and message size (Patel et al., 2010).

Enumeration

WSDL (Web Services Definition Language) provides key information about methods and how to invoke those methods (Tiwari & Singh, 2011). This information can be exploited by the attackers can cause potential disaster to web services WSDL file must be provided with limited access as WSDL scanning makes it possible to identify several vulnerabilities in the application. WSDL Scanning can be avoided by providing a separate access WSDL to external clients that contain the external operations only, so the malicious user could try to guess the omitted operations and call them. Below is an example of a WSDL where the <portType> element defines "glossaryTerms" as the name of the port, and "getTerm" as the name of an operation. The "getTerm" operation has an input message called "getTermRequest" and an output message called "getTermResponse". The <message> elements define the parts of each message and the associated data types.

Figure 5. WSDL file

```
<message name="getTermRequest">
  <part name="term" type="xs:string"/>
</message>

<message name="getTermResponse">
  <part name="value" type="xs:string"/>
</message>

<portType name="glossaryTerms">
  <operation name="getTerm">
    <input message="getTermRequest"/>
    <output message="getTermResponse"/>
  </operation>
</portType>

<binding type="glossaryTerms" name="b1">
  <soap:binding style="document"
  transport="http://schemas.xmlsoap.org/soap/http" />
  <operation>
    <soap:operation soapAction="http://example.com/getTerm"/>
    <input><soap:body use="literal"/></input>
    <output><soap:body use="literal"/></output>
  </operation>
</binding>
```

BPEL Workflow

BPEL State Deviation

In Business Process Execution Language (BPEL) state deviation attacks the attackers make Web Service requests that are syntactically valid, but are violating the existing workflow contexts. This is performed as a flooding attack and each incoming request massively consumes the BPEL engine's CPU and memory resources. Let consider BPEL engine running one BPEL Process which have a sequence of two receive activities first and second. Only first activity can initiate a new process instance. The attacker may use several SOAP messages invoking second operation and contains correlated properties which does not match to any of the currently running process instance. Since a second activity cannot invoke new process instance, therefore the sequence of all such message will be discarded by BPEL engine which in turn may cause full memory and CPU consumption. Countermeasure for BPEL state deviation attacks is possible, if the state of the workflow context can be determined by the intermediate firewall system.

Workflow Engine Hijacking

BPEL engines are powerful machines which can become target of Denial of Service attacks. Thus, the attacker uses the power of the workflow engine's host system to tear down the target system. This kind of attack uses the WSAddressing but the attackers point to the target system URL. So, the target system receives a heavy number of requests, providing a Denial of Service. The countermeasure against this is verification of the caller's endpoint URL, ideally at the beginning of a process execution (Havrikov, H"oschele, Galeotti, & Zeller, 2014).

Cross Site Request Forgery

This is an attack that forces a user to execute unwanted actions on a web application in which they are currently authenticated. This attack specifically targets state-changing requests, the attacker has no way to see the response of the forged request. An attacker may attempt to trick a user into a CSRF attack by using Social engineering in a chat or email. By placing a well-crafted GET request in the body of an unsolicited email that prompts the users to log into their bank account. If the user clicks this link while authenticated in the online banking web application, then the browser will submit the malicious GET request to the online bank web application. Cross-Site Request Forgery does require that the attacker know how the Web browser behavior regarding the handling of session-related information such as cookies and http authentication information. Knowledge by the attacker of valid web application URLs. Application session management relying only on information which is known by the browser. Existence of HTML tags whose presence cause immediate access to an http[s] resource; for example, the image tag img.

If a user were authenticated with their online banking web application and the browser did not block cross site sharing. Another method that can be employed is to put the malicious code in a HTML form or as a JavaScript script. In this case there is malicious code in the anchor href tag in the HTML that would transfer an amount of money into the listed account number. To trick an unwitting victim, they would have crafted this HTML malicious code into an email with an offer to see their photos. See an example in Figure 6.

Figure 6. Cross-site request forgery

```
<a
href="http://bank.com/transfer.do?acct=1001997643&amount=100000">Vie
w my Pictures!</a>
Or
It may be a link for an image.
<img src="http://bank.com/transfer.do?acct=1001997643&amount=100000"
width="0" height="0" border="0">
```

Table 1. Category of attacks for SOAP and RESTFul web services

CATEGORY	ATTACK	SOAP	RESTFUL
Injection	SQL	Yes	No
	XPath	Yes	No
	XML	Yes	No
	SOAP action overriding	Yes	No
Privilege escalation	Code execution	Yes	No
	Parameter tempering	Yes	Yes
Disclosure attacks	Username/password	Yes	No
	Server path disclosure	No	Yes
Denial of service attacks	Buffer Overflow	Yes	No
	Resource Exhaustion attack	Yes	No
	Oversized cryptography	Yes	No
	Enumeration	Yes	No
BPEL	BPEL State Deviation	Yes	No
	Workflow Engine Hijacking	No	Yes
Cross Site Request Forgery	Cross Site Request Forgery	No	Yes

TOOLS AND TECHNIQUES FOR MITIGATION

Usage of Security Scanner Tools (M1)

Vieira, M., Antunes, N., Vieira, H. M., and Madeira, H., (2009) conducted a study to understand effectiveness of traditional web application security scanner tools for detecting web service related vulnerabilities. They have identified two major issues in four commercial web scanner tools: higher false positive rates and lower rate for attack coverage (two of the tools detected less than 20% known attacks). They conducted testing on over 300 publicly available services. Some of these services involved different technologies including .NET, Java and Delphi. To choose the list of web services to test they used a set of generic keywords, and keywords related to company names such as Microsoft, Oracle, Google and

Acunetix. Out of a rather large list of web services they choose 300 to test. The scanners they used could detect six types of vulnerabilities (SQL Injection, XPath Injection, Code Execution, Buffer Overflow, Username/Password Disclosure, and Server Path Disclosure).

Fuzz Testing Tool (M2)

In their paper, Automated and Effective Testing of Web Services for XML Injection Attacks (Jan, S., Nguyen, C. D., & Briand, L. C., 2016) proposed an automated testing approach and tool for XMLi. They propose a new tool called SOLMI. The authors propose that SOLMI is much better than Fuzz testing tools (WSFuzzer, ReadyAPI) fuzz testing tools. Fuzz testing or fuzzing is a software testing technique used to discover coding errors and security loopholes in software, operating systems or networks by inputting massive amounts of random data, called fuzz, to the system in an attempt to make it crash. Fuzz testing tools work by injecting XML meta-characters(e.g.>, <) into the message attempting to alter the structure of the message to detect if a System Under Test (SUT) is vulnerable. Usually these meta characters are discarded by the XML Gateway or the SUT itself when it parses and validates the data. These methods are largely ineffective in detecting vulnerabilities in detecting subtle vulnerabilities in the XML processing. There are problems with fuzz testing tools, they generate invalid XML messages, and many false positives, as well as no dedicated testing tool for XML injection.

SOLMI is a tool and testing approach that makes use of a constraint solver to automatically generate well-formed and valid XML messages with respect to give domain constraints, which also carrying malicious content. By doing this the generated messages are not easily recognized. This makes it easier for the message to make it past the XML Gateway and into the SUT. The authors tested the fuzz testing tools (ReadyAPI) and SOLMI against the 44 web services they were testing. Of the two SOLMI had the higher success rate. SOLMI was able to reach the web services on the average of 76.86% of the time.

Schema Validation (M3)

Tiwari and Singh (2011) advise in their paper "Survey of Potential Attacks on Web Services and Web Service Compositions", that the simplest approach is Schema Validation. Using Schema Validation all messages are validated with the XML schema and any SOAP messages that deviate from web services specification will be rejected. This does have the drawback of increasing CPU and memory consumption. They recommend that this be used as a supporting measure with other countermeasures. Schema Hardening is also discussed, this approach involves restricting the XML tree to limit the memory needed for processing the message. For instance, if the WS description defines an infinite list of elements, the list is changed into a list with finite number of elements. Another measure they recommend includes the Strict enforcement of WS-Security protocol. WS-Security can also provide some types of security to a SOA application. It is a joint specification by IBM, Microsoft, RSA Security, and VeriSign. It describes how to sign SOAP messages to ensure integrity, and provide non-repudiation. How to encrypt SOAP messages to assure confidentiality, and how to attach security tokens to ascertain the sender's identity. Networks are generally protected by firewalls, however, many of these firewalls allow XML to pass thru, and malicious SOAP messages can cause damage. The firewall for web services is different from typical application level gateways. The main difference between a web service firewall and other firewalls is that this firewall focuses on data payload and contents at application level. To prevent this an XML firewall should be installed as part of the DMZ.

Instrumentation and Interception (M4)

Antunes, Laranjeiro, Vieira, and Madeira, (2009) proposed a new automatic approach for the detection of SQL Injection and XPath Injection vulnerabilities in "Effective Detection of SQL/XPath Injection Vulnerabilities in Web Services." They proposed a tool designed and built to implement the steps to their approach called CIVS-WS (Command Injection Vulnerability Scanner for Web Services). Their approach contains five steps.

1. Instrument the web service to intercept all SQL/XPath Commands executed.
2. Generate a workload based on the web service operations, parameters, data types, and input domains.
3. Execute the workload to learn SQL commands and XPath queries issued by the service.
4. Generate an Attack load based on a large set of SQL Injection and XPath Injection attacks.
5. Execute the Attack load the detect vulnerabilities by comparing the SQL and XPath commands executed with valid ones previously learned.

This approach is based on the learning of SQL and XPath commands and queries, this is accomplished by intercepting all commands and hashing them. Once a command has been intercepted and parsed in order to remove the variant part and a hash code is generated to uniquely identify each command. Vulnerability detection starts by automatically identifying all the locations in the web service code where the SQL and XPath commands are executed. The authors had a lot of success rate with 100% coverage and 0% false positive rates.

Knowledge-Based and Signature-Based (M5)

Rosa, Santin, and Malucelli, (2012) discussed in their article *"Mitigating xml injection 0-day attacks through strategy-based Detection systems,"* a XML injection Strategy-based detection system approach called XID, to mitigate the time gap for zero-day attacks. They stated because many new and unknown attacks are derived from known attack strategies—there should be low false-positive detection rates. They suggested a hybrid approach that supports knowledge-based detection derived from a signature-based approach. XID is a hybrid approach that supports knowledge-based detection derived from a signature-based detection approach. They created an ontology that was queried by SPARQL (SQL like query engine. XID would detect a possible attack in a network packet using snort and snort rules then examine the packet against the ontology using SPARQL to query to look for an instance of exactly the set of attack actions. If no identical instance is found then the prototype would infer that it is a new attack and could be a new variation. The prototype then creates a new attack action in the ontology for future events. The prototype then alerts of a new attack.

Application Layer Gateway/Web Service Firewall (M6)

Gruschka and Luttenberger, (2006) discussed the usage of an Application Layer Gateway and Firewalls for Web Services in *Protecting Web Services from DoS Attacks by SOAP Message Validation*. Firewalls can be used to filter packets by protocol as well as prevent access to services using the target IP address and target port. Application Layer gateways can understand simple application protocols such as HTTP. ALG can protect against attacks using malformed HTTP requests and poison cookie requests. One way of preventing the oversized payload attack is to limit the size of the SOAP message and reject it before it reaches the server. The authors designed a prototype Web Service Firewall called *CheckWay*. This firewall validates the SOAP message XML Documents using the WSDL and creates a schema based on the WSDL. Once *CheckWay* validates a SOAP message against the schema it then forwards the SOAP message to the web service. SOAP messages that contain an unlimited number of elements do not match the XML schema created by *CheckWay* and are rejected, and any long simple type elements do not match the schema and are dropped.

Schema Validation/Self-Adaptive Schema Hardening (M7)

Patel et al., (2010) discussed in *Attacks on Web Services and Mitigation Schemes,* some of the attacks facing Web Services such as XML Injection, XSS Injection and SOAP header Manipulations. They offered some mitigation techniques as well. The writers discussed the use of schema validation as well as a Self-adaptive schema hardening and Thwarting SOAP attachment attacks. The writers created a prototype extension that works with IIS Internet Information Services, that scans through a WSDL file to identify SOAP ports and then associated operations with the value of SOAPAction. It then generates a XML Schema Definition used for Validation. For self-adaptive schema hardening they recommend using an algorithm to automate XSD's based on the fact that the good SOAP requests are either the same or would not differ significantly. These good schemas can be merged together and to obtain a single schema to validate all SOAP messages against.

Thwarting SOAP Attachments Attacks they recommend scanning all attachments with a SOAP message interceptor and Anti-Virus. Also, ensuring that each attachment is properly signed.

Table 2. Mapping of tools and attack types

CATEGORY	ATTACK	Technique/Tool
Injection	SQL	M1, M4
	XPath	M1, M2, M3, M4, M5, M6, M7
	XML	M1, M2, M3, M4, M5, M6, M7
	SOAP action overriding	M1, M3. M4
Privilege escalation	Code execution	M1
	Parameter tempering	M4
Disclosure attacks	Username/password	M1
	Server path disclosure	M1
Denial of service attacks	Buffer Overflow	M7
	Resource Exhaustion attack	M6, M7
	Oversized cryptography	M6. M7
	Enumeration	M6, M7
BPEL	BPEL State Deviation	M6, M7
	Workflow Engine Hijacking	M6, M7
Cross Site Request Forgery	Cross Site Request Forgery	M6, M7

BEST PRACTICES FOR SECURING WEB SERVICES

Injection Attack Mitigation

One method of protecting web services from Injection Attacks is using signature-based detection systems. Signatures identify attacks through some malicious content. Signature-based detection leads to a low false positive rate. There is a limitation on Signature-based detection systems is that it does not detect any new unknown attacks. It is also vulnerable to zero-day attacks (Rosa et al., 2012).

Another method is through knowledge-based systems that detect some previously known and cataloged behavior. It does detect new attacks; however, it is limited due to high false positive detection rates (Rosa et al., 2012).

SQL Injection Mitigation

SQL injection mitigation is performed by considering all input information as malicious and sanitizing all user inputs so only known good values are accepted. Prepared Statements or parameterized queries are the most efficient and easy way to avoid SQL Injection Attacks. Another preferred method is the use of Stored Procedures, certain stored procedure programming constructs have the same effect as parameterized queries.

XPath Injection Mitigation

XPath injection attacks are very similar to SQL Injections attacks in fact they use the same syntax in the form fields that an SQL injection Attack uses. One best practice to prevent XPath Injection Attack is to sanitize the information in the fields before it is submitted to the server. By using a parameterization technique that removes all single or double quotes from the username and password fields an attacker cannot use ' or 1=1 or ' to create a true condition that could lead to an erroneous log in. Another important method of preventing an XPath Injection Attack in a web application is use SQL Database instead of XML Database to authenticate users and passwords (Antunes, N., Laranjeiro, N., Vieira, M., & Madeira, H., 2009).

XML Injection

XML injections can be mitigated by applying a very strict schema validation on the SOAP message aimed at discovering and rejecting invalid data types and messages. Sanitizing any user input data before it reaches the main program and consider all user input to be unsafe. The most effective method is to sanitize all quotation marks from the user input. Data Validation where the data is validated to ensure that it contains only permitted characters within length boundaries.

SOAP Action Overriding Attacks

Utilizing a XML Schema Validator to detect malicious SOAP messages on a Web Service Firewall using a WSDL compiler to compile the schemas and an XML validator to filter potential dangerous SOAP messages. Determining the operation based on the SOAP body content ("XML WSDL," 2017).

Parameter Tampering

HTTP headers tampering can be mitigated by only trusting server sided originated header that is cryptographically protected by a server-side generated cookie. If a HTTP header originated client side it should not be used to make any security decisions. Verification mechanisms such as the establishment of constraints on type and format in the WSDL file, then verifying that the correct type and format was received by the web service (Gruschka & Luttenberger, 2006). OWASP recommends using Data Validation by checking that numbers are within range boundaries to mitigate Parameter Tampering.

Disclosure Mitigation

Verify that all password fields do not echo the user's password when it is entered. Utilize hidden fields in the inputs for username and password. Ensure that user names are not used in the server path. If a user's name is in the path an attacker could use brute force hacking to hack the password and gain control of the server. If the server path contains a path outside of the webroot folder then an attacker would know where to look for other files if he gains control of the server.

Denial of Service Attacks

Ye (2008) developed a defense against DoS attacks on web services (XDoS) based on the Service Oriented Architecture approach. The scheme has two modes, i.e. the normal mode and the under-attack mode. The operations provider decides which mode the system is working in. If the operation provider detects no attacks then the system operates in the normal mode. Otherwise, the system operates in the under-attack mode. Operation Providers subscribe to ServiceHub, the operations provided by the operation provider binds the operations to the ServiceHub as described in the WSDL file. This causes the operations to be perceived as being provided by the ServiceHub, this results in the all service requests send directly to the ServiceHub. This saves the operations provider from being attacked because the operation provider's address is not known to the public. Attackers cannot exhaust the network bandwidth of the operations provider easily. If the system is operation in the normal mode then clients' service requests do not need to be authenticated and validated. When running the under-attack mode all clients' service request must be authenticated and validated before they can be processed. The operations provider only processes a serviced request if it has been authenticated and validated, by doing this it does not waste any resources on an attackers' request. An attacker can cause an operations provider to consume a large amount of system resources by sending large numbers of requests that force the victim to authenticate and validate. To help prevent this kind of attack operations providers subscribe to the services of other service providers to delegate the authentication and validation tasks. These service providers are called verifiers, they carry out the task of authentication and validation and the attackers cannot exhaust the operations provider system. Both the operations provider and the verifiers provide their services though the ServiceHub, they send messages through the ServiceHub and only the ServiceHub knows their addresses, because of this they cannot directly message each other. In the under-attack mode, the operations provider informs the ServiceHub of the authentication and validation services that it subscribes to.

Buffer Overflow

There are four basic approaches to defending against buffer overflow attacks. The first approach involves the programming of the web service code. This should be done in a programming language that automatically performs input validation. Java and C# perform these tasks. If you must write in C or C++, all expected input lengths should be explicitly specified.

The second approach is Memory Allocation Countermeasures, this is allocating only non-executable storage areas for input buffers. This is effective against malicious code execution but may not counteract buffer overflow DoS attacks.

The third approach is Compiler-based countermeasures. Some C and C++ compilers have anti-overflow countermeasures to ensure that the source code has arrays bounds checks performed at compile time on all array accesses. This does cause overhead on the compilation process. Other countermeasures include integrity checks on code pointers to buffers before dereferencing those pointers.

The fourth approach is Library-based countermeasures. Safe libraries that replace commonly used but overflow prone standard C and C++ functions (Gruschka & Luttenberger, 2006).

Resource Exhaustion Attack

Resource Exhaustion Attacks can be prevented by proper configuration of the web service system. One method to prevent oversized XML documents can be prevented by configuring the Web server on which the Web service is running to only accept messages up to a certain size. If an oversized XML Document is passed to the web server it will be ignored, and will not the web service.

Another method is to use a XML gateway. XML gateways provide a robust system for detecting and validating XML traffic before it reaches the Web service and can be conFigured to notify appropriate personnel when such an attack has been attempted (Gruschka & Luttenberger, 2006).

Oversized Cryptography

Oversized Cryptography is also known as Recursive Cryptography attack. The attack can be stopped from working by applying "Strict WS-Security Policy Enforcement". That means that only SOAP Messages are accepted that are explicitly required by the security policy. Usually a WS-Security Policy defines only the minimum requirements of a SOAP message in regard to security features. However, when using "Strict WS-Security Policy Enforcement" the security features of the Policy are to be considered not only as the minimum requirement but as the maximum requirement. Any SOAP Message that doesn't apply to the policy gets discarded and doesn't reach the XML parser. "Strict WS-Security Policy Enforcement" has to be implemented by hand by the web service developer (Gruschka & Luttenberger, 2006).

Enumeration

WSDL enumeration is difficult to defend against, however, the security of the web service should not rely on the secrecy of the WSDL file but, other actions such as integrity, confidentiality and access control features should be used to secure the wen service. Proper configuration of those actions makes the disclosure of WSDL not an issue at all.

BPEL State Deviation

BPEL State Deviation attacks can be mitigated through the use of a stateful packet firewall that fends correlational-invalid and state-invalid messages. It is necessary to identify and reject correlation-invalid and state-invalid messages using as computational resources as possible.

Cross Site Request Forgery

Some of the best practices for preventing CSRF attacks are to check standard headers to verify the request is same origin. This is done by determining the origin of the request is coming from (source origin) and determining the origin the request is going to (target origin). Check that the origin header matches the target origin. Origin HTTP Header standard was introduced as a method of defending against CSRF and other Cross Domain Attacks.

Other methods include requiring any state changing operation have a secure random token, double submit cookie and encrypted token pattern.

LIMITATIONS OF APPROACHES AND BEST PRACTICES

In 2009 when (Antunes, N., Laranjeiro, N., Vieira, M., & Madeira, H., 2009) tested four commercial web vulnerability scanners widely used (including two different versions of a specific brand), they found that two major issues in the commercial web scanner tools: higher false positive rates and lower rate for attack coverage (two of the tools detected less than 20% known attacks).

Using the SOLMI tool authors Jan, Nguyen and Briand tested against other Fuzz testing tools that generate invalid XML messages and cause many false positives. The SOLMI tool had a higher success rate of reaching the web services on the average of 76.86% of the time.

Tiwari and Singh (2011) suggest that XML Schema hardening and Schema Validation of SOAP messages as a countermeasure against many XMLi Attacks. Usage of a Web Services Firewall that can prevent malicious Soap messages from reaching the web services. This is a very effective countermeasure.

Rosa et al., (2012) discussed knowledge-based and signature-based detection, their ideas and techniques are very effective, only for those attacks that are like attacks that currently exist. Any attack that falls outside of the known attack types would not be detected. But, it would have to be an attack that is totally unknown, it would be a true zero-day vulnerability.

Gruschka and Luttenberger (2006) discussed the usage of an Application Layer Gateway and Firewalls for Web Services, these are very good practices to use. If an invalid or ill formed SOAP message is blocked at the firewall there is less chance of an attack being successful.

Patel et al.(2010) discussed in *"Attacks on Web Services and Mitigation Schemes"*, using schema hardening, and schema validation and scanning of SOAP message attachments. The self-adaptive schema hardening could work, but may be difficult to initiate. Schema validation is still a good idea.

The countermeasures and best practices for the attacks are effective to date. There is more work to be done in the areas of BPEL state deviation and workflow engine hijacking.

CONCLUSION

There are many types of attacks that attackers/criminal can use against a computer system. This research was focused on Web Services SOAP and RESTFul, and the attacks that can be used against them. These attacks are categorized as Injection Attacks, Privilege Escalation Attacks, Disclosure Attacks, Denial of Service Attacks and Business Process Execution Language Attacks. Knowing the vulnerabilities and exploits that Web Services are susceptible to is important to finding the best practice for the mitigation of the attacks that can be used against Web Services.

This paper covers many of the attacks and mitigation techniques to prevent and defend against those attacks. In the future, we intend to develop an attack signature generation approach that can be used for signature-based intrusion detection systems (IDS).

REFERENCES

Antunes, N., Laranjeiro, N., Vieira, M., & Madeira, H. (2009). Effective detection of SQL/XPath Injection vulnerabilities in web services. *SCC 2009 - 2009 IEEE International Conference on Services Computing*, 260–267. 10.1109/SCC.2009.23

Gruschka, N., & Luttenberger, N. (2006). Protecting web services from DoS attacks by SOAP message validation. *IFIP International Federation for Information Processing, 201*, 171–182. doi:10.1007/0-387-33406-8_15

Havrikov, N., H''oschele, M., Galeotti, J. P., & Zeller, A. (2014). XMLMate: Evolutionary XML Test Generation. *Proceedings of the 22nd ACM SIGSOFT International Symposium on Foundations of Software Engineering*, 719–722. 10.1145/2635868.2661666

Jan, S., Nguyen, C. D., & Briand, L. (2015). Known XML Vulnerabilities Are Still a Threat to Popular Parsers and Open Source Systems. *Proceedings - 2015 IEEE International Conference on Software Quality, Reliability and Security*, 233–241. 10.1109/QRS.2015.42

Jan, S., Nguyen, C. D., & Briand, L. C. (2016). Automated and effective testing of web services for XML injection attacks. *Proceedings of the 25th International Symposium on Software Testing and Analysis - ISSTA 2016*, 12–23. 10.1145/2931037.2931042

Patel, V., Mohandas, R., & Pais, A. R. (2010). Attacks on Web Services and mitigation schemes. *Security and Cryptography (SECRYPT), Proceedings of the 2010 International Conference on*, 1–6.

Qiang, L., Li, L., & Wang, C. (2014). Automatic fuzz testing of web service vulnerability. *2014 International Conference on Information and Communications Technologies (ICT 2014)*, 1.035-1.035. 10.1049/cp.2014.0589

Rosa, T. M., Santin, A. O., & Malucelli, A. (2012). *Mitigating XML Injection Zero - Day Attack through Strategy - based Detection System*. Academic Press.

Tiwari, S., & Singh, P. (2011). Survey of potential attacks on web services and web service compositions. *Electronics Computer Technology (ICECT), 2011 3rd International Conference on, 2*, 47–51. 10.1109/ICECTECH.2011.5941653

Vieira, M., Antunes, N., Vieira, H. M., & Madeira, H. (2009). *Using Web Security Scanners to Detect Vulnerabilities in Web Services*. Using Web Security Scanners to Detect Vulnerabilities in Using Web Security Scanners to Detect Vulnerabilities in Web Services. doi:10.1109/DSN.2009.5270294

XML WSDL. (2017). Retrieved from https://www.w3schools.com/xml/xml_wsdl.asp

Ye, X. (2008). Countering DDoS and XDoS attacks against web services. *Proceedings of The 5th International Conference on Embedded and Ubiquitous Computing, EUC 2008, 1*, 346–352. 10.1109/EUC.2008.61

Compilation of References

Abdullah, K., Lee, C., Conti, G., & Copeland, J. A. (2005). Visualizing network data for intrusion detection. In *Proceedings from the Sixth Annual IEEE SMC Informational Assurance Workshop* (pp. 100-108). West Point, NY: IEEE. 10.1109/IAW.2005.1495940

Abdullah, K., Lee, C., Conti, G., Copeland, J. A., & Stasko, J. (2005). Ids rainstorm: Visualizing ids alarms. In *Proceedings of the IEEE Workshops on Visualization for Computer Security* (p. 1). Washington, DC: IEEE Computer Society.

Abimbola, A. A., Munoz, J. M., & Buchanan, W. J. (2007). Investigating false positive reduction in http via procedure analysis. In ICNS '06: proceedings of the international conference on networking and services (pp. 87–93). Washington, DC: IEEE Computer Society.

Abou-Assaleh, T., Cercone, N., Keselj, V., & Sweidan, R. (2004). N-Gram-Based Detection of New Malicious Code. *Proceedings of the 28th Annual International Computer Software and Applications Conference, 2*(1).

Abramson, N. 1970. The aloha system: Another alternative for computer communications. In *Proceedings of the November 17-19, 1970, fall joint computer conference*, 281–285.

Abusalah, L., Khokhar, A., & Guizani, M. (2008). A survey of secure mobile ad hoc routing protocols. *IEEE Communications Surveys and Tutorials, 10*(4), 78–93. doi:10.1109/SURV.2008.080407

AC, Y. (1986). How to generate and exchange secrets. In *27th IEEE symposium on foundations of computer science*, (pp. 162–167). Los Alamitos, CA: IEEE Press.

Aggarwal, C., & Yu, P. S. (2008). A Survey of Randomization Methods for Privacy-Preserving Data Mining. *Advances in Database Systems, Springer, 34*, 137–156. doi:10.1007/978-0-387-70992-5_6

Agrawal, S. (2006). FRAPP: A framework for high-accuracy privacy-preserving mining. Data Mining and Knowledge Discovery, 101-139.

Agrawal, T. I. s., & Swami, A. (1993). Mining association rules between sets of items in large databases. *SIGMOD Rec., 22*(2). 10.1145/170035.170072

Agrawal, D., & Aggarwal, C. (2001). On the design and quantification of privacy preserving data mining algorithms. In *Twentieth ACM SIGACT-SIGMOD-SIGART Symposium on Principles of Database Systems* (pp. 247-255). Santa Barbara, CA: ACM. 10.1145/375551.375602

Agrawal, R. S. (2000). *Privacy-preserving data mining. In 2000 ACM SIGMOD conference on management of data* (pp. 439–450). Dallas, TX: ACM.

Agrawal, R., & Srikant, R. (2000). Privacy-preserving data mining. In *Proceedings of the 2000 ACM SIGMOD international conference on Management of data* (pp. 439-450). New York: ACM. 10.1145/342009.335438

Ahmad, A., & Ruighavar, A. (2003). *Improved Event Logging for security and Forensics: developing audit management infrastructure requirements*. Paper presented at the Security Conference.

Ahmed, E. G., Shaaban, E., & Hashem, M. (2010). *Lightweight Mutual Authentication Protocol for Low Cost RFID Tags. International Journal of Network Security & Its Application (IJNSA)*.

Aikaterini, M., & Christos, D. (2005). Detecting Denial of Service Attacks Using Emergent Self-Organizing Maps. *2005 IEEE International Symposium on Signal Processing and Information Technology*.

Airehrour, D., Gutierrez, J., & Ray, S. K. (2015). GradeTrust: A secure trust based routing protocol for MANETs. *IEEE Symposium conducted at the meeting of the Telecommunication Networks and Applications Conference (ITNAC), 2015 International*.

Akowuah, F., Yuan, X., Xu, J., & Wang, H. (2012). An Overview of Laws and Standards for Health Information Security and Privacy. In *Security & Management International Conference* (pp. 403-408). Las Vegas, NV: CSREA Press.

Akyildiz, I. F., Su, W., Sankarasubramaniam, Y., & Cayirci, E. (2002). Wireless sensor networks: A survey. *Computer Networks, 38*(4), 393–422. doi:10.1016/S1389-1286(01)00302-4

Al Ghamdi, A., Aseeri, M., & Ahmed, M. R. (2013). A Novel Trust and Reputation Model Based WSN Technology to Secure Border Surveillance. *International Journal of Future Computer and Communication, 2*(3), 263–265. doi:10.7763/IJFCC.2013.V2.164

Alka, G. R. (2013). Privacy Preserving Three-Layer Naive Bayes Classifier for Vertically Partitioned Databases. *Journal of Information and Computational Science*, 119–129.

Alsaleh, M., Alarifi, A., Alqahtani, A., & Al-Salman, A. (2015). Visualizing web server attacks: Patterns in PHPIDS logs. *Security and Communication Networks, 8*(11), 1991–2003. doi:10.1002ec.1147

Alsaleh, M., Barrera, D., & Van Oorschot, P. C. (2008). Improving security visualization with exposure map filtering. In *Annual Computer Security Applications Conference* (pp. 205-214). IEEE. 10.1109/ACSAC.2008.16

Alshammari, R., Sonamthiang, S., Teimouri, M., & Riordan, D. (2007). Using neuro-fuzzy approach to reduce false positive alerts. In *CNSR '07: proceedings of the fifth annual conference on communication networks and services research* (pp. 345-349). Washington, DC: IEEE Computer Society.

Al-Yaseen, W. L., Othman, Z. A., & Nazri, M. Z. (2015). *Hybrid Modified K-Means with C4.5 for Intrusion Detection Systems in Multiagent Systems* (Vol. 2015). The Scientific World Journal.

Andem, V. R. (2003). *A cryptanalysis of the tiny encryption algorithm*. Citeseer.

Anderson, J. (1980). *Computer security threat monitoring and surveillance*. Academic Press.

Anderson, B. (2011). Graph-Based Malware Detection Using Dynamic Analysis. *Journal in Computer Virology, 7*(4), 247–258.

Anderson, P. (1990). A Theory of Computer Semiotics: Semiotic Approaches to Construction and Assessment of Computer Systems. *Computational Linguistics, 18*(4), 555–562.

Anne Sabourin, J. S. (2015). *Méthodes des k-plus proches voisins*. Paris: Travaux Pratiques, Telecom Paristech.

Antunes, N., Laranjeiro, N., Vieira, M., & Madeira, H. (2009). Effective detection of SQL/XPath Injection vulnerabilities in web services. *SCC 2009 - 2009 IEEE International Conference on Services Computing*, 260–267. 10.1109/SCC.2009.23

Archibugi, D., & Michie, J. (1995). Technology and Innovation: An Introduction. *Cambridge Journal of Economics*, *19*. 10.1093/oxfordjournals.cje.a035298

Arik, F. S. A. (2006). k-Anonymous Decision Tree Induction. In Knowledge Discovery in Databases, PKDD (pp. 151-162). ACM.

ARM Ltd. (2009a). *Keil C51 Compiler Basics*. Available at: http://www.esacademy.com/automation/docs/c51primer/c02.htm

ARM Ltd. (2009b). *LX51 User's Guide: Code Banking*. Available at: http://www.keil.com/support/man/docs/lx51/lx51_codebanking.htm

Arndt, R. Z. (2017). *Emory Healthcare cyberattack affects 80,000 patient records*. Retrieved from http://www.modernhealthcare.com/article/20170302/NEWS/170309983/emory-healthcare-cyberattack-affects-80000-patient-records

Ashwin, M., Daniel, K., & Johannes, G. (2007). L-diversity: Privacy beyond k-anonymity. *ACM Transactions on Knowledge Discovery from Data*, 3.

Atkins, B., & Huang, W. (2013). A Study of Social Engineering in Online Frauds. *Open Journal of Social Sciences*, *1*(03), 23–32. doi:10.4236/jss.2013.13004

Austin, A., & Williams, L. (2011). One Technique is Not Enough: A Comparison of Vulnerability Discovery Techniques. *2011 International Symposium on Empirical Software Engineering and Measurement*, 97–106. 10.1109/ESEM.2011.18

Axelsson, S. (2000). The Base-Rate Fallacy and the Difficulty of Intrusion Detection. *ACM Transactions on Information and System Security*, *3*(3), 186–205. doi:10.1145/357830.357849

Aycock, J. (2006). *Computer Viruses and Malware*. Springer Science & Business Media.

Backhouse, J. (2000). *Searching for Meaning – Performatives and Obligations in Public Key Infrastructures*. Paper presented at the International Workshop on the Language-Action Perspective on Communication Modelling.

Backhouse, J. (1992). *The use of semantic analysis in the development of information systems*. London: London School of Economics.

Backhouse, J., & Dhillon, G. (1996). Structures of Responsibility and Security of Information Systems. *European Journal of Information Systems*, *5*(1), 2–9. doi:10.1057/ejis.1996.7

Badrul, N. A., & Hasimi, S. (2008). Identifying false alarm for network intrusion detection system using data mining and decision tree. In *DNCOCO'08: Proceedings of the 7th conference on Data networks, communications, computers* (pp. 22-28). Bucharest, Romania: World Scientific and Engineering Academy and Society (WSEAS).

Ballora, M., & Hall, D. L. (2010). Do you see what I hear: experiments in multi-channel sound and 3D visualization for network monitoring? Proceedings: Vol. 7709. *Cyber Security, Situation Management, and Impact Assessment II; and Visual Analytics for Homeland Defense and Security II*. Orlando, FL: SPIE.

Ball, R., Fink, G. A., & North, C. (2004). Home-centric visualization of network traffic for security administration. In *Proceedings of the 2004 ACM workshop on Visualization and Data Mining for Computer Security* (pp. 55-64). ACM. 10.1145/1029208.1029217

Bansal, A., Chen, T., & Zhong, S. (2013). Privacy Preserving Back-Propagation Neural Network Learning over Arbitrarily Partitioned Data. *Neural Computing & Applications*, *20*(1), 143–150. doi:10.100700521-010-0346-z

Bárász, M., Boros, B., Ligeti, P., Lója, K., & Nagy, D. (2007a). Breaking LMAP. *Proc. of RFIDSec*, 7. Available at: http://www.cs.elte.hu/~turul/pubs/lmap.pdf

Bárász, M., Boros, B., Ligeti, P., Lója, K., & Nagy, D. (2007b). Passive attack against the M2AP mutual authentication protocol for RFID tags. *Proc. of First International EURASIP Workshop on RFID Technology.* Available at: http://www.cs.elte.hu/~turul/pubs/mmap.pdf

Barford, P., Jha, S., & Yegneswara, V. (2004). Fusion and Filtering in Distributed Intrusion Detection Systems. *The 42nd Annual Allerton Conference on Communication, Control and Computing.*

Baronas, A., & Louis, M. (1988). Restoring a Sense of Control During Implementation: How User Involvement Leads to System Acceptance. *Management Information Systems Quarterly, 12*(1), 329–336. doi:10.2307/248811

Baskerville, R., Stucke, C., Kim, J., & Sainsbury, R. (2013). The information security risk estimation engine. A tool for possibility based risk assessment. In Proceedings of 2013 IFIP 8.11/11.13 Dewald Roode Information Security Research Workshop. Niagara Falls, NY: IFIP.

Baskerville, R. (1993). Information Systems Security Design Methods: Implications for Information Systems Development. *ACM Computing Surveys, 35*(4), 375–414. doi:10.1145/162124.162127

Baskerville, R., & Siponen, M. (2002). An information security meta-policy for emergent organizations. *Logistics Information Management, 15*(5/6), 337–346. doi:10.1108/09576050210447019

Bass, T. (2000). Intrusion detection systems and multisensor data fusion. *Communications of the ACM, 43*(4), 99–105. doi:10.1145/332051.332079

Bayer, U., Moser, A., Kruegel, C., & Kirda, E. (2006). Dynamic Analysis of Malicious Code. *Journal in Computer Virology, 2*(1), 67–77. doi:10.100711416-006-0012-2

Beck, R., & Franke, J. (2009). Designing reputation and trust management systems. *E-Commerce Trends for Organizational Advancement: New Applications and Methods: New Applications and Methods, 118.*

Bello, A., Liu, W., Bai, Q., & Narayanan, A. (2015a). Exploring the Role of Structural Similarity in Securing Smart Metering Infrastructure. *Symposium conducted at the meeting of the Data Science and Data Intensive Systems (DSDIS), 2015 IEEE International Conference on Data Science and Data Intensive Systems (DSDIS).* 10.1109/DSDIS.2015.95

Bello, A., Liu, W., Bai, Q., & Narayanan, A. (2015b). Revealing the Role of Topological Transitivity in Efficient Trust and Reputation System in Smart Metering Network. *Symposium conducted at the meeting of the Data Science and Data Intensive Systems (DSDIS), 2015 IEEE International Conference on Data Science and Data Intensive Systems (DSDIS).* 10.1109/DSDIS.2015.114

Benaloh, J. (1986). Lecture notes in computer science: Vol. 263. *Secret sharing homomorphisms: Keeping shares of a secret secret.* Berlin: Springer-Verlag.

Benjamin, C. M. F. W. (2010). Privacy-Preserving Data Publishing: A Survey of Recent Developments. ACM Computing Surveys, 42(4).

Bertino, E. L. (2008). A Survey of Quantification of Privacy Preserving Data Mining Algorithms. In Models and Algorithms. Springer.

Best, D. M., Hafen, R. P., Olsen, B. K., & Pike, W. A. (2011). Atypical behavior identification in large-scale network traffic. In *IEEE Symposium on Large Data Analysis and Visualization* (pp. 15-22). IEEE. 10.1109/LDAV.2011.6092312

Bhuyan, M. H., Bhattacharyya, D. K., & Kalita, J. K. (2014). Network Anomaly Detection: Methods, Systems and Tools. *IEEE Communications Surveys and Tutorials, 16*(1), 303–336. doi:10.1109/SURV.2013.052213.00046

Bilar, D. (2007). Opcodes as Predictor for Malware. *International Journal of Electronic Security and Digital Forensics*, *1*(2), 156. doi:10.1504/IJESDF.2007.016865

Blum, M., & Goldwasser, S. (1984). An efficient probabilistic public-key encryption that hides all partial information. In R. Blakely (Ed.), *Advances in cryptology—Crypto 84 proceedings* (pp. 289–299). Berlin: Springer-Verlag.

Boehmer, W. (2009). Cost-Benefit Trade-Off Analysis of an ISMS Based on ISO 27001. In *International Conference on Availability, Reliability and Security (ARES '09)* (pp. 392- 399). Fukuoka: CPS. 10.1109/ARES.2009.128

Bogdanov, A., Knudsen, L. R., Leander, G., Paar, C., Poschmann, A., Robshaw, M. J., ... Vikkelsoe, C. (2007). PRESENT: An ultra-lightweight block cipher. *Lecture Notes in Computer Science*, *4727*, 450–466. doi:10.1007/978-3-540-74735-2_31

Bogen, A. C., Dampier, D. A., & Carver, J. C. (2007). Support for computer forensics examination planning with domain: a report of one experiment trial. In *40th. Annual Hawaii International Conference on System Sciences* (pp. 267b-267b). IEEE. 10.1109/HICSS.2007.505

Bonfante, G. (2007). *Control Flow Graphs as Malware Signatures To Cite This Version: Control Flow Graphs as Malware Signatures*. Academic Press.

Boudaoud, K. (2000). *Détection d'intrusions: Une nouvelle approche par systèmes multi-agents* (Thèse de doctorat). l'école Polytechnique Fédérale de Lausanne.

Boudaoud, K. (2000). *Détection d'intrusions: Une nouvelle approche par systèmes multi-agents* (PhD thesis). Ecole Polytechnique Fédérale de Lausanne.

Boukerch, A., Xu, L., & El-Khatib, K. (2007). Trust-based security for wireless ad hoc and sensor networks. *Computer Communications*, *30*(11), 2413–2427. doi:10.1016/j.comcom.2007.04.022

Bousquet, A., Clemente, P., & Lalande, J. F. (2011). SYNEMA: Visual monitoring of network and system security sensors. In *Proceedings of the International Conference on Security and Cryptography* (pp. 375-378). IEEE.

Bowen, P., Chew, E., & Hash, J. (2007). *Information Security Guide For Government Executives Information Security Guide For Government Executives*. National Institute of Standards and Technology NIST. doi:10.6028/NIST.IR.7359

Bowers, D. (2001). The Health Insurance Portability and Accountability Act: Is it really all that bad? *Proceedings - Baylor University. Medical Center*, *14*(4), 347–348. Retrieved from http://www.pubmedcentral.nih.gov/articlerender.fcgi?artid=1305898&tool=pmcentrez&rendertype=abstract PMID:16369644

Bregant, J., & Bregant, R. (2014). Cybercrime and Computer Crime. The Encyclopedia of Criminology and Criminal Justice.

Breiman, L. (2001). Random Forests. *Machine Learning*, 1–33.

Brotby, W. K. (2006). *Information security management metrics: A definitive guide to effective security monitoring and measurement*. Boca Raton, FL: Taylor & Francis Group.

Brunk, C., Kelly, J., & Kohavi, R. (1997). MineSet: An Integrated System for Data Mining. In *Proceedings of the Fourth International Conference on Knowledge Discovery and Data Mining* (pp. 135-138). Academic Press.

Bulgurcu, B., Cavusoglu, H., & Benbasat, I. (2010). Information Security Policy Compliance: An Empirical Study of Rationality-Based Beliefs and Information Security Awareness. *Management Information Systems Quarterly*, *34*(3), 523–548. doi:10.2307/25750690

Burrell, J. (2012). *Invisible Users: Youth in the Internet Cafes of Urban Ghana*. MIT Press. doi:10.7551/mitpress/9780262017367.001.0001

Cadger, F., Curran, K., Santos, J., & Moffett, S. (2016). Location and mobility-aware routing for improving multimedia streaming performance in MANETs. *Wireless Personal Communications, 86*(3), 1653-1672. DOI:10.1007/s11277-015-3012-z

Cannady, J. (1998). Articial neural networks for misuse detection. *Proceedings of the 1998 National Information Systems Security Conference (NISSC'98)*, 443-456.

Cao, T., Bertino, E., & Lei, H. (2009). Security Analysis of the SASI Protocol. *IEEE Transactions on Dependable and Secure Computing*, 73–77.

Carb'o, J., Orfila, A., & Ribagorda, A. (2003). Adaptive Agents Applied to Intrusion Detection. LNAI 2691, 445–453. doi:10.1007/3-540-45023-8_43

Center For Disease Control and Prevention. (2007). Retrieved from https://www.cdc.gov/ehrmeaningfuluse/introduction.html

Chabot, C. (2009, March/April). Demystifying Visual Analytics. *IEEE Computer Graphics and Applications, 29*(2), 84–87. doi:10.1109/MCG.2009.23 PMID:19462638

Chang, B. H., & Jeong, C. Y. (2011). An efficient network atack visualization using security quad and cube. *Electronics and Telecommunications Research Institute Journal, 33*(5), 770–779.

Cheikh, M., Hacini, S., & Boufaida, Z. (2014). Classification of DOS Attacks Using Visualization Technique. *International Journal of Information Security and Privacy, 8*(2), 19–32. doi:10.4018/IJISP.2014040102

Chen, T., & Zhong, S. (2009). Privacy-Preserving Backpropagation Neural Network Learning. *IEEE Transactions on Neural Networks, 20*(10), 1554–1564. doi:10.1109/TNN.2009.2026902 PMID:19709975

Chen, W., & Cai, S. (2005). Ad hoc peer-to-peer network architecture for vehicle safety communications. *IEEE Communications Magazine, 43*(4), 100–107. doi:10.1109/MCOM.2005.1421912

Cheung, S., Crawford, R., Dilger, M., Frank, J., Hoagland, J., Levitt, K. N., . . . Zerkle, D. (1999). The Design of GrIDS: A Graph-Based Intrusion Detection System. CSE-99-2.

Chiang, E., & Assane, D. (2007). Determinants of Music Copyright Violations on the University Campus. *Journal of Cultural Economics, 31*(3), 187–204. doi:10.100710824-007-9042-y

Chien, H. (2007). SASI: A New Ultralightweight RFID Authentication Protocol Providing Strong Authentication and Strong Integrity. *IEEE Transactions on Dependable and Secure Computing, 4*(4), 337–340. doi:10.1109/TDSC.2007.70226

Chien, H., & Huang, C. W. (2007). Security of ultra-lightweight RFID authentication protocols and its improvements. *Operating Systems Review, 41*(4), 86. doi:10.1145/1278901.1278916

Chirkova, R. A. D., Ozsu, M. T., & Sellis, T. K. (Eds.). (2007). *Proceedings of the 23rd International Conference on Data Engineering*. Istanbul, Turkey: Academic Press.

Chittur, A. (2001). *Model generation for an intrusion detection system using genetic algorithms* (PhD thesis). Ossining High School in cooperation with Columbia Univ.

Cho, J.-H., Swami, A., & Chen, R. (2011). A survey on trust management for mobile ad hoc networks. *IEEE Communications Surveys and Tutorials, 13*(4), 562–583. doi:10.1109/SURV.2011.092110.00088

Chouchane, M. R., & Lakhotia, A. (2006). Using Engine Signature to Detect Metamorphic Malware. *Proceedings of the 4th ACM workshop on Recurring malcode - WORM '06*, 73. 10.1145/1179542.1179558

Chouchane, M. R., Walenstein, A., & Lakhotia, A. (2007). Statistical Signatures for Fast Filtering of Instruction-Substituting Metamorphic Malware. *Proceedings of the 2007 ACM workshop on Recurring malcode - WORM '07*, 31. 10.1145/1314389.1314397

Christianini, N. S.-T. J. (2000). An introduction to support vector machines and other kernel-based learning methods. Cambridge University Press.

Chung, C., Hsieh, Y., Wang, Y., & Chang, C. (2016). Aware and smart member card: RFID and license plate recognition systems integrated applications at parking guidance in shopping mall. In *2016 Eighth international conference on advanced computational intelligence (ICACI)* (pp. 253–256). Academic Press.

Chyssler, T., Burschka, S., Semling, M., Lingvall, T., & Burbeck, K. (2004). Alarm Reduction and Correlation in Intrusion Detection Systems. *Proceedings of Detection of Intrusions and Malware & Vulnerability Assessment, GI SIG SIDAR Workshop (DIMVA 2004)*.

Clifton, G. (2000). Developing custom intrusion detection filters using data mining. *21st Century Military Communications Conference Proceedings*. 10.1109/MILCOM.2000.904991

Cohen, W. W. (1995). Fast effective rule induction. In *Machine Learning: the 12th International Conference*. Morgan Kaufmann. 10.1016/B978-1-55860-377-6.50023-2

Cohen, F. (2006). *IT Security Governance Guidebook With Security Program Metrics*. Pennsauken, NJ: Auerbach Publishers Inc.

Colitti, L., Di Battista, G., Mariani, F., Patrignani, M., & Pizzonia, M. (2005). Visualizing Interdomain Routing with BGPlay. *Journal of Graph Algorithms and Applications*, *9*(1), 117–148. doi:10.7155/jgaa.00102

Collotta, M., Pau, G., & Tirrito, S. (2015). A preliminary study to increase baggage tracking by using a RFID solution. In *Proceedings of the international conference on numerical analysis and applied mathematics 2014 (ICNAAM-2014)* (Vol. 1648). AIP Publishing. 10.1063/1.4912985

Conti, G., & Abdullah, K. (2004). Passive visual fingerprinting of network attack tools. In *Proceedings of the 2004 ACM workshop on Visualization and data mining for computer security* (pp. 45-54). ACM. 10.1145/1029208.1029216

Conti, G., Abdullah, K., Grizzard, J., Stasko, J., Copeland, J. A., Ahamad, M., ... Lee, C. (2006). Countering Security Analyst and Network Administrator Overload Through Alert and Packet Visualization. *IEEE Computer Graphics and Applications*, *26*(2), 60–70. doi:10.1109/MCG.2006.30 PMID:16548461

Cordella, L. P., Limongiello, A., & Sansone, C. (2004). Network intrusion detection by a multi-stage classification system. *Lecture Notes in Computer Science*, *3077*, 324–333. doi:10.1007/978-3-540-25966-4_32

Cotroneo, D., Paudice, A., & Pecchia, A. (2016). Automated root cause identification of security alerts: Evaluation in a SaaS Cloud. *Future Generation Computer Systems*, *56*(Supplement C), 375–387. doi:10.1016/j.future.2015.09.009

Coyne, J., & Kluksdahl, N. (1994). *"Mainstreaming" Automated Information Systems Security Engineering (A Case Study in Security Run Amok)*. Paper presented at the ACM Conference.

Cremonini, M., & Riccardi, M. (2009). The Dorothy Project: An Open Botnet Analysis Framework for Automatic Tracking and Activity Visualization. In *Proceedings of the 3rd European Conference on Computer Network Defense* (pp. 52-54). Milano, Italy: Academic Press. 10.1109/EC2ND.2009.15

D'Arco, P., & De Santis, A. (2008). *From Weaknesses to Secret Disclosure in a Recent Ultra-Lightweight RFID Authentication Protocol*. Cryptology ePrint Archive. Retrieved from http://eprint. iacr. org/2008/470

Daemen, J., & Rijmen, V. (1999). *AES proposal*. Rijndael.

Dai, H., Jia, Z., & Qin, Z. (2009). Trust evaluation and dynamic routing decision based on fuzzy theory for manets. *Journal of Software, 4*(10), 1091–1101. doi:10.4304/jsw.4.10.1091-1101

Dang, T. T., & Dang, T. K. (2014). Visualizing Web Attack Scenarios in Space and Time Coordinate Systems. *Transactions on Large-Scale Data and Knowledge Centered Systems*, 1-14.

Dang, T. T., & Dang, T. K. (2014). An Extensible Framework for Web Application Vulnerabilities Visualization and Analysis. In *Future Data and Security Engineering* (pp. 86–96). Basel, Switzerland: Springer. doi:10.1007/978-3-319-12778-1_7

Daoud, E. A., Jebril, I., & Zaqaibeh, B. (2008). Computer Virus Strategies and Detection Methods. *International Journal Open Problems Computer and Mathematics, 1*(2), 122–129.

De Haes, S., & Van Grembergen, W. (2006). Information technology governance best practices in Belgian organisations. *Proceedings of the Annual Hawaii International Conference on System Sciences, 8*. 10.1109/HICSS.2006.222

Debar, H., Becker, M., & Siboni, D. (1992). A neural network component for an intrusion detection system. In *SP '92: Proceedings of the 1992 IEEE Symposium on Security and Privacy*. IEEE Computer Society. 10.1109/RISP.1992.213257

Deepa, A. J., & Kavitha, V. (2012). A comprehensive survey on approaches to intrusion detection system. *Procedia Engineering, 38*, 2063–2069. doi:10.1016/j.proeng.2012.06.248

Deleersnyder, S., De Win, B., Glas, B., Arciniegas, F., Bartoldus, M., & Carter, J. (2009). *Glas, B*. Software Assurance Maturity Model.

Demetrescu, C., & Italiano, G. F. (2006). Dynamic shortest paths and transitive closure: Algorithmic techniques and data structures. *Journal of Discrete Algorithms, 4*(3), 353–383. doi:10.1016/j.jda.2005.12.003

Denning, D. (1987). An intrusion-detection model. *IEEE Transactions on Software Engineering, 13*, 222–232.

Dhillon, G. (2007). *Principles of Information Systems Security: Text and Cases*. Hoboken, NJ: John Wiley & Sons.

Dhillon, G., & Backhouse, J. (2000). Information System Security Management in the New Millennium. *Communications of the ACM, 43*(7), 125–128. doi:10.1145/341852.341877

Dhillon, G., & Backhouse, J. (2001). Current Directions in IS Security Research: Towards Socio-Organizational Perspectives. *Information Systems Journal, 11*(2), 127–153. doi:10.1046/j.1365-2575.2001.00099.x

Dhillon, G., & May, J. (2006). Interpreting Security in Human-Computer Interactions: A Semiotic Analysis. In P. Zhang & D. Galletta (Eds.), *Human-Computer Interaction and Management Information Systems: Foundations*. Armonk, NY: M.E. Sharp.

Dhillon, G., Syed, R., & Pedron, C. (2016). Interpreting Information Security Culture: An Organizational Transformation Case Study. *Computers & Security, 56*, 63–69. doi:10.1016/j.cose.2015.10.001

Dickerson, J. E., & Dickerson, J. A. (2000). Fuzzy network proling for intrusion detection. In *Proc. of NAFIPS 19th International Conference of the North American Fuzzy Information Processing Society* (pp. 301-306). North American Fuzzy Information Processing Society (NAFIPS).

Doherty, J., Curran, K., & McKevitt, P. (2017). Streaming Audio Using MPEG–7 Audio Spectrum Envelope to Enable Self-similarity within Polyphonic Audio. *TELKOMNIKA (Telecommunication Computing Electronics and Control), 15*(1), 190-202. DOI: 10.12928/telkomnika.v15i1.4581

Dolev, S., & Tzachar, N. (2008). *Malware Signature Builder and Detection for Executable Code*. Academic Press.

Duffield, M. (2014). *Global governance and the new wars: The merging of development and security*, Z. B. Ltd.

Dumas, M. (2011). *Alertwheel: Visualisation radiale de graphes bipartis appliquée aux systèmes de détection d'intrusions sur des réseaux informatiques*. Mémoire de l'école de technologie supérieure, université du Québec.

Duquea, S. (2015). Nizam bin Omar, M. (2015). Using Data Mining Algorithms for Developing a Model for Intrusion Detection System (IDS). *Procedia Computer Science*, *6*, 46–51. doi:10.1016/j.procs.2015.09.145

DuW. Z. Z. (2002). Building decision tree classifier on private data. In IEEE international conference on data mining workshop on privacy, security and data mining (pp. 1-8). Maebashi City, Japan: IEEE.

Earl, M. (1993). Experiences in Strategic Information Systems Planning. *Management Information Systems Quarterly*, *17*(1), 1–24. doi:10.2307/249507

Eastlake, D., & Jones, P. (2001). *US secure hash algorithm 1 (SHA1)*. RFC 3174, September 2001.

Edwards, M., Peersman, C., & Rashid, A. (2017). Scamming the scammers: towards automatic detection of persuasion in advance fee frauds. In *Proceedings of the 26th International Conference on World Wide Web Companion* (pp. 1291-1299). International World Wide Web Conferences Steering Committee.

Eisenbarth, T., Kumar, S., Paar, C., Poschmann, A., & Uhsadel, L. (2007). A survey of lightweight-cryptography implementations. *IEEE Design & Test of Computers*, *24*(6), 522–533. doi:10.1109/MDT.2007.178

el Ruptor, M. (2007). *File:XXTEA.png - Wikipedia, the free encyclopedia*. Available at: http://en.wikipedia.org/wiki/File:XXTEA.png

Elfeshawy, N. A., & Faragallah, O. S. (2013). Divided two-part adaptive intrusion detection system. *Wireless Netw, 19*, 301-321.

Elisa, B., Dan, L., & Wei, J. (2008). *Privacy-Preserving Data Mining*. Chicago: Springer US.

Elshoush, H. T., & Osman, I. M. (2011). Alert correlation in collaborative intelligent intrusion detection systems - A survey. *Applied Soft Computing*, *11*(7), 4349–4365. doi:10.1016/j.asoc.2010.12.004

Endert, A., North, C., Chang, R., & Zhou, M. (2014). Toward usable interactive analytics: Coupling cognition and computation. In *Proceedings of the ACM SIGKDD Workshop on Interactive Data Exploration and Analytics* (pp. 52-56). New York: ACM.

ENISA - European Network and Information Security Agency. (2005). *Inventory of risk management/risk assessment methods*. Heraklion, Greece: European Union Agency for Network and Information Security.

ENISA - European Network and Information Security Agency. (2006). *Inventory of risk management/risk assessment tools*. Heraklion, Greece: European Union Agency for Network and Information Security.

ENISA - European Network and Information Security Agency. (2009). *Cloud computing: Benefits, risk and recommendation*. Heraklion, Greece: European Union Agency for Network and Information Security.

EPCGlobal. (2008). *EPCglobal UHF Class 1 Gen 2*. Available at: http://www.epcglobalinc.org/standards/uhfc1g2

Erbacher, R. F. (2003). Intrusion behavior detection through visualization. *IEEE International Conference on Systems, Man and Cybernetics*, *3*, 2507-2513.

Erbacher, R. F., Christensen, K., & Sundberg, A. (2005). Designing visualization capabilities for ids challenges. In *IEEE Workshop on Visualization for Computer Security* (pp. 121-127). Minneapolis, MN: IEEE.

Erbacher, R. F., Walker, K. L., & Frincke, D. A. (2002). Intrusion and misuse detection in large-scale systems. *IEEE Computer Graphics and Applications*, *22*(1), 38–47. doi:10.1109/38.974517

Evfimievski, A. S. R. (2002). Privacy preserving mining of association rules. In *Eighth ACM SIGKDD international conference on knowledge discovery and data mining* (pp. 217-228). Edmonton, Canada: ACM.

Examples of PHI Identifiers Health information. (n.d.). Retrieved from http://www.irb.emory.edu/documents/phi_identifiers.pdf

Fady, H. (2007). *Détection de fraudes et Extraction de Connaissances* (Master's thesis). Montpellier 2 Univ.

FakeNameGenerator. (n.d.). Retrieved from: http://www.fakenamegenerator.com/

Falcone, R., & Castelfranchi, C. (2012). Trust and transitivity: how trust-transfer works. *Highlights on Practical Applications of Agents and Multi-Agent Systems*, 179-187.

Falcone, R., & Castelfranchi, C. (2009). Socio-cognitive model of trust. In *Encyclopedia of Information Science and Technology* (2nd ed.; pp. 3508–3512). IGI Global. doi:10.4018/978-1-60566-026-4.ch558

Fawcett. (2006). *Pattern recognition*. Academic Press.

Fayyad, P. U. G. P.-s. (1996). *Knowledge discovery and data mining: Towards a unifying framework*. AAAI Press.

Fazlali, M., Khodamoradi, P., Mardukhi, F., Nosrati, M., & Dehshibi, M. M. (2016). Metamorphic Malware Detection Using Opcode Frequency Rate and Decision Tree. *International Journal of Information Security and Privacy*, *10*(3), 67–86. doi:10.4018/IJISP.2016070105

FBI. (2015). *2015 Internet crime report*. Federal Bureau of Investigation. US Department of Justice. Retrieved from: https://pdf.ic3.gov/2015_IC3Report.pdf

Federal Information Processing Standards. (1993). *FIPS 46-2 - (DES), Data Encryption Standard*. Available at: http://www.itl.nist.gov/fipspubs/fip46-2.htm

Fenz, S., Heurix, J., Neubauer, T., & Pechstein, F. (2014). Current challenges in information security risk management. *Information Management & Computer Security*, *22*(5), 410–430. doi:10.1108/IMCS-07-2013-0053

Ferebee, D., & Dasgupta, D. (2008). Security Visualization Survey. In *Proceedings of the 12th Colloquium for Information Systems Security Education* (pp. 119-126). Dallas, TX: CISSE.

Fernandes, D. A. B., Soares, L. F. B., Gomes, J. V., Freire, M. M., & Inácio, P. R. M. (2014). Security Issues in Cloud Environments: A Survey. *International Journal of Information Security*, *13*(2), 113–170. doi:10.100710207-013-0208-7

Ferry, E., O'Raw, J., & Curran, K. (2016). Security Evaluation of the OAuth 2.0 Framework. *Information & Computer Security, 23*(1), 73-101. doi: 10.1108/ICS-12-2013-0089

Fink, G. A., Muessig, P., & North, C. (2005). Visual correlation of host processes and network traffic. In *IEEE Workshop on Visualization for Computer Security* (pp. 11-19). IEEE.

Fischer, F., Mansmann, F., Keim, D. A., Pietzko, S., & Waldvogel, M. (2008). Large-scale network monitoring for visual analysis of attacks. In *Visualization for Computer Security* (pp. 111–118). Berlin: Springer. doi:10.1007/978-3-540-85933-8_11

Fitzgerald, B. (1998). An empirical investigation into the adoption of systems development methodologies. *Information & Management*, *34*(6), 317–328. doi:10.1016/S0378-7206(98)00072-X

Forrest, S., Hofmeyr, S. A., & Somayaji, A. (1997). Computer immunology. *Communications of the ACM, 40*(10), 88–96. doi:10.1145/262793.262811

Fox, Henning, Reed, & Simonian. (1990). A neural network approach towards intrusion detection. *Proceedings of the 13th national computer security conference*, 125-34.

Fraser, R. (2006, June 6). *Canada Health Infoway.* Academic Press.

FSA - Swedish Financial Supervisory Authority. (2014a). Regulations and general guidelines regarding governance, risk management and control at credit institutions. Stockholm, Sweden: Finansinspektionen.

FSA - Swedish Financial Supervisory Authority. (2014b). Regulations and general guidelines regarding governance, risk management of operational risks. Stockholm, Sweden: Finansinspektionen.

Fullam, K., & Barber, K. (2007). *Dynamically learning sources of trust information: experience vs. reputation.* ACM. doi:10.1145/1329125.1329325

Fung, G. M. O. (2001). Proximal support vector machine classifiers. In *Proceedings of the ACM SIGKDD international conference knowledge discovery and data mining* (pp. pp 77–86). ACM. 10.1145/502512.502527

Furnell, S., Dowland, P., Illingworth, H., & Reynolds, P. (2000). Authentication and Supervision: A Survey of User Attitudes. *Computers & Security, 19*(6), 529–539. doi:10.1016/S0167-4048(00)06027-2

Galliers, R. D., & Leidner, D. E. (2014). Strategic information management: challenges and strategies in managing information systems. *Information Strategy, 625.* Retrieved from http://www.worldcat.org/isbn/0750656190

Garcı'a-Teodoro, P., Dı'az-Verdejo, J., Macia´-Ferna'ndez, G., & Va'zquez, E. (2009). Anomaly-based network intrusion detection: Techniques, systems and challenges. *Computers & Security, 28*(1-2), 18–28. doi:10.1016/j.cose.2008.08.003

Garner, S. R. W. (2007). *The Waikato Environment for Knowledge Analysis.* Waikato ML Group.

Geolocation Map. (2009). *SecViz- Security Visualization.* Retrieved May 2016, 19, from http://secviz.org/content/geolocation-map

George, R. (2013). How Cybercriminals Choose Their Targets and Tactics. *Information Week.*

Ghoniem, M., Shurkhovetskyy, G., Bahey, A., & Otjacques, B. (2014). VAFLE: visual analytics of firewall log events. Proceedings: Vol. 9017. *Visualization and Data Analysis 2014. 9017* (p. 901704). San Francisco, CA: International Society for Optics and Photonics. doi:10.1117/12.2037790

Giacinto, G., Perdidci, R., & Roli, R. (2005). Network Intrusion Detection by Combining One-class Classifiers. *International Conference on Image Analysis and Processing, ICIAP*, 58-65. 10.1007/11553595_7

Giacinto, G., Perdisci, R. M., Del Rio, M., & Roli, F. (2008). Intrusion detection in computer networks by a modular ensemble of one-class classifiers. *Inf. Fusion, 9*(1), 69–82.

Giordana, A., Neri, F., & Saitta, L. (1995). Search-intensive concept induction. *Evolutionary Computation, 3*(4), 375-416.

Girardin, L. (1999). An Eye on Network Intruder-Administrator Shootouts. *Workshop on Intrusion Detection and Network Monitoring*, 19-28.

Glasgow, J., Macewen, G., & Panangaden, P. (1992). A Logic for Reasoning about Security. *ACM Transactions on Computer Systems, 10*(3), 226–264. doi:10.1145/146937.146940

Goeschel, K. (2016). *Reducing false positives in intrusion detection systems using data-mining techniques utilizing support vector machines, decision trees, and naive Bayes for off-line analysis.* Paper presented at the SoutheastCon 2016.

Goldreich, O., & Micali, S., & Wigderson. (1987). A How to play any mental game—a completeness theorem for protocols with honest majority. *19th ACM symposium on the theory of Computing*, 218–229.

Goodall, J. R., Lutters, W. G., Rheingans, W. G., & Komlodi, A. (2005). Preserving the big picture: Visual network traffic analysis with tnv. In *IEEE Workshop on InVisualization for Computer Security* (pp. 47-54). IEEE. 10.1109/VIZSEC.2005.1532065

Goodall, J. R., Radwan, H., & Halseth, L. (2010). Visual Analysis of Code Security. In *Proceedings of the Seventh International Symposium on Visualization for Cyber Security* (pp. 46-51). New York, NY: ACM. 10.1145/1850795.1850800

Goodhue, D., & Straub, D. (1991). Security concerns of system users: A study of perceptions of the adequacy of security. *Information & Management, 20*. 10.1016/0378-7206(91)90024-V

Grandison, T., & Sloman, M. (2000). A survey of trust in internet applications. *IEEE Communications Surveys and Tutorials, 3*(4), 2–16. doi:10.1109/COMST.2000.5340804

Grill, M., Pevný, T., & Rehak, M. (2017). Reducing false positives of network anomaly detection by local adaptive multivariate smoothing. *Journal of Computer and System Sciences, 83*(1), 43–57. doi:10.1016/j.jcss.2016.03.007

Gruschka, N., & Luttenberger, N. (2006). Protecting web services from DoS attacks by SOAP message validation. *IFIP International Federation for Information Processing, 201*, 171–182. doi:10.1007/0-387-33406-8_15

Gugelmann, D., Gasser, F., Ager, B., & Lenders, V. (2015). Hviz: HTTP(S) traffic aggregation and visualization for network forensics. In *Proceedings of the Second Annual DFRWS Europe*. Dublin, Ireland: Elsevier. 10.1016/j.diin.2015.01.005

Hacini, S., Guessoum, Z., & Cheikh, M. (2013). False Alarm Reduction Using Adaptive Agent-Based Profiling. *International Journal of Information Security and Privacy, 7*(4), 53–74. doi:10.4018/ijisp.2013100105

Haigh, T., & Landwehr, C. (2014). *Building Code for Medical Device Software Security*. Retrieved October 10, 2017, from IEEE Cybersecurity: https://www.computer.org/cms/CYBSI/docs/BCMDSS.pdf

Hall, M., Witten, I., & Frank, E. (2011). *Data Mining: Practical Machine Learning Tools and Techniques*. Kaufmann.

Hang, C.-W., & Singh, M. P. (2010). Trust-based recommendation based on graph similarity. *Proceedings of the 13th International Workshop on Trust in Agent Societies (TRUST)*.

Harary, F., & Kommel, H. J. (1979). Matrix measures for transitivity and balance. *The Journal of Mathematical Sociology, 6*(2), 199–210. doi:10.1080/0022250X.1979.9989889

Harran, M., Farrelly, W., & Curran, K. (2017) A Method for Verifying Integrity & Authenticating Digital Media. *Applied Computing and Informatics, 13*(2), 34-40. DOI: 10.1016/j.aci.2017.05.006

Harrison, L., Spahn, R., Iannacone, M., Downing, & Goodall, J. R. (2012). NV: Nessus vulnerability visualization for the web. In *Proceedings of the Ninth International Symposium on Visualization for Cyber Security* (pp. 25-32). Seattle, WA: ACM. 10.1145/2379690.2379694

Harrison, L., & Lu, A. (2012). The future of security visualization: Lessons from network visualization. *Network, 26*(6), 6–11.

Hartung, C., Balasalle, J., & Han, R. (2005). *Node compromise in sensor networks: The need for secure systems*. Department of Computer Science University of Colorado at Boulder. Available at: http://citeseerx.ist.psu.edu/viewdoc/download?doi=10.1.1.134.8146&rep=rep1&type=pdf

Havrikov, N., H''oschele, M., Galeotti, J. P., & Zeller, A. (2014). XMLMate: Evolutionary XML Test Generation. *Proceedings of the 22nd ACM SIGSOFT International Symposium on Foundations of Software Engineering*, 719–722. 10.1145/2635868.2661666

Health Infoway Website. (n.d.). Retrieved from http://sl.infoway-inforoute.ca/downloads/Ross_Fraser_-_ISO_27799.pdf

HealthIT.gov. (2013). *Guide to Privacy and Security of Health Information*. Author.

Hegazy, A.E., Darwish, A.M., & El-Fouly, R. (2007). *Reducing νTESLA memory requirements*. Academic Press.

Helms, E., & Williams, L. (2011). Evaluating access control of open source electronic health record systems. *Proceeding of the 3rd Workshop on Software Engineering in Health Care - SEHC '11*, 63. 10.1145/1987993.1988006

Henner, M. (2014). Scambaiters. *G-L.* Retrieved from: http://zkm.de/event/2015/09/globale-infosphare/g-l#mischka-henner

Hernandez-Castro, J. C., Tapiador, J. M., Peris-Lopez, P., & Quisquater, J. J. (2008). *Cryptanalysis of the SASI Ultra-lightweight RFID Authentication Protocol with Modular Rotations*. Arxiv preprint arXiv:0811.4257

Hernandez-Castro, J. C., Estevez-Tapiador, J. M., Ribagorda-Garnacho, A., & Ramos-Alvarez, B. (2006). Wheedham: An automatically designed block cipher by means of genetic programming. *Proc. of CEC*, 192–199. 10.1109/CEC.2006.1688308

HINT Project. (2010). *Research Project: HINT Project*. Letterkenny Institute of Technology.

HIPAA Background. (2010). Retrieved from http://hipaa.bsd.uchicago.edu/background.html

HITECH Act Summary. (2009). Retrieved from http://www.hipaasurvivalguide.com/hitech-act-summary.php%09

HITRUST. (2012, March). Retrieved from Health Information Trust Alliance: http://www.hitrustalliance.net/csf/

HKSAR. (2008, February). *An Overview of Information Security Standards*. Retrieved September 17, 2012, from Info Sec Website: http://www.infosec.gov.hk/english/technical/files/overview.pdf

Hong, K., Chi, Y., Chao, L. R., & Tang, J. (2006). An empirical study of information security policy on information security elevation in Taiwan. *Information Management & Computer Security*, *14*(2), 104–115. doi:10.1108/09685220610655861

Hong, S., Hong, D., Ko, Y., Chang, D., Lee, W., & Lee, S. (2004). Differential Cryptanalysis of TEA and XTEA. *Information Security and Cryptology-ICISC*, *2003*, 402–417.

Hooper, E. (2006). An intelligent detection and response strategy to false positives and network attacks. *Proc. fourth IEEE International Workshop on Information Assurance IWIA*, 12-31. 10.1109/IWIA.2006.4

Howcroft & Trauth. (2005). *Handbook of Critical Information Systems Research*. Northampton, UK: Edward Elgar Publishing, Inc.

Humphreys, E. (2008). Information security management standards: Compliance, governance and risk management. *Information Security Technical Report*, *13*(4), 247–255. doi:10.1016/j.istr.2008.10.010

Humphrey, W., Edwards, R., LaCroix, G., Owens, M., & Schulz, H. (1987). *A method for assessing the software engineering capability of contractors (Technical Report, Software Engineering Institute, Carnegie Mellon University)*. Springfield, VA: National Technical Information Services, U.S. Department of Commerce.

Huston, T. (2001). Security Issues for Implementation of E-Medical Records. *Communications of the ACM*, *44*(9), 89–94. doi:10.1145/383694.383712

Hwanjo, Y., & Jaideep, V., & J, X. (2006). Privacy-Preserving SVM Classification on Vertically Partitioned Data. In *10th Pacific-Asia Conference, PAKDD 2006* (pp. 647-656). Singapore: Springer Berlin Heidelberg.

IEEE CyberSecurity. (2014). *About*. Retrieved October 10, 2017, from IEEE Cybersecurity: https://cybersecurity.ieee.org/about/

ISACA. (2009). *The risk IT framework*. Rolling Meadows, IL: ISACA.

ISACA. (2012). Retrieved July 03, 2012, from ISACA Website: http://www.isaca.org

ISECT. (2012). *ISO 27001 Security*. Retrieved September 2012, from ISO 27001 Security: http://www.iso27001security.com/html/27002.html#HistoryOfISO17799

ISO - International Organization for Standardization. (2008). *Information technology – process assessment; assessment of organizational maturity* (ISO/IEC Technical Report 15504-7). Geneva, Switzerland: ISO/IEC.

ISO - International Organization for Standardization. (2011a). *Information technology – Information security risk management (ISO/IEC 27005)*. Geneva, Switzerland: ISO/IEC.

ISO - International Organization for Standardization. (2011b). *Information technology – security techniques — information security incident management (ISO/IEC 27035)*. Geneva, Switzerland: ISO/IEC.

ISO - International Organization for Standardization. (2013). *Information technology –Information security management system Requirements. (ISO/IEC 27001)*. Geneva, Switzerland: ISO/IEC.

ISO. (2013). *Home: Standards*. Retrieved March 24, 2013, from ISO Website: http://www.iso.org/iso/home/standards.htm

ISO/IEC. (2013). *ISO/IEC 27002:2013*. Retrieved March 24, 2014 from http://www.iso.org/iso/home/store/catalogue_ics/catalogue_detail_ics.htm?csnumber=54533

ISO27000. (2007). *ISO 27000 Standards*. Retrieved September 16, 2012, from The ISO 27000 Directory Website: http://www.27000.org/iso-27799.htm

IT Governance Institute. (2006). *Information Security Governance: Guidance for Boards of Directors and Executive Management Guidance for Boards of Directors and Executive Management*. Author.

ITGI - IT Security Institute. (2008). *Guidance for information security managers*. Rolling Meadows, IL: IT Security Institute.

Ivan, D., Mads, J., & Jesper, B. N. (2010, September). A generalization of Paillier's public-key system with applications to electronic voting. *International Journal of Information Security*, 371–385.

Jabez, J., & Muthukumar, B. (2015). Intrusion Detection System (IDS): Anomaly Detection using Outlier Detection Approach. *Procedia Computer Science*, *48*, 338–346. doi:10.1016/j.procs.2015.04.191

Jaideep, V., Murat, K., & Clifton, C. (2008). Privacy-preserving Naïve Bayes classification. *The VLDB Journal — The International Journal on Very Large Data Bases*, 879-898.

Jaideep, V., Chris, C., Murat, K., & Scott, P. (2008). Privacy-Preserving Decision Trees over Vertically Partitioned Data. *ACM Transactions on Knowledge Discovery from Data*.

Jaideep, V., Hwanjo, Y., & Xiaoqian, J. (2008). Privacy-preserving SVM classification. *Knowledge and Information Systems*, 161–178.

Jaiwei, H., & Micheline, K. (2011). *Data Mining –Concepts and Techniques*. Morgan Kaufmann.

Jan, S., Nguyen, C. D., & Briand, L. (2015). Known XML Vulnerabilities Are Still a Threat to Popular Parsers and Open Source Systems. *Proceedings - 2015 IEEE International Conference on Software Quality, Reliability and Security*, 233–241. 10.1109/QRS.2015.42

Janies, J. (2008). Existence plots: A low-resolution time series for port behavior analysis. *Visualization for Computer Security*, 161-18.

Jan, S., Nguyen, C. D., & Briand, L. C. (2016). Automated and effective testing of web services for XML injection attacks. *Proceedings of the 25th International Symposium on Software Testing and Analysis - ISSTA 2016*, 12–23. 10.1145/2931037.2931042

JC, B. (1986). Secret sharing homomorphisms: Keeping shares of a secret secret. In Advances in cryptography—CRYPTO86 vol 263, Lecture notes in computer science (pp. 251–260). Berlin: Springer-Verlag.

Jiang, S., Song, X., Wang, H., Han, J.-J., & Li, Q.-H. (2006). A clustering-based method for unsupervised intrusion detections. *Pattern Recognition Letters*, 27(7), 802–810. doi:10.1016/j.patrec.2005.11.007

Jiang, W., Song, H., & Dai, Y. (2005). Real-time intrusion detection for high-speed networks. *Computers & Security*.

Jiawei, Y. (2013). *Privacy Preserving Back-Propagation Neural Network Learning Made Practical with Cloud Computing. IEEE Transactions on Parallel and Distributes Systems*.

Jim Finkle, T. F. a. J. W. (2016, December). *Cyber saudi-shamoon-targets*. Academic Press.

Jinwala, D.C., Patel, D.R. & Dasgupta, K.S. (2008). *Investigating and Analyzing the Light-weight ciphers for Wireless Sensor Networks*. Academic Press.

Jirapummin, C., Wattanapongsakorn, N., & Kanthamanon, P. (2002). Hybrid neural networks for intrusion detection system. *2002 International Technical Conference on Circuits/Systems,Computers and Communications (ITC-CSCC 2002)*, 928–931.

Johnson, B. G. (2014). *Measuring ISO 27001 ISMS processes*. ISO.

Johnson, B., & Shneiderman, B. (1991). Tree-maps: A space-filling approach to the visualization of hierarchical information structures. In *IEEE Conference on Visualization Proceedings* (pp. 284-291). San Diego, CA: IEEE. 10.1109/VISUAL.1991.175815

Jøsang, A., Ismail, R., & Boyd, C. (2007). A survey of trust and reputation systems for online service provision. *Decision Support Systems*, 43(2), 618–644. doi:10.1016/j.dss.2005.05.019

Josephsen, D. (2007). *Building a monitoring infrastructure with Nagios*. Upper Saddle River, NJ: Prentice Hall.

Joshi, J., Ghafoor, A., Aref, W. G., & Spafford, E. H. (2001). Digital Government Security Infrastructure Design Challenges. *Computer*, 34(2), 66–72. doi:10.1109/2.901169

Juels, A. (2005). Strengthening EPC tags against cloning. *Proceedings of the 4th ACM workshop on Wireless security*, 76. Available at: http://citeseerx.ist.psu.edu/viewdoc/download?doi=10.1.1.68.6553&rep=rep1&type=pdf

Juels, A. (2006). RFID security and privacy: A research survey. *IEEE Journal on Selected Areas in Communications*, 24(2), 381–394. doi:10.1109/JSAC.2005.861395

Julisch, K. (2000). Dealing with False Positives in Intrusion Detection. *3rd Intl. Workshop on the Recent Advances in Intrusion Detection*.

Julisch, K. (2001). Mining Alarm Clusters to Improve Alarm Handling Efficiency. *Proceedings of the 17th Annual Conference on Computer Security Application*, 12-21. 10.1109/ACSAC.2001.991517

Julish, K. (2001). *Mining alarm clustering to improve alarm handling efficiency*. Paper presented at the Computer Security Applications Conference.

Jyothsna, V., Rama Prasad, V. V., & Munivara Prasad, K. (2011). A Review of Anomaly based *Intrusion Detection Systems*. *International Journal of Computers and Applications, 28*(7), 26–35. doi:10.5120/3399-4730

Kafali, O., Jones, J., Petruso, M., Williams, L., & Singh, M. P. (2017). How Good Is a Security Policy against Real Breaches? A HIPAA Case Study. *Proceedings - 2017 IEEE/ACM 39th International Conference on Software Engineering, ICSE 2017*, 530–540. 10.1109/ICSE.2017.55

Kahn, H. (1986). *On escalation: Metaphors and scenarios*. Santa Barbara, CA: Praeger.

KairUs Art+Research. (n.d.). Retrieved from: http://kairus.org/

KairUs. (2011). RE: Dakar arts festival. *KairUs Art+Research*. Retrieved from: http://kairus.org/re-dakar-arts-festival-2011/

Kam, R. (2012). *Top 3 issues facing patient privacy*. Retrieved from http://www.healthcareitnews.com/news/top-3-issues-facing-patient-privacy

Kamble, P., Kshirsagar, R. V., & Mankar, K. (2007). *Wireless Sensor Network Architecture*. Available at: http://www.ieee-spce.org/colloquium/proceedings/Communication_and_Networking/spit-1.pdf

Kam, H. T. (1995). Random Decision Forest. *3rd Int'l Conf. on Document Analysis and Recognition*, 14–18.

Kamsties, E. (2005). Understanding ambiguity in requirements engineering. *Engineering and Managing Software Requirements*, 245–266. 10.1007/3-540-28244-0_11

Kannadiga, P., & Zulkernine, M. (2005). DIDMA: A Distributed Intrusion Detection System Using Mobile Agents. *First ACIS International Workshop on Self-Assembling Wireless Networks (SNPD/SAWN'05)*, 12-21. 10.1109/SNPD-SAWN.2005.31

Kan, Z., Hu, C., Wang, Z., Wang, G., & Huang, X. (2010). NetVis: A network security management visualization tool based on treemap. In *2010 2nd International Conference on Advanced Computer Control*. Shenyang, China: IEEE.

Kaplantzis, S., & Mani, N. (2006). A study on classification techniques for network intrusion detection. *IASTED Conference on Networks and Communication Systems (NCS 2006)*.

Karahana, E., Straub, D., & Chervany, N. (1999). Information Technology Adoption Across Time: A Cross-Sectional Comparison of Pre-Adoption and Post-Adoption Beliefs. *Management Information Systems Quarterly, 23*(2), 183–213. doi:10.2307/249751

Karlof, C., Sastry, N., & Wagner, D. (2004). TinySec: a link layer security architecture for wireless sensor networks. *Proceedings of the 2nd international conference on Embedded networked sensor systems*, 162–175. Available at: http://citeseerx.ist.psu.edu/viewdoc/download?doi=10.1.1.61.4930&rep=rep1&type=pdf

Karnik, A., Goswami, S., & Guha, R. (2007). Detecting Obfuscated Viruses Using Cosine Similarity Analysis. *Modelling & Simulation, 2007. AMS'07. First Asia International Conference on IEEE*, 165–70. 10.1109/AMS.2007.31

Karokola, G. (2012). *A framework for securing e-government services*. (Unpublished doctoral thesis). Department of Computer and System Sciences, Stockholm University, Sweden.

Katz, J. (1970). *Semantic Theory*. New York: Harper and Row.

Kaushal, K., Swadas, P., & Prajapati, N. (2012). Metamorphic Malware Detection Using Statistical Analysis. *International Journal of Soft Computing and Engineering, 2*(3), 49–53.

Kayacik, G. (2006). A hierarchal SOM-based intrusion detection system. *Engineering Applications of Artificial Intelligence*. doi:10.1016/j.engappai.2006.09.005

Kayacık, H. G., Zincir-Heywood, A. N., & Heywood, M. I. (2005). Selecting Features for Intrusion Detection: A Feature Relevance Analysis on KDD 99 Intrusion Detection Datasets. *Proceeding of the Third Annual Conference on Privacy, Security and Trust PST2005*, 3-8.

Kayacık, H. G., Zincir-Heywood, A. N., & Heywood, M. I. (2005). Selecting Features for Intrusion Detection: A Feature Relevance Analysis on KDD 99 Intrusion Detection Datasets. *Third Annual Conference on Privacy, Security and Trust*.

Keerthi, S. S. E. G. (2002). Convergence of a Generalized SMO Algorithm for SVM Classifier Design. Machine Learning, 351-360.

Keim, D. A., Mansmann, F., Schneidewind, J., & Schreck, T. (2006). Monitoring network traffic with radial traffic analyzer. In *IEEE Symposium On Visual Analytics Science And Technology* (pp. 123-128). Baltimore, MD: IEEE. 10.1109/VAST.2006.261438

Kelsey, J., Schneier, B. & Wagner, D. (1997). Related-key cryptanalysis of 3-way, biham-des, cast, des-x, newdes, rc2, and tea. *Information and Communications Security*, 233–246.

Khodamoradi, P., Fazlali, M., Mardukhi, F., & Nosrati, M. (2015). Heuristic Metamorphic Malware Detection Based on Statistics of Assembly Instructions Using Classification Algorithms. *2015 18th CSI International Symposium on Computer Architecture and Digital Systems (CADS)*. 10.1109/CADS.2015.7377792

Khosravifar, B., & Bentahar, J. (2008). An Experience Improving Intrusion Detection Systems False Alarm Ratio by Using Honeypot. *22nd International Conference on Advanced Information Networking and Application: AINA 2008*, 997-1004. 10.1109/AINA.2008.44

Kim, D. S., & Park, J. S. (2003). Lecture Notes in Computer Science: Vol. 2662. *Network-based Intrusion Detection with Support Vector Machines*. Berlin: Springer-Verlag. doi:10.1007/978-3-540-45235-5_73

Kim, S., & Lee, J. (2007). A system architecture for high-speed deep packet inspection in signature-based network intrusion prevention. *Journal of Systems Architecture*, *53*(5-6), 310–320. doi:10.1016/j.sysarc.2006.10.005

King, J., & Williams, L. (2014). Log Your CRUD: Design Principles for Software Logging Mechanisms. *Proceedings of the 2014 Symposium and Bootcamp on the Science of Security*, 5:1--5:10. 10.1145/2600176.2600183

Kingsford, K. M., Zhang, F., Ayeh, M. D. N., & MaryMargaret, A. (2017). A Mathematical Model for a Hybrid System Framework for Privacy Preservation of Patient Health Records. *2017 IEEE 41st Annual Computer Software and Applications Conference (COMPSAC)*, 119–124. 10.1109/COMPSAC.2017.21

Kintzel, C., Fuchs, J., & Mansmann, F. (2011). Monitoring large ip spaces with clockview. In *Proceedings of the 8th international symposium on visualization for cyber security* (p. 2). Pittsburgh, PA: ACM.

Klimov, A., & Shamir, A. (2004). Cryptographic Applications of T-functions. *Lecture Notes in Computer Science*, *3006*, 248–261. doi:10.1007/978-3-540-24654-1_18

Knapp, K., Marshall, T., Rainer, R. Jr, & Ford, N. (2007). Information Security Effectiveness: Conceptualization and Validation of a Theory. *International Journal of Information Security and Privacy*, *1*(2), 37–60. doi:10.4018/jisp.2007040103

Ko, Y., Hong, S., Lee, W., Lee, S., & Kang, J. S. (2004). Related key differential attacks on 27 rounds of XTEA and full-round GOST. Fast Software Encryption, 299–316. doi:10.1007/978-3-540-25937-4_19

Koike, H., & Ohno, K. (2004). SnortView: visualization system of snort logs. In *Proceedings of the 2004 ACM workshop on Visualization and data mining for computer security* (pp. 143-147). Washington, DC: ACM.

Koike, H., Ohno, K., & Koizumi, K. (2005). Visualizing cyber attacks using IP matrix. In *IEEE Workshop on Visualization for Computer Security* (pp. 91-98). Minneapolis, MN: IEEE.

Kolter, J. Z., & Maloof, M. A. (2004). Learning to Detect Malicious Executables in the Wild. *Proceedings of the 2004 ACM SIGKDD international conference on Knowledge discovery and data mining - KDD '04*, 470. 10.1145/1014052.1014105

Komlodi, A., Rheingans, P., Ayachit, U., Goodall, J. R., & Joshi, A. (2005). A user-centered look at glyph-based security visualization. In *IEEE Workshop on Visualization for Computer Security* (pp. 21-28). Minneapolis, MN: IEEE.

Konstantinou, E., & Wolthusen, S. (2008). Metamorphic Virus: Analysis and Detection. Royal Holloway University of London.

Korba, A. A., Nafaa, M., & Ghanemi, S. (2016). Hybrid Intrusion Detection Framework for Ad hoc networks. *International Journal of Information Security and Privacy*, *10*(4), 1–32. doi:10.4018/IJISP.2016100101

Krasser, S., Conti, G., Grizzard, J., Gribschaw, J., & Owen, H. (2005). Real-time and forensic network data analysis using animated and coordinated visualization. *Proceedings from the Sixth Annual IEEE SMC Information Assurance Workshop*, 42-49. 10.1109/IAW.2005.1495932

Krebs, B. (2013). *The Value of a Hacked Email Account*. Available: http://krebsonsecurity.com/2013/06/the-value-of-a-hacked-email-account/

Kronman, L., & Zingerle, A. (2013). Humiliating Entertainment or Social Activism? Analyzing Scambaiting Strategies against Online Advance Fee Fraud. In *Cyberworlds (CW), 2013 International Conference on*. IEEE.

Ksiazak, P., Farrelly, W., & Curran, K. (2015). A Lightweight Authentication Protocol for Secure Communications between Resource-Limited Devices and Wireless Sensor Networks. *International Journal of Information Security and Privacy*, *8*(4), 62-102. DOI: 10.4018/IJISP.2014100104

Kühnhauser, W. (1999). Policy Groups. *Computers & Security*, *18*(4), 351–363. doi:10.1016/S0167-4048(99)80081-9

Kumar, S., & Spafford, E. G. (1995). *A Software Architecture to support Misuse Intrusion Detection*. Technical Report CSD-TR-95-009, Purdue University.

Kumar, M., Hanumanthappa, M., & Suresh Kumar, T. V. (2011). Intrusion Detection System - False Positive Alert Reduction Technique. *ACEEE International Journal of Network Security*, *2*(3), 37–40.

Kumawat, A., Sharma, A. K., & Kumawat, S. (2017). Identification of Cryptographic Vulnerability and Malware Detection in Android. *International Journal of Information Security and Privacy*, *11*(3), 15–28. doi:10.4018/IJISP.2017070102

Kuncheva, L. I. (2004). Combining Pattern Classifiers: Methods and Algorithms. John Wiley & Sons.

Laboratory, M. L. (1998-1999). *Darpha Intrusion Detection Data Sets*. Lincoln: Author.

Lad, M., Massey, D., & Zhang, L. (2006). Visualizing internet routing changes. *IEEE Transactions on Visualization and Computer Graphics*, *12*(6), 1450–1460. doi:10.1109/TVCG.2006.108 PMID:17073368

Lai, Q., Zhou, C., Ma, H., Wu, Z., & Chen, S. (2015). Visualizing and characterizing DNS lookup behaviors via log-mining. *Neurocomputing*, *169*, 100–109. doi:10.1016/j.neucom.2014.09.099

Lakkaraju, K., Yurcik, W., & Lee, A. J. (2004). NVisionIP: netflow visualizations of system state for security situational awareness. In *Proceedings of the 2004 ACM workshop on Visualization and data mining for computer security* (pp. 65-72). Washington, DC: ACM. 10.1145/1029208.1029219

Lambodar, J. N. (2013). Privacy Preserving Distributed Data Mining with Evolutionary Computing. In *International Conference on Frontiers of Intelligent Computing: Theory and Applications* (pp. 259-267). Springer.

Landim, F. L. P., Fernandes, A. M., Mesquita, R. B., Collares, P. M. C., & Frota, M. A. (2010). Interpersonal network analysis: Application to the reality of a nursing team working in a hematology unit. *Saúde e Sociedade, 19*(4), 828–837. doi:10.1590/S0104-12902010000400010

Langton, J. T., & Newey, B. (2010, April). Evaluation of current visualization tools for cyber security. In *SPIE Defense, Security, and Sensing*. International Society for Optics and Photonics.

Latanya, S. (2002). k-ANONYMITY: A Model For Protecting Privacy. *International Journal of Uncertainty, Fuzziness and Knowledge-based Systems*, 557–570.

Lau, S. (2004). The Spinning Cube of Potential Doom. *Communications of the ACM - Wireless Sensor Networks, 47*(6), 25-26.

Law, K., & Kwok, L. F. (2004). IDS False Alarm Filtering Using KNN Classifier. LNCS, 3325, 114-121.

Lee, W., Stolfo, S. J., & Mok, K. W. (1999). A data mining framework for building intrusion detection models. *IEEE Symposium on Security and Privacy*, 120-132.

Lee, Y. C., Hsieh, Y. C., You, P. S., & Chen, T. C. (2009). A New Ultralightweight RFID Protocol with Mutual Authentication. *Information Engineering, 2009. ICIE'09. WASE International Conference on*, 58–61. 10.1109/ICIE.2009.24

Lee, C. P., Tros, J., Gibbs, N., Beyah, R., & Copeland, J. A. (2005). Visual firewall: real-time network security monitor. In *IEEE Workshop on Visualization for Computer Security* (pp. 129-136). IEEE.

Lee, S., Lee, S.-G., & Yoo, S. (2003). An integrative model of computer abuse based on social control and general deterrence theories. *Information & Management, 41*(6), 707–718. doi:10.1016/j.im.2003.08.008

Lee, W., & Stolfo, S. (1998). Data mining approaches for intrusion detection. *Proceedings of the 7th USENIX Security Symposium.*

Lee, W., & Stolfo, S. J. (2000). A framework for constructing features and models for intrusion detection systems. *Information and System Security, 3*(4), 227261.

Lee, W., Stolfo, S. J., & Mok, K. W. (2000). Adaptive intrusion detection, a data mining approach. *Artificial Intelligence Review, 14*(6), 533567. doi:10.1023/A:1006624031083

Legal Information Institute. (1992). Retrieved from https://www.law.cornell.edu/cfr/text/45/164.308

Lei, X. C. (2014). Information Security in Big Data: Privacy and Data Mining. *IEEE Access: Practical Innovations, Open Solutions, 2*, 1149–1174. doi:10.1109/ACCESS.2014.2362522

Leong, K. S., Ng, M.L., & Engels, D.W. (2006). EPC Network Architecture. *Auto-ID Labs: EPC Network Architecture.* Available at: http://www.autoidlabs.org/uploads/media/AUTOIDLABS-WP-SWNET-012.pdf

Levin, D., Lee, Y., Valenta, L., Li, Z., Lai, V., Lumezanu, C., . . . Bhattacharjee, B. (2015). Alibi Routing. *Proceedings of the 2015 ACM Conference on Special Interest Group on Data Communication.*

Li Sin, W.-S. M.-J. (2014). *A new privacy preserving proximal support vector machine for classification of vertically partitioned data. International Journal Machine Learning and Cybernetics.*

Li, T., & Deng, R. (2007). Vulnerability analysis of EMAP-an efficient RFID mutual authentication protocol. *Proc. of AReS*, 7. Available at: http://citeseerx.ist.psu.edu/viewdoc/download?doi=10.1.1.63.6430&rep=rep1&type=pdf

Liang, H., Taihui, L., Nannan, X., & Jiejun, H. (2015). *False positive elimination in intrusion detection based on clustering*. Paper presented at the 2015 12th International Conference on Fuzzy Systems and Knowledge Discovery (FSKD).

Liao, Q., Blaich, A., Striegel, A., & Thain, D. (2008). ENAVis: Enterprise Network Activities Visualization. In *Proceedings of the 22nd conference on Large installation system administration conference* (pp. 59-74). San Diego, CA: Usenix.

Liebenau, J., & Backhouse, J. (1990). *Understanding Information: An Introduction.* London: Macmillan. doi:10.1007/978-1-349-11948-6

Lin, Da, & Stamp. (2011). Hunting for Undetectable Metamorphic Viruses. *Journal in Computer Virology, 7*(3), 201–14.

Li, T., & Wang, G. (2007). Security analysis of two ultra-lightweight RFID authentication protocols. *International Federation for Information Processing, 232*, 109.

Liu, G., Wang, Y., & Orgun, M. A. (2011). Trust Transitivity in Complex Social Networks. *Symposium conducted at the meeting of the AAAI.*

Liu, D., & Ning, P. (2004). Multilevel μTESLA: Broadcast authentication for distributed sensor networks. *ACM Transactions on Embedded Computing Systems, 3*(4), 800–836. doi:10.1145/1027794.1027800

Livnat, Y., Agutter, J., Moon, S., Erbacher, R. F., & Foresti, S. (2005). A visualization paradigm for network intrusion detection. In *Proceedings from the Sixth Annual IEEE SMC Information Assurance Workshop* (pp. 92-99). West Point, NY: IEEE. 10.1109/IAW.2005.1495939

Li, X., Wang, Q., Yang, L., & Luo, X. (2012). The research on network security visualization key technology. In *Fourth International Conference on Multimedia Information Networking and Security* (pp. 983-988). Nanjing, China: IEEE. 10.1109/MINES.2012.236

Lock, R., Sommerville, I., & Storer, T. (2009). *Responsibility modelling for risk analysis*. Retrieved June 2017 from http://archive.cs.st-andrews.ac.uk/STSE-Handbook/Papers/ResponsibilityModellingforRiskAnalysis-Lock.pdf

Lu, A., Wang, W., Dnyate, A., & Hu, X. (2011). Sybil Attack Detection through Global Topology Pattern Visualization. *Information Visualization, 10*(1), 32–46. doi:10.1057/ivs.2010.1

Lue, J. (1999). *Integrating fuzzy logic with data mining methods for intrusion detection* (Master's thesis). Mississippi State Univ.

Luethi, M., & Knolmayer, G. F. (2009). Security in Health Information Systems: An Exploratory Comparison of U.S. and Swiss Hospitals. In *42nd Hawaii International Conference on System Sciences* (pp. 1-10). Waikoloa, HI: CPS.

Lu, J. (2009). Related-key rectangle attack on 36 rounds of the XTEA block cipher. *International Journal of Information Security, 8*(1), 1–11. doi:10.100710207-008-0059-9

Lu, L. F., Zhang, J. W., Huang, M. L., & Fu, L. (2010). A new concentric-circle visualization of multi-dimensional data and its application in network security. *Journal of Visual Languages and Computing, 21*(4), 194–208. doi:10.1016/j.jvlc.2010.05.002

Luo, B., & Xia, J. (2014). A novel intrusion detection system based on feature generation with visualization strategy. *Expert Systems with Applications, 41*(9), 4139–4147. doi:10.1016/j.eswa.2013.12.048

Luse, A. (2009). *Exploring utilization of visualization for computer and network security.* Ames, IA: Iowa State University.

Lusher, D., Robins, G., Pattison, P. E., & Lomi, A. (2012). "Trust Me": Differences in expressed and perceived trust relations in an organization. *Social Networks, 34*(4), 410–424. doi:10.1016/j.socnet.2012.01.004

Maarouf, I., Baroudi, U., & Naseer, A. R. (2009). Efficient monitoring approach for reputation system-based trust-aware routing in wireless sensor networks. *IET Communications*, 3(5), 846–858. doi:10.1049/iet-com.2008.0324

Machanavajjhala, A. (2007). L-diversity: Privacy beyond k-anonymity. *Journal of ACM Transactions on Knowledge Discovery from Data*, 1(1).

Manganaris, S., Christensen, M., Zerkle, D., & Hermiz, K. (2000). A data mining analysis of RTID alarms. *Computer Networks*, 34(4), 571–577. doi:10.1016/S1389-1286(00)00138-9

Mangasarian, O. L. E. W. (2008). Privacy-Preserving Classification of Vertically Partitioned Data via Random Kernels. ACM Transactions on Knowledge Discovery from Data, 2(3).

Mann, I. (2010). *Hacking the human: Social engineering techniques and security countermeasures*. Gower Publishing, Ltd.

Manoranjan, P., Nayak, C. K., & Pradhan, S. D. K. (2016). Intrusion Detection System (IDS) and Their Types. *Network Security Attacks and Countermeasures*, 228–244.

Mansman, F., Meier, L., & Keim, D. A. (2008). Visualization of Host Behavior for Network Security. In *Proceedings of the Workshop on Visualization for Computer Security* (pp. 187-202). Berlin: Springer. 10.1007/978-3-540-78243-8_13

Mansmann, F., Keim, D. A., North, S. C., Rexroad, B., & Sheleheda, D. (2007). Visual Analysis of Network Traffic for Resource Planning, Interactive Monitoring, and Interpretation of Security Threats. *IEEE Transactions on Visualization and Computer Graphics*, 13(6), 1105–1112. doi:10.1109/TVCG.2007.70522 PMID:17968053

Markus, M. (1983). Power, Politics, and MIS Implementation. *Communications of the ACM*, 26(6), 430–444. doi:10.1145/358141.358148

Mármol, F. G., & Pérez, G. M. (2009). TRMSim-WSN, trust and reputation models simulator for wireless sensor networks. *Symposium conducted at the meeting of the Communications, 2009. ICC'09. IEEE International Conference on.*

Marty, R. (2009). *Applied security visualization*. Addison Wesley Professional.

Mashima, D., & Ahamad, M. (2012). Enhancing accountability of electronic health record usage via patient-centric monitoring. *Proceedings of the 2nd ACM SIGHIT International Health Informatics Symposium*, 409–418. 10.1145/2110363.2110410

Mathieu-Dupas, E. (2010). *Algorithme des K plus proches voisins pondérés (WKNN) et Application en diagnostic*. Montpellier: SysDiag, Unité Mixte de Recherche CNRS-BIO-RAD.

Mathur, K., & Hiranwal, S. (2013). A Survey on Techniques in Detection and Analyzing Malware Executables. *International Journal of Advanced Research in Computer Science and Software Engineering*, 3(4), 422–428.

McBrearty, S., Farrelly, W., & Curran, K. (2016). The Performance Cost of Preserving Data/Query Privacy Using Searchable Symmetric Encryption. *Security and Communication Networks*, 9(18), 5311–5332. doi:10.1002ec.1699

McPherson, J., Ma, K. L., Krystosk, P., Bartoletti, T., & Christensen, M. (2004). Portvis: a tool for port-based detection of security events. In *Proceedings of the 2004 ACM workshop on Visualization and data mining for computer security* (pp. 73-81). Washington, DC: ACM. 10.1145/1029208.1029220

McRee, R. (2008). Security Visualization: What you don't see can hurt you. Information Systems Security Association, 38-41.

Mechtri, L., Tolba, F. D., & Ghanemi, S. (2016). Agents for Intrusion Detection in MANET: A Survey and Analysis. In W. Awad, E. El-Alfy, & Y. Al-Bastaki (Eds.), *Improving Information Security Practices through Computational Intelligence* (pp. 126–147). Hershey, PA: IGI Global; doi:10.4018/978-1-4666-9426-2.ch006

MegaCorp. (n.d.). *KairUs Art+Research.* Retrieved from: http://megacorp.kairus.org

Menezes, A. J., Oorschot, P. C. V., & Vanstone, S. A. (1997). *Handbook of applied cryptography.* CRC Press.

Meng, W., Li, W., & Kwok, L.-F. (2015). Design of intelligent KNN-based alarm filter using knowledge-based alert verification in intrusion detection. *Security and Communication Networks, 8*(18), 3883–3895. doi:10.1002ec.1307

Mielikainen, T. (2004). Privacy Problems with Anonymized Transaction Databases. *7th International Conference, DS 2004* (pp. 219-229). Padova, Italy: Springer Berlin Heidelberg.

Milgo, E. C. (2009). *Statistical Tools for Linking Engine-Generated Malware to Its Engine.* Columbus State University.

Mintzberg, H. (1983). *Structures in Fives: Designing Effective Organizations.* Englewood Cliffs, NJ: Prentice Hall.

Mintzberg, H., Lampel, J., Quinn, J., & Goshal, S. (2003). *The Strategy Process.* Prentice Hall.

Mitaim, S., & Kosko, B. (1998). Neural Fuzzy Agents for Profile Learning and Adaptive Object Matching. *Presence (Cambridge, Mass.), 7*(6), 617–637. doi:10.1162/105474698565965

Mitchell, R., Marcella, R., & Baxter, G. (1999). Corporate information security management. *New Library World* (Vol. 100). 10.1108/03074809910285888

Mittelstädt, S., Stoffel, A., & Keim, D. A. (2014). Methods for Compensating Contrast Effects in Information Visualization. *Computer Graphics Forum, 33*(3), 231–240. doi:10.1111/cgf.12379

Mohamed, N., & Singh, J. K. (2012). A conceptual framework for information technology governance effectiveness in private organizations. *Information Management & Computer Security, 20*(2), 88–106. doi:10.1108/09685221211235616

Mollin, R. A. (2007). *An introduction to cryptography.* CRC Press.

Moon, D., Hwang, K., Lee, W., Lee, S., & Lim, J. (2002). Impossible differential cryptanalysis of reduced round XTEA and TEA. Fast Software Encryption, 117–121. doi:10.1007/3-540-45661-9_4

Morimoto, S. (2009). Application of COBIT to Security Management in Information Systems Development. *Fourth International Conference on Frontier of Computer Science and Technology,* 625-630. 10.1109/FCST.2009.38

Morin, B. (2004). *Corrélation d'alertes issues d'outils de détection d'intrusions avec prise en compte d'informations sur le système surveillé* (PhD thesis). Institut National des Sciences Appliquées de Rennes, France.

Morin, B., & Debar, H. (2003). Correlation of intrusion symptoms: an application of chronicles. *Proceedings of the 6th international conference on Recent Advances in Intrusion Detection (RAID'03),* 94-112. 10.1007/978-3-540-45248-5_6

Morris, C. (1970). *Foundations of the Unity Of Science: Toward an International Encyclopedia of Unified Science.* Chicago: University of Chicago Press.

Moskovitch, R., Stopel, D., Feher, C., Nissim, N., Japkowicz, N., & Elovici, Y. (2009). Unknown Malcode Detection and the Imbalance Problem. *Journal in Computer Virology, 5*(4), 295–308. doi:10.100711416-009-0122-8

Moulton, R., & Coles, R. S. (2003). Applying Information Security Governance. *Computers & Security, 22*(7), 580–584. doi:10.1016/S0167-4048(03)00705-3

Muelder, C., Ma, K.-L., & Bartoletti, T. (2005). Interactive Visualization for Network and Port Scan Detection. In *International Workshop on Recent Advances in Intrusion Detection* (pp. 265-283). Seattle, WA: Springer Berlin Heidelberg.

Mukkamala, Sung, & Abraham. (2003). *Intrusion detection using ensemble of soft computing paradigms.* Academic Press.

Nadiammai, G. V., Krishnaveni, S., & Hemalatha, M. (2011). A Comprehensive Analysis and study in Intrusion Detection System using Data Mining Techniques. *International Journal of Computers and Applications, 35*(8), 51–56.

Nakamura, L. (2014). 'I WILL DO EVERYthing That Am Asked': Scambaiting, Digital Show-Space, and the Racial Violence of Social Media. *Journal of Visual Culture*, 258–273.

Naoum, R.S.. Abdula Abid, N., & Namh Al-Sultani, Z. (2012). An Enhanced Resilient Backpropagation Artificial Neural Network for Intrusion Detection System. *International Journal of Computer Science and Network Security, 12*(3).

Narsingyani, D., & Kale, O. (2015). *Optimizing false positive in anomaly based intrusion detection using Genetic algorithm*. Paper presented at the 2015 IEEE 3rd International Conference on MOOCs, Innovation and Technology in Education (MITE).

Nataraj, L., Karthikeyan, S., Jacob, G., & Manjunath, B. S. (2011). Malware images: visualization ad automatic classification. In *Proceedings of the 8th international symposium on visualization for cyber security* (p. 4). Pittsburgh, PA: ACM.

Nations, U. (2008). *International Standard Industrial Classification of All Economic Activities (Revision 4)*. New York: United Nations Publication.

Needham, R.M. & Wheeler, D.J. (1997). *eXtended Tiny Encryption Algorithm*. Prentice Hall.

Neri, F. (2000). Comparing local search with respect to genetic evolution to detect in-trusion in computer networks. In *Proceedings of the 2000 Congress on Evolutionary Computation CEC00* (pp. 238-243). IEEE Press.

Nguyen, H. A., & Choi, D. (2008). Application of Data Mining to Network Intrusion Detection: Classifier Selection Model Challenges for Next Generation Network Operations and Service Management Lecture Notes. *Computer Science, 5297*, 399–408.

Ni, S. Y., Tseng, Y. C., Chen, Y. S., & Sheu, J. P. (1999). The broadcast storm problem in a mobile ad hoc network. *Proceedings of the 5th annual ACM/IEEE international conference on Mobile computing and networking*, 162. Available at: http://citeseerx.ist.psu.edu/viewdoc/download?doi=10.1.1.123.5000&rep=rep1&type=pdf

Nielsen, J. (1995). *10 usability heuristics for user interface design*. Fremont, CA: Nielsen Norman Group.

Nilsson, G., Petkovski, P., & Räihä, T. (2005). *The implementation and the effects on Swedish companies* (Unpublished master's thesis). School of Business, Economics and Law, University of Gothenburg, Sweden.

NIST - National Institute of Standard and Technology. (2012b). *Computer Security Incident Handling Guide (NIST Special Publication 800-61 Revision 2)*. Gaithersburg, MD: U.S. Department of Commerce.

NIST - National Institute of Standards and Technology. (2002). *Risk management guide for information technology systems (NIST Special Publication 800-30)*. Gaithersburg, MD: U.S. Department of Commerce.

NIST - National Institute of Standards and Technology. (2010). *Guide for applying risk management framework to federal information systems (NIST Special Publication 800-37 Revision 1)*. Gaithersburg, MD: U.S. Department of Commerce.

NIST - National Institute of Standards and Technology. (2011a). *Guide for conducting risk assessment (NIST Special Publication 800-30 Revision 1)*. Gaithersburg, MD: U.S. Department of Commerce.

NIST - National Institute of Standards and Technology. (2011b). *Managing information security risk (NIST Special Publication 800-39)*. Gaithersburg, MD: U.S. Department of Commerce.

NIST - National Institute of Standards and Technology. (2011c). *Information security continuous monitoring (ISCM) for federal information system and organizations (NIST Special Publication 800-137)*. Gaithersburg, MD: U.S. Department of Commerce.

NIST - National Institute of Standards and Technology. (2012a). *CAESARS framework extension: An enterprise continuous monitoring reference model (NIST Interagency Report 7756 – Second Draft)*. Gaithersburg, MD: U.S. Department of Commerce.

NIST. (2009, August). *NIST Special Publication 800-53*. Retrieved September 16, 2012, from National Institute of Standards and Technology: http://csrc.nist.gov/publications/nistpubs/800-53-Rev3/sp800-53-rev3-final.pdf

NIST. (2015, July). *NIST Special Publication 1800-1*. Retrieved October 7, 2017, from National Institute of Standards and Technology: https://nccoe.nist.gov/projects/use-cases/health-it/ehr-on-mobile-devices

NIST. (2017, May). *NIST Special Publication 1800-8*. Retrieved October 10, 2017, from National Institute of Standards and Technology: https://nccoe.nist.gov/sites/default/files/library/sp1800/hit-infusion-pump-nist-sp1800-8-draft.pdf

Nolan, R. (1973). Managing the computer resource: A stage hypothesis. *Communications of the ACM, 16*(7), 399–405. doi:10.1145/362280.362284

Nordic Semiconductors. (2009a). *Nordic Semiconductor - nRF905 Multiband Transceiver*. Available at: http://www.nordicsemi.com/index.cfm?obj=product&act=display&pro=83

Nordic Semiconductors. (2009b). *Nordic Semiconductor - nRF9E5 Multiband Transceiver/MCU/ADC*. Available at: http://www.nordicsemi.com/index.cfm?obj=product&act=display&pro=82

Nunnally, T., Chi, P., Abdullah, K., Uluagac, A. S., Copeland, J. A., & Beyah, R. (2013). P3D: a parallel 3D coordinate visualization for advanced network scans. In *2013 IEEE International Conference on Communications* (pp. 2052-2057). London: IEEE.

Nunnally, T., Uluagac, A. S., Copeland, J. A., & Beyah, R. (2012). 3DSVAT: a 3D stereoscopic vulnerability assessment tool for network security. In *2012 IEEE 37th Conference on Local Computer Networks* (pp. 111-118). Clearwater, FL: IEEE.

Nyarko, K., Capers, T., Scott, C., & Ladeji-Osias, K. (2002). Network intrusion visualization with NIVA, an intrusion detection visual analyzer with haptic integration. In *10th Symposium on Haptic Interfaces for Virtual Environment and Teleoperator Systems* (pp. 277-284). Orlando, FL: IEEE. 10.1109/HAPTIC.2002.998969

Oberheide, J., Goff, M., & Karir, M. (2006). Flamingo: Visualizing internet traffic. In *10th. IEEE/IFIP Network Operations and Management Symposium* (pp. 150-161). Vancouver, Canada: IEEE.

Ohta, S., Kurebayashi, R., & Kobayashi, K. (2008). Minimizing False Positives of a Decision Tree Classifier for Intrusion Detection on the Internet. *Journal of Network and Systems Management, 16*(4), 399–419. doi:10.100710922-008-9102-4

Oladimeji, E. a., Chung, L., Jung, H. T., & Kim, J. (2011). Managing security and privacy in ubiquitous eHealth information interchange. *Proceedings of the 5th International Confernece on Ubiquitous Information Management and Communication - ICUIMC '11*, 1. 10.1145/1968613.1968645

Oliveira, S. Z. O. (2003). Privacy preserving clustering by data transformation. *18th Brazilian symposium on databases*, 304–318.

Oliynyk, M. (2016). *Why is healthcare data security so important?* Retrieved from https://www.protectimus.com/blog/why-is-healthcare-data-security-so-important/

Olson, M., & Chervaney, N. (1980). The Relationship between Organizational Characteristics and the Structure of the Information Services Function. *Management Information Systems Quarterly, 4*(2), 57–68. doi:10.2307/249337

Olzak, T. (2013, September). *COBIT 5 for Information Security: The Underlying Principles*. Retrieved March 23, 2014, from TechRepublic: http://www.techrepublic.com/blog/it-security/cobit-5-for-information-security-the-underlying-principles/

Onut, I. V., & Ghorbani, A. A. (2007). Svision: A novel visual netwok-anomaly identification technique. *Computers & Security, 26*(3), 201–212. doi:10.1016/j.cose.2006.10.001

Orfila, A., Carb'o, J., & Ribagorda, A. (2005). Intrusion Detection Effectiveness Improvement by a Multiagent System. *International Journal of Computer Science & Applications, 2*(1), 1–6.

Orlikowski, W. (1993). CASE Tools as Organizational Change: Investigating Incremental and Radical Changes in Systems Development. *Management Information Systems Quarterly, 17*(3), 309–340. doi:10.2307/249774

Ouafi, K., & Vaudenay, S. (2009). Smashing SQUASH-0. Advances in Cryptology - EUROCRYPT 2009, 300-312. doi:10.1007/978-3-642-01001-9_17

P, P. (1999). Public key cryptosystems based on composite degree residuosity classes. In *Advances in Cryptology—Eurocrypt '99 proceedings, lecture notes in computer science* (vol. 1592, pp. 223–238). Berlin: Springer-Verlag.

Paillier, P. (1999). Public-Key Cryptosystems Based on Composite Degree Residuosity Classes. EUROCRYPT, 223–238.

Pari, P. (2011-2013). *Classification consensuelle*. Retrieved from http://pari.ai.univ-paris8.fr/?author=1

Parker, J. (2012, March). Retrieved July 3, 2012, from Enfocus Solutions Inc.: http://blog.enfocussolutions.com/Powering_Requirements_Success/bid/131740/COBIT-5-is-Coming

Patel, K. S., & Shah, J. S. (2016). Analysis of Existing Trust Based Routing Schemes Used in Wireless Network. *International Journal of Information Security and Privacy, 10*(2), 26–40. doi:10.4018/IJISP.2016040103

Patel, V., Mohandas, R., & Pais, A. R. (2010). Attacks on Web Services and mitigation schemes. *Security and Cryptography (SECRYPT), Proceedings of the 2010 International Conference on*, 1–6.

Pathak, J. (2005). Information Technology Governance and COBIT. In J. Pathak (Ed.), Information Technology Auditing: An Evolving Agenda (pp. 151-156). Springer Berlin Heidelberg.

Pathan, A.-S. K. (2016). *Security of self-organizing networks: MANET, WSN, WMN, VANET*. CRC Press.

Peltier, T. R. (2013). *Information Security Fundamentals* (2nd ed.). Taylor & Francis. doi:10.1201/b15573

Peng, D., Chen, W., & Peng, Q. (2012). TrustVis: Visualizing Trust towards Attack Identification in Distributed Computing Environments. *Security and Communication Networks, 6*(12), 1445–1459. doi:10.1002ec.521

Peng, H., Long, F., & Ding, C. (2005). Feature Selection Based on Mutual Information: Criteria of Max-Dependency, Max-Relevance, and Min-Redundancy. *IEEE Transactions on Pattern Analysis and Machine Intelligence, 27*(8), 1226–1238. doi:10.1109/TPAMI.2005.159 PMID:16119262

Perdisci, R., Giacinto, G., & Roli, F. (2006). Alarm clustering for intrusion detection systems in computer networks. *Engineering Applications of Artificial Intelligence, 19*(4), 429–438. doi:10.1016/j.engappai.2006.01.003

Peris-Lopez, P., Hernandez-Castro, J. C., Estevez-Tapiador, J. M., & Ribagorda, A. (2006b). LMAP: A real lightweight mutual authentication protocol for low-cost RFID tags. *Workshop on RFID Security*, 12–14. Available at: http://citeseerx.ist.psu.edu/viewdoc/download?doi=10.1.1.110.2082&rep=rep1&type=pdf

Peris-Lopez, P., Hernandez-Castro, J. C., Tapiador, J. M., van der Lubbe, J. C., Singh, M. K., Liang, G., . . . Kish, L. L. (2008). *Security Flaws in a Recent Ultralightweight RFID Protocol*. Arxiv preprint arXiv:0910.2115

Peris-Lopez, P., Hernandez-Castro, J., Tapiador, J., & Ribagorda, A. (2009). Advances in Ultralightweight Cryptography for Low-Cost RFID Tags: Gossamer Protocol. Information Security Applications, 56–68.

Peris-Lopez, P., Hernandez-Castro, J. C., Estevez-Tapiador, J. M., & Ribagorda, A. (2006a). EMAP: An efficient mutual-authentication protocol for low-cost RFID tags. *Lecture Notes in Computer Science*, *4277*, 352–361. doi:10.1007/11915034_59

Peris-Lopez, P., Hernandez-Castro, J. C., Estevez-Tapiador, J. M., & Ribagorda, A. (2006c). M^2AP: A Minimalist Mutual-Authentication Protocol for Low-Cost RFID Tags. *Lecture Notes in Computer Science*, *4159*, 912–923. doi:10.1007/11833529_93

Perrig, A., Canetti, R., Song, D., & Tygar, J. D. (2001). Efficient and secure source authentication for multicast. In *Network and Distributed System Security Symposium* (pp. 35–46). NDSS. Available at http://citeseerx.ist.psu.edu/viewdoc/download?doi=10.1.1.18.1680&rep=rep1&type=pdf

Perrig, A., Szewczyk, R., Tygar, J. D., Wen, V., & Culler, D. E. (2002). SPINS: Security protocols for sensor networks. *Wireless Networks*, *8*(5), 521–534. doi:10.1023/A:1016598314198

Philips, M. (2003). *Using a capability maturity model to derive security requirements*. Bethesda, MD: SANS Institute.

Pietraszek, T., & Tanner, A. (2005). Data mining and machine learning– towards reducing false positives in intrusion detection'. *Information Security Technical Report*, *10*(3), 169–183. doi:10.1016/j.istr.2005.07.001

Pigeau, R., & McCann, C. (2002). Re-conceptualizing command and control. *Canadian Military Journal*, *3*(1), 53–64.

Platt, J. C. (1998). *Fast Training of Support Vector Machines using Sequential Minimal Optimization*. Academic Press.

Plonk, A., & Carblanc, A. (2008). *Malicious Software (Malware): A Security Threat to the Internet Economy*. Academic Press.

Pokrywka, R. (2008). Reducing False Alarm Rate in Anomaly Detection with Layered Filtering. LNCS, 5101, 396-404.

Ponemon, L. (2017). *2017 Cost of Data Breach Study*. IBM Security and Ponemon Institute LLC.

Popescu, D., Rugaber, S., Medvidovic, N., & Berry, D. M. (2008). Reducing ambiguities in requirements specifications via automatically created object-oriented models. Lecture Notes in Computer Science), 5320, 103–124. doi:10.1007/978-3-540-89778-1_10

Pöppelbuß, J., & Röglinger, M. (2011). What makes a useful maturity model? A framework of general design principles for maturity models and its demonstration in business process management. In *Proceedings of the Nineteenth European Conference on Information Systems (ECIS 2011)*. Association for Information Systems Electronic Library (AISeL).

Portia, C. (2011). *Data mining and Neural Networks from Commercial Perspective*. Academic Press.

Poschmann, A., Leander, G., Schramm, K., & Paar, C. (2007). New light-weight crypto algorithms for RFID. *Proceedings of The IEEE International Symposium on Circuits and Systems*, 1843–1846. Available at: http://citeseerx.ist.psu.edu/viewdoc/download?doi=10.1.1.80.1217&rep=rep1&type=pdf

Posthumus, S., & von Solms, R. (2004). A framework for the governance of information security. *Computers & Security*, *23*(8), 638–646. doi:10.1016/j.cose.2004.10.006

PRGL. (2011, December 22). Retrieved March 4, 2012, from Praxiom Research Group Limited: http://www.praxiom.com/iso-17799-intro.htm

Protecting Your Privacy & Security, Your Health Information Privacy. (n.d.). Retrieved from https://www.healthit.gov/patients-families/your-health-information-privacy

Purkait, S. (2012). Phishing Counter Measures and Their Effectiveness - Literature Review. *Information Management & Computer Security*, *20*(5), 382–420. doi:10.1108/09685221211286548

Qasim Ali, M., Al-Shaer, E., Khan, H., & Khayam, S. A. (2013). Automated Anomaly Detector Adaptation using Adaptive Threshold Tuning. *ACM Transactions on Information and System Security*, *15*(4), 1–30. doi:10.1145/2445566.2445569

Qassim, Q., Patel, A., & Mohd-Zin, A. (2014, September). Strategy to Reduce False Alarms in Intrusion Detection and Prevention Systems. *The International Arab Journal of Information Technology*, *11*(5).

Qiang, L., Li, L., & Wang, C. (2014). Automatic fuzz testing of web service vulnerability. *2014 International Conference on Information and Communications Technologies (ICT 2014)*, 1.035-1.035. 10.1049/cp.2014.0589

Quattrociocchi, W., Caldarelli, G., & Scala, A. (2014). Self-healing networks: Redundancy and structure. *PLoS One*, *9*(2), e87986. doi:10.1371/journal.pone.0087986 PMID:24533065

Quinlan, J. R. (1986). Induction of Decision Trees. *Machine Learning*, *1*(1), 81–106. doi:10.1007/BF00116251

Quinlan, J. R. (2014). *C4. 5: Programs for Machine Learning*. Elsevier.

Qureshi, B., Min, G., & Kouvatsos, D. (2012). A distributed reputation and trust management scheme for mobile peer-to-peer networks. *Computer Communications*, *35*(5), 608–618. doi:10.1016/j.comcom.2011.07.008

Rabin, M.O. (1979). *Digitalized signatures and public-key functions as intractable as factorization*. MtT/LCS/TR-212.

Ragsdale, D., Carver, C., Humphries, J., & Pooch, U. (2000). Adaptation techniques for intrusion detection and intrusion response system. *SMC 2000 Conference Proceedings 2000 IEEE International Conference on Systems, Man, and Cybernetics Evolving to Systems Humans Organizations and their Complex Interactions*, 2344-2349.

Raisonance, S. A. S. (2010). *Raisonance, Corporate home page*. Available at: http://www.raisonance.com/

Ramaki, A. A., Khosravi-Farmad, M., & Bafghi, A. G. (2015). *Real time alert correlation and prediction using Bayesian networks*. Paper presented at the 2015 12th International Iranian Society of Cryptology Conference on Information Security and Cryptology (ISCISC).

Ranasinghe, D. C., & Cole, P. H. (2008). *Networked RFID Systems and Lightweight Cryptography*. Springer Berlin Heidelberg. doi:10.1007/978-3-540-71641-9

Rasmussen, J. (1997). Risk management in a dynamic society: A modeling problem. *Safety Science*, *27*(2), 183–213. doi:10.1016/S0925-7535(97)00052-0

Raymond Chi-Wing Wong, J. L.-C. (2006). (α, k)-anonymity: an enhanced k-anonymity model for privacy preserving data publishing. In *12th ACM SIGKDD international conference on Knowledge discovery and data mining* (pp. 754-759). New York: ACM.

RedCard Security. (2008). *ISO 27799:2008*. Retrieved September 16, 2012, from RedCard Security Website: http://www.redcardsecurity.com/pages/resources_files/ISO27799-2008.pdf

Rees, J., Subhajyoti, S., & Spafford, E. (2003). PFIRES: A Policy Framework for Information Security. *Communications of the ACM*, *46*(7), 101–106. doi:10.1145/792704.792706

Reich, B., & Benbasat, I. (2000). Factors that influence the social dimension of alignment between business and information technology objectives. *Management Information Systems Quarterly*, *24*(1), 81–113. doi:10.2307/3250980

Reinsmidt, E., Schwab, D., & Yang, L. (2016). Securing a Connected Mobile System for Healthcare. *Proceedings of IEEE International Symposium on High Assurance Systems Engineering*, 19–22. 10.1109/HASE.2016.53

Ren, P., Gao, Y., Li, Z., Chen, Y., & Watson, B. (2005). IDGraphs: intrusion detection and analysis using histograms. In *IEEE Workshop on Visualization for Computer Security* (pp. 39-46). Minneapolis, MN: IEEE.

Ren, P., Kristoff, J., & Gooch, B. (2006). Visualizing DNS traffic. In *Proceedings of the 3rd international wrkshop on Visualization for computer security* (pp. 23-30). Alexandria, VA: ACM.

Rezgui, A., & Eltoweissy, M. (2007). TARP: A Trust-Aware Routing Protocol for Sensor-Actuator. *Networks Symposium conducted at the meeting of the Mobile Adhoc and Sensor Systems, 2007. MASS 2007. IEEE International Conference on.* doi:10.1109/MOBHOC.2007.4428674

Richardson, R. (2008). *2008 CSI Computer Crime & Security Survey.* Computer Security Institute.

Riel, J.-P., & Irwin, B. (2006). InetVis, a visual tool for network telescope traffic analysis. In *Proceedings of the 4th international conference on Computer graphics, virtual reality, visualisation and interaction in Africa* (pp. 85-89). Cape Town, South Africa: ACM.

Rinne, S., Eisenbarth, T., & Paar, C. (2007). *Performance analysis of contemporary light-weight block ciphers on 8-bit microcontrollers.* ECRYPT.

Rivest, R. L. (1995). The RC5 encryption algorithm. *Dr. Dobb's Journal of Software Tools for the Professional Programmer, 20*(1), 146–149.

Rizvi, S., & Haritsa, J. (2002). Maintaining data privacy in association rule mining. In *28th Very Large Database Conference.* Hong Kong, China: Academic Press. 10.1016/B978-155860869-6/50066-4

Rockart, J., & Crescenzi, A. (1984). Engaging top management in information technology. *Sloan Management Review, 25.*

Rode, J., Johansson, C., DiGioia, P., Filho, R. S., Nies, K., Nguyen, D. H., ... Redmiles, D. (2006). Seeing Further: Extending Visualization as a Basis for Usable Security. In *Proceedings of the second symposium on Usable privacy and security* (pp. 145-155). New York: ACM. 10.1145/1143120.1143138

Rosa, T. M., Santin, A. O., & Malucelli, A. (2012). *Mitigating XML Injection Zero - Day Attack through Strategy - based Detection System.* Academic Press.

Runwal, N., Low, R. M., & Stamp, M. (2012). Opcode Graph Similarity and Metamorphic Detection. *Journal in Computer Virology, 8*(1–2), 37–52. doi:10.100711416-012-0160-5

Russell, M.D. (2004). *Tinyness: an overview of TEA and related ciphers.* Draft v0.3, 3.

Ryan, J., Lin, M.-J., & Miikkulainen, R. (1998). Intrusion detection with neural networks. In M. I. Jordan, M. J. Kearns, & S. A. Solla (Eds.), Advances in Neural Information Processing Systems: Vol. 10. *The MIT Press.*

Saarinen, M. J. (1998). *Cryptanalysis of Block Tea.* Unpublished manuscript.

Saeed, S. A. (2012). Privacy-preserving back-propagation and extreme learning machine algorithms. Data and Knowledge Engineering, 40-61.

Sammany, M., Sharawi, M., El-Beltagy, M., & Saroit, I. (2007). Artificial Neural Networks Architecture for Intrusion Detection Systems and Classification of Attacks. *Fifth international conference- INFO 2007.*

Saneifar, H. (2008). *Clustering de motifs séquentiels Application à la détection d'intrusions* (Master's thesis). Montpellier 2 Univ.

Santo, I. (2013). Idea: Opcode-Sequence-Based Malware Detection. *Information Sciences.*

Santos, I. (2011). Opcode-Sequence-Based Semi-Supervised Unknown Malware Detection. Lecture Notes in Computer Science, 6694, 50–57. doi:10.1007/978-3-642-21323-6_7

Santos, I., Brezo, F., Sanz, B., Laorden, C., & Bringas, P. G. (2011). Using Opcode Sequences in Single-Class Learning to Detect Unknown Malware. *IET Information Security, 5*(4), 220. doi:10.1049/iet-ifs.2010.0180

Santos, & Laorden, & Bringas. (2009, January). Collective Classification for Unknown Malware Detection. *Learning*.

Sarkar, S., & Datta, R. (2012). A trust based protocol for energy-efficient routing in self-organized manets. *IEEE Symposium conducted at the meeting of the India Conference (INDICON), 2012 Annual.*

Sarma, S. E. (2001). *Towards the five-cent tag*. Technical Report MIT-AUTOID-WH-006, MIT Auto ID Center. Available at: http://www.autoidlabs.org/uploads/media/mit-autoid-wh-006.pdf

Sarma, S. E., Weis, S. A., & Engels, D. W. (2003). RFID systems and security and privacy implications. *Lecture Notes in Computer Science, 2523*, 454–469. doi:10.1007/3-540-36400-5_33

Schiffman, M. (2010). *A Brief History of Malware Obfuscation: Part 2 of 2*. Cisco Blog.

Schneier, B. (1996). *Applied Cryptography: Protocols, Algorithms, and Source Code in C* (2nd ed.). Wiley.

Schou, C., & Shoemaker, D. P. (2006). *Information Assurance for the Enterprise: A Roadmap to Information Security*. McGraw-Hill, Inc.

Schultz, E. (2004). The case for one-time credentials. *Computers & Security, 23*(6), 441–442. doi:10.1016/j.cose.2004.08.001

Schultz, M. G., Eskin, E., Zadok, E., & Stolfo, S. J. (2001). Data Mining Methods for Detection of New Malicious Executables. *Proceedings of the 2001 IEEE Symposium on Security and Privacy*, 38–49. 10.1109/SECPRI.2001.924286

Schwarz, C. (n.d.). *Spamming back*. Retrieved from: http://www.christophschwarz.net

Scott, J. (2017). Social network analysis. *Sage (Atlanta, Ga.)*.

SecureWorks. (2017). *State of Cybercrime: Exposing the threats, techniques and markets that fuel the economy of cybercriminals*. Atlanta, GA: SecureWorks.

Seo, I., Lee, H., & Han, S. C. (2014). Cylindrical Coordinates Security Visualization for multiple domain and control botnet detection. *Computers & Security, 46*, 141–153. doi:10.1016/j.cose.2014.07.007

Services, D. o. (2002). *Standard for privacy of individually identifiable health information*. Available: http://www.hhs.gov/ocr/ privacy/hipaa/administrative/privacyrule/privruletxt.txt

Shabtai, A., Moskovitch, R., Feher, C., Dolev, S., & Elovici, Y. (2012). Detecting Unknown Malicious Code by Applying Classification Techniques on OpCode Patterns. *Security Informatics, 1*(1), 1. doi:10.1186/2190-8532-1-1

Shamir, A. (2008). SQUASH – A New MAC with Provable Security Properties for Highly Constrained Devices Such as RFID Tags. Fast Software Encryption, 144-157. doi:10.1007/978-3-540-71039-4_9

Shankarapani, M. K., Ramamoorthy, S., Movva, R. S., & Mukkamala, S. (2011). Malware Detection Using Assembly and API Call Sequences. *Journal in Computer Virology, 7*(2), 107–119. doi:10.100711416-010-0141-5

Shen, J. (2016). A practical RFID grouping authentication protocol in multiple-tag arrangement with adequate security assurance. In *2016 18th international conference on advanced communication technology (ICACT)*. IEEE.

Shiakallis, O., Mavromoustakis, C. X., Mastorakis, G., Bourdena, A., & Pallis, E. (2015). Traffic-based S-MAC: A novel scheduling mechanism for optimized throughput in mobile peer-to-peer systems. *International Journal of Wireless Networks and Broadband Technologies, 4*(1), 62–80. doi:10.4018/ijwnbt.2015010105

Shipra, A., & Jayant, R. H., & P, A. B. (2009). FRAPP: A framework for high-accuracy privacy-preserving mining. *Data Mining and Knowledge Discovery*, 101–139.

Shiravi, H., Shiravi, A., & Ghorbani, A. A. (2010). IDS alert visualization and monitoring through heuristic host selection. *Information and Communications Security*, 445-458.

Shiravi, H., Shiravi, A., & Ghorbani, A. A. (2011). Situational assessment of intrusion alerts: A multi attack scenario evaluation. *Information and Communications Security*, 399-413.

Shiravi, H., Shiravi, A., & Ghorbani, A. A. (2012). *A survey of visualization systems for network security*. Academic Press.

Shittu, R., Healing, A., Ghanea-Hercock, R., Bloomfield, R., & Rajarajan, M. (2015). Intrusion alert prioritisation and attack detection using post-correlation analysis. *Computers & Security*, *50*, 1–15. doi:10.1016/j.cose.2014.12.003

Shruti, G., Umang, S., Reddy, B. V. R., & Hoda, M. N. (2012). Analytical Study of Existing Methodologies of IDS for False Alarm Rate - A Survey and Taxonomy. *International Journal of Emerging Technology and Advanced Engineering*, *2*(4), 393–399.

Sinclair, C., Pierce, L., & Matzner, S. (1999). An application of machine learning to network intrusion detection. In *ACSAC '99: Proceedings of the 15th Annual Computer Security Applications Conference*. Washington, DC: IEEE Computer Society. 10.1109/CSAC.1999.816048

Singh, S. K., Kumar, P., & Singh, J. P. (2017). Localization in Wireless Sensor Networks Using Soft Computing Approach. *International Journal of Information Security and Privacy*, *11*(3), 42–53. doi:10.4018/IJISP.2017070104

Singh, U., & Gupta, S. (2012). Incorporation of IDS in Real World Applications. *Journal of Emerging Trends in Computing and Information Sciences*, *3*(1), 15–20.

Siponen, M. (2000). A conceptual foundation for organizational information security awareness. *Information Management & Computer Security*, *8*(1), 31–41. doi:10.1108/09685220010371394

Siponen, M., & Willison, R. (2009). Information security management standards: Problems and solutions. *Information & Management*, *46*(5), 267–270. doi:10.1016/j.im.2008.12.007

Slater, D. (2004, January 4). *Numbers: ITIL, COBIT and More: Who Uses What?* Retrieved March 23, 2014 from http://www.csoonline.com/article/216935/numbers-itil-cobit-and-more-who-uses-what-

Smallridge, J., Wagner, P., & Crowl, J. N. (2016). Understanding cyber-vigilantism: A conceptual framework. *Journal of Theoretical & Philosophical Criminology*, *8*(1), 57.

Smith, B., Austin, A., Brown, M., King, J. T., Lankford, J., Meneely, A., & Williams, L. (2010). Challenges for protecting the privacy of health information. *Proceedings of the Second Annual Workshop on Security and Privacy in Medical and Home-Care Systems - SPIMACS '10*, 1. 10.1145/1866914.1866916

Sohrabi Safa, N., Von Solms, R., & Furnell, S. (2016). Information security policy compliance model in organizations. *Computers & Security*, *56*, 1–13. doi:10.1016/j.cose.2015.10.006

Solli-Sæther, H., & Gottschalk, P. (2010). The modelling process for stage models. *Journal of Organizational Computing and Electronic*, *20*(3), 279–293. doi:10.1080/10919392.2010.494535

Sommer, P. (1998). Intrusion detection systems as evidence. *Proceedings of the RAID 98 Conference*.

Sommestad, T., Karlzén, H., & Hallberg, J. (2015). A Meta-Analysis of Studies on Protection Motivation Theory and Information Security Behaviour. *International Journal of Information Security and Privacy*, *9*(1), 26–46. doi:10.4018/IJISP.2015010102

Song, H. T., Okabe, Y., Eto, M., Inoue, D., & Nakao, K. (2011). Statistical analysis of honeypot data and building of kyoto 2006+ dataset for nids evaluation. *Proceedings of the First Workshop on Building Analysis Datasets and Gathering Experience Returns for Security.* 10.1145/1978672.1978676

Spamscamscam. (n.d.). *Urgent & confidential.* Retrieved from: http://www.spamscamscam.com/

Srivastava, V., Neel, J. O., MacKenzie, A. B., Menon, R., DaSilva, L. A., Hicks, J. E., ... Gilles, R. P. (2005). Using game theory to analyze wireless ad hoc networks. *IEEE Communications Surveys and Tutorials, 7*(1-4), 46–56. doi:10.1109/COMST.2005.1593279

Staheli, D., Yu, T., Crouser, J. R., Damodaran, S., Nam, K., O'Gwynn, D., ... Harrison, L. (2014). Visualization Evaluation for Cyber Security: Trends and Future Directions. In *Proceedings of the Eleventh Workshop on Visualization for Cyber Security* (pp. 49-56). New York: ACM. 10.1145/2671491.2671492

Stamper, R. (1973). *Information in Business and Administrative Systems.* New York: Halstead Press.

Standaert, F., Piret, G., Gershenfeld, N., & Quisquater, J. (2006). SEA: A scalable encryption algorithm for small embedded applications. *Lecture Notes in Computer Science, 3928,* 222–236. doi:10.1007/11733447_16

Stephenson, P. (2000). The application of intrusion detection systems in a forensic environment. *Proceedings of the RAID 2000 Conference.*

Stolfo, J., Wei, F., Lee, W., Prodromidis, A., & Chan, P. K. (2000). Mining with Application to Fraud and Intrusion Detection: Results from the JAM Project. *Proceedings of DARPA Information Survivability Conference and Exposition,* 130-144.

Straub, D. Jr. (1990). Effective IS Security: An Empirical Study. *Information Systems Research, 1*(3), 255–276. doi:10.1287/isre.1.3.255

Straub, D., & Welke, R. (1998). Coping with Systems Risk: Security Planning Models for Management Decision Making. *Management Information Systems Quarterly, 22*(4), 441–469. doi:10.2307/249551

Subba, B., Biswas, S., & Karmakar, S. (2016). A Neural Network based system for Intrusion Detection and attack classification. In *Communication (NCC), 2016 Twenty Second National Conference on* (pp. 1-6). IEEE.

Sun, H. M., Ting, W. C., & Wang, K. H. (2008). *On the security of chien's ultralightweight RFID authentication protocol.* Cryptology ePrint Archive, Report 2008/083. Available at: http://eprint.iacr.org/2008/083.pdf

Sundaram, A. (1996). An Introduction to Intrusion Detection. Technical Report, Purdue University.

Sun, L., Wei-Song, M., Biao, Q., & Zhi-Jian, Z. (2014). A new privacy-preserving proximal support vector machine for classification of vertically partitioned data. *International Journal of Machine Learning and Cybernetics,* 109–118.

Swedish Bankers' Association. (2016). *Banks in Sweden.* Retrieved March 2016 from www.swedishbankers.se

Swedish Civil Contingencies Agency. (2014). *International case report on cyber security incidents – Reflections on three cyber incidents in the Netherlands, Germany and Sweden.* Stockholm, Sweden: Myndigheten för Samhällsskydd och Beredskap.

Swedish National Audit Office. (2014). Information security in the civil public administration. Stockholm, Sweden: Riksrevisionen.

Symantec. (2014). *Symantec Internet Security Threat Report 2014.* Retrieved April 5, 2016, from http://www.symantec.com/content/en/us/enterprise/other_resources/b-istr_main_report_v19_21291018.en-us.pdf

Symantec. (2017). *Ransom.Wannacry. Security Response.* Author.

Szor, P. (2005). *The Art of Computer Virus Research and Defense*. Pearson Education.

T, M. (2004). Privacy problems with anonymized transaction databases. In*7th international conference proceedings, Lecture notes in computer science* (vol. 3245, pp. 219–229). Berlin: Springer-Verlag.

Takada, T., & Koike, H. (2002). Tudumi: Information visualization system for monitoring and auditing computer logs. In *Sixth International Conference on Information Visualization* (pp. 570-576). London, UK: IEEE. 10.1109/IV.2002.1028831

Tambe Ebot, A. C. (2017). Explaining two forms of Internet crime from two perspectives: toward stage theories for phishing and Internet scamming. *Jyväskylä Studies in Computing, 259.*

Tanwar, S., & Kumar, A. (2017). A Proposed Scheme for Remedy of Man-In-The-Middle Attack on Certificate Authority. *International Journal of Information Security and Privacy, 11*(3), 1–14. doi:10.4018/IJISP.2017070101

Tavallaee, M., Bagheri, E., Lu, W., & Ghorbani, A. A. (2009). A Detailed Analysis of the KDD CUP 99 Data Set. *Proceedings of 2009 IEEE Symposium on Computational Intelligence in Security and Defense Applications (CISDA 2009),* 53-58. 10.1109/CISDA.2009.5356528

Taylor, T., Brooks, S., & McHugh, J. (2008). NetBytes viewer: An entity-based netflow visualization utility for identifying intrusive behavior. In *Proceedings of the Workshop on Visualization for Computer Security* (pp. 101-114). Berlin: Springer. 10.1007/978-3-540-78243-8_7

Teoh, S. T., Ma, K. L., Wu, S. F., Mankin, A., Massey, D., Zhao, X., . . . Bush, R. (2003). ELISHA: A Visual-Based Anomaly Detection System for the BGP Routing Protocol. *IFIP/IEEE DistributedSystems: Operations and Management,* 155-168.

Teoh, S. T., Ma, K. L., Wu, S. F., & Jankun-Kelly, T. J. (2004). Detecting flaws and intruders with visual data analysis. *IEEE Computer Graphics and Applications, 24*(5), 27–35. doi:10.1109/MCG.2004.26 PMID:15628098

Teoh, S. T., Ma, K. L., Wu, S. F., & Zhao, X. (2002). Case study: Interactive visualization for internet security. In *Proceedings of the conference on Visualization'02* (pp. 505-508). Boston: IEEE Computer Society.

Teoh, S. T., Ranjan, S., Nucci, A., & Chuah, C. N. (2006). BGP eye: a new visualization tool for real-time detection and analysis of BGP anomalies. In *Proceedings of the 3rd international workshop on Visualization for computer security* (pp. 81-90). Alexandria, VA: ACM. 10.1145/1179576.1179593

Teoh, S. T., Zhang, K., Tseng, S. M., Ma, K. L., & Wu, S. F. (2004). Combining visual and automated data mining for near-real time anomaly detection and analysis in BGP. In *Proceedings of the 2004 ACM workshop on Visualization and data mining for computer security* (pp. 35-44). Washington, DC: ACM. 10.1145/1029208.1029215

ThreatConnect. (n.d.). *Security Operations and Analytics Platform. Author.*

Tiwari, S., & Singh, P. (2011). Survey of potential attacks on web services and web service compositions. *Electronics Computer Technology (ICECT), 2011 3rd International Conference on, 2,* 47–51. 10.1109/ICECTECH.2011.5941653

Tran, T., Al-Shaer, E., & Boutaba, R. (n.d.). PolicyVis: Firewall Security Policy Visualization and Inspection. *21st Large Installation System Administration Conference, 7,* 1-16.

Tricaud, S. (2008). Picviz: Finding a needle in a Haystack. In *Proceedings of the First USENIX conference on Analysis of system logs* (pp. 3-3). Berkeley, CA: USENIX Association.

Tri, D. T., & Dang, T. K. (2009). Security Visualization For Peer-To-Peer Resource. *International Journal on Computer Science and Engineering, 1*(2), 47–55.

Trompeter, C., & Eloff, J. (2001). A Framework for the Implementation of Socio-ethical Controls in Information Security. *Computers & Security*, *20*(5), 384–391. doi:10.1016/S0167-4048(01)00507-7

Tuikka, A.-M., Rantanen, M. M., Heimo, O. I., Koskinen, J., Sachdeva, N., & Kimppa, K. K. (2016). Where is patient in EHR project? *ACM SIGCAS Computers and Society*, *45*(3), 73–78. doi:10.1145/2874239.2874250

Ula, M., Ismail, Z., & Sidek, Z. (2011). A Framework for the Governance of Information Security in Banking System. *Journal of Information Assurance & Cybersecurity*, *23*(8), 1–12. doi:10.5171/2011.726196

Ulrich, W. (2001). A Philosophical Staircase for Information Systems Definition, Design, and Development. *Journal of Information Technology Theory and Application*, *3*, 55–84.

Usman, A. B., & Gutierrez, J. (2016). A Reliability-Based Trust Model for Efficient Collaborative Routing in Wireless Networks. *Proceedings of the 11th International Conference on Queueing Theory and Network Applications*.

Uysal, M. (2009). *Cooperative communications for improved wireless network transmission: Framework for virtual antenna array applications: Framework for virtual antenna array applications*. IGI Global.

Vaarandi, R. (2009). Real-time classification of ids alerts with data mining techniques. *Proceedings of the 2009 IEEE MILCOM Conference*. 10.1109/MILCOM.2009.5379762

Vaarandi, R. (2010). Network ids alert classification with frequent itemset mining and data clustering. *Proceedings of the 2010 IEEE Conference on Network and Service Management*. 10.1109/CNSM.2010.5691262

Vaidya, J. H. (2008). Privacy-preserving SVM classification. Knowledge and Information Systems, 14(2), 161-178.

Vaidya, J. M. K. (2008). Privacy Preserving Naïve Bayes Classification. The VLDB Journal, 879-898.

Vaishnavi, V., & Kuechler, W. (2004). *Design research information systems*. Retrieved March 2016 from http://desrist. org/design-research-in-information-systems

Van Grembergen, W., & De Haes, S. (2009). COBIT as a Framework for Enterprise Governance of IT. In *Enterprise Governance of Information Technology* (pp. 137–164). Springer US. doi:10.1007/978-0-387-84882-2_5

Vance, P., Prasad, G., Harkin, J., & Curran, K. (2015). Designing a Compact Wireless Network based Device-free Passive Localisation System for Indoor Environments. *International Journal of Wireless Networks and Broadband Technologies*, *4*(2), 28–43. doi:10.4018/IJWNBT.2015040103

Vapnik, V. N. (1998). *Statistical learning theory. Adaptive and learning systems for signal processing, communications, and control*. New York: Wiley.

Varadharajan, B. M. V. (2014). *Design and Analysis of Security Attacks against Critical Smart Grid Infrastructures*. Paper presented at the 19th International Conference on Engineering of Complex Computer Systems, Tianjin.

Vault Information Services. (2009). *8052.com - The Online 8051/8052 Microcontroller Resource - 8052.com*. Available at: http://www.8052.com/

Verdenius, F., & van Someren, M. W. (1997). Applications of inductive learning techniques: a survey in the Netherlands. *Journal of AI Communications*, *10*(1), 3-20.

Verizon. (2016). 2016 Data Breach Investigations Report. *Verizon Business Journal*, (1), 1–65. 10.1017/CBO9781107415324.004

Vice. (2013). Welcome to the skammerz ishu. *Vice*. Retrieved from: https://www.vice.com/en_us/article/kwp8zz/welcome-to-the-skammerz-ishu

Vieira, M., Antunes, N., Vieira, H. M., & Madeira, H. (2009). *Using Web Security Scanners to Detect Vulnerabilities in Web Services*. Using Web Security Scanners to Detect Vulnerabilities in Using Web Security Scanners to Detect Vulnerabilities in Web Services. doi:10.1109/DSN.2009.5270294

Viinikka, J. D. H., Mé, L., Séguier, R., & Tarvainen, M. (2006). *Time series modeling for ids alert management*. Paper presented at the ACM Symposium on Information Computer and Communications Security. 10.1145/1128817.1128835

Viinikka, J. D., Mé, L., Lehikoinen, A., & Tarvainen, M. (2009). Processing intrusion detection alert aggregates with time series modeling. *Information Fusion Journal*, 312–324.

Viinikka, J., & Debar, H. (2004). Monitoring IDS background noise using EWMA control charts and alert information. LNCS, 3224, 166-187.

Vinod, P., Jaipur, R., Laxmi, V., & Gaur, M. (2009). Survey on Malware Detection Methods. *Proceedings of the 3rd Hackers' Workshop on Computer and Internet Security (IITKHACK'09)*, 74–79.

VN, V. (1998). Statistical learning theory. New York: Wiley.

von Solms, R., & van Niekerk, J. (2013). From information security to cyber security. *Computers & Security, 38*, 97–102. doi:10.1016/j.cose.2013.04.004

Von Solms, S. H. (2005). Information Security Governance - Compliance Management vs Operational Management. *Computers & Security, 24*(6), 443–447. doi:10.1016/j.cose.2005.07.003

Waddock, S. A., & Graves, S. B. (1997). The Corporate Social Performance-Financial Performance Link. *Strategic Management Journal, 18*(4), 303–319. doi:

Wahlgren, G. (2004). Use of risk analysis in large Swedish organizations. Department of Computer and System Sciences, University of Stockholm and Royal Institute of Technology Sweden, Report Series No. 06-019.

Wahlgren, G., & Kowalski, S. (2014). Evaluation of escalation maturity model for IT security risk management: A design science work in progress. Proceedings of 2014 IFIP 8.11/11.13 Dewald Roode Information Security Research Workshop.

Wahlgren, G., & Kowalski, S. (2016). A maturity model for measuring organizations escalation capability of IT-related security incidents in Sweden. In *Proceedings of the 11th Pre-ICIS Workshop on Information Security and Privacy*. Association for Information Systems Electronic Library (AISeL).

Wahlgren, G., Fedotova, A., Musaeva, A., & Kowalski, S. (2016). IT security incidents escalation in the Swedish financial sector: A maturity model study. In *Proceedings of the Tenth International Symposium on Human Aspects of Information Security & Assurance (HAISA 2016) Frankfurt, Germany*. (pp 45-55). Plymouth, UK: Plymouth University

Wahlgren, G., & Kowalski, S. (2013). IT security risk management model for cloud computing: A need for a new escalation approach. *International Journal of E-Entrepreneurship and Innovation, 4*(4), 1–19. doi:10.4018/ijeei.2013100101

Walsham, G. (1993). *Interpreting Information Systems in Organizations*. Chichester, UK: Wiley.

Wang, K., & Stolfo, S. J. (2004). Anomalous Payload-Based Network Intrusion Detection. LNCS, 3224, 203-222.

Wang, Y., & Vassileva, J. (2003). Trust and reputation model in peer-to-peer networks. *Symposium conducted at the meeting of the Peer-to-Peer Computing, 2003 Proceedings. Third International Conference on*.

Warner, J. (2011). Understanding cyber-crime in Ghana: A view from below. *The International Journal of Cyber Criminology, 5*, 736–749.

Watts, D., & Strogatz, S. (1998). Collective dynamics of small-world networks. *Nature, 393*, 440–442. doi:10.1038/30918

Wenliang, D., & Zhijun, Z. (2002). Building decision tree classifier on private data. *CRPIT '14 Proceedings of the IEEE international conference on Privacy, security and data mining* (vol. 14, pp. 1-8). ACM.

What are the differences between electronic medical records, electronic health records, and personal health records? (2015). Retrieved from https://www.healthit.gov/providers-professionals/faqs/what-are-differences-between-electronic-medical-records-electronic

What is 2FA? An extra layer of security that is known as multi factor authentication. (n.d.). Retrieved from https://www.securenvoy.com/two-factor-authentication/what-is-2fa.shtm

What is an electronic health record (EHR)? (n.d.). Retrieved from https://www.healthit.gov/providers-professionals/faqs/what-electronic-health-record-ehr

What is Protected Health Information. (n.d.). Retrieved from https://www.truevault.com/protected-health-information.html

Wheeler, D., & Needham, R. (1994). TEA, a tiny encryption algorithm. Fast Software Encryption, 363–366.

Wheeler, D., & Needham, R. (1998). *XXTEA: Correction to XTEA. Technical report*. Computer Laboratory, University of Cambridge.

Whitaker, R. B., & Erbacher, R. F. (2011). A tri-linear visualization for network anomaly detection. In *SPIE Proceedings of Visualization and Data Analysis 2011*. San Francisco, CA: The Society for Imaging Science and Technology.

Wi-Fi Alliance. (2003). *Wi-Fi Protected Access: Strong, standards-based, interoperable security for today's Wi-Fi networks*. Author.

Williams, M. J., & Musolesi, M. (2016). Spatio-temporal networks: Reachability, centrality and robustness. *Open Science*, *3*(6), 160196. PMID:27429776

Willison, R. (2002). *Opportunities for Computer Abuse: Assessing a Crime Specific Approach in the Case of Barings Bank* (Unpublished Dissertation). London School of Economics, London, UK.

Wilson, M., & Howcroft, D. (2002). Re-conceptualising failure: Social shaping meets IS research. *European Journal of Information Systems*, *11*(4), 236–250. doi:10.1057/palgrave.ejis.3000437

Witten, I. H., & Frank, E. (1999). *Data Mining: Practical Machine Learning Tools and Techniques with Java Implementations*. Academic Press.

Wohlgemuth, J. (2012). *Small World Properties of Facebook Group Networks*. University of Nebraska at Omaha.

Wong, D. H., Chai, K. S., Ramadass, S., & Vavasseur, N. (2010). Expert-Aware Approach: A New Approach to Improve Network Security Visualization Tool. In *Second International Conference on Computational Intelligence, Communication Systems and Networks* (pp. 227-231). Liverpool, UK: IEEE. 10.1109/CICSyN.2010.64

Wong, T., Jacobson, V., & Alaettinoglu, C. (2005). Internet routing anomaly detection and visualization. In *Proceedings of International Conference on Dependable Systems and Networks* (pp. 172-181). Yokohama, Japan: IEEE.

Xiao, F. J., S. (2010). A novel data mining-based method for alert reduction and analysis. *Journal of Networks*.

Xiao, L., Gerth, J., & Hanrahan, P. (2006). Enhancing visual analysis of network traffic using a knowledge representation. In *IEEE Symposium On Visual Analytics Science And Technology* (pp. 107-114). Palo Alto, CA: IEEE. 10.1109/VAST.2006.261436

XML WSDL. (2017). Retrieved from https://www.w3schools.com/xml/xml_wsdl.asp

Yacoub, M. B. Y. (1997). *Hvs: A heuristic for variable selection in multilayer artificial neural network classifier.* Paper presented at the International Conference on Artificial Neural Networks and Intelligent Engineering.

Yang, Y. (1997). *An evaluation of statistical approach to text categorization.* Rapport interne Technichal Report CMU-CS-97-127, Carnegie Mellon University.

Yao, A. C.-C. (1986). How to generate and exchange secrets. In *Foundations of Computer Science, 1986., 27th Annual Symposium* (pp. 162 - 167). Toronto, Canada: IEEE.

Yarrkov, E. (2010). *Cryptanalysis of XXTEA.* Available at: http://eprint.iacr.org/2010/254

Ye, W., Heidemann, J., & Estrin, D. (2002). An energy-efficient MAC protocol for wireless sensor networks. IEEE INFOCOM, 1567–1576.

Yehuda, L., & Benny, P. (2007). An Efficient Protocol for Secure Two-Party Computation in the Presence of Malicious Adversaries. In *26th Annual International Conference on the Theory and Applications of Cryptographic Techniques* (pp. 52-78). Barcelona, Spain: Springer Berlin Heidelberg.

Ye, X. (2008). Countering DDoS and XDoS attacks against web services. *Proceedings of The 5th International Conference on Embedded and Ubiquitous Computing, EUC 2008, 1,* 346–352. 10.1109/EUC.2008.61

Yin, X., Yurcik, W., Treaster, M., Li, Y., & Lakkaraju, K. (2004). VisFlowConnect: netflow visualizations of link relationships for security situational awareness. In *Proceedings of the 2004 ACM Workshop on Visualization and Data Mining for Computer Security* (pp. 26-34). Washington, DC: ACM. 10.1145/1029208.1029214

You, C., Wang, T., Zhou, B., Dai, H., & Sun, B. (2010). A distributed energy-aware trust topology control algorithm for service-oriented wireless mesh networks. *Advances in Swarm Intelligence,* 276-282.

You, I., & Yim, K. (2010). Malware Obfuscation Techniques: A Brief Survey. *Proceedings - 2010 International Conference on Broadband, Wireless Computing Communication and Applications,* 297–300. 10.1109/BWCCA.2010.85

Yuan, Y., & Guanzhong, D. (2007). An Intrusion Detection Expert System with Fact-Base. *Asian Journal of Information Technology, 6*(5), 614–617.

Yuan, Z., & Sheng, Z. (2013). A privacy-preserving algorithm for distributed training of neural network ensembles. *Neural Computing & Applications,* 269–282.

Yuil, J. F. S. (1999). *Intrusion detection for an ongoing attack.* Paper presented at the International Workshop on Recent Advances in Intrusion Detection RAID 99.

Yu-Long, S., Qing-Qi, P.E.I., & Jian-Feng, M.A. (2007). *microTESLA: Broadcast Authentication Protocol for Multiple-Base-Station Sensor Networks.* Academic Press.

Zahariadis, T., Leligou, H. C., Trakadas, P., & Voliotis, S. (2010). Trust management in wireless sensor networks. *European Transactions on Telecommunications, 21*(4), 386–395.

Zanero, S. (2004). Behavioural intrusion detection. In *Proceedings of the 19th ISCIS Symposium* (pp. 657-666). Springer-Verlag.

Zanero, S. (2004). Behavioural Intrusion Detection. *Proceedings of the 19th ISCIS Symposium,* 657-666.

Zanero, S., & Savaresi, S. M. (2004). Unsupervised Learning Techniques for an Intrusion Detection System. *Proceedings of the ACM Symposium on Applied Computing, ACM SAC,* 412-419. 10.1145/967900.967988

Zhang, J., Wen, Y., Nguyen, Q. V., Lu, L., Huang, M., Yang, J., & Sun, J. (2009). Multi-dimensional Data Visualization using Concentric Coordinates. *Visual Information Communication*, 95-118.

Zhang, N. W. (2004). A new scheme on privacy-preserving association rule mining. In PKDD Proceedings of the 8th European Conference on Principles and Practice of Knowledge Discovery in Databases, Lecture Notes in Computer Science (vol. 3202, pp. 484-495). Academic Press, Pisa, Italy: Springer Berlin Heidelberg.

Zhang, X., Liu, C., Nepal, S., & Chen, J. (2013). An efficient quasi-identifier index based approach for privacy preservation over incremental data sets on cloud. *Journal of Computer and System Sciences*, *79*(5), 542–555. doi:10.1016/j.jcss.2012.11.008

Zhang, Y., Xiao, Y., Chen, M., Zhang, J., & Deng, H. (2012). A survey of security visualization for computer network logs. *Security and Communication Networks*, *5*(4), 404–421. doi:10.1002ec.324

Zhao, Y., Zhou, F., & Shi, R. (2012). NetSecRadar: A real-time visualization system for network security: VAST 2012 Mini Challenge Award: Honorable mention for interesting use of radial visualization technique. In *IEEE Conference on Visual Analytics Science and Technology* (pp. 281-282). Seattle, WA: IEEE. 10.1109/VAST.2012.6400516

Zhong, S. Z. (2011). A Privacy-Preserving Algorithm for Distributed Training of Neural Network Ensembles. *Neural Computing & Applications*, *22*(1), 269–282.

Zhou, R., & Hwang, K. (2007). Powertrust: A robust and scalable reputation system for trusted peer-to-peer computing. *IEEE Transactions on Parallel and Distributed Systems*, *18*(4), 460–473. doi:10.1109/TPDS.2007.1021

Zubair, A. B. (2012). Multi-agent systems for protecting critical infrastructures: A survey. *Journal of Network and Computer Applications*, *35*(3), 1151–1161. doi:10.1016/j.jnca.2012.01.006

About the Contributors

Yassine Maleh is from Morocco. He is a PhD of the University Hassan 1st in Settat Morocco, since 2016. He received his Master degree (2012) in Network and IT Security from Faculty of Science and Technology Settat, Morocco, and his Bachelor in Networks and IT Systems (2009) from Hassan 1st University Morocco. He is IT Project Manager at the National Port Agency in Morocco. He is Member of IEEE Communications Society and European Microwave Association. and International Association of Engineers IAENG. His research interests include Wireless Sensor Networks, Virtual Laboratory, Internet of Things, and Networks Security. He has served and continues to serve on the executive and technical program committees of numerous international conference and journals such as International Journal of Networks Security and International Journal of Sensor Networks and Data Communications.

* * *

Sahid Abdelkbir is from Morocco. He is a PhD Student at the University Hassan 1st in Settat Morocco, since 2014. He received his Master degree (2012) in Computer Sciences from the Faculty of Science and Technology Settat, Morocco, and his Bachelor in Networks and IT Systems (2009) from Hassan 1st University Morocco. His research interests include Information Systems, IT Service Management, IT Security and IT Agility.

Francis Enoch Akowuah obtained his Bachelor of Science Computer Science degree from the Kwame Nkrumah University of Science and Technology, Kumasi, Ghana. He worked at the University of Mines and Technology, Tarkwa, Ghana from October 2008 to December 2011 as Senior ICT Assistant. In January 2012, he enrolled at the North Carolina A & T State University, Greensboro, US, to pursue Master of Science Computer Science degree. He has played roles as both Teaching Assistant and Research Assistant. Currently, he is a PhD student and Teaching Assistant at Syracuse University. His research interests include cyber security, computer networks, Android security and health informatics.

Aymen Akremi received his Ph.D. in Computer Science and information systems at CES Laboratory, University of Sfax, Tunisia in 2016. He received his Master's degree from High Institute of Engineers, Sfax, Tunisia in 2012. He is an assistant professor in college of Computer Science and Information Systems, and member of the Scientific and Technology Unit at Umm Al-Qura University, Saudi Arabia. His main research topics of interest are digital forensics investigation properties, description, and requirements within service oriented architecture (SOA), definition and design of digital forensics aware policies within SOA, network information security, network intrusion detection system management in high speed networks, and Data mining techniques.

William Bond, MSIT Graduate Student, Department of Information Technology, College of Computing and Software Engineering, Kennesaw State University. He will be receiving his Master of Science Information Technology from Kennesaw State University in the Fall of 2017. He received his Bachelor of Applied Science in Information Technology from Kennesaw State University in 2016. He received an Associates of Applied Science Degree in Network Specialist from North Georgia Technical College in Clarkesville, Georgia in 2012. His research interests include Web Services vulnerabilities and mitigations, Information Security and Data Analytics. He served in the United States Army as a Field Artilleryman and as a Non-Commissioned Officer. He is a member the Upsilon Pi Epsilon International Honor Society for the Computing and Information Disciplines.

Zizette Boufaïda is a Professor of Computer Science at University of Constantine 2-Abdelhamid Mehri, Algeria, and the Co-Head of the SI&BC research group at the LIRE Laboratory. Her research interests include knowledge representation and reasoning formal knowledge representation for semantic web, ontology development.

Mohamed Cheikh received his engineer degree on computer sciences in 2005 and MSc from University of Menturi Constantine (Algeria) in 2009, MSc dissertation was in Adaptive intrusion detection based agents, he is currently a PhD student in the Department of Computer Science in the same university (from 2010) and assistant professor at August 20, 1955 university at Skikda (Algeria). His research interests include network intrusion detection, artificial intelligence, IA, Multi agent systems, Classification and Pattern Recognition, consensual classification.

Victor Clincy is currently a Full Professor of Computer Science at Kennesaw State University. He held various engineering and management positions in the telecommunications industry for 15 years with such companies as AT&T Bell Labs, Scientific-Atlanta (a CISCO Systems company), Nortel and Texas Instruments. Dr. Clincy holds post-graduate and graduate degrees in engineering from Columbia University, Southern Methodist University, North Carolina State University and the University of Pittsburgh.

Kevin Curran is a Reader in Computer Science and group leader for the Ambient Intelligence Research Group. Dr Curran has made significant contributions to advancing the knowledge of computer networking evidenced by over 800 published works. He is a regular contributor to BBC radio & TV news in the UK and quoted in trade and consumer IT magazines on a regular basis. He is an IEEE Technical Expert for Security and a member of the EPSRC Peer Review College.

Abdellah Ezzati is a Professor and researcher Scientist in Faculty of Science and Technology in Morocco. He obtained his PHD in 1997 in Faculty of science of University Mohamed V in Rabat and member of the Computer commission in the same Faculty. Now is an associate professor in Hassan 1st University in Morocco and he is the Head of Bachelor of Computer Science. He participates to several project as the project Palmes, which elaborate a Moroccan Education Certification. His research spans various aspects of computer architecture, computer communications (networks), computer Security and Reliability. He was also a member of the Organizing and the Scientific Committees of several international symposia and conferences dealing with topics related Networks, Security and Information and Communication technologies and their applications. He is the author and co-author of more than 70 papers included journals, conferences, chapters and books, which appeared in refereed specialized journals and symposia.

Maryam Farhadi is currently pursuing her MSCS at Kennesaw State University. Her research interests lie in application security, electronic health record, HIPAA. She is a student member of ACM.

Mahmood Fazlali received BSc degree in 2001 from Shahid Beheshti University (SBU), MSc. degree in 2004 from University of Isfahan, and PhD degree in 2010 from SBU in computer architecture. He performed researches on reconfigurable computing systems in computer engineering lab of Delft University of Technology, TUDelft. Now, he is an assistant professor in computer science department at SBU. His research interest includes, multicore and parallel systems and malware detection.

Zahia Guessoum is a "Maître de Conférences" (Associate Professor) at the University of Reims Champagne Ardenne in France. She received her doctorship/PhD (1996) and then her "habilitation à diriger des recherches" (2003), both in computer science and from University Pierre & Marie Curie (Paris 6), France. She is a member of the Multi-Agent System (MAS) Team of "Laboratoire d'Informatique de Paris 6" (LIP6). Her general research interests are about adaptive agents and multi-agent systems, fault-tolerant MAS, multi-agent oriented software engineering, coordination mechanism and complex system.

Banu Gunel is an associate professor at the Informatics Institute, Middle East Technical University, Ankara, Turkey since October 2010. She received her BSc degree in Electrical and Electronic Engineering of the same university in 2000, MSc degree in Communication Systems and Signal Processing from the University of Bristol, UK in 2001 and PhD degree in Computer Science from the Queen's University of Belfast, UK in 2004. Between 2004 and 2010, she worked as a post-doctoral researcher at the Center for Vision, Speech and Signal Processing, University of Surrey, UK. Her research interests include audio signal processing, security and surveillance systems.

Jairo A. Gutiérrez is the Deputy Head of the School of Engineering, Computer and Mathematical Sciences at Auckland University of Technology in New Zealand. He received a Systems and Computing Engineering degree from Universidad de Los Andes in Colombia, a Master's degree in Computer Science from Texas A &M University, and a Ph.D. in Information Systems from the University of Auckland. His current research is on viable business models for IT-enabled enterprises, next-generation networks and security issues in wireless networks.

Salima Hacini graduated in computer sciences engineering at Mentouri University of Constantine (Algeria) where she received a Magister and a Ph.D degrees. She is actually an associate professor at TLSI department of Abdehamid Mehri University. She is also a permanent member of LIRE Laboratory. Her research interests include Mobile agents security, information systems security, intrusion detection systems, trust computing, fault detection and tolerance in context-aware systems. Actually, she has about 20 of published papers in scientific journals and proceedings of international conferences.

Hisham M. Haddad, Professor of Computer Science, received his Ph.D. in Computer Science from Oklahoma State University in Stillwater, Oklahoma, in 1992. He served at Marshall University, Huntington, WV, for 9 years as Assistant and Associate Professor of Computer Science. Before joining Kennesaw State University in 2001, he worked in the private sector as Senior Software Architect and Project Manager. Dr. Haddad is active member of the professional community, active participant in professional activities, and is a member the Association for Computing Machinery (ACM). His research interests include Software Engineering, Software Reuse, Software Security, Component-Based Development, Programming Languages, Object-Oriented Technologies, and Undergraduate CS Education. He is active in involving students in research activities. He participated in many funded research and development projects from different agencies, and published in professional journals and refereed International and National conferences.

Hareesha K. S. has been working as Professor in MIT, Manipal University. His research interests encompass privacy preservation in data mining, spatial data mining and its relevance in society as a whole, bio-informatics, biologically inspired algorithms, soft computing and computer vision. He has published quite a good number of research papers in these areas. He has got fellowship award from Boston University to present his research contributions. Dr. Hareesha K.S. has been a member of IEEE society and life member of ISTE, India IACSIT, Singapore. He has been a member of numerous program committee of IEEE, IACSIT conferences in the area of Data Mining, Bioinformatics, Digital Image Processing and Artificial Intelligence. Also, received a grant from BIRAC-DBT, Govt.of India, for a start up for design and development of diagnostic tool for spinal disorders.

P. Kamakshi is Professor & Head of the Department of Information Technology Kakatiya Institute of Technology and Science Warangal.

Peyman Khodamoradi received his B.Sc. in computer engineering from Islamic Azad University, Kermanchah Branch in 2012 and M.Sc in software engineering from Islamic Azad University Kermanchah branch in 2015. His research interest includes computer security specially malware detection.

Stewart Kowalski has over 35 years of industry and academic experience in information security and has worked for a number of large international companies including Ericsson, Telia Research, Huawei, Digital and HP. He has also taught and researched information security at a number of universities, including the Royal Institute of Technology (KTH), Stockholm School of Economics, and Stockholm University Department of Computer and Systems Sciences. He is currently Professor of Information Security at the Department of Information Security and Communication Technology, Norwegian University of Science and Technology, Norway. He is also the current head of the Information Security Management Group at the Center for Cyber and Information Security, CCIS.

Linda Kronman is a media artist and designer from Helsinki, Finland currently living and working in Daejeon, South Korea. Since year 2000 she has worked as Graphic Designer, Art Director and Animation Designer and taken part in several multidisciplinary Research & Design projects. In her artistic work she explores interactive and transmedial methods of storytelling with a special focus on digital fiction. Since 2010 she has been a part of the KairUs Art+ Research collective and her current research includes topics such as anti-fraud activism, electronic waste, rare earth minerals, smart cities and visualizing data for advocacy. She has organized several participatory workshops and attended international exhibitions including Moscow Young Arts Biennale, Siggraph ASIA, NEMAF, WRO Biennale and Ars Electronica.

Piotr Ksiazak is a graduate of Letterkenny Institute of Technology, Donegal, Ireland and is currently working in the IT industry.

Sampath Kumar, Associate Professor, Department of Electronics and Communication Engineering, Manipal Institute of Technology, Manipal. Research interests include medical image processing and computer vision. Received a grant under "Fast Track Scheme for Young Scientists" from SERB-DST, Govt. of India. Also, received grant from BIRAC-DBT, Govt. of India, for a start-up for design and development of diagnostic tool for spinal disorders.

Jonathan Land is currently a Masters Student in the Department of Computer Science and Engineering at the University of Tennessee at Chattanooga.

Michael Lapke is an Assistant Professor of Management Information Systems at the University of Mary Washington in Fredericksburg, VA. He joined UMW in 2012 and is excited to be a part of the new College of Business and a dynamic institution. He previously held positions at East Carolina University, Rhode Island College, and the Florida Institute of Technology.Dr. Lapke earned his doctorate at Virginia Commonwealth University in Richmond, Virginia under the guidance of Dr. Gurpreet Dhillon. His primary research area was Information Systems Security, specifically IS Security Policy Formulation and Implementation. He has presented research at the America's Conference for Information Systems (AMCIS), the European Conferences for Information Systems (ECIS) and The Information Institute's Security Conference. He has papers pending at the Journal of Strategic Information Systems, Computers & Security, and the Journal of Information Systems Security.

Sumana M. was born in Karnataka, India. She has received the B.E. degree in Computer Science and engineering from Manipal Institute of Technology, Karnataka, India, in 2000, and the M.Tech. degree from VTU University in 2007, Karnataka, India . She has obtained her Ph.D. degree in privacy preserving data mining in computer science and Engineering from the Manipal University, Karnataka, India. She is presently working as an Associate Professor in the department of Information Science and Engineering in M S Ramaiah Institute of Technology since 2007. Previously she has worked as a lecturer in the Manipal Institute of Technology. Her current research interests include data mining, cryptography and secure multiparty computations. She is a Life Member of the Indian Society for Technical Education (ISTE), the System Society of India. She is also an IEEE member.

Mohsen Rouached is currently acting as an associate professor in the Computers and Information Technology department at Qabus University, Oman. He received his M.S and Ph.D in computer science from Nancy University in 2005 and 2008 respectively. His research interests span over several areas related to Service Oriented Computing, Business Processes, Security, Privacy, and Forensics Management, Services Semantics, and Wireless Sensors Networks. He has published over 50 research papers in these domains. He serves as program committee member and reviewer at many international journals and conferences and has been participating in several research projects.

Hassen Sallay received his Ph.D in computer science from Nancy University, France, in 2004. He is currently an associate professor in the College of Computer Science and Information Systems at Umm Al-Qura University, Saudi Arabia. He is the leader of the Aman system research team focusing on excellence in building security technical intelligence to support academic institutions and professional bodies. His research interests are mainly in Security and Digital Forensics, Networking and Machine Learning. He has conducted and participated in several research projects concerning these fields. He has published several research papers in international journals, conference proceedings as well as book chapters.

Hossain Shahriar is an Assistant Professor of Information Technology at Kennesaw State University, Georgia, USA since Fall 2012. He received his PhD in Computing from Queen's University, Canada in 2012. His research interests include cyber security, particularly application (web, mobile) security vulnerabilities and mitigation approaches, risk assessment techniques, and metric-based attack detection. He also teaches cyber security courses in BSIT and MSIT degree programs such as Ethical Hacking. Dr. Shahriar has published more than 60 peer reviewed articles on various research topics within cyber security in International Journals, Conferences, and Book Chapters including ACM SIN, ACM SAC, IEEE HASE, IEEE COMPSAC, Computer & Security, and ACM Computing Survey. He has been a reviewer for many international journals and PC member of international conferences on software, computer, and application security. He served as Fast Abstract Chair in IEEE COMPSAC 2015-2017, Program Chair in ACM SIN 2016, Publicity Chair in IEEE COMPSAC 2017, Publication Chair in ACM SAC 2017 -2018, and Student Research Competition Chair in ACM SAC 2016. Currently, he is also a Co-PI of a funded research project from National Science Foundation on Secure Mobile Application Development aiming to develop open source labware resources. Dr. Shahriar is a professional member of ACM, SIGAPP, and IEEE.

Ferda Özdemir Sönmez is a doctoral candidate at the Informatics Institute, Middle East Technical University (METU), Ankara, Turkey. She received her B.Sc. degree in Electrical and Electronics Engineering department in 1997. After graduation, she worked in the private sector for 15 years as software specialist, software development consultant, project manager and IT manager. She is holding the PMP degree since 2009. The projects she worked with include mainly e-government and Telco projects. She started her graduate study in Informatics Institute, METU, in 2012 in information systems and got M.Sc. She proceeded with a Ph.D. in 2014, in the same department. Her research interests involve: security requirements engineering, security cost management, and security visualization.

Aminu Bello Usman is a PhD student in the School of Engineering, Computer and Mathematical Sciences at Auckland University of Technology in New Zealand. He received a Bachelor in computer Science Bayero University, kano Nigeria, a Master in Network Security, Middlesex University, London. His current research is on Secure Wireless Mobile Networks, Network Security, Ethical Hacking and Cloud Computing Security.

Gunnar Wahlgren is a PhD student in the IT Security field at Department of Computer and System Science, Stockholm University. His research topic is IT Security Risk Management focusing on risk monitoring and risk communication. Gunnar received a licentiate degree from Stockholm University

1996. Gunnar has more than 50 years of broad IT-experience working as a programmer, systems analyst and project leader. The last 33 years he has been working in the IT Security field as an IT Security consultant and project leader for different kinds of IT Security projects. Gunnar took up his PhD studies again 2012 after his retirement.

Hong Wang is an Associate Professor of Management Information Systems at North Carolina A&T State University, USA. He holds a Ph.D. in MIS from Ohio State University. He is also a Visiting Professor at Yunnan University of Finance and Economics and Dalian Maritime University in China. His research interests include Information Systems, Enterprise Systems, System Security and Information Assurance, Business Intelligence, Artificial Intelligence, Networking, and Business Process Reengineering. He has published more than 20 articles in refereed academic journals such as Expert Systems with Applications, Expert Systems, Enterprise Information Systems, Systems Research and Behavioral Science, Electronic Government, International Journal of Management and Enterprise Development, Computers and Industrial Engineering, International Journal of Production Research, Computers and Operations Research, Information Technology and Management, among others. He has also secured grants from the US National Science Foundation (NSF) and other sources.

Jinsheng Xu is an Associate Professor in the Department of Computer Science at North Carolina A&T State University (NC A&T). He holds a Ph.D. in computer science from Michigan State University. His research interests include cyber security, social networks, data mining, simulation, and parallel computing. He implemented several interactive and animated information assurance (IA) educational tools, which are used in IA courses to enhance learning experience. Dr. Xu participated in several funded projects in IA education and research. He successfully mapped courseware of the Department of Computer Science to the Committee on National Security Systems (CNSS) National Standards 4011 and 4013E in 2008 and successfully lead NC A&T's application for National Centers of Academic Excellence in IA Education (CAE/IAE) designated by the National Security Agency and the Department of Homeland Security.

Li Yang is a Guerra Professor and Assistant Dean in the College of Engineering and Computer Science. She is the Director of the UTC Information Security (InfoSec) Center, a National Center of Academic Excellence in Information Assurance/Cyber Defense (CAE-IA/CD). Her research interests include network and information security, cryptography, intrusion detection, bioinformatics, and engineering techniques for complex software system design.

Xiaohong Yuan is a Professor in the Department of Computer Science at North Carolina A&T State University (NC A&T) and the Director of the University's Center for Cyber Defense, a Center of Academic Excellence in Information Assurance Education (CAE/IAE). She holds a Ph.D. in computer science from Florida Atlantic University. Her research interests include information security, software security, visualization and health informatics security and privacy. Dr. Yuan has led the establishment of the Secure Software Engineering program in the Department of Computer Science at NC A&T. She also led the establishment of the Health Informatics Security and Privacy program at NC A&T.

Mounia Zaydi is from Morocco. She is a PhD student at The Faculty of Science and Technology in Settat Morocco, since 2016. She received his Master degree (2012) in Network and IT Security from Faculty of Science and Technology Settat, Morocco, and his Bachelor in Networks and IT Systems (2010) from Hassan 1st University Morocco. She is a part-time professor at the Mohamed 6 international academy of civil aviation in Casablanca Morocco and at University Hassan 1st in Settat Morocco teaching information system security subjects and information technology services management. Her research interests include, Information Systems, Security Governance, risk assessment and Management.

Andreas Zingerle is a media artist from Innsbruck, Austria. He received his PhD from the University of Art and Design Linz (Austria) researching topics such as internet crime, fraud and scam, vigilante counter-movements and anti-fraud activism. He implements social engineering strategies that emerge in his research into interactive narratives, artistic installations, data visualisations and creative media competence trainings. In the last years he worked on several installations exploring a creative misuse of technology and alternative ways of Human Computer Interaction. Since 2004 he takes part in international conferences and exhibitions, among others Ars Electronica, Siggraph, Japan Media Arts Festival, File, WRO Biennial.

Index

A

Accuracy 47, 49, 57, 59-62, 66, 68, 87-88, 90-91, 215, 255-256, 264, 267-272, 277-279, 286-287, 291-293, 309, 312, 332, 337, 339-342, 344, 347, 349-350, 355-356
Adaptive intrusion detection 292-293, 296, 314
Alert Reduction 257
Anomaly-based detection 292
Anti-fraud 322-323, 326, 333, 336
ARRA 200
Attack-Type 193
authentication 1, 3-7, 9-10, 12-15, 19, 21, 25-27, 29, 31, 36, 39, 47, 57, 59, 200, 202, 209, 245, 368, 374

B

Big Data 154

C

Capability 48, 51-52, 59, 98, 109-110, 113-114, 129-130, 137-139, 141, 156, 175, 178, 211, 256, 293
Case Study 99, 181, 237, 242-243, 246-247
classification 66-69, 71, 75, 81-82, 90, 99, 104, 107, 154, 156, 162-163, 165, 174, 179, 182, 184, 207, 245, 256-257, 260, 267, 276-281, 284, 286-287, 294, 308, 313, 337-344, 346, 350-352, 360
Classifications 152, 156, 167, 355-356
Classifiers 66-68, 72-73, 82, 86-88, 90-91, 276, 279, 282-283, 287, 312-313, 339-340, 350, 353
Cloud Computing 138-139, 144
COBIT 97, 131, 214-218, 221, 225, 233-234
Collaborative Routing 53
Compliance 102-106, 131, 199, 201, 211, 225-226, 229, 233-234, 239, 246-247
computer security 104, 226, 276
Consensual algorithms 312

C (continued)

Cryptography 1-2, 5, 12, 15, 20, 50, 68, 90, 223-224, 367, 375
CSF 214-215, 225-226, 233-234
Cybercrime 237-238, 322

D

Data Collection 99, 134, 182, 184, 193
Data mining 66-68, 90, 256-260, 265, 270, 293, 338-339, 345
Digital Storytelling 335
Display Types 152-154, 156-157, 165, 172, 174-177, 179, 183-184

E

EHR 199-202, 205-211, 223, 233-234
Engagement 96-97
Escalation 129-130, 132, 135-136, 138-141, 144-145, 149, 364, 377

F

Fake Profiles 331
False alarms 159, 276, 279, 291-295, 301, 310, 314-315
Forensics readiness 255-256, 259, 270
Formulation 99, 237-239, 241-247, 249
Fraud 51, 67, 215, 322-324, 327, 329-330, 333, 335

G

Governance 96-99, 101-105, 107-110, 113, 115, 122-123, 130-131, 144, 217-218, 225

H

Health Informatics 222-224, 233
Health Information Systems 215, 220, 233-234

High Speed Network 257
HIPAA 199-202, 208-209, 211, 225
HITECH 200, 211, 225
Homomorphic Property 72, 78, 85

I

Implementation 1, 4, 14-15, 17, 20, 25-27, 29, 31, 38-40, 57, 59-60, 62, 68, 98-99, 102-103, 105-106, 122, 131, 157, 180, 184, 202, 205-208, 211, 214-215, 220, 223, 225-226, 231, 234, 237-238, 240, 242-249, 256, 285, 292, 301, 346
Incident 129-130, 132, 135-137, 141, 144, 149, 200
Incident Management 136, 149
Information Visualization 153, 156-157, 170, 174, 184, 193
Injection Attacks 50, 361, 363, 370, 373, 377
Interactive Narratives 335
Intrusion Alert 255
Intrusion Detection 153, 159, 162, 165, 168, 170, 172, 174, 176, 193, 255-256, 276-279, 282, 287, 291-297, 301, 309-310, 312-314, 377
Intrusion Detection Systems 255-256, 276, 291, 294, 309, 377
ISO 97-98, 105, 108, 113, 130, 132-133, 136-137, 214-215, 219-225, 233-235, 332
IT Risk 130, 149

K

KDD 276-277, 279-282, 284, 286-287, 301, 305, 315

L

Lifecycle 20, 237, 249

M

machine learning 257, 293, 338-340, 344
Malware detection 337-345, 356
Maturity 96-99, 105-110, 113-115, 122-123, 129, 134, 137-145, 149
Maturity Attribute 140-141, 143
Maturity Levels 113, 115, 137-140, 142-144
Maturity Models 108, 137-138
metamorphic malware 337-342, 344, 346, 349, 353, 355
Multi-Agent System 314

N

Naive Bayesian Classification 69
Network Performance Metrics 53

Network Traffic 154-155, 159-160, 162-163, 166, 171-175, 179-180, 183, 193, 266, 270, 276-277, 279, 282, 284, 292, 295, 312
Nigerian 419-Scam 335
NIST Special Publication 136, 202, 214-215, 226-227, 229, 233-234

O

obfuscation 339, 341-342, 346
Open Source Intelligence 330, 335
Organization 97-99, 102, 104-110, 113-115, 122-123, 129-139, 141-142, 144-145, 149, 160, 216, 218-223, 226, 230, 233-234, 237, 239-240, 244, 246-249, 256, 362
Organizational Levels 132, 144, 149

P

Paillier 66, 72-73, 75, 82, 85-86, 90
PHI 199-202
Phishing 206, 330, 336
Privacy 4-5, 12, 66, 68, 73, 75-79, 81-82, 86-88, 90-91, 199-202, 208-211, 214, 223-227, 231, 234-235, 246, 323
Privacy Preserving Data Mining 66-68, 90
Privilege Escalation attacks 377

R

RESTful 361-362, 377
Review 105, 122, 142, 152, 154, 157, 159, 178-179, 184-185, 201, 209, 293
Risk Communication 132, 134-135
Risk Management 104-106, 108, 129-134, 149, 217, 227, 234
Risk Monitoring 104, 132-134
Risk Treatment 132-133, 135-136, 234

S

Scambaiting 322-326, 333, 336
Scambaiting/Scambaiters 336
security 1, 3-5, 7, 10, 12, 14-17, 19-23, 25-27, 39-40, 47-48, 50-51, 55, 68, 86, 90, 96-99, 101-110, 112-115, 122-123, 129-142, 144, 149, 152-157, 159-163, 166, 168, 170, 172, 174-184, 193, 199-202, 205-211, 214-215, 217-231, 233-235, 237-243, 245-249, 255-257, 276, 291, 293, 297, 309, 311-312, 330, 333, 337, 365, 367, 369-370, 374-375
Security Data Source 193

Security Management 96, 98, 104, 108-110, 113, 115, 130, 174, 193, 219-222, 233
Security Policy 98, 210, 237-249, 309, 375
Security Visualization 152-157, 159, 161-162, 165-166, 168, 170, 177-180, 182-184, 193
Self-Assessment 129, 141-142, 144
Semantic Analysis 244-247
Semantically Secure 66, 68, 73, 75
Semiotic Theory 240
sensors 15, 18-19, 39, 134, 175-176, 295
SOAP 360-361, 364-365, 368, 370-373, 375-377
Standards 16, 20, 96-97, 101, 112, 130, 136, 139, 202, 208-209, 214-215, 218-219, 221-222, 225-227, 229, 231, 233-234, 237
Storytelling 323, 326, 333, 335
Support Vector Machine 81-82, 86, 88, 91, 341

T

Taxonomies 156

U

Use-Cases 154, 156, 159-160, 162

V

Vigilante 322-323
Vigilante Communities 323
Visualization 152-157, 159-170, 172, 174-185, 193, 276, 279-281, 283, 312-313

W

Web Services 360-363, 365-367, 369-374, 376-377
Workshop 138, 231, 323-324, 326-328, 330, 332
WSDL 367, 372-375

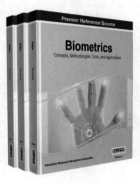

Stay Current on the Latest Emerging Research Developments

Become an IGI Global Reviewer for Authored Book Projects

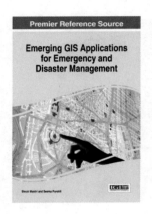

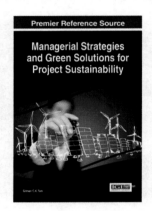

The overall success of an authored book project is dependent on quality and timely reviews.

In this competitive age of scholarly publishing, constructive and timely feedback significantly decreases the turnaround time of manuscripts from submission to acceptance, allowing the publication and discovery of progressive research at a much more expeditious rate. Several IGI Global authored book projects are currently seeking highly qualified experts in the field to fill vacancies on their respective editorial review boards:

Applications may be sent to:
development@igi-global.com

Applicants must have a doctorate (or an equivalent degree) as well as publishing and reviewing experience. Reviewers are asked to write reviews in a timely, collegial, and constructive manner. All reviewers will begin their role on an ad-hoc basis for a period of one year, and upon successful completion of this term can be considered for full editorial review board status, with the potential for a subsequent promotion to Associate Editor.

If you have a colleague that may be interested in this opportunity,
we encourage you to share this information with them.

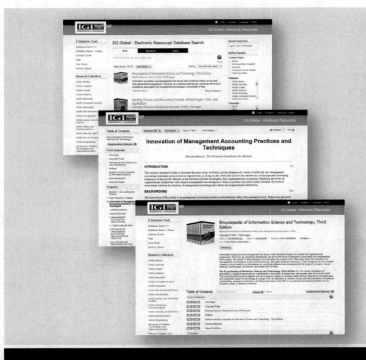

Information Resources Management Association

Advancing the Concepts & Practices of Information Resources Management in Modern Organizations

Become an IRMA Member

Members of the **Information Resources Management Association (IRMA)** understand the importance of community within their field of study. The Information Resources Management Association is an ideal venue through which professionals, students, and academicians can convene and share the latest industry innovations and scholarly research that is changing the field of information science and technology. Become a member today and enjoy the benefits of membership as well as the opportunity to collaborate and network with fellow experts in the field.

IRMA Membership Benefits:

- **One FREE Journal Subscription**

- **30% Off Additional Journal Subscriptions**

- **20% Off Book Purchases**

- Updates on the latest events and research on Information Resources Management through the IRMA-L listserv.

- Updates on new open access and downloadable content added to Research IRM.

- A copy of the Information Technology Management Newsletter twice a year.

- A certificate of membership.

IRMA Membership $195

Scan code or visit **irma-international.org** and begin by selecting your free journal subscription.

Membership is good for one full year.

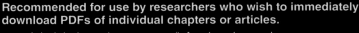